"Convenient, Indispensable, Admirable"

Here in a compact new form is one of the most famous books of all times. Based on the world-famous treasury of wit and wisdom, BARTLETT'S FAMILIAR QUOTATIONS, it has been specially edited and revised for greater enjoyment and easier reference. THE SHORTER BARTLETT'S FAMILIAR QUOTATIONS contains over 10,000 quotations by nearly 2,000 authors.

Unique in the field of pocket-size books, this giant little volume contains 500 pages with entries arranged alphabetically by author for quick reference. It has an easy-to-use index compiled by subject, by author and by key words.

Here at your fingertips is a rich and varied treasury of information on every subject which will bring you the fascinating and rewarding pleasure of reading the most memorable passages of all times.

The Shorter Bartlett's

FAMILIAR
QUOTATIONS

A collection of Passages, Phrases, and Proverbs
Traced to Their Sources
in Ancient and Modern Literature by

JOHN BARTLETT

CHRISTOPHER MORLEY, *Editor*
LOUELLA D. EVERETT, *Associate Editor*

Permabook Edition edited by KATHLEEN SPROUL

A POCKET CARDINAL® EDITION published by
POCKET BOOKS, INC. • NEW YORK

THE SHORTER BARTLETT'S FAMILIAR QUOTATIONS

A Pocket *Cardinal* edition
1st printing.........January, 1953
17th printing......December, 1964

The Shorter Bartlett's Familiar Quotations is an abridged edition of *Familiar Quotations*, published by Little, Brown and Company in 1937, and has been arranged in this compact Pocket *Cardinal* format for convenient, easy reference.

Pocket *Cardinal* editions are published by Pocket Books, Inc., and are printed and distributed in the U.S.A. by Affiliated Publishers, a division of Pocket Books, Inc., 630 Fifth Avenue, New York, N.Y. 10020. Trademark registered in the United States and other countries.

L

THE SHORTER
BARTLETT'S
FAMILIAR QUOTATIONS

PREFACE

The first edition of *Bartlett's Familiar Quotations* was published a century ago, in 1855. Since then, under the editorship of John Bartlett and in recent years that of Christopher Morley and Louella D. Everett, it has been revised, enlarged, and brought up to date no less than a dozen times. With each edition Bartlett's has grown in reputation, in stature, and in importance, until today it is comparable only to the dictionary as a household institution.

The criteria of selection laid down by Bartlett have been changed and modified somewhat as the times required. The broad principles upon which the work is based, however, remain now as they were when the first editor wrote his brief and now famous preface:

The object of this work is to show, to some extent, the obligations our language owes to various authors for numerous phrases and familiar quotations which have become "household words."

This Collection, originally made without any view of publication, has been considerably enlarged by additions from an English work on a similar plan, and is now sent forth with the hope that it may be found a convenient book of reference.

Though perhaps imperfect in some respects, it is be-

lieved to possess the merit of accuracy, as the quotations have been taken from the original sources.

Should this be favorably received, endeavors will be made to make it more worthy of the approbation of the public in a future edition.

CAMBRIDGE, MAY, 1855.

Time added material inexorably, and in later years Bartlett felt the weight of accumulation sorely. As he said in his preface to the fourth edition:

. . . It is not easy to determine in all cases the degree of familiarity that may belong to phrases and sentences which present themselves for admission; for what is familiar to one class of readers may be quite new to another. Many maxims of the most famous writers of our language, numberless curious and happy turns from orators and poets, have knocked at the door, and it was hard to deny them. But to admit these simply on their own merits, without assurance that the general reader would readily recognize them as old friends, was aside from the purpose of this collection. Still, it has been thought better to incur the risk of erring on the side of fulness . . .

In 1947 Christopher Morley echoed Bartlett's cry:

Man may be condemned as much by what he remembers as by what he forgets. The editors are anxiously aware of probable errors, premature inclusions, regrettable omissions. It is not easy to be a bottleneck for the flood of print. What the great editor C. E. Montague called "the supreme tribute of perfect quotation" is rare. It is as double-divinely opportune as the seeding of wildflowers by the muting of birds. For this kind of vivarium as good a motto as any is the late Mr. Justice Holmes's description of his Legal Papers (1920): "Fragments of my fleece left on the hedges of life." The thornier the hedges, the more scraps of wool . . .

The Shorter Bartlett's is the first and only abridged edition of *Familiar Quotations*. It must be evident that in no sense is it intended to supplant the larger volume, any more than the desk dictionary is designed to serve the purposes of the more complete unabridged. *The Shorter Bartlett's* will provide the user with a conveniently compact reference book which, while not as inclusive as the parent volume, will still be an authoritative guide to the great and memorable passages of ancient and modern literature. It has the very considerable virtues of brevity and convenience. Those who require a fuller and more exhaustive compendium will, of course, turn to *Familiar Quotations*, which now, more than ever, is recognized as the standard work in the field.

The problems of selection and deletion have plagued the editor of the present volume, as they did her predecessors, through every stage of the work. Much that is good and great was necessarily sacrificed to the requirements of space. But that was inevitable in a volume in which the editors had for years selected and winnowed each passage with such infinite care. It is hoped, however, that this shorter version represents, as truly as the source book, the flavor and spirit of the hundreds of great thinkers whose wise and witty words have been included.

The arrangement of the material in the present volume differs somewhat from that in *Familiar Quotations*. Because the new edition was designed to serve different purposes, and because of the change in its format, it seemed wise to make certain changes for the convenience of the user.

Quotations from known writers appear under the names of the authors, which are arranged alphabetically. In the case of pen names, which sometimes may be better known than real names, both are listed in their correct alphabetical place with cross references from one to the other. Dates of birth and death follow the names except in those few cases in which accurate dates have never been ascertained.

When more than one quotation appear under an author's name, they are given in the order of the date of writing, except the Shakespeare material, which follows the usual order of the early folio editions of the plays published in the 1600s.

Familiar and well-loved phrases often come down to us without specific authorship. These have been grouped at the end of the author section in the following order:

   a. Unknown Authorship, which includes an Addenda section of slogans and other phrases traced to their origin, curious epitaphs, miscellaneous translations, etc.
   b. The King James Bible, including the Old Testament, New Testament, Apocrypha; other religious books, including the Douay Bible, the Koran, and the Book of Common Prayer.

The index at the back of the book is based primarily on subject classifications. Sometimes the subject entry will apply to the meaning of a quotation, sometimes to an actual key word. Such a system makes for ease of reference. For example, if the reader wants a quotation on *Christmas,* he has only to turn to that subject in the index. There he will find a succession of page numbers, each with a letter (as 125b) for quick location on the page. If he remembers the sense of a quotation but only vaguely its wording, the index can help to track it down through its meaning. He will find classifications as inclusive as "Greatness" and "Mankind," and as precise as "Aviation," "Baseball," and "Abraham Lincoln."

The major subjects—such as "Age," "Life," "Love," "Death," etc.—have been divided into sub-categories under the entry itself. Often the reader is also directed by cross references to one or more related classifications.

Some quotations, even brief ones, refer to more than a single subject, and in such cases are indexed under each subject. The meaning of some quotations often differs from their key word, but it will always be possible to find those quotations under the proper subject listing.

Proverbs and maxims have not been indexed as such but appear under the subjects to which they refer. The reader in search of the apt proverbial expression will do well, however, to consult a few well-known sources such as Aesop, Cervantes, Chaucer, Dryden, John Heywood, Shakespeare, and, of course, the Bible.

The arrangement of the material in *The Shorter Bartlett's* has been determined by one consideration—the convenience of the reader. If he will take a few moments to master the simple system employed throughout the book, he will find that he has at his finger tips in this handy volume the finest thoughts and words of all mankind.

BARTLETT'S
FAMILIAR QUOTATIONS

Lascelles Abercrombie
[1881–1938]

[a] But here's the happiest light
can lie on ground,
Grass sloping under trees
Alive with yellow shine of daffodils!   *Ryton Firs*

[b] Crumble, crumble,
Voiceless things;
No faith can last
That never sings.

For the last hour
To joy belongs;
The steadfast perish,
But not the songs.
        The Stream's Song.
        Stanzas 6 and 7

John Emerich Edward
Dalberg, Lord Acton
[1834–1902]

[c] Power tends to corrupt; absolute power corrupts absolutely.
        Letter to Bishop Mandell
        Creighton, 1887

Louis Adamic
[1899–1951]

[d] There is a certain blend of
courage, integrity, character and
principle which has no satisfactory dictionary name but has been
called different things at different times in different countries.
Our American name for it is
"guts."   *A Study in Courage*

Charles Follen Adams
[1842–1918]

[e] I haf von funny leedle poy
Vot gomes schust to mine knee;
Der queerest schap, der createst
rogue,
As efer you dit see.
He runs, und schumps, und
schmashes dings
In all barts off der house;
But vot off dot? He vas mine son,
Mine leedle Yawcob Strauss.
        Yawcob Strauss. Stanza 1

[f] I vants to gondradict dot shap
Dot made dis leedle shoke:
"A woman vas der glinging vine,
Und man der shturdy oak."
        Der Oak und der Vine. Stanza 1

Franklin Pierce Adams
("F.P.A.")
[1881–1960]

[g] Christmas is over and Business is Business.
        For the Other 364 Days

[h] "Up, to the office, . . . and so
to bed."
        A Ballade of Mr. Samuel Pepys.
        Refrain

[i] "Oh, why do you gaze, my
dear, my dear,   .
And muse on the misty sky?"
"I'm afraid that it isn't going to
clear,
And we won't get the washing
dry."   *Sehnsucht. Stanza 5*

[j] If, my dear, you seek to slum-
ber,
Count of stars an endless number;
If you still continue wakeful,
Count the drops that make a lake-
ful,
Then, if vigilance yet above you
Hover, count the times I love you;
And if slumber still repel you,
Count the times I do not tell you.
        Lullaby

[k] Ruthlessly pricking our gon-
falon bubble,
Making a Giant hit into a double,
Words that are weighty with
nothing but trouble:
"Tinker to Evers to Chance."
        Baseball's Sad Lexicon

[l] The rich man has his motor-
car,
His country and his town estate.
He smokes a fifty-cent cigar
And jeers at Fate.

Yet though my lamp burn low and
dim,
Though I must slave for livelihood—
Think you that I would change
with him?
You bet I would!
        The Rich Man. Stanzas 1 and 3

[m] O bards of rhyme and metre
free,
My gratitude goes out to ye
For all your deathless lines—
ahem!
Let's see now. . . . What *is* one of
them?   *To a Vers Librist*

[n] Prints, approaches the well-
known date;
Time to wallop and stigmatize;

Time for the wearisome old debate;
Why did it win the Pulitzer Prize?
Ballade of the Annual Query.
L'Envoi

[o] Echo again the words of Paine,
Clear as a mountain stream is clear,
Sane as a prairie breeze is sane.
Sound again on the listening ear . . .
"These are the times that try men's souls."
Ballade of the American Crisis
[1942]

Henry Brooks Adams
[1838–1918]

[p] Accident counts for much in companionship as in marriage.
The Education of Henry Adams.
Chap. 4

[q] Women have, commonly, a very positive moral sense; that which they will, is right; that which they reject, is wrong; and their will, in most cases, ends by settling the moral.
Ibid. Chap. 6

[r] All experience is an arch, to build upon. *Ibid.*

[s] Although the Senate is much given to admiring in its members a superiority less obvious or quite invisible to outsiders, one Senator seldom proclaims his own inferiority to another, and still more seldom likes to be told of it.
Ibid. Chap. 7

[t] Friends are born, not made. *Ibid.*

[u] Young men have a passion for regarding their elders as senile.
Ibid. Chap. 11

[v] Knowledge of human nature is the beginning and end of political education. *Ibid. Chap. 12*

[w] His first struggle with a sleeping-car made him doubt the value—to him—of a Pullman civilization. *Ibid. Chap. 16*

[x] Chaos often breeds life, when order breeds habit. *Ibid.*

[y] The difference is slight, to the influence of an author, whether he is read by five hundred readers, or by five hundred thousand; if he can select the five hundred, he reaches the five hundred thousand. *Ibid. Chap. 17*

[z] The newspaper-man is, more than most men, a double personality; and his person feels best satisfied in its double instincts when writing in one sense and thinking in another. *Ibid.*

[a] A teacher affects eternity; he can never tell where his influence stops. *Ibid. Chap. 20*

[b] One friend in a lifetime is much; two are many; three are hardly possible. Friendship needs a certain parallelism of life, a community of thought, a rivalry of aim. *Ibid.*

[c] Morality is a private and costly luxury. *Ibid. Chap. 22*

[d] He too serves a certain purpose who only stands and cheers.
Ibid. Chap. 24

[e] Practical politics consists in ignoring facts. *Ibid.*

[f] Nothing in education is so astonishing as the amount of ignorance it accumulates in the form of inert facts. *Ibid. Chap. 25*

[g] Power is poison. Its effect on Presidents had been always tragic, chiefly as an almost insane excitement at first, and a worse reaction afterwards; but also because no mind is so well balanced as to bear the strain of seizing unlimited force without habit or knowledge of it; and finding it disputed with him by hungry packs of wolves and hounds whose lives depend on snatching the carrion. *Ibid. Chap. 28*

[h] We combat obstacles in order to get repose, and, when got, the repose is insupportable.
Ibid. Chap. 29

[i] Simplicity is the most deceitful mistress that ever betrayed man. *Ibid. Chap. 30*

[j] No one means all he says, and yet very few say all they mean, for words are slippery and thought is viscous. *Ibid. Chap. 31*

[k] The Indian Summer of life should be a little sunny and a little sad, like the season, and infinite in wealth and depth of tone —but never hustled.
Ibid. Chap. 35

John Adams
[1735–1826]

[l] Yesterday the greatest question was decided which ever was debated in America; and a greater perhaps never was, nor will be, decided among men. A resolution was passed without one dissenting colony, that those United Colonies are, and of right ought to be, free and independent States.
Letter to Mrs. Adams
[July 3, 1776]

John Quincy Adams
[1767–1848]

[m] My wants are many, and, if told,

Would muster many a score;
And were each wish a mint of
      gold,
I still should long for more.
      *The Wants of Man, Stanza 1
      In The Quincy [Massachu-
      setts] Patriot, September 25,
      1841*

[n] This is the last of earth! I am
      content.   *His Last Words*

Sarah Flower Adams
[1805–1848]

[o] Though like the wanderer,
      The sun gone down,
Darkness be over me,
      My rest a stone;
Yet in my dreams I'd be
Nearer, my God, to Thee,
      Nearer to Thee.
Nearer, My God, to Thee. Stanza 2

[p] Once have a priest for enemy;
      good bye
To peace.
      Vivia Perpetua. Act III, Sc. 2

Harold Adamson

[q] Comin' in on a Wing and a
      Prayer.   *Title of popular
      song of World War II*

Jane Addams
[1860–1935]

[r] Private beneficence is totally
inadequate to deal with the vast
numbers of the city's disinherited.
      Twenty Years at Hull House

[s] The common stock of intellectual enjoyment should not be difficult of access because of the
economic position of him who
would approach it.   *Ibid.*

Joseph Addison
[1672–1719]

[t] Unbounded courage and com-
      passion join'd,
Tempering each other in the vic-
      tor's mind,
Alternately proclaim him good
      and great,
And make the hero and the man
      complete.   *The Campaign
      [written in honor of the battle of
      Blenheim]. Line 219*

[u] The spacious firmament on
      high,
With all the blue ethereal sky,
And spangled heavens, a shining
      frame,
Their great Original proclaim . . .
And all the planets in their turn,
Confirm the tidings as they roll,
And spread the truth from pole to
      pole. . . .

For ever singing as they shine,
The hand that made us is divine.
      *Ode [in The Spectator, No 465,
      August 23, 1712]*

[v] 'Tis not in mortals to com-
      mand success.
But we'll do more, Sempronius,—
      we'll deserve it
      Cato Act I, Sc. 2

[w] Beauty soon grows familiar
      to the lover,
Fades in his eye, and palls upon
      the sense.   *Ibid. Sc. 4*

[x] My voice is still for war.
Gods! can a Roman senate long
      debate
Which of the two to choose, slav-
      ery or death?
      Ibid. Act II, Sc. 1

[y] The woman that deliberates
      is lost.   *Ibid. Act IV, Sc. 1*

[z] It must be so,—Plato, thou
      reasonest well!
Else whence this pleasing hope,
      this fond desire,
This longing after immortality?
Or whence this secret dread, and
      inward horror
Of falling into naught? Why
      shrinks the soul
Back on herself, and startles at
      destruction?
'Tis the divinity that stirs within
      us;
'Tis Heaven itself that points out
      an hereafter,
And intimates eternity to man.
Eternity! thou pleasing, dreadful
      thought!   *Ibid. Act V, Sc. 1*

[a] Sweet are the slumbers of the
      virtuous man.   *Ibid. Sc. 4*

[b] I shall endeavour to enliven
morality with wit, and to temper
wit with morality.
      *The Spectator, No. 10,
      March 11, 1711*

[c] True happiness is of a retired
nature, and an enemy to pomp
and noise; it arises, in the first
place, from the enjoyment of
one's self; and, in the next, from
the friendship and conversation
of a few select companions.
      Ibid. No. 15, March 17, 1711

[d] A man that has a taste of
musick, painting, or architecture,
is like one that has another sense,
when compared with such as have
no relish of those arts.
      Ibid. No. 93, June 16, 1711

[e] Of all the diversions of life,
there is none so proper to fill up
its empty spaces as the reading of
useful and entertaining authors
      Ibid

[f] There is not so variable thing
in nature as a lady's head-dress.
      Ibid. No. 98, June 21, 1711

[g] There is no defence against reproach but obscurity.
Ibid. No. 101, June 26, 1711

[h] Authors have established it as a kind of rule, that a man ought to be dull sometimes; as the most severe reader makes allowances for many rests and nodding-places in a voluminous writer.
Ibid. No. 124, July 23, 1711

[i] Books are the legacies that a great genius leaves to mankind, which are delivered down from generation to generation, as presents to the posterity of those who are yet unborn.
Ibid. No. 166, September 10, 1711

[j] Good-nature is more agreeable in conversation than wit, and gives a certain air to the countenance which is more amiable than beauty.
Ibid. No. 169, September 13, 1711

[k] Were I to prescribe a rule for drinking, it should be formed upon a saying quoted by Sir William Temple: the first glass for myself, the second for my friends, the third for good humour, and the fourth for mine enemies.
Ibid. No. 195, October 13, 1711

[l] I consider an human soul without education like marble in the quarry, which shows none of its inherent beauties till the skill of the polisher fetches out the colours, makes the surface shine, and discovers every ornamental cloud, spot and vein that runs through the body of it.
Ibid. No. 215, November 6, 1711

[m] Death only closes a man's reputation, and determines it as good or bad.
Ibid. No. 349, April 10, 1712

[n] Mirth is like a flash of lightning, that breaks through a gloom of clouds, and glitters for a moment; cheerfulness keeps up a kind of daylight in the mind, and fills it with a steady and perpetual serenity.
Ibid. No. 381, May 17, 1712

[o] Sir Roger made several reflections on the greatness of the British Nation; as, that one Englishman could beat three Frenchmen; . . . with many other honest prejudices which naturally cleave to the heart of a true Englishman.
Ibid. No. 383, May 20, 1712

[p] The Fraternity of the Henpeck'd.
Ibid. No. 482, September 12, 1712

[q] A man should always consider how much he has more than he wants and how much more

unhappy he might be than he really is.
Ibid. No. 574, July 30, 1714

[r] We are always doing something for Posterity, but I would fain see Posterity do something for us.
Ibid. No. 574, July 30, 1714

George Ade
[1866–1944]

[s] Last night at twelve I felt immense,
But now I feel like thirty cents. . . .
But, R-E-M-O-R-S-E!
The water-wagon is the place for me;
It is no time for mirth and laughter,
The cold, gray dawn of the morning after!
The Sultan of Sulu. Remorse

[t] A good folly is worth what you pay for it.   *Fables in Slang.*
A Lot for Three Dollars

[u] Only the more rugged mortals should attempt to keep up with current literature.
Ibid. Didn't Care for Story-books

[v] Never put off until To-morrow what should have been Done early in the Seventies.
Forty Modern Fables. The Third and Last Call

[w] If it were not for the Presents, an Elopement would be Preferable.   *Ibid. The General Manager of the Love Affair*

[x] The Time to enjoy a European trip is about Three Weeks after Unpacking.
Ibid. The Hungry Man

[y] Draw your Salary before Spending it.
Ibid. The People's Choice

[z] For Parlor Use the Vague Generality is a Life-Saver.
Ibid. The Wise Piker

"AE"
see George W. Russell

Aeschylus
[525–456 B.C.]

[a] "Honor thy father and thy mother" stands written among the three laws of most revered righteousness.   *Suppliants (tr. Morris Hickey Morgan). Nauck's Edition, No. 707*

[b] Words are the physicians of a mind diseased.   *Prometheus (tr. Morris Hickey Morgan). Nauck's Edition, No. 378*

[c] Too lightly opened are a woman's ears;

Her fence downtrod by many trespassers. *Agamemnon (tr. Sir Gilbert Murray). Line 486*

[d] I think the slain
Care little if they sleep or rise again;
And we, the living, wherefore should we ache
With counting all our lost ones?
Ibid. Line 595

[e] Sweet is a grief well ended.
Ibid. Line 805

[f] For not many men, the proverb saith,
Can love a friend whom fortune prospereth
Unenvying. *Ibid. Line 832*

[g] Him who pitieth suffering men
Zeus pitieth, and his ways are sweet on earth.
The Eumenides (tr. Sir Gilbert Murray). Line 91

[h] Pleasantest
Of all ties is the tie of host and guest. *The Choëphoroe (tr. Sir Gilbert Murray). Line 699*

[i] O Death the Healer, scorn thou not, I pray,
To come to me: of cureless ills thou art
The one physician. Pain lays not its touch
Upon a corpse.
Fragment 250 (tr. Plumptre)

[j] Bronze is the mirror of the form; wine, of the heart.
Fragment 384

[k] It is not the oath that makes us believe the man, but the man the oath.
Fragment 385

Aesop
[*Floruit* 550 B.C.]

[l] Any excuse will serve a tyrant.
The Wolf and the Lamb

[m] Beware lest you lose the substance by grasping at the shadow.
The Dog and the Shadow

[n] You may share the labors of the great, but you will not share the spoil. *The Lion's Share*

[o] Better beans and bacon in peace than cakes and ale in fear.
The Town Mouse and the Country Mouse

[p] Little friends may prove great friends.
The Lion and the Mouse

[q] Better no rule than cruel rule.
The Frogs Desiring a King

[r] A huge gap appeared in the side of the mountains. At last a tiny mouse poked its little head out of the gap.
Much outcry, little outcome.
The Mountains in Labor

[s] There is always someone worse off than yourself.
The Hares and the Frogs

[t] It is easy to be brave from a safe distance.
The Wolf and the Kid

[u] Outside show is a poor substitute for inner worth.
The Fox and the Mask

[v] It is not only fine feathers that make fine birds.
The Jay and the Peacock

[w] Gratitude is the sign of noble souls. *Androcles*

[x] They found that even the Belly, in its dull quiet way, was doing necessary work for the Body, and that all must work together or the Body will go to pieces.
The Belly and the Members

[y] I am sure the grapes are sour. . . .
It is easy to despise what you cannot get.
The Fox and the Grapes

[z] Familiarity breeds contempt.
The Fox and the Lion

[a] The little Reed, bending to the force of the wind, soon stood upright again when the storm had passed over. . . .
Obscurity often brings safety.
The Tree and the Reed

[b] Appearances are deceptive.
The Wolf in Sheep's Clothing

[c] The boy called out "Wolf, Wolf!" and the villagers came out to help him. A few days afterward he tried the same trick, and again they came to his help. Shortly after this a Wolf actually came, but this time the villagers thought the boy was deceiving them again and nobody came to his help. . . .
A liar will not be believed, even when he speaks the truth.
The Shepherd's Boy

[d'] Example is the best precept.
The Two Crabs

[e'] Never trust a friend who deserts you at a pinch.
The Two Fellows and the Bear

[f'] United we stand, divided we fall.
The Four Oxen and the Lion

[g'] A little thing in hand is worth more than a great thing in prospect.
The Fisher and the Little Fish

[h'] I will have nought to do with a man who can blow hot and cold with the same breath.
The Man and the Satyr

[i'] Put your shoulder to the wheel.
Hercules and the Waggoner

[j] The gods help them that help
themselves.   *Ibid.*

[k] Please all, and you will please
none.   *The Man, the Boy, and
the Donkey*

[l] Who is to bell the Cat? It is
easy to propose impossible remedies.   *Belling the Cat*

[m] Plodding wins the race.
The Hare and the Tortoise

[n] The haft of the arrow had
been feathered with one of the
eagle's own plumes. We often give
our enemies the means of our own
destruction.
The Eagle and the Arrow

[o] Do not count your chickens
before they are hatched.
The Milkmaid and Her Pail

[p] Never trust the advice of a
man in difficulties.
The Fox and the Goat

Charles Hamilton Aïdé
[1830–1906]

[q] I sit beside my lonely fire
And pray for wisdom yet:
For calmness to remember
Or courage to forget.
Remember or Forget

[r] When we are parted, let me
lie
In some far corner of thy heart,
Silent, and from the world
apart,
Like a forgotten melody.
When We Are Parted

Conrad Aiken
[1889–   ]

[s] Music I heard with you was
more than music,
And bread I broke with you was
more than bread.   *Music I
Heard with You. Stanza 1*

[t] I arise, I face the sunrise,
And do the things my fathers
learned to do.
Stars in the purple dusk above
the rooftops
Pale in a saffron mist and seem to
die,
And I myself on a swiftly tilting
planet
Stand before a glass and tie my
tie.   *Senlin. Morning Song*

[u] Rock meeting rock can know
love better
Than eyes that stare or lips that
touch.
All that we know in love is bitter,
And it is not much.
Annihilation. Stanza 8

[v] How shall we praise the mag-
nificence of the dead,

The great man humbled, the
haughty brought to dust?
Is there a horn we should not
blow as proudly
For the meanest of us all, who
creeps his days,
Guarding his heart from blows,
to die obscurely?   *Tetélestai*

[w] All lovely things will have an
ending,
All lovely things will fade and
die,
And youth, that's now so bravely
spending,
Will beg a penny by and by.
*All Lovely Things Will Have
an Ending*

[x] Ice is the silent language of
the peak;
and fire the silent language of the
star.   *And in the Human
Heart. Sonnet X*

[y] For brief as water falling will
be death,
and brief as flower falling, or a
leaf,
brief as the taking, and the giving, breath;
thus natural, thus brief, my love,
is grief.   *Ibid. Sonnet XVIII*

[z] So, in the morning, when the
east is strung
with the bright harp-strings of
another day:
against whose glistening golden
cords are sung
all things that birds can sing or
words can say:
like a great page of music,
whereto leaning
even the dark trees with their
cordage sing.
Ibid. Sonnet XXIII

John Aikin
[1747–1822]

[a] And what is a conqueror?
Have not you, too, gone about the
earth like an evil genius, blasting
the fair fruits of peace and industry; plundering, ravaging, killing,
without law, without justice,
merely to gratify an insatiable
lust for dominion? All that I have
done to a single district with a
hundred followers, you have done
to whole nations with a hundred
thousand. If I have stripped individuals, you have ruined kings
and princes. If I have burned a
few hamlets, you have desolated
the most flourishing kingdoms
and cities of the earth. What is,
then, the difference, but that as
you were born a king and I a private man, you have been able to
become a mightier robber than I?
*Alexander the Great and a
Thracian Robber*

Zoë Akins
[1886-   ]

[b] So much do I love wandering,
So much I love the sea and sky,
That it will be a piteous thing
In one small grave to lie.
The Wanderer. Stanza 2

[c] Nothing seems so tragic to
one who is old as the death of one
who is young, and this alone
proves that life is a good thing.
The Portrait of Tiero

Alcaeus
[611-580 B.C.]

*Translation by J. M. Edmonds.
Loeb Classical Library, Lyra
Graeca, Vol. 1*

[d] Not houses finely roofed or
the stones of walls well-builded,
nay nor canals and dockyards,
make the city, but men able to use
their opportunity.
Aristides: Rhodian Oration

[e] 'Tis said that wrath is the
last thing in a man to grow old.
Scholiast on Sophocles

[f] One that hath wine as a chain
about his wits, such an one lives
no life at all.
Demetrius: On Poems.

Amos Bronson Alcott
[1799-1888]

[g] The true teacher defends his
pupils against his own personal
influence. He inspires self-dis-
trust. He guides their eyes from
himself to the spirit that quickens
him. He will have no disciple.
Orphic Sayings. The Teacher

[h] Who loves a garden still his
Eden keeps,
Perennial pleasures plants, and
wholesome harvests reaps.
Tablets. Page 6

Louisa May Alcott
[1832-1888]

[i] I had a pleasant time with
my mind, for it was happy.   *Life,
Letters and Journals, Chap. 3*

[j] Resolved to take Fate by the
throat and shake a living out of
her.   *Ibid. Chap. 5*

[k] Life is my college. May I
graduate well, and earn some
honors!   *Ibid.*

[l] Above man's aims his nature
rose.
The wisdom of a just content
Made one small spot a continent,
And tuned to poetry Life's prose.
*Ibid. Chap. 7, Thoreau's Flute
[Atlantic Monthly, September
1863], Stanza 2*

[m] To smooth the rough and
thorny way
Where other feet begin to tread;
To feed some hungry soul each
day
With sympathy's sustaining
bread.   *Ibid. Chap. 11, My
Prayer, Stanza 4*

[n] Now I am beginning to live
a little, and feel less like a sick
oyster at low tide.
Ibid. Chap. 11

[o] Death, the stern sculptor,
with a touch
No earthly power can stay,
Changes to marble in an hour
The beautiful, pale clay.
Our Madonna. Stanza 6

[p] Philosophers sit in their syl-
van hall
And talk of the duties of man,
Of Chaos and Cosmos, Hegel and
Kant,
With the Oversoul well in the van;
All on their hobbies they amble
away
And a terrible dust they make;
Disciples devout both gaze and
adore,
As daily they listen and bake.
Philosophers

Richard Aldington
[1892-   ]

[q] The moon,
With a rag of gauze about her
loins.   *Evening*

Dorothy Keeley Aldis
[1897-   ]

[r] Why, when I was told the
news,
I felt wings upon my shoes
And gallivanted down the street
Wanting to be indiscreet
And shout to all the world that I
Was about to multiply.
Maternity

Henry Aldrich
[1647-1710]

[s] If all be true that I do think,
There are five reasons we should
drink:
Good wine—a friend—or being
dry—
Or lest we should be by and by—
Or any other reason why.
*Five Reasons for Drinking.
From Causae Bibendi, by
John Sirmond [1589-1649]*

James Aldrich
[1810-1856]

[t] Her suffering ended with the
day,
Yet lived she at its close,

And breathed the long, long night
    away
In statue-like repose.

But when the sun in all his state
    Illumed the eastern skies,
She passed through Glory's morn-
    ing-gate,
And walked in Paradise.
    A Death-Bed. Stanzas 1 and 2

Thomas Bailey Aldrich
[1836–1907]

[u] So precious life is! Even to
    the old
    The hours are as a miser's coins!
        Broken Music. Stanza 4

[v] We knew it would rain, for
    the poplars showed
    The white of their leaves.
        Before the Rain. Stanza 3

[w] You do poets and their song
A grievous wrong,
If your own soul does not bring
To their high imagining
As much beauty as they sing.
        Appreciation. Stanza 2

[x] When were December and
    May known to be happy to-
    gether?   *Thalia. Stanza 4*

[y] Black Tragedy lets slip her
    grim disguise
And shows you laughing lips and
    roguish eyes;
But when, unmasked, gay Comedy
    appears,
How wan her cheeks are, and what
    heavy tears!   *Masks*

[z] Some weep because they part,
And languish broken-hearted,
And others—O my heart!—
Because they never parted.
        The Difference

[a] Sweet courtesy has done its
    most
If you have made each guest for-
    get
That he himself is not the host.
        Hospitality

[b] My mind lets go a thousand
    things,
Like dates of wars and deaths of
    kings.   *Memory*

[c] The folk who lived in Shake-
    speare's day
And saw that gentle figure pass
By London Bridge, his frequent
    way—
They little knew what man he
    was.
        Guilielmus Rex. Stanza 1

[d] They fail, and they alone,
    who have not striven.
    Enamored Architect of Airy
        Rhyme

[e] I vex me not with brooding
    on the years

That were ere I drew breath: why
    should I then
Distrust the darkness that may
    fall again
When life is done?
        I Vex Me Not

[f] What is more cheerful, now,
in the fall of the year, than an
open-woodfire? Do you hear those
little chirps and twitters coming
out of that piece of apple-wood?
Those are the ghosts of the robins
and blue-birds that sang upon the
bough when it was in blossom
last spring. In Summer whole
flocks of them come fluttering
about the fruit-trees under the
window: so I have singing birds
all the year round.
        Miss Mehitabel's Son

Joseph Addison Alexander
[1800–1860]

[g] There is a time, we know not
    when,
    A point we know not where,
That marks the destiny of men,
    For glory or despair.
        The Doomed Man. Stanza 1

[h] There is a line, by us unseen,
    That crosses every path;
The hidden boundary between
    God's patience and His wrath.
        Ibid. Stanza 2

Henry Alford
[1810–1871]

[i] Life is so short, so fast the
    lone hours fly,
We ought to be together, you and
    I.   *You and I. Stanza 4*

Ali Ben Abou Taleb
(Son-in-law of Mahomet)
[? –660]

[j] Believe me, a thousand
    friends suffice thee not;
In a single enemy thou hast more
    than enough.

Elizabeth Akers Allen
[1832–1911]

[k] Backward, turn backward, O
    Time, in your flight,
Make me a child again just for to-
    night!   *Rock Me to Sleep*
    [*Saturday Evening Post,*
    June 9, 1860]. *Stanza 1*

[l] How much the heart may
    bear, and yet not break!
How much the flesh may suffer
    and not die!

    Life inflicts its worst
On soul and body—but we can
    not die,

Though we be sick, and tired, and
faint, and worn,—
Lo, all things can be borne!
Endurance. Stanzas 1 and 5

[m] And all the pain of lonely
days,
And nights with sleepless sorrow
wild,
Hides in the quaint and stilted
phrase,
"An amiable child."
"An Amiable Child." Stanza 15
[*On the stone marking the grave
of St. Clair Pollock, near Grant's
Tomb, on Riverside Drive, New
York, is inscribed: "Erected to
the memory of an amiable child."
The boy died July 15, 1797, at the
age of five years.*]

[n] Carve not upon a stone when
I am dead
The praises which remorseful
mourners give
To women's graves—a tardy rec-
ompense—
But speak them while I live.
Till Death. Stanza 6

Hervey Allen
[1889–1949]

[o] Christ Jesus, when I come to
die
Grant me a clean, sweet, summer
sky,
Without the mad wind's panther
cry.
Send me a little garden breeze
To gossip in magnolia trees.
*The Priest and the Pirate:
A Ballad of Theodosia Burr.
Stanza 3*

[p] Grow up as soon as you can.
It pays. The only time you really
live fully is from thirty to sixty.
. . . The young are slaves to
dreams; the old servants of regrets. Only the middle-aged have
all their five senses in the keeping
of their wits.
Anthony Adverse. Chap. 31

[q] What is even a wise book but
a blast from the lungs made
visible to the eyes? *Ibid.*

James Lane Allen
[1849–1925]

[r] The finest music in the room
is that which streams out to the
ear of the spirit in many an exquisite strain from the little shelf
of books on the opposite wall.
Every volume there is an instrument which some melodist of the
mind created and set vibrating
with music.
A Kentucky Cardinal

[s] The birds are moulting. If
man could only moult also—his

mind once a year its errors, his
heart once a year its useless passions. *Ibid.*

[t] I have yet to encounter that
common myth of weak men, an
insurmountable barrier.
The Choir Invisible. Chap. 3

William Allen
[1806–1879]

[u] Fifty-four forty, or fight.
[*The challenge of Senator Allen
(of Ohio) became the slogan of
the expansionists who claimed for
the United States the region, now
Oregon, as far north as the south-
ern boundary of Alaska, latitude
54° 40'. It was the campaign cry
of James K. Polk, who was elected
President.*]

William Allingham
[1828–1889]

[v] Up the airy mountain,
Down the rushy glen,
We daren't go a-hunting
For fear of little men.
The Fairies. Stanza 1

[w] Robin's here in coat of
brown,
And scarlet breast-knot gay.
Robin Redbreast. Stanza 1

Alphonso the Learned
[1221–1284]

[x] Had I been present at the
creation, I would have given some
useful hints for the better order-
ing of the universe.

Henri-Frédéric Amiel
[1821–1881]

[y] Truth is the secret of eloquence and of virtue, the basis of
moral authority; it is the highest
summit of art and of life.
Journal

[z] Doing easily what others find
difficult is talent; doing what is
impossible for talent is genius.
Ibid.

[a] A man without passion is
only a latent force, only a possibility, like a stone waiting for the
blow from the iron to give forth
sparks. *Ibid.*

Harold MacDonald
Anderson
[1876–1940]

[b] Alone?
Is he alone at whose right side
rides Courage, with Skill within
the cockpit and Faith upon the
left? Does solitude surround the

brave when Adventure leads the
way and Ambition reads the dials?
Is there no company with him for
whom the air is cleft by Daring
and the darkness is made light by
Emprise? . . .
Alone? With what other companions would that man fly to
whom the choice were given?
*"Lindbergh Flies Alone," Edi-
torial, New York Sun, May 21,
1927 [Included by permission
of Mr. Anderson and The Sun]*

Persis Greely Anderson
[1901–1932]

[c] Behold the wicked little barb
Which catches fish in human garb
And yanks them back when they
feel gay
With "Will it last?" or "Does it
pay?"
The Question Mark. Stanza 1

Sherwood Anderson
[1876–1941]

[d] Everyone in the world is
Christ and they are all crucified.
Winesburg, Ohio. The Philosopher

[e] I am a lover and have not
found my thing to love.
Ibid. Tandy

Elmer Frank Andrews
[1890–   ]

[f] If a man has an office with a
desk on which there is a buzzer,
and if he can press that buzzer
and have somebody come dashing
in response—then he's an executive. *Address before the Trade
Association Executives' Forum
of Chicago [December 9, 1938]*

Sir Norman Angell
[1874–   ]

[g] The Great Illusion. *Title
of book on the futility of war*

[h] The power of words is such
that they have prevented our
learning some of the most important events in the world's history. *Let the People Know.
Chap. 7: Words That Are
Assassins*

Louis Kaufman Anspacher
[1878–1947]

[i] Marriage is that relation between man and woman in which
the independence is equal, the
dependence mutual, and the obligation reciprocal. *Address,
Boston [December 30, 1934]*

Mary Antin
[1881–1949]

[j] So at last I was going to
America! Really, really going, at
last! The boundaries burst. The
arch of heaven soared. A million
suns shone out for every star. The
winds rushed in from outer space,
roaring in my ears, "America!
America!" *The Promised Land*

Everard Jack Appleton
[1872–1931]

[k] Somewhere she waits to make
you win,
Your soul in her firm white
hands;
Somewhere the gods have made
for you
The woman who understands.
The Woman Who Understands

Aristophanes
[446–380 B.C.]

[l] He works and blows the coals
And has plenty of other irons in
the fire. *The Acharnians
(tr. B. B. Rogers)*

[m] Exalted ideas of fancy require
To be clothed in a suitable vesture
of phrase. *The Frogs (tr.
John Hookham Frere)*

[n] I laugh'd till I cried. *Ibid.*

[o] If we withdraw the confidence we placed
In these our present statesmen,
and transfer it
To those whom we mistrusted
heretofore,
This seems I think our fairest
chance for safety:
If with our present counsellors
we fail,
Then with their opposites we
might succeed. *Ibid.*

[p] Shame is the apprehension of
a vision
Reflected from the surface of
opinion—
The opinion of the public.
Ibid.

[q] Perhaps death is life, and life
is death,
And victuals and drink an illusion
of the senses;
For what is Death but an eternal
sleep?
And does not Life consist in sleeping and eating? *Ibid.*

[r] I commend the old proverb,
"For we must look about under
every stone, lest an orator bite
us." *The Trial of Euripides
(tr. William James Hickie)*

[s] Old age is but a second childhood. *The Clouds (tr. Thomas
Mitchell)*

[t] Throw fear to the wind.
The Wasps (tr. Richard Cumberland)

[u] O the days that are gone by,
O the days that are no more,
When my eye was bold and fearless, and my hand was on the oar. *Ibid.*

Aristotle
[384-322 B.C.]

[v] Poverty is the parent of revolution and crime. *Politics (tr. Benjamin Jowett). Book II*

[w] Even when laws have been written down, they ought not always to remain unaltered. *Ibid.*

[x] That judges of important causes should hold office for life is not a good thing, for the mind grows old as well as the body. *Ibid.*

[y] If liberty and equality, as is thought by some, are chiefly to be found in democracy, they will be best attained when all persons alike share in the government to the utmost. *Ibid. Book IV*

[z] Those States are likely to be well administered in which the middle class is large, and larger if possible than both the other classes, or at any rate than either singly; for the addition of the middle class turns the scale and prevents either of the extremes from being dominant. *Ibid.*

[a] Inferiors revolt in order that they may be equal, and equals that they may be superior. Such is the state of mind which creates revolutions. *Ibid. Book V*

[b] It is not enough to know about Virtue, then, but we must endeavor to possess it, and to use it, or to take any other steps that may make us good.
Nicomachean Ethics. X, 9, 1

[c] The generality of men are naturally apt to be swayed by fear rather than by reverence and to refrain from evil rather because of the punishment that it brings, than because of its own foulness. *Ibid.*

John Stanhope Arkwright
[1872-]

[d] O valiant Hearts, who to your glory came
Through dust of conflict and through battle-flame;
Tranquil you lie, your knightly virtue proved,

Your memory hallowed in the land you loved. *The Supreme Sacrifice. [Sung at the dedication of the Tomb of the Unknown Soldier, Washington, D.C., November 11, 1921]. Stanza 1*

"Peleg Arkwright"
see **David Law Proudfit**

Peter Arno
[1904-]

[e] I consider your conduct unethical and lousy.
Caption for cartoon

Sir Edwin Arnold
[1832-1904]

[f] And ye say, "Abdallah's dead!"
Weeping at the feet and head.
I can see your falling tears,
I can hear your sighs and prayers;
Yet I smile and whisper this:
I am not the thing you kiss.
Cease your tears and let it lie;
It was mine—it is not I.
After Death in Arabia

[g] Not a face below the sun
But is precious—unto one!
Not an eye, however dull,
But seems—somewhere—beautiful.
Facies non Omnibus Una

[h] God can't be always everywhere: and, so,
Invented Mothers.
Mothers. Stanza 6

[i] Somewhere there waiteth in this world of ours
For one lone soul, another lonely soul—
Each chasing each through all the weary hours,
And meeting strangely at one sudden goal;
Then blend they—like green leaves with golden flowers,
Into one beautiful and perfect whole—
And life's long night is ended, and the way
Lies open onward to eternal day.
Destiny

[j] Lo! as the wind is, so is mortal life,
A moan, a sigh, a sob, a storm, a strife. *The Deva's Song*

[k] The end of birth is death; the end of death is birth: this is ordained. *The Song Celestial (Translated from The Bhagavad-Gita)*

George Arnold
[1834-1865]

[l] "Learn while you're young," he often said,
"There is much to enjoy down here below;

Life for the living, and rest for
the dead!"
Said the jolly old pedagogue, long
ago.   *The Jolly Old*
       Pedagogue. Stanza 2
"The living need charity more
than the dead."
       Ibid. Stanza 3

[m] I,
Being dry,
Sit, idly sipping here
My Beer.   *Beer*

[n] O, finer far
Than fame, or riches, are
The graceful smoke-wreaths of
this free cigar!   *Ibid.*

Matthew Arnold
[1822–1888]

[o]   Be his
My special thanks, whose even-
balanced soul, . . .
Business could not make dull, nor
Passion wild:
Who saw life steadily and saw it
whole.
     Sonnet 2, To a Friend

[p]   The will is free:
Strong is the Soul, and wise, and
beautiful:
The seeds of godlike power are in
us still:
Gods are we, Bards, Saints,
Heroes, if we will.   *Sonnet
4, Written in Emerson's Essays*

[q] France, famed in all great
arts, in none supreme.
    *Sonnet 10, To a Republican
Friend, 1848*

[r] Strew on her roses, roses,
And never a spray of yew.
In quiet she reposes:
Ah! would that I did too.
     Requiescat. Stanza 1

[s] Tonight it doth inherit
The vasty Hall of Death.
     Ibid. Stanza 4

[t] Yet they, believe me, who
await
No gifts from Chance, have conquered Fate.   *Resignation*

[u] Resolve to be thyself: and
know, that he
Who finds himself, loses his misery.
     Self-Dependence. Stanza 8

[v] Calm Soul of all things! make
it mine
To feel, amid the city's jar,
That there abides a peace of thine,
Man did not make, and can not
mar.   *Lines Written in
Kensington Gardens. Stanza 10*

[w] So Tiberius might have sat,
Had Tiberius been a cat.
     Poor Matthias

[x] Ah, love, let us be true
To one another!   *Dover Beach*

[y] And we are here as on a
darkling plain
Swept with confused alarms of
struggle and flight,
Where ignorant armies clash by
night.   *Ibid.*

[z] The foot less prompt to meet
the morning dew,
The heart less bounding to emotion new,
And hope, once crush'd, less quick
to spring again.
     Thyrsis. Stanza 14

[a] We do not what we ought;
What we ought not, we do;
And lean upon the thought
That Chance will bring us
through.
     Empedocles on Etna

[b] Is it so small a thing
To have enjoy'd the sun,
To have lived light in the spring,
To have loved, to have thought, to
have done?   *Ibid.*

[c] With women the heart argues,
not the mind.   *Merope*

[d] This strange disease of modern life.   *The Scholar
     Gypsy. Stanza 21*

[e] Most men eddy about
Here and there—eat and drink,
Chatter and love and hate,
Gather and squander, are raised
Aloft, are hurl'd in the dust,
Striving blindly, achieving
Nothing; and then they die.
     Rugby Chapel

[f] Was Christ a man like us?
Oh, let us try
*If we then, too, can be such men
as he!*   *The Better Part*

[g] Spare me the whispering,
crowded room,
The friends who come and gape
and go,
The ceremonious air of gloom—
All, which makes death a hideous show.   *A Wish*

[h] Poetry is simply the most
beautiful, impressive and widely
effective mode of saying things,
and hence its importance.
     Essays. Heinrich Heine

[i] *Philistine* must have originally meant, in the mind of those
who invented the nickname, a
strong, dogged, unenlightened op-
ponent of the children of the
light.   *Ibid.*

[j] On the breast of that huge
Mississippi of falsehood called
history, a foam-bell more or less
is of no consequence.   *Ibid.*
   Literary Influence of Academies

[k] The pursuit of the perfect,
then, is the pursuit of sweetness
and light.
     Ibid. Culture and Anarchy

[1] Whispering from her towers the last enchantments of the Middle Age . . . home of lost causes, and forsaken beliefs, and unpopular names, and impossible loyalties! *Essays in Criticism. Oxford*

Joseph Ashby-Sterry
[1838–1917]

[m] When the glass is at ninety
  a man is a fool
Who directs not his efforts to try
  to keep cool.
        Ninety in the Shade

[n] The ruddy ripe tomata
  In china bowl of ice,
And grouse worth a sonata
  Undoubtedly are nice.
        The Riparian Philosopher

[o] It's much too hot for reason,
  And far too warm for rhyme.
        Ibid.

[p] There are people, I'm told—
  some say there are heaps—
Who speak of the talkative Sam-
  uel as Peeps;
And some so precise and pedantic
  their step is,
Who call the delightful old diarist
  Pepys;
But those I think right, and I
  follow their steps,
Ever mention the garrulous gossip
  as Pepys. *Pepys*

Athenaeus
[*Circa* A.D. 200]
Translation by Charles Duke Yonge

[q] It was a saying of Demetrius Phalereus, that "Men having often abandoned what was visible for the sake of what was uncertain, have not got what they expected, and have lost what they had,—being unfortunate by an enigmatical sort of calamity."
        The Deipnosophists. VI, 23

[r] Every investigation which is guided by principles of Nature fixes its ultimate aim entirely on gratifying the stomach.
        Ibid. VII, 11

Gertrude Franklin Atherton
[1857–1948]

[s] Women love the lie that saves their pride, but never an unflattering truth. *The Conqueror. Book III, Chap. 6*

[t] The perfect friendship of two men is the deepest and highest sentiment of which the finite mind is capable; women miss the best in life. *Ibid. Chap. 12*

[u] No matter how hard a man may labour, some woman is always in the background of his mind. She is the one reward of virtue. *Ibid. Book IV, Chap. 3*

Roy Atwell
[1880–   ]

[v] In these days of indigestion
It is oftentimes a question
As to what to eat and what to
  leave alone;
For each microbe and bacillus
Has a different way to kill us,
And in time they always claim us
  for their own.

Some little bug is going to find
  you some day,
Some little bug will creep behind
  you some day. *Some Little Bug Is Going to Find You Some Day. Stanzas 1 and 3*

John Aubrey
[1626–1697]
From the Brief Lives, edited by Andrew Clark

[w] He [Thomas Hobbes] walked much and contemplated, and he had in the head of his staffe a pen and ink-horne, carried alwayes a note-booke in his pocket, and as soon as a thought darted, he presently entred it into his booke, or otherwise he might perhaps have lost it. *I, 334*

[x] He had read much, but his contemplation was much more than his reading. He was wont to say that if he had read as much as other men, he should have knowne no more than other men. *Ibid. 349*

Wystan Hugh Auden
[1907–   ]

[y] A host of columbines and pathics
Who show the poor by mathematics
    In their defence
That wealth and poverty are merely
Mental pictures, so that clearly
Every tramp's a landlord really
    In mind-events
Let fever sweat them till they tremble
Cramp rack their limbs till they resemble
    Cartoons by Goya:
Their daughters sterile be in rut,
May cancer rot their herring gut,
The circular madness on them shut,
    Or paranoia.
        On This Island. XIV

[z] Cathedrals,
Luxury liners laden with souls,
Holding to the east their hulls of
stone.   *Ibid. XVII*

[a] The poet reciting to Lady
Diana
While the footmen whisper 'Have
a banana,'
The judge enforcing the obsolete
law,
The banker making the loan for
the war,
The expert designing the long-
range gun
To exterminate everyone under
the sun,
Would like to get out but can only
mutter:—
'What can I do? It's my bread and
butter.'   *Ibid. XVIII*

[b] In the nightmare of the dark
All the dogs of Europe bark,
And the living nations wait,
Each sequestered in its hate.
In Memory of W. B. Yeats [1939]

[c] And the seas of pity lie
Locked and frozen in each eye.
Ibid.

[d] Master of nuance and scruple,
Pray for me and for all writers
living or dead;
Because there are many whose
works
Are in better taste than their
lives, because there is no end
To the vanity of our calling.
*At the Grave of Henry James.
Stanza 27*

St. Augustine
[A.D. 354–430]

[e] When I am here, I do not fast
on Saturday; when at Rome, I do
fast on Saturday.
Epistle 36, To Casulanus

[f] The spiritual virtue of a
sacrament is like light,—although
it passes among the impure, it is
not polluted.   *Tract on St.
John. Chap. 5, 15*

Joseph Auslander
[1897–   ]

[g] This man is dead.
Everything you can say
Is now quite definitely said:
This man held up his head
And had his day,
Then turned his head a little to
one way
And slept instead.   *Steel*

[h]   Spring had come
Like the silver needle-note of a
fife,
Like a white plume and a green
lance and a glittering knife
And a jubilant drum.   *Ibid.*

[i] Three things filled this day
for me,

Three common things filled this
day;
Each had, for me, a word to say;
Said it in beauty, and was done:
Cows on a hillside all one way,
A buttercup tilted seductively,
And a lark arguing with the sun.
Three Things. Stanza 1

Jane Austen
[1775–1817]

[j] Everything nourishes what is
strong already.
Pride and Prejudice. Chap. 9

[k] Those who do not complain
are never pitied.   *Ibid. Chap. 20*

[l] What dreadful hot weather we
have! It keeps me in a continual
state of inelegance.
*Letters to her sister Cassandra.
September 18, 1796*

[m] I do not want people to be
very agreeable, as it saves me the
trouble of liking them a great
deal.   *Ibid. December 24, 1798*

[n] "Only a novel" . . . in short,
only some work in which the
greatest powers of the mind are
displayed, in which the most
thorough knowledge of human
nature, the happiest delineation
of its varieties, are conveyed to
the world in the best chosen language.
Northanger Abbey. Chap. 5

Alfred Austin
[1835–1913]

[o] So long as Faith with Free-
dom reigns,
And loyal Hope survives,
And gracious Charity remains
To leaven lowly lives;
While there is one untrodden
tract
For intellect or will,
And men are free to think and act,
Life is worth living still.
Is Life Worth Living?

[p] Why should we lodge in
marble or in bronze
Spirits more vast than earth, or
sea, or sky?
Wiser the silent worshiper who
cons
Their page for Wisdom that will
never die. . . .
Gods for themselves are monu-
ments enough.   *On the
Proposal to Erect a Statue to
Shakespeare in London*

Henry Willard Austin
[1858–1912]

[q] Genius, that power which
dazzles mortal eyes,
Is oft but perseverance in disguise.
Perseverance Conquers All

Mary Hunter Austin
[1868–1934]

[r] What need has he of clocks
    who knows
When highest peaks are gilt and
    rose
Day has begun?
    Clocks and Calendars. Stanza 1

[s] Whisper of the wind along the
    sage,
Only wait till I can get the word—
Never was it printed in a page,
Never was it spoken, never heard.
    Whisper of the Wind

William Edmondstoune Aytoun
[1813–1865]

[t] News of battle!—news of
    battle!
Hark! 'tis ringing down the
    street;
And the archways and the pave-
    ment
Bear the clang of hurrying feet.
Edinburgh after Flodden. Stanza 1

Maltbie Davenport Babcock
[1858–1901]

[u] Back of the loaf is the snowy
    flour,
And back of the flour the mill,
And back of the mill is the wheat
    and the shower,
And the sun and the Father's
    will.   *"Give Us This Day
        Our Daily Bread"*

Bertha Adams Backus
[*Floruit* 1911]

[v] Build for yourself a strong-
    box,
Fashion each part with care;
When it's strong as your hand can
    make it,
Put all your troubles there;
Hide there all thought of your
    failures,
And each bitter cup that you
    quaff;
Lock all your heartaches within it,
Then sit on the lid and laugh.
    *Then Laugh [Munsey's Maga-
    zine, February 1911]. Stanza 1*

Francis Bacon
[1561–1626]

[w] I hold every man a debtor to
his profession; from the which as
men of course do seek to receive
countenance and profit, so ought
they of duty to endeavour themselves by way of amends to be a
help and ornament thereunto.
    Maxims of the Law. Preface

[x] No pleasure is comparable to
the standing upon the vantage-
ground of truth.   *Of Truth*

[y] Men fear death as children
fear to go in the dark; and as that
natural fear in children is increased with tales, so is the other
    Of Death

[z] Revenge is a kind of wild justice, which the more man's nature
runs to, the more ought law to
weed it out.   *Of Revenge*

[a] Prosperity is not without
many fears and distastes; and adversity is not without comforts
and hopes.   *Of Adversity*

[b] He that hath wife and children hath given hostages to fortune; for they are impediments to
great enterprises, either of virtue
or mischief.
    Of Marriage and Single Life

[c] Wives are young men's mis-
tresses, companions for middle
age, and old men's nurses.
    Ibid.

[d] A good name is like a precious
ointment; it filleth all around
about; and will not easily away;
for the odors of ointments are
more durable than those of flowers.   *Of Praise*

[e] Mahomet made the people believe that he would call a hill to
him, . . . The people assembled.
Mahomet called the hill to come
to him, again and again; and
when the hill stood still he was
never a whit abashed, but said,
"If the hill will not come to Mahomet, Mahomet will go to the
hill."   *Of Boldness*

[f] The desire of power in excess
caused the angels to fall; the desire of knowledge in excess caused
man to fall.   *Of Goodness*

[g] A little philosophy inclineth
man's mind to atheism, but depth
in philosophy bringeth men's
minds about to religion.
    Of Atheism

[h] Fortune is like the market,
where many times, if you can stay
a little, the price will fall.
    Of Delays

[i] There is a cunning which we
in England call "the turning of
the cat in the pan"; which is,
when that which a man says to
another, he lays it as if another
had said it to him.   *Of Cunning*

[j] There is a wisdom in this beyond the rules of physic. A man's
own observation, what he finds
good of and what he finds hurt of,
is the best physic to preserve
health.   *Of Regimen of Health*

[k] Discretion of speech is more than eloquence; and to speak agreeably to him with whom we deal is more than to speak in good words or in good order.
Of Discourse

[l] If a man look sharply and attentively, he shall see Fortune; for though she is blind, she is not invisible.   *Of Fortune*

[m] Young men are fitter to invent than to judge, fitter for execution than for counsel, and fitter for new projects than for settled business.
Of Youth and Age

[n] Virtue is like a rich stone,—best plain set.   *Of Beauty*

[o] There is no excellent beauty that hath not some strangeness in the proportion.   *Ibid.*

[p] God Almighty first planted a garden.   *Of Gardens*

[q] Some books are to be tasted, others to be swallowed, and some few to be chewed and digested.
Of Studies

[r] Reading maketh a full man, conference a ready man, and writing an exact man.   *Ibid.*

[s] Books must follow sciences, and not sciences books.
Proposition touching Amendment of Laws

[t] Knowledge is power.   *Meditationes Sacræ, De Hæresibus*

[u] Cleanness of body was ever deemed to proceed from a due reverence to God.
Advancement of Learning

[v] States as great engines move slowly.   *Ibid.*

[w] The world's a bubble, and the life of man
Less than a span.   *The World*

[x] Who then to frail mortality shall trust
But limns on water, or but writes in dust.   *Ibid.*

[y] My Lord St. Albans said that Nature did never put her precious jewels into a garret four stories high, and therefore that exceeding tall men had ever very empty heads.   *Apothegms. No. 17*

[z] Sir Henry Wotton used to say that critics are like brushers of noblemen's clothes.
Ibid. No. 64

[a] Age appears to be best in four things,—old wood best to burn, old wine to drink, old friends to trust, and old authors to read.   *Ibid. No. 97*

[b] Pyrrhus, when his friends congratulated to him his victory over the Romans under Fabricius, but with great slaughter of his own side, said to them, "Yes; but if we have such another victory, we are undone." [Hence, a "Pyrrhic victory."]   *Ibid. No. 193*

[c] Cosmus, Duke of Florence, was wont to say of perfidious friends, that "We read that we ought to forgive our enemies; but we do not read that we ought to forgive our friends."   *Ibid. No. 206*

[d] I bequeath my soul to God. . . . My body to be buried obscurely. For my name and memory, I leave it to men's charitable speeches, and to foreign nations, and the next age.   *From his Will*

Leonard Bacon
[1887–   ]

[e] Technique! The very word is like the shriek
Of outraged Art. It is the idiot name
Given to effort by those who are too weak,
Too weary, or too dull to play the game.
The mighty have no theory of technique.
Ph.D's. Sophia Trenton

[f] Interpreting the simplest symbol wrong,
Missing the gold and treasuring the tin,
Dwelling upon the trivial so long.
Ibid.

[g] Those who dwell upon ivory towers
Have heads of the same materials.
Tower of Ivory

[h] Go forth, my book, and take whatever pounding
The heavy-fisted destinies prepare.
I know you are not anything astounding,
And, to be quite sincere, I don't much care.
Ulug Beg. Introduction

Philip James Bailey
[1816 1902]

[i] Let each man think himself an act of God.
His mind a thought, his life a breath of God;
And let each try, by great thoughts and good deeds,
To show the most of Heaven he hath in him.   *Festus. Proem*

[j] Evil and good are God's right hand and left.   *Ibid.*

[k'] Art is man's nature; nature is God's art.   *Ibid.*

[l'] Men might be better if we better deemed

Of them. The worst way to improve the world
Is to condemn it.
Ibid. A Mountain, Sunrise

[m] The first and worst of all frauds is to cheat
Oneself.   *Ibid. Anywhere*

[n] Who never doubted never half believed.
Where doubt there truth is—'tis her shadow.
Ibid. A Country Town

[o] Envy's a coal comes hissing hot from hell.   *Ibid.*

[p] The sole equality on earth is death.   *Ibid.*

[q] America, half-brother of the world!
With something good and bad of every land. *Ibid. The Surface*

[r] Worthy books
Are not companions—they are solitudes:
We lose ourselves in them and all our cares.
Ibid. A Village Feast

[s] Respect is what we owe; love, what we give.   *Ibid.*

[t] The worst men often give the best advice.   *Ibid.*

[u] Poets are all who love, who feel great truths,
And tell them; and the truth of truths is love. *Ibid. Another and a Better World*

[v] There is no disappointment we endure
One half so great as that we are to ourselves. *Ibid. The Sun*

[w] It is folly to tell women truth!
They would rather live on lies, so they be sweet.   *The Devil's Advice on Love-Making*

Joanna Baillie
[1762–1851]

[x] Oh, swiftly glides the bonnie boat,
Just parted from the shore,
And to the fisher's chorus-note
Soft moves the dipping oar.
Oh, Swiftly Glides the Bonnie Boat

[y] Oh, who shall lightly say that fame
Is nothing but an empty name,
When but for those, our mighty dead,
All ages past a blank would be.
The Worth of Fame. Stanza 2

Bruce Bairnsfather
[1887–   ]

[z] If you know a better 'ole, go to it. *Caption of famous cartoon during the first World War*

Karle Wilson
(Mrs. Thomas Ellis) Baker
[1878–   ]

[a] Brother, the creed would stifle me
That shelters you.
Creeds. Stanza 2

[b] Let me grow lovely, growing old—
So many fine things do:
Laces, and ivory, and gold,
And silks need not be new.
Old Lace: Let Me Grow Lovely

[c] To-day I have grown taller from walking with the trees.
Good Company

[d] I love the friendly faces of old sorrows;
I have no secrets that they do not know.
I Love the Friendly Faces. Stanza 1

Faith Baldwin
[1893–   ]

[e] I think that Life has spared those mortals much—
And cheated them of more—who have not kept
A breathless vigil by the little bed
Of some beloved child.   *Vigil*

Arthur James Balfour
[1848–1930]

[f] Biography should be written by an acute enemy.
Quoted by S. K. Ratcliffe in The London Observer, January 30, 1927

Honoré de Balzac
[1799–1850]

[g] Manufacturing industry depends solely on itself, competition is its life. Protect it, and it goes to sleep; it dies from monopoly as well as from the tariff. The nation that succeeds in making all other nations its vassals will be the one which first proclaims commercial liberty; it will have enough manufacturing power to supply its productions at a cheaper price than those of its rivals.   *The Country Doctor (tr. Katherine Prescott Wormeley). Chap. 1*

[h] I believe in the incomprehensibility of God.
Letter to Madame de Hanska [1837]

John Kendrick Bangs
[1862–1922]

[i] Be sure to keep a mirror always nigh
In some convenient, handy sort of place,

And now and then look squarely
in thine eye,
And with thyself keep ever face
to face.
    Face to Face. Stanza 1

[j] I think mankind by the
would be less bored
If only thou wert not thine own
reward.   *A Hint to Virtue*

[k] I have no dog, but it must be
Somewhere there's one belongs to
me—
A little chap with wagging tail,
And dark brown eyes that never
quail.   *My Dog. Stanza 1*

[l] I love to watch the rooster
crow,
He's like so many men I know
Who brag and bluster, rant and
shout
And beat their manly breasts,
without
The first damn thing to crow
about.   *The Rooster*

[m] To dig and delve in nice
clean dirt
Can do a mortal little hurt.
    Gardening

[n] "I'm just as big for me," said
he,
"As you are big for you!"
   The Little Elfman. Stanza 2

Kendall Banning
[1879–1944]

[o] The world has but one song
to sing,
And it is ever new;
The first and last of all the songs,
For it is ever true;
A little song, a tender song,
The only song it hath:
"There was a youth of Ascalon
Who loved a girl of Gath."
    Once on a Time. Stanza 2

Ewald Hermann Auguste Banse
[1883–]

[p] The English, once they have
adopted an objective, never let it
out of sight for a moment, and
use absolutely any means of getting to it without the slightest
compunction
Germany Prepares for War [1934]

[q] The psychological error lay
in our conception of the American
as a self-important boaster, a
shoddy manufacturer of shoddy
goods and an unscrupulous over-
reacher in business, whose word
could not be trusted. Such Americans there certainly were, but
there is the other type of American, who is conspicuously efficient
in all industrial and technical
undertakings, the American who

builds the highest houses, produces most motor-cars, attains
record economic output, who built
the Panama Canal and whose
spirit of enterprise knows no
bounds.   *Ibid.*

[r] The Russians are only for-
midable when they retire into
their own geographical and psychological interior.   *Ibid.*

Bertrand Barère
[1755–1841]

[s] The tree of liberty only grows
when watered by the blood of
tyrants.   *Speech in the French
National Convention* [1792]

Richard Harris Barham
[1788–1845]

[t] Right as a trivet.
    *Ingoldsby Legends.
Auto-da-fè*

[u] The Cardinal rose with a dig-
nified look,
He call'd for his candle, his bell,
and his book!
In holy anger, and pious grief,
He solemnly cursed that rascally
thief!
He cursed him at board, he
cursed him in bed;
From the sole of his foot to the
crown of his head;
He cursed him in sleeping, that
every night
He should dream of the devil,
and wake in a fright;
He cursed him in living, he
cursed him in drinking, he
He cursed him in coughing, in
sneezing, in winking;
He cursed him in sitting, in
standing, in lying;
He cursed him in walking, in
riding, in flying,
He cursed him in living, he
cursed him dying!—
Never was heard such a terrible
curse! But what gave rise to
no little surprise,
Nobody seem'd one penny the
worse!
    The Jackdaw of Rheims

Maurice Baring
[1874–1945]

[v] I do not need you changed,
dissolved in air,
Nor rarefied,
I need you all imperfect, as you
were.   *For His Dead Nephew*

[w] All theories of what a good
play is, or how a good play should
be written, are futile. A good play
is a play which when acted upon
the boards makes an audience

interested and pleased. A play that
fails in this is a bad play.
Have You Anything to Declare?

Sabine Baring-Gould
[1834–1924]

[x] Crowns and thrones may
    perish,
Kingdoms rise and wane,
But the church of Jesus
Constant will remain.
Onward, Christian Soldiers

[y] Now the day is over,
Night is drawing nigh;
Shadows of the evening
Steal across the sky.
Now the Day Is Over. Stanza 1

David Barker
[1816–1874]

[z] One night, as old St. Peter
    slept,
He left the door of Heaven ajar,
When through, a little angel crept,
And came down with a falling
    star.
My Child's Origin. Stanza 1

George Barker
[1913–   ]

[a] What is it all but a Wool-
    worth welter of things?
Seven Munich Elegies. 5

[b] Life is torpedoed and like a
    Titanic goes under
Threshing her ensigns
Against the dreadnought seas of
    blood and thunder
That flood our visions.   *Ibid. 6*

[c] Most near, most dear, most
    loved and most far,
Under the window where I often
    found her
Sitting as huge as Asia, seismic
    with laughter,
Gin and chicken helpless in her
    Irish hand,
Irresistible as Rabelais but most
    tender for
The lame dogs and hurt birds that
    surround her,—
She is a procession no one can fol-
    low after
But be like a little dog following
    a brass band.   *To My Mother*

Charlotte Alington Barnard ("Claribel")
[1830–1869]

[d] I cannot sing the old songs I
    sang long years ago,
For heart and voice would fail me,
    and foolish tears would flow.
I Cannot Sing the Old Songs

[e] Take back the heart that thou
gavest,

What is my anguish to thee?
Take back the freedom thou
    cravest,
Leaving the fetters to me.
Take Back the Heart

Richard Barnfield
[1574–1627]

[f] Every one that flatters thee
Is no friend in misery.
Words are easy, like the wind;
Faithful friends are hard to find.
Every man will be thy friend
Whilst thou hast wherewith to
    spend:
But, if store of crowns be scant,
No man will supply thy want.
Address to the Nightingale

[g] He that is thy friend indeed,
He will help thee in thy need.
Ibid.

Phineas Taylor Barnum
[1810–1891]

[h] There's a sucker born every
minute.

Matthias Barr
[1831– ?]

[i] Only a baby small,
Dropt from the skies;
Small, but how dear to us,
God knoweth best.
Only a Baby Small

[j] Come, give me your hand, sir,
    my friend and my brother:
If honest, why sure that's
    enough.
One hand, if it's true, is as good
    as another,
No matter how brawny or rough.
Give Me Your Hand

Alfred Barrett, S.J.
[1906–   ]

[k] Smiled Christ—"Thus do I
    treat My friends,
So must I thus treat you."
"No wonder, Lord," sighed Teresa,
"No wonder You have so few!"
Repartee. Stanza 3

[l] See how in God's design,
Layette to mound,
A lifetime of linen
Laps us round.   *Linen*

Eaton Stannard Barrett
[1786–1820]

[m] Not she with trait'rous kiss
    her Saviour stung,
Not she denied him with unholy
    tongue,
She, while apostles shrank, could
    danger brave,

Last at his cross, and earliest at
his grave.   *Woman. Part I*

Sir James Matthew Barrie
[1860–1937]

[n] The life of every man is a
diary in which he means to write
one story, and writes another; and
his humblest hour is when he
compares the volume as it is with
what he vowed to make it.
    The Little Minister. Chap. 1

[o] The most gladsome thing in
the world is that few of us fall
very low; the saddest that, with
such capabilities, we seldom rise
high.   *Ibid. Chap. 3*

[p] Has it ever struck you that
the trouts bite best on the sabbath? God's critters tempting
decent men.   *Ibid. Chap. 8*

[q] You canna expect to be baith
grand and comfortable.
    Ibid. Chap. 10

[r] A house is never still in darkness to those who listen intently.
. . . Ghosts were created when the
first man woke in the night.
    Ibid. Chap. 22

[s] Let no one who lives be called
altogether unhappy. Even love un-
returned has its rainbow.
    Ibid. Chap. 24

[t] Those who bring sunshine to
the lives of others cannot keep it
from themselves.
    A Window in Thrums. Chap. 18

[u] So much of what is great in
Scotland has sprung from the
closeness of the family ties.
    Margaret Ogilvy. Chap. 2

[v] Do you believe in fairies?
    Peter and Wendy. Chap. 13

[w] Eyes that say you never
must, nose that says why don't
you? and a mouth that says I
rather wish you could: such is the
portrait of Mary A———.
    The Little White Bird. Chap. 1

[x] Shall we make a new rule of
life from tonight: always to try to
be a little kinder than is necessary?   *Ibid. Chap. 4*

[y] The only ghosts, I believe,
who creep into this world, are
dead young mothers, returned to
see how their children fare. There
is no other inducement great
enough to bring the departed
back.   *Ibid.*

[z] The reason birds can fly and
we can't is simply that they have
perfect faith, for to have faith is
to have wings.   *Ibid. Chap. 14*

[a] Poets are people who despise
money except what you need for
today.   *Ibid. Chap. 15*

[b] When a great man dies . . .
the immortals await him at the
top of the nearest hill.
    George Meredith

[c] *Alick:* What *is* charm, exactly,
Maggie?
    Maggie: Oh, it's—it's a sort of
bloom on a woman. If you have it,
you don't need to have anything
else; and if you don't have it, it
doesn't much matter what else
you have. Some women, the few,
have charm for all; and most
have charm for one. But some
have charm for none.
    What Every Woman Knows. Act I

[d] Every man who is high up
loves to think that he has done it
all himself; and the wife smiles,
and lets it go at that.
    Ibid. Act IV

Michael Joseph Barry
[1817–1889]

[e] But whether on the scaffold
    high
Or in the battle's van,
The fittest place where man can
    die
Is where he dies for man!
    *The Place Where Men Should Die.
        Stanza 5*

Ethel Barrymore
[1879–   ]

[f] That's all there is; there isn't
any more.
    *Added, with the author's per-
    mission, as the curtain line of
    "Sunday" [1906]*

Guillaume de Salluste,
Seigneur du Bartas
[1544–1590]

*From Divine Weekes and Workes,
translated [1606] by J. Sylvester*

[g] The world's a stage, where
God's omnipotence,
His justice, knowledge, love, and
    providence
Do act the parts.
    First Week. First Day

[h] What is well done is done
soon enough.   *Ibid.*

[i] And swans seem whiter if
swart crowes be by.   *Ibid.*

[j] Night's black mantle covers
all alike.   *Ibid.*

[k] Much like the French (or like
    ourselves, their apes),
Who with strange habit do dis-
    guise their shapes;
Who loving novels, full of affecta-
    tion,
Receive the manners of each other
nation.   *Ibid. Second Day*

[l] With tooth and nail.   *Ibid.*

[m] Bright-flaming, heat-full fire,
The source of motion.   *Ibid.*

[n] To man the earth seems altogether
No more a mother, but a step-
dame rather.
    Ibid. Third Day

[o] For where's the state beneath
the firmament
That doth excel the bees for government?
    Ibid. Fifth Day, Part I

[p] These lovely lamps, these
windows of the soul.
    Ibid. Sixth Day

[q] Even as a surgeon, minding
off to cut
Some cureless limb,—before in
ure he put
His violent engins on the vicious
member,
Bringeth his patient in a senseless slumber,
And grief-less then (guided by
use and art ,
To save the whole, sawes off th'
infested part.   *Ibid.*

[r] Living from hand to mouth
    Second Week. First Day, Part 4

[s] Who well lives, long lives; for
this age of ours
Should not be numbered by years,
daies, and hours.
    Ibid. Fourth Day, Book 2

[t] Made no more bones.
    The Maiden Blush

Bernard Mannes Baruch
[1870-   ]

[u] America has never forgotten
—and will never forget—the
nobler things that brought her
into being and that light her path
—the path that was entered upon
only one hundred and fifty years
ago. . . . How young she is! It will
be centuries before she will adopt
that maturity of custom—that
clothing of the grave—that some
people believe she is already fitted
for.
    *Address on Accepting The
    Churchman Award, New York.
    May 23, 1944*

David Bates
[1810-1876]

[v] Is Dr. Jones, the dentist in?
An aching tooth has made me
fret;

The tooth is out . . .
Reader, would you avoid this
pain?

Then have your crumbling teeth
well filled.
    The Toothache. Stanzas 8 and 11

Katharine Lee Bates
[1859-1929]

[w] O beautiful for patriot dream
That sees beyond the years
Thine alabaster cities gleam
Undimmed by human tears!
    America! America!
God shed His grace on thee,
And crown thy good with brother-
hood
From sea to shining sea!
    America the Beautiful. Stanza 4

Clifford Bax
[1886-   ]

[x] All we had of joy endures, a
joy within us;
All the rest of life is lovelier for
those years.
    Musician. Stanza 13

Thomas Haynes Bayly
[1797-1839]

[y] Those who have wealth must
be watchful and wary,
Power, alas! naught but misery
brings!
    I'd Be a Butterfly. Stanza 2

[z] Why don't the men propose,
Mamma?
Why don't the men propose?
    Why Don't the Men Propose?

[a] Friends depart, and memory
takes them
To her caverns, pure and deep.
    Teach Me to Forget

[b] Tell me the tales that to me
were so dear,
Long, long ago, long, long ago.
    Long, Long Ago

[c] Oh pilot, 'tis a fearful night!
There's danger on the deep.
    The Pilot

[d] Absence makes the heart
grow fonder:
Isle of Beauty, fare thee well!
    Isle of Beauty

Charles Austin Beard
[1874-1948]
and
Mary Ritter Beard
[1876-   ]

[e] At no time, at no place, in
solemn convention assembled,
through no chosen agents, had the
American people officially proclaimed the United States to be a
democracy. The Constitution did
not contain the word or any word

lending countenance to it, except possibly the mention of "We, the people," in the preamble . . when the Constitution was framed no respectable person called himself or herself a democrat.
America in Midpassage. Chap. 17

James Beattie
[1735–1803]

[f] At the close of the day when the hamlet is still,
And mortals the sweets of forgetfulness prove,
When naught but the torrent is heard on the hill,
And naught but the nightingale's song in the grove.
The Hermit

Robert Brewster Beattie
[1875–1946]

[g] To leave the old with a burst of song,
To recall the right and forgive the wrong;
To forget the thing that binds you fast
To the vain regrets of the year that's past.
A Way to a Happy New Year

Pakenham Beatty
[*Floruit* 1881]

[h] By thine own soul's law learn to live,
And if men thwart thee, take no heed,
And if men hate thee, have no care;
Sing thou thy song, and do thy deed,
Hope thou thy hope, and pray thy prayer.
Self-Reliance. Stanza 1

Pierre de Beaumarchais
[1732–1799]

[i] If you assure me that your intentions are honorable.
Le Barbier de Séville. Act IV, Sc. 6

Francis Beaumont
[1584–1616]

[j] What things have we seen
Done at the Mermaid! heard words that have been
So nimble and so full of subtile flame
As if that every one from whence they came
Had meant to put his whole wit in a jest,
And resolved to live a fool the rest
Of his dull life.
Letter to Ben Jonson

Beaumont and Fletcher
FRANCIS BEAUMONT [1584–1616]
JOHN FLETCHER [1579–1625]

[k] All your better deeds
Shall be in water writ, but this in marble.
Philaster. Act V, Sc. 3

[l] Then, my good girls, be more than women wise;
At least be more than I was; and be sure
You credit any thing the light gives life to,
Before a man.
The Maid's Tragedy. Act II, Sc. 2

[m] A soul as white as heaven.
Ibid. Act IV, Sc. 1

[n] There is a method in man's wickedness,—
It grows up by degrees.
A King and No King. Act V, Sc. 4

[o] As cold as cucumbers.
Cupid's Revenge. Act I, Sc. 1

[p] Kiss till the cow comes home.
Scornful Lady. Act III, Sc. 1

[q] Beggars must be no choosers.
Ibid. Act V, Sc. 3

[r] One foot in the grave.
*The Little French Lawyer.
Act I, Sc. 1*

[s] Go to grass.
Ibid. Act IV, Sc. 7

[t] There is no jesting with edge tools.   *Ibid.*

[u] Death hath so many doors to let out life.   *The Custom of
the Country. Act II, Sc. 2*

[v] Of all the paths [that] lead to a woman's love
Pity's the straightest.   *The
Knight of Malta. Act I, Sc. 1*

[w] What's one man's poison, signor,
Is another's meat or drink.
Love's Cure. Act III, Sc. 2

Michael Wentworth Beck
[1815–1843]

[x] This world is not so bad a world
As some would like to make it;
Though whether good, or whether bad,
Depends on how we take it.
The World as It Is. Stanza 1

Carl Lotus Becker
[1873–1945]

[y] Economic distress will teach men, if anything can, that realities are less dangerous than fancies, that fact-finding is more effective than fault-finding.
Progress and Power

[z] The significance of man is that he is that part of the universe that asks the question, What is the significance of Man? He alone can stand apart imaginatively and, regarding himself and the universe in their eternal aspects, pronounce a judgment. The significance of man is that he is insignificant and is aware of it. *Ibid.*

Thomas Lovell Beddoes
[1803–1849]

[a] If there were dreams to sell,
What would you buy?
Some cost a passing-bell:
Some a light sigh.
Dream-Pedlary

[b] Tell me how many beads
there are
In a silver chain
Of evening rain,
Unravell'd from the tumbling main,
And threading the eye of a yellow star:
So many times do I love, again.
Song. Stanza 2

Bernard Elliott Bee
[1823–1861]

[c] See, there is Jackson, standing like a stone-wall.
Of General T. J. Jackson, at the Battle of Bull Run [July 21, 1861]

Henry Ward Beecher
[1813–1887]

[d] A thoughtful mind, when it sees a Nation's flag, sees not the flag only, but the Nation itself; and whatever may be its symbols, its insignia, he reads chiefly in the flag the Government, the principles, the truths, the history which belongs to the Nation that sets it forth.
The American Flag

[e] Nothing marks the increasing wealth of our times and the growth of the public mind toward refinement, more than the demand for books. *Star Papers. Subtleties of Book Buyers*

[f] You cannot forget if you would, those golden kisses all over the cheeks of the meadow, queerly called dandelions. *Ibid. A Discourse on Flowers*

Sir Max Beerbohm
[1872–1956]

[g] Most women are not so young as they are painted.
A Defence of Cosmetics

[h] To make oneself beautiful is an universal instinct *Ibid*

[i] She was hardly more affable than a cameo. *Zuleika Dobson. Chap 3*

[j] The dullard's envy of brilliant men is always assuaged by the suspicion that they will come to a bad end *Ibid. Chap 4*

[k] Ordinary saints grow faint to posterity, whilst quite ordinary sinners pass vividly down the ages. *Ibid. Chap 6*

[l] Of all the objects of hatred, a woman once loved is the most hateful *Ibid. Chap. 13*

[m] I have known no man of genius who had not to pay, in some affliction or defect either physical or spiritual, for what the gods had given him.
No. 2, The Pines

[n] It seems to be a law of nature that no man ever is loth to sit for his portrait. *Quia Imperfectum*

[o] To say that a man is vain means merely that he is pleased with the effect he produces on other people. A conceited man is satisfied with the effect he produces on himself. *Ibid.*

[p] Strange, when you come to think of it, that of all the countless folk who have lived before our time on this planet not one is known in history or in legend as having died of laughter.
Laughter

Ethel Lynn Beers
[1827–1879]

[q] All quiet along the Potomac to-night,
No sound save the rush of the river,
While soft falls the dew on the face of the dead,—
The picket's off duty forever
The Picket Guard [Harper's Weekly September 30, 1861]. Stanza 6

[r] Where are the dear, old-fashioned posies,
Quaint in form and bright in hue,
Such as grandma gave her lovers
When she walked the garden through?

Will the modern florist's triumph
Look so fair or smell so sweet?
Old-Fashioned Fowers. Stanzas 1 and 9

Harold Begbie
[1871–1929]

[s] She is a wall of brass,
You shall not pass! You shall not pass!

Spring up like summer grass,
Surge on her, mass on mass,
Still shall you break like glass.
    *Verdun. Written for the French
        Red Cross, London [1916]*

[t] "The Christian ideal," it is
said, "has not been tried and
found wanting; it has been found
difficult, and left untried."
    Life of William Booth

Arthur W. Bell
[1875–1945]

[u] Myself grown old do fearfully
    frequent
Grim hospitals and hear great
    argument
About me, but with luck have
    heretofore
Come out by the same door
    wherein I went.
    Omar Is X-Rayed

Henry Glassford Bell
[1805–1874]

[v] The blood of beauty, wealth,
    and power—the heart-blood
    of a Queen,
The noblest of the Stuart race—
    the fairest earth has seen—
Lapped by a dog! Go think of it
    in silence and alone!
Then weigh against a grain of
    sand the glories of a throne.
    Mary, Queen of Scots

John Joy Bell
[1871–1934]

[w] I've never traveled for more
    'n a day,
I never was one to roam,
But I likes to sit on the busy quay,
Watchin' the ships that says to
    me—
"Always somebody goin' away,
    Somebody gettin' home."
    On the Quay. Stanza 1

Edward Bellamy
[1850–1898]

[x] If we could have devised an
arrangement for providing everybody with music in their homes,
perfect in quality, unlimited in
quantity, suited to every mood,
and beginning and ceasing at will,
we should have considered the
limit of human felicity already attained.   *Looking Backward*

Francis Bellamy
[1855–1931]

[y] I pledge allegiance to the flag
of the United States and to the
republic for which it stands, one
nation, indivisible, with liberty
and justice for all.   *The Pledge
of Allegiance to the Flag [1892]*

Hilaire Belloc
[1870–   ]

[z] Child, do not throw this book
    about,
Refrain from the unholy pleas-
    ure
Of cutting all the pictures out,
Regard it as your choicest treas-
    ure.   *A Bad Child's Book of
        Beasts. Foreword*

[a] I shoot the Hippopotamus
    With bullets made of platinum,
Because if I use leaden ones
    His hide is sure to flatten 'em.
    Ibid. The Hippopotamus

[b] Here richly, with ridiculous
    display,
The Politician's corpse was laid
    away.
While all of his acquaintance
    sneered and slanged,
I wept; for I had longed to see
    him hanged.   *Epitaph on
        the Politician Himself*

[c] The Tipple's aboard and the
    night is young,
The door's ajar and the Barrel is
    sprung,
I am singing the best song ever
    was sung
And it has a rousing chorus.
    *West Sussex Drinking Song.
        Chorus*

[d] How slow the Shadow creeps:
    but when 'tis past
How fast the Shadows fall. How
    fast! How fast!
    For a Sundial

[e] The moon on the one hand,
    the dawn on the other:
The moon is my sister, the dawn
    is my brother.
The moon on my left and the
    dawn on my right.
My brother, good morning: my
    sister, good night.
    The Early Morning

[f] He does not die that can be-
    queath
Some influence to the land he
    knows,
Or dares, persistent, interwreath
Love permanent with the wild
    hedgerows;
He does not die, but still re-
    mains
Substantiate with his darling
    plains.
    Duncton Hill. Stanza 1

[g] There's nothing worth the
    wear of winning
But laughter and the love of
    friends.   *Dedicatory Ode*

[h] For no one, in our long de-
    cline,

So dusty, spiteful and divided,
Had quite such pleasant friends as
  mine,
Or loved them half as much as
  I did.   *Ibid.*

[i] Of Courtesy, it is much less
Than Courage of Heart or Holi-
  ness,
Yet in my walks it seems to me
That the Grace of God is in Cour-
  tesy.   *Courtesy*

[j] Drinking when I had a mind
  to,
Singing when I felt inclined to.
                The Path to Rome

[k] Most holy Night, that still
  dost keep
The keys of all the doors of sleep,
To me when my tired eyelids close
  Give thou repose.
            The Night. Stanza 1

[l] When I am dead, I hope it
  may be said:
"His sins were scarlet, but his
  books were read."
                On His Books

Robert Charles Benchley
[1889–1945]

[m] I haven't been abroad in so
long that I almost speak English
without an accent.
        The Old Sea Rover Speaks

[n] *Enter first Lady-in-Waiting
(Flourish,[1] Hautboys[2] and[3]
torches).[4]
First Lady-in-Waiting*—What[5]
ho![6] Where[7] is[8] the[9] music?[10]

NOTES

1. *Flourish:* The stage direction
here is obscure. Clarke claims it
should read "flarish," thus changing the meaning of the passage to
"flarish" (that is, the King's), but
most authorities have agreed that
it should remain "flourish," sup-
plying the predicate which is to be
flourished. There was at this time
a custom in the countryside of
England to flourish a mop as a
signal to the passing vender of
berries, signifying that in that
particular household there was a
consumer-demand for berries, and
this may have been meant in this
instance. That Shakespeare was
cognizant of this custom of flourishing the mop for berries is
shown in a similar passage in the
second part of *King Henry IV,*
where he has the Third Page enter and say, "Flourish." Cf. also
Hamlet, IV, 7:4.   *Of All Things.
            Shakespeare Explained*

[o] An Austrian scientist has
come out with the announcement
that there is no such thing as a
hundred per cent male or a hundred per cent female. If this is
true, it is really a big step forward.
*Inside Benchley. A Talk to
Young Men: Graduation Ad-
dress on "The Decline of Sex"*

Laura Benét
[1884–   ]

[p] Lost in the spiral of his conscience, he
Detachedly takes rest.
            The Snail. Stanza 1

[q] He spoke: she teetered up
  On pink rheumatic feet;
"Go forth, my dove," he said,
  "That we may eat."
            Noah's Dove. Stanza 6

Stephen Vincent Benét
[1898–1943]

[r] I died in my boots like a
  pioneer
With the whole wide sky above
  me.   *The Ballad
            of William Sycamore*

[s] He could fiddle all the bugs
  off a sweetpotato-vine.
    *The Mountain Whippoorwill.
                    Stanza 22*

[t] Down where the taproots of
  New England trees
Suck bare existence from the
  broken stones.
        The Golden Corpse. Sonnet 4

[u] American Muse, whose strong
  and diverse heart
So many men have tried to understand
But only made it smaller with
  their art,
Because you are as various as your
  land.
    John Brown's Body. Invocation

[v] Lincoln, six feet one in his
  stocking feet,
The lank man, knotty and tough
  as a hickory rail,
Whose hands were always too big
  for white-kid gloves,
Whose wit was a coonskin sack of
  dry, tall tales,
Whose weathered face was homely
  as a plowed field.
            Ibid. Book 2

[w] Honesty rare as a man without self-pity,
Kindness as large and plain as a
  prairie wind.   *Ibid.*

[x] The Union's too big a horse to
  keep changing the saddle
Each time it pinches you. As long
  as you're sure
The saddle fits, you're bound to
  put up with the pinches
And not keep fussing the horse.
            Ibid.

[**y**] The trees in the streets are old trees used to living with people,
Family-trees that remember your grandfather's name.
                              Ibid. Book 4

[**z**] Stonewall Jackson, wrapped in his beard and his silence.
                              Ibid.

[**a**] They bred such horses in Virginia then,
Horses that were remembered after death
And buried not so far from Christian ground.   *Ibid.*

[**b**] The ant finds kingdoms in a foot of ground.   *Ibid.*

[**c**] The quiet, equable, deadly holder-on,
Faded-brown as a cinnamon-bear in Spring. [Of General Grant.]
                              Ibid. Book 6

[**d**] "Let us cross the river," he said, "and rest under the shade of the trees." [*General "Stonewall" Jackson's last words (May 10, 1863.)*]   *Ibid.*

[**e**]   Oh, singing tongue!
Great tongue of bronze and salt and the free grasses,
Tongue of America, speaking for the first time.
                    Ode to Walt Whitman. I

[**f**] Rolling, rolling from Arkansas, Kansas, Iowa,
Rolling from Ohio, Wisconsin, Illinois,
Rolling and shouting:
Till, at last, it is Mississippi,
The Father of Waters; the matchless; the great flood
Dyed with the earth of States; with the dust and the sun and the seed of half the States.
                              Ibid.

[**g**] I have fallen in love with American names,
The sharp names that never get fat,
The snakeskin-titles of mining-claims,
The plumed war-bonnet of Medicine Hat,
Tucson and Deadwood and Lost Mule Flat.
                    American Names

[**h**] Now grimy April comes again,
Maketh bloom the fire-escapes,
Maketh silvers in the rain,
Maketh winter coats and capes
Suddenly all worn and shabby
Like the fur of winter bears.
                    For City Spring

[**i**] If two New Hampshiremen aren't a match for the devil, we might as well give the country back to the Indians.
          The Devil and Daniel Webster

[**j**] Books are not men and yet they are alive,
They are man's memory and his aspiration,
The link between his present and his past,
The tools he builds with.
                    They Burned the Books

[**k**] Our earth is but a small star in the great universe. Yet of it we can make, if we choose, a planet unvexed by war, untroubled by hunger or fear, undivided by senseless distinctions of race, color or theory.   *Prayer, written for and read by President Franklin D. Roosevelt to the United Nations on Flag Day, June 14, 1942*

[**l**] Grant us brotherhood, not only for this day but for all our years—a brotherhood not of words but of acts and deeds. We are all of us children of earth—grant us that simple knowledge. If our brothers are oppressed, then we are oppressed. If they hunger we hunger. If their freedom is taken away our freedom is not secure.
                              Ibid.

[**m**] That queer sense of relief and shame
Which comes to those who make sensible decisions.
          Western Star. Book I. Page 128

[**n**] There were human beings aboard the Mayflower,
Not merely ancestors.
                    Ibid. Page 133

[**o**] Remember that when you say
"I will have none of this exile and this stranger
For his face is not like my face and his speech is strange,"
You have denied America with that word.   *Ibid. Page 180*

William Rose Benét
[1886–1950]

[**p**] How at the corners of streets
It seems one suddenly meets
The unforgotten face, the long-dead moment living!
"No, they were—they are gone,"
We murmur. "We live on."
          Persistent Instant. Stanza 1

[**q**] A million brains of weary folk are throbbing through the hours
With wishes tremendous—from some of which defend us—
But most are longings old for the country to enfold
And drown them in its purple and greenery and gold.
          Wish-Horses. Stanza 2

[**r**] I flung my soul to the air like a falcon flying. . . .

I shall start a heron soon
In the marsh beneath the
    moon—
A strange white heron rising with
    silver on its wings.
    The Falconer of God. Stanza 1

[s] Neither will I put myself for-
    ward as others may do,
Neither, if you wish me to flatter,
    will I flatter you;
I will look at you grimly, and so
    you will know I am true.
    Eternal Masculine. Stanza 1

[t] Ocean, wherein the whale
Swims minnow-small.

For the Lord said, "Let Whale Be!"
And there was Whale!
    Whale. Stanzas 1 and 22

[u] Times she'll be docile as the
    gentlest thing
That ever blinked in fur or folded
    wing,
And then, like lightning in the
    dead of night,
Fill with wild, crackling, intermit-
    ting light
My mind and soul and senses—
    and next be
Aloof askance as a dryad in a tree.
    The Woodcutter's Wife. Stanza 2

[v] O Love, a thousand, thousand
    voices,
From night to dawn, from dawn
    to night,
Have cried the passion of their
    choices
To orb your name and keep it
    bright.
    The Name of Love. Stanza 1

[w] Jesse James was a two-gun
    man
    (Roll on, Missouri!) . . .
In seven states he cut up dadoes.
He's gone with the buffler an' the
    desperadoes.
    Jesse James: American Myth

[x] Who writes poetry imbibes
honey from the poisoned lips of
life.   *Man Possessed. Preface*

[y] Chilled Martini like Ithuriel's
    spear
Transfixing all dubiety within,
Oiled by an olive and shred of
    lemonpeel!   *The Martini*

[z] Like flame, like wine, across
    the still lagoon
The colors of the sunset stream.
Spectral in heaven as climbs the
    frail veiled moon,
So climbs my dream.
    Gaspara Stampa. Stanza 1

[a] One speck within vast star-
    space lying
Awoke, arose, resumed its cloth-
    ing,
And crawled another day toward
    dying.
    Animalcule. Stanza 7

[b] Voice of the forum loud and
    harsh
Full of frog-rhetoric of the
    marsh; . . .
Whose every utterance is base—
Yearlong the nations cry to thee,
God of our gods, Stupidity!
    Hymn to Stupidity

[c] When at our history men
    stand amazed . . .
Our captains may have grown as
    quaint
And crazed as any medieval saint.
    Ode for an Epoch

[d] Of the first of such from
    Gloucester,
    'twas the word, "See how she
    scoons!"
Cried Captain Andrew the builder,
"Then a scooner let her be!"
    Gloucester Schooner. Stanza 2

[e] How we exult when aught
    within us
draws approbation from the eye.
What oily unguents still can win
    us.
How little truth we perish by.

By God but I was born to laugh-
    ter
and merry comrades make me
    glow
until the merciless moment after
chilled to the heart I know I
    know . . .
    *The Dust Which Is God.
    Wild Harp Slung Behind Him*

[f] What did your body say to
    mine
deep in velvet night's delight?
*On heaven's wall a golden vine
    clambers bright.*
    Ibid. That Rin Sae Deep

Park Benjamin
[1809–1864]

[g] I'm king of the dead— . . .
And my scepter of rule is the
    spade I hold:
Come they from cottage or come
    they from hall,
Mankind are my subjects, all, all,
    all!
Let them loiter in pleasure or toil-
    fully spin—
I gather them in, I gather them
    in!   *The Old Sexton*

Enoch Arnold Bennett
[1867–1931]

[h] Pessimism, when you get used
to it, is just as agreeable as optimism.
    Things That Have Interested Me

[i] The price of justice is eternal
publicity.   *Ibid. Second Series*

Henry Holcomb Bennett
[1863–1924]

[j] Hats off!
Along the street there comes
A blare of bugles, a ruffle of
    drums,
A flash of color beneath the sky:
    Hats off!
The flag is passing by.
        The Flag Goes By. Stanza 1

John Bennett
[1865–   ]

[k] God made memory cruel, that
men might know remorse; but the
Devil devised forgetfulness, ano-
dyne of regret.
        Madame Margot. Page 82

[l] If Life's a lie, and Love's a
    cheat,
As I have heard men say,
Then here's a health to fond de-
    ceit—
God bless you, dear, to-day!
        *God Bless You, Dear, To-day.
        Stanza 3*

[m] I want men to remember,
When gray Death sets me free,
I was a man who had many
    friends,
And many friends had me.
        I Want an Epitaph

William Cox Bennett
[1820–1895]

[n] "God wills but ill," the
    doubter said,
"Lo, time doth evil only bear;
Give me a sign His love to prove,
His vaunted goodness to de-
    clare!"
The poet pointed where a flower,
    A simple daisy, starred the sod,
And answered, "Proof of love and
    power
Behold, behold a smile of God!"
        A Thought

Isaac de Benserade
[1612–1691]

[o] In bed we laugh, in bed we
    cry;
And, born in bed, in bed we die.
The near approach a bed may
    show
Of human bliss to human woe.
    Translated by Dr. Samuel Johnson

Arthur Christopher Benson
[1862–1925]

[p] Faith hath a fleeting breath,
Hopes may be frail but fond,
But Love shall be Love till death,
And perhaps beyond.
        The Gift

[q] If it be well with him,
If it be well, I say,
I will not try with a childish cry
To draw him thence away:
Only my day is dim,
Only I long for him,
Where is my friend to-day?
        My Friend

[r] Edward Fitzgerald said that
he wished we had more lives of
obscure persons; one wants to
know what other people are
thinking and feeling about it all.
. . . If the dullest person in the
world would only put down sin-
cerely what he or she thought
about his or her life, about work
and love, religion and emotion, it
would be a fascinating document.
        From a College Window

Stella Benson (Mrs. J. C. O'Gorman Anderson)
[1892–1933]

[s] Call no man foe, but never
    love a stranger.
Build up no plan, nor any star
    pursue.
Go forth with crowds; in loneli-
    ness is danger.
        To the Unborn. Stanza 3

[t] It was young David mocked
    the Philistine,
It was young David laughed be-
    side the river.
There came his mother—his and
    yours and mine—
With five smooth stones, and
    dropped them in his quiver.
        Five Smooth Stones. Stanza 3

[u] The first stone is love, and
    that shall fail you.
The second stone is hate, and that
    shall fail you.
The third stone is knowledge, and
    that shall fail you.
The fourth stone is prayer, and
    that shall fail you.
The fifth stone shall not fail you.

The fifth stone is a magic stone,
    my David,
Made up of fear and failure, lies
    and loss.
        Ibid. Stanzas 5 and 10

[v] Sling your fifth stone, O son
    of mine, and win.
Grief do I give you, grief and
    dreadful laughter;
Sackcloth for banner, ashes in
    your wine.

Go forth, go forth, nor ask me
    what comes after;
The fifth stone shall not fail you,
    son of mine.
*Go forth, go forth, and slay the
    Philistine.*
        Ibid. Stanzas 12 and 13

[w] Family jokes, though rightly
cursed by strangers, are the bond
that keeps most families alive.
Pipers and a Dancer. Chap. 9

Edmund Clerihew Bentley
[1875–   ]

[x] George the Third
Ought never to have occurred.
One can only wonder
At so grotesque a blunder.
Biography for Beginners

Ralph Bergengren
[1871–1947]

[y] Christmas itself may be called
    into question
If carried so far it creates indiges-
    tion.
The Unwise Christmas

George Berkeley,
Bishop of Cloyne
[1685–1753]

[z] Westward the course of em-
    pire takes its way;
The four first acts already past,
A fifth shall close the drama with
    the day:
Time's noblest offspring is the
    last.
*On the Prospect of Planting
Arts and Learning in America.
Stanza 6*

[a] Our youth we can have but
    to-day,
We may always find time to grow
    old.   *Can Love Be
    Controlled by Advice?*

[b] He who says there is no such
thing as an honest man, you may
be sure is himself a knave.
Maxims Concerning Patriotism

Irving Berlin
[1888–   ]

[c] God bless America,
Land that I love;
Stand beside her and guide her
Through the night with a light
    from above.   *God Bless
America [Written in 1917, first
sung by Kate Smith Armistice
Day, 1938]*

Mademoiselle Bertin
[1744–1813]

[d] There is nothing new except
what is forgotten. [Mlle. Bertin
was milliner to Marie Antoinette.]

Albert Jeremiah Beveridge
[1862–1927]

[e] This party comes from the
grass roots. It has grown from the
soil of the people's hard necessities.   *Address as Temporary
Chairman of the Bull Moose Convention, Chicago [August 5, 1912]*

Sir William Beveridge
[1879–   ]

[f] The object of government in
peace and in war is not the glory
of rulers or of races, but the happiness of the common man.
Social Insurance

Ernest Bevin
[1884–1951]

[g] There has never been a war
yet which, if the facts had been
put calmly before the ordinary
folk, could not have been prevented. The common man is the
greatest protection against war.
*Speech in the House of
Commons, November 1945*

Martha Gilbert
Dickinson Bianchi
[1866–1943]

[h] The fatal realm of Memory,—
Men call it heaven—and hell.
The Haunted Kingdom

Elizabeth Asquith Bibesco
[1897–1945]

[i] I have made a great discovery.
What I love belongs to me. Not
the chairs and tables in my house,
but the masterpieces of the world.
It is only a question of loving
them enough.   *Balloons*

[j] It is never any good dwelling
on goodbyes. It is not the being
together that it prolongs, it is the
parting.
The Fir and the Palm. Chap. 15

Isaac Bickerstaff
[1735–1812?]

[k] There was a jolly miller once
    lived on the River Dee;
He worked and sung from mourn
    till night, no lark so blithe
    as he. . . .
And this the burden of his song
    forever used to be,—
"I care for nobody, no, not I, if no-
    body cares for me."
Love in a Village. Act. I, Sc. 2

Edward Henry Bickersteth,
Bishop of Exeter
[1825–1906]

[l] Our years are like the shadows
    The sunny hills that lie,
Or grasses in the meadows
    That blossom but to die;
A sleep, a dream, a story
    By strangers quickly told,

An unremaining glory
  Of things that soon are old.
      O God, the Rock of Ages.
                  Stanza 2

Ambrose Bierce
[1842–1914?]

[m] He damned his fellows for
    his own unworth,
And, bad himself, thought noth-
    ing good on earth.
                  An Epitaph

[n] To men a man is but a mind.
    Who cares
What face he carries or what form
    he wears?
But woman's body is the woman.
          The Devil's Dictionary

[o] *Bore:* a person who talks
    when you wish him to listen.
                  Ibid.

[p] *Marriage:* a community con-
    sisting of a master, a mistress, and
    two slaves, making in all, two.
                  Ibid.

[q] Woman would be more
    charming if one could fall into
    her arms without falling into her
    hands.   *Epigrams*

[r] You are not permitted to kill
    a woman who has injured you, but
    nothing forbids you to reflect that
    she is growing older every minute.
    You are avenged 1440 times a day.
                  Ibid.

"Josh Billings"
(Henry Wheeler Shaw)
[1818–1885]

[s] It is better to know nothing
    than to know what ain't so.
                  Proverb

[t] A sekret ceases tew be a sekret
    if it iz once confided—it iz like a
    dollar bill, once broken, it iz never
    a dollar agin.   *Affurisms (from
        Josh Billings: His Sayings)*

[u] Love iz like the meazles; we
    kant have it bad but onst, and the
    later in life we have it the tuffer it
    goes with us.   *Ibid.*

[v] Better make a weak man
    your enemy than your friend.
                  Ibid.

[w] Poverty iz the step-mother
    ov genius.   *Ibid.*

[x] The wheel that squeaks the
    loudest
Is the one that gets the grease.
                  The Kicker

Guy Willis Bilsland
[1882–   ]

[y] Three thousand miles of bor-
    der line—nor fort nor arméd
    host

On all this frontier neighbor-
    ground, from east to western
    coast; . . .
A living proof to all the world of
    faith in brotherhood.

God speed that surely dawning
    day—that coming hour di-
    vine—
When all the nations of the earth
    shall boast such border line.
      Ou, Border Line. Stanzas 4 and 6

Laurence Binyon
[1869–1943]

[z] For Mercy, Courage, Kindness,
    Mirth,
There is no measure upon earth
Nay, they wither, root and stem,
If an end be set to them.   *A Song*

[a] They shall grow not old, as
    we that are left grow old:
Age shall not weary them, nor the
    years condemn.
At the going down of the sun and
    in the morning
We will remember them.
          For the Fallen. Stanza 4

George Birdseye
[1844–1919]

[b] The longest day is in June,
    they say;
    The shortest in December.
They did not come to me that
    way:
    The shortest I remember
You came a day with me to stay,
    And filled my heart with laugh-
    ter;
The longest day—you were away—
    The very next day after.
              *Shortest and Longest
      [Century Magazine, June 1889]*

[c] "He has married been,
And so on earth has suffered for
    all sin."
"Married? 'Tis well; for I've been
    married twice!"
"Begone! We'll have no fools in
    Paradise."
              The Hindoo's Paradise

John Peale Bishop
[1892–1944]

[d] Things I have hated: A cer-
    tain shade of brown
Which elder ladies love; wet roofs
    that drip
Their huge drops on your neck;
    short sheets that slip
And leave your ankles freezing;
    fires that smoke;
Carved, heavy furniture of var-
    nished oak.   *The Great Hater*

Morris Bishop
[1893–   ]

[e] And on the pedestal these
words appear:
"My name is Ozymandias, king of
kings!
Look on my works, ye Mighty, and
despair!"
Also the names of Emory P. Gray,
Mr. and Mrs. Dukes, and Oscar
Baer,
Of 17 West 4th Street, Oyster Bay.
Ozymandias Revisited

[f] Things did not vibrate so
when I was young . . .
But now all rattles, beats, drums,
bombinates.
My ears are shaken with an in-
cessant whir.
The air-drill chatters, the riveter
palpitates.
"Brrr!" goes the world; "Brr-rrr-
rrr!"
*Lines Written in a Moment of
Vibrant Ill-health*

[g] There I stood, and humbly
scanned
The miracle that sense appals,
And I watched the tourists stand
Spitting in Niagara Falls.
*Public Aid for Niagara Falls.
Stanza 4*

Thomas Brigham Bishop
[1835–1905]

[h] John Brown's body lies
a-mouldering in the grave,
His soul goes marching on.
John Brown's Body

[i] Shoo, fly! don't bodder me! I
belong to Company G,
I feel like a morning star.
Shoo, Fly. Refrain

Alexandre Charles
Auguste Bisson
[1848–1912]

[j] Our life is like some vast lake
that is slowly filling with the
stream of our years. As the waters
creep surely upward the land-
marks of the past are one by one
submerged But there shall always
be memory to lift its head above
the tide until the lake is overflowing.   *Madame X*
(tr. J. W. McConaughy)

Colonel Valentine Blacker
[1778–1823]

[k] Put your trust in God, my
boys, and keep your powder
dry!   *Oliver's Advice*

Richard Doddridge Blackmore
[1825–1900]

[l] Women, who are, beyond all
doubt, the mothers of all mischief,
also nurse that babe to sleep when
he is too noisy.
Lorna Doone. Chap. 57

Sir William Blackstone
[1723–1780]

[m] The royal navy of England
hath ever been its greatest defence
and ornament; it is its ancient
and natural strength,—the floating bulwark of our island.
*Commentaries. Vol. I, Book I,
Chap. XIII, § 418*

Frederick Temple
Hamilton Blackwood,
Lord Dufferin
[1826–1902]

[n] In the market-place lay a
dead dog. Of the group gathered
around it, one said: "This carcass
is disgusting." Another said, "The
sight of it is torment." Every man
spoke in this strain. But Jesus
drew near and said, "Pearls are
not equal in whiteness to his
teeth. Look not on the failures of
others and the merits of thyself;
cast thine eye on thine own
fault."
*Installation Address as Lord
Rector of St. Andrews University [1891]*

James W. Blake
[1862–1935]

[o] East Side, West Side, all
around the town,
The tots sang "Ring-a-rosie,"
"London Bridge is falling
down";
Boys and girls together, me and
Mamie Rorke,
Tripped the light fantastic on the
sidewalks of New York.
*The Sidewalks of New York
[1894]*

William Blake
[1757–1827]

[p] Little lamb, who made thee?
Dost thou know who made thee,
Gave thee life, and bid thee feed
By the streams and o'er the mead?
The Lamb. Stanza 1

[q] Piping down the valleys wild,
Piping songs of pleasant glee,
On a cloud I saw a child.
Songs of Innocence. Introduction

[r] The moon, like a flower
In heaven's high bower,
With silent delight
Sits and smiles on the night.
Night. Stanza 1

[s] Love seeketh not itself to
please,
Nor for itself hath any care,

But for another gives its ease,
And builds a heaven in hell's de-
    spair.   *The Clod and the*
                  Pebble. Stanza 1

[t] Tiger, tiger, burning bright
In the forests of the night.
What immortal hand or eye
Could frame thy fearful sym-
    metry?   *The Tiger. Stanza 1*

[u] To see the world in a grain of
    sand,
And a heaven in a wild flower;
Hold infinity in the palm of your
    hand,
And eternity in an hour.
Auguries of Innocence. Stanza 1

[v] He who doubts from what he
    sees
Will ne'er believe, do what you
    please.
If the Sun and Moon should
    doubt,
They'd immediately go out.
                  Ibid. Stanza 6

[w] He who bends to himself a
    Joy
Doth the wingèd life destroy;
But he who kisses the Joy as it
    flies
Lives in Eternity's sunrise.
                  Eternity

[x] I was angry with my friend:
I told my wrath, my wrath did
    end.
I was angry with my foe:
I told it not, my wrath did grow.
        A Poison Tree. Stanza 1

[y] Tools were made, and born
    were hands,
Every farmer understands.
        Proverbs. Line 83

[z] A truth that's told with bad
    intent
Beats all the lies you can invent.
                  Ibid. Line 95

[a] Seek Love in the pity of
    others' woe,
In the gentle relief of another's
    care,
In the darkness of night and the
    winter's snow,
With the naked and outcast—
    see Love there.
        William Bond. Stanza 13

[b] The door of Death is made of
    gold
That mortal eyes cannot behold.
    Dedication of the Designs for
    Robert Blair's The Grave. To
    Queen Charlotte

[c] The busy bee has no time for
    sorrow.   *Proverbs of Hell*

[d] Think in the morning, act in
the noon, eat in the evening, sleep
in the night.   *Ibid.*

[e] Poetry fettered, fetters the
human race.
Jerusalem. Preface to Chapter 1

[f] And did those feet in ancient
    time
Walk upon England's mountain
    green?
And was the holy Lamb of God
On England's pleasant pastures
    seen?   *Milton*

[g] Bring me my bow of burning
    gold!
Bring me my arrows of desire!
                  Ibid.

[h] I will not cease from mental
    fight,
Nor shall my sword sleep in my
    hand,
Till we have built Jerusalem
In England's green and pleasant
    land.   *Ibid.*

Laman Blanchard
[1803–1845]

[i] Give me to live with Love
    alone
And let the world go dine and
    dress;
For Love hath lowly haunts. . . .
If life's a flower, I choose my
    own—
'Tis "love in Idleness."
    Dolce far Niente. Stanza 4

Don Blanding
[1894–   ]

[j] There are times when only a
    dog will do
For a friend . . . when you're
    beaten sick and blue
And the world's all wrong, for he
    won't care
If you break and cry, or grouch
    and swear,
For he'll let you know as he licks
    your hands
That he's downright sorry . . . and
    understands.
    Vagabond's House. Stanza 5

[k] Hollywood . . . Hollywood . . .
Fabulous Follywood . . .
Celluloid Babylon, glorious, glam-
    orous.   *Hollywood. Stanza 1*

Mathilde Blind
[1841–1896]

[l] We are so tired; my heart and
    I.
Of all things here beneath the sky
Only one thing would please us
    best—
Endless, unfathomable rest.
                  Rest. Stanza 1

Léon Blum
[1872–1950]

[m] Life does not give itself to
one who tries to keep all its advantages at once. I have often
thought morality may perhaps

consist solely in the courage of making a choice.

> Quoted in The Practical Cogitator (Selected and arranged by Charles P. Curtis, Jr. and Ferris Greenslet). Page 97

[n] No government can remain stable in an unstable society and an unstable world.

> A L'Echelle Humaine. Page 54

Wilfrid Scawen Blunt
[1840–1922]

[o] He who has once been happy is for aye
Out of destruction's reach.
> Sonnet, With Esther

[p] Nor has the world a better thing,
Though one should search it round,
Than thus to live one's own sole king,
Upon one's own sole ground.
> The Old Squire. Stanza 14

John B. Bogart
[1845–1921]

[q] When a dog bites a man, that is not news, because it happens so often. But if a man bites a dog, that is news.
> Quoted by Frank M. O'Brien in The Story of The Sun

Nicholas Boileau-Despréaux
[1636–1711]

[r] Plague on the fool who taught us to confine
The swelling thought within a measured line;
Who first in narrow thraldom fancy pent,
And chained in rhyme each pinioned sentiment.
> Satire 2. Line 55

[s] In spite of every sage whom Greece can show,
Unerring wisdom never dwelt below;
Folly in all of every age we see,
The only difference lies in the degree.
> Satire 4. Line 37

[t] Of all the creatures that creep, swim, or fly,
Peopling the earth, the waters, and the sky,
From Rome to Iceland, Paris to Japan,
I really think the greatest fool is man.
> Satire 8. Line 1

[u] Follows his wife like fringe upon her gown.
> Ibid. Line 47

[v] The terrible burden of having nothing to do.
> Epistle XI

George Henry Boker
[1823–1890]

[w] Lay him low, lay him low,
In the clover or the snow!
What cares he? he cannot know.
> Dirge for a Soldier. Stanza 1

[x] I am that blessing which men fly from—Death.
> Countess Laura. Stanza 13

[y] Love is that orbit of the restless soul
Whose circle grazes the confines of space,
Bounding within the limits of its race
Utmost extremes.
> Sonnet, Love

William Bolitho
[1890–1930]

[z] The adventurer is within us, and he contests for our favour with the social man we are obliged to be. These two sorts of life are incompatibles; one we hanker after, the other we are obliged to. There is no other conflict so deep and bitter as this.
> Twelve Against the Gods. Introduction

[a] We, like the eagles, were born to be free. Yet we are obliged, in order to live at all, to make a cage of laws for ourselves and to stand on the perch.
> Ibid.

[b] His real glory is that of all adventurers: to have been the tremendous outsider.
> Ibid. Christopher Columbus

[c] The most dangerous enterprise in the world, the foundation of a religion.
> Ibid. Mahomet

[d] That great bourn of all common sense: compromise.
> Ibid.

[e] You need more tact in the dangerous art of giving presents than in any other social action.
> Ibid. Lola Montez

[f] Contrary to male sentimentality and psychology, the confrontation of a hostile crowd, to a woman, is like a tonic.
> Ibid.

[g] The historic moment is always simple and brief; it belongs to one man and one alone, without possibility (if it be truly ripe) of any confusion of rights.
> Ibid. Charles XII of Sweden

[h] The voice of the people needs a whole art of harmonic transcription to be understood.
> Ibid. Woodrow Wilson

[i] Wilson's adventure was the world's, and one day the world will know it, even the fools.
> Ibid.

[j] Like Arthur and the legendary Alexander, and many other lesser men, he [Woodrow Wilson]

left, even though defeated, a hope,
a promise, that League, which is
as it were a symbol of his perished
flesh and blood, a fragment torn
out of his heart and left with us,
to serve for one who will come
after in a retaking up of his adventure.   *Ibid.*

Napoleon Bonaparte
[1769–1821]

[k] Go, sir, gallop, and don't forget that the world was made in six
days. You can ask me for anything
you like, except time.
     *To one of his aides. Quoted in
     R. M. Johnston: The Corsican*

[l] What is the throne?—a bit of
wood gilded and covered with velvet. I am the state—I alone am
here the representative of the
people. Even if I had done wrong
you should not have reproached
me in public—people wash their
dirty linen at home. France has
more need of me than I of France.
          To the Senate [1814]

[m] The bullet that will kill me
is not yet cast.
          At Montereau [1814]

[n] The Allied Powers having proclaimed that the Emperor Napoleon is the sole obstacle to the re-
establishment of peace in Europe,
he, faithful to his oath, declares
that he is ready to descend from
the throne, to quit France, and
even to relinquish life, for the
good of his country.
     Act of Abdication [April 4, 1814]

[o] Whatever shall we do in that
remote spot? Well, we will write
our Memoirs. Work is the scythe
of time.   *On board H. M. S.
               Bellerophon [1815]*

[p] I generally had to give in
[speaking of his relations with the
Empress Josephine].
          On St. Helena [1816]

[q] Our body is a watch, intended
to go for a given time. The watch-
maker cannot open it, and must
work at random. For once that he
relieves or assists it by his crooked
instruments, he injures it ten
times, and at last destroys it.
          *To Dr. Antommarchi
          [October 14, 1820]*

[r] Our hour is marked, and no
one can claim a moment of life beyond what fate has predestined.
     To Dr. Arnott [April 1821]

[s] Madame Montholon having
inquired what troops he considered the best, "Those which are
victorious, Madame," replied the
Emperor.   *Bourrienne:
          Memoirs, Vol. 10, Page 399*

[t] Tête d'armée (Head of the
army.)   *Last words [May 5, 1821]*

Horatius Bonar
[1808–1889]

[u] The star is not extinguished
when it sets
   Upon the dull horizon; it but
     goes
To shine in other skies, then re-
     appear
In ours, as fresh as when it first
     arose.
          Life from Death. Stanza 1

[v] Beyond the smiling and the
     weeping I shall be soon;
Beyond the waking and the sleep-
     ing,
Beyond the sowing and the reap-
     ing.   *A Little While. Stanza 1*

Carrie Jacobs Bond
[1862–1946]

[w] For Memory has painted this
     perfect day
With colors that never fade,
And we find at the end of a perfect
     day
   The soul of a friend we've made.
          A Perfect Day. Stanza 2

Sir David William Bone
[1874–   ]

[x] We sailors are jealous for our
vessels. Abuse us if you will, but
have a care for what you may say
of our ships. We alone are entitled
to call them bitches, wet brutes,
stubborn craft, but we will stand
for no such liberties from the
beach.   *Merchantmen-at-Arms*

Gavin Bone
[1907–1942]

[y] In translation it is more important to produce poetical acid
of the same formula than to preserve any strict equivalence of
words.   *Anglo-Saxon Poetry*

James Bone
[1872–   ]

[z] 'London!' It has the sound of
distant thunder.
          The London Perambulator

[a] The City of Dreadful Height.
          *Description of New York
          [Manchester Guardian]*

[b] To make a cliché is to make
a classic. [Apropos the phrase
"ocean greyhound," first said by
his father, David Drummond
Bone, of S.S. *Alaska*, the first ship
to cross the Atlantic in less than
a week (1881).]
     *Farewell speech on Fleet Street,
          December 29, 1945*

George Borrow
[1803–1881]

[c] Trust not a man's words if
you please, or you may come to
very erroneous conclusions; but at
all times place implicit confidence
in a man's countenance in which
there is no deceit; and of necessity
there can be none. If people would
but look each other more in the
face, we should have less cause to
complain of the deception of the
world; nothing so easy as physiog-
nomy nor so useful.
Lavengro. Chap. 22

[d] Translation is at best an
echo. *Ibid. Chap. 25*

[e] There's night and day,
brother, both sweet things; sun,
moon, and stars, brother, all sweet
things; there's likewise a wind on
the heath. Life is very sweet,
brother; who would wish to die?
Ibid.

[f] Youth is the only season for
enjoyment, and the first twenty-
five years of one's life are worth all
the rest of the longest life of man,
even though those five-and-
twenty be spent in penury and
contempt, and the rest in the possession of wealth, honours, respectability.
The Romany Rye. Chap. 30

General Pierre Bosquet
[1810–1861]

[g] It is magnificent, but it is not
war.
*Said of the charge of the Light
Brigade at the battle of Bala-
klava [October 25, 1854]*

John Collins Bossidy
[1860–1928]

[h] And this is good old Boston,
The home of the bean and the
cod,
Where the Lowells talk to the
Cabots
And the Cabots talk only to God.
*Toast, Midwinter Dinner,
Holy Cross Alumni [1910]*

James Boswell
[1740–1795]
*See also under
Samuel Johnson*

[i] That favourite subject, Myself. *Letter to Temple
[July 26, 1763]*

[j] We cannot tell the precise moment when friendship is formed.
As in filling a vessel drop by drop,
there is at last a drop which
makes it run over; so in a series
of kindnesses there is at last one

which makes the heart run over.
*Life of Dr Johnson Everyman
edition, Vol. II. Page 122*

Gordon Bottomley
[1874 1948]

[k] Many deaths have place in
men
Before they come to die;
Joys must be used and spent, and
then
Abandoned and passed by.
New Year's Eve, 1913

[l] Poetry is founded on the
hearts of men: . . .
And, when mankind is dead and
the world cold,
Poetry's immortality will pass.
Atlantis

[m] When you destroy a blade of
grass
You poison England at her roots.
To Iron Founders and Others

Dion Boucicault
[1822–1890]

[n] Then take the shamrock from
your hat and cast it on the
sod,
It will take root and flourish still,
though under foot it's trod.
*The Wearing of the Green
[adapted from the tradi-
tional Irish ballad]. Stanza 2*

Harold Edwin Boulton
[1859–1935]

[o] Speed, bonnie boat, like a bird
on the wing;
Onward, the sailors cry:
Carry the lad that's born to be
King
Over the sea to Skye.
Skye Boat Song. Stanza 1

Francis William Bourdillon
[1852–1921]

[p] The night has a thousand
eyes,
And the day but one;
Yet the light of the bright world
dies,
With the dying sun.
Light. Stanza 1

[q] The mind has a thousand
eyes,
And the heart but one;
Yet the light of a whole life dies,
When love is done.
Ibid. Stanza 2

Pauline Carrington
Rust Bouvé
[1860–1928]

[r] In the land of the Island
Kingdom,

'Mid Shinto temple and shrine,
. . .
There is carved an odd, quaint les-
son,
Wondrously cut in the wood—
The three wise monkeys of Nikko,
Who see, speak, hear, but the
good!   *The Three Wise*
Monkeys. Stanza 1

Gamaliel Bradford
[1863–1932]

[s] I sometimes wish that God
were back
In this dark world and wide;
For though some virtues he might
lack,
He had his pleasant side.
          Exit God

[t] Youth is alive, and once we
too were young,
Dreamed we could make the
world all over new,
Tossed eager projects lightly from
the tongue,
And hoped the hurrying years
would prove them true.
Wellesley at Fifty, 1881–1931

John Bradford
[1510–1555]

[u] The familiar story, that, on
seeing evil-doers taken to the
place of execution, he was wont to
exclaim: "But for the grace of God
there goes John Bradford," is a
universal tradition, which has
overcome the lapse of time.
*Biographical Notice, Parker
Society edition, The Writings
of John Bradford, Page 43*

Mary Emily Bradley
[1835–1898]

[v] Of all the flowers that come
and go
The whole twelve months together,
This little purple pansy brings
Thoughts of the sweetest, saddest
things.
          Heart's Ease. Stanza 1

Edward Stuyvesant Bragg
[1827–1912]

[w] They love him most for the
enemies he has made.
*Speech seconding the nomina-
tion of Grover Cleveland for
the Presidency, Democratic
National Convention, Chicago
[July 9, 1884]*

John Gardiner Calkins
Brainard
[1795–1828]

[x] Death has shaken out the
sands of thy glass.
          Lament for Long Tom

[y] I saw two clouds at morning,
Tinged with the rising sun,
And in the dawn they floated on,
And mingled into one.
I thought that morning cloud was
blest,
It moved so sweetly to the West.
          Epithalamium. Stanza 1

Mary Gardiner Brainard
[1837–1905]

[z] I see not a step before me as
I tread on another year;
But I've left the Past in God's
keeping,—the Future His
mercy shall clear;
And what looks dark in the distance, may brighten as I draw
near.
          Not Knowing. Stanza 2

Harry Braisted

[a] You're Not the Only Pebble
on the Beach. *Title of song* [1896]

Berton Braley
[1882-   ]

[b] Got any river they say isn't
crossable?
Got any mountains that can't
be cut through?

Trained by a task that's the big-
gest in history:
Who has a job for this Panama
Gang?
At Your Service. Stanzas 2 and 3

[c] The grammar has a rule ab-
surd
Which I would call an outworn
myth:
"A preposition is a word
You mustn't end a sentence
with!"
No Rule to be Afraid of. Stanza 1

[d] This is not I . . .
Retouched and smoothed and
prettified to please;
Put back the wrinkles and the
lines I know;
I have spent blood and brain
achieving these.
Out of the pain, the struggle and
the wrack,
These are my scars of battle—put
them back!
          Sonnet: To a Photographer

[e] With doubt and dismay you
are smitten,
You think there's no chance for
you, son?
Why, the best books haven't been
written,
The best race hasn't been run.
          Opportunity. Stanza 1

[f] If with pleasure you are viewing any work a man is doing,

If you like him or you love him,
tell him now.

Do not wait till life is over and
he's underneath the clover,
For he cannot read his tombstone when he's dead!
Do It Now. Stanzas 1 and 2

[g] If I should lose, let me stand
by the road
And cheer as the winners go by!
Prayer of a Sportsman. Stanza 1

[h] Give the boy a dog and you've
furnished him a playmate
Always true and faithful as can
be.   *A Gift. Stanza 1*

Anna Hempstead Branch
[1875-1937]

[i] Order is a lovely thing;
On disarray it lays its wing,
Teaching simplicity to sing.
The Monk in the Kitchen

[j] God wove a web of loveliness,
Of clouds and stars and birds,
But made not anything at all
So beautiful as words.
Songs for My Mother: Her Words.
Stanza 5

[k] Oh, grieve not, ladies, if at
night
Ye wake to feel your beauty
going.
It was a web of frail delight,
Inconstant as an April snowing.
Grieve Not, Ladies. Stanza 1

William Cowper Brann
[1855-1898]

[l] Boston runs to brains as well
as to beans and brown bread. But
she is cursed with an army of
cranks whom nothing short of a
straight-jacket or a swamp-elm
club will ever control.
The Iconoclast. Beans and Blood

[m] No man can be a patriot on
an empty stomach.
Ibid. Old Glory

Robert Bridges
[1844-1930]

[n] Beauty being the best of all
we know
Sums up the unsearchable and
secret aims
Of nature.
The Growth of Love. Sonnet 8

[o] I live on hope and that I
think do all
Who come into this world.
Ibid. Sonnet 63

[p] Behind the western bars
The shrouded day retreats,
And unperceived the stars
Steal to their sovran seats.
The Clouds Have Left the Sky.
Stanza 3

[q] I have loved flowers that fade,
Within whose magic tents
Rich hues have marriage made
With sweet unmemoried scents.
I Have Loved Flowers that Fade.
Stanza 1

[r] Ah! little at best can all our
hopes avail us
To lift this sorrow, or cheer us,
when in the dark,
Unwilling, alone we embark,
And the things we have seen and
have known and have heard
of, fail us.
On a Dead Child. Stanza 7

[s] When first we met we did not
guess
That Love would prove so hard a
master.
Of more than common friendli-
ness
When first we met we did not
guess.   *Triolet*

[t] So sweet love seemed that
April morn,
When first we kissed beside the
thorn,
So strangely sweet, it was not
strange
We thought that love could never
change.
Shorter Poems. Book V, 5

[u] Love, from whom the world
begun,
Hath the secret of the sun.
Love can tell, and love alone,
Whence the million stars were
strewn,
Why each atom knows its own.
New Poems. Number 9

[v] The nightingale
as amorous of his art as of his
brooding mate
practiseth every phrase of his
espousal lay,
and still provoketh envy of the
lesser songsters.
The Testament of Beauty

[w] Wisdom will repudiate thee,
if thou think to enquire
WHY things are as they are or
whence they came: thy task
is first to learn WHAT IS.
Ibid.

[x] Our hope is ever livelier than
despair, our joy
livelier and more abiding than our
sorrows are.   *Ibid.*

John Bright
[1811-1889]

[y] The Angel of Death has been
abroad throughout the land; you
may almost hear the beating of
his wing.   *Speech, House of*
Commons [February 23, 1855]

[z] Force is no remedy.
On the Irish Troubles [1880]

[a] Had they [the Tories] been in the wilderness they would have complained of the Ten Commandments.   *Remark*

Anthelme Brillat-Savarin
[1755–1826]

[b] Tell me what you eat, and I will tell you what you are.
Physiologie du Goût. Aphorism 4

Mary Dow Brine

[c] She's somebody's mother, boys, you know,
For all she's aged and poor and slow.   *Somebody's Mother*

Denis William Brogan
[1900–   ]

[d] American social fences have to be continually repaired; in England they are like wild hedges; they grow if left alone.
The English People

[e] Man does not live by bread alone, even pre-sliced bread.
The American Character

[f] Any well-established village in New England or the northern Middle West could afford a town drunkard, a town atheist, and a few Democrats.   *Ibid.*

Charlotte Brontë
[1816–1855]

[g] Oft a little morning rain
Foretells a pleasant day.
Life. Stanza 1

[h] The human heart has hidden treasures,
In secret kept, in silence sealed;—
The thoughts, the hopes, the dreams, the pleasures,
Whose charms were broken if revealed.
Evening Solace. Stanza 1

Emily Brontë
[1818–1848]

[i] Bliss like thine is bought by years
Dark with torment and with tears.
Sleep Not. Stanza 1

[j] Love is like the wild rose-briar;
Friendship like the holly-tree.
The holly is dark when the rose-briar blooms,
But which will bloom most constantly?
Love and Friendship. Stanza 1

[k] I'll walk where my own nature would be leading—
It vexes me to choose another guide—

Where the grey flocks in ferny glens are feeding,
Where the wild wind blows on the mountain-side.
Often Rebuked. Stanza 4

[l] No coward soul is mine,
No trembler in the world's storm-troubled sphere:
I see Heaven's glories shine,
And faith shines equal, arming me from fear.
Last Lines. Stanza 1

[m] There is not room for Death.
Ibid. Stanza 7

Rupert Brooke
[1887–1915]

[n] And in that Heaven of all their wish,
There shall be no more land, say fish.
Heaven

[o] Say, is there Beauty yet to find?
And Certainty? and Quiet kind?
Deep meadows yet, for to forget
The lies, and truths, and pain? . . . oh! yet
Stands the Church clock at ten to three?
And is there honey still for tea?
The Old Vicarage, Grantchester

[p] For what they'd never told me of,
And what I never knew,
It was that all the time, my love,
Love would be merely you.
Song

[q] Breathless, we flung us on the windy hill,
Laughed in the sun, and kissed the lovely grass.   *The Hill*

[r] I have been so great a lover: filled my days
So proudly with the splendor of Love's praise. . . .
These I have loved:
White plates and cups, clean-gleaming . . .
The cool kindliness of sheets, that soon
Smooth away trouble; and the rough male kiss
Of blankets; grainy wood; live hair that is
Shining and free; blue-massing clouds; the keen
Unpassioned beauty of a great machine;
The benison of hot water; furs to touch,
The good smell of old clothes.
The Great Lover

[s] If I should die, think only this of me:
That there's some corner of a foreign field
That is for ever England.
The Soldier

[t] Blow out, you bugles, over the rich dead!
There's none of these so lonely and poor of old,
But, dying, has made us rarer gifts than gold.
    The Dead. I

Noah Brooks
[1830–1903]

[u] Conductor, when you receive a fare,
Punch in the presence of the passenjare.
A blue trip slip for an eight cent fare,
A buff trip slip for a six cent fare,
A pink trip slip for a five cent fare,
Punch in the presence of the passenjare.
Punch, brothers, punch with care,
Punch in the presence of the passenjare.
    Inspired by a notice to conductors, posted in New York horsecars [Attributed to Mark Twain, and included by him in A Literary Nightmare]

Phillips Brooks
[1835–1893]

[v] O little town of Bethlehem!
How still we see thee lie;
Above thy deep and dreamless sleep
The silent stars go by;
Yet in thy dark streets shineth
The everlasting Light;
The hopes and fears of all the years
Are met in thee to-night.
    O Little Town of Bethlehem. Stanza 1

[w] Everywhere, everywhere, Christmas tonight!
Christmas in lands of the fir-tree and pine,
Christmas in lands of the palm-tree and vine;
Christmas where snow-peaks stand solemn and white,
Christmas where corn-fields lie sunny and bright.
    A Christmas Carol. Stanza 1

[x] Life comes before literature, as the material always comes before the work. The hills are full of marble before the world blooms with statues.
    Literature and Life

[y] May I try to tell you again where your only comfort lies? It is not in forgetting the happy past. People bring us well-meant but miserable consolation when they tell what time will do to help our grief. We do not want to lose our grief, because our grief is bound up with our love and we could not cease to mourn without being robbed of our affections.
    Letter to a friend on the death of his mother [November 19 1891]

Van Wyck Brooks
[1886–   ]

[z] His wife not only edited his works but edited him.   *The Ordeal of Mark Twain. Chap. 5*

[a] Emerson advised his fellow-townsmen to manufacture school-teachers and make them the best in the world.   *The Flowering of New England. Chap. 13*

[b] As against having beautiful workshops, studies, etc., one writes best in a cellar on a rainy day.   *Epigram*

Robert Barnabas Brough
[1828–1860]

[c] Christians were on the earth ere Christ was born. . . .
Thousands of years ago men dared to die
Loving their enemies—and wondered why!
    An Early Christian

Henry Peter, Lord Brougham
[1779–1868]

[d] Let the soldier be abroad if he will, he can do nothing in this age. There is another personage,— a personage less imposing in the eyes of some, perhaps insignificant. The schoolmaster is abroad, and I trust to him, armed with his primer, against the soldier in full military array.   *Speech, Opening of Parliament [January 29, 1828]*

Heywood Campbell Broun
[1888–1939]

[e] The ability to make love frivolously is the chief characteristic which distinguishes human beings from the beasts.
    It Seems to Me. A Spring Sunday

[f] Life is a copycat and can be bullied into following the master artist who bids it come to heel.
    Ibid. Nature the Copycat

[g] The Irish are the cry-babies of the Western world. Even the mildest quip will set them off into resolutions and protests.
    Ibid. The Piece That Got Me Fired

[h] The swaggering underemphasis of New England.   *Heywood Broun: Collected Edition [1941]*

Alice Brown
[1857–1948]

[i] Of this round earth whereon
  I stand,
I do not own one inch of land;
I shall not lose upon the day
When Gaffer Death drags me
  away.   *Autolycus. Stanza 1*

[j] You shall lie by living waters,
  you shall walk with laughing
  heroes,
You are garnered up in safety in a
  large and lofty room.
  *On the Death of Louise Imogen
    Guiney [Atlantic Monthly,
      March 1921]*

Frances Brown
[1816–1864]

[k] Sad losses have ye met,
  But mine is heavier yet,
For a believing heart hath gone
  from me.   *Losses. Stanza 5*

[l] Oh! those blessed times of
  old! with their chivalry and
  state;
I love to read their chronicles,
  which such brave deeds relate;
I love to sing their ancient
  rhymes, to hear their legends
  told—
But, Heaven be thanked! I live not
  in those blessed times of old!
  *Oh! the Pleasant Days of Old.
    Stanza 7*

John Mason Brown
[1900–   ]

[m] To many people dramatic
criticism must seem like an attempt to tattoo soap bubbles.
      Broadway in Review

[n] Death re-creates an individual out of someone who has fallen
singly from the ranks. In his loneliness by a foreign roadside, this
man or that ceases to be Government Issue, a mass commodity
produced by a mass response out
of a mass need and hope. He once
again becomes man's issue, and
woman's, too.
      Many a Watchful Night

Roscoe Conkling Ensign Brown
[1867–1946]

[o] With equal care weigh well
the record of the wisdom and the
folly of mankind.   *Inscription
  for the wall of the Central
  Library, Brooklyn, New York*

[p] Farther than the arrow,
higher than wings, fly poet's song
and prophet's word.
  *Inscription for a door of the
    Library*

Thomas (Tom) Brown
[1663–1704]

[q] I do not love thee, Doctor Fell,
The reason why I cannot tell;
But this alone I know full well,
I do not love thee, Doctor Fell.
  *Written while a student at
    Christ Church, Oxford*

[r] To treat a poor wretch with a
bottle of Burgundy, and fill his
snuff-box, is like giving a pair of
laced ruffles to a man that has
never a shirt on his back.
      Laconics

Thomas Edward Brown
[1830–1897]

[s] A Garden is a lovesome thing,
    God wot!
  Rose plot,
  Fringed pool,
  Ferned grot—
  The veriest school
Of Peace; and yet the fool
Contends that God is not—
Not God! in Gardens! when the
    eve is cool?
Nay, but I have a sign:
'Tis very sure God walks in mine.
      My Garden

Charles Farrar Browne
see "Artemus Ward"

Sir Thomas Browne
[1605–1682]

[t] The thousand doors that lead
to death.   *Religio Medici. Part I,
              Sect. XLIV*

[u] The heart of man is the place
the Devil dwells in: I feel sometimes a hell within myself.
      Ibid. Sect. LI

[v] There is no road or ready way
to virtue.   *Ibid. Sect. LV*

[w] It is the common wonder of
all men, how among so many millions of faces there should be none
alike.   *Ibid. Part II, Sect. II*

[x] There is music wherever there
is harmony, order, or proportion;
and thus far we may maintain the
music of the spheres.
      Ibid. Sect. IX

[y] Sleep is a death; oh, make me
    try
By sleeping, what it is to die,
And as gently lay my head
On my grave, as now my bed!
      Ibid. Sect. XII

[z] Oblivion is not to be hired:
the greater part must be content
to be as though they had not been.
      Urn-Burial. Chapter 5

[a] Man is a noble animal, splendid in ashes and pompous in the
grave.   *Ibid.*

[b] When we desire to confine our words, we commonly say they are spoken under the rose.
Vulgar Errors

[c] An old and gray-headed error.
Ibid.

William Browne
[1591–1643]

[d] There is no season such delight can bring,
As summer, autumn, winter, and the spring.   *Variety*

Elizabeth Barrett Browning
[1806–1861]

[e] Of all the thoughts of God that are
Borne inward into souls afar,
Along the Psalmist's music deep,
Now tell me if that any is,
For gift or grace, surpassing this:
"He giveth his beloved—sleep?"
The Sleep. Stanza 1

[f] The child's sob in the silence curses deeper
Than the strong man in his wrath.
The Cry of the Children. Stanza 13

[g] Therefore to this dog will I,
Tenderly not scornfully,
Render praise and favor:
With my hand upon his head,
Is my benediction said
Therefore and for ever.
To Flush, My Dog. Stanza 14

[h] Unless you can muse in a crowd all day
On the absent face that fixed you;
Unless you can love, as the angels may,
With the breadth of heaven betwixt you;
Unless you can dream that his faith is fast,
Through behoving and unbehoving;
Unless you can die when the dream is past—
Oh, never call it loving!
*A Woman's Shortcomings.
Stanza 5*

[i] "Yes," I answered you last night;
"No," this morning, sir, I say:
Colors seen by candle-light
Will not look the same by day.
The Lady's "Yes." Stanza 1

[j] How do I love thee? Let me count the ways.   *Sonnets from the Portuguese. XLIII*

[k] When the dust of death has choked
A great man's voice, the common words he said
Turn oracles.   *Casa Guidi Windows. Part I, Line 250*

[l]   But so fair,
She takes the breath of men away
Who gaze upon her unaware.
*Bianca Among the Nightingales.
Stanza 12*

[m] Grief may be joy misunderstood.
De Profundis. Stanza 21

[n] Women know
The way to rear up children (to be just),
They know a simple, merry, tender knack
Of tying sashes, fitting baby-shoes,
And stringing pretty words that make no sense.
Aurora Leigh. Book I, Line 47

[o] Life, struck sharp on death,
Makes awful lightning.
Ibid. Line 210

[p]   When
We gloriously forget ourselves and plunge
Soul-forward, headlong, into a book's profound,
Impassioned for its beauty and salt of truth—
'Tis then we get the right good from a book.
Ibid. Line 705

[q] A woman's always younger than a man
At equal years.
Ibid. Book II, Line 329

[r]   Men do not think.
Of sons and daughters, when they fall in love.   *Ibid. Line 608*

[s]   Every wish
Is like a prayer, with God.
Ibid. Line 954

[t] Girls have curious minds
And fain would know the end of everything.   *Ibid. Line 1194*

[u]   Pay the income-tax
And break your heart upon 't.
Ibid. Book III, Line 566

[v] How many desolate creatures on the earth
Have learnt the simple dues of fellowship
And social comfort, in a hospital.
Ibid. Line 1122

[w] A good neighbour, even in this
Is fatal sometimes,—cuts your morning up
To mincemeat of the very smallest talk.
Ibid. Book IV, Line 488

[x] A little sunburnt by the glare of life.   *Ibid. Line 1140*

[y]   Every age
Appears to souls who live in 't . . .
Most unheroic.
Ibid. Book V, Line 155

[z] Men get opinions as boys
learn to spell,
By reiteration chiefly.
Ibid. Book VI, Line 6

[a] Surgeons . . .
Spend raptures upon perfect
specimens
Of indurated veins, distorted
joints,
Or beautiful new cases of curved
spine. *Ibid. Line 173*

[b] Since when was genius found
respectable? *Ibid. Line 275*

[c] Earth's crammed with
heaven,
And every common bush afire
with God;
But only he who sees takes off his
shoes—
The rest sit round it and pluck
blackberries.
Ibid. Book VII, Line 820

Robert Browning
[1812–1889]

[d] For music (which is earnest
of a heaven,
Seeing we know emotions strange
by it,
Not else to be revealed,) is like a
voice,
A low voice calling fancy, as a
friend,
To the green woods in the gay
summer time. *Pauline*

[e] Heap logs and let the blaze
laugh out!
Paracelsus. Part III

[f] Respect all such as sing when
all alone! *Ibid.*

[g]   I detest all change,
And most a change in aught I
loved long since. *Ibid.*

[h]   Every joy is gain
And gain is gain, however small.
Ibid. Part IV

[i] 'Twere too absurd to slight
For the hereafter the to-day's delight! *Sordello. VI*

[j] Any nose
May ravage with impunity a rose.
Ibid.

[k] Day!
Faster and more fast,
O'er night's brim, day boils at last.
Pippa Passes. Introduction

[l] The year's at the spring
And day's at the morn.
Ibid. Part I

[m] God's in his heaven:
All's right with the world.
Ibid.

[n] May's warm slow yellow
moonlit summer nights.
Ibid Part III

[o] In the morning of the world,
When earth was nigher heaven
than now. *Ibid.*

[p] June reared that bunch of
flowers you carry,
From seeds of April's sowing.
Ibid.

[q] All service ranks the same
with God:
With God, whose puppets, best
and worst,
Are we: there is no last nor first.
Ibid. Part IV

[r] Just for a handful of silver he
left us,
Just for a riband to stick in his
coat. *The Lost Leader*

[s] What a man's work comes to!
So he plans it,
Performs it, perfects it, makes
amends
For the toiling and moiling, and
then, *sic transit!   Old Pictures in Florence. Stanza 10*

[t] Oh, to be in England,
Now that April's there.
*Home-Thoughts from Abroad.
Stanza 1*

[u] That's the wise thrush; he
sings each song twice over,
Lest you should think he never
could recapture
The first fine careless rapture!
Ibid. Stanza 2

[v] God is seen God
In the star, in the stone, in the
flesh, in the soul and the clod.
Saul. XVII

[w] Oh, the little more, and how
much it is!
And the little less, and what
worlds away!
By the Fireside. Stanza 39

[x] To dry one's eyes and laugh at
a fall,
And baffled, get up and begin
again.
Life in a Love. Stanza 2

[y] Ah, did you once see Shelley
plain,
And did he stop and speak to
you,
And did you speak to him again?
How strange it seems and new!
Memorabilia. I

[z'] There's a woman like a dewdrop, she's so purer than the
purest. *A Blot in the
'Scutcheon. Act I, Sc. 3*

[a'] When is man strong until he
feels alone?
Colombe's Birthday, Act III

[b'] "You're wounded!" "Nay,"
the soldier's pride
Touched to the quick, he said:
"I'm killed, Sire!" And his chief
beside,
Smiling the boy fell dead.
*Incident of the French Camp.
Stanza 5*

[c] When a man's busy, why,
    leisure
Strikes him as wonderful pleas-
    ure:
'Faith, and at leisure once is he?
Straightway he wants to be busy
        The Glove Stanza 1

[d] It's a long lane that knows
    no turnings.
    The Flight of the Duchess. XVII

[e] Ah, but a man's reach should
    exceed his grasp,
Or what's a heaven for?
        Andrea del Sarto.

[f]   You call for faith:
I show you doubt, to prove that
    faith exists.
The more of doubt, the stronger
    faith, I say,
If faith o'ercomes doubt.
        Bishop Blougram's Apology

[g] God be thanked, the meanest
    of his creatures
Boasts two soul-sides, one to face
    the world with,
One to show a woman when he
    loves her!
        One Word More. XVII

[h] Grow old along with me!
The best is yet to be,
The last of life, for which the first
    was made.
        Rabbi Ben Ezra. Stanza 1

[i] Progress, man's distinctive
    mark alone,
Not God's, and not the beasts':
    God is, they are;
Man partly is, and wholly hopes to
    be.   *A Death in the Desert.*

[j] O Lyric Love, half angel and
    half bird,
And all a wonder and a wild de-
    sire.
        The Ring and the Book. I

[k] Call in law when a neighbor
    breaks your fence,
Cribs from your field, tampers
    with rent or lease,
Touches the purse or pocket,—but
    woos your wife?
No: take the old way trod when
    men were men!
        Ibid. II, Half-Rome

[l] "The serpent tempted me and
    I did eat."
So much of paradisal nature,
    Eve's!
Her daughters ever since prefer to
    urge
"Adam so starved me I was fain
    accept
The apple any serpent pushed my
    way."
        Ibid. IV, Tertium Quid

[m] 'Twas a thief that said the
    last kind word to Christ:
Christ took the kindness and for-
    gave the theft.
        Ibid. VI, Giuseppe Caponsacchi

[n] There's a blessing on the
    hearth
A special providence for father-
    hood!
    *Ibid. VIII, Dominus Hyacinthus
    de Archangelis*

[o]   What I call God,
And fools call Nature.
        Ibid X The Pope

[p] Why comes temptation, but
    for man to meet
And master and make crouch be-
    neath his foot
And so be pedestaled in triumph?
        Ibid.

[q] White shall not neutralize
    the black, nor good
Compensate bad in man, absolve
    him so:
Life's business being just the
    terrible choice   *Ibid.*

[r] A man in armor is his armor's
    slave   *Herakles*

[s] So absolutely good is truth,
    truth never hurts
The teller.
        Fifine at the Fair. XXXII

[t]   That far land we dream
    about,
Where every man is his own archi-
    tect.   *Red Cotton Night-
        Cap Country. II*

[u] A secret's safe
'Twixt you, me, and the gate-post!
        The Inn Album. II

[v] Because a man has shop to
    mind
In time and place, since flesh
    must live,
Needs spirit lack all life behind,
    All stray thoughts, fancies fugi-
    tive,
All love except what trade can
    give?   *Shop. Stanza 20*

[w] Good, to forgive;
Best, to forget!
Living, we fret;
Dying, we live.   *La Saisiaz.
        Introduction, Stanza 1*

[x] Such a starved bank of moss
Till, that May-morn,
Blue ran the flash across:
Violets were born!
        *The Two Poets of Croisic.
        Introduction, Stanza 1*

[y]   As if true pride
Were not also humble!
        In an Album

[z] What Youth deemed crystal,
    Age finds out was dew
Morn set a-sparkle, but which
    noon quick dried.
Jochanan Hakkadosh Stanza 101

[a] Help me with knowledge—
for Life's Old—Death's New!
Epitaph on Levi Lincoln Thaxter
        [1824–1884]

[b] A minute's success pays the failure of years. *Apollo and the Fates. Stanza 42*

[c] There is no truer truth obtainable
By Man than comes of music.
Parleyings with Certain People. With Charles Avison, VI

Jean de la Bruyère
[1645–1696]

[d] Liberality consists less in giving a great deal than in gifts well-timed. *Les Caractères. Du Cœur*

[e] To laugh at men of sense is the privilege of fools.
Ibid. De la Société

[f] Everything has been said.
Ibid. Des Ouvrages de l'Esprit

George Sands Bryan
[1879–1943]

[g] "What has upheld you on your way?
What has supported you when faint?
On what have you for strength relied?"
"My vittles," said the dear old saint.
Aunt Phoebe. Stanza 4

William Jennings Bryan
[1860–1925]

[h] The humblest citizen of all the land, when clad in the armor of a righteous cause is stronger than all the hosts of Error.
Speech at the National Democratic Convention, Chicago [1896]

[i] You shall not press down upon the brow of labor this crown of thorn. You shall not crucify mankind upon a cross of gold.
Ibid.

[j] If matter mute and inanimate, though changed by the forces of Nature into a multitude of forms, can never die, will the spirit of man suffer annihilation when it has paid a brief visit, like a royal guest, to this tenement of clay? No. I am as sure that there is another life as I am that I live to-day. *The Prince of Peace*

William Cullen Bryant
[1794–1878]

[k] To him who in the love of Nature holds
Communion with her visible forms, she speaks
A various language. . . .
Go forth, under the open sky, and list
To Nature's teachings.
Thanatopsis

[l]   The hills,
Rock-ribbed, and ancient as the sun.   *Ibid.*

[m] Old ocean's gray and melancholy waste.   *Ibid*

[n] So live, that when thy summons comes . . .
Thou go not, like the quarry-slave at night,
Scourged to his dungeon, but, sustained and soothed
By an unfaltering trust, approach thy grave,
Like one that wraps the drapery of his couch
About him, and lies down to pleasant dreams.   *Ibid.*

[o] He who, from zone to zone,
Guides through the boundless sky thy certain flight,
In the long way that I must tread alone,
Will lead my steps aright.
To a Waterfowl. Stanza 8

[p] The stormy March has come at last,
With wind, and cloud, and changing skies;
I hear the rushing of the blast,
That through the snowy valley flies.   *March. Stanza 1*

[q] The groves were God's first temples.   *A Forest Hymn*

[r] Rogue's Island once—but when the rogues were dead,
Rhode Island was the name it took instead.   *A Meditation on Rhode Island Coal. Stanza 1*

[s] The melancholy days are come, the saddest of the year,
Of wailing winds, and naked woods, and meadows brown and sere.   *The Death of the Flowers. Stanza 1*

[t] Loveliest of lovely things are they,
On earth, that soonest pass away.
The rose that lives its little hour
Is prized beyond the sculptured flower.   *A Scene on the Banks of the Hudson. Stanza 3*

[u] These are the gardens of the Desert, these
The unshorn fields, boundless and beautiful,
For which the speech of England has no name—
The Prairies.   *The Prairies*

[v] Truth, crushed to earth, shall rise again;
The eternal years of God are hers;
But Error, wounded, writhes in pain,
And dies among his worshippers.
The Battle-Field. Stanza 9

[w] The fiercest agonies have shortest reign.   *Mutation*

x] Tender pauses speak
The overflow of gladness, when
words are all too weak.
The Damsel of Peru. Stanza 7

y] Man foretells afar
The courses of the stars; the very
hour
He knows when they shall darken
or grow bright;
Yet doth the eclipse of Sorrow and
of Death
Come unforewarned.
An Evening Revery

[z] We plant, upon the sunny lea,
A shadow for the noontide hour,
A shelter from the summer
shower,
When we plant the apple-tree.
*The Planting of the Apple-Tree.
Stanza 2*

[a] The horrid tale of perjury and
strife,
Murder and spoil, which men call
history.   *Earth*

[b] Lord, who ordainest for mankind
Benignant toils and tender
cares!
We thank Thee for the ties that
bind
The mother to the child she
bears.
The Mother's Hymn. Stanza 1

James Bryce
[1838–1922]

[c] The greatest liberty that man
has taken with Nature.
*South America [Of the Panama
Canal]*

[d] What you want [in Washing-
ton] is to have a city which every
one who comes from Maine, Texas,
Florida, Arkansas, or Oregon can
admire as being something finer
and more beautiful than he had
ever dreamed of before; something
which makes him even more
proud to be an American.   *The
Nation's Capital [National Geo-
graphic Magazine, 1913]*

[e] To most people nothing is
more troublesome than the effort
of thinking.   *Studies in History
and Jurisprudence, Vol. 2, Page 7*

John Buchan,
Lord Tweedsmuir
[1875–1940]

[f] We can only pay our debt to
the past by putting the future in
debt to ourselves.   *Address to
the People of Canada, on the
Coronation of King George VI,
May 12, 1937*

Robert Buchanan
[1841–1901]

[g]   Alone at night,
I read my Bible more and Euclid
less.
An Old Dominie's Story

[h] I saw the starry Tree
Eternity
Put forth the blossom Time.
Proteus

[i] I say, the world is lovely,
And that loveliness is enough.
Artist and Model

Pearl S. Buck
(Mrs. Richard J. Walsh)
[1892–   ]

[j] How could an actual person
fit into the covers of a book? The
book is not a continent, not a
definite geographical measure, it
cannot contain so huge a thing as
an actual full-size person. Any
person has to be scaled by elim-
inations to fit the book world.
Advice to Unborn Novelists

James Buckham
("Paul Pastnor")
[1858–1908]

[k] King Hassan, well beloved,
was wont to say
When aught went wrong, or any
project failed:
"To-morrow, friends, will be another day!"
And in that faith he slept and
so prevailed.
To-morrow. Stanza 1

Arthur Henry Reginald Buller
[1874–1944]

[l] There was a young lady
named Bright,
Whose speed was far faster than
light;
She set out one day
In a relative way,
And returned home the previous
night.   *Limerick
[Punch, December 19, 1923]*

George W. Bungay
[1826–1892]

[m] The merchant who for silk
would sell
The cotton woven in,
Something that is not truth will
tell,
And think it little sin.
The False and the True. Stanza 4

Alfred Bunn
[1796–1860]

[n] I dreamt that I dwelt in
marble halls,
With vassals and serfs at my side.

But—I also dreamt, which pleas'd
me most,
That you loved me still the same.
The Bohemian Girl. Act 2, Song

Henry Cuyler Bunner
[1855–1896]

[o] Off with your hat as the flag
goes by!
And let the heart have its say;
You're man enough for a tear in
your eye
That you will not wipe away.
The Old Flag. Stanza 1

[p] It was an old, old, old, old
lady,
And a boy that was half-past
three;
And the way that they played to-
gether
Was beautiful to see.
"One, Two, Three." Stanza 1

[q] What does he plant who
plants a tree?
He plants the friend of sun and
sky;
He plants the flag of breezes free;
The shaft of beauty towering
high.
The Heart of the Tree. Stanza 1

[r] Happy the mortal free and
independent,
Master of the mainspring of his
own volition!
Look on us with the eye of sweet
compassion:
We are Cook's Tourists.
*The Wail of the "Personally
Conducted." Stanza 6*

John Bunyan
[1628–1688]

[s] The name of the slough was
Despond.
Pilgrim's Progress. Part I

[t] Dark as pitch.   *Ibid.*

[u] The pilgrim they laid in a
large upper chamber, whose window opened toward the sun-ris-
ing; the name of the chamber was
Peace.   *Ibid.*

[v] It beareth the name of Vanity
Fair, because the town where 'tis
kept is lighter than vanity.
Ibid.

[w] A castle called Doubting
Castle, the owner whereof was
Giant Despair.   *Ibid.*

[x] They came to the Delectable
Mountains.   *Ibid.*

[y] Some things are of that na-
ture as to make
One's fancy chuckle, while his
heart doth ache. *Ibid. The
Author's Way of Sending Forth
His Second Part of the Pilgrim*

[z] A man that could look no way
but downwards with a muck-rake
in his hand.   *Ibid. Part I*

[a] He that is down needs fear no
fall.
Ibid. The Shepherd Boy's Song

[b] So he passed over, and all the
trumpets sounded for him on the
other side.   *Ibid*

Robert Jones Burdette
[1844–1914]

[c] I love the man who knows it
all,
From east to west, from north to
south,
Who knows all things, both great
and small,
And tells it with his tiresome
mouth.
He Knows It All. Stanza 1

[d] The shadows soft and gray
the pearly light
Of summer twilight deep'ning
into night.
Bartimeus. Stanza 1

[e] There are two days in the
week about which and upon
which I never worry. Two care-
free days, kept sacredly free from
fear and apprehension. One of
these days is Yesterday. . . . And
the other . . . is Tomorrow.
The Golden Day

Gelett Burgess
[1866–1951]

[f] I'd rather have Fingers than
Toes,
I'd rather have Eyes than a Nose;
And as for my Hair
I'm glad it's all there,
I'll be awfully sad when it goes.
Nonsense Verses

[g] I never saw a Purple Cow,
I never hope to see one;
But I can tell you, anyhow,
I'd rather see than be one.
The Purple Cow

[h] Ah, yes, I wrote the "Purple
Cow"—
I'm sorry, now, I wrote it!
But I can tell you, anyhow,
I'll kill you if you quote it.
Cinq Ans Après

[i] Not the quarry, but the chase,
Not the laurel, but the race,
Not the hazard, but the play,
Make me, Lord, enjoy alway.
A Prayer

Edmund Burke
[1729–1797]

[j] The writers against religion,
whilst they oppose every system,

are wisely careful never to set up any of their own.   *Works. Vol. I, Preface, A Vindication of Natural Society*

[k] I am convinced that we have a degree of delight, and that no small one, in the real misfortunes and pains of others.   *On the Sublime and Beautiful. Sect. XIV*

[l] Custom reconciles us to everything.   *Ibid. Sect. XVIII*

[m] There is, however, a limit at which forbearance ceases to be a virtue.   *Observations on a Late Publication on the Present State of the Nation* [1769]

[n] So to be patriots as not to forget we are gentlemen.
      Thoughts on the Cause of the Present Discontents

[o] It ought to be the happiness and glory of a representative to live in the strictest union, the closest correspondence, and the most unreserved communication with his constituents. . . . It is his duty to sacrifice his repose, his pleasures, his satisfaction, to theirs; and above all, ever, and in all cases, to prefer their interests to his own.   *Speech to the Electors of Bristol* [*November 3, 1774*]

[p] Your representative owes you, not his industry only, but his judgment; and he betrays instead of serving you if he sacrifices it to your opinion.   *Ibid.*

[q] There is America, which at this day serves for little more than to amuse you with stories of savage men and uncouth manners, yet shall, before you taste of death, show itself equal to the whole of that commerce which now attracts the envy of the world.   *Speech on Conciliation with America* [*March 22, 1775*]

[r] The march of the human mind is slow.   *Ibid.*

[s] All government,—indeed every human benefit and every prudent act,—is founded on compromise and barter.   *Ibid.*

[t] What shadows we are, and what shadows we pursue.
      Speech at Bristol on Declining the Poll [*September 9, 1780*]

[u] People will not look forward to posterity who never look backward to their ancestors.
      Reflections on the Revolution in France

[v] You had that action and counteraction which, in the natural and in the political world, from the reciprocal struggle of discordant powers draws out the harmony of the universe.   *Ibid.*

[w] The age of chivalry is gone; that of sophisters, economists, and calculators has succeeded.   *Ibid.*

[x] That chastity of honour which felt a stain like a wound.
      Ibid.

[y] Vice itself lost half its evil by losing all its grossness.   *Ibid.*

[z] Kings will be tyrants from policy, when subjects are rebels from principle.   *Ibid.*

[a] Because half-a-dozen grasshoppers under a fern make the field ring with their importunate chink, whilst thousands of great cattle, reposed beneath the shadow of the British oak, chew the cud and are silent, pray do not imagine that those who make the noise are the only inhabitants of the field.   *Ibid.*

[b] He that wrestles with us strengthens our nerves and sharpens our skill. Our antagonist is our helper.   *Ibid.*

[c] You can never plan the future by the past.   *Letter to a Member of the National Assembly*

[d] The cold neutrality of an impartial judge.
      Preface to Brissot's Address

[e] And having looked to Government for bread, on the very first scarcity they will turn and bite the hand that fed them.
      Thoughts and Details on Scarcity

[f] Example is the school of mankind, and they will learn at no other.   *Letter I, On a Regicide Peace*

[g] The people never give up their liberties but under some delusion.
      Speech at County Meeting of Bucks [1784]

[h] Mere parsimony is not economy. . . . Expense, and great expense, may be essential part of true economy.
      Letter to a Noble Lord [1796]

[i] He was not merely a chip of the old block, but the old block itself.
      On Pitt's First Speech. From Wraxall's Memoirs, First Series, Vol. I, Page 342

Dana Burnet

[1888-   ]

[j] I'd rather have an inch of dog than miles of pedigree.
      The Road to Vagabondia. Stanza 3

Robert Burns

[1759–1796]

[k] Auld Nature swears the lovely dears
      Her noblest work she classes, O;

Her 'prentice han' she tried on
man,
And then she made the lasses,
O!   *Green Grow the Rashes.*
Stanza 5

[l] Some books are lies frae end
to end.   *Death and*
Dr. Hornbook. Stanza 1

[m] The best laid schemes o' mice
and men
Gang aft a-gley;
An' lea'e us nought but grief and
pain,
For promis'd joy.
To a Mouse, Stanza 7

[n] When chill November's surly
blast
Made fields and forests bare.
Man Was Made to Mourn.
Stanza 1

[o] Man's inhumanity to man
Makes   countless   thousands
mourn.   *Ibid. Stanza 7*

[p] Princes and lords are but the
breath of kings,
"An honest man's the noblest
work of God."
The Cotter's Saturday Night.
Stanza 19

[q] Gie me ae spark o' Nature's
fire,
That's a' the learning I desire.
First Epistle to J. Lapraik.
Stanza 13

[r] The social, friendly, honest
man,
Whate'er he be,
'Tis he fulfils great Nature's plan,
And none but he.
Second Epistle to J. Lapraik.
Stanza 15

[s] Morality, thou deadly bane,
Thy tens o' thousands thou hast
slain!
A Dedication to Gavin Hamilton

[t] It's hardly in a body's pow'r,
To keep, at times, frae being sour.
Epistle to Davie. Stanza 2

[u] God knows, I'm no the thing
I should be,
Nor am I even the thing I could
be.   *To the Reverend*
John M'Math, Stanza 8

[v] O Life! how pleasant, in thy
morning,
Young Fancy's rays the hills
adorning!
Cold-pausing   Caution's   lesson
scorning,
We frisk away,
Like schoolboys, at th' expected
warning,
To joy an' play.
Epistle to James Smith.
Stanza 15

[w] Oh wad some power the giftie
gie us
To see oursels as others see us!

It wad frae monie a blunder free
us,
An' foolish notion.
To a Louse. Stanza 8

[x] Then   gently   scan   your
brother man,
Still gentler sister woman;
Though they may gang a kennin
wrang,
To step aside is human.
Address to the Unco Guid.
Stanza 7

[y] What's done we partly may
compute,
But know not what's resisted.
Ibid. Stanza 8

[z] O life! thou art a galling
load,
Along a rough, a weary road,
To wretches such as I!
Despondency. Stanza 1

[a] To catch Dame Fortune's
golden smile,
Assiduous wait upon her;
And gather gear by ev'ry wile
That's justified by honor:
Not for to hide it in a hedge,
Nor for a train-attendant;
But for the glorious privilege
Of being independent.
Epistle to a Young Friend.
Stanza 7

[b] If there's another world, he
lives in bliss;
If there is none, he made the best
of this.
Epitaph on William Muir

[c] When Nature her great masterpiece design'd,
And fram'd her last, best work,
the human mind,
Her eye intent on all the wondrous
plan,
She form'd of various stuff the
various Man.
To Robert Graham. Stanza 1

[d] Flow   gently,   sweet   Afton,
among thy green braes;
Flow gently, I'll sing thee a song
in thy praise.
Flow Gently, Sweet Afton.
Stanza 1

[e] Naebody cares for me,
I care for naebody.
I Hae a Wife o' my Ain.
Stanza 4

[f] Should auld acquaintance be
forgot,
And never brought to mind?
Should auld acquaintance be for-
got,
And auld lang syne?

We'll tak a cup o' kindness yet
For auld lang syne!
Auld Lang Syne.
Stanzas 1 and 5

[g] John Anderson my jo, John,
When we were first acquent,

Your locks were like the raven,
Your bonny brow was brent
        John Anderson Stanza 1

[h] This day Time winds th' exhausted chain,
To run the twelvemonth's length
again.   *New Year's Day 1791.*
        Stanza 1

[i] The voice of Nature loudly
cries,
And many a message from the
skies,
That something in us never dies.
        Ibid. Stanza 3

[j] My heart's in the Highlands,
my heart is not here;
My heart's in the Highlands
a-chasing the deer.
        My Heart's in the Highlands.
        Chorus

[k] She is a winsome wee thing,
She is a handsome wee thing,
She is a lo'esome wee thing,
This sweet wee wife o' mine.
        My Wife's a Winsome Wee Thing
        Chorus

[l] The golden hours on angel
wings
Flew o'er me and my dearie;
For dear to me as light and life
Was my sweet Highland Mary
        Highland Mary Stanza 2

[m] But, oh! fell death's untimely frost,
That nipt my flower sae early.
        Ibid. Stanza 3

[n] Liberty's in every blow!
Let us do, or die.
Scots, Wha Hae [*Bannockburn*].
        Stanza 6

[o] Oh, my luve is like a red, red
rose,
That's newly sprung in June;
Oh, my luve is like the melodie,
That's sweetly played in tune.
        A Red, Red Rose Stanza 1

[p] Nursing her wrath to keep it
warm.
        Tam o' Shanter. Stanza 1

[q] Ah, gentle dames! it gars me
greet
To think how monie counsels
sweet,
How monie lengthened, sage ad-
vices,
The husband frae the wife despises.   *Ibid. Stanza 4*

[r] But pleasures are like poppies
spread,
You seize the flower, its bloom is
shed;
Or like the snow falls in the river,
A moment white, then melts forever.   *Ibid. Stanza 7*

[s] That hour, o' night's black
arch the keystane.   *Ibid.*

[t] Inspiring bold John Barley-
corn,

What dangers thou canst make us
scorn!   *Ibid. Stanza 11*

[u] The mirth and fun grew fast
and furious.   *Ibid. Stanza 13*

[v] But to see her was to love her,
Love but her, and love forever
        Ae Fond Kiss. Stanza 2

[w] Had we never loved sae
kindly
Had we never loved sae blindly,
Never met—or never parted—
We had ne'er been broken-
hearted!   *Ibid.*

[x] Ye banks and braes o' bonny
Doon,
How can ye bloom sae fresh and
fair?
How can ye chant, ye little birds,
And I sae weary fu' o' care?
        The Banks o' Doon. Stanza 1

[y] The rank is but the guinea's
stamp,
The man's the gowd for a' that.
        Is There for Honest Poverty.
        Stanza 1

[z] Some hae meat and canna eat,
And some wad eat that want it;
But we hae meat, and we can eat,
And sae the Lord be thankit.
        The Selkirk Grace

Amelia Josephine Burr
[1878-   ]

[a] As one who looks on a face
through a window through
life I have looked on God.
Because I have loved life, I shall
have no sorrow to die.
        A Song of Living Stanza 3

John Burroughs
[1837-1921]

[b] In sorrow he learned this
truth—
One may return to the place of his
birth,
He cannot go back to his youth.
        The Return. Stanza 3

[c] Serene, I fold my hands and
wait,
Nor care for wind, nor tide, nor
sea;
I rave no more 'gainst time or fate,
For lo! my own shall come to
me.   *Waiting. Stanza 1*

[d] Literature is an investment
of genius which pays dividends to
all subsequent times.
        Literary Fame

[e] Time does not become sacred
to us until we have lived it
        The Spell of the Past

[f] Nature teaches more than she
preaches There are no sermons
in stones It is easier to get a spark
out of a stone than a moral
        Time and Change.
        The Gospel of Nature

[g] I go to books and to nature as a bee goes to the flower, for a nectar that I can make into my own honey. *The Summit of the Years*

[h] Life is a struggle, but not a warfare. *Ibid.*

[i] How far are we from home?
Last words [March 29, 1921], on a train crossing Ohio, homeward bound from California

Henry Burton
[1840–1930]

[j] Have you had a kindness shown?
Pass it on. *Pass It On*
[*Official poem of the International Sunshine Society*].
Stanza 1

Richard Burton
[1861–1940]

[k] From their folded mates they wander far,
Their ways seem harsh and wild;
They follow the beck of a baleful star,
Their paths are dream-beguiled.
Black Sheep

[l] I sit in mine house at ease,
Moving nor foot nor hand;
Yet sail through uncharted seas
And wander from land to land.
Travel

Robert Burton
[1577–1640]

[m] Naught so sweet as melancholy. *Anatomy of Melancholy. The Author's Abstract*

[n] They lard their lean books with the fat of others' works.
Ibid. Democritus to the Reader

[o] A dwarf standing on the shoulders of a giant may see farther than a giant himself.
Ibid.

[p] Women wear the breeches.
Ibid.

[q] Cookery is become an art, a noble science; cooks are gentlemen. *Ibid. Part I, Sect. 2, Memb 2 Subsect. 2*

[r] No rule is so general, which admits not some exception.
Ibid. Subsect. 3

[s] A nightingale dies for shame if another bird sings better.
Ibid. Memb. 3, Subsect. 6

[t] [Desire] is a perpetual rack, or horsemill, according to Austin, still going round as in a ring.
Ibid. Subsect. 11

[u] [The rich] are indeed rather possessed by their money than possessors. *Ibid. Subsect. 12*

[v] I may not here omit those two main plagues and common dotages of human kind, wine and women, which have infatuated and besotted myriads of people; they go commonly together.
Ibid. Subsect. 13

[w] All our geese are swans.
Ibid. Subsect. 14

[x] They are proud in humility; proud in that they are not proud.
Ibid.

[y] See one promontory (said Socrates of old), one mountain, one sea, one river, and see all.
Ibid. Memb. 4, Subsect. 7

[z] Aristotle said melancholy men of all others are most witty.
Ibid. Sect. 3, Memb. 1, Subsect. 3

[a] Seneca thinks the gods are well pleased when they see great men contending with adversity.
Ibid. Part II, Sect. 1, Memb. 1, Subsect. 1

[b] Machiavel says virtue and riches seldom settle on one man.
Ibid. Memb. 2

[c] Set a beggar on horseback and he will ride a gallop. *Ibid.*

[d] Who cannot give good counsel? 'Tis cheap, it costs them nothing. *Ibid. Memb. 2*

[e] All places are distant from heaven alike. *Ibid. Memb. 4*

[f] Every man, as the saying is, can tame a shrew but he that hath her. *Ibid. Memb. 6*

[g'] Divers have been relieved [of melancholy] by exonerating themselves to a faithful friend. *Ibid.*

[h'] Tobacco, divine, rare, superexcellent tobacco, which goes far beyond all the panaceas, potable gold and philosopher's stones, a sovereign remedy to all diseases.
Ibid. Sect. 4, Memb. 2, Subsect. 2

[i'] Birds of a feather will gather together. *Ibid. Part III, Sect. 1, Memb. 1, Subsect. 2*

[j'] Every man for himself, his own ends, the Devil for all.
Ibid. Memb. 3

[k'] No cord nor cable can so forcibly draw, or hold so fast, as love can do with a twined thread.
Ibid. Sect. 2, Memb. 1, Subsect. 2

[l'] Marriage and hanging go by destiny; matches are made in heaven. *Ibid. Memb. 2, Subsect. 5*

[m'] Diogenes struck the father when the son swore. *Ibid.*

[n'] Though it rain daggers with their points downward.
Ibid. Memb. 3

[o] Going as if he trod upon eggs.
Ibid.

[p] As clear and as manifest as
the nose in a man's face.
Ibid. Sect. 3, Memb. 4, Subsect. 1

[q] Make a virtue of necessity.
Ibid.

[r] Where God hath a temple,
the Devil will have a chapel.
Ibid. Sect. 4, Memb. 1. Subsect. 2

[s] The fear of some divine and
supreme powers keeps men in
obedience. *Ibid.*

[t] Out of too much learning become mad. *Ibid.*

[u] The Devil himself, which is
the author of confusion and lies.
Ibid. Subsect 3

[v] When they are at Rome, they
do there as they see done.
Ibid. Memb. 2, Subsect. 1

[w] One religion is as true as another. *Ibid.*

Wilhelm Busch
[1832–1908]

[x] Youth should heed the older-
witted
When they say, don't go too
far—
Now their sins are all committed,
Lord, how virtuous they are'
Pious Helen (Die fromme Helene)

Ellis Parker Butler
[1869–1937]

[y] Pigs is Pigs. *Title of story*

[z] It is other folks' dogs and
children that make most of the
bad feelin's between neighbors.
*The Confessions of a Daddy.
Chap 1*

Nicholas Murray Butler
[1862–1947]

[a] An expert is one who knows
more and more about less and
less. *Commencement Address.
Columbia University*

Samuel Butler
[1600–1680]

[b] We grant, although he had
much wit,
He was very shy of using it.
Hudibras, Part I, Canto I. Line 45

[c] Whatever sceptic could inquire for,
For every why he had a wherefore. *Ibid. Line 131*

[d] Compound for sins they are
inclined to,
By damning those they have no
mind to. *Ibid. Line 215*

[e] He ne'er consider'd it, as loth
To look a gift-horse in the mouth.
Ibid. Line 489

[f] Quoth Hudibras, "I smell a
rat!
Ralpho, thou dost prevaricate."
Ibid. Line 821

[g] And bid the devil take the
hin'most. *Ibid. Canto II,
Line 633*

[h] I'll make the fur
Fly 'bout the ears of the old cur.
Ibid. Canto III, Line 277

[i] Love is a boy by poets styl'd;
Then spare the rod and spoil the
child. *Ibid. Part II, Canto I,
Line 843*

[j] The sun had long since in the
lap
Of Thetis taken out his nap,
And, like a lobster boil'd the morn
From black to red began to turn.
Ibid Canto II, Line 29

[k] For truth is precious and
divine,—
Too rich a pearl for carnal swine.
Ibid. Line 257

[l] He that imposes an oath
makes it,
Not he that for convenience takes
it;
Then how can any man be said
To break an oath he never made?
Ibid. Line 377

[m] As the ancients
Say wisely, have a care o' th' main
chance,
And look before you ere you leap;
For as you sow. ye are like to reap.
Ibid. Line 501

[n] Doubtless the pleasure is as
great
Of being cheated as to cheat.
Ibid. Canto III, Line 1

[o'] To swallow gudgeons ere
they're catch'd,
And count their chickens ere
they're hatch'd.
Ibid. Line 923

[p'] What makes all doctrines
plain and clear?
About two hundred pounds a year.
And that which was prov'd true
before
Prove false again? Two hundred
more. *Ibid. Part III, Canto
I, Line 1277*

[q'] With crosses, relics, crucifixes,
Beads, pictures, rosaries, and
pixes,—
The tools of working our salvation
By mere mechanic operation.
Ibid. Line 1495

[r'] True as the dial to the sun,
Although it be not shin'd upon.
Ibid. Canto II, Line 175

[s'] For those that fly may fight
again,

Which he can never do that's
slain.
           Ibid. Canto III, Line 243

[t] He that complies against his
will
Is of his own opinion still.
           Ibid. Line 547

[u] And poets by their sufferings
grow,
As if there were no more to do,
To make a poet excellent,
But only want and discontent.
           Fragments

Samuel Butler
[1835–1902]

[v] It is far safer to know too
little than too much. People will
condemn the one, though they
will resent being called upon to
exert themselves to follow the
other.
           The Way of All Flesh. Chap. 5

[w] It is our less conscious
thoughts and our less conscious
actions which mainly mould our
lives and the lives of those who
spring from us.   *Ibid.*

[x] To me it seems that youth is
like spring, an over-praised season
—delightful if it happen to be a
favoured one, but in practice . . .
more remarkable   for biting
east winds than genial breezes.
           Ibid. Chap. 6

[y] In old age we live under the
shadow of Death, which, like a
sword of Damocles, may descend
at any moment, but we have so
long found life to be an affair of
being rather frightened than hurt
that we have become like the people who live under Vesuvius, and
chance it without much misgiv-
ing.   *Ibid.*

[z] A virtue, to be serviceable,
must, like gold, be alloyed with
some commoner but more durable
metal.   *Ibid. Chap. 19*

[a] One great reason why clergymen's households are generally
unhappy is because the clergyman is so much at home and close
about the house.   *Ibid. Chap. 24*

[b] The best liar is he who makes
the smallest amount of lying go
the longest way.   *Ibid. Chap. 39*

[c] When people get it into their
heads that they are being specially favoured by the Almighty,
they had better as a general rule
mind their p's and q's.
           Ibid. Chap. 71

[d] An empty house is like a stray
dog or a body from which life has
departed.   *Ibid. Chap. 72*

[e] A man's friendships are, like
his will, invalidated by marriage

—but they are also no less invalidated by the marriage of his
friends.   *Ibid. Chap. 75*

[f] I reckon being ill as one of the
great pleasures of life, provided
one is not too ill and is not obliged
to work till one is better.
           Ibid. Chap. 80

[g] A hen is only an egg's way of
making another egg.
           Life and Habit. Chap. 8

[h] Life is the art of drawing
sufficient conclusions from in-
sufficient premises.
           Note-Books. Lord, What Is Man?

[i] All progress is based upon a
universal innate desire on the
part of every organism to live beyond its income.   *Ibid.*

[j] I do not think America is a
good place in which to be a genius.
A genius can never expect to
have a good time anywhere, but
America is about the last place in
which life will be endurable at all
for an inspired writer.
           Ibid. Cash and Credit

[k] I have gone in for posthumous fame. . . Posterity will give
a man a fair hearing; his own
times will not do so if he is attacking vested interests.
           Ibid. Homo Unius Libri

[l] The public buys its opinions
as it buys its meat, or takes in its
milk, on the principle that it is
cheaper to do this than to keep a
cow. So it is, but the milk is more
likely to be watered.   *Ibid.*
Sequel to "Alps and Sanctuaries"

[m] How holy people look when
they are sea-sick!
           Ibid. The Channel Passage

[n] The man who lets himself be
bored is even more contemptible
than the bore.
           The Fair Haven. Memoir, Chap. 3

[o] You will think you are better
    than the people who, when I
    was alive, swore that what-
    ever I did was wrong,
And damned my books for me as
    fast as I could write them;
But you will not be better, you
    will be just the same, neither
    better nor worse,
And you will go for some future
    Butler as your fathers have
    gone for me;
Oh, how I should have hated you!
           To Critics and Others

William Allen Butler
[1825–1902]

[p] We read Virginia's blazoned
    roll
  Of heroes, and forthwith

Greets us upon the starry scroll
That homeliest name,—*John
Smith!*
Virginia's Virgin. Part I, Stanza 1

[q] Dresses for breakfasts, and
dinners, and balls;
Dresses to sit in, and stand in, and
walk in;
Dresses to dance in, and flirt in.
and talk in;
Dresses in which to do nothing at
all;
Dresses for Winter, Spring, Sum-
mer, and Fall.
*Nothing to Wear [Harper's
Weekly, February 7 1857]*

[r] This same Miss McFlimsey of
Madison Square,
The last time we met was in utter
despair,
Because she had nothing what-
ever to wear!   *Ibid.*

Hezekiah Butterworth
[1839–1905]

[s] Methinks when I stand in
life's sunset,
As I stood when we parted at
school,
I shall see the bright faces of
children
I loved in the village of Yule.
*The Beautiful Village of Yule.
Stanza 9*

Witter Bynner
[1881–   ]

[t] Name me no names for my
disease,
With uninforming breath;
I tell you I am none of these,
But homesick unto death.
*The Patient to the Doctors.
Stanza 1*

[u] I am a miser of my memories
of you
And will not spend them.
Coins

[v] What's the use of a new-born
child? . . .
To raise the dead heart?—to set
wild
The fettered hope?
Poor Richard

[w] A leader is best
When people barely know that he
exists.   *The Way of Life
According to Laotzu*

[x] The biggest problem in the
world
Could have been solved when it
was small.   *Ibid.*

John Byrom
[1692–1763]

[y] Take time enough: all other
graces

Will soon fill up their proper
places.
Advice to Preach Slow

[z] As clear as a whistle.
Epistle to Lloyd

[a] The point is plain as a pike-
staff.   *Epistle to a Friend*

[b] Bone and Skin, two millers
thin,
Would starve us all, or near it:
But be it known to Skin and Bone
That Flesh and Blood can't bear
it.
Epigram on Two Monopolists

George Noel Gordon,
Lord Byron
[1788–1824]

[c] I only know we loved in vain;
I only feel—farewell! farewell!
*Farewell! If Ever Fondest Prayer.
Stanza 2*

[d] 'Tis pleasant, sure, to see
one's name in print;
A book's a book, although there's
nothing in 't.
*English Bards and Scotch
Reviewers Line 51*

[e] With just enough of learning
to misquote.   *Ibid Line 66*

[f]   As soon
Seek roses in December, ice in
June;
Hope constancy in wind, or corn
in chaff;
Believe a woman or an epitaph,
Or any other thing that's false,
before
You trust in critics.
Ibid. Line 75

[g] Maid of Athens, ere we part,
Give, oh give me back my heart!
Maid of Athens. Stanza 1

[h] Near this spot are deposited
the remains of one who possessed
Beauty without Vanity, Strength
without Insolence, Courage without Ferocity, and all the Virtues
of Man, without his Vices. This
Praise, which would be unmeaning Flattery if inscribed over human ashes, is but a just tribute to
the Memory of Boatswain, a Dog.
*Inscription on the Monument of
a Newfoundland Dog*

[i] Vex'd with mirth the drowsy
ear of night.
*Childe Harold's Pilgrimage.
Canto I, Stanza 2*

[j] Had sigh'd to many, though
he loved but one.
Ibid. Stanza 5

[k] Maidens, like moths, are ever
caught by glare,
And Mammon wins his way where
seraphs might despair.
Ibid. Stanza 9

[1] In hope to merit heaven by making earth a hell.
Ibid. Stanza 20

[m] Gone, glimmering through the dream of things that were.
Ibid. Canto II, Stanza 2

[n] There was a sound of revelry by night,
And Belgium's capital had gather'd then
Her beauty and her chivalry, and bright
The lamps shone o'er fair women and brave men.
A thousand hearts beat happily; and when
Music arose with its voluptuous swell,
Soft eyes look'd love to eyes which spake again,
And all went merry as a marriage bell.
But hush! hark! a deep sound strikes like a rising knell!
Ibid. Canto III, Stanza 21

[o] On with the dance! let joy be unconfined;
No sleep till morn, when Youth and Pleasure meet
To chase the glowing hours with flying feet. *Ibid. Stanza 22*

[p] He who surpasses or subdues mankind
Must look down on the hate of those below.
Ibid. Stanza 45

[q] All tenantless, save to the crannying wind.
Ibid. Stanza 47

[r] History's purchased page to call them great.
Ibid. Stanza 48

[s] High mountains are a feeling, but the hum
Of human cities torture.
Ibid. Stanza 72

[t] For his mind
Had grown Suspicion's sanctuary.
Ibid. Stanza 80

[u] This quiet sail is as a noiseless wing
To waft me from distraction.
Ibid. Stanza 85

[v] On the ear
Drops the light drip of the suspended oar. *Ibid. Stanza 86*

[w] In solitude, where we are least alone. *Ibid. Stanza 90*

[x] The sky is changed,—and such a change! O night
And storm, and darkness! ye are wondrous strong,
Yet lovely in your strength, as is the light
Of a dark eye in woman! Far along,
From peak to peak, the rattling crags among,
Leaps the live thunder.
Ibid. Stanza 9.

[y] The morn is up again, the dewy morn,
With breath all incense.
Ibid. Stanza 98

[z] Fame is the thirst of youth.
Ibid. Stanza 112

[a] I stood
Among them, but not of them; in a shroud
Of thoughts which were not their thoughts. *Ibid. Stanza 113*

[b] Where Venice sate in state, throned on her hundred isles.
Ibid. Canto IV, Stanza 1

[c] The thorns which I have reap'd are of the tree
I planted; they have torn me, and I bleed.
I should have known what fruit would spring from such a seed.
Ibid. Stanza 10

[d] Parting day
Dies like the dolphin, whom each pang imbues
With a new colour as it gasps away,
The last still loveliest, till—'tis gone, and all is gray.
Ibid. Stanza 29

[e] Italia! O Italia! thou who hast
The fatal gift of beauty.
Ibid. Stanza 42

[f] O Rome! my country! city of the soul! *Ibid. Stanza 78*

[g] I speak not of men's creeds—they rest between
Man and his Maker.
Ibid. Stanza 95

[h] Yet, Freedom! yet thy banner, torn, but flying,
Streams like the thunder-storm against the wind.
Ibid. Stanza 98

[i] Heaven gives its favourites—early death.
Ibid. Stanza 102

[j] Death, the sable smoke where vanishes the flame.
Ibid. Stanza 124

[k] "While stands the Coliseum, Rome shall stand;
When falls the Coliseum, Rome shall fall;
And when Rome falls—the world."
Ibid. Stanza 145

[l'] There is a pleasure in the pathless woods,
There is a rapture on the lonely shore,
There is society, where none intrudes,
By the deep sea, and music in its roar:

I love not man the less, but Nature more. *Ibid. Stanza 178*

[m] Roll on, thou deep and dark blue ocean, roll!
Ten thousand fleets sweep over thee in vain;
Man marks the earth with ruin,—his control
Stops with the shore.
Ibid. Stanza 179

[n] He sinks into thy depths with bubbling groan,
Without a grave, unknell'd, uncoffin'd, and unknown.
Ibid. Stanza 179

[o] Thou glorious mirror, where the Almighty's form
Glasses itself in tempests.
Ibid. Stanza 183

[p] And I have loved thee, Ocean! and my joy
Of youthful sports was on thy breast to be
Borne, like thy bubbles, onward; from a boy
I wantoned with thy breakers, . . .
And trusted to thy billows far and near,
And laid my hand upon thy mane,—as I do here.
Ibid. Stanza 184

[q] Such is the aspect of this shore;
'Tis Greece, but living Greece no more! . . .
Shrine of the mighty! can it be
That this is all remains of thee?
The Giaour. Line 90

[r] For freedom's battle, once begun,
Bequeath'd by bleeding sire to son,
Though baffled oft, is ever won.
Ibid. Line 123

[s] Better to sink beneath the shock
Than moulder piecemeal on the rock. *Ibid. Line 969*

[t] The morning-star of memory!
Ibid. Line 1130

[u] Who hath not proved how feebly words essay
To fix one spark of beauty's heavenly ray? *The Bride of Abydos. Canto I, Stanza 6*

[v] The light of love, the purity of grace,
The mind, the music breathing from her face,
The heart whose softness harmonized the whole,—
And oh, that eye was in itself a soul! *Ibid.*

[w] She walks in beauty, like the night
Of cloudless climes and starry skies;

And all that's best of dark and bright
Meet in her aspect and her eyes;
Thus mellow'd to that tender light
Which Heaven to gaudy day denies. *Hebrew Melodies. She Walks in Beauty, Stanza 1*

[x] The Assyrian came down like the wolf on the fold,
And his cohorts were gleaming in purple and gold. *The Destruction of Sennacherib. Stanza 1*

[y] Sighing that Nature form'd but one such man,
And broke the die. *Monody on the Death of Sheridan. Line 117*

[z] O God! it is a fearful thing
To see the human soul take wing
In any shape, in any mood.
The Prisoner of Chillon. Stanza 8

[a] Here's a sigh to those who love me,
And a smile to those who hate;
And, whatever sky's above me,
Here's a heart for every fate.
To Thomas Moore. Stanza 2

[b] So we'll go no more a-roving
So late into the night.
Letter to Thomas Moore [February 26, 1817]

[c] Mont Blanc is the monarch of mountains;
They crowned him long ago
On a throne of rocks, in a robe of clouds,
With a diadem of snow.
Manfred. Act I, Sc. 1

[d] All farewells should be sudden. *Sardanapalus. Act V*

[e] She was not old, nor young, nor at the years
Which certain people call a "certain age,"
Which yet the most uncertain age appears. *Beppo. Stanza 22*

[f] For most men (till by losing rendered sager)
Will back their own opinions by a wager. *Ibid. Stanza 27*

[g] One hates an author that's all author. *Ibid. Stanza 75*

[h] What's drinking?
A mere pause from thinking!
The Deformed Transformed. Act III, Sc. 1

[i] He seems
To have seen better days, as who has not
Who has seen yesterday?
Werner. Act I, Sc. 1

[j] The patient search and vigil long
Of him who treasures up a wrong.
Mazeppa. Stanza 10

[k] The "good old times"—all times when old are good.
The Age of Bronze. Stanza 1

[l] Whose game was empires and
whose stakes were thrones,
Whose table earth, whose dice
were human bones.
Ibid. Stanza 3

[m] Sublime tobacco! which from
east to west
Cheers the tar's labour or the
Turkman's rest.
The Island. Canto II, Stanza 19

[n] Divine in hookas, glorious in
a pipe
When tipp'd with amber, mellow,
rich, and ripe; . . .
Yet thy true lovers more admire
by far
Thy naked beauties—give me a
cigar! *Ibid.*

[o] My days are in the yellow leaf;
The flowers and fruits of love
are gone;
The worm, the canker, and the
grief
Are mine alone!
On My Thirty-sixth Year. Stanza 2

[p] But, oh! ye lords of ladies
intellectual,
Inform us truly,—have they not
henpeck'd you all?
Don Juan. Canto I, Stanza 22

[q] Her stature tall,—I hate a
dumpy woman.
Ibid. Stanza 61

[r] Christians have burnt each
other, quite persuaded
That all the Apostles would have
done as they did.
Ibid. Stanza 83

[s] And whispering, "I will ne'er
consent,"—consented.
Ibid. Stanza 117

[t] 'Tis sweet to know there is an
eye will mark
Our coming, and look brighter
when we come.
Ibid. Stanza 123

[u] Sweet is revenge—especially
to women. *Ibid. Stanza 124*

[v] Man's love is of man's life a
thing apart;
'Tis woman's whole existence.
Ibid. Stanza 194

[w] There's nought, no doubt, so
much the spirit calms
As rum and true religion.
Ibid. Canto II, Stanza 34

[x] 'Tis said that persons living
on annuities
Are longer lived than others.
Ibid. Stanza 65

[y]   All who joy would win
Must share it,—happiness was
born a twin.
Ibid. Stanza 172

[z] Let us have wine and women,
mirth and laughter,
Sermons and soda-water the day
after. *Ibid. Stanza 178*

[a] In her first passion woman
loves her lover,
In all the others, all she loves is
love. *Ibid. Canto III,
Stanza 3*

[b] All tragedies are finished by a
death,
All comedies are ended by a marriage. *Ibid. Stanza 9*

[c] The isles of Greece, the isles
of Greece!
Where burning Sappho loved and
sung. . . .
Eternal summer gilds them yet,
But all, except their sun, is set.
Ibid. Stanza 86, 1

[d] But words are things, and a
small drop of ink,
Falling like dew upon a thought,
produces
That which makes thousands,
perhaps millions, think.
Ibid. Stanza 88

[e] And glory long has made the
sages smile,
'Tis something, nothing, words,
illusion, wind—
Depending more upon the historian's style
Than on the name a person
leaves behind.
Ibid. Stanza 90

[f] Ah, surely nothing dies but
something mourns.
Ibid. Stanza 108

[g] And if I laugh at any mortal
thing,
'Tis that I may not weep.
Ibid. Canto IV, Stanza 4

[h]   And her face so fair
Stirr'd with her dream, as rose-
leaves with the air.
Ibid. Stanza 29

[i] These two hated with a hate
Found only on the stage.
Ibid. Stanza 93

[j] I've stood upon Achilles'
tomb,
And heard Troy doubted: time
will doubt of Rome.
Ibid. Stanza 101

[k] That all-softening, over-
powering knell,
The tocsin of the soul—the dinner
bell.
Ibid. Canto V, Stanza 49

[l'] The women pardon'd all except her face.
Ibid. Stanza 113

[m'] Polygamy may well be held
in dread,
Not only as a sin, but as a bore.
Ibid. Canto VI, Stanza 12

[n'] He scratch'd his ear, the infallible resource
To which embarrass'd people have
recourse. *Ibid. Stanza 100*

[o] 'Mongst them were several
Englishmen of pith,
Sixteen were called Thompson and
nineteen Smith.
Ibid. Canto VII, Stanza 18

[p] The drying up a single tear
has more
Of honest fame than shedding
seas of gore.
Ibid. Canto VIII, Stanza 3

[q] Indigestion is—that inward
fate
Which makes all Styx through one
small liver flow.
Ibid. Canto IX, Stanza 15

[r] "Gentlemen farmers"—a race
worn out quite.
Ibid. Stanza 32

[s]   He said
Little, but to the purpose.
Ibid. Stanza 83

[t] And wrinkles (the damned
democrats) won't flatter.
Ibid. Canto X, Stanza 24

[u] Ready money is Aladdin's
lamp.   *Ibid. Canto XII,
Stanza 12*

[v] Cervantes   smil'd   Spain's
chivalry away.   *Ibid. Canto
XIII, Stanza 11*

[w] Society is now one polish'd
horde,
Formed of two mighty tribes, the
Bores and *Bored*.
Ibid. Stanza 95

[x]   All human history attests
That happiness for man,—the
hungry sinner!—
Since Eve ate apples, much de-
pends on dinner.
Ibid. Stanza 99

[y] Death, so called, is a thing
which makes men weep,
And yet a third of life is passed
in sleep.   *Ibid. Canto XIV,
Stanza 3*

[z] 'Tis strange, but true; for
truth is always strange,—
Stranger than fiction.
Ibid. Stanza 101

[a] The Devil hath not, in all his
quiver's choice,
An arrow for the heart like a
sweet voice.   *Ibid. Canto
XV, Stanza 13*

[b] Friendship is Love without
his wings.   *L'Amitié est
l'Amour sans Ailes*

[c] I awoke one morning and
found myself famous.
*Quoted by Thomas Moore in
his Life of Byron, Chap. 14*

[d] The world is a bundle of hay,
Mankind are the asses that pull,
Each tugs in a different way,—
And the greatest of all is John
Bull!   *Letter to Thomas
Moore [June 22, 1821]*

James Branch Cabell
[1879-   ]

[e] I shall marry in haste, and
repeat at leisure.
Jurgen. Chap. 38

[f] There is no faith stronger
than that of a bad-tempered
woman in her own infallibility.
Ibid. Chap. 39

[g] Poetry is man's rebellion
against being what he is.
Ibid. Chap. 44

George Washington Cable
[1844-1925]

[h] There came to port last Sun-
day night
The queerest little craft,
Without an inch of rigging on;
I   looked   and   looked—and
laughed!

She has no manifest but this,
No flag floats o'er the water;
She's too new for the British
Lloyd's—
My daughter! O my daughter!
The New Arrival. Stanzas 1 and 2

Caedmon
*[Floruit 670, earliest
English Christian poet]
From the text of
Benjamin Thorpe*

[i] Light was first
Through the Lord's word
Named day:
Beauteous, bright creation!
Creation. The First Day

[j] The fiend with all his com-
rades
Fell then from heaven above,
Through as long as three nights
and days,
The angels from heaven into hell;
And them all the Lord trans-
formed to devils,
Because they his deed and word
Would not revere.   *Ibid. The
Fall of the Rebel Angels*

Hall Caine
[1853-1931]

[k] I reject the monstrous theory
that while a man may redeem the
past a woman never can.   *The
Eternal City. Part VI, Chap. 18*

Arthur Wallace Calhoun
[1885-   ]

[l] Gentlemen of the old régime
in the South used to say: "A
woman's name should appear in
print but twice—when she marries and when she dies."
*Social History of the American
Family. Vol. II, page 326*

John C. Calhoun
[1782–1850]

[m] The very essence of a free
government consists in considering offices as public trusts, bestowed for the good of the country, and not for the benefit of an
individual or a party.
Speech [February 13, 1835]

[n] A power has risen up in the
government greater than the
people themselves, consisting of
many and various and powerful
interests, combined into one mass,
and held together by the cohesive
power of the vast surplus in the
banks.   *Speech [May 27, 1836]*

Charles Stuart Calverley
[1831–1884]

[o] I have a liking old
For thee, though manifold
Stories, I know, are told,
   Not to thy credit!
      Ode to Tobacco. Stanza 2

[p] I can not sing the old songs
      now!
It is not that I deem them low;
'Tis that I can't remember how
      They go.   *Changed*

[q] The farmer's daughter hath
      soft brown hair
(*Butter and eggs and a pound
      of cheese*)
And I met with a ballad, I can't
      say where,
   That wholly consisted of lines
      like these.   *Ballad, after
William Morris [The Auld Wife].
   Part I, Stanza 6*

[r] But ah! disasters have their
      use;
And life might e'en be too sun-
      shiny.   *Disaster, after
            Moore. Stanza 5*

[s] As the flight of a bird in the
      air
Is the flight of a joke.
      Flight. Stanza 10

[t] Ere the morn the East has
      crimsoned,
   When the stars are twinkling
      there
(As they did in Watts' hymns, and
   Made him wonder what they
      were)
When   the   forest-nymphs   are
      beading
   Fern and flower with silvery
      dew
My infallible proceeding
   Is to wake, and think of you.
      The 14th of February

Anne Campbell
(Mrs. George W. Stark)
[1888–   ]

[u] You are the trip I did not
      take;

You are the pearls I cannot buy;
You are my blue Italian lake;
You are my piece of foreign sky.
      To My Child

[v] It isn't that we talk so
      much,—
   Sometimes the evening through
You do not say a word to me,
   I do not talk to you.
You sit beside your reading lamp,
   I like my easy chair,
And it is joy enough for me
   To know that you are there.
      Companionship. Stanza 1

Bartley Campbell
[1843–1888]

[w] Rags are royal raiment when
worn for virtue's sake. [*Carved on
Campbell's monument in Pitts-
burgh.*]   *The White Slave*

Joseph Campbell
[1881–   ]

[x] As a white candle
In a holy place,
So is the beauty
Of an aged face.
      The Old Woman. Stanza 1

[y] Her thoughts as still
As the waters
Under a ruined mill.
      Ibid. Stanza 3

Roy Campbell
[1902–   ]

[z] Far in the desert we have been
Where Nature, still to poets kind,
Admits no vegetable green
To soften the determined mind.
      Poets in Africa. Stanza 2

[a] Not with so glutinous a syrup
As moonlight shall we grease our
      speech.   *Ibid. Stanza 4*

[b] I love to see, when leaves de-
      part,
The clear anatomy arrive,
Winter, the paragon of art,
That kills all forms of life and
      feeling
Save what is pure and will survive.
      Autumn. Stanza 1

Thomas Campbell
[1777–1844]

[c] 'Tis distance lends enchant-
      ment to the view,
And robes the mountain in its
      azure hue.   *Pleasures of
            Hope. Part I, Line 7*

[d] The world was sad, the gar-
      den was a wild,
And man, the hermit, sigh'd—till
      woman smiled.
      Ibid. Part II, Line 37

THOMAS CAMPION—KAREL ČAPEK 59

[e] O star-eyed Science! hast
thou wandered there,
To waft us home the message of
despair? *Ibid. Line 325*

[f] But, sad as angels for the good
man's sin,
Weep to record, and blush to give
it in. *Ibid. Line 357*

[g] Cease, every joy, to glimmer
on my mind,
But leave, oh leave the light of
Hope behind!
Ibid. Line 375

[h] And rustic life and poverty
Grow beautiful beneath his touch.
*Ode to the Memory of Burns.
Stanza 5*

[i] Whose lines are mottoes of
the heart,
Whose truths electrify the sage.
Ibid. Stanza 14

[j] Britannia needs no bulwarks,
No towers along the steep;
Her march is o'er the mountain
waves,
Her home is on the deep.
Ye Mariners of England. Stanza 3

[k] Few, few shall part where
many meet!
The snow shall be their winding-
sheet
And every turf beneath their feet
Shall be a soldier's sepulchre.
Hohenlinden. Stanza 8

[l] Star that bringeth home the
bee,
And sett'st the weary labourer
free! *Song to the Evening
Star. Stanza 1*

[m] Triumphal arch, that fill'st
the sky
When storms prepare to part,
I ask not proud Philosophy
To teach me what thou art.
To the Rainbow. Stanza 1

[n] To live in hearts we leave be-
hind
Is not to die.
Hallowed Ground. Stanza 6

Thomas Campion
[1575?–1620?]

[o] Good thoughts his only
friends,
His wealth a well-spent age,
The earth his sober inn
And quiet pilgrimage.
*Integer Vitae, after Horace.
Stanza 6*

[p] Never love unless you can
Bear with all the faults of man:
Men will sometimes jealous be,
Though but little cause they see.
Never Love. Stanza 1

[q] There is a garden in her face
Where roses and white lilies
blow;

A heavenly paradise that place,
Wherein all pleasant fruits do
grow;
There cherries grow that none
may buy,
Till Cherry-Ripe themselves do
cry. *Cherry-Ripe. Stanza 1*

[r] The summer hath his joys,
And winter his delights;
Though love and all his pleasures
are but toys,
They shorten tedious nights.
Winter Nights. Stanza 2

Henry Seidel Canby
[1878–   ]

[s] Arrogance, pedantry, and dogmatism are the occupational diseases of those who spend their
lives directing the intellects of the
young. *Alma Mater*

[t] [Walt Whitman] remembered
things impossible for us, impossible but intelligible, and which
will become unintelligible at our
peril. *Classic Americans.
Walt Whitman*

George Canning
[1770–1827]

[u] And finds, with keen, dis-
criminating sight,
Black's not so black,—nor white so
very white. *New Morality*

[v] Give me the avowed, the
erect, the manly foe,
Bold I can meet,—perhaps may
turn his blow!
But of all plagues, good Heaven,
thy wrath can send,
Save, save, oh save me from the
candid friend! *Ibid.*

[w] In matters of commerce the
fault of the Dutch
Is offering too little and asking
too much.
*Dispatch to Sir Charles Bagot,
British Minister at The Hague
[January 31, 1826]*

Karel Čapek
[1890–1938]

[x] Rossum's Universal Robots
[mechanical men].
"R. U. R.," a play

[y] O Lord, grant that in some
way it may rain every day, say
from about midnight until three
o'clock in the morning, . . .
gentle and warm so that it can
soak in; . . . that there may be
plenty of dew and little wind,
enough worms, no plant-lice and
snails, no mildew, and that once
a week thin liquid manure and
guano may fall from heaven.
*The Gardener's Year: The Gar-
dener's Prayer*

Thomas Carew
[1595–1639]

[z] Ask me no more where Jove
bestows,
When June is past, the fading
rose.   *To Celia. Stanza 1*

[a] He that loves a rosy cheek,
Or a coral lip admires,
Or from star-like eyes doth seek
Fuel to maintain in his fires;—
As old Time makes these decay,
So his flames must waste away.
          Disdain Returned. Stanza 1

[b] Then fly betimes, for only
they
Conquer Love that run away.
          Conquest by Flight

Henry Carey
[1663–1743]

[c] God save our gracious king!
Long live our noble king!
God save the king!
          God Save the King

[d] Of all the girls that are so
smart,
There's none like pretty Sally.
She is the darling of my heart,
And she lives in our alley.
          Sally in Our Alley. Stanza 1

[e] Of all the days that's in the
week
I dearly love but one day,
And that's the day that comes be-
twixt
A Saturday and Monday.
          Ibid. Stanza 4

Will Carleton
[1845–1912]

[f] Worm or beetle—drought or
tempest—on a farmer's land
may fall,
Each is loaded full o' ruin, but a
mortgage beats 'em all.
          The Tramp's Story

[g] I've watched my duty,
straight an' true,
An' tried to do it well;
Part of the time kept heaven in
view,
An' part steered clear of hell.
          *The New Church Doctrine.
          Stanza 2*

[h] If there's a heaven upon the
earth, a fellow knows it when
He's been away from home a week,
and then gets back again.
          Goin' Home To-day. Stanza 7

[i] "Careful with fire," is good
advice, we know;
"Careful with words," is ten times
doubly so.
Thoughts unexpressed may sometimes fall back dead;
But God himself can't kill them
when they're said.
          The First Settler's Story

[j] The kind old country doctor
Whom the populace considered
with a mingled love and
dread.
          The Country Doctor. Stanza 1

[k] He has seen old views and
patients disappearing, one by
one,
He has learned that Death is master both of Science and of Art.
          Ibid. Stanza 3

[l] But ships long time together
Can better the tempest weather
Than any other two.
          One and Two. Stanza 3

[m] Betsey, like all good women,
had a temper of her own.
          Betsey and I Are Out. Stanza 4

[n] Now he didn't give you that
baby, by a hundred thousand
mile;
He just think you need some sunshine, and he lent him for a
while.
          The Funeral. Stanza 6

[o] To appreciate heaven well
'Tis good for a man to have some
fifteen minutes of hell.
          *Gone with a Handsomer Man.
          Stanza 20*

[p] Over the hill to the poor-
house I'm trudgin' my weary
way.   *Over the Hill to the
          Poorhouse. Stanza 1*

Francis Carlin (James Francis Carlin MacDonnell)
[1881–1945]

[q] My love is o'er a Water,
A calm and tideless sea,
And I would that I had taught her
To come in dreams to me.
          The Stilly Sea. Stanza 2

[r] That which is in disorder
Has neither rule nor rhyme,
Like the stars at Heaven's border
And the troubled laughter of
Time.
          The Ravelled Edge. Stanza 3

[s] May you never know the
sweetness of a bitter tear, may you
learn that a rainy day is never
dull, and may you vision Nature
as a sacramental of Beauty itself.
May you live long in health on the
green side of the grave, and be
welcomed in the Land of Other-
where by Him whose arms are
ever outstretched to little ones,
and to those who are as such.
          *To an Unknown, Waiting for
          a Birthday*

Jane Welsh (Mrs. Thomas) Carlyle
[1801–1866]

[t] Medical men all over the
world having merely entered into

a tacit agreement to call all sorts of maladies people are liable to, in cold weather, by one name; so that one sort of treatment may serve for all, and their practice be thereby greatly simplified.
Letter to John Welsh
[March 4, 1837]

[u] Never does one feel oneself so utterly helpless as in trying to speak comfort for great bereavement. I will not try it. Time is the only comforter for the loss of a mother. *Letter to Thomas Carlyle [December 27, 1853]*

[v] Of all God's creatures, man Alone is poor. *To a Swallow Building Under Our Eaves*

Thomas Carlyle
[1795–1881]

[w] May blessings be upon the head of Cadmus or the Phoenicians, or whoever invented books! . . . . An art that carries the voice of man to the extremities of the earth, and to the latest generations. *Early Letters.*
To Mr. R. Mitchell

[x] True humour springs not more from the head than from the heart; it is not contempt, its essence is love; it issues not in laughter, but in still smiles, which lie far deeper.
Richter [In Edinburgh Review, June 1827]

[y] He who would write heroic poems should make his whole life a heroic poem. *Life of Schiller*

[z] Literary men are . . . a perpetual priesthood. *State of German Literature. Fichte*

[a] Fame, we may understand, is no sure test of merit, but only a probability of such. *Goethe*
[In Edinburgh Review, 1828]

[b] Clever men are good, but they are not the best. *Ibid.*

[c] We are firm believers in the maxim that, for all right judgment of any man or thing, it is useful, nay essential, to see his good qualities before pronouncing on his bad. *Ibid.*

[d] An educated man stands, as it were, in the midst of a boundless arsenal and magazine, filled with all the weapons and engines which man's skill has been able to devise from the earliest time. *Burns*

[e] A poet without love were a physical and metaphysical impossibility. *Ibid.*

[f] His religion, at best, is an anxious wish;—like that of Rabelais, "a great Perhaps." *Ibid.*

[g] Whoso belongs only to his own age, and reverences only its gilt Popinjays or soot-smeared Mumbojumbos, must needs die with it.
On Boswell's Life of Johnson

[h] There is tolerable travelling on the beaten road, run how it may; only on the new road not yet levelled and paved, and on the old road all broken into ruts and quagmires, is the travelling bad or impracticable. *Ibid.*

[i] Of all outward evils Obscurity is perhaps in itself the least. *Ibid.*

[j] All work is as seed sown; it grows and spreads, and sows itself anew. *Ibid.*

[k] Silence is deep as Eternity; speech is shallow as Time.
Sir Walter Scott [In London and Westminster Review, November 12, 1838]

[l] No man lives without jostling and being jostled; in all ways he has to elbow himself through the world, giving and receiving offence. *Ibid.*

[m] The uttered part of a man's life, let us always repeat, bears to the unuttered, unconscious part a small unknown proportion. He himself never knows it, much less do others. *Ibid.*

[n] Ill-health, of body or of mind, is defeat. . . . Health alone is victory. Let all men, if they can manage it, contrive to be healthy! *Ibid.*

[o] The lightning-spark of Thought, generated or say rather heaven-kindled, in the solitary mind, awakens its express likeness in another mind, in a thousand other minds, and all blaze up together in combined fire. *Ibid.*

[p] Considered as a whole, the Christian religion of late ages has been continually dissipating itself into Metaphysics; and threatens now to disappear, as some rivers do, in deserts of barren sand. *Ibid.*

[q] Nothing that was worthy in the past departs; no truth or goodness realized by man ever dies, or can die; but is all still here, and, recognized or not, lives and works through endless changes. *Ibid.*

[r] The barrenest of all mortals is the sentimentalist. *Ibid.*

[s] Love is ever the beginning of Knowledge, as fire is of light.
Essays. Death of Goethe

[t] Music is well said to be the speech of angels.
Ibid. The Opera

[u] Everywhere the human soul stands between a hemisphere of light and another of darkness on the confines of two everlasting hostile empires,—Necessity and Free Will. *Ibid.*

[v] History is the essence of innumerable biographies.
On History

[w] The Public is an old woman. Let her maunder and mumble.
Journal [1835]

[x] "A fair day's-wages for a fair day's-work": it is as just a demand as governed men ever made of governing. It is the everlasting right of man. *Past and Present. Book I, Chap. 3*

[y] Fire is the best of servants; but what a master!
Ibid. Book II, Chap. 9

[z] All work, even cotton-spinning, is noble; work is alone noble. . . . A life of ease is not for any man, nor for any god.
Ibid. Book III, Chap. 4

[a] Blessed is he who has found his work; let him ask no other blessedness. *Ibid. Chap 11*

[b] The fine arts once divorcing themselves from *truth* are quite certain to fall mad, if they do not die.
Latter Day Pamphlets. No. 8

[c] A healthy hatred of scoundrels. *Ibid. No. 12*

[d] Genius . . . which is the transcendent capacity for taking trouble first of all.
Life of Frederick the Great. Book IV, Chap. 3

[e] Happy the people whose annals are blank in history-books.
Ibid. Book XVI, Chap. 1

[f] No man who has once heartily and wholly laughed can be altogether irreclaimably bad.
Sartor Resartus. Book I, Chap. 4

[g] He who first shortened the labor of Copyists by device of *Movable Types* was disbanding hired Armies, and cashiering most Kings and Senates, and creating a whole new Democratic world: he had invented the Art of printing. *Ibid. Chap. 5*

[h] Be not the slave of Words.
Ibid. Chap. 8

[i] What you see, yet can not see over, is as good as infinite.
Ibid. Book II, Chap. 1

[j] Sarcasm I now see to be, in general, the language of the Devil; for which reason I have, long since, as good as renounced it. *Ibid. Chap. 4*

[k] That there should one man die ignorant who had capacity for knowledge, this I call a tragedy.
Ibid. Book III, Chap. 4

[l] In good-breeding, which differs, if at all, from high-breeding, only as it gracefully remembers the rights of others, rather than gracefully insists on its own rights, I discern no special connection with wealth or birth.
Ibid. Chap. 6

[m] No sadder proof can be given by a man of his own littleness than disbelief in great men.
Heroes and Hero-Worship. The Hero as Divinity

[n] The history of the world is but the biography of great men.
Ibid.

[o] We must get rid of Fear.
Ibid.

[p] The greatest of faults, I should say, is to be conscious of none.
Ibid. The Hero as Prophet

[q] Adversity is sometimes hard upon a man; but for one man who can stand prosperity, there are a hundred that will stand adversity.
Ibid. The Hero as a Man of Letters

[r] The oak grows silently, in the forest, a thousand years; only in the thousandth year, when the woodman arrives with his axe is there heard an echoing through the solitudes; and the oak announces itself when, with far-sounding crash, it falls.
The French Revolution. Vol. I, Book II, Chap. 1

[s] O poor mortals, how ye make this earth bitter for each other.
Ibid. Book V, Chap. 5

[t'] Men that can have communion in nothing else, can sympathetically eat together, can still rise into some glow of brotherhood over food and wine.
Ibid. Book VII, Chap. 2

[u'] Battles, in these ages, are transacted by mechanism; with the slightest possible development of human individuality or spontaneity; men now even die, and kill one another, in an artificial manner. *Ibid. Chap 4*

[v'] Is man's civilization only a wrappage, through which the savage nature of him can still burst, infernal as ever? *Ibid. Vol. III, Book V, Chap. 7*

[w'] What is Man? A foolish baby, Vainly strives, and fights, and frets.

Demanding all, deserving nothing,
One small grave is what he gets.
Cui Bono. Stanza 3

[x] The unspeakable Turk.
In public letter [1877]

Bliss Carman
[1861–1929]

[y] An open hand, an easy shoe,
And a hope to make the day go
through.
The Joys of the Road

[z] A comrade neither glum nor
merry.
No fidget and no reformer, just
A calm observer of ought and
must. *Ibid.*

[a] These are the joys of the open
road—
For him who travels without a
load. *Ibid.*

[b] Over the shoulders and slopes
of the dune
I saw the white daisies go down
to the sea.
Daisies. Stanza 1

[c] The scarlet of the maples can
shake me like a cry
Of bugles going by.
A Vagabond Song. Stanza 2

[d] There is something in October sets the gypsy blood astir.
Ibid. Stanza 3

[e] Hack and Hew were the sons
of God
In the earlier earth than now;
One at his right hand, one at his
left,
To obey as he taught them how.
Hack and Hew. Stanza 1

[f] Hem and Haw were the sons
of sin,
Created to shally and shirk;
Hem lay 'round and Haw looked
on.
While God did all the work.
Hem and Haw. Stanza 1

[g] Heaven is no larger than
Connecticut;
No larger than Fairfield County.
A Measure of Heaven

[h] There is virtue in the open;
there is healing out of doors;
The great Physician makes his
rounds along the forest floors.
*An Open Letter, Christmas, 1920
[written at Lake Placid, N. Y.,
while Carman was a patient
there]. Stanza 4*

[i] I took a day to search for God,
And found Him not. But as I trod
By rocky ledge, through woods
untamed,
Just where one scarlet lily
flamed,
I saw His footprint in the sod.
Vestigia. Stanza 1

Dale Carnegie
[1888–   ]

[j] How to Win Friends and Influence People. *Title of book*

Julia A. Fletcher Carney
[1823–1908]

[k] Little drops of water, little
grains of sand,
Make the mighty ocean and the
pleasant land.
Little Things

[l] Little deeds of kindness, little
words of love,
Help to make earth happy like the
heaven above. *Ibid.*

Edward Carpenter
[1844–1929]

[m] Motherhood is, after all,
woman's great and incomparable
work. *Love's Coming-of-Age.
Woman in Freedom*

[n] When Death comes, breaking
into the circle of our friends,
words fail us, our mental ma-
chinery ceases to operate, all our
little stores of wit and wisdom,
our maxims, our mottoes, accu-
mulated from daily experience,
evaporate and are of no avail.
These things do not seem to touch
or illuminate in any effective way
the strange vast Presence whose
wings darken the world for us.
*The Drama of Love and Death.
Chap. 1*

[o] Love is an Art, and the
greatest of the Arts. *Ibid. Chap. 4*

[p] Every new movement or man-
ifestation of human activity,
when unfamiliar to people's
minds, is sure to be misrepre-
sented and misunderstood.
Ibid. Chap. 8, Note

[q] In Man, the positive content
of religion is the instinctive sense
. . . of an inner unity and con-
tinuity with the world around.
This is the stuff out of which religion is made. *Pagan and
Christian Creeds. Chap. 4*

[r] There is a presence and an influence in Nature and the Open
which expands the mind and
causes brigand cares and worries
to drop off—whereas in confined
places foolish and futile thoughts
of all kinds swarm like microbes
and cloud and conceal the soul.
*Lecture I, The Teaching of the
Upanishads. Rest*

Henry Bernard Carpenter
[1840–1887]

[s] The time will come when this,
our Holy Church,

Shall melt away in ever widening
    walls,
And be for all mankind. And in
    its place
Shall rise another church, whose
    covenant word
Shall be the act of love. Not *Credo*
    then
But *Amo* shall be the watchword
    through its gate.
          Liber Amoris

"Lewis Carroll"
(Charles Lutwidge Dodgson)
[1832–1898]

[t] Alice! a childish story take
    And with a gentle hand
Lay it where childhood's dreams
    are twined
In Memory's mystic band,
Like pilgrim's withered wreath of
    flowers
Plucked in a far-off land.
      *Alice's Adventures in
      Wonderland. Introduction*

[u] "You are old, Father Wil-
    liam," the young man said,
"And your hair has become very
    white;
And yet you incessantly stand on
    your head—
    Do you think, at your age, it is
    right?"   *Ibid. Chap. 5*

[v] "Really, now you ask me,"
said Alice, very much confused, "I
don't think—"
    "Then you shouldn't talk," said
the Hatter.   *Ibid. Chap. 7*

[w] "Tut, tut, child," said the
Duchess. "Everything's got a
moral if only you can find it."
          Ibid. Chap. 9

[x] Take care of the sense and
the sounds will take care of themselves.   *Ibid.*

[y] Child of the pure, unclouded
    brow
And dreaming eyes of wonder!
    *Through the Looking-Glass and
    What Alice Found There. In-
    troduction*

[z] He chortled in his joy.
          *Ibid. Chap. 1
      (Jabberwocky. Stanza 6)*

[a] "The horror of that moment,"
the King went on, "I shall never,
never forget!"
    "You will, though," the Queen
said, "if you don't make a memorandum of it."   *Ibid.*

[b] "A slow sort of country," said
the Queen. "Now, *here*, you see, it
takes all the running you can do,
to keep in the same place. If you
want to get somewhere else, you
must run at least twice as fast as
that!"   *Ibid. Chap. 2*

[c] "The time has come," the
    Walrus said,
"To talk of many things:
Of shoes—and ships—and sealing-
    wax—
Of cabbages—and kings—
And why the sea is boiling hot—
    And whether pigs have wings."
    *Ibid. Chap. 4 (The Walrus and
    the Carpenter, Stanza 11)*

[d] "The rule is, jam to-morrow,
and jam yesterday—but never jam
today."
    "It *must* come sometimes to
'jam today,'" Alice objected.
    "No, it can't," said the Queen.
"It's jam every *other* day: to-day
isn't any *other* day, you know."
          Ibid. Chap. 5

[e] "When I use a word,"
Humpty-Dumpty said, "it means
just what I choose it to mean—
neither more nor less."
          Ibid. Chap 6

[f] As large as life and twice as
natural.   *Ibid. Chap. 7*

[g] He had bought a large map
    representing the sea,
Without the least vestige of
    land:
And the crew were much pleased
    when they found it to be
A map they could all under-
    stand.
    *The Hunting of the Snark.
    Fit the Second, Stanza 2*

[h] You may charge me with
    murder—or want of sense—
(We are all of us weak at
    times):
But the slightest approach to a
    false pretence
Was never among my crimes!
    Ibid. Fit the Fourth, Stanza 4

[i] There are certain things—as,
    a spider, a ghost,
The income-tax, gout, an um-
    brella for three—
That I hate, but the thing that I
    hate the most
Is a thing they call the Sea.
      A Sea Dirge. Stanza 1

William Herbert Carruth
[1859–1924]

[j] A haze on the far horizon,
    The infinite, tender sky,
The ripe, rich tint of the corn-
    fields,
    And the wild geese sailing
    high—
And all over upland and lowland
    The charm of the golden-rod,
Some of us call it Autumn,
    And others call it God.
      *Each in His Own Tongue.
      Stanza 2*

Charles Edward Carryl
[1841–1920]

[k] The night was thick and hazy
When the *Piccadilly Daisy*
Carried down the crew and Captain in the sea;
And I think the water drowned
'em,
For they never, never found 'em,
And I know they didn't come
ashore with me.
Robinson Crusoe. Stanza 1

[l] Canary birds feed on sugar
and seed,
Parrots have crackers to crunch;
And as for the poodles, they tell
me the noodles
Have chicken and cream for
their lunch.
　　But there's never a question
　　About my digestion—
Anything does for me!
The Camel's Complaint. Stanza 1

[m] A capital ship for an ocean
trip
Was the "Walloping Windowblind."
No gale that blew dismayed her
crew
Or troubled the Captain's mind.
The man at the wheel was taught
to feel
Contempt for the wildest blow,
And it often appeared, when the
weather had cleared,
　　That he'd been in his bunk below.
*Davy and the Goblin,
A Nautical Ballad. Stanza 1*

Guy Wetmore Carryl
[1873–1904]

[n] You call it a waste of time,
this taste
For popular tunes, and yet
Good-bye to care when you
whistle the air
Of the song that you can't forget. *The Organ Man. Stanza 3*

[o] How imposing it would be
If pumpkins grew upon a tree!
*The Iconoclastic Rustic and the
Apropos Acorn. Stanza 1*

[p] And in his dim, uncertain
sight
Whatever wasn't must be right,
From which it follows he had
strong
Convictions that what was, was
wrong, *Ibid. Stanza 2*

[q] In every new and smart disease,
From housemaid's knee to heart
disease,
She recognized the symptoms as
her own!
*How Jack Found That Beans May
Go Back on a Chap. Stanza 2*

William Lorenzo Carter
[1813–1860]

[r] "O daughter, dear," her
mother said,
　"this blanket round you fold,
'Tis such a dreadful night abroad
　you will catch your death of
　cold."

Young ladies, think of this fair
girl and always dress aright,
And never venture thinly clad on
such a wintry night.
*Young [or Fair] Charlotte.
Stanza 3 and last stanza*

Pierre Cartier
[1878–　]

[s] While in France we consider
it takes three generations to go
from shirtsleeves to wealth, here,
in America, where accelerated
speed is an important element of
success, it takes but one generation to complete the same process.
*Address, French Chamber of
Commerce of the United States.
New York, September 27, 1940*

William Cartwright
[1611–1643]

[t] St. Francis and St. Benedight,
Bless this house from wicked
wight,
From the nightmare and the
Goblin
That is hight Good Fellow Robin.
Keep it from all evil spiretes,
Fairies, Wezles, Bats, and Ferrytes
From Curfew Time to the next
Prime. *A House Blessing*

Alice Cary
[1820–1871]

[u] There must be rough, cold
weather,
And winds and rains so wild;
Not all good things together
Come to us here, my child.
November

[v] Kiss me, though you make
believe;
Kiss me, though I almost know
You are kissing to deceive.
Make Believe. Stanza 1

Phoebe Cary
[1824–1874]

[w] I think true love is never
blind,
But rather brings an added
light,
An inner vision quick to find
The beauties hid from common
sight. *True Love. Stanza 1*

[x] Her washing ended with the
day,
Yet lived she at its close,
And passed the long, long night
away
In darning ragged hose.
*The Wife (Parody on James
Aldrich's A Death-Bed)*

[y] But when the sun in all its
state
Illumed the Eastern skies,
She passed about the kitchen
grate
And went to making pies. *Ibid.*

Lizzie York Case
[1840–1911]

[z] There is no unbelief;
Whoever plants a seed beneath
the sod
And waits to see it push away the
clod,
He trusts in God.
Unbelief. Stanza 1

Phila Henrietta Case
[*Floruit* 1864]

[a] Oh! why does the wind blow
upon me so wild?
Is it because I'm nobody's child?
Nobody's Child. Stanza 1

Willa Sibert Cather
[1876–1947]

[b] Oh, this is the joy of the rose:
That it blows,
And goes. *In Rose-Time*

[c] Where are the loves that we
have loved before
When once we are alone, and shut
the door? *L'Envoi*

[d] Fireflies gleam in the damp
and mould,—
All that is left of the Caesars' gold.
The Palatine. Stanza 3

[e] How smoothly the trains run
beyond the Missouri.
Going Home, Burlington Route

[f] I like trees because they seem
more resigned to the way they
have to live than other things do.
O Pioneers! Part II, Chap. 8

[g] Winter lies too long in country towns; hangs on until it is
stale and shabby, old and sullen.
My Antonia. Book II, Chap. 7

[h] That irregular and intimate
quality of things made entirely
by the human hand.
*Death Comes for the Arch-
bishop. Book I, Chap. 3*

[i] The Miracles of the Church
seem to me to rest not so much
upon faces or voices or healing
power coming suddenly near to us

from afar off, but upon our per-
ceptions being made finer, so that
for a moment our eyes can see and
our ears can hear what is there
about us always. *Ibid. Chap. 4*

[j] Only solitary men know the
full joys of friendship.
*Shadows on the Rock.
Book III, Part V*

[k] Sometimes a neighbor whom
we have disliked a lifetime for his
arrogance and conceit lets fall a
single commonplace remark that
shows us another side, another
man, really; a man uncertain, and
puzzled, and in the dark like ourselves. *Ibid. Epilogue*

Madison Julius Cawein
[1865–1914]

[l] Here is the place where Loveliness keeps house,
Between the river and the wooded
hills.
Here Is the Place

[m] An old Spanish saying is that
"a kiss without a moustache is
like an egg without salt."
Nature-Notes. Page 119

Henri Cazalis
(Jean Lahors)
[1840–1909]

[n] Click, click, click . . . Death is
prancing;
Death, at midnight, goes a-danc-
ing,
Tapping on a tomb with talon
thin,
Click, click, click, goes the grisly
violin.
". . . Equality, Fraternity" (tr.
Bertram Galbraith).
Stanza 1

Susannah Centlivre
[1667–1723]

[o] The real Simon Pure.
*A Bold Stroke for a Wife.
Act. V, Sc. 1*

Miguel de Cervantes
[1547–1616]

*From Don Quixote, translated by
Peter Anthony Motteux [died
1718]. Page numbers of the Modern Library Giant edition.*

[p] You are a King by your own
Fireside, as much as any Monarch
in his Throne.
The Author's Preface. Page xix

[q] As ill-luck would have it.
Part I. Book I, Chap. 2, Page 12

[r] The brave man carves out his
fortune. *Ibid. Chap. 4, Page 22*

[s] Which I have earned with the sweat of my brows. *Ibid.*

[t] Can we ever have too much of a good thing?
Ibid. Chap. 6, Page 37

[u] Fortune may have yet a better success in reserve for you, and they who lose to-day may win to-morrow.
Ibid. Chap. 7, Page 39

[v] Those two fatal words, Mine and Thine.
Ibid. Book II, Chap. 3, Page 63

[w] The eyes those silent tongues of Love. *Ibid. Page 65*

[x] As good-natured a soul as e'er trod on shoe of leather.
Ibid. Chap. 4, Page 69

[y] And had a face like a blessing. *Ibid.*

[z] There's not the least thing can be said or done, but people will talk and find fault.
Ibid. Page 70

[a] It is a true saying, that a man must eat a peck of salt with his friend, before he knows him.
Ibid. Book III, Chap. 1, Page 92

[b] Thank you for nothing.
Ibid. Page 94

[c] No limits but the sky.
Ibid. Page 110

[d] To give the devil his due.
Ibid. Page 111

[e] A peck of troubles.
Ibid. Chap. 4, Page 112

[f] Lest we leap out of the frying-pan into the fire; or, out of God's blessing into the warm sun.
Ibid.

[g] Paid him in his own coin.
Ibid. Page 119

[h] Every tooth in a man's head is more valuable than a diamond.
Ibid. Page 121

[i] You are come off now with a whole skin. *Ibid. Page 127*

[j] Get out of harm's way.
Ibid. Chap. 6, Page 130

[k] Fear is sharp-sighted, and can see things under ground, and much more in the skies.
Ibid. Page 131

[l] A finger in every pie.
Ibid. Page 133

[m] No better than she should be. *Ibid.*

[n] Every dog has his day. *Ibid.*

[o] That's the nature of women, ...not to love when we love them, and to love when we love them not. *Ibid.*

[p] You may go whistle for the rest. *Ibid. Page 134*

[q] Why do you lead me a wild-goose chase? *Ibid. Page 136*

[r] Experience, the universal Mother of Sciences.
Ibid. Chap. 7, Page 140

[s'] Ne'er cringe nor creep, for what you by force may reap.
Ibid. Page 149

[t'] 'Tis an office of more trust to shave a man's beard than to saddle a horse. *Ibid. Page 151*

[u'] I know it all by heart.
Ibid. Chap. 8, Page 157

[v'] Let every man mind his own business. *Ibid.*

[w'] Those who'll play with cats must expect to be scratched.
Ibid. Page 159

[x'] 'Tis the part of a wise man to keep himself to-day for to-morrow, and not venture all his eggs in one basket.
Ibid. Chap. 9, Page 162

[y'] I know what's what. *Ibid.*

[z'] Absence, that common cure of love. *Ibid. Page 177*

[a'] Lovers are commonly industrious to make themselves uneasy.
Ibid. Page 179

[b'] 'Tis the only comfort of the miserable to have partners in their woes. *Ibid. Chap. 10, Page 173*

[c'] I never thrust my nose into other men's porridge. It is no bread and butter of mine; every man for himself, and God for us all. *Ibid. Chap. 11, Page 183*

[d'] Naked came I into the world, and naked must I go out. *Ibid.*

[e'] Little said is soon amended.
Ibid. Page 184

[f'] A close mouth catches no flies. *Ibid.*

[g'] Mere flim-flam stories, and nothing but shams and lies.
Ibid. Page 187

[h'] There's no need to make an enquiry about a woman's pedigree, as there is of us men, when some badge of honour is bestowed on us. *Ibid. Page 194*

[i'] There are but two things that chiefly excite us to love a woman, an attractive beauty, and unspotted fame. *Ibid. Page 195*

[j'] 'Tis ill talking of halters in the house of a man that was hanged. *Ibid.*

[k'] My memory is so bad, that many times I forget my own name! *Ibid.*

[l'] Ready to split his sides with laughing. *Ibid. Chap. 13, Page 208*

[m'] As much a fool as he was, he loved money, and knew how to keep it when he had it, and was wise enough to keep his own counsel.   *Ibid.*

[n] What man has assurance enough to pretend to know thoroughly the riddle of a woman's mind, and who could ever hope to fix her mutable nature?
Ibid. Page 216

[o] Demonstrations of love are never altogether displeasing to women, and the most disdainful, in spite of all their coyness, reserve a little complaisance in their hearts for their admirers.
Ibid. Book IV, Chap. 1, Page 226

[p] My honour is dearer to me than my life.   *Ibid. Page 228*

[q] Let things go at sixes and sevens.   *Ibid. Chap. 3, Page 250*

[r] I must speak the truth, and nothing but the truth.
Ibid. Page 255

[s] The ornament of her sex.
Ibid. Chap. 7, Page 287

[t] He that gives quickly gives twice.   *Ibid. Page 291*

[u] Required in every good lover ... the whole alphabet ... Agreeable, Bountiful, Constant, Dutiful, Easy, Faithful, Gallant, Honourable, Ingenious, Kind, Loyal, Mild, Noble, Officious, Prudent, Quiet, Rich, Secret, True, Valiant, Wise ... Young and Zealous.
Ibid. Page 292

[v] Virtue is the truest nobility.
Chap. 9, Page 314

[w] The proof of the pudding is in the eating.
Ibid. Chap. 10, Page 322

[x] Let none presume to tell me that the pen is preferable to the sword.   *Ibid. Page 325*

[y] It is past all controversy, that what costs dearest, is, and ought most to be valued.
Ibid. Chap. 11, Page 328

[z] It seldom happens that any felicity comes so pure as not to be tempered and allayed by some mixture of sorrow.
Ibid. Chap. 14, Page 359

[a] There's no striving against the stream; and the weakest still goes to the wall.
Ibid. Chap. 20, Page 404

[b] I would have nobody to control me, I would be absolute; and who but I? Now, he that is absolute can do what he likes; he that can do what he likes, can take his pleasure; he that can take his pleasure, can be content; and he that can be content, has no more to desire. So the matter's over;

and come what will come, I am satisfied. *Ibid. Chap. 23, Page 423*

[c] Even a worm when trod upon, will turn again. *Part II. Book III, Author's Preface, Page 440*

[d] While there's life there's hope.   *Ibid. Chap. 3, Page 463*

[e] Miracle me no miracles.
Ibid. Page 464

[f] He has done like Orbaneja, the painter of Ubeda; ... when he had scrawled out a misshapen cock, was forced to write underneath in Gothic letters, "This is a cock."   *Ibid.*

[g] He that publishes a book runs a very great hazard, since nothing can be more impossible than to compose one that may secure the approbation of every reader.   *Ibid. Page 466*

[h] Ready cash.
Ibid. Chap. 4, Page 468

[i] Every man is as Heaven made him, and sometimes a great deal worse.   *Ibid.*

[j] There's no sauce in the world like hunger.
Ibid. Chap. 5, Page 473

[k] Birds of a feather flock together.   *Ibid. Page 474*

[l] Journey over all the universe in a map, without the expense and fatigue of travelling, without suffering the inconveniences of heat, cold, hunger, and thirst.
Ibid. Chap. 6, Page 479

[m] Presume to put in her oar.
Ibid. Page 480

[n'] A little in one's own pocket is better than much in another man's purse. 'Tis good to keep a nest-egg. Every little makes a mickle. *Ibid. Chap. 7, Page 486*

[o'] Fore-warned fore-armed.
Ibid. Chap. 10, Page 502

[p'] As well look for a needle in a bottle of hay.   *Ibid.*

[q'] The very pink of courtesy.
Ibid. Chap. 13, Page 521

[r'] Neither fish, flesh, nor good red-herring.   *Ibid.*

[s'] I'll turn over a new leaf.
Ibid. Page 524

[t'] Let every man look before he leaps.   *Ibid. Chap. 14, Page 528*

[u'] The pen is the tongue of the mind.   *Ibid. Chap. 16, Page 543*

[v'] Modesty is a virtue not often found among poets, for almost every one of them thinks himself the greatest in the word.
Ibid. Chap. 18, Page 555

[w'] Sings like a lark.
Ibid. Chap. 19, Page 564

[x] Marriage is a noose.   *Ibid.*

[y] There were but two families in the world, Have-much and Have-little.
Ibid. Chap. 20, Page 574

[z] He preaches well that lives well, quoth Sancho, that's all the divinity I understand.
Ibid. Page 575

[a] Love and War are the same thing, and stratagems and policy are as allowable in the one as in the other. *Ibid. Chap. 21, Page 580*

[b] A private sin is not so prejudicial in this world as a public indecency.
Ibid. Chap. 22, Page 582

[c] Patience, and shuffle the cards.   *Ibid. Chap. 23, Page 592*

[d] Old . . . that's an affront no woman can well bear.
Ibid. Chap. 31, Page 644

[e] One of the most considerable advantages the great have over their inferiors, is to have servants as good as themselves.
Ibid. Page 645

[f] Great persons are able to do great kindnesses.
Ibid. Chap. 32, Page 662

[g] An honest man's word is as good as his bond.
Ibid. Book IV, Chap. 34, Page 674

[h] Heaven's help is better than early rising.   *Ibid.*

[i] There's a time for some things, and a time for all things; a time for great things, and a time for small things.   *Ibid. Page 682*

[j] With a grain of salt.
Ibid. Chap. 37, Page 690

[k] They cover a dunghill with a piece of tapestry when a procession goes by.   *Ibid. Page 691*

[l] Good wits jump; a word to the wise is enough.   *Ibid. Page 692*

[m] My understanding has forsook me, and is gone a wool-gathering.   *Ibid. Chap. 38, Page 692*

[n] Diligence is the mother of good fortune.
Ibid. Chap. 43, Page 724

[o] What a man has, so much he's sure of.   *Ibid. Page 725*

[p] When a man says, "Get out of my house! what would you have with my wife?" there's no answer to be made.   *Ibid. Page 726*

[q] The pot calls the kettle black.
Ibid. Page 727

[r] Mum's the word.
Ibid. Chap. 44, Page 729

[s] Walls have ears.
Ibid. Chap. 48, Page 763

[t] Man appoints, and God disappoints. *Ibid. Chap. 55, Page 816*

[u] Many count their chickens before they are hatched; and where they expect bacon meet with broken bones.   *Ibid.*

[v] I shall be as secret as the grave.   *Ibid. Chap. 62, Page 862*

[w] Now blessings light on him that first invented this same sleep! It covers a man all over, thoughts and all, like a cloak; 'tis meat for the hungry, drink for the thirsty, heat for the cold, and cold for the hot. 'Tis the current coin that purchases all the pleasures of the world cheap; and the balance that sets the king and the shepherd, the fool and the wise man even.
Ibid. Chap. 68, Page 898

[x'] The ass will carry his load, but not a double load; ride not a free horse to death.
Ibid. Chap. 71, Page 917

[y'] I thought it working for a dead horse, because I am paid beforehand.   *Ibid.*

[z'] He . . . got the better of himself, and that's the best kind of victory one can wish for.
Ibid. Chap. 72, Page 924

[a'] Every man was not born with a silver spoon in his mouth.
Ibid. Chap. 73, Page 926

[b'] Ne'er look for birds of this year in the nests of the last.
Ibid. Chap. 74, Page 933

[c'] There is a strange charm in the thoughts of a good legacy, or the hopes of an estate, which wondrously alleviates the sorrow that men would otherwise feel for the death of friends.   *Ibid. Page 934*

[d'] For if he like a madman lived, At least he like a wise one died.
Ibid. Page 935 (Don Quixote's Epitaph)

[e'] Don't put too fine a point to your wit for fear it should get blunted.   *The Little Gypsy (La Gitanilla)*

John White Chadwick
[1840–1904]

[f'] If good men were only better, Would the wicked be so bad?
A Timely Question. Stanza 1

Patrick Reginald Chalmers

[g'] "I find," said 'e, "things very much as 'ow I've always found, For mostly they goes up and down or else goes round and round."
Roundabouts and Swings. Stanza 2

[h] A little dog
Walked out that day with These,
Round eyes agog
For butterflies and bees,
Wet nose for smells that please.
A Chosen Saint. Stanza 3

[i] Little garden gods,
Bless the time of sowing,
Watering and growing; . . .
Bless our garden that it may
Beat our next-door neighbor's.
Cottage Garden Prayer. Stanza 2

(Arthur) Neville Chamberlain
[1869–1940]

[j] Peace for our time . . . peace with honor.
Report [October 1, 1937] on his return to London after a conference at Munich with Hitler, Daladier, and Mussolini

[k] Hitler has missed the bus.
Speech in the House of Commons [April 4, 1940]

Joseph Chamberlain
[1836–1914]

[l] London is the clearing-house of the world.
Speech, Guildhall, London [January 19, 1904]

[m] The day of small nations has passed away; the day of Empires has come. *Speech, Birmingham [May 13, 1904]*

Robert William Chambers
[1865–1933]

[n] Sez Corporal Madden to Private McFadden:
"Yer figger wants padd'n—
Sure, man, ye've no shape!
Behind ye yer shoulders
Stick out like two bowlders;
Yer shins are as thin
As a pair of pen-holders!"
The Recruit. Stanza 3

Sébastien R. N. Chamfort
[1741–1794]

[o] The most useless day of all is that in which we have not laughed.
Maxims and Thoughts. 1

William Ellery Channing
[1780–1842]

[p] The office of government is not to confer happiness, but to give men opportunity to work out happiness for themselves.
The Life and Character of Napoleon Bonaparte

[q] I do and I must reverence human nature. I bless it for its kind affections. I honor it for its achievements in science and art, and still more for its examples of heroic and saintly virtue. These are marks of a divine origin and the pledges of a celestial inheritance; and I thank God that my own lot is bound up with that of the human race.
Inscription, from his writings, on Channing Memorial, Public Garden, Boston

William Ellery Channing
[1818–1901]

[r] Habitant of castle gray,
Creeping thing in sober way,
Visible sage mechanician,
Skilfulest arithmetician.
The Spider [The New England Magazine, October 1835]

[s] Beneath the endless surges of the deep,
Whose green content o'erlaps them evermore,
A host of mariners perpetual sleep,
Too hushed to heed the wild commotion's roar.
Death. Stanza 1

[t] I laugh, for hope hath happy place with me,—
If my bark sinks, 'tis to another sea. *A Poet's Hope*

[u] I sing New England, . . .
She still is there, the guardian on the tower,
To open for the world a purer hour. *New England*

[v] The hills are reared, the seas are scooped in vain
If learning's altar vanish from the plain. *Inscription for the Alcott House, Concord [This couplet remains over the mantelpiece in Alcott House, Concord, Mass., just as it was painted by May Alcott]*

William Henry Channing
[1810–1884]

[w] To live content with small means; to seek elegance rather than luxury, and refinement rather than fashion; to be worthy, not respectable, and wealthy, not rich; to study hard, think quietly, talk gently, act frankly; to listen to stars and birds, to babes and sages, with open heart; to bear all cheerfully, do all bravely, await occasions, hurry never. In a word, to let the spiritual, unbidden and unconscious, grow up through the common. This is to be my symphony. *My Symphony*

Arthur Chapman
[1873–1935]

x] Out where the handclasp's a
    little stronger,
Out where the smile dwells a little
    longer,
That's where the West begins.
        Out Where the West Begins.
            Stanza 1

y] Where there's more of singing
    and less of sighing,
Where there's more of giving and
    less of buying,
And a man makes friends without
    half trying.   *Ibid. Stanza 3*

George Chapman
[1559–1634]

z] Exceeding fair she was not;
    and yet fair
In that she never studied to be
    fairer
Than Nature made her.
        All Fools. Act I, Sc. 1

a] I tell thee Love is Nature's
    second sun,
Causing a spring of virtues where
    he shines.   *Ibid.*

b] *Cornelia.* What flowers are
    these?
Gazetta. The pansy this.
Cornelia. Oh, that's for lovers'
    thoughts.   *Ibid. Act II, Sc. 1*

c] Young men think old men are
    fools; but old men know young
    men are fools.   *Ibid. Act V, Sc. 1*

d] For one heat, all know, doth
    drive out another,
One passion doth expel another
    still.
        Monsieur D'Olive. Act V, Sc. 1

e] Who to himself is law no law
    doth need,
Offends no law, and is a king in-
    deed.
        Bussy D'Ambois. Act II, Sc. 1

f] They're only truly great who
    are truly good.
        Revenge for Honour. Act V, Sc. 2

g] I will neither yield to the song
    of the siren nor the voice of the
    hyena, the tears of the crocodile
    nor the howling of the wolf.
        Eastward Ho. Act V, Sc. 1

h] Promise is most given when
    the least is said.
        Musœus of Hero and Leander

Robert William Chapman
[1881–   ]

i] A house is infinitely communicative and tells many things
besides the figure of its master's
income. There are houses that
confess intellectual penury, and
houses that reek of enlighten-
ment.
        The Portrait of a Scholar

j] A quotation, like a pun,
should come unsought, and then
be welcomed only for some propriety or felicity justifying the
intrusion.
        Ibid. The Art of Quotation

Elizabeth Rundle Charles
[1828–1896]

k] To know how to say what
other people only think, is what
makes men poets and sages; and
to dare to say what others only
dare to think, makes men martyrs
or reformers.   *Chronicles of the
        Schönberg-Cotta Family, XIV*

Salmon Portland Chase
[1808–1873]

l] The Constitution, in all its
provisions, looks to an indestruct-
ible Union composed of inde-
structible States.   *Decision in
    Texas v. White, 7 Wallace, 725*

Geoffrey Chaucer
[1340–1400]
*From the text of Walter William
Skeat [Oxford University Press,
1933] and also the Globe Edition
[Macmillan, 1907]*

m] Hard is his herte that loveth
    nought
In May.
    The Romaunt of the Rose. Line 85

n] The tyme, that may not so-
    journe,
But goth, and never may retourne,
As water that doun renneth ay,
But never drope retourne may.
        Ibid. Line 381

o] As round as appel was his
    face.   *Ibid. Line 819*

p] Morpheus,
Thou knowest him wel, the god of
    sleep.   *The Book of the
        Duchesse. Line 136*

q] Nature, the vicaire of th'
    almyghty lorde.
The Parlement of Foules. Line 379

r] A fool can noght be stille.
        Ibid. Line 574

s] Now welcom somer, with thy
    sonne soft,
That hast this wintres weders
    overshake.   *Ibid. Line 680*

t] A fool may eek a wys man
    ofte gyde.   *Troilus and
        Criseyde. Book I, Line 630*

u] Lord, this is an huge rayn!
This were a weder for to slepen
    inne!
        Ibid. Book III, Line 656

v] Right as an aspen leef she
    gan to quake.
        Ibid. Line 1200

[w] He that nought n'assayeth,
nought n'acheveth.
Ibid. Book V, Line 1786

[x] Of alle the floures in the
mede,
Than love I most these floures
white and rede,
Swiche as men callen daysies in
our toun.   *The Legend of
Good Women, Prologue, Line 41*

[y] Whan that Aprille with his
shoures sote
The droghte of Marche hath
perced to the rote.
*The Canterbury Tales, Prologue.
Line 1*

[z] And smale fowles maken
melodye,
That slepen al the night with open
yë,
(So priketh hem nature in hir
corages):
Than longen folk to goon on pil-
grimages.   *Ibid. Line 9*

[a] He was a verray parfit gentil
knight.   *Ibid. Line 72*

[b] Therfore, in stede of weping
and preyeres,
Men moot yeve silver to the povre
freres.   *Ibid. Line 231*

[c] And gladly wolde he lerne,
and gladly teche.
Ibid. Line 308

[d] For May wol have no slogar-
dye a-night.
The sesoun priketh every gentil
herte,
And maketh him out of his sleep
to sterte.
Ibid. The Knightes Tale. Line 1042

[e] Ech man for himself.
Ibid. Line 1182

[f] What is this world? what
asketh man to have?
Now with his love, now in his
colde grave
Allone, with-outen any companye.
Ibid. Line 2777

[g] This world nis but a thurgh-
fare full of wo,
And we ben pilgrimes, passing to
an fro;
Deeth is an ende of every worldly
sore.   *Ibid. Line 2847*

[h] So was hir joly whistle wel
y-wet.
Ibid. The Reves Tale. Line 4155

[i] Ful wys is he that can him-
selven knowe.
Ibid. The Monkes Tale. Line 3329

[j] For dronkenesse is verray
sepulture
Of mannes wit and his discre-
cioun.
Ibid. The Pardoner's Tale. Line 448

[k] Gret swering is a thing ab-
hominable,

And false swering is yet more re
prevable.   *Ibid. Line 63*

[l] In his owene grece I made hin
frye.   *Ibid. The Wife o
Bath's Prologue. Line 48*

[m] What thing we may na
lightly have,
Ther-after wol we crye al-day and
crave.   *Ibid. Line 51*

[n] Loke who that is most vertu
ous alway,
Privee and apert, and most en
tendeth ay
To do the gentil dedes that he can
And tak him for the grettest genti
man.   *Ibid. The Tale of th
Wyf of Bathe. Line 111*

[o] For though we slepe or wake
or rome, or ryde,
Ay fleeth the tyme, it nil no mar
abyde.
Ibid. The Clerkes Tale. Line 11

[p] No wedded man so hardy be
t'assaille
His wyves pacience, in hope te
finde
Grisildes, for in certein he shal
faille!   *Ibid. Line 118*

[q] It is no childes pley
To take a wyf with-oute avyse-
ment.   *Ibid
The Marchantes Tale. Line 153*

[r] Pacience is an heigh vertu
certeyn.   *Ibid
The Frankeleyns Tale. Line 773*

[s] Trouthe is the hyeste thing
that men may kepe.
Ibid. Line 1479

[t] But al thing which that shy-
neth as the gold
Nis nat gold, as that I have herd
it told.   *Ibid. The Chanouns
Yemannes Tale. Line 962*

[u] The firste vertu, sone, if thou
wolt lere,
Is to restreyne and kepe wel thy
tonge.   *Ibid.
The Maunciples Tale. Line 332*

[v] Thing that seyd, is seyd; and
forth it gooth.
Ibid. Line 355

John Vance Cheney

[1848–1922]

[w'] Who drives the horses of the
sun
Shall lord it but a day;
Better the lowly deed were done,
And kept the humble way.
The Happiest Heart. Stanza 1

Philip Dormer Stanhope,
Earl of Chesterfield

[1694–1773]

[x'] Whatever is worth doing at
all, is worth doing well.
Letters. March 10, 1746

[y] Do as you would be done by, is the surest method of pleasing.
Ibid. October 16, 1747

[z] Manners must adorn knowledge, and smooth its way through the world. Like a great rough diamond, it may do very well in a closet by way of curiosity, and also for its intrinsic value.
Ibid. July 1, 1748

[a] Without some dissimulation no business can be carried on at all.
Ibid. May 22, 1749

[b] Style is the dress of thoughts.
Ibid. November 24, 1749

[c] I assisted at the birth of that most significant word "flirtation," which dropped from the most beautiful mouth in the world.
The World. No. 101

[d] The dews of the evening most carefully shun,—
Those tears of the sky for the loss of the sun.
Advice to a Lady in Autumn

[e] Women, and young men, are very apt to tell what secrets they know, from the vanity of having been trusted.
Letters to His Son

Gilbert Keith Chesterton
[1874–1936]

[f] Nothing sublimely artistic has ever arisen out of mere art, any more than anything essentially reasonable has ever arisen out of the pure reason. There must always be a rich moral soil for any great aesthetic growth.
A Defence of Nonsense

[g] The whole difference between construction and creation is exactly this: that a thing constructed can only be loved after it is constructed; but a thing created is loved before it exists.
Preface to Dickens's Pickwick Papers

[h] A good joke is the one ultimate and sacred thing which cannot be criticized. Our relations with a good joke are direct and even divine relations.
Ibid.

[i] The world will never starve for wonders; but only for want of wonder.
Inscription on General Motors Building, A Century of Progress Exposition, Chicago

[j] Thieves respect property. They merely wish the property to become their property that they may more perfectly respect it.
The Man Who Was Thursday

[k] You can free things from alien or accidental laws, but not from the laws of their own nature. . . . Do not go about as a demagogue, encouraging triangles to break out of the prison of their three sides. If a triangle breaks out of its three sides, its life comes to a lamentable end.
Orthodoxy. Chap. 3

[l] Heights were made to be looked at, not to be looked from.
The Innocence of Father Brown.
(The Hammer of God)

[m] I think I will not hang myself to-day.
A Ballade of Suicide

[n] St. George he was for England,
And before he killed the dragon
He drank a pint of English ale
Out of an English flagon.
The Englishman

[o] And Noah he often said to his wife when he sat down to dine,
"I don't care where the water goes if it doesn't get into the wine."
Wine and Water

[p] Before the Roman came to Rye or out to Severn strode,
The rolling English drunkard made the rolling English road.
The Rolling English Road

[q] Tea is like the East he grows in,
A great yellow Mandarin
With urbanity of manner
And unconsciousness of sin. . . .

And, like all the East he grows in,
He is Poison when he's strong.
The Song of Right and Wrong

[r] Cocoa is a cad and coward.
Ibid.

[s] Heaven sent us Soda Water
As a torment for our crimes.
Ibid.

[t] For the great Gaels of Ireland
Are the men that God made mad,
For all their wars are merry,
And all their songs are sad.
The Ballad of the White Horse.
Book II

[u] Step softly, under snow or rain,
To find the place where men can pray;
The way is all so very plain
That we may lose the way.
The Wise Men

[v] I also had my hour;
One far fierce hour and sweet:
There was a shout about my ears,
And palms before my feet.
The Donkey

[w] The Yankee is a dab at electricity and crime,
He tells you how he hustles and it takes him quite a time,
I like his hospitality that's cordial and frank,

I do not mind his money but I do
not like his swank.
    A Song of Self-Esteem

[x] The face of Father Brown . . .
could shine with ignorance as well
as with knowledge.
    The Wisdom of Father Brown

Lydia Maria Child
[1802–1880]

[y] Genius hath electric power
Which earth can never tame,
Bright suns may scorch and dark
    clouds lower,
Its flash is still the same.
    *Marius Amid the Ruins of
    Carthage*

[z] Over the river and through
    the wood,
To grandfather's house we'll go;
    The horse knows the way
    To carry the sleigh,
Through the white and drifted
    snow.
    Thanksgiving Day. Stanza 1

George William Childs
[1829–1894]

[a] Do not keep the alabaster
boxes of your love and tenderness
sealed up until your friends are
dead. Fill their lives with sweetness. Speak approving, cheering
words while their ears can hear
them, and while their hearts can
be thrilled and made happier by
them.   *A Creed*

Thomas Holley Chivers
[1807–1858]

[b] As the diamond is the crystalline Revelator of the achromatic
white light of Heaven, so is a perfect poem the crystalline revelation of the Divine Idea.
    Preface to Eonchs of Ruby

[c] As an egg, when broken, never
Can be mended, but must ever
Be the same crushed egg for ever—
So shall this dark heart of mine!
    To Allegra Florence in Heaven

Rufus Choate
[1799–1859]

[d] The courage of New England
was the "courage of Conscience."
It did not rise to that insane and
awful passion, the love of war for
itself.   *Address at Ipswich
    Centennial [1834]*

[e] The final end of Government
is not to exert restraint but to do
good.   *Speech, The Necessity of
Compromise in American Politics,
U. S. Senate [July 2, 1841]*

[f] We join ourselves to no party
that does not carry the flag and
keep step to the music of the
Union.   *Letter to the Whig Convention, Worcester [October 1,
    1855]*

Henry Fothergill Chorley
[1808–1872]

[g] Then here's to the oak, the
    brave old oak,
Who stands in his pride alone!
And still flourish he, a hale green
    tree,
When a hundred years are gone!
    The Brave Old Oak. Refrain

Agatha Christie

[h] It is completely unimportant.
That is why it is so interesting.
    The Murder of Roger Ackroyd

Dio Chrysostom
[A.D. 40–120]
*Translation by J. W. Cohoon.
Loeb Classical Library*

[i] Idleness and lack of occupation are the best things in the
world to ruin the foolish.
    *Tenth Discourse On Servants.
    Chap. 7*

[j] Like men with sore eyes: they
find the light painful, while the
darkness, which permits them to
see nothing, is restful and agreeable.   *Eleventh, or Trojan, Discourse. Chap. 2*

Edward A. Church
[1844–1929]

[k] Of all the words the Evange-
    lists record,
To comfort souls perplexèd and
    distressed,
This ever seems to me divinest,
    best—
The thought that Peter spoke—
    "Thou knowest, Lord."
    Sonnet, Thou Knowest

[l] Come, holy fire, consume this
    clay,
Ashes to ashes now return;
An outworn garment here we lay,
As on thine Altar, Lord, to burn.

Not to corruption and the worm
    Our shrinking spirits yield the
    claim,
But give this well-beloved form
    The cleanly burial of the flame.
    Cremation Hymn. Stanzas 1 and 2

Francis Pharcellus Church
[1839–1906]

[m] Virginia, your little friends
are wrong. They have been
affected by the skepticism of a

skeptical age. They do not believe except they see. They think that nothing can be which is not comprehensible by their little minds. All minds, Virginia, whether they be men's or children's, are little. In this great universe of ours man is a mere insect, an ant, in his intellect, as compared with the boundless world about him, as measured by the intelligence capable of grasping the whole of truth and knowledge. . . .
Not believe in Santa Claus? You might as well not believe in fairies. . . .
No Santa Claus! Thank God, he lives, and he lives forever. A thousand years from now, Virginia, nay, ten times ten thousand years from now, he will continue to make glad the heart of childhood.
Editorial: Is There a Santa Claus? [First published in The New York Sun, September 21, 1897, in reply to an inquiry from Virginia O'Hanlon. These extracts are included by permission of The New York Sun]

Charles Churchill
[1731–1764]

[n] He mouths a sentence as curs mouth a bone.
The Rosciad. Line 322

[o] Apt alliteration's artful aid.
The Prophecy of Famine. Line 86

[p] With curious art the brain, too finely wrought,
Preys on herself, and is destroyed by thought.
Epistle to William Hogarth. Line 645

[q] Be England what she will,
With all her faults she is my country still.
The Farewell. Line 27

Winston Spencer Churchill
[1874–   ]
See also Franklin D. Roosevelt

[r] Nothing in life is so exhilarating as to be shot at without result.
The Malakand Field Force [1898]

[s] Terminological inexactitude.
Speech, House of Commons, February 22, 1906

[t] By being so long in the lowest form [at Harrow] I gained an immense advantage over the cleverer boys. . . . I got into my bones the essential structure of the ordinary British sentence—which is a noble thing. Naturally I am biassed in favor of boys learning English; and then I would let the clever ones learn Latin as an honor, and Greek as a treat.
Roving Commission: My Early Life

[u] Dictators ride to and fro upon tigers which they dare not dismount. And the tigers are getting hungry.   *While England Slept*

[v] I cannot forecast to you the action of Russia. It is a riddle wrapped in a mystery inside an enigma.
Broadcast, October 1, 1939

[w] I have nothing to offer but blood, toil, tears and sweat.
First Statement as Prime Minister, House of Commons, May 13, 1940

[x] Victory at all costs, victory in spite of all terror, victory however long and hard the road may be; for without victory there is no survival.   *Ibid.*

[y] We shall fight on the beaches, we shall fight on the landing grounds, we shall fight in the fields and in the streets, we shall fight in the hills; we shall never surrender.   *Speech on Dunkirk, House of Commons, June 4, 1940*

[z] If we open a quarrel between the past and the present, we shall find that we have lost the future.
Speech, House of Commons, and later broadcast, June 18, 1940

[a] If the British Empire and its Commonwealth last for a thousand years, men will still say, "This was their finest hour."
Ibid.

[b] Never in the field of human conflict was so much owed by so many to so few.   *Tribute to the Royal Air Force, House of Commons, August 20, 1940*

[c] The only guide to a man is his conscience; the only shield to his memory is the rectitude and sincerity of his actions.
Tribute to Neville Chamberlain, former Prime Minister, House of Commons, November 12, 1940

[d] To die at the height of a man's career, the highest moment of his effort here in this world, universally honored and admired, to die while great issues are still commanding the whole of his interest, to be taken from us at a moment when he could already see ultimate success in view—is not the most unenviable of fates.
Report on the War Situation. House of Commons, December 19, 1940

[e] The British nation is unique in this respect. They are the only people who like to be told how bad things are, who like to be told the worst.   *Report on the War Situation, House of Commons, June 10, 1941*

[f] A vile race of quislings—to use the new word which will carry

the scorn of mankind down the centuries—is hired to fawn upon the conqueror [referring to Vidkun Quisling, head of the Nasjonal Samling party in Norway, who co-operated and collaborated with the Nazis when Germany invaded Norway, April 9, 1940], to collaborate in his designs, and to enforce his rule upon their fellow-countrymen, while grovelling low themselves.   *Speech at St. James's Palace, London, June 12, 1941*

[g] The destiny of mankind is not decided by material computation. When great causes are on the move in the world . . . we learn that we are spirits, not animals, and that something is going on in space and time, and beyond space and time, which, whether we like it or not, spells duty.
Radio Broadcast to America on receiving the Honorary Degree of Doctor of Laws from the University of Rochester, New York, June 16, 1941

[h] In the past we have had a light which flickered, in the present we have a light which flames, and in the future there will be a light which shines over all the land and sea.
Speech on War with Japan, House of Commons, December 8, 1941, and later broadcast

[i] We have not journeyed all this way across the centuries, across the oceans, across the mountains, across the prairies, because we are made of sugar candy.
Speech to the Canadian Senate and House of Commons, Ottawa, broadcast, December 30, 1941

[j] When I warned [the French] that Britain would fight on alone whatever they did, their generals told their Prime Minister and his divided Cabinet, "In three weeks England will have her neck wrung like a chicken." Some chicken; some neck.   *Ibid.*

[k] The late M. Venizelos observed that in all her wars England—he should have said Britain, of course—always wins one battle —the last.
Speech at the Lord Mayor's Day Luncheon, London, November 10, 1942

[l] There is no finer investment for any community than putting milk into babies.   *Radio Broadcast (A Four Years' Plan), March 21, 1943*

[m] The House of Commons thrives on criticism, it is perfectly impervious to newspaper abuse or taunts from any quarter, and it is capable of digesting almost anything or almost any body of gentlemen, whatever be the views with which they arrive.
Speech on Rebuilding the House of Commons, October 28, 1943

[n] He died in harness, and we may well say in battle harness, like his soldiers, sailors and airmen who died side by side with ours and carrying out their tasks to the end all over the world. What an enviable death was his. . . .
In Franklin Roosevelt there died the greatest American friend we have ever known—and the greatest champion of freedom who has ever brought help and comfort from the new world to the old.   *Tribute to President Franklin D. Roosevelt in the House of Commons, April 17, 1945*

[o] An iron curtain has descended across the Continent.
Address at Westminster College, Fulton, Missouri, March 5, 1946

Colley Cibber
[1671–1757]

[p] As good be out of the world as out of the fashion.
Love's Last Shift. Act II

[q] We shall find no fiend in hell can match the fury of a disappointed woman.   *Ibid. Act IV*

[r] Old houses mended,
Cost little less than new before they're ended.
The Double Gallant. Prologue

[s] Possession is eleven points in the law.   *Woman's Wit. Act I*

Marcus Tullius Cicero
[106–43 B.C.]

[t] He is never less at leisure than when at leisure.
De Officiis. IX, 10

[u] For how many things, which for our own sake we should never do, do we perform for the sake of our friends.   *De Amicitia (tr. Cyrus R. Edmonds). XVI*

[v] There is no greater bane to friendship than adulation, fawning, and flattery.   *Ibid. XXV*

[w] Crimes are not to be measured by the issue of events, but from the bad intentions of men.
Paradox III

[x] There is no place more delightful than home.
Epistolae. IV, 8

[y] While the sick man has life there is hope.   *Ibid. IX, 10*

[z] For as I like a young man in
whom there is something of the
old, so I like an old man in whom
there is something of the young;
and he who follows this maxim, in
body will possibly be an old man,
but he will never be an old man
in mind.   *De Senectute* (tr.
        Cyrus R. Edmonds). XI

[a] Intelligence, and reflection,
and judgment, reside in old men,
and if there had been none of
them, no states could exist at all.
        Ibid. XIX

[b] Old age is the consummation
of life, just as of a play.
        Ibid. XXIII

Raymond Clapper
[1892–1945]

[c] It's a wise crack that knows
its own father.
        *Quoted in Washington Tapestry
        by Olive Ewing Clapper*

John Clare
[1793–1864]

[d] My friends forsake me like a
        memory lost.   *Written in
        Northampton County Asylum*

[e] The daisy lives, and strikes
        its little root
Into the lap of time: centuries
        may come,
And pass away into the silent
        tomb,
And still the child, hid in the
        womb of time,
Shall smile and pluck them, when
        this simple rhyme
Shall be forgotten.
        The Daisy's Eternity

[f]   The world was on thy page
Of victories but a comma.
        To Napoleon

[g] The wind and clouds, now
        here, now there,
Hold no such strange dominion
As woman's cold, perverted will,
And soon estranged opinion.
        When Lovers Part

[h] If life had a second edition,
how I would correct the proofs.
        *In a letter to a friend. Quoted
        in Foreword to J. W. and Anne
        Tibble's John Clare: A Life*

Badger Clark, Jr.
[1883–   ]

[i] I waste no thought on my
        neighbor's birth
Or the way he makes his prayer.
I grant him a white man's room
        on earth
If his game is only square.
While he plays it straight I'll call
        him mate;
If he cheats I drop him flat.
        The Westerner. Stanza 3

[j] O Lord, I've never lived where
        churches grow,
I love creation better as it stood
That day You finished it so long
        ago,
And looked upon Your work and
        called it good.
        A Cowboy's Prayer. Stanza 1

[k] Oh, stranger, tell my pards
        below
I took a rampin' dream in tow,
And if I never lay him low,
I'll never turn him loose!
        *The Glory Trail [also known
        as High-Chin Bob]*

Thomas Curtis Clark
[1877–   ]

[l] We need the comrade heart
That understands,
And the warmth, the living
        warmth
Of human hands.   *The Touch
        of Human Hands. Stanza 1*

James Freeman Clarke
[1810–1888]

[m] Beneath the shadow of the
        Great Protection,
The soul sits, hushed and calm.
        The Shadow. Stanza 2

[n] Every inmost aspiration is
        God's angel undefiled;
And in every "O my Father!"
        slumbers deep a "Here, my
        child!"   *Prayer Its Own
        Answer (translated from Jelal-
        el-Deen). Couplet 8*

Joseph Ignatius Constantine Clarke
[1846–1925]

[o] "Wherever there's Kellys
        there's trouble," said Burke.
   "Wherever fighting's the game,
Or a spice of danger in grown
        man's work,"
Said Kelly, "you'll find my
        name."

"Oh, the fighting races don't die
        out,
If they seldom die in bed."
        *The Fighting Race.
        Stanzas 2 and 5*

MacDonald Clarke
[1798–1842]

[p] Whilst twilight's curtain
        spreading far,
Was pinned with a single star.
        Death in Disguise. Line 227

[q] Ha! see where the wild-blaz-
        ing Grog-shop appears,
As the red waves of wretched-
        ness swell;
The horrible Light-house of
        Hell!   *The Rum-hole*

Henry Clay
[1777–1852]

[r] It would not be thought very just or wise to arraign the honorable professions of law and physic because the one produces the pettifogger and the other the quack. *Speech on the Protection of Home Industry, U. S. House of Representatives [April 26, 1820]*

[s] Government is a trust, and the officers of the government are trustees; and both the trust and the trustees are created for the benefit of the people.
Speech at Ashland, Kentucky [March 1829]

[t] The arts of power and its minions are the same in all countries and in all ages. It marks its victim; denounces it; and excites the public odium and the public hatred, to conceal its own abuses and encroachments. *Speech on the State of the Country, U. S. Senate [March 14, 1834]*

[u] Sir, I would rather be right than be President.
Speech [1850], referring to the compromise measures

[v] General Alexander Smyth, a tedious speaker in Congress, observed: "You, sir, speak for the present generation; but I speak for posterity."
"Yes," said Mr. Clay, "and you seem resolved to speak until the arrival of your audience."
Quoted by Epes Sargent in Life of Henry Clay

Elizabeth Hannah Jocelyn Cleaveland
[1824–1911]

[w] I'm bound for heaven and when I'm there
I shall want my Book of Common Prayer,
And though I put on a starry crown,
I should feel quite lost without my gown. *No Sects in Heaven. Stanza 4*

Sarah Norcliffe Cleghorn
[1876–   ]

[x] The golf links lie so near the mill
That almost every day
The laboring children can look out
And watch the men at play.
Quatrain [First published in The Conning Tower of The New York Tribune, January 23, 1915.]

[y] Thanks to Saint Matthew, who had been

At mass-meetings in Palestine,
We know whose side was spoken for
When Comrade Jesus had the floor.
Comrade Jesus. Stanza 1

Samuel Langhorne Clemens
see "Mark Twain"

Grover Cleveland
[1837–1908]

[z] Public officers are the servants and agents of the people, to execute the laws which the people have made. *Letter accepting the nomination for Governor of New York [October 1882]*

[a] Your every voter, as surely as your chief magistrate, exercises a public trust. *Inaugural Address [March 4, 1885]*

[b] When more of the people's sustenance is exacted through the form of taxation than is necessary to meet the just obligations of Government and expenses of its economical administration, such exaction becomes ruthless extortion and a violation of the fundamental principles of a free Government. *Second Annual Message [December 1886]*

[c] I have tried so hard to do the right. *Last Words*

John Clifford
[1836–1923]

[d] Last evening I paused beside a blacksmith's door
And heard the anvil ring the vesper chime.

"How many anvils have you had," said I,
"To wear and batter all these hammers so?"
"Just one," said he; then said with twinkling eye,
"The anvil wears the hammers out, you know." *Hammer and Anvil. Stanzas 1 and 2*

[e] And so, I thought, the anvil of God's Word
For ages skeptic blows have beat upon;
Yet, though the noise of falling blows was heard,
The anvil is unharmed—the hammers gone. *Ibid. Stanza 3*

Arthur Hugh Clough
[1819–1861]

[f] It fortifies my soul to know That, though I perish, Truth is so.
"With Whom Is no Variableness"

[g] This world is very odd we see,
We do not comprehend it;
But in one fact we all agree,
God won't, and we can't, mend
it.   *Dipsychus. Part II, Sc. 2*

[h] Grace is given of God, but
knowledge is bought in the
market.   *The Bothie of
Tober-na-Vuolich. Part IV*

[i] Where lies the land to which
the ship would go?
Far, far ahead, is all her seamen
know.   *Songs of Absence*

[j] That out of sight is out of
mind
Is true of most we leave behind;
It is not sure, nor can be true,
My own and only love, of you.
          Ibid.

[k] How in God's name did Columbus get over
Is a pure wonder to me.
          Columbus. Stanza 1

[l] What if wise men had, as far
back as Ptolemy,
Judged that the earth, like an
orange was round,
None of them ever said, Come
along, follow me,
Sail to the West, and the East will
be found.   *Ibid. Stanza 3*

Florence Earle Coates
[1850–1927]

[m] There is always room for
beauty: memory
A myriad lovely blossoms may
enclose,
But, whatsoe'er hath been, there
still must be
Room for another rose.
          The Poetry of Earth. Stanza 1

[n] How living are the dead!
Enshrined, but not apart,
How safe within the heart
We hold them still—our dead,
Whatever else be fled!
          Immortal. Stanza 1

[o] Think not of love as a debt—
Due in May or in December.
          Mother-Love. Stanza 1

Elizabeth Coatsworth
(Mrs. Henry Beston)
[1893–   ]

[p] Let it be understood that I
am Don Juan Gomez!
My saddle cloth is fringed with
scalps of Indians I have slain,
And when I see a girl and knock
upon her shutter,
Though it be dawn or dark, I need
not knock again.
          Announcement. Stanza 2

[q] To a life that seizes
Upon content,
Locality seems
But accident.   *To Daughters,
Growing Up. Stanza 7*

[r] Cat, if you go outdoors you
must walk in the snow.
You will come back with little
white shoes on your feet,
Little white slippers of snow that
have heels of sleet.
Stay by the fire, my Cat. Lie still,
do not go.
          On a Night of Snow

Irvin Shrewsbury Cobb
[1876–1944]

[s] It smells like gangrene starting in a mildewed silo, it tastes
like the wrath to come, and when
you absorb a deep swig of it you
have all the sensations of having
swallowed a lighted kerosene
lamp. A sudden, violent jolt of it
has been known to stop the victim's watch, snap his suspenders
and crack his glass eye right
across.   *Definition of "Corn
Licker" given to the Distillers'
Code Authority, N. R. A.*

[t] I charge my family . . . that
they shall put on none of the
bogus habiliments of so-called
mourning. Folds of black crepe
never ministered to the memory
of the departed.   *Letter of Instructions to be opened after
his death*

[u] Lay my ashes at the roots of a
dogwood tree in Paducah at the
proper planting season. Should
the tree live, that will be monument enough for me.   *Ibid.*

Robert Peter Tristram Coffin
[1892–   ]

[v] Life and death upon one
tether
And running beautiful together.
          Crystal Moment

[w] I, the new owner of this ancient house,
Take over more than walls and
hearths and stairs;
There has been sorrow here and
human pride,
And I am taking over things like
prayers.
          Taking Over an Old House

[x] A man should choose with
careful eye
The things to be remembered by.
          The Weather Vane

George Michael Cohan
[1878–1942]

[y] Hurried and worried until
we're buried, and there's no
curtain call,
Life's a funny proposition, after
all.
          Life's a Funny Proposition

[z] Always leave them laughing
when you say good-bye.
Title of Song

[a] Give my regards to Broadway,
Remember me to Herald Square,
Tell all the gang at Forty-second
Street
That I will soon be there.
Give My Regards to Broadway

[b] What's all the shootin' for?
The Tavern

Sir Edward Coke
[1552–1634]

[c] Reason is the life of the law;
nay, the common law itself is
nothing else but reason. . . . The
law, which is perfection of reason.
First Institute

[d] The house of every one is to
him as his castle and fortress, as
well for his defence against injury
and violence as for his repose.
Semayne's Case. 5 Rep. 91

[e] They (corporations) cannot
commit treason, nor be outlawed
nor excommunicated, for they have
no souls.   *Case of Sutton's
Hospital. 10 Rep. 32*

Frank Moore Colby
[1865–1925]

[f] Men will confess to treason,
murder, arson, false teeth, or a
wig. How many of them will own
up to a lack of humor?
Essays. Vol. 1

[g] Nobody can describe a fool to
the life, without much patient
self-inspection.   *Ibid.*

[h] Every man ought to be in-
quisitive through every hour of
his great adventure down to the
day when he shall no longer cast a
shadow in the sun. For if he dies
without a question in his heart,
what excuse is there for his continuance?   *Ibid.*

[i] Were it not for the presence
of the unwashed and the half-
educated, the formless, queer and
incomplete, the unreasonable and
absurd, the infinite shapes of the
delightful human tadpole, the
horizon would not wear so wide a
grin.   *Imaginary Obligations*

[j] In public we say the race is to
the strongest; in private we know
that a lopsided man runs the fastest along the little side-hills of
success.   *Constrained Attitudes*

[k] Journalists have always been
our most old-fashioned class,
being too busy with the news of
the day to lay aside the mental
habits of fifty years before.
Constrained Attitudes

Samuel Valentine Cole
[1851–1925]

[l] Where'er men go, in heaven,
or earth, or hell,
They find themselves, and that is
all they find.
The Difference

[m] The man who knows and
knows he knows,
To him your homage bring;
He wields the power that waits
and wins,
And he is rightful king.
An Old Saw Reset. Stanza 1

[n] In April Rome was founded;
Shakespeare died;
The shot whose sound rang out
from Concord town
And brought an avalanche of
echoes down,
Shaking all thrones of tyranny
and pride,
Was fired in April; . . .
'Twas April when they laid the
martyr's crown
On Lincoln's brow.   *In April*

Hartley Coleridge
[1796–1849]

[o] Be not afraid to pray; to pray
is right.
Pray, if thou canst, with hope, but
ever pray,
Though hope be weak, or sick with
long delay.
Pray in the darkness if there be
no light.   *Prayer*

[p]   On this hapless earth
There's small sincerity of mirth,
And laughter oft is but an art
To drown the outcry of the heart.
Address to Certain Gold-fishes

[q] Her very frowns are fairer far
Than smiles of other maidens are.
Song. She Is Not Fair

Samuel Taylor Coleridge
[1772–1834]

[r] We were the first that ever
burst
Into that silent sea.
*The Ancient Mariner.
Part II, Stanza 5*

[s] As idle as a painted ship
Upon a painted ocean.
Ibid. Stanza 8

[t] Water, water, everywhere,
Nor any drop to drink.
Ibid. Stanza 9

[u] Without a breeze, without a
tide,
She steadies with upright keel.
Ibid. Part III, Stanza 6

[v] The nightmare Life-in-Death
was she.   *Ibid. Stanza 11*

[w] The sun's rim dips, the stars
     rush out :
At one stride comes the dark ;
          Ibid. Stanza 13

[x] Fear at my heart, as at a cup,
My life-blood seem'd to sip.
          Ibid. Stanza 14

[y] And thou are long, and lank,
     and brown,
As is the ribbed sea-sand.
          Ibid. Part IV, Stanza 1

[z] Alone, alone, all, all alone ;
Alone on a wide, wide sea.
          Ibid. Stanza 3

[a] The moving moon went up
     the sky,
And nowhere did abide ;
Softly she was going up,
And a star or two beside.
          Ibid. Stanza 10

[b] Oh sleep ! it is a gentle thing,
Beloved from pole to pole.
          Ibid. Part V, Stanza 1

[c] A noise like of a hidden brook
In the leafy month of June,
That to the sleeping woods all
     night
Singeth a quiet tune.
          Ibid. Stanza 17

[d] So lonely 'twas, that God
     himself
Scarce seemed there to be.
          Ibid. Part VII, Stanza 19

[e] He prayeth well who loveth
     well
Both man and bird and beast.

He prayeth best who loveth best
All things both great and small.
          Ibid. Stanzas 22 and 23

[f] To be wroth with one we love
Doth work like madness in the
     brain.   *Christobel. Part II*

[g] In Xanadu did Kubla Khan
A stately pleasure-dome decree ;
Where Alph, the sacred river, ran
Through caverns measureless to
     man,
Down to a sunless sea.
          Kubla Khan

[h] A savage place ! as holy and
     enchanted
As e'er beneath a waning moon
     was haunted
By woman wailing for her demon
     lover !   *Ibid.*

[i] For he on honey-dew hath
     fed,
And drunk the milk of Paradise.
          Ibid.

[j] What is an Epigram ? A drawf-
     ish whole,
Its body brevity, and wit its soul.
          An Epigram

[k] Ere sin could blight or sorrow
     fade,
Death came with friendly care ;

The opening bud to heaven con-
     veyed,
And bade it blossom there.
          Epitaph on an Infant

[l] Forth from his dark and
     lonely hiding-place
(Portentous sight !) the owlet
     Atheism,
Sailing on obscene wings athwart
     the noon,
Drops his blue-fring'd lids, and
     holds them close,
And hooting at the glorious sun
     in heaven
Cries out, "Where is it ?"
          Fears in Solitude

[m] And the Devil did grin, for
     his darling sin
Is pride that apes humility.
          The Devil's Thoughts. Stanza 6

[n] All thoughts, all passions, all
     delights,
Whatever stirs this mortal frame,
All are but ministers of Love,
     And feed his sacred flame.
          Love. Stanza 1

[o] Tranquillity !   thou   better
     name
Than all the family of Fame.
          Ode to Tranquillity

[p] Aloof with hermit-eye I scan
The present work of present
     man—
A wild and dream-like trade of
     blood and guile,
Too foolish for a tear, too wicked
     for a smile.   *Ibid.*

[q] A mother is a mother still,
The holiest thing alive.
          The Three Graves

[r] How seldom, friend ! a good
     great man inherits
Honor or wealth, with all his
     worth and pains ! . . .
Greatness and goodness are not
     means, but ends !
Hath he not always treasures,
     always friends,
The good great man ? Three treas-
     ures,—love, and light,
And calm thoughts, regular as in-
     fant's breath ;—
And three firm friends, more sure
     than day and night,—
Himself, his Maker, and the angel
     Death.   *Complaint* [*Edition
     of 1852*]—*The Good Great Man*
          [*Edition of 1893*]

[s] Nought cared this body for
     wind or weather,
When youth and I lived in 't to-
     gether.
          Youth and Age. Stanza 1

[t] I counted two-and-seventy
     stenches,
All well defined, and several
     stinks. . . .
The river Rhine, it is well known,
Doth wash your city of Cologne ;

But tell me, nymphs! what power
　　divine
Shall henceforth wash the river
　　Rhine?　　　　　　*Cologne*

[u] Clothing the palpable and
　　familiar
With golden exhalations of the
　　dawn.　　*Wallenstein. Part II,
　The Death of Wallenstein, Act
　V, Sc. 1 (tr. from Schiller)*

[v] Often do the spirits
Of great events stride on before
　　the events,
And in to-day already walks to-
　　morrow.　　　　　　*Ibid.*

[w] The happiness of life is made
up of minute fractions—the little
soon forgotten charities of a kiss
or smile, a kind look, a heartfelt
compliment, and the countless in-
finitesimals of pleasurable and
genial feeling.　　*The Friend.
　　　　　　　The Improvisatore*

[x] Not the poem which we have
read, but that to which we *return*,
with the greatest pleasure, possesses the genuine power, and
claims the name of *essential
poetry.*
　　Biographia Literaria. Chap. 1

[y] Every reform, however necessary, will by weak minds be carried to an excess, that itself will
need reforming.　　　　*Ibid.*

[z] Men whose dearest wishes are
fixed on objects wholly out of
their own power, become in all
cases more or less impatient and
prone to anger.　　　　*Ibid.*

[a] The lamentable difficulty I
have always experienced in saying "No."　　*Ibid. Chap. 10*

[b] Good sense is the body of
poetic genius, fancy its drapery,
motion its life, and imagination
the soul.　　*Ibid. Chap. 14*

[c] Our myriad-minded Shakespeare.　　　*Ibid. Chap. 15*

[d] Talk of the devil, and his
horns appear, says the proverb.
　　　　　　　Ibid. Chap. 23

[e] I wish our clever young poets
would remember my homely definitions of prose and poetry; that
is, prose,—words in their best
order; poetry,—the best words in
their best order.　　*Table Talk*

[f] Beneath this sod
A poet lies, or that which once
　　seemed he—
Oh, lift a thought in prayer for
　　S.T.C.!
That he, who many a year, with
　　toil of breath,
Found death in life, may here find
　　life in death.
　　Epitaph written for himself

Daniel Clement Colesworthy
[1810–1893]

[g] A little word in kindness
　　spoken,
A motion or a tear,
Has often healed the heart that's
　　broken,
And made a friend sincere.
　　　A Little Word. Stanza 1

John Churton Collins
[1848–1908]

[h] Mistrust a subordinate who
never finds fault with his superior.　　*Aphorisms. Quoted by
　Logan Pearsall Smith: English
　Aphorists*

[i] The secret of success in life is
known only to those who have not
succeeded.　　　　　*Ibid.*

[j] If men were as unselfish as
women, women would very soon
become more selfish than men.
　　　　　　　　　　Ibid.

Mortimer Collins
[1827–1876]

[k] There was an Ape in the days
　　that were earlier;
Centuries passed, and his hair
　　became curlier;
Centuries more gave a thumb to
　　his wrist—
Then he was Man—and a Posi-
　　tivist.　　*The Positivists*

[l] A man is as old as he's feeling,
A woman as old as she looks.
　　　　　How Old Are You?

William Collins
[1721–1759]

[m] Well may your hearts believe
　　the truths I tell:
'Tis virtue makes the bliss,
　　where'er we dwell.
　　*Oriental Eclogues. I, Selim, or
　　The Shepherd's Moral, Line 5*

[n] Curst be the gold and silver
　　which persuade
Weak men to follow far-fatiguing
　　trade.
　　*Ibid. II, Hassan, or The Camel
　　　　　　　　Driver, Line 31*

[o] Now air is hush'd, save where
　　the weak-eyed bat,
With short shrill shriek, flits by on
　　leathern wing,
Or where the beetle winds
His small but sullen horn.
　　Ode to Evening. Stanza 3

[p] How sleep the brave, who
　　sink to rest
By all their country's wishes
　　bless'd!
　　*Ode Written in the Year 1746.
　　　　　　　　　Stanza 1*

[q] O Music, sphere-descended maid,
Friend of Pleasure, Wisdom's aid! *The Passions. Line 95*

George Colman, the Younger
[1762-1836]

[r] On their own merits modest men are dumb.
Epiloque to the Heir at Law

[s] Three stories high, long, dull, and old,
As great lords' stories often are.
The Maid of the Moor

[t] But when ill indeed,
E'en dismissing the doctor don't always succeed.
Lodgings for Single Gentlemen

Charles Caleb Colton
[1780-1832]

[u] Imitation is the sincerest flattery. *The Lacon*

Padraic Colum
[1881-   ]

[v] Oh, to have a little house!
To own the hearth and stool and all! *An Old Woman of the Roads. Stanza 1*

[w] A tune is more lasting than the voice of the birds.
A song is more lasting than the riches of the world.
Polonius and the Ballad-Singers

Isabel Fiske Conant
[1874-   ]

[x] He who loves an old house
Never loves in vain,
How can an old house
Used to sun and rain,
To lilac and larkspur,
And an elm above,
Ever fail to answer
The heart that gives it love?
Old House. Stanza 1

James Bryant Conant
[1893-   ]

[y] Slogans are both exciting and comforting, but they are also powerful opiates for the conscience. *Baccalaureate Address, Harvard College [June 17, 1934]*

[z] Some of mankind's most terrible misdeeds have been committed under the spell of certain magic words or phrases. *Ibid.*

[a] Liberty like charity must begin at home.
Our Fighting Faith. Our Unique Heritage [address at Harvard June 30, 1942]

[b] The primary concern of American education today is . . .

to cultivate in the largest number of our future citizens an appreciation both of the responsibilities and the benefits which come to them because they are American and free. *General Education in a Free Society*

Helen Gray Cone
[1859-1934]

[c] Dash the bomb on the dome of Paul's,—
Deem ye the fame of the Admiral falls?
Pry the stone from the chancel floor,—
Dream ye that Shakespeare shall live no more?
Where is the giant shot that kills Wordsworth walking the old green hills?
A Chant of Love for England

William Congreve
[1670-1729]

[d] Thus grief still treads upon the heels of pleasure;
Married in haste, we may repent at leisure.
The Old Bachelor. Act V, Sc. 1

[e] Music hath charms to soothe the savage breast,
To soften rocks, or bend a knotted oak.
The Mourning Bride. Act I, Sc. 1

[f] Heaven has no rage like love to hatred turned,
Nor hell a fury like a woman scorned. *Ibid. Act III, Sc. 8*

[g] Love's but a frailty of the mind. *Ibid. Sc. 12*

[h] If there's delight in love, 'tis when I see
That heart which others bleed for, bleed for me. *The Way of the World. Act IV, Sc. 9*

[i] Defer not till to-morrow to be wise,
To-morrow's sun to thee may never rise. *Letter to Cobham*

Grace Hazard Conkling
[1878-   ]

[j] I have an understanding with the hills
At evening when the slanted radiance fills
Their hollows, and the great winds let them be,
And they are quiet and look down at me. *After Sunset*

[k] Invisible beauty has a word so brief
A flower can say it or a shaken leaf,
But few may ever snare it in a song. *Ibid.*

Roscoe Conkling
[1829–1888]

[1] He will hew to the line of right, let the chips fall where they may.
> Speech nominating General Grant for a third term, National Republican Convention, Chicago [June 5, 1880]

Marcus Cook Connelly
[1890–   ]

[m] Gangway for de Lawd God Jehovah!   *The Green Pastures*

[n] God. I'll jest r'ar back an' pass a miracle.   *Ibid.*

[o] Gabriel. How about cleanin' up de whole mess of 'em and sta'tin all over ag'in wid some new kind of animal?
> God. An' admit I'm licked?
>   *Ibid.*

[p] Even bein' Gawd ain't a bed of roses.   *Ibid.*

Cyril Connolly

[q] Spring is a call to action, hence to disillusion, therefore April is called "the cruellest month."   *The Unquiet Grave*

[r] There is no fury like a woman searching for a new lover. *Ibid.*

[s] Obesity is a mental state, a disease brought on by boredom and disappointment.   *Ibid.*

[t] Melancholy and remorse form the deep leaden keel which enables us to sail into the wind of reality; we run aground sooner than the flat-bottomed pleasure-lovers, but we venture out in weather that would sink them.
> *Ibid.*

Obadiah Milton Conover
[1825–1884]

[u] Alone I walk the peopled city,
Where each seems happy with his own;
O friends, I ask not for your pity—
I walk alone.   *Via Solitaria*

Joseph Conrad
[1857–1924]

[v] But the artist appeals to that part of our being which is not dependent on wisdom; to that in us which is a gift and not an acquisition—and, therefore, more permanently enduring. He speaks to our capacity for delight and wonder, to the sense of mystery surrounding our lives: to our sense of pity, and beauty, and pain.   *The Nigger of the Narcissus. Preface*

[w] The ship, a fragment detached from the earth, went on lonely and swift like a small planet.   *Ibid. Chap. 2*

[x] She . . . was strong and upright like an obelisk, had a beautiful face, a candid brow, pure eyes, and not a thought of her own in her head.
> *Tales of Unrest. The Return*

[y] What greatness had not floated on the ebb of that river [the Thames] into the mystery of an unknown earth! . . . The dreams of men, the seed of commonwealths, the germs of empires.   *Heart of Darkness*

[z] The sea never changes and its works, for all the talk of men, are wrapped in mystery.
> *Typhoon. Falk: A Reminiscence*

[a] I have known the sea too long to believe in its respect for decency.   *Ibid.*

[b] The East Wind, an interloper in the dominions of Westerly Weather, is an impassive-faced tyrant with a sharp poniard held behind his back for a treacherous stab.   *Rulers of East and West*

[c] The autocratic sway of the West Wind, whether forty north or forty south of the equator, is characterized by an open, generous, frank, barbarous recklessness. For he is a great autocrat, and to be a great autocrat you must be a great barbarian. *Ibid.*

[d] What all men are really after is some form, or perhaps only some formula, of peace.
> *Under Western Eyes. Part I*

[e] The belief in a supernatural source of evil is not necessary; men alone are quite capable of every wickedness.
> *Ibid. Part II, 4*

[f] Why should a man certain of immortality think of his life at all?   *Ibid.*

[g] No woman is ever completely deceived.   *Ibid. 5*

[h] You can't ignore the importance of a good digestion. The joy of life . . . depends on a sound stomach, whereas a bad digestion inclines one to skepticism, incredulity, breeds black fancies and thoughts of death.
> *Ibid. Part III*

[i] All ambitions are lawful except those which climb upward on the miseries or credulities of mankind.   *A Personal Record. Preface*

[j] For Englishmen especially, of all the races of the earth, a task, any task, undertaken in an ad-

venturous spirit acquires the merit of romance. *Ibid. Chap. 5*

[k] Only a moment; a moment of strength, of romance, of glamour —of youth! . . . A flick of sunshine upon a strange shore, the time to remember, the time for a sigh, and—goodbye!—Night—Goodbye . . . ! *Youth*

[l] There is a weird power in a spoken word. . . . And a word carries far—very far—deals destruction through time as the bullets go flying through space.
Lord Jim. Chap. 15

[m] You shall judge of a man by his foes as well as by his friends.
Ibid. Chap. 34

[n] Vanity plays lurid tricks with our memory. *Ibid. Chap. 41*

[o] Some great men owe most of their greatness to the ability of detecting in those they destine for their tools the exact quality of strength that matters for their work. *Ibid. Chap. 42*

[p] In plucking the fruit of memory one runs the risk of spoiling its bloom. *The Arrow of Gold. Author's Note*

Eliza Cook
[1817–1889]

[q] There's a magical tie to the land of our home,
Which the heart cannot break, though the footsteps may roam. *The Land of My Birth. Stanza 1*

[r] I love it, I love it; and who shall dare
To chide me for loving that old armchair?
The Old Arm-Chair

[s] How cruelly sweet are the echoes that start
When memory plays an old tune on the heart!
Old Dobbin. Stanza 16

[t] Better build schoolrooms for "the boy"
Than cells and gibbets for "the man."
A Song for the Ragged Schools. Stanza 12

[u] Whenever you find your heart despair
Of doing some goodly thing,
Con over this strain, try bravely again,
And remember the Spider and King. *Try Again. Stanza 16*

Edmund Vance Cooke
[1866–1932]

[v] Well, did you hear? Tom Lincoln's wife to-day,

The devil's luck for folk as poor as they!
Poor Tom! poor Nance!
Poor youngun born without a chance!
Born Without a Chance. Stanza 1

[w] The Woman tempted me— and tempts me still!
Lord God, I pray You that she ever will! *Adam*

[x] 'Tis not the weight of jewel or plate,
Or the fondle of silk and fur;
'Tis the spirit in which the gift is rich,
As the gifts of the wise ones were;
And we are not told whose gift was gold
Or whose was the gift of myrrh.
The Spirit of the Gift

[y] My pa held me up to the moo-cow-moo,
So clost I could almost touch,
En' I fed him a couple of times or two,
En' I wasn't a fraid-cat—much.
The Moo-Cow-Moo. Stanza 1

[z] I and only I
Fling the bold banner of untruth on high
And sing the full, free candour of the lie! *Ananias*

Rose Terry Cooke
[1827–1892]

[a] Three things never come again. . . .
Never to the bow that bends
Comes the arrow that it sends.
. . .
Never comes the chance that passed,
That one moment was its last.
. . .
Never shall thy spoken word
Be again unsaid, unheard.
Unreturning

Calvin Coolidge
[1872–1933]

[b] There is no right to strike against the public safety by anybody, anywhere, any time.
Telegram to Samuel Gompers, president of the American Federation of Labor [September 14, 1919], on the occasion of the Boston police strike

[c] I love Vermont because of her hills and valleys, her scenery and invigorating climate, but most of all because of her indomitable people. They are a race of pioneers who have almost beggared themselves to serve others. If the spirit of liberty should vanish in other parts of our Union . . . it could all

be replenished from the generous store held by the people of this brave little State of Vermont.
Address from train platform; Bennington, Vermont [September 21, 1928]

[d] To my friend, in recollection of his son, and my son, who, by the grace of God, have the privilege of being boys throughout Eternity.
Inscription in a friend's book after the death of Calvin Coolidge, Jr.

George Cooper
[1838–1927]

[e] October gave a party;
The leaves by hundreds came:
The ashes, oaks, and maples,
And those of every name.
October's Party. Stanza 1

[f] Sweet Genevieve,
The days may come, the days may go,
But still the hands of memory weave
The blissful dreams of long ago.
Sweet Genevieve

Charles Townsend Copeland
[1860–1952]

[g] A man is always better than a book.
Tribute to Nathaniel Southgate Shaler. Copeland Reader

[h] To eat is human; to digest, divine.
Epigram

Alfred Edgar Coppard
[1878–   ]

[i] Truth is truth and love is love,
Give us grace to taste thereof;
But if truth offend my sweet,
Then I will have none of it.
Mendacity. Stanza 1

Bishop Richard Corbet
[1582–1635]

[j] Nor too much wealth nor wit come to thee,
So much of either may undo thee.
To His Son, Vincent Corbet

[k] I wish thee all thy mother's graces,
Thy father's fortunes and his places.
Ibid.

Pierre Corneille
[1606–1684]

[l] We easily believe that which we wish. *Le Baron. Act I, Sc. 3*

[m] Do your duty, and leave the rest to heaven.
Horace. Act II, Sc. 8

[n] Who is all-powerful should fear everything.
Cinna. Act. IV, Sc. 2

[o] A service beyond all recompense
Weighs so heavy that it almost gives offence.
Suréna. Act III, Sc. 1

Frances Cornford
[1886–   ]

[p] I had a little dog and my dog was very small;
He licked me in the face, and he answered to my call;
Of all the treasures that were mine I loved him most of all.
A Child's Dream. Stanza 1

[q] Deep in my heart I thought with pride,
"I know a person who has died."
A Recollection

[r] O why do you walk through the fields in gloves,
Missing so much and so much?
O fat white woman whom nobody loves,
Why do you walk through the fields in gloves
When the grass is as soft as the breast of doves
And shivering-sweet to the touch? *To a Fat Lady Seen from the Train*

Norman Corwin
[1910–   ]

[s] So they've given up.
They're finally done in, and the rat is dead in an alley back of the Wilhelmstrasse.
Take a bow, G.I.,
Take a bow, little guy.
The superman of tomorrow lies at the feet of you common men of his afternoon.
On a Note of Triumph [1945]

[t] This is It, kid, this is The Day, all the way from Newburyport to Vladivostok.
You had what it took and you gave it, and each of you has a hunk of rainbow 'round your helmet.
Seems like free men have done it again. *Ibid.*

William Johnson Cory
[1823–1892]

[u] All beauteous things for which we live
By laws of time and space decay.
But oh, the very reason why
I clasp them, is because they die.
Mimnermus in Church. Stanza 4

[v] You come not, as aforetime, to the headstone every day,

And I, who died, I do not chide
because, my friend, you play;
Only, in playing, think of him
who once was kind and dear,
And, if you see a beauteous thing,
just say, he is not here.
Remember

[w] They told me, Heraclitus,
they told me you were dead;
They brought me bitter news to
hear and bitter tears to shed.
I wept, as I remembered, how
often you and I
Had tired the sun with talking
and sent him down the sky.
And now that thou art lying, my
dear old Carian guest,
A handful of grey ashes, long long
ago at rest,
Still are thy pleasant voices, thy
Nightingales, awake,
For Death, he taketh all away, but
them he cannot take.
*Heraclitus, Paraphrase
from Callimachus*

Nathaniel Cotton
[1705–1788]

[x] If solid happiness we prize,
Within our breasts this jewel lies,
And they are fools who roam.
The world has nothing to bestow;
From our own selves our joys must
flow,
And that dear hut, our home.
The Fireside. Stanza 3

Margaret Courtney
[1822–1862]

[y] Be kind to thy father, for
when thou wert young,
Who loved thee so fondly as he?
He caught the first accents that
fell from thy tongue,
And joined in thy innocent
glee. *Be Kind. Stanza 1*

Noel Coward
[1899–   ]

[z] Mad dogs and Englishmen go
out in the mid-day sun;
The Japanese don't care to, the
Chinese wouldn't dare to;
Hindus and Argentines sleep
firmly from twelve to one,
But Englishmen detest a siesta.
Mad Dogs and Englishmen

Abraham Cowley
[1618–1667]

[a] The thirsty earth soaks up the
rain,
And drinks, and gapes for drink
again.
The plants suck in the earth, and
are
With constant drinking fresh and
fair. . . .

Fill all the glasses there, for why
Should every creature drink but
I?
Why, man of morals, tell me why?
From Anacreon, II. Drinking

[b] A mighty pain to love it is,
And 'tis a pain that pain to miss;
But of all pains, the greatest pain
It is to love, but love in vain.
Ibid. VII. Gold

[c] Th' adorning thee with so
much art
Is but a barb'rous skill;
'Tis like the pois'ning of a dart,
Too apt before to kill.
The Waiting Maid

[d] Let but thy wicked men from
out thee go,
And all the fools that crowd thee
so,
Even thou, who dost thy millions
boast,
A village less than Islington wilt
grow,
A solitude almost.
Of Solitude. VII

[e] God the first garden made,
and the first city Cain.
Ibid. II

[f] Words that weep and tears
that speak. *The Prophet*

[g] Thus would I double my life's
fading space;
For he that runs it well, runs
twice his race.
*Discourse XI, Of Myself.
Stanza XI*

[h] Ah yet, ere I descend to the
grave
May I a small house and large
garden have;
And a few friends, and many
books, both true,
Both wise, and both delightful
too! *The Wish*

William Cowper
[1731–1800]

[i] Happiness depends, as Nature
shows,
Less on exterior things than most
suppose. *Table Talk. Line 246*

[j] Freedom has a thousand
charms to show,
That slaves, howe'er contented,
never know. *Ibid. Line 260*

[k] Manner is all in all, whate'er
is writ,
The substitute for genius, sense,
and wit. *Ibid. Line 542*

[l] The sounding jargon of the
schools.
Truth. Line 367

[m] A fool must now and then be
right by chance.
Conversation. Line 96

[n] Pernicious weed! whose scent
the fair annoys,

88 WILLIAM COWPER

Unfriendly to society's chief joys:
Thy worst effect is banishing for
hours
The sex whose presence civilizes
ours. *Ibid. Line 251*

[o] His wit invites you by his
looks to come,
But when you knock, it never is at
home. *Ibid. Line 303*

[p] Absence of occupation is not
rest,
A mind quite vacant is a mind
distress'd. *Retirement. Line 623*

[q] An idler is a watch that wants
both hands,
As useless if it goes as if it stands.
Ibid. Line 681

[r] How sweet, how passing sweet,
is solitude!
But grant me still a friend in my
retreat,
Whom I may whisper, Solitude is
sweet. *Ibid. Line 740*

[s] How fleet is a glance of the
mind!
Compared with the speed of its
flight
The tempest itself lags behind,
And the swift-winged arrows of
light.
*Verses Supposed to be Written
by Alexander Selkirk. Stanza 6*

[t] I shall not ask Jean Jacques
Rousseau
If birds confabulate or no.
Pairing Time Anticipated

[u] Misses! the tale that I relate
This lesson seems to carry,—
Choose not alone a proper mate,
But proper time to marry. *Ibid. Moral*

[v] That though on pleasure she
was bent,
She had a frugal mind.
History of John Gilpin. Stanza 8

[w] God made the country, and
man made the town.
*The Task. Book I, The Sofa,
Line 749*

[x] Oh for a lodge in some vast
wilderness,
Some boundless contiguity of
shade,
Where rumour of oppression and
deceit,
Of unsuccessful or successful
war,
Might never reach me more.
*Ibid. Book II, The Timepiece,
Line 1*

[y] Slaves cannot breathe in England; if their lungs
Receive our air, that moment they
are free!
They touch our country, and their
shackles fall. *Ibid. Line 40*

[z] Riches have wings, and grandeur is a dream. *Ibid. Book
III, The Garden, Line 265*

[a] Now stir the fire, and close the
shutters fast,
Let fall the curtains, wheel the
sofa round,
And while the bubbling and loud-
hissing urn
Throws up a steamy column, and
the cups
That cheer but not inebriate wait
on each,
So let us welcome peaceful evening in. *Ibid. Book IV,
The Winter Evening, Line 36*

[b] While fancy, like the finger
of a clock,
Runs the great circuit, and is still
at home. *Ibid. Line 118*

[c] O Winter, ruler of the inverted year! *Ibid. Line 120*

[d] But war's a game, which, were
their subjects wise,
Kings would not play at.
*Ibid. Book V, The Winter
Morning Walk, Line 187*

[e] There is in souls a sympathy
with sounds; . . . .
How soft the music of those vil-
lage bells
Falling at intervals upon the ear
In cadence sweet!
*Ibid. Book VI, Winter
Walk at Noon, Line 1*

[f] Here the heart
May give a useful lesson to the
head,
And Learning wiser grow without
his books. *Ibid. Line 85*

[g] Knowledge is proud that he
has learn'd so much;
Wisdom is humble that he knows
no more. *Ibid. Line 96*

[h] I would not enter on my list
of friends,
(Though graced with polish'd
manners and fine sense,
Yet wanting sensibility), the
man
Who needlessly sets foot upon a
worm. *Ibid. Line 560*

[i] God moves in a mysterious
way
His wonders to perform;
He plants his footsteps in the sea
And rides upon the storm.
Light Shining out of Darkness

[j] Behind a frowning providence
He hides a shining face. *Ibid.*

[k] Beware of desperate steps!
The darkest day,
Live till to-morrow, will have
pass'd away.
The Needless Alarm. Moral

[l] Oh that those lips had language! Life has pass'd

With me but roughly since I
heard thee last.
> *On the Receipt of
> My Mother's Picture*

[m] The man that hails you Tom
or Jack,
And proves, by thumping on your
back,
His sense of your great merit,
Is such a friend that one had need
Be very much his friend indeed
To pardon or to bear it.
> *On Friendship. Stanza 26*

[n] For 'tis a truth well known to
most,
That whatsoever thing is lost,
We seek it, ere it come to light,
In every cranny but the right.
> *The Retired Cat*

[o] He that holds fast the golden
mean,
And lives contentedly between
The little and the great,
Feels not the wants that pinch the
poor,
Nor plagues that haunt the rich
man's door.
> *Translation of Horace. Book II,
> Ode X, To Licinius, Stanza 2*

Kenyon Cox
[1856–1919]

[p] Work thou for pleasure—
paint, or sing, or carve
The thing thou lovest, though the
body starve—
Who works for glory misses oft the
goal;
Who works for money coins his
very soul.
Work for the work's sake, then,
and it may be
That these things shall be added
unto thee.   *Work*

Arthur Cleveland Coxe
[1818–1896]

[q] I never can see the old
churchyard
But I breathe to God a prayer,
That, sleep as I may in this
fevered life,
I may rest when I slumber there.
> *St. George's Churchyard,
> Hempstead, Long Island*

George Crabbe
[1754–1832]

[r] In this fool's paradise he
drank delight. *The Borough.
> Letter XII, Players*

[s] Books cannot always please,
however good;
Minds are not ever craving for
their food.
> *Ibid. Letter XXIV, Schools*

[t] Time has touched me gently
in his race,

And left no odious furrows in my
face.
> *Ibid. Book XVII, The Widow*

[u] The ring, so worn as you behold,
So thin, so pale, is yet of gold.
> *A Marriage Ring*

[v] He tried the luxury of doing
good.   *Tales of the Hall.
> Book III, Boys at School*

Dinah Maria Mulock Craik
[1826–1887]

[w] God rest ye, merry gentlemen! let nothing you dismay,
For Jesus Christ, our Saviour, was
born on Christmas day.
> *A Christmas Carol. Stanza 1*

[x] A friend stands at the door;
In either tight-closed hand
Hiding rich gifts, three hundred
and three-score. *A Psalm for
> New Year's Eve. Stanza 1*

[y] Oh, my son's my son till he
gets him a wife,
But my daughter's my daughter
all her life. *Young and Old*

[z] Oh, the comfort, the inexpressible comfort of feeling safe with
a person, having neither to weigh
thoughts nor measure words, but
pouring them all right out, just as
they are, chaff and grain together;
certain that a faithful hand will
take and sift them, keep what is
worth keeping, and then with the
breath of kindness blow the rest
away.
> *A Life for a Life. Page 169*

Christopher Pearse Cranch
[1813–1892]

[a] No night so wild but brings
the constant sun
With love and power untold;
No time so dark but through its
woof there run
Some blessed threads of gold.
> *Oh, Love Supreme*

Hart Crane
[1899–1932]

[b] Damp tonnage and alluvial
march of days . . .
Tortured with history, its one will
—flow.
> *The River (Mississippi)*

[c] Thin squeaks of radio static,
The captured fume of space foams
in our ears.   *Ibid.*

[d] Bunched in mutual glee
The bearings glint,—O murmur-
less and shined
In oilrinsed circles of blind
ecstasy! *The Power House*

[e] O, early following thee, I
    searched the hill
Blue-writ and odor-firm with vio-
    lets.   *To Walt Whitman*

Nathalia Crane
[1913–   ]

[f] Oh, I'm in love with the jani-
    tor's boy,
And the janitor's boy loves me;
He's going to hunt for a desert isle
In our geography.
          The Janitor's Boy. Stanza 1

[g] Every gaudy color
Is a bit of truth.
          The Vestal. Stanza 5

[h] In the darkness, who would
    answer for the color of a rose,
Or the vestments of the May moth
    and the pilgrimage it goes?
          The Blind Girl. Stanza 1

[i] I sat down on a bumble bee,
    But I arose again;
And now I know the tenseness of
    Humiliating pain.
          Suffering. Stanza 3

[j] The steps of the paper-box
    factory,
As well as the gardens of kings
Are only the blue-print devices
Of love, and the commonplace
    things.
          The Commonplace. Stanza 6

[k] When the moon comes over
    Brooklyn
On time with the borough clock,
'Tis the same that saw Palmyra
And the walls of Antioch.
          The Moon of Brooklyn. Stanza 1

[l] There is a glory
In a great mistake.
          Imperfection

Stephen Crane
[1871–1900]

[m] He had fought like a pagan
who defends his religion.
          *The Red Badge of Courage.
                    Chap. 17*

[n] Within him, as he hurled
himself forward, was born a love,
a despairing fondness for this flag
which was near him. It was a creation of beauty and invulnerability.
          Ibid. Chap. 19

[o] None of them knew the color
of the sky.   *The Open Boat*

[p] Presently, God said,
"And what did you do?"
The little blade answered, "Oh,
    my Lord,
Memory is bitter to me,
For, if I did good deeds,
I know not of them."
Then God, in all His splendor,
Arose from His throne.
"O best little blade of grass!" He
    said.   *The Blades of Grass*

[q] A man said to the universe:
    "Sir, I exist!"
"However," replied the universe,
"That fact has not created in me
A sense of obligation."
          War Is Kind. Fragment

Helen D'Arcy Cranstoun
(Mrs. Dugald Stewart)
[1765–1838]

[r] I weep not for the silent dead,
Their pains are past, their sorrows
    o'er.   *The Song of Genius*

Adelaide Crapsey
[1878–1914]

[s] These be
Three silent things:
The falling snow . . . the hour
Before the dawn . . . the mouth
    of one
Just dead.   *Cinquain: Triad*

Richard Crashaw
[1613–1649]

[t] The conscious water saw its
God and blushed.
          *Epigrammata Sacra. Aquae in
                    Vinum Versae*

[u] Two went to pray? Oh, rather
    say
One went to brag, the other to
    pray;
One stands up close and treads on
    high
Where the other dares not send
    his eye;
One nearer to God's altar trod,
The other to the altar's God.
          *Two Went up to the Temple to
                    Pray*

[v] Whoe'er she be,
That not impossible she,
That shall command my heart
    and me.
          Wishes to his Supposed Mistress

[w] A happy soul, that all the
    way
To heaven hath a summer's day.
          *In Praise of Lessius's Rule of
                    Health*

Mrs. Edward Craster

[x] The centipede was happy
    quite
Until a toad in fun
Said, "Pray, which leg goes after
    which?"
That worked her mind to such a
    pitch,
She lay distracted in a ditch,
Considering how to run.
          *Credited, in Cassell's Weekly,
                    to Pinafore Poems [1871]*

Francis Marion Crawford
[1854–1909]

[y] The sea is Death's garden, and
  he sows dead men in the loam,
When the breast of the waters is
  ploughed like a field by the
  gale,
When the ocean is turned up and
  rent in long furrows of foam
By the coulter and share of the
  wind and the harrow of hail.
  The Song of the Sirens. Stanza 7

[z] What is charm? It is what the
violet has and the camellia has
not.   *Children of the King.*
                    Chap. 5

John Wallace
("Captain Jack")
Crawford
[1847–1917]

[a] When a bit of sunshine hits
  ye,
After passing of a cloud,
When a fit of laughter gits ye
An' yer spine is feelin' proud,
Don't fergit to up and fling it
  At a soul that's feelin' blue,
For the minute that ye sling it,
  It's a boomerang to you.
                    The Boomerang

Julia Crawford
[1800–1885]

[b] Kathleen mavourneen! the
  grey dawn is breaking,
The horn of the hunter is heard
  on the hill.
  Kathleen Mavourneen. Stanza 1

[c] Hast thou forgotten how soon
  we must sever?
Oh! hast thou forgotten this day
  we must part?
It may be for years, and it may be
  forever;
Then why art thou silent, thou
  voice of my heart?   *Ibid.*

Benedetto Croce
[1866–1952]

[d] What constitutes history may
be thus described: It is the act of
comprehending and understanding induced by the requirements
of practical life. . . . Every serious
history, and every serious philosophy, ought to be a history and a
philosophy "for the occasion," as
Goethe said of genuine poetry,
though the occasion of poetry is in
the passions, that of history in the
conduct of life and in morality.
  History: Its Theory and Practice

David Crockett
[1786–1836]

[e] I leave this rule for others
  when I'm dead,

Be always sure you're right—then
  go ahead.   *Autobiography*

[f] Don't shoot, colonel, I'll come
  down:
I know I'm a gone coon.
  *Story told by Crockett of a treed
                    raccoon*

Oliver Cromwell
[1599–1658]

[g] The State, in choosing men
to serve it, takes no notice of their
opinions. If they be willing faithfully to serve it, that satisfies.
  *Before the Battle of Marston
          Moor [July 2, 1644]*

[h] A few honest men are better
than numbers. If you choose
godly, honest men to be captains
of horse, honest men will follow
them.   *Reorganization of the
                    Army [1645]*

Thomas William
Hodgson Crosland
[1868–1924]

[i] God's infinite mercy, how that
  child did cry,
In spite of bottle, bauble, pepper-
  mint, nurse!
  The Baby in the Ward

Marian Evans Cross
see "George Eliot"

Grace Noll
(Mrs. Norman H.)Crowell
[1877–   ]

[j] I hold to my heart when the
  geese are flying—
A wavering wedge on the high,
  bright blue—
I tighten my lips to keep from crying:
"Beautiful birds, let me go with
  you."   *Wild Geese. Stanza 1*

[k] God wrote His loveliest poem
  on the day
He made the first tall silver poplar
  tree,
And set it high upon a pale-gold
  hill
For all the new enchanted earth
  to see.
  Silver Poplars. Stanza 1

William Ulick O'Connor
Cuffe (Lord Desart)
[1845–1898]

[l] Mother Hubbard, you see, was
old: there being no mention of
others, we may presume she was
alone, a widow—a friendless, old,
solitary widow. Yet did she despair? Did she sit down and weep,

or read a novel, or wring her hands? No! She went to the cupboard.   *Mock Sermon: Old Mother Hubbard*

Ely Culbertson
[1891–   ]

[m] The bizarre world of cards . . . a world of pure power politics where rewards and punishments were meted out immediately. A deck of cards was built like the purest of hierarchies, with every card a master to those below it a lackey to those above it. And there were "masses"—long suits—which always asserted themselves in the end, triumphing over the kings and aces.   *Total Peace. Chap. 1*

[n] Power politics the diplomatic name for the law of the jungle.   *Must We Fight Russia? Chap. 2*

[o] God and the politicians willing, the United States can declare peace upon the world, and win it.   *Ibid. Chap. 5*

Countee Cullen
[1903–1946]

[p] Not for myself I make this prayer,
But for this race of mine
That stretches forth from shadowed places
    Dark hands for bread and wine.
        Pagan Prayer. Stanza 1

[q] She thinks that even up in heaven
Her class lies late and snores,
While poor black cherubs rise at seven
To do celestial chores.
        Epitaph: A Lady I Know

[r] They lie not easy in a grave
Who once have known the sea.
        Epitaph for Joseph Conrad

Bishop Richard Cumberland
[1632–1718]

[s] It is better to wear out than to rust out.
    Quoted by Bishop George Horne [1730–1792]: Sermon on the Duty of Contending for the Truth

Edward Estlin Cummings
[1894–   ]

[t] when the proficient poison of sure sleep bereaves us of our slow tranquilities   *When the Proficient Poison of Sure Sleep*

[u] nobody, not even the rain, has such small hands.
        Somewhere I Have Never Travelled

[v] "next to of course god america i
love you land of the pilgrims and so forth oh
say can you see by the dawn's early my
country 'tis of centuries come and go
and are no more what of it we should worry
in every language even deafanddumb
thy sons acclaim your glorious name by gorry
by jingo by gee by gosh by gum
why talk of beauty what could be more beautiful than these heroic happy dead
who rushed like lions to the roaring slaughter
they did not stop to think they died instead
then shall the voices of liberty be mute?"
He spoke. And drank rapidly a glass of water.
        Next To Of Course God

[w] this is the garden: colours come and go,
frail azures fluttering from night's outer wing
strong silent greens serenely lingering,
absolute lights like baths of golden snow.
        This Is The Garden

[x] open your thighs to fate and (if you can
withholding nothing) World, conceive a man.
        Collected Poems, 293

William Thomas Cummings
[1903–1944?]

[y] There are no atheists in the foxholes.
    Field Sermon on Bataan [1942]

Allan Cunningham
[1784–1842]

[z] A wet sheet and a flowing sea,
    A wind that follows fast,
And fills the white and rustling sail,
    And bends the gallant mast;
And bends the gallant mast, my boys,
    While, like the eagle free,
Away the good ship flies, and leaves
    Old England on the lee.
        A Wet Sheet and a Flowing Sea. Stanza 1

[a] John Grumlie swore by the light o' the moon,
And the green leaves on the tree,
That he could do more work in a day

Than his wife could do in three.
*John Grumlie (adapted from
the old ballad, The Wife of
Auchtermuchty). Stanza 1*

Sir Andrew Browne Cunningham
[1883–   ]

[b] We are so outnumbered
there's only one thing to do. We
must attack. *Before attacking
the Italian fleet at Taranto,
November 1940. Quoted in
"British Commanders," published by British Information
Services*

Will Cuppy
[1884–1949]

[c] Let's not be too quick to
blame the human race for everything. A great many species of
animals became extinct before
man ever appeared on earth.
How to Become Extinct

[d] The Dodo never had a chance.
He seems to have been invented
for the sole purpose of becoming
extinct and that was all he was
good for. *Ibid.*

George William Curtis
[1824–1892]

[e] In that calm Syrian afternoon, memory, a pensive Ruth,
went gleaning the silent fields of
childhood and found the scattered
grain still golden and the morning
sunlight fresh and fair.
The Howadji in Syria. Ave Maria

[f] While we read history we
make history.
The Call of Freedom

[g] Imagination is as good as
many voyages—and how much
cheaper. *Prue and I. Preface*

[h] Every mother who has lost an
infant, has gained a child of immortal youth. *Ibid. Chap. 3*

[i] Happiness is speechless.
Ibid. Chap. 4

[j] The pride of ancestry increases in the ratio of distance.
Ibid. Chap. 6

[k] It is a great pity that men
and women forget that they have
been children. Parents are apt to
be foreigners to their sons and
daughters. *Ibid. Chap. 7*

[l] Love is the coldest of critics.
Ibid.

Charlotte Cushman
[1816–1876]

[m] God conceived the world,
that was poetry;

He formed it, that was sculpture;
He colored it; that was painting;
He peopled it with living beings;
that was the grand, divine,
eternal drama.
*On the Curtain of Ford's Opera
House, Baltimore, Maryland*

Julian Stearns Cutler
[1854–1930]

[n] A common thing is a grass
blade small,
Crushed by the feet that pass,
But all the dwarfs and giants tall,
Working till doomsday shadows
fall
Can't make a blade of grass.
Wonderful. Stanza 1

George Washington Cutter
[1801–1865]

[o] Harness me down with your
iron bands,
Be sure of your curb and rein:
For I scorn the power of your
puny hands,
As the tempest scorns a chain.
Song of Steam. Stanza 1

Édouard Daladier
[1884–   ]

[p] If French and German blood
is now to be spilled, as it was
twenty-five years ago . . . then
each of the two peoples will fight
confident of its own victory. But
surely Destruction and Barbarism
will be the real victors.
*Letter to Adolf Hitler,
August 26, 1939*

[q] A phrase has spread from
civilians to soldiers and back
again: "This is a phony war."
*Speech to the Deputies,
December 22, 1939*

Mary Kyle Dallas
[1837–1897]

[r] Man never quite forgets his
very first love,
Unless she's true.
After Ten Years. Stanza 4

Ormonde Maddock Dalton
see "W. Compton Leith"

Thomas Augustine Daly
[1871–1948]

[s] I gotta love for Angela,
I love Carlotta, too.
I no can marry both o' dem,
So w'at I gona do?
Between Two Loves. Stanza 1

[t] Up to the breeze of the morning I fling you,

Blending your folds with the
    dawn in the sky;
There let the people behold you,
    and bring you
    Love and devotion that never
        shall die.
Proudly, agaze at your glory, I
    stand,
Flag o' my land! flag o' my land!
            Flag o' My Land. Stanza 1

[u] Sing clear, O! throstle,
Thou golden-tongued apostle
And little brown-frocked brother
Of the loved Assisian!
                To a Thrush

[v] W'at good eesa wife eef she
    don'ta be fat?
            Da Styleesha Wife

[w] I'm Home's heart! Warmth I
    give and light,
If you but feed me.
I blossom in the winter night,
    When most you need me.
    Inscription for a Fireplace

[x] The green and gold of my de-
    light—
Asparagus, with Hollandaise!
    Ballade by a Glutton. Stanza 1

[y] The Man, the One and Only
    One—
First Gentleman on Earth—
Said: "How about a little fun?
    Come! let us have some mirth!"

"To some swell Night Club we
    must roam,"
Said he, "and drink cham-
    pagne."
But she said: "We can stay at
    home,
And still be raising Cain."
        *The First New Year's Eve.
            Stanzas 1 and 3*

Richard Henry Dana
[1787–1879]

[z] It is an impression, of which
we can not rid ourselves if we
would, when sitting by the body
of a friend, that he has still a consciousness of our presence; that,
though he no longer has a concern
in the common things of the
world, love and thought are still
there. The face which we had been
familiar with so long, when it was
all life and motion, seems only in
a state of rest. We know not how
to make it real to ourselves that
in the body before us there is not
a something still alive.
                Mother and Son

Richard Henry Dana
[1815–1882]

[a] Six days shalt thou labor and
do all thou art able,

And on the seventh—holystone
    the decks and scrape the cable.
    *Two Years Before the Mast
    Chap. 3, Philadelphia Catechism*

Samuel Daniel
[1562–1619]

[b] Care-charmer Sleep, son o
    the sable Night,
Brother to Death, in silent dark
    ness born.
            Sonnet: To Deli

[c] Make me to say when all my
    griefs are gone,
Happy the heart that sighed fo
    such a one!
        Sonnet: I Must Not Griev

[d] Love is a sickness full of woes
All remedies refusing.
            Hymen's Triumpl

Dante Alighieri
[1265–1321]
*Translation by Henry Francis
        Cary*

[e] All hope abandon, ye who
    enter here.
            Hell. Canto III, Line

[f] The wretched souls of those
    who lived
Without or praise or blame.
            Ibid. Line 34

[g] Who knows most, him loss o
    time most grieves.
    Purgatory. Canto I, Line 7

[h] If prayer do not aid me first
That riseth up from heart which
    lives in grace,
What other kind avails, not heard
    in heaven?
        Ibid. Canto IV, Line 129

[i] I am Virgil; for no sin
Deprived of heaven, except for
    lack of faith.
        Ibid. Canto VII, Line 6

[j] Now was the hour that wakens
    fond desire
In men at sea, and melts their
    thoughtful heart
Who in the morn have bid sweet
    friends farewell.
        Ibid. Canto VIII, Line 1

[k] The noise
Of worldly fame is but a blast of
    wind,
That blows from diverse points,
    and shifts its name,
Shifting the point it blows from.
        Ibid. Canto XI, Line 97

[l] Consider that this day ne'er
    dawns again.
        Ibid. Canto XII, Line 78

[m] Woman, the creature of an
    hour.
        Ibid. Canto XXIX, Line 25

[n] Between two kinds of food,
    both equally

Remote and tempting, first a man
    might die
Of hunger, ere he one could freely
    choose.
        Paradise. Canto IV, Line 1

[o] As one, who from a dream
    awaken'd, straight,
All he hath seen forgets; yet still
    retains
Impression of the feeling in his
    dream.
        Ibid. Canto XXXIII, Line 55

Hugh Antoine D'Arcy
[1843–1925]

[p] With chalk in hand the vaga-
    bond began
To sketch a face that well might
    buy the soul of any man.
Then as he placed another lock
    upon the shapely head,
With a fearful shriek he leaped
    and fell across the picture—
    dead!
    *The Face Upon the Floor [often
    misquoted as "The Face on the
    Barroom Floor"]*

George Darley
[1795–1846]

[q] A little cross
To tell my loss;
A little bed
To rest my head;
A little tear is all I crave
Under my very little grave.

With nothing more upon it than—
Here lies the Little Friend of Man!
    Robin's Cross. Stanzas 1 and 2

Charles Robert Darwin
[1809–1882]

[r] I have called this principle,
by which each slight variation, if
useful, is preserved, by the term
Natural Selection.
    The Origin of Species. Chap. 3

[s] The expression often used by
Mr. Herbert Spencer, of the Survival of the Fittest, is more accurate, and is sometimes equally
convenient.   *Ibid. Chap. 3*

[t] Even when we are quite alone,
how often do we think with pleasure or pain of what others think
of us—of their imagined approbation or disapprobation.
    The Descent of Man. Chap. 4

[u] The highest possible stage in
moral culture is when we recognize that we ought to control our
thoughts.   *Ibid.*

[v] The Simiadae then branched
off into two great stems, the New
World and Old World monkeys;
and from the latter at a remote
period, Man, the wonder and the
glory of the universe, proceeded.
    Ibid. Chap 6

[w] Physiological experiment on
animals is justifiable for real investigation, but not for mere
damnable and detestable curiosity.
    Letter to E. Ray Lankester

[x] Believing as I do that man in
the distant future will be a far
more perfect creature than he now
is, it is an intolerable thought
that he and all other sentient
beings are doomed to complete
annihilation after such long-con-
tinued slow progress. To those
who fully admit the immortality
of the human soul, the destruction of our world will not appear
so dreadful.   *Life and Letters*

[y] Among the scenes which are
deeply impressed on my mind,
none exceed in sublimity the
primeval forests undefaced by the
hand of man. No one can stand in
these solitudes unmoved, and not
feel that there is more in man
than the mere breath of his body.
    *Journal during the Voyage of
    H.M.S. Beagle. Chap. 21*

Erasmus Darwin
[1731–1802]

[z] Soon shall thy arm, uncon-
    quer'd steam! afar
Drag the slow barge, or drive the
    rapid car;
Or on wide-waving wings ex-
    panded bear
The flying chariot through the
    field of air.   *The Botanic
    Garden. Part I, Canto I, Line 289*

Harry Micajah Daugherty
[1860–1941]

[a] In a smoke-filled room in
    some hotel.
    *Republican National Convention,
        Chicago, June 1920*

Sir William Davenant
[1606–1668]

[b] For angling-rod he took a
    sturdy oake;
For line, a cable that in storm
    ne'er broke;
His hooke was such as heads the
    end of pole
To pluck down house ere fire con-
    sumes it whole;
The hook was baited with a
    dragon's tale,—
And then on rock he stood to bob
    for whale.
    Britannia Triumphans. Page 15

[c] Since knowledge is but sor-
    row's spy,
It is not safe to know.
    The Just Italian. Act V, Sc. 1

[d] I shall ask leave to desist,
when I am interrupted by so great
an experiment as dying.
> *His apology, in illness, for not*
> *having finished Gondibert*

Russell Wheeler Davenport
[1899–]

[e]   Her flag
The strong, oracular emblem of
     her will—
The spangled cloth of peace—the
     bloody rag
Above embattled gulch and smok-
     ing hill,
Like freedom nailed in pain
     against the sky.
> *My Country*

Norman Davey
[1888–]

[f] By the canal in Flanders I
     watched a barge's prow
Creep slowly past the poplar-trees;
     and there I made a vow
That when these wars are over
     and I am home at last
However much I travel I shall not
     travel fast.
Horses and cars and yachts and
     planes: I've no more use for
     such:
For in three years of war's alarms
     I've hurried far too much;
And now I dream of something
     sure, silent and slow and
     large;
So when the War is over—why, I
     mean to buy a barge.
> *By the Canal in Flanders*

John Davidson
[1857–1909]

[g] That minister of ministers,
     Imagination, gathers up
The undiscovered Universe,
     Like jewels in a jasper cup.
> *There Is a Dish to Hold the Sea*

[h] Dance and sing, we are
     eternal;
Let us still be mad with drink-
     ing:
'Tis a madness less infernal
     Than the madness caused by
     thinking.
> *Song of Bacchantes and Satyrs.*
> *Stanza 1*

[i] A vagrant bee twanged like an
     airy lyre
Of one rich-hearted chord.
> *The Ordeal*

[j] Some diplomat no doubt
Will launch a heedless word,
And lurking war leap out.
> *War-Song*

[k] And blood in torrents pour
In vain—always in vain,
For war breeds war again.
> *Ibid.*

[l] The hostess of the sky, the
     moon.
> *Afternoon. Stanza 1*

[m] Do I believe in Heaven and
     Hell? I do;
We have them here; the world is
     nothing else.
> *Dedication to the Generation*
> *Knocking at the Door*

[n] Men should no longer degrade
themselves under such appella-
tions as Christian, Mohammedan,
Agnostic, Monist, etc. Men are the
Universe become conscious: the
simplest man should consider
himself too great to be called after
any name.
> *Fleet Street and*
> *Other Poems. Foreword*

Sir John Davies
[1569–1626]

[o] What can we know? or what
     can we discern,
When error chokes the windows of
     the mind?   *The Vanity of*
> *Human Learning. Stanza 15*

[p] I know my life's a pain, and
     but a span;
I know my sense is mock'd in
     ev'ry thing:
And to conclude, I know myself a
     man,
Which is a proud, and yet a
     wretched thing.
> *Ibid. Stanza 45*

[q] Wedlock, indeed, hath oft
     compared been
To public feasts, where meet a
     public rout,—
Where they that are without
     would fain go in,
And they that are within would
     fain go out.   *Contention*
> *Betwixt a Wife, etc.*

Mary Carolyn Davies

[r] Women are door-mats and
     have been—
The years those mats applaud—
They keep their men from going
     in
With muddy feet to God.
> *Door-Mats*

Scrope Davies
[1771–1852]

[s] Babylon in all its desolation
is a sight not so awful as that of
the human mind in ruins.
> *Letter to Thomas Raikes*
> *[May 25, 1835]*

William Henry Davies
[1871–1940]

[t] A poor life this if, full of care,
We have no time to stand and
     stare.
> *Leisure*

[u] They sniffed, poor things, for
their green fields,
They cried so loud I could not
sleep:
For fifty thousand shillings down
I would not sail again with
sheep.   *Sheep. Stanza 5*

[v] Look, there's a rainbow now!
See how that lovely rainbow
throws
Her jewelled arm around
This world, when the rain goes.
        The Rainbow. Stanza 2

[w] Fools have their second
childhood, but the Great
Still keep their first, and have no
second state.
        Men That Think

[x] The finest scarf or collar
made,
To keep a woman warm,
By night or day, on sea or land,
Is still a lover's arm.
        Space. Stanza 3

[y] Nature's real king, to whom
the power was given
To make an inkdrop scent the
world for ever.   *Shakespeare*

[z] I had Ambition, by which sin
The angels fell;
I climbed and, step by step, O
Lord,
Ascended into Hell.   *Ambition*

[a] I'll make my Joy a secret
thing,
My face shall wear a mask of
care;
And those who hunt a Joy to
death,
Shall never know what sport is
there!
        Hunting Joy, Stanza 3

[b] No matter where this body is,
The mind is free to go elsewhere.
        The Mind's Liberty

Leonardo da Vinci
[1452–1519]
*From his Note-Books, translated
by Edward McCurdy*

[c] In rivers, the water that you
touch is the last of what has
passed and the first of that which
comes: so with time present.

[d] Whoever in discussion ad-
duces authority uses not intellect
but memory.

[e] No counsel is more trustworthy than that which is given
upon ships that are in peril.

[f] Intellectual passion drives
out sensuality.

[g] No member needs so great a
number of muscles as the tongue;
this exceeds all the rest in the
number of its movements.

[h] As a well-spent day brings
happy sleep, so life well used
brings happy death.

Charles Thomas Davis
[1888–1945]

[i] Who walks a road with love
will never walk
That road alone again.
Old lonely things will garb them
in the guise
Of beauty glowing with remem-
bered eyes.   *Who Walks a
Road with Love*

Elmer Davis
[1890–   ]

[j] Atomic warfare is bad enough;
biological warfare would be worse;
but there is something that is
worse than either. The French can
tell you what it is; or the Czechs,
or the Greeks, or the Norwegians,
or the Filipinos; it is subjection
to an alien oppressor.
        *No World, If Necessary [The
Saturday Review of Literature,
March 30, 1946]*

Robert Hobart ("Bob") Davis
[1869–1942]

[k] I am the printing-press, born
of the mother earth. My heart is
of steel, my limbs are of iron, and
my fingers are of brass.
I sing the songs of the world,
the oratorios of history, the sym-
phonies of all time.
I am the voice of to-day, the
herald of to-morrow. I weave into
the warp of the past the woof of
the future. I tell the stories of
peace and war alike.
I make the human heart beat
with passion or tenderness. I stir
the pulse of nations, and make
brave men do better deeds, and
soldiers die. . . .
I am the laughter and tears of
the world, and I shall never die
until all things return to the immutable dust.
I am the printing-press.
        I Am the Printing-Press.

Christopher Dawson
[1889–   ]

[l] Religion has withdrawn into
isolated strongholds, where it remains on the defensive, surveying
the land through the narrow loop-
holes in the fortifications.
        The Judgment of the Nations

Beth Day
[*Circa* 1855]

[m] If you are tempted to reveal
A tale to you someone has told

About another, make it pass,
Before you speak, three gates of
  gold:
These narrow gates. First, "Is it
  true?"
Then, "Is it needful?" In your
  mind
Give truthful answer. And the
  next
Is last and narrowest, "Is it
  kind?"
                    Three Gates of Gold

Clarence Day
[1874–1935]

[n] The parting injunctions
Of mothers and wives
Are one of those functions
That poison their lives.
                    Scenes from the Mesozoic

[o] It is possible that our race
may be an accident, in a meaningless universe, living its brief life
uncared-for, on this dark, cooling
star: but even so—and all the
more—what marvelous creatures
we are! What fairy story, what tale
from the Arabian Nights of the
jinns, is a hundredth part as wonderful as this true fairy story of
simians! It is so much more heart-
ening, too, than the tales we invent. A universe capable of giving
birth to many such accidents is—
blind or not—a good world to live
in, a promising universe.
                    This Simian World. XIX

[p] Father declared he was going
to buy a new plot in the cemetery,
a plot all for himself. "And I'll
buy one on a corner," he added
triumphantly, "where I can get
out!"
Mother looked at him, startled
but admiring, and whispered to
me, "I almost believe he could do
it."   *Life with Father*

Holman Francis Day
[1865–1935]

[q] The purest affection the heart
  can hold
Is the honest love of a nine-year-
  old.   *That May-
              basket for Mabel Fry*

Eugene Victor Debs
[1855–1926]

[r] While there is a lower class I
am in it, while there is a criminal
element I am of it; while there is
a soul in prison, I am not free.
    *Quoted by the Very Reverend
    Hewlett Johnson, who said:
    "Noble words, and they find
    echoes down the ages."*

Stephen Decatur
[1779–1820]

[s] Our country! In her intercourse with foreign nations may
she always be in the right; but our
country, right or wrong. *Toast,
Norfolk, Virginia [April 1816]*

Daniel Defoe
[1661–1731]

[t] Wherever God erects a house
  of prayer,
The Devil always builds a chapel
  there;
And 'twill be found, upon examination,
The latter has the largest congregation.   *The True-Born
      Englishman. Part I, Line 1*

[u] He bade me observe it, and I
should always find, that the calamities of life were shared among
the upper and lower part of mankind; but that the middle station
had the fewest disasters.
              Robinson Crusoe. Page 23

[v] I let him know his name
should be Friday, which was the
day I saved his life.
                    Ibid. Page 234

[w] I took my man Friday with
me.   *Ibid.*

Charles André Joseph
Marie de Gaulle
[1890–   ]

[x] France has lost a battle. But
France has not lost the war.
    *Broadcast from London to the
    French people after the fall of
    France [June 18, 1940]*

[y] France will fight this battle
with passion, but she will fight it
with discipline.   *Broadcast to
    France [June 6, 1944]*

[z] It is not tolerable, it is not
possible, that from so much death,
so much sacrifice and ruin, so
much heroism, a greater and better humanity shall not emerge.
    *Speech in Ottawa, Canada
              [July 11, 1944]*

Thomas Dekker
[1570?–1641]

[a] The reason why fond women
  love to buy
Adulterate complexion: here 'tis
  read,—
False colours last after the true be
  dead.   *A Description of a
          Lady by Her Lover*

[b] We are ne'er like angels till
  our passion dies.   *The Hon-
    est Whore. Part II, Act I, Sc. 2*

[c] Turn over a new leaf.
              Ibid. Act II, Sc. 1

[d] Honest labour bears a lovely
face.   *Patient Grissell.*
                      Act I, Sc. 1

Walter De la Mare
[1873-   ]

[e] Slowly, silently, now the
moon
Walks the night in her silver
shoon.   *Silver*

[f] When all at peace, two friends
at ease alone
Talk out their hearts; yet still
Between the grace notes of
The voice of love
From each to each
Trembles a rarer speech,
And with its presence every pause
doth fill.   *Silence*

[g] Look thy last on all things
lovely
Every hour. Let no night
Seal thy sense in deathly slumber
Till to delight
Thou have paid thy utmost bless-
ing.   *Farewell. Stanza 3*

[h] Here lies, but seven years old,
our little maid,
Once of the darkness, oh, so sore
afraid.
Light of the World—remember
that small fear,
And when nor moon nor stars do
shine—draw near!
                      An Epitaph

[i] Nay, nay, sweet England, do
not grieve!
Not one of these poor men who
died
But did within his soul believe
That death for thee was glori-
fied.
"How Sleep the Brave." Stanza 1

[j] Hi! handsome hunting man,
Fire your little gun.
Bang! Now the animal
Is dead and dumb and done.
Nevermore to peep again, creep
again, leap again,
Eat or sleep or drink again, oh,
what fun!   *Hi!*

[k] Memory—that strange de-
ceiver!
Who can trust her? How believe
her—
While she hoards with equal care
The poor and trivial, rich and
rare;
Yet flings away, as wantonly,
Grave fact and loveliest fantasy?
                      Memory

[l] Poor Jim Jay
Got stuck fast
In Yesterday.   *Jim Jay*

[m] Whatever Miss T. eats
Turns into Miss T.   *Miss T.*

[n] Be not too wildly amorous of
the far,

Nor lure thy fantasy to its utmost scope.
            The Imagination's Pride

[o] Not the briefest moment—
yours or mine—
Can ever come again.
                Not One. Stanza 2

[p] I met at eve the Prince of
Sleep,
His was a still and lovely face,
He wandered through a valley
steep,
Lovely in a lonely place.
                    I Met at Eve

[q] And Conscience less my mind
indicts
For idle days than dreamless
nights.
              Dreams. Stanza 37

Margaret Wade Deland
[1857-1945]

[r] Alas! that men must see
Love, before Death!
Else they content might be
With their short breath.
                  Love and Death

Jacques Delille
[1738-1813]

[s] Fate makes our relatives,
choice makes our friends.
                La Pitié. Canto I

Walter De Map
[1140-1210]

[t] Die I must, but let me die
drinking in an inn!
Hold the wine-cup to my lips
sparkling from the bin!
So, when angels flutter down to
take me from my sin,
"Ah, God have mercy on this sot,"
the cherubs will begin.
*Quoted by J. R. Green, in A
Short History of the English
People, Chap. 3, Sect. 1*

Augustus De Morgan
[1806-1871]

[u] Great fleas have little fleas
upon their backs to bite 'em,
And little fleas have lesser fleas,
and so *ad infinitum.*
And the great fleas themselves, in
turn, have greater fleas to go
on;
While these again have greater
still, and greater still, and so
on.   *A Budget of Paradoxes*

Demosthenes
[384-322 B.C.]

*Translation by C. A. and J. H.
Vince. Loeb Classical Library*

[v] Like the diet prescribed by
doctors, which neither restores the

strength of the patient nor allows
him to succumb, so these doles
that you are now distributing
neither suffice to ensure your
safety nor allow you to renounce
them and try something else.
Third Olynthiac. 33

[w] To remind the man of the
good turns you have done him is
very much like a reproach.
De Corona. 269

Sir John Denham
[1615–1669]

[x] I can no more believe old
Homer blind,
Than those who say the sun hath
never shined:
The age wherein he lived was
dark, but he
Could not want sight who taught
the world to see.
Progress of Learning

[y] Nor needs thy juster title the
foul guilt
Of Eastern kings, who, to secure
their reign,
Must have their brothers, sons,
and kindred slain.
On Mr. John Fletcher's Works

Thomas, Lord Denman
[1779–1854]

[z] A delusion, a mockery, and a
snare.
*O'Connell v. The Queen (in 11
Clark and Finnelly Reports)*

Clarence James Dennis
[1876–1938]

[a] Me name is Mud.
*The Sentimental Bloke: A
Spring Song. Stanza 2*

[b] A suddin notion stops me wiv
a jar—
Wot if Doreen, I thinks, should
grow to be
A fat ole weepin' willer like 'er
Mar!   *Ibid. Mar. Stanza 24*

John Dennis
[1657–1734]

[c] A man who could make so vile
a pun would not scruple to pick a
pocket.   *The Gentleman's Magazine. Vol. LI, Page 324*

[d] Our author, for the advantage of this play ("Appius and
Virginia"), had invented a new
species of thunder, which was approved of by the actors, and is the
very sort that at present is used in
the theatre. The tragedy however
was coldly received, notwith-
standing such assistance, and
was acted but a short time. Some
nights after, Mr. Dennis, being in

the pit at the representation of
"Macbeth," heard his own thunder made use of; upon which he
rose in a violent passion, and exclaimed, with an oath, that it was
his thunder. "See," said he, "how
the rascals use me! They will not
let my play run, and yet they
steal my thunder!"
*Biographia Britannica. Vol. V,
Page 103*

Thomas De Quincey
[1785–1859]

[e] If once a man indulges himself in murder, very soon he
comes to think little of robbing;
and from robbing he next comes
to drinking and Sabbath-break-
ing, and from that to incivility
and procrastination.
On Murder

[f] Call for the grandest of all
earthly spectacles, what is that?
It is the sun going to his rest.
Call for the grandest of all human
sentiments, what is that? It is
that man should forget his anger
before he lies down to sleep.
*Confessions of an English Opium-
Eater (Everyman edition). Page 86*

[g] Mails from the North—the
East—the West—the South—
whence, according to some curious
etymologists, comes the magical
word NEWS.   *Ibid. Page 145*

[h] Worlds of fine thinking lie
buried in that vast abyss [news-
papers], never to be disentombed
or restored to human admiration.
*Reminiscences of the English
Lake Poets. Coleridge*

[i] Dyspepsia is the ruin of most
things: empires, expeditions, and
everything else.
Letter to Hessey [1823]

Gabriel Romanovitch
Derzhavin
[1743–1816]

[j] Thou from primeval nothing-
ness didst call
First chaos, then existence.
*Ode to God (tr. Sir John
Bowring). Stanza 3*

Marc Antoine Désaugiers
[1772–1827]

[k] When we are dead, it's for a
long time.
Song. Le Délire Bacchique

Frank Desprez
[1853–1916]

[l] And I wonder why I do not
care

For the things that are, like the
  things that were.
Does half my heart lie buried
  there,
In Texas, down by the Rio
  Grande?   *Lasca*

Aubrey Thomas de Vere
[1814–1902]

[m] Count each affliction,
  whether light or grave,
God's messenger sent down to
  thee; do thou
With courtesy receive him.
                          Sorrow

[n] Grief should be
Like joy, majestic, equable, sedate,
Confirming, cleansing, raising,
  making free;
Strong to consume small troubles;
  to commend
Great thoughts, grave thoughts,
  thoughts lasting to the end.
                          Ibid.

Mary Ainge De Vere
("Madeline Bridges")
[1844–1920]

[o] Then give to the world the
  best you have,
And the best will come back to
  you.   *Life's Mirror. Stanza 1*

[p] For life is the mirror of king
  and slave,
'Tis just what we are and do.
                  Ibid. Stanza 5

Bernard De Voto
[1897–   ]

[q] The West begins where the
average annual rainfall drops below twenty inches. When you
reach the line which marks that
drop—for convenience, the one
hundredth meridian—you have
reached the West.
          The Plundered Province

[r] New England is a finished
place. Its destiny is that of Florence or Venice, not Milan, while
the American empire careens onward toward its unpredicted end.
. . . It is the first American section to be finished, to achieve
stability in the conditions of its
life. It is the first old civilization,
the first permanent civilization in
America.
New England: There She Stands

[s] Pessimism is only the name
that men of weak nerves give to
wisdom.
  Mark Twain: The Ink of History

George Dewey
[1838–1917]

[t] You may fire when ready,
Gridley.   *At battle of Manila
                Bay [May 1, 1898]*

Thomas Edmund Dewey
[1902–   ]

[u] That's why it's time for a
change.   *Campaign speech, San
Francisco [September 21, 1944]*

Charles Dibdin
[1745–1814]

[v] Spanking Jack was so comely,
  so pleasant, so jolly,
Though winds blew great guns,
  still he'd whistle and sing;
Jack loved his friend, and was
  true to his Molly,
And if honour gives greatness,
  was great as a king.
          The Sailor's Consolation

[w] Did you ever hear of Captain
  Wattle?
He was all for love, and a little for
  the bottle.
    Captain Wattle and Miss Roe

Thomas Dibdin
[1771–1841]

[x] Oh, it's a snug little island!
A right little, tight little island.
          The Snug Little Island

Charles Dickens
[1812–1870]

[y] Be wery careful o' vidders all
your life.
        Pickwick Papers. Chap. 20

[z] Please, sir, I want some more.
            Oliver Twist. Chap. 2

[a] There are books of which the
backs and covers are by far the
best parts.   *Ibid. Chap. 14*

[b] There is something about a
roused woman, especially if she
add to all her other strong passions, the fierce impulses of recklessness and despair, which few
men like to provoke.
                  Ibid. Chap. 16

[c] "If the law supposes that,"
said Mr. Bumble, . . . "the law is
a ass, a idiot."   *Ibid. Chap. 51*

[d] A demd, damp, moist, unpleasant body!
      Nicholas Nickleby. Chap. 34

[e] He has gone to the demnition
bow-wows.   *Ibid. Chap. 64*

[f] My life is one demd horrid
grind.   *Ibid.*

[g] What is the odds, so long as
the wing of friendship never
moults a feather.   *The Old
                Curiosity Shop. Chap. 2*

[h] That vague kind of penitence
which holidays awaken next
morning.   *Ibid. Chap. 40*

[i] The memory of those who lie
below passes away so soon. At first

they tend them, morning, noon, and night; they soon begin to come less frequently; from once a day, to once a week; from once a week to once a month; then at long and uncertain intervals; then, not at all. *Ibid. Chap. 54*

[j] Any man may be in good spirits and good temper when he's well dressed. There ain't much credit in that.
Martin Chuzzlewit. Chap. 5

[k] Regrets are the natural property of gray hairs. *Ibid. Chap. 10*

[l] Leave the bottle on the chimley-piece, and don't ask me to take none, but let me put my lips to it when I am so dispoged. *Ibid. Chap. 19*

[m] Here are all kinds of employers wanting all sorts of servants, and all sorts of servants wanting all kinds of employers, and they never seem to come together. *Ibid. Chap. 36*

[n] Old Marley was as dead as a doornail. *A Christmas Carol. Stave One*

[o] Secret, and self-contained, and solitary as an oyster. *Ibid.*

[p] As good as gold. *Ibid. Stave Three*

[q] "God bless us every one!" said Tiny Tim. *Ibid.*

[r] It was always said of him, that he knew how to keep Christmas well. *Ibid. Stave Five*

[s] The New Year, like an Infant Heir to the whole world, was waited for, with welcomes, presents, and rejoicings. *The Chimes. Second Quarter*

[t] Oh the nerves, the nerves; the mysteries of this machine called Man! Oh the little that unhinges it: poor creatures that we are! *Ibid. Third Quarter*

[u] I want to know what it says. . . . The sea, Floy, what it is that it keeps on saying. *Dombey and Son. Chap. 8*

[v] You'll find us rough, Sir, but you'll find us ready. *David Copperfield. Chap. 3*

[w] I am a lone lorn creetur . . . and everythink goes contrary with me. *Ibid.*

[x] Barkis is willin'. *Ibid. Chap. 5*

[y] Annual income twenty pounds, annual expenditure nineteen nineteen six, result happiness. Annual income twenty pounds, annual expenditure twenty pounds ought and six, result misery. *Ibid. Chap. 12*

[z] It's a mad world. Mad as Bedlam. *Ibid. Chap. 14*

[a] It was as true . . . as turnips is. It was as true . . . as taxes is. And nothing's truer than them. *Ibid. Chap. 21*

[b] Accidents will occur in the best regulated families. *Ibid. Chap. 28*

[c] People can't die, along the coast . . . except when the tide's pretty nigh out. They can't be born, unless it's pretty nigh in—not properly born, till flood. He's going out with the tide. *Ibid.*

[d] There wasn't room to swing a cat there. *Ibid. Chap. 35*

[e] I ate umble pie with an appetite. *Ibid. Chap. 39*

[f] Skewered through and through with office-pens, and bound hand and foot with red tape. *Ibid. Chap. 43*

[g] The dreams of childhood—its airy fables; its graceful, beautiful, humane, impossible adornments of the world beyond: so good to be believed in once, so good to be remembered when outgrown. *Hard Times. Book II, Chap. 9*

[h] A person who can't pay, gets another person who can't pay, to guarantee that he can pay. *Little Dorrit. Book I, Chap. 23*

[i] Papa, potatoes, poultry, prunes, and prism, are all very good words for the lips: especially prunes and prism. *Ibid. Book II, Chap. 5*

[j'] It is at least as difficult to stay a moral infection as a physical one. *Ibid. Chap. 13*

[k'] It was the best of times, it was the worst of times, it was the age of wisdom, it was the age of foolishness, it was the epoch of belief, it was the epoch of incredulity, it was the season of Light, it was the season of Darkness, it was the spring of hope, it was the winter of despair. *A Tale of Two Cities. Book I, Chap. 1*

[l'] Detestation of the high is the involuntary homage of the low. *Ibid. Book II, Chap. 9*

[m'] Dead as mutton. *Ibid. Chap. 14*

[n'] He's as thin as a lath. *Ibid.*

[o'] It is a far, far better thing that I do, than I have ever done; it is a far, far better rest that I go to, than I have ever known. *Ibid. Book III, Chap. 15*

[p'] I have known a vast quantity of nonsense talked about bad men not looking you in the face. Don't trust that conventional idea. Dishonesty will stare honesty out of countenance, any day in the week, if there is anything to be got by it.   *Hunted Down. Chap. 2*

[q] In the little world in which children have their existence, whosoever brings them up, there is nothing so finely perceived and so finely felt, as injustice.
Great Expectations. Chap. 9

[r] Probably every new and eagerly expected garment ever put on since clothes came in, fell a trifle short of the wearer's expectation.   *Ibid. Chap. 19*

[s] Heaven knows we need never be ashamed of our tears, for they are rain upon the blinding dust of earth, overlying our hard hearts.   *Ibid.*

[t] And I *do* come home at Christmas. We all do, or we all should. We all come home, or ought to come home, for a short holiday—the longer, the better—from the great boarding-school, where we are forever working at our arithmetical slates, to take, and give a rest.
A Christmas Tree

Charles Monroe Dickinson
[1842–1924]

[u] If the days grow dark, if care and pain
Press close and sharp on heart and brain,
Then lovely pictures still shall bloom
Upon the walls of memory's room.
My Burdens

Emily Dickinson
[1830–1886]

(*Centenary Edition of The Poems of Emily Dickinson, published by Little, Brown and Company, Boston, 1930.*)

[v] Success is counted sweetest
By those who ne'er succeed.
First Series. Life, I, Success, Stanza 1

[w] Here a star, and there a star,
Some lose their way.
Here a mist, and there a mist:
Afterwards—day!
Ibid. IV, Stanza 2

[x] A precious, mouldering pleasure 'tis
To meet an antique book,
In just the dress his century wore.
Ibid. X, In a Library, Stanza 1

[y] The soul selects her own society,
Then shuts the door.
Ibid. XIII, Exclusion, Stanza 1

[z] To fight aloud is very brave,
But gallanter, I know,

Who charge within the bosom
The cavalry of woe.
Ibid. XVI, Stanza 1

[a] Inebriate of air am I,
And debauchee of dew,
Reeling, through endless summer days,
From inns of molten blue.
Ibid. XX, Stanza 2

[b] Alter? When the hills do.
Falter? When the sun
Question if his glory
Be the perfect one.
Ibid. Love, III, Stanza 1

[c] The pedigree of honey
Does not concern the bee;
A clover, any time, to him
Is aristocracy.   *Ibid. Nature, V*

[d] Some keep the Sabbath going to church;
I keep it staying at home,
With a bobolink for a chorister,
And an orchard for a dome.
Ibid. A Service of Song, VI, Stanza 1

[e] These are the days when birds come back,
A very few, a bird or two,
To take a backward look.
Ibid. Nature, XXVII, Indian Summer, Stanza 1

[f] The morns are meeker than they were,
The nuts are getting brown;
The berry's cheek is plumper,
The rose is out of town.
Ibid. XXVIII, Autumn, Stanza 1

[g] That short, potential stir
That each can make but once,
That bustle so illustrious
'Tis almost consequence,
Is the *éclat* of death.
Ibid. Time and Eternity, XIII, The Funeral

[h] Afraid? Of whom am I afraid?
Not death; for who is he?
The porter of my father's lodge
As much abasheth me.
Ibid. XXIV, Stanza 1

[i] Because I could not stop for Death,
He kindly stopped for me;
The carriage held but just ourselves
And Immortality.   *Ibid. XXVII, The Chariot, Stanza 1*

[j] If I shouldn't be alive
When the robins come,
Give the one in red cravat
A memorial crumb.
Ibid. XXXVII, Stanza 1

[k] How dreary to be somebody!
How public, like a frog
To tell your name the livelong day
To an admiring bog!
Second Series Life, I, Stanza 2

[l] One of the ones that Midas touched,

Who failed to touch us all,
Was that confiding prodigal,
The blissful oriole. *Ibid. Nature,*
XIII, The Oriole, Stanza 1

[**m**] A bird came down the walk:
He did not know I saw;
He bit an angle-worm in halves
And ate the fellow, raw. *Ibid.*
XXIII, In the Garden, Stanza 1

[**n**] God made a little gentian;
It tried to be a rose
And failed, and all the summer
laughed.
Ibid. XLVIII, Fringed Gentian

[**o**] A few prosaic days
A little this side of the snow
And that side of the haze.
Ibid. XLIX, November, Stanza 1

[**p**] One need not be a chamber
to be haunted;
One need not be a house;
The brain has corridors surpassing
Material place. *Ibid. Time and*
Eternity, XXIX, Ghosts, Stanza 1

[**q**] A word is dead
When it is said,
Some say.
I say it just
Begins to live
That day.   *Third Series.*
Life, VI, A Word

[**r**] There is no frigate like a book
To take us lands away,
Nor any courses like a page
Of prancing poetry.
Ibid. XVI, A Book

[**s**] Reverse cannot befall that
fine Prosperity
Whose sources are interior.
The Single Hound. VIII

[**t**] This quiet dust was Gentle-
men and Ladies,
And Lads and Girls;
Was laughter and ability and sigh-
ing,
And frocks and curls.
Ibid. LXXIV

[**u**] If I read a book and it makes
my whole body so cold no fire can
ever warm me, I know that is
poetry. If I feel physically as if the
top of my head were taken off, I
know that is poetry. These are the
only ways I know it. Is there any
other way?   *Life and Letters of*
Emily Dickinson, by Martha
Gilbert Dickinson Bianchi

Goldsworthy Lowes Dickinson
[1862–1932]

[**v**] Consider the American continent! How simple it is! How
broad! How large! How grand in
design! A strip of coast, a range
of mountains, a plain, a second
range, a second strip of coast!
That is all! Contrast the com-

plexity of Europe, its lack of symmetry, its variety, irregularity,
disorder and caprice! The geography of the two continents
already foreshadows the differences in their civilizations.
A Modern Symposium

[**w**] To the man who has the religion of peace, the supreme value
is love. To the man who has the
religion of war, the supreme value
is strife. *The Choice Before Us.*
Chap. 3

[**x**] War is not "inevitable," but
proceeds from definite and re-
movable causes.   *Ibid. Chap. 9*

[**y**] Nations are quite capable of
starving every other side of life—
education, sanitation, housing,
public health, everything that
contributes to life, physical, intellectual, moral, and spiritual,
in order to maintain their arma-
ments.   *Ibid. Chap. 11*

[**z**] A fundamental, and as many
believe, the most essential part of
Christianity, is its doctrine of reward and punishment in the
world beyond; and a religion
which had nothing at all to say
about this great enigma we should
hardly feel to be a religion at all.
The Greek View of Life. Chap 1,
Sect. 11

[**a**] Dissatisfaction with the world
in which we live and determina-
tion to realize one that shall be
better, are the prevailing characteristics of the modern spirit.
Ibid. Chap. 5

Sir Kenelm Digby
[1603–1665]

[**b**] The hot water is to remain
upon it [the tea] no longer than
whiles you can say the Miserere
Psalm very leisurely.
The Closet Opened. Tea with Eggs

[**c**] All Matter is indifferent to
Form.
Of the Vegetation of Plants

Kenelm Henry Digby
[1800–1880]

[**d**] Island of Saints, still constant, still allied
To the great truths opposed to
human pride.   *Erin*

George Dillon
[1907–   ]

[**e**] When love was false and I was
full of care,
And friendship cold and I was sick
with fear,
Music, the beautiful disturber of
the air,

Drew near,
Saying: Come with me into my
    country of air
Out of the querulous and uncivil
    clay;
Fling down its aching members
    into a chair,
And come away.   *The Constant*
            One. Stanzas 1 and 2

Wentworth Dillon,
Earl of Roscommon
[1633–1685]

[f] Men ever had, and ever will
    have, leave
To coin new words well suited to
    the age.
Words are like leaves, some wither
    ev'ry year,
And ev'ry year a younger race suc-
    ceeds.   *Translation of*
        Horace's Ars Poetica. Line 73

[g] Old men are only walking
    hospitals.   *Ibid. Line 202*

[h] True friends appear less
    mov'd than counterfeit;
As men that truly grieve at fu-
    nerals
Are not so loud, as those that cry
    for hire.   *Ibid. Line 484*

[i] Immodest words admit of no
    defence,
For want of decency is want of
    sense.   *Essay on Trans-*
            lated Verse. Line 113

Thomas Parke D'Invilliers

[j] Then wear the gold hat, if
    that will move her;
If you can bounce high, bounce
    for her too,
Till she cry "Lover, gold-hatted,
    high-bouncing lover,
I must have you!"
        Quoted on title page
        of The Great Gatsby,
        by F. Scott Fitzgerald

Diogenes Laertius
[Circa A.D. 200]

From The Lives and Opinions of
Eminent Philosophers, translated
by Charles Duke Yonge. Bohn
Classical Library

[k] When Thales was asked what
was difficult, he said, "To know
one's self." And what was easy,
"To advise another."   *Thales. 9*

[l] Solon used to say . . . that laws
were like cobwebs,—for that if any
trifling or powerless thing fell into
them, they held it fast; while if it
were something weightier, it broke
through them and was off.
            Solon. 10

[m] Solon gave the following advice: "Consider your honour, as a

gentleman, of more weight than
an oath."   *Ibid. 12*

[n] Chilo advised, "not to speak
evil of the dead."   *Chilo. 2*

[o] Pittacus, when he had got
Alcaeus into his power, released
him, saying, "Forgiveness is better
than revenge."   *Pittacus. 3*

[p] Anarcharsis, on learning that
the sides of a ship were four
fingers thick, said that "the passengers were just that distance
from death."   *Anarcharsis. 5*

[q] It was a common saying of
Myson that men ought not to investigate things from words, but
words from things; for that things
are not made for the sake of
words, but words for things.
            Myson. 3

[r] Socrates said, "Those who
want fewest things are nearest to
the gods."   *Socrates. 11*

[s] He said that there was one
only good, namely, knowledge;
and one only evil, namely, ignorance.   *Ibid. 14*

[t] Being asked whether it was
better to marry or not, he replied,
"Whichever you do, you will repent it."   *Ibid. 16*

[u] Time is the image of eternity.
            Plato. 41

[v] There is a written and an unwritten law. The one by which we
regulate our constitutions in our
cities is the written law; that
which arises from custom is the
unwritten law.   *Ibid. 51*

[w] The question was put to him,
what hope is; and his answer was,
"The dream of a waking man."
            Aristotle. 11

[x] He used to say that personal
beauty was a better introduction
than any letter; but others say
that it was Diogenes who gave this
description of it, while Aristotle
called beauty "the gift of God";
that Socrates called it "a short-
lived tyranny"; Theophrastus, "a
silent deceit"; Theocritus, "an
ivory mischief."   *Ibid.*

[y] On one occasion Aristotle was
asked how much educated men
were superior to those unedu-
cated: "As much," said he, "as the
living are to the dead."   *Ibid.*

[z] He was once asked what a
friend is, and his answer was,
"One soul abiding in two bodies."
            Ibid.

[a] Asked what he gained from
philosophy, he answered, "To do
without being commanded what
others do from fear of the laws."
            Ibid.

[b] It was a favourite expression of Theophrastus that time was the most valuable thing that a man could spend.
Theophrastus. 10

[c] Antisthenes used to say that envious people were devoured by their own disposition, just as iron is by rust.   *Antisthenes. 4*

[d] A man once asked Diogenes what was the proper time for supper, and he made answer, "If you are a rich man, whenever you please; and if you are a poor man, whenever you can."   *Diogenes. 6*

[e] Diogenes lighted a candle in the daytime, and went round saying, "I am looking for a man."
Ibid.

[f] When asked what wine he liked to drink, he replied, "That which belongs to another." *Ibid.*

[g] When Zeno was asked what a friend was, he replied, "Another I."   *Zeno. 19*

[h] They say that the first inclination which an animal has is to protect itself.   *Ibid. 52*

[i] He calls drunkenness an expression identical with ruin.
Pythagoras. 6

Dionysius, the Elder
[430–367 B.C.]

[j] Let thy speech be better than silence, or be silent.   *Fragment 6*

Benjamin Disraeli, Earl of Beaconsfield
[1804–1881]

[k] Yes, I am a Jew, and when the ancestors of the right honourable gentleman were brutal savages in an unknown island, mine were priests in the temple of Solomon.   *Reply to a taunt by Daniel O'Connell*

[l] A conservative government is an organized hypocrisy.
Speech on Agricultural Interests [March 17, 1845]

[m] Justice is truth in action.
Speech [February 11, 1851]

[n] It is much easier to be critical than to be correct.
Speech [January 24, 1860]

[o] Posterity is a most limited assembly. Those gentlemen who reach posterity are not much more numerous than the planets.
Speech [June 3, 1862]

[p] In the character of the victim [Lincoln], and even in the accessories of his last moments, there is something so homely and innocent that it takes the question, as it were, out of all the pomp of history and the ceremonial of diplomacy—it touches the heart of nations and appeals to the domestic sentiment of mankind.
Address, House of Commons [May 1, 1865]

[q] The secret of success is constancy to purpose.
Speech [June 24, 1870]

[r] The author who speaks about his own books is almost as bad as a mother who talks about her own children.
Speech [November 19, 1870]

[s] Increased means and increased leisure are the two civilizers of man.
Speech to the Conservatives of Manchester [April 3, 1872]

[t] A university should be a place of light, of liberty, and of learning.   *Speech, House of Commons [March 8, 1873]*

[u] The health of the people is really the foundation upon which all their happiness and all their powers as a State depend.
Speech [July 24, 1877]

[v] Experience is the child of Thought, and Thought is the child of Action. We can not learn men from books.
Vivian Grey. Book V, Chap. I

[w] Variety is the mother of Enjoyment.   *Ibid. Chap. IV*

[x] I repeat . . . that all power is a trust; that we are accountable for its exercise; that from the people and for the people all springs, and all must exist.
Ibid. Book VI, Chap. VII

[y] Youth is a blunder; manhood a struggle; old age a regret.
Coningsby. Book III, Chap. I

[z] Property has its duties as well as its rights.
Sybil. Book II, Chap. XI

[a] Little things affect little minds.   *Ibid. Book III, Chap. II*

[b'] That when a man fell into his anecdotage, it was a sign for him to retire. *Lothair. Chap. XXVIII*

[c'] Every woman should marry—and no man.   *Ibid. Chap. XXX*

[d'] "My idea of an agreeable person," said Hugo Bohun, "is a person who agrees with me."
Ibid. Chap. XXXV

Charles Divine
[1889–1950]

[e'] I wonder who is haunting the little snug café,
That place, half restaurant and home, since we have gone away;

The candled dimness, smoke and talk, and tables brown and bare—
But no one thinks of tablecloths when love and laughter's there.   *At the Lavender Lantern. Stanza 1*

[f] Where hearts were high and fortunes low, and onions in the stew.   *Ibid. Stanza 3*

Richard Watson Dixon
[1833–1900]

[g] Forth comes the moon, the sweet surprise of heaven.
    The Spirit Wooed

[h] There is a soul above the soul of each,
A mightier soul, which yet to each belongs:
There is a sound made of all human speech,
And numerous as the concourse of all songs.   *Humanity*

William Croswell Doane
[1832–1913]

[i] I am quite sure he thinks that I am God—
Since he is God on whom each one depends
For life and all things that His bounty sends—
My dear old dog, most constant of all friends.   *Cluny*

Henry Austin Dobson
[1840–1921]

[j] Once at the Angelus
(Ere I was dead),
Angels all glorious
Came to my bed.
    "Good-Night, Babette!"

[k] Time goes, you say? Ah no!
Alas, Time stays, *we* go.
    The Paradox of Time. Stanza 1

[l] All passes. Art alone
Enduring stays to us;
The Bust outlasts the throne,—
The Coin, Tiberius.
    Ars Victrix (Imitated from Théophile Gautier). Stanza 8

[m] The ladies of St. James's!
They're painted to the eyes;
Their white it stays for ever,
Their red it never dies:
But Phyllida, my Phyllida!
Her color comes and goes;
It trembles to a lily,—
It wavers to a rose.   *The Ladies of St. James's. Stanza 4*

[n] Ye gods! how he talk'd! What a torrent of sound,
His hearers invaded, encompass'd and—drown'd!
    A Postscript to "Retaliation"

[o] He made little fishes talk vastly like whales.   *Ibid.*

[p] But little lore of loving can any flagon teach,
For when my tongue is loosed most, then most I lose my speech.   *The Maltworm's Madrigal. Stanza 6*

[q] In the work-a-day world,—
for its needs and woes,
There is place and enough for the pains of prose;
But whenever the May-bells clash and chime,
Then hey!—for the ripple of laughing rhyme!   *The Ballad of Prose and Rhyme. Envoy*

[r] Old books, old wine, old Nankin blue;—
All things, in short, to which belong
The charm, the grace that Time makes strong,—
All these I prize, but (*entre nous*) Old friends are best!
    To Richard Watson Gilder. Stanza 3

[s] Fame is a food that dead men eat,—
I have no stomach for such meat.
    Fame is a Food that Dead Men Eat. Stanza 1

[t] The Press is too much with us: small and great;
We are undone of chatter and *on dit*,
Report, retort, rejoinder, repartee,
Mole-hill and mare's nest, fiction up-to-date.   *A Pleasant Invective Against Printing*

[u] I shall not see the morning sky;
I shall not hear the night-wind sigh;
I shall be mute, as all men must In after days!   *In After Days*

Lee Wilson Dodd
[1879–1933]

[v] You steal green apples from the Tree
Of Life, miscalling greenness pleasure.
    To the Younger Generation

[w] Much that I sought, I could not find:
Much that I found, I could not bind;
Much that I bound, I could not free;
Much that I freed returned to me.
    Ronde Macabre

[x] Furious Propaganda, with her brand,
Fires the dry prairies of our wide Waste Land;
Making the Earth, Man's temporal station, be
One stinking altar to Publicity.
    The Great Enlightenment

Philip Doddridge
[1702–1751]

[y] Awake, my soul! stretch every
nerve,
And press with vigour on;
A heavenly race demands thy zeal,
And an immortal crown.
*Zeal and Vigour in the Christian
Race. Stanza 1*

Mary Abigail Dodge
("Gail Hamilton")
[1838–1896]

[z] The moment an audacious
head is lifted one inch above the
general level, pop! goes the unerring rifle of some biographical
sharpshooter, and it is all over
with the unhappy owner.
*Skirmishes and Sketches. The
New School of Biography*

[a] What's virtue in man can't
be vice in a cat.   *Both Sides*

Mary Mapes Dodge
[1838–1905]

[b] Grandma told me all about it,
Told me, so I couldn't doubt it,
How she danced—my Grandma
danced!—
Long ago.
The Minuet. Stanza 1

[c] Whenever a snowflake leaves
the sky,
It turns and turns to say "Good-
by!"
Good-by, dear clouds, so cool and
gray!"
Then lightly travels on its way.
Snowflakes

Samuel Dodge
[*Floruit* 1868]

[d] You may go through this
world, but 'twill be very slow
If you listen to all that is said as
you go;
You'll be worried and fretted and
kept in a stew,
For meddlesome tongues must
have something to do,
For people will talk, you know.
People Will Talk. Stanza 1

Charles Lutwidge Dodgson
see "Lewis Carroll"

Robert Dodsley
[1703–1764]

[e] No state of life but must to
patience bow:
The tradesman must have
patience for his bill;
He must have patience who to law
will go;

And should he lose his right,
more patience still;
Yea, to prevent or heal full many
a strife,
How oft, how long must man have
patience with his wife.
To Patience

Digby Mackworth Dolben
[1848–1867]

[f] The years of gold
When all the months were May.
A Song

[g] As fresh as when the first
sunrise
Awoke the lark in Paradise.
The Shrine

Charles Fletcher Dole
[1845–1927]

[h] Good Will is the mightiest
practical force in the universe.
Cleveland Address

Nathan Haskell Dole
[1852–1935]

[i] What other State compares
with Maine
In glorious coasts, where ocean
tides
Have for long ages beat in vain
To storm the coves where safety
hides;
Where pillared cliffs like sentries
stand
To guard the entries to the land,
From Kittery to Calais!
The State of Maine. Stanza 1

John Donne
[1573–1631]

[j] I have done one braver thing
Than all the Worthies did;
And yet a braver thence doth
spring,
Which is, to keep that hid.
The Undertaking. Stanza 1

[k] Stay, O sweet, and do not
rise!
The light that shines comes from
thine eyes;
The day breaks not: it is my heart,
Because that you and I must part.
Daybreak. Stanza 1

[l] No spring nor summer beauty
hath such grace
As I have seen in one autumnal
face.
*Elegie IX, The Autumnal:
To Lady Magdalen Herbert*

[m] The snail, which everywhere
doth roam
Carrying his own house still, still
is at home,
Follow (for he is easy paced) this
snail,

Be thine own palace, or the
world's thy jail. *Verse Letter
to Sir Henry Wotton*

[n] Go and catch a falling star.
Song

[o] I long to talk with some old
lover's ghost,
Who died before the god of love
was born. *Love's Deity*

[p] No man is an Iland, intire of
itselfe; every man is a peece of the
Continent, a part of the maine; if
a Clod bee washed away by the
Sea, Europe is the lesse, as well
as if a Promontorie were, as well
as if a Mannor of thy friends or of
thine owne were, any man's death
diminishes me, because I am involved in Mankinde; And therefore never send to know for whom
the bell tolls; it tolls for thee.
Devotions. XVII

[q] Death, be not proud, though
some have called thee
Mighty and dreadful, for thou art
not so;
For those whom thou think'st
thou dost overthrow
Die not, poor Death; nor yet canst
thou kill me. *Sonnet: Death*

"Mr. Dooley"
(Finley Peter Dunne)
[1867–1936]

[r] Life'd not be worth livin' if
we didn't keep our inimies.
On New Year's Resolutions

[s] Ivrything that's worth havin'
goes to th' city; th' counthry takes
what's left.
The City as a Summer Resort

[t] Th' dimmycratic party ain't
on speakin' terms with itsilf.
*Mr. Dooley Discusses Party
Politics*

[u] Th' raypublican party broke
ye, but now that ye're down we'll
not turn a cold shoulder to ye.
Come in an' we'll keep ye broke.
Ibid.

[v] When ye build yer triumphal
arch to yer conquerin' hero, Hin-
nissey, build it out of bricks so
the people will have somethin'
convanient to throw at him as he
passes through. *Fame*

[w] Vice . . . is a creature of such
heejus mien, . . . that the more ye
see it th' better ye like it.
The Crusade Against Vice

[x] I don't know what a chamber
iv commerce is onless 'tis a place
where business men go to sleep.
On the Amateur Ambassadors

[y] "Ye know a lot about mar-
riage, but ye niver married," said
Mr. Hennessy.
"No," said Mr. Dooley. "No, say

I, givin' three cheers, I know
about marriage th' way an astronomer knows about th' stars."
Marriage

John Roderigo
Dos Passos
[1896–   ]

[z] The chilly December day
two shivering bicycle mechanics
from Dayton, Ohio,
first felt their homemade contrap-
tion
whittled out of hickory sticks,
gummed together with Arnstein's
bicycle cement,
stretched with muslin they'd sewn
on their sister's sewingma-
chine in their own backyard
on Hawthorn Street in Dayton, Ohio,
soar into the air
above the dunes and the wide
beach
at Kitty Hawk.
The Big Money. [*The Campers
at Kitty Hawk*]
[*Celebrating the Wright brothers'
first flight*]

Fyodor Dostoyevsky
[1821–1881]

[a] Man is a pliable animal, a being who gets accustomed to everything!
*The House of the Dead (Prison
Life in Siberia)* [*Everyman
edition*]. *Part I, Chap. 2*

[b] It is acknowledged that
neither convict prisons, nor the
hulks, nor any system of hard
labour ever cured a criminal.
Ibid.

[c] Tyranny is a habit capable of
being developed, and at last becomes a disease. . . . The man and
the citizen disappear for ever in
the tyrant. *Ibid. Part II, Chap. 3*

[d] Even those who have renounced Christianity and attack
it, in their inmost being still follow the Christian ideal, for hitherto neither their subtlety nor the
ardour of their hearts has been
able to create a higher ideal of
man and of virtue than the ideal
given by Christ of old.
*The Brothers Karamazov (tr.
Constance Garnett). Part II,
Book IV, Chap. 1*

[e] Until you have become really,
in actual fact, a brother to every
one, brotherhood will not come to
pass. *Ibid. Book VI, Chap. 2*

[f] Be not forgetful of prayer.
Every time you pray, if your prayer
is sincere, there will be new feeling and new meaning in it, which

will give you fresh courage, and you will understand that prayer is an education.   *Ibid. Chap. 3*

[g] Love all God's creation, the whole and every grain of sand in it. Love every leaf, every ray of God's light. Love the animals, love the plants, love everything. If you love everything, you will perceive the divine mystery in things. Once you perceive it, you will begin to comprehend it better every day. And you will come at last to love the whole world with an all-embracing love.   *Ibid.*

[h] Men reject their prophets and slay them, but they love their martyrs and honour those whom they have slain.   *Ibid.*

Sarah Doudney
[1843–1926]

[i] Oh, the wasted hours of life
That have drifted by!
Oh, the good that might have
been,
Lost without a sigh!
        The Lesson of the Water-Mill

[j] Sleep on, beloved, sleep, and take thy rest;
Lay down thy head upon thy Saviour's breast;
We love thee well, but Jesus loves thee best—
Good-night!
        Good-Night. Stanza 1

(George) Norman Douglas
[1868–1952]

[k] You can tell the ideals of a nation by its advertisements.
        South Wind. Chap. 7

[l] A love-match is generally a failure and a money-match is always a mistake. The heroes, the saints and sages—they are those who face the world alone.
        Ibid. Chap. 11

[m] No great man is ever born too soon or too late. When we say that the time is not ripe for this or that celebrity, we confess by implication that this very man, and no other, is required.
        Ibid. Chap. 13

[n] Many a man who thinks to found a home discovers that he has merely opened a tavern for his friends.   *Ibid. Chap. 24*

"Marion Douglas"
(Annie Douglas
Green Robinson)
[1842–1913]

[o] Said old Gentleman Gay, "On a Thanksgiving Day,

If you want a good time, then giv
something away."
        A Good Thanksgivin

Bartholomew Dowling
[1823–1863]

[p] There's a mist on the glas
congealing,
'Tis the hurricane's sultr
breath;
And thus does the warmth of feel
ing
Turn ice in the grasp of Death
        The Revel. Stanza

Fairfax Downey
[1893–   ]

[q] Alas, air travel is so swift an
always getting shorter,
On long train trips one got
chance to know the Pullma
porter.
Soon after you have favored m
with smiles, some gum, a pil
low,
We land, and vanishes your form
so trim, sylphlike and willow
        Love On a High Plan

Ernest Dowson
1867–1900]

[r] They are not long, the weepin
and the laughter,
Love and desire and hate:
I think they have no portion i
us after
We pass the gate.
        Vitae Summa Brevis. Stanza

[s] I have been faithful to thee
Cynara! in my fashion.
        *None Sum Qualis Eram Bona
        Sub Regno Cynara*

[t] I have forgot much, Cynara
gone with the wind,
Flung roses, roses, riotously with
the throng.   *Ibid. Stanza*

[u] What is the use of speech
Silence were fitter:
Lest we should still be wishing
things unsaid.   *You Would
Have Understood Me. Stanza*

[v] Before my light goes out forever if God should give me a
choice of graces,
I would not reck of length of days,
nor crave for things to be;
But cry: "One day of the great
lost days, one face of all the
faces,
Grant me to see and touch once
more and nothing more to
see."
        Impenitentia Ultima. Stanza 1

Sir Arthur Conan Doyle
[1859–1930]

[w] When you have eliminated
the impossible, whatever remains,

however improbable, must be the truth. *Sherlock Holmes: The Sign of the Four. Chap. 6*

[x] You know my methods, Watson. *Ibid. The Crooked Man*

[y] Come, Watson, come! The game is afoot. *Ibid. The Adventure of the Abbey Grange*

[z] Elementary, my dear Watson. *Ibid. The Crooked Man*

[a] No British autobiography has ever been frank, and consequently no British autobiography has ever been good. Of all forms of literature it is the one least adapted to the national genius. You could not imagine a British Rousseau, still less a British Benvenuto Cellini. *Through the Magic Door*

[b] Several incidents in my life have convinced me of spiritual interposition—of the promptings of some beneficent force outside ourselves, which tries to help us where it can. *Ibid.*

Sir Francis Hastings Doyle
[1810–1888]

[c] Vain, mightiest fleets of iron framed;
Vain, those all-shattering guns;
Unless proud England keep, untamed,
The strong heart of her sons.
The Private of the Buffs. Stanza 5

Joseph Rodman Drake
[1795–1820]

[d] Flag of the free heart's hope and home!
By angel hands to valour given;
Thy stars have lit the welkin dome,
And all thy hues were born in heaven.
Forever float that standard sheet!
Where breathes the foe but falls before us,
With Freedom's soil beneath our feet,
And Freedom's banner streaming o'er us?
The American Flag. Stanza 5 (New York Evening Post, May 29, 1819)

Michael Drayton
[1563–1631]

[e] For that fine madness still he did retain
Which rightly should possess a poet's brain.
(Said of Marlowe) To Henry Reynolds, of Poets and Poesy

[f] Since there's no help, come let us kiss and part.
Sonnet: Love's Farewell

John Drinkwater
[1882–1937]

[g] Great hills that fold above the sea,
Ecstatic airs and sparkling skies,
Sing out your words to master me,
Make me immoderately wise.
Invocation

[h] And not a girl goes walking
Along the Cotswold lanes
But knows men's eyes in April
Are quicker than their brains.
Cotswold Love

[i] When the high heart we magnify,
And the clear vision celebrate,
And worship greatness passing by,
Ourselves are great.
Abraham Lincoln

Louise Driscoll
[1875–   ]

[j] There you will find what Every man needs,
Wild religion
Without any creeds.
Spring Market. Stanza 5

[k] You can't forget a garden
When you have planted seed—
When you have watched the weather
And know a rose's need.
You Can't Forget a Garden

[l] Villon among the birds is he,
A bold, bright rover, bad and free;
Yet not without such loveliness
As makes the curse upon him less.
The Blue Jay. Stanza 1

William Driver
[1803–1886]

[m] On August 10, 1831, a large American flag was presented to Captain William Driver of the brig *Charles Doggett* by a band of women, in recognition of his humane service in bringing back the British mutineers of the ship *Bounty* from Tahiti to their former home, Pitcairn Island. As the flag was hoisted to the masthead, Captain Driver proclaimed, "I name thee the Old Glory." The flag is now in the Smithsonian Institution, Washington, D.C.

William Henry Drummond
[1854–1907]

[n] De win' can blow lak hurricane
An' s'pose she blow some more,
You can't get drown on Lac St. Pierre
So long you stay on shore.
The Wreck of the "Julie Plante." Stanza 6

[o] Do w'at you lak wit' your old gran'pere

For w'en you're beeg feller he
won't be dere—
Leetle Bateese!
Little Bateese. Stanza 7

John Dryden
[1631–1700]

[p] Great wits are sure to madness near allied,
And thin partitions do their
bounds divide. *Absalom and
Achitophel. Part I, Line 163*

[q] And all to leave what with his
toil he won
To that unfeather'd two-legged
thing, a son.   *Ibid. Line 169*

[r] Who think too little, and who
talk too much. *Ibid. Line 534*

[s] A man so various, that he
seem'd to be
Not one, but all mankind's epit-
ome;
Stiff in opinions, always in the
wrong,
Was everything by starts, and
nothing long;
But, in the course of one revolv-
ing moon
Was chymist, fiddler, statesman,
and buffoon.   *Ibid. Line 545*

[t] So over violent, or over civil,
That every man with him was God
or Devil.   *Ibid. Line 557*

[u] Of ancient race by birth, but
nobler yet
In his own worth. *Ibid. Line 900*

[v] Beware the fury of a patient
man.   *Ibid. Line 1005*

[w] For truth has such a face and
such a mien,
As to be lov'd needs only to be
seen.   *The Hind and the
Panther. Part I, Line 33*

[x] Of all the tyrannies on human kind
The worst is that which persecutes
the mind.   *Ibid. Line 239*

[y] And kind as kings upon their
coronation day.
Ibid. Line 271

[z] Too black for heaven, and yet
too white for hell.
Ibid. Line 343

[a] When the cause goes hard,
the guilty man
Excepts, and thins his jury all he
can. *Ibid. Part II, Line 242*

[b] War seldom enters but where
wealth allures. *Ibid. Line 706*

[c] Jealousy, the jaundice of the
soul.   *Ibid. Part III, Line 73*

[d] Let the guiltless person throw
the stone.
Ibid. Line 684

[e] Secret guilt by silence is betrayed.   *Ibid. Line 763*

[f] Possess your soul with
patience.   *Ibid. Line 839*

[g] For those whom God to ruin
has design'd,
He fits for fate, and first destroys
their mind.   *Ibid. Line 1093*

[h] Our vows are heard betimes!
and Heaven takes care
To grant, before we can conclude
the prayer:
Preventing angels met it half the
way,
And sent us back to praise, who
came to pray.
Britannia Rediviva. Line 1

[i] Genius must be born, and
never can be taught.
Epistle to Congreve. Line 60

[j] Be kind to my remains; and
oh defend,
Against your judgment, your
departed friend! *Ibid. Line 72*

[k] Better to hunt in fields, for
health unbought,
Than fee the doctor for a nauseous draught.
The wise, for cure, on exercise depend;
God never made his work for man
to mend.   *Epistle to John
Dryden of Chesterton. Line 92*

[l] So softly death succeeded life
in her,
She did but dream of heaven, and
she was there.
Eleonora. Line 315

[m] He was exhal'd; his great
Creator drew
His spirit, as the sun the morning
dew.   *On the Death of a
Very Young Gentleman*

[n] None but the brave deserves
the fair.
Alexander's Feast. Line 15

[o] Sweet is pleasure after pain.
Ibid. Line 60

[p′] Sooth'd with the sound, the
king grew vain;
Fought all his battles o'er again;
And thrice he routed all his foes,
and thrice he slew the slain.
Ibid. Line 66

[q′] For pity melts the mind to
love.   *Ibid. Line 96*

[r′] Softly sweet, in Lydian
measures,
Soon he sooth'd his soul to pleas-
ures.
War, he sung, his toil and trouble;
Honour but an empty bubble;
Never ending, still beginning,
Fighting still, and still destroying.
If all the world be worth thy
winning,
Think, oh think it worth enjoy-
ing:
Lovely Thais sits beside thee,
Take the good the gods provide
thee.   *Ibid. Line 97*

s] A very merry, dancing, drinking,
Laughing, quaffing, and unthinking time.
The Secular Masque. Line 38

t] The sword within the scabbard keep,
And let mankind agree.
Ibid. Line 61

u] Fool, not to know that love endures no tie,
And Jove but laughs at lovers' perjury. *Palamon and Arcite. Book II, Line 758*

v] For Art may err, but Nature cannot miss.   *The Cock and the Fox. Line 452*

w] He trudg'd along unknowing what he sought,
And whistled as he went, for want of thought.
Cymon and Iphigenia. Line 84

x] Not heaven itself upon the past has power;
But what has been, has been, and I have had my hour.
Imitation of Horace. Book III, Ode 29, Line 71

y] I can enjoy her while she's kind;
But when she dances in the wind,
And shakes the wings and will not stay,
I puff the prostitute away.
Ibid. Line 81

z] And virtue, though in rags, will keep me warm.
Ibid. Line 87

a] Arms and the man I sing, who, forced by fate
And haughty Juno's unrelenting hate. *Virgil, Æneid. Line 1*

b] Ill habits gather by unseen degrees,—
As brooks make rivers, rivers run to seas.
Ovid, Metamorphoses. Book XV, The Worship of Æsculapius, Line 155

c] Our souls sit close and silently within,
And their own web from their own entrails spin;
And when eyes meet far off, our sense is such,
That, spider-like, we feel the tenderest touch.
Marriage à la Mode. Act II, Sc. 1

d] Errors, like straws, upon the surface flow;
He who would search for pearls must dive below.
All for Love. Prologue

e] Men are but children of a larger growth. *Ibid. Act IV, Sc. 1*

f] I am as free as Nature first made man,

Ere the base laws of servitude began,
When wild in woods the noble savage ran. *The Conquest of Granada. Part I, Act I, Sc. 1*

g] Death in itself is nothing; but we fear
To be we know not what, we know not where.
Aurengzebe. Act IV, Sc. 1

h] When I consider life, 'tis all a cheat.
Yet fool'd with hope, men favour the deceit;
Trust on, and think to-morrow will repay.
To-morrow's falser than the former day;
Lies worse, and while it says we shall be blest
With some new joys, cuts off what we possess.
Strange cozenage! none would live past years again,
Yet all hope pleasure in what yet remain,
And from the dregs of life think to receive
What the first sprightly running could not give.
Ibid.

i] All delays are dangerous in war. *Tyrannic Love. Act I, Sc. 1*

j] Pains of love be sweeter far
Than all other pleasures are.
Ibid. Act IV, Sc. 1

k] Of no distemper, of no blast he died,
But fell like autumn fruit that mellow'd long,—
Even wonder'd at, because he dropp'd no sooner.
Fate seem'd to wind him up for four-score years,
Yet freshly ran he on ten winters more;
Till like a clock worn out with eating time,
The wheels of weary life at last stood still.
Œdipus. Act IV, Sc. 1

l] There is a pleasure sure
In being mad which none but madmen know.
The Spanish Friar. Act II, Sc. 1

m] He [Shakespeare] was the man who of all Modern, and perhaps Ancient Poets, had the largest and most comprehensive soul. . . .

He needed not the spectacles of Books to read Nature; he looked inwards, and found her there.
Essay of Dramatic Poesy

William Edward Burghardt DuBois
[1868-   ]

n] Herein lies the tragedy of the age: not that men are poor—all

men know something of poverty;
not that men are wicked—who is
good? Not that men are ignorant
—what is truth? Nay, but that
men know so little of men.
The Souls of Black Folk

Stephen Duck
[1705–1756]

[o] Would you, my friend, a finished sceptic make,
To form his nature these materials take:
A little learning; twenty grains
of sense
Joined with a double share of
ignorance;
Infuse a little wit into the skull,
Which never fails to make a
mighty fool;
Two drams of faith; a tun of
doubting next;
Let all be with the dregs of reason
mixt:
When in his mind these jarring
seeds are sown,
He'll censure all things but approve of none.   *Proper Ingredients to Make a Sceptic*

Alexandre Dumas,
the Elder
[1802–1870]

[p] All for one, one for all, that
is our device.
The Three Musketeers. Chap. 9

[q] There are virtues which be-
come crimes by exaggeration.
*The Count of Monte Cristo.
Chap. 90*

[r] Look for the woman [Cher-
chez la femme.]   *The Mohicans
of Paris. Vol. III, Chaps. 10 and 11*

Alexandre Dumas,
the Younger
[1824–1895]

[s] Business? It's quite simple.
It's other people's money.
*La Question d'Argent.
Act II, Sc. 7*

George Louis Palmella
Busson du Maurier
[1834–1896]

[t] He had never heard such
music as this, never dreamt such
music was possible. He was conscious, while it lasted, that he saw
deeper into the beauty, the sadness of things, the very heart of
them, and their pathetic evanes-
cence, as with a new inner eye—
even into eternity itself, beyond
the veil.   *Trilby. Part I*

[u] Lovely female shapes are terrible complicators of the difficulties and dangers of this earthly
life, especially for their owner.
Ibid.

[v] That is the worst of those
dear people who have charm; they
are so terrible to do without, when
once you have got accustomed to
them and all their ways.
Ibid. Part V

[w] She was one of those rarely
gifted beings who cannot look or
speak or even stir without waking
up (and satisfying) some vague
longing that lies dormant in the
hearts of most of us.
Ibid. Part VII

[x] There can be prayers without
words just as well as songs, I suppose.   *Ibid. Part VIII*

[y] Grief tires more than anything, and brings a deeper slumber.   *Ibid.*

[z] A little work, a little play,
To keep us going—and so, good-
day!

A little warmth, a little light,
Of love's bestowing—and so, good-
night!

A little fun, to match the sorrow
Of each day's growing—and so,
good-morrow!

A little trust that when we die
We reap our sowing! and so—
good-by!   *Ibid.*

[a] The wretcheder one is, the
more one smokes; and the more
one smokes, the wretcheder one
gets—a vicious circle!
Peter Ibbetson. Page 135

[b] I do not know if little dogs
cause as large griefs when they die
as big ones.   *Ibid. Page 152*

[c] What matter if it be a fool's
paradise? Paradise is paradise, for
whoever owns it!   *Ibid. Page 265*

[d] I have no talent for making
new friends, but oh, such a genius
for fidelity to old ones!
Ibid. Page 276

[e] There is both an impertinence
and a lack of taste in any man's
laying bare to the public eye—to
any eye—the bliss that has come
to him through the love of a devoted woman, with whose life his
own has been bound up.
Ibid. Page 305

Florence French Dunbar
[1916–   ]

[f] The Spring comes truly when,
between the rains,

The stiff new wasps ascend the window panes.   *Wasp Time*

Paul Laurence Dunbar
[1872–1906]

[g] Folks ain't got no right to censuah otha folks about dey habits;
Him dat giv' de squir'ls de bush-tails made de bobtails fu' de rabbits.   *Accountability*

[h] There is a heaven, for ever, day by day,
The upward longing of my soul doth tell me so.
There is a hell, I'm quite as sure; for pray,
If there were not, where would my neighbours go?   *Theology*

[i] An' you couldn't he'p f'om dancin' ef yo' feet was boun' wif twine,
When Angelina Johnson comes a-swingin' down de line.
    Angelina

[j] Sweetah den de music of a lovesick mockin'-bird,
Comin' f'om de gal you loves bet-ter den yo' kin,
'Howdy, honey, howdy, won't you step right in?"
    "Howdy, Honey, Howdy!"

[k] It's easy 'nough to titter w'en de stew is smokin' hot,
But hit's mighty ha'd to giggle w'en dey's nuffin' in de pot.
    Philosophy

Finley Peter Dunne
see "Mr. Dooley"

Edward John Moreton Drax Plunkett, Lord Dunsany
[1878–   ]

[l] We shall be with you in your distant time,
Shall lean towards you across many a year,
Shall bring you courage with a way-worn rhyme:
We were not wholly here.
    To Those That Come After. Stanza 3

Will Durant
[1885–   ]

[m] A statesman cannot afford to be a moralist.
    What is Civilization?

[n] Civilization exists by geologi-cal consent, subject to change without notice.   *Ibid.*

[o] The finger that turns the dial rules the air.   *Ibid.*

[p] The health of nations is more important than the wealth of nations.   *Ibid.*

John Sullivan Dwight
[1813–1893]

[q] Rest is not quitting
The busy career,
Rest is the fitting
Of self to its sphere.

'Tis the brook's motion,
Clear without strife,
Fleeing to ocean
After its life.
    Rest. Stanzas 4 and 5

[r] Work, and thou wilt bless the day
Ere the toil be done;
They that work not, can not pray,
Can not feel the sun.   *Working*

Edward Dyer
[*Circa* 1540–1607]

[s] My mind to me a kingdom is;
Such present joys therein I find,
That it excels all other bliss
That earth affords or grows by kind   *MS. Rawl. 85, P. 17*

John Dyer
[*Floruit* 1714]

[t] While wine and friendship crown the board,
We'll sing the joys that both afford;
And he that won't with us comply,
Down among the dead men let him lie.   *Down Among the Dead Men. Stanza 3*

Max Eastman
[1883–   ]

[u] I don't know why it is we are in such a hurry to get up when we fall down. You might think we would lie there and rest a while.
    The Enjoyment of Laughter. Part III, Chap. 4

[v] Modernity is a poor thing to feel priggish about. . . . No man can keep up with the times for more than seventy years, and after that his frantic efforts to do so look silly forever.
    Ibid. Part V, Chap. 4

Arthur Wentworth Hamilton Eaton
[1859–1937]

[w] His heart was breaking, breaking,
'Neath loads of care and wrong;
Who blames the man for taking
What life denied so long?
    The Suicide. Stanza 1

Sir Arthur Stanley Eddington
[1882–1944]

[x] It is one thing for the human mind to extract from the phenomena of nature the laws which it has itself put into them; it may be a far harder thing to extract laws over which it has no control. It is even possible that laws which have not their origin in the mind may be irrational, and we can never succeed in formulating them.
Space, Time, and Gravitation

(Robert) Anthony Eden
[1897–   ]

[y] Every succeeding scientific discovery makes greater nonsense of old-time conceptions of sovereignty. *House of Commons* [*November 22, 1945*]

Mary Baker Eddy
[1821–1910]

[z] The prayer that reforms the sinner and heals the sick is an absolute faith that all things are possible to God,—a spiritual understanding of Him, an unselfed love.
Science and Health with Key to the Scriptures. Page 1

[a] The basis of all health, sinlessness, and immortality is the great fact that God is the only Mind; and this Mind must be not merely believed, but it must be understood. *Ibid.*

[b] Divine Love always has met and always will meet every human need. *Ibid. Page 494*

[c] How would you define Christian Science?
As the law of God, the law of good, interpreting and demonstrating the divine Principle and rule of universal harmony.
Rudimental Divine Science. Page 1

[d] Blest Christmas morn, though murky clouds
Pursue thy way,
Thy light was born where storm enshrouds
Nor dawn nor day!
Christmas Morn. Stanza 1

[e] O'er waiting harp-strings of the mind
There sweeps a strain,
Low, sad, and sweet, whose measures bind
The pow'r of pain.
O'er Waiting Harp-strings of the Mind. Stanza 1

Edwin Francis Edgett
[1867–1946]

[f] He may have a message
For the world,
But he is welcome
To no editorial haunts
If he rolls his manuscript.
The Manuscript Roller

Irwin Edman
[1896–   ]

[g] Whene'er with wild elation
Tremblingly I smite the lyre,
Comes the swift and kind damnation:
"He's a clever versifier."
The Curse of Faint Praise

[h] Whichever way I turn the dial,
Somebody's asking someone something,
Somebody's learning is on trial,
Someone is being proved a dumb thing.
Intermission, Please! Stanza 3

Amanda M. Edmond
[1824–1862]

[i] There are rich and proud men there, mother,
With wondrous wealth to view,
And the bread they fling to their dogs to-night
Would give life to me and you.
Give Me Three Grains of Corn. Stanza 6

Jonathan Edwards
[1703–1758]

[j] Resolved, never to do anything which I should be afraid to do if it were the last hour of my life. *Seventy Resolutions*

[k] I assert that nothing ever comes to pass without a cause.
The Freedom of the Will

[l] This dictate of common sense. *Ibid.*

John Edwin
[1749–1790]

[m] A man's ingress into the world is naked and bare,
His progress through the world is trouble and care;
And lastly, his egress out of the world, is nobody knows where.
If we do well here, we shall do well there:
I can tell you no more if I preach a whole year.
The Eccentricities of John Edwin [second edition, London, 1791]. Vol. I, Page 74

Albert Einstein
[1879-   ]

[n] Some recent work by E. Fermi and L. Szilard, which has been communicated to me in manuscript, leads me to expect that the element uranium may be turned into a new and important source of energy in the immediate future.
Letter to Franklin D. Roosevelt
[August 2, 1939]

[o] Since I do not foresee that atomic energy is to be a great boon for a long time, I have to say that for the present it is a menace. Perhaps it is well that it should be. It may intimidate the human race into bringing order into its international affairs, which, without the pressure of fear, it would not do.
Einstein on the Atomic Bomb. Atlantic Monthly, November 1945

Dwight David Eisenhower
[1890-   ]

[p] Abilene, Kansas, and Denison, Texas, would together add in size to possibly one-five-hundredth part of Greater London. Yet kinship among nations is not determined in such measurements as proximity, size, and age. Rather we should turn to those inner things, call them what you will—I mean those intangibles that are the real treasures free men possess.
Address at Guildhall on the occasion of his receiving the Freedom of the City of London [July 12, 1945]

[q] As long as there are sovereign nations possessing great power, war is inevitable.   *Ibid.*

[r] Neither London nor Abilene, sisters under the skin, will sell her birthright for physical safety, her liberty for mere existence.   *Ibid.*

Charles William Eliot
[1834-1926]

[s] Carrier of news and knowledge
Instrument of trade and commerce
Promoter of mutual acquaintance
Among men and nations and hence
Of peace and good will.

Carrier of love and sympathy
Messenger of friendship
Consoler of the lonely
Servant of the scattered family
Enlarger of the public life.
Inscriptions for the East and West Pavilions, Post Office, Washington, D.C.

(These inscriptions were edited by Woodrow Wilson, to read:
Carrier of news and knowledge
Instrument of trade and
Promoter of mutual acquaintance
Of peace and good will
Among men and nations.

Messenger of sympathy and love
Servant of parted friends
Consoler of the lonely
Bond of the scattered family
Enlarger of the common life.)

"George Eliot"
(Marian Evans Cross)
[1819-1880]

[t] 'Tis God gives skill,
But not without men's hands: He could not make
Antonio Stradivari's violins
Without Antonio.   *Stradivarius*

[u] Boots and shoes are the greatest trouble of my life. Everything else one can turn and turn about, and make old look like new; but there's no coaxing boots and shoes to look better than they are.   *Amos Barton. Chap. 2*

[v] It's no trifle at her time of life to part with a doctor who knows her constitution.
Janet's Repentance. Chap. 3

[w] He was like a cock who thought the sun had risen to hear him crow.   *Adam Bede. Chap. 33*

[x] I've never any pity for conceited people, because I think they carry their comfort about with them.   *The Mill on the Floss. Book V, Chap. 4*

[y] Below their names it was written: "In their death they were not divided."
Ibid. Last line of book

[z] Blessed is the man who, having nothing to say, abstains from giving in words evidence of the fact.   *Impressions of Theophrastus Such*

[a] Life is too precious to be spent in this weaving and unweaving of false impressions, and it is better to live quietly under some degree of misrepresentation than to attempt to remove it by the uncertain process of letter-writing.
Life and Letters. Letter to Mrs. Peter Taylor [June 8, 1856]

Thomas Stearns Eliot
[1888-   ]

[b] April is the cruelest month, breeding
Lilacs out of dead land, mixing
Memory and desire, stirring
Dull roots with spring rain.
The Waste Land

[c] When lovely woman stoops to folly and
Paces about her room again, alone,
She smooths her hair with automatic hand,
And puts a record on the gramophone.   *Ibid.*

[d] We are the hollow men
We are the stuffed men
Leaning together
Headpiece filled with straw. Alas!
Our dried voices, when
We whisper together
Are quiet and meaningless
As wind in dry grass
Or rats' feet over broken glass
In our dry cellar.
        The Hollow Men. I

[e] This is the way the world ends
Not with a bang but a whimper.
        Ibid. V

[f] Where is the Life we have lost in living?
Where is the wisdom we have lost in knowledge?
Where is the knowledge we have lost in information?
The cycles of Heaven in twenty centuries
Bring us farther from God and nearer to the Dust.   *The Rock*

[g] Uncorseted, her friendly bust
Gives promise of pneumatic bliss.
        Whispers of Immortality

[h] The evening is spread out against the sky
Like a patient etherized upon a table.   *The Love Song of J. Alfred Prufrock*

[i] But though I have wept and fasted, wept and prayed,
Though I have seen my head (grown slightly bald) brought in upon a platter,
I am no prophet—and here's no great matter;
I have seen the moment of my greatness flicker,
And I have seen the eternal Footman hold my coat, and snicker,
And in short, I was afraid.   *Ibid.*

[j] I grow old. . . . I grow old.

I shall wear the bottoms of my trousers rolled.   *Ibid.*

[k] The broad-backed hippopotamus
Rests on his belly in the mud;
Although he seems so firm to us
He is merely flesh and blood.
        The Hippopotamus

[l] We have been, let us say, to hear the latest Pole
Transmit the Preludes, through his hair and finger-tips.
        Portrait of a Lady. I

[m] I am aware of the damp souls of housemaids
Sprouting despondently at area gates. *Morning at the Window*

[n] The last temptation is the greatest treason:
To do the right deed for the wrong reason.   *Murder in the Cathedral. Part I*

[o] Poetry is not a turning loose of emotion, but an escape from emotion.   *Tradition and the Individual Talent*

[p] Human kind
Cannot bear very much reality.
        Four Quartets: Burnt Norton [1943]

[q] What the dead had no speech for, when living,
They can tell you, being dead: the communication
Of the dead is tongued with fire beyond the language of the living. *Ibid. The Dry Salvages*

Elizabeth, Queen of England
[1533–1603]

[r] The use of the sea and air is common to all; neither can a title to the ocean belong to any people or private persons, forasmuch as neither nature nor public use and custom permit any possession thereof.   *To the Spanish Ambassador [1580]*

[s] My care is like my shadow in the sun—
Follows me flying—flies when I pursue it.   *On the Departure of Alençon [1582]*

[t] Monarchs ought to put to death the authors and instigators of war, as their sworn enemies and as dangers to their states.
        To Fénélon

[u] I am no lover of pompous title, but only desire that my name may be recorded in a line or two, which shall briefly express my name, my virginity, the years of my reign, the reformation of religion under it, and my preservation of peace.   *To her ladies, discussing her epitaph*

Ebenezer Elliott
[1781–1849]

[v] When wilt Thou save the people?
O God of mercy, when?
Not kings and lords, but nations!
Not thrones and crowns, but men!
Flowers of Thy heart, O God are they;
Let them not pass, like weeds, away—
God save the people!
        Corn Law Rhymes. When Wilt Thou Save the People?, Stanza 1

Havelock Ellis
[1859–1939]

[**w**] To be a leader of men one must turn one's back on men.
Introduction to J. K. Huysmans' Against the Grain

[**x**] God is an Unutterable Sigh in the Human Heart, said the old German mystic.
Impressions and Comments

[**y**] Without an element of the obscene there can be no true and deep aesthetic or moral conception of life. . . . It is only the great men who are truly obscene. If they had not dared to be obscene they could never have dared to be great.
Ibid.

[**z**] The omnipresent process of sex, as it is woven into the whole texture of our man's or woman's body, is the pattern of all the process of our life.
The New Spirit

[**a**] "Charm"—which means the power to effect work without employing brute force—is indispensable to women. Charm is a woman's strength just as strength is a man's charm.
The Task of Social Hygiene. Chap. 3

[**b**] The larger our great cities grow, the more irresistible becomes the attraction which they exert on the children of the country, who are fascinated by them, as the birds are fascinated by the lighthouse or the moths by the candle.
Chap. 5

[**c**] An urban life saps that calm and stolid strength which is necessary for all great effort and stress, physical or intellectual.
Ibid.

[**d**] The German feels nothing of that sensitive jealousy with which the French seek to guard private life and the rights of the individual.
Ibid. Chap. 9

[**e**] Holland is one of the traditional lands of freedom; it was the home of independent intellect, of free religion, of autonomous morals, when every other country in Europe was closed to these manifestations of the spirit.
Ibid.

[**f**] When Charles V retired in weariness from the greatest throne in the world to the solitude of the monastery at Yuste, he occupied his leisure for some weeks in trying to regulate two clocks. It proved very difficult. One day, it is recorded, he turned to his assistant and said: "To think that I attempted to force the reason and conscience of thousands of men into one mould, and I cannot make two clocks agree!"
Ibid.

[**g**] Conquest brings self-conceit and intolerance, the reckless inflation and dissipation of energies. Defeat brings prudence and concentration; it ennobles and fortifies.
Ibid. Chap. 10

[**h**] A nation's art-products and its scientific activities are not mere national property; they are international possessions, for the joy and service of the whole world. The nations hold them in trust for humanity.
Ibid.

[**i**] The family only represents one aspect, however important an aspect, of a human being's functions and activities. . . . A life is beautiful and ideal, or the reverse, only when we have taken into our consideration the social as well as the family relationship.
Little Essays of Love and Virtue. Chap. 1

[**j**] That indeed were a world fit to perish, wherein the moralist had set up the ignoble maxim: Safety first.
Ibid. Chap. 2

[**k**] The by-product is sometimes more valuable than the product.
Ibid. Chap. 3

[**l**] The greatest task before civilization at present is to make machines what they ought to be, the slaves, instead of the masters of men.
Ibid. Chap. 7

[**m**] The art of dancing stands at the source of all the arts that express themselves first in the human person. The art of building, or architecture, is the beginning of all the arts that lie outside the person; and in the end they unite. . . .
Dancing is the loftiest, the most moving, the most beautiful of the arts, because it is no mere translation or abstraction from life; it is life itself.
The Dance of Life. Chap. 2

[**n**] The place where optimism most flourishes is the lunatic asylum.
Ibid. Chap. 3

[**o**] Thinking in its lower grades is comparable to paper money, and in its higher forms it is a kind of poetry.
Ibid.

[**p**] If at some period in the course of civilization we seriously find that our science and our religion are antagonistic, then there must be something wrong either with our science or with our religion.
Ibid. Chap. 5

[**q**] A man must not swallow more beliefs than he can digest.
Ibid.

[r] The Promised Land always lies on the other side of a wilderness.   *Ibid.*

[s] What we call "morals" is simply blind obedience to words of command.   *Ibid. Chap. 6*

[t] The prevalence of suicide, without doubt, is a test of height in civilization; it means that the population is winding up its nervous and intellectual system to the utmost point of tension and that sometimes it snaps. *Ibid. Chap. 7*

[u] The more rapidly a civilization progresses, the sooner it dies for another to arise in its place.   *Ibid.*

[v] The sun and the moon and the stars would have disappeared long ago . . . had they happened to be within the reach of predatory human hands.   *Ibid.*

[w] Had there been a Lunatic Asylum in the suburbs of Jerusalem, Jesus Christ would infallibly have been shut up in it at the outset of his public career. That interview with Satan on a pinnacle of the Temple would alone have damned him, and everything that happened after could but have confirmed the diagnosis. The whole religious complexion of the modern world is due to the absence from Jerusalem of a Lunatic Asylum.
          Impressions and Comments.
          Series III

Henry Ellis
[1777–1869]

[x] To make a mountain of a mole-hill.   *Original Letters.*
          Second Series, Page 312

Ralph Waldo Emerson
[1803–1882]

[y] Nor knowest thou what argument
Thy life to thy neighbor's creed has lent.
All are needed by each one;
Nothing is fair or good alone.
          Each and All. Stanza 1

[z] I wiped away the weeds and foam,
I fetched my sea-born treasures home;
But the poor, unsightly, noisome things
Had left their beauty on the shore,
With the sun and the sand and the wild uproar.
          Ibid. Stanza 3

[a] He builded better than he knew;—
The conscious stone to beauty grew. *The Problem. Stanza 2*

[b]   Enclosed
In a tumultuous privacy of storm.
          The Snow-Storm

[c] Life is too short to waste
In critic peep or cynic bark,
Quarrel or reprimand:
'Twill soon be dark.   *To J. W.*

[d] But in the mud and scum of things
There alway, alway something sings.   *Fragments*

[e] If eyes were made for seeing,
Then Beauty is its own excuse for being.   *The Rhodora*

[f] Heartily know,
When half-gods go,
The gods arrive.
          Give All to Love. Stanza 4

[g] Love not the flower they pluck, and know it not,
And all their botany is Latin names.   *Blight*

[h] By the rude bridge that arched the flood,
  Their flag to April's breeze unfurled,
Here once the embattled farmers stood,
  And fired the shot heard round the world.
          Hymn sung at the Completion of the Battle Monument, Concord [April 19, 1836]. Stanza 1

[i] God said, I am tired of kings,
I suffer them no more.
          Boston Hymn [January 1, 1863].
          Stanza 1

[j] So nigh is grandeur to our dust,
  So near is God to man,
When Duty whispers low, *Thou must,*
  The youth replies, *I can.*
          Voluntaries. III

[k] Fear not, then, thou child infirm,
There's no god dare wrong a worm.
          Compensation. I

[l] He thought it happier to be dead,
To die for Beauty, than live for bread.   *Beauty*

[m] Damsels of Time, the hypocritic Days,
Muffled and dumb like Barefoot dervishes,
And marching single in an endless file,
Bring diadems and fagots in their hands.   *Days*

[n] Go where he will, the wise man is at home,
His hearth the earth,—his hall the azure dome.
          Wood-Notes. I, 3

[o] That book is good
Which puts me in a working mood.

Unless to Thought is added Will,
Apollo is an imbecile.   *The Poet*

[p] In the vaunted works of Art
The master-stroke is Nature's
part.   *Art*

[q] The music that can deepest
reach,
And cure all ill, is cordial speech.
                        Merlin's Wisdom

[r] A day for toil, an hour for
sport,
But for a friend is life too short.
                                  Ibid.

[s] Time dissipates to shining
ether the solid angularity of facts.
                                History

[t] There is properly no History;
only Biography.   *Ibid.*

[u] To be great is to be misunderstood.   *Self-Reliance*

[v] An institution is the lengthened shadow of one man.   *Ibid.*

[w] Nothing can bring you peace
but yourself.   *Ibid.*

[x] Everything in Nature contains all the powers of Nature.
Everything is made of one hidden
stuff.   *Compensation*

[y] It is as impossible for a man
to be cheated by any one but himself, as for a thing to be, and not
to be, at the same time.   *Ibid.*

[z] All mankind love a lover.
                                   Love

[a] No man ever forgot the visitations of that power to his heart
and brain, which created all
things new; which was the dawn
in him of music, poetry, and art.
                                  Ibid.

[b] A friend is a person with
whom I may be sincere. Before
him, I may think aloud. . . .
   A friend may well be reckoned
the masterpiece of Nature.
                            Friendship

[c] Two may talk and one may
hear, but three cannot take part
in a conversation of the most sincere and searching sort.   *Ibid.*

[d] I do then with my friends as
I do with my books. I would have
them where I can find them, but
I seldom use them.   *Ibid.*

[e] In skating over thin ice our
safety is our speed.   *Prudence*

[f] Heroism feels and never reasons and therefore is always right.
                                Heroism

[g] Nothing great was ever
achieved without enthusiasm.
                                 Circles

[h] Nothing astonishes men so
much as common sense and plain
dealing.   *Art*

[i] The only gift is a portion of
thyself.   *Gifts*

[j] The less government we have,
the better—the fewer laws, and
the less confided power. *Politics*

[k] Money, which represents the
prose of life, and which is hardly
spoken of in parlors without an
apology, is, in its effects and laws,
as beautiful as roses.
                    Nominalist and Realist

[l] He is great who is what he is
from Nature, and who never re-
minds us of others.
                        *Representative Men.
                        Uses of Great Men*

[m] Every hero becomes a bore
at last.   *Ibid.*

[n] [Napoleon] directed Bourrienne to leave all his letters un-
opened for three weeks, and then
observed with satisfaction how
large a part of the correspondence
had thus disposed of itself, and no
longer required an answer.
                  *Ibid. Napoleon; or,
                  The Man of the World*

[o] I find the Englishman to be
him of all men who stands firmest
in his shoes.
                  English Traits. Manners

[p'] Coal is a portable climate.
                  Conduct of Life. Wealth

[q'] The world is his, who has
money to go over it.   *Ibid.*

[r'] The farmer is covetous of his
dollar, and with reason. . . . He
knows how many strokes of labor
it represents. His bones ache with
the day's work that earned it.
                                  Ibid.

[s'] Art is a jealous mistress, and,
if a man have a genius for painting, poetry, music, architecture, or
philosophy, he makes a bad husband, and an ill-provider.   *Ibid.*

[t'] One of the benefits of a college education is to show the boy
its little avail.   *Ibid. Culture*

[u'] There is always a best way of
doing everything, if it be to boil
an egg. Manners are the happy
ways of doing things.
                          Ibid. Behavior

[v'] The highest compact we can
make with our fellow is,—"Let
there be truth between us two
forevermore."   *Ibid.*

[w'] It is sublime to feel and say
of another, I need never meet, or
speak, or write to him: we need
not reinforce ourselves, or send
tokens of remembrance: I rely on
him as on myself: if he did thus
or thus, I know it was right.
                                  Ibid.

[x'] We must be as courteous to a
man as we are to a picture, which

we are willing to give the advantage of a good light.   *Ibid.*

[y] There is one topic peremptorily forbidden to all wellbred, to all rational mortals, namely, their distempers. If you have not slept, or if you have slept, or if you have headache, or sciatica, or leprosy, or thunderstroke, I beseech you, by all angels, to hold your peace.   *Ibid.*

[z] Beauty without grace is the hook without the bait.
     Ibid. Beauty

[a] Never read any book that is not a year old.
     Ibid. In Praise of Books

[b] God may forgive sins, he said, but awkwardness has no forgiveness in heaven or earth.
     Society and Solitude

[c] The most advanced nations are always those who navigate the most.   *Ibid. Civilization*

[d] Hitch your wagon to a star.
     Ibid.

[e] The true test of civilization is, not the census, nor the size of cities, nor the crops—no, but the kind of man the country turns out.   *Ibid.*

[f] Raphael paints wisdom; Handel sings it, Phidias carves it, Shakespeare writes it, Wren builds it, Columbus sails it, Luther preaches it, Washington arms it, Watt mechanizes it.   *Ibid. Art*

[g] Every genuine work of art has as much reason for being as the earth and the sun.   *Ibid.*

[h] We boil at different degrees.
     Ibid. Eloquence

[i] We have the newspaper, which does its best to make every square acre of land and sea give an account of itself at your breakfast-table.
     Ibid. Works and Days

[j] Can anybody remember when the times were not hard and money not scarce?   *Ibid.*

[k] A man builds a fine house; and now he has a master, and a task for life; he is to furnish, watch, show it, and keep it in repair the rest of his days.   *Ibid.*

[l] We do not count a man's years until he has nothing else to count.
     Ibid. Old Age

[m] I have heard with admiring submission the experience of the lady who declared that the sense of being well-dressed gives a feeling of inward tranquillity which religion is powerless to bestow.
     *Letters and Social Aims.
     Social Aims*

[n] Abraham Lincoln . . . who was at home and welcome with the humblest, and with a spirit and a practical vein in the times of terror that commanded the admiration of the wisest. His heart was as great as the world, but there was no room in it to hold the memory of a wrong.
     Greatness

[o] Next to the originator of a good sentence is the first quoter of it.   *Quotation and Originality*

[p] A good poem goes about the world offering itself to reasonable men, who read it with joy and carry it to their reasonable neighbors.   *Morals*

[q] Wit makes its own welcome, and levels all distinctions.
     The Comic

[r] The perception of the comic is a tie of sympathy with other men.
     Ibid.

[s] What is a weed? A plant whose virtues have not yet been discovered.
     Fortune of the Republic

[t] Great men are they who see that spiritual is stronger than any material force; that thoughts rule the world.
     *Progress of Culture, Phi Beta
     Kappa Address [July 18, 1867]*

[u] Four snakes gliding up and down a hollow for no purpose that I could see—not to eat, not for love, but only gliding.
     Journal, April 11, 1834

[v] I hate quotations. Tell me what you know.   *Ibid. May 1849*

[w] I trust a good deal to common fame, as we all must. If a man has good corn, or wood, or boards, or pigs to sell, or can make better chairs or knives, crucibles or church organs than anybody else, you will find a broad, hardbeaten road to his house, though it be in the woods.   *Ibid. 1855*

Gilbert Emery
[1875–1945]

[x] They're a poor lot, the men, all of 'em, and dirty, too—but the thing is, darlin', to get one that cleans easy.   *Tarnish. Act III*

Daniel Decatur Emmet
[1815–1904]

[y'] In Dixie land, I'll took my stand,
To lib an' die in Dixie,
     Away, away,
Away down South in Dixie.
     *I Wish I Was in Dixie's Land
     [1859]*

Friedrich Engels
[1820–1895]

[z] By bourgeoisie is meant the class of modern capitalists, owners of the means of social production and employers of wage-labor. By proletariat, the class of modern wage-laborers who, having no means of production of their own, are reduced to selling their labor-power in order to live.
Footnote to Manifesto of the Communist Party. Part I, Bourgeois and Proletarians

George Allan England
[1877–1936]

[a] He yawned, and laid his cigaret aside,
And on the baggage-check, grimly stamped "Body," wrote
Two simple words. Scrawled words, with careless fingers. Just a note
Of this poor shipment's worthlessness.
She who had died,
Two days before, was sunshine, joy, and life.
To all of us. . . . .
"No Value!" And the world had ceased to turn:
And all the gold from here to Babylon might burn
To dross, unminded, for we bore our dead.   *"No Value"*

Paul Engle
[1908–   ]

[b] Wytham, Water Eaton, Wolvercote,
Old names worn water-smooth under the tongue.   *Corn*

[c] The tense American nerve relaxed, I lived
With a gray quietness that let the mind
Grow inward like a root.
          [At Oxford] Ibid.

[d] I heard, down the long valley of my bones,
The cry of home run like a calling hound . . .
Belly and brain, I lived America.   *Ibid.*

Thomas Dunn English
[1819–1902]

[e] Don't you remember sweet Alice, Ben Bolt?
Sweet Alice, whose hair was so brown;
Who wept with delight when you gave her a smile,
And trembled with fear at your frown!   *Ben Bolt*

[First published in *The New York Mirror*, Sept. 2, 1843. It was set to music, an adaptation of an old German melody, by Nelson Kneass, and sung in a play, *The Battle of Buena Vista*. In 1894, George Du Maurier used the song in his novel, *Trilby*, and it became popular at once.]

[f] Though little dangers they may fear,
When greater dangers men environ
Then women show a front of iron;
And, gentle in their manner, they
Do bold things in a quiet way.
          Betty Zane. Stanza 1

Quintus Ennius
[239–169 B.C.]

[g] No sooner said than done—so acts your man of worth.
          Annals. Book 9 (Quoted by Priscianus)

[h] I never indulge in poetics
Unless I am down with rheumatics.   *Fragment of a Satire (Quoted by Priscianus)*

Epictetus
[Circa A.D. 60]

Translation [1865] by Thomas Wentworth Higginson, based on that [1758] of Elizabeth Carter

[i] When you have shut your doors, and darkened your room, remember never to say that you are alone, for you are not alone; but God is within, and your genius is within,—and what need have they of light to see what you are doing?   *Discourses. Chap. 14*

[j] No great thing is created suddenly, any more than a bunch of grapes or a fig. If you tell me that you desire a fig, I answer you that there must be time. Let it first blossom, then bear fruit, then ripen.   *Ibid. Chap. 15*

[k] Why, then, do you walk as if you had swallowed a ramrod?
          Ibid. Chap. 21

[l] Difficulties are things that show what men are.
          Ibid. Chap. 24

[m] Appearances to the mind are of four kinds. Things either are what they appear to be; or they neither are, nor appear to be; or they are, and do not appear to be; or they are not, and yet appear to be. Rightly to aim in all these cases is the wise man's task.
          Ibid. Chap. 27

[n] What is the first business of one who studies philosophy? To part with self-conceit. For it is

impossible for any one to begin to learn what he thinks that he already knows.

How to Apply General Principles to Particular Cases. 17

[o] Every habit and faculty is preserved and increased by correspondent actions,—as the habit of walking, by walking; or running, by running.

How the Semblances of Things Are to Be Combated. 18

[p] Whatever you would make habitual, practise it; and if you would not make a thing habitual, do not practise it, but habituate yourself to something else.

Ibid.

[q] Reckon the days in which you have not been angry. I used to be angry every day; now every other day; then every third and fourth day; and if you miss it so long as thirty days, offer a sacrifice of thanksgiving to God.   *Ibid.*

[r] And if any is unhappy, remember that he is for himself; for God made all men to enjoy felicity and peace.

That We Ought Not to Be Affected by Things Not in Our Own Power. 24

Desiderius Erasmus
[1465–1536]

[s] No one is injured save by himself.   *Adages*

John Erskine
[1879–1951]

[t] The Moral Obligation to Be Intelligent.   *Title of book*

[u] The body travels more easily than the mind, and until we have limbered up our imagination we continue to think as though we had stayed home. We have not really budged a step until we take up residence in someone else's point of view.   *The Complete Life. Chap. 8. Foreigners*

Euclid
[*Circa* 300 B.C.]

[v] There is no royal road to geometry.

Quoted by Proclus: Commentaria in Euclidem. Book 2, Chap. 4

[Ptolemy I, King of Egypt, wished to study geometry, without going over the thirteen parts of Euclid's *Elements*. He said that a short-cut would be agreeable, whereupon Euclid answered. Often misquoted as "no royal road to learning."]

Euripides
[484–406 B.C.]

[w] I care for riches, to make gifts
To friends, or lead a sick man back to health
With ease and plenty. Else small aid is wealth
For daily gladness; once a man be done
With hunger, rich and poor are all as one.   *Electra. (tr. Sir Gilbert Murray) Line 539*

[x] Danger gleams
Like sunshine to a brave man's eyes.   *Iphigenia in Tauris. (tr. Sir Gilbert Murray) Line 115*

[y] How oft the darkest hour of ill
Breaks brightest into dawn.
          Ibid. Line 723

(*The following translations by Morris Hickey Morgan*)

[z] Old men's prayers for death are lying prayers, in which they abuse old age and long extent of life. But when death draws near, not one is willing to die, and age no longer is a burden to them.
          Alcestis. Line 669

[a] A bad beginning makes a bad ending.   *Aeolus. Fragment 32*

[b] Time will explain it all. He is a talker, and needs no questioning before he speaks.
          Ibid. Fragment 38

[c] Woman is woman's natural ally.   *Alope. Fragment 109*

[d] Man's best possession is a sympathetic wife.
          Antigone. Fragment 164

[e] Toil, says the proverb, is the sire of fame.
          Licymnius. Fragment 477

[f] Cowards do not count in battle; they are there, but not in it.   *Meleager. Fragment 523*

[g] A woman should be good for everything at home, but abroad good for nothing.
          Ibid. Fragment 525

[h] Where two discourse, if the one's anger rise,
The man who lets the contest fall is wise.
          Protesilaus. Fragment 656

[i] When good men die their goodness does not perish,
But lives though they are gone. As for the bad,
All that was theirs dies and is buried with them.
          Temenidae. Fragment 734

[j] Who knows but life be that which men call death,
And death what men call life?
          Phrixus. Fragment 830

[k] Whoso neglects learning in his youth, loses the past and is dead for the future.
Ibid. Fragment 927

[l] The gods visit the sins of the fathers upon the children.
Ibid. Fragment 970

[m] Those whom God wishes to destroy, he first deprives of their senses. *Fragment, Greek Iambic*

Laurence Eusden
[1688–1730]

[n] A woman's work, grave sirs, is never done.
*At a Cambridge Commencement
[second edition, 1714]*

Anthony Euwer
[1877–   ]

[o] As a beauty I'm not a great star.
Others are handsomer far;
But my face—I don't mind it
Because I'm behind it;
It's the folks out in front that I jar. *Limerick [Often quoted by Woodrow Wilson]*

Abbie Huston Evans

[p] He carries deathlessness about his person
As others carry money, left and right
Conferring it, on a woman, on a weed. *The Poet*

[q] Hay-barn or planet—does it signify?
An ancient inmost frame gone down the wind,
Become a puff of smoke; given back; at one . . .
Annihilation getting in its work
At top-speed, unmasked, is no sight for children.
The Passing of the Hay Barn

William Maxwell Evarts
[1818–1901]

[r] The pious ones of Plymouth, who, reaching the Rock, first fell upon their own knees and then upon the aborigines.
Quoted by Henry Watterson in The Louisville Courier-Journal [July 4, 1913]

David Everett
[1770–1813]

[s] You'd scarce expect one of my age
To speak in public on the stage;
And if I chance to fall below
Demosthenes or Cicero,
Don't view me with a critic's eye,
But pass my imperfections by.
Large streams from little fountains flow,
Tall oaks from little acorns grow.
Lines written for a school declamation for Ephraim H. Farrar, aged seven, New Ipswich, New Hampshire [1791]

Edward Everett
[1794–1865]

[t] As a work of art, I know few things more pleasing to the eye, or more capable of affording scope and gratification to a taste for the beautiful, than a well-situated, well-cultivated farm.
Address at Buffalo, New York [October 9, 1857]

[u] When I contemplate the extent to which the moral sentiments, the intelligence, the affections of so many millions of people,—sealed up by a sacred charm within the cover of a letter,—daily circulate through a country, I am compelled to regard the Post-office, next to Christianity, as the right arm of our modern civilization.
Mount Vernon Papers. No. 27

Joseph Warren Fabens
[1821–1875]

[v] But I've never known a sorrow
That could with that compare,
When off the blue Canaries
I smoked my last cigar.
My Last Cigar. Stanza 4

Frederick William Faber
[1814–1863]

[w] The sea, unmated creature, tired and lone,
Makes on its desolate sands, eternal moan.
The Sorrowful World

[x] Hark! Hark! my soul, angelic songs are swelling
O'er earth's green fields, and ocean's wave-beat shore;
How sweet the truth those blessed strains are telling
Of that new life when sin shall be no more!
Pilgrims of the Night

Georgius Fabricius
[1516–1571]

[y] Death comes to all
But great achievements raise a monument
Which shall endure until the sun grows cold.
In Praise of Georgius Agricola [1494–1555]. Quoted by Her-

bert Clark Hoover and Lou Henry Hoover in their transla- tion of Agricola's De Re Metal- lica, Page XXIV

Clifton Fadiman
[1904–   ]

[z] Ennui, felt on the proper oc- casions, is a sign of intelligence.
Reading I've Liked

Charles B. Fairbanks
("Aguecheek")
[1827–1859]

[a] I have a profound respect for the sea as a moral teacher. No man can be tossed about upon it with- out feeling his impotence and in- significance.
My Unknown Chum. A Passage Across the Atlantic

[b] Cleanliness is a great virtue; but when it is carried to such an extent that you cannot find your books and papers which you left carefully arranged on your table— when it gets to be a monomania with man or woman—it becomes a bore.
Ibid. Antwerp and Brussels

[c] The genuine human boy may, I think, safely be set down as the noblest work of God. . . . There is a generous instinct in boys which is far more trustworthy than those sliding, and unreliable, and de- ceptive ideas which we call settled principles.
Ibid. Boyhood and Boys

[d] The sewing-circle—the Prot- estant confessional, where each one confesses, not her own sins, but the sins of her neighbors.
Ibid. Memorials of Mrs. Grundy

"Michael Fairless"
(Margaret Fairless Barber)
[1869–1901]

[e] The people who make no roads are ruled out from intelli- gent participation in the world's brotherhood.
The Roadmender. I, 5

Francis E. Falkenbury

[f] As I came down to South Street by the soft sea-water, I saw long ships, their mast-heads ever bowing:
Sweet slender maids in clinging gowns of golden,
Curtseying stately in a fashion olden,
Bowing sweetly—each a king's fair daughter—

To me, their millionth, millionth lover,
I, the seventh son of the old sea- rover,
As I came down to South Street by the myriad moving water.
South Street

Hans Fallada
[1893–1947]

[g] Little Man, What Now?
Title of novel on Germany, post World War I

Catherine Maria Fanshawe
[1765–1834]

[h] 'Twas whisper'd in heaven, 'twas mutter'd in hell,
And echo caught faintly the sound as it fell;
On the confines of earth 'twas per- mitted to rest,
And the depths of the ocean its presence confess'd.
Enigma: The Letter H

George Farquhar
[1678–1707]

[i] Like hungry guests, a sitting audience looks.
The Inconstant. Prologue

[j]   The prologue is the grace,
Each act, a course, each scene, a different dish.   *Ibid.*

David Glasgow Farragut
[1801–1870]

[k] Damn the torpedoes! Go ahead!
At Mobile Bay [August 5, 1864]

Edgar Fawcett
[1847–1904]

[l] She remembers so many graves
That no one else will remember.
The Grass. Stanza 3

[m] In some blithe moment, was it Nature's choice
To dower a scrap of sunset with a voice?   *To an Oriole*

Mark Fenderson
[1873–1944]

[n] What's the use? Yesterday an egg, to-morrow a feather duster.
Caption of Cartoon, The Dejected Rooster

François de Salignac de la Mothe Fénelon
[1651–1715]

[o] That weary listlessness, which renders life unsupportable to the

voluptuous and the indolent, is unknown to those who can employ themselves by reading.
Telemachus. Book II

[p] Commerce is a kind of spring, which, diverted from its natural channel, ceases to flow.
Ibid. Book III

[q] There were some who said that a man at the point of death was more free than all others, because death breaks every bond, and over the dead the united world has no power.
Ibid. Book V

[r] By labor Wisdom gives poignancy to pleasure, and by pleasure she restores vigor to labor.
Ibid. Book VII

[s] Do not men die fast enough without being destroyed by each other? Can any man be insensible of the brevity of life? and can he who knows it, think life too long!
Ibid.

[t] The art of cookery is the art of poisoning mankind, by rendering the appetite still importunate, when the wants of nature are supplied.
Ibid. Book X

[u] To be always ready for war, said Mentor, is the surest way to avoid it.
Ibid.

[v] Some of the most dreadful mischiefs that afflict mankind proceed from wine; it is the cause of disease, quarrels, sedition, idleness, aversion to labour, and every species of domestic disorder.
Ibid.

[w] The number of diseases is a disgrace to mankind.
Ibid. Book XIII

Arthur Davison Ficke
[1883–1945]

[x] No man of elder years than fifty
Should be empowered with lands and gold.
It turns them shrewd and over-thrifty,
It makes them cruel and blind and cold.
Youth and Age. Stanza 1

[y] Old men in impotence can beget
New wars to kill the lusty young.
Young men can sing: old men forget
That any song was ever sung.
Ibid. Stanza 3

[z] Those great obscure momentous souls
Whom fame does not record,
Whose impulse still our fate controls
With deathless deed or word.

... the snivelling servant maid
With injured peevish look,
Who on the lagging fire-coals laid
Carlyle's long-labored book.

Men who perhaps down wells have thrown
Plays of Euripides.

Or sold some budding Shakespeare drink,
Or shut in cells some Blake,
Or forced some Shelley to death's brink
For true religion's sake.
Immortals in Exile. Stanzas 2, 4, 7, 8

[a] She stood as noble as a tower
Pure of impeachment as the sky,
As much an earth-bloom as the flower;
The slow winds flowed austerely by,
And she was of their harmony.
Naked Girl on Hilltop

Eugene Field
[1850–1895]

[b] He could whip his weight in wildcats.
Modjesky as Cameel. Stanza 10

[c] No matter what conditions
Dyspeptic come to feaze,
The best of all physicians
Is Apple-pie and cheese!
Apple-Pie and Cheese. Stanza 5

[d] I'm sure no human heart goes wrong
That's told "Good-by—God bless you!"
"Good-by—God Bless You!" Stanza 2

[e] I never lost a little fish—yes, I am free to say
It always was the biggest fish I caught that got away.
Our Biggest Fish. Stanza 2

[f] How gracious those dews of solace that over my senses fall
At the clink of the ice in the pitcher the boy brings up the hall!
The Clink of the Ice. Stanza 1

[g] When one's all right, he's prone to spite
The doctor's peaceful mission;
But when he's sick, it's loud and quick
He bawls for a physician.
Doctors. Stanza 2

[h] Have you ever heard of the Sugar-Plum Tree?
'Tis a marvel of great renown!
It blooms on the shore of the Lollipop sea
In the garden of Shut-Eye Town.
The Sugar-Plum Tree. Stanza 1

[i] I pray that, risen from the dead,
I may in glory stand—

A crown, perhaps, upon my head,
But a needle in my hand.
Grandma's Prayer. Stanza 1

[j] Wynken, Blynken, and Nod
  one night
Sailed off in a wooden shoe—
Sailed on a river of crystal light
  Into a sea of dew.   *Wynken,
  Blynken, and Nod. Stanza 1*

[k] The little toy dog is covered
  with dust,
But sturdy and stanch he
  stands;
And the little toy soldier is red
  with rust,
And his musket moulds in his
  hands;
Time was when the little toy dog
  was new,
And the soldier was passing fair;
And that was the time when our
  Little Boy Blue
  Kissed them and put them
  there.
    Little Boy Blue. Stanza 1

[l] The Rock-a-By Lady from
  Hushaby street
Comes stealing; comes creeping.
  The Rock-a-By Lady. Stanza 1

[m] Have you ever heard the
  wind go "Yooooo"?
'Tis a pitiful sound to hear!
It seems to chill you through and
  through
With a strange and speechless
  fear.
    The Night Wind. Stanza 1

[n] The gingham dog went
  "Bow-wow-wow!"
And the calico cat replied "Mee-
  ow!"
The air was littered, an hour or
  so,
With bits of gingham and calico.
    The Duel. Stanza 2

[o] Father calls me William, sister
  calls me Will,
Mother calls me Willie, but the
  fellers call me Bill!
  Jest 'Fore Christmas. Stanza 1

[p] 'Most all the time, the whole
  year round, there ain't no flies
  on me,
But jest 'fore Christmas I'm as
  good as I kin be!   *Ibid.*

[q] Mother tells me "Happy
  dreams!" and takes away the
  light,
An' leaves me lyin' all alone an'
  seein' things at night.
    Seein' Things. Stanza 1

[r] Be sure the salve of flattery
  soaps all you do and say;
Herein the only royal road to fame
  and fortune lies:
Put not your trust in vinegar—
  molasses catches flies!
    Uncle Eph. Stanza 4

Kate Field
[1838–1896]

[s] They talk about a woman's
  sphere as though it had a
  limit;
There's not a place in earth or
  heaven,
There's not a task to mankind
  given,
There's not a blessing or a woe,
There's not a whispered "yes" or
  "no,"
There's not a life, or death, or
  birth,
That has a feather's weight of
  worth
Without a woman in it.
    Woman's Sphere

"Michael Field"
(Katharine Bradley)
[1846–1914]
(Edith Cooper)
[1862–1913]

[t] The enchanting miracles of
change.   *Renewal*

[u] Praying and sighing through
  the London streets
While my heart beats
To do some miracle, when sud-
  denly
At curve of Regent Circus I espy,
Sit 'mid a jeweller's trays of
  spangleglitter,
A tiny metal insect-pin, a fly.
This utter trifle for my love I buy,
And thinking of it on her breast
My heart has rest.   *A Miracle*

[v] Quiet as a plough laid at the
  furrow's end.   *Old Age*

Rachel Field
[1894–1942]

[w] Doorbells are like a magic
  game,
Or the grab-bag at a fair—
You never know when you hear
  one ring
Who may be waiting there.
    Doorbells

Henry Fielding
[1707–1754]

[x] I am as sober as a judge.
    *Don Quixote in England.
    Act. III, Sc. 14*

[y] When I'm not thank'd at all,
  I'm thank'd enough;
I've done my duty, and I've done
  no more.   *Tom Thumb the
  Great. Act I, Sc. 3*

[z] We must eat to live and live
to eat.   *The Miser. Act III, Sc. 3*

[a] Penny saved is a penny got.
    Ibid. Sc. 12

[b] Oh, the roast beef of England,
And old England's roast beef!
  The Grub Street Opera.
    Act III, Sc. 2

[c] The dusky night rides down
  the sky,
And ushers in the morn;
The hounds all join in glorious
  cry,
The huntsman winds his horn,
And a-hunting we will go.
  A-hunting We Will Go. Stanza 1

[d] Can any man have a higher
notion of the rule of right and the
eternal fitness of things?
  The History of Tom Jones.
    Book IV, Chap. 4

[e] Wisdom, whose lessons have
been represented as so hard to
learn by those who never were at
her school, only teaches us to extend a simple maxim universally
known. And this is, not to buy at
too dear a price.
  Ibid. Book VI, Chap. 3

James Thomas Fields
[1816–1881]

[f] It [courtesy] transmutes
aliens into trusting friends,
And gives its owner passport
 round the globe. *Courtesy*

[g] No wonder skies upon you
 frown;
You've nailed the horse-shoe up-
 side down!
Just turn it round, and soon you'll
 see
How you and Fortune will agree.
  The Lucky Horse-shoe. Stanza 6

[h] Oh, to be home again, home
 again, home again!
Under the apple-boughs, down
 by the mill!
  In a Strange Land

[i] 'Tis a fearful thing in winter
To be shattered in the blast,
And to hear the rattling trumpet
Thunder, "Cut away the mast!"
  Ballad of the Tempest. Stanza 2

[j] Is not God upon the ocean,
Just the same as on the land?
  Ibid. Stanza 5

Millard Fillmore
[1800–1874]

[k] Let us remember that revolutions do not always establish freedom. *Third Annual Address*
    [December 6, 1852]

Francis Miles Finch
[1827–1907]

[l] These in the robings of glory,
Those in the gloom of defeat,
All with the battle-blood gory,
In the dusk of eternity meet:

Under the sod and the dew,
 Waiting the judgment-day;
Under the laurel, the Blue,
 Under the willow, the Gray.
  The Blue and the Gray. Stanza 2

Oscar W. Firkins
[1864–1932]

[m] My state is contentment
within despair.
  Letter [December 29, 1922]

[n] The great art includes much
that the small art excludes:
humor, pain, and evil. Much that
is repulsive when alone becomes
beautiful in its relation. To find
the ennobling relation is the task
of life and of art. *Lecture Notes*

[o] A classic is produced by the
cooperation of the public with the
author. A classic is a work which
is fit to enter into permanent relations with a large section of
mankind. *Ibid.* [*The quotations are from Memoirs and Letters of O. W. Firkins, University
of Minnesota Press.*]

Williston Fish
[1858–1939]

[p] A will is a solemn matter,
even with men whose life is given
up to business, and who are by
habit mindful of the future.
    A Last Will
[*Harper's Weekly, September 3,
1898, and repeated by request of
many readers, December 12, 1908*]

[q] I leave to children exclu-
sively, but only for the life of their
childhood, all and every the dandelions of the fields and the
daisies thereof, with the right to
play among them freely. *Ibid.*

[r] To lovers I devise their imaginary world, with whatever they
may need, as the stars of the sky,
the red, red roses by the wall, the
snow of the hawthorn, the sweet
strains of music, or aught else
they may desire to figure to each
other the lastingness and beauty
of their love. *Ibid.*

[s] To those who are no longer
children, or youths, or lovers, I
leave, too, the knowledge of what
a rare, rare world it is. *Ibid.*

Margaret Fishback
(Mrs. Alberto G. Antolini)
[1904–]

[t] Christmas cards confuse me
 so—
Why the kittens? Why the doe?
Why the little coal-black Scottie?
  • • •

Something simple now and then,
Saying just "Good will to men."
                          Moderns

[u] The same old charitable lie
Repeated as the years scoot by
Perpetually makes a hit—
"You really haven't changed a
    bit!"   *The Lie of the Land*

Dorothy Canfield Fisher
[1879–   ]

[v] A mother is not a person to
lean on but a person to make
leaning unnecessary.
                    Her Son's Wife

Herbert Albert
Laurens Fisher
[1865–1940]

[w] Purity of race does not exist.
Europe is a continent of energetic
mongrels.
       A History of Europe. Chap. 1

[x] Politics is the art of human
happiness.   *Ibid. Chap. 31*

[y] Taine pointed out that history was made by men, that men
had bodies, that bodies were now
healthy, now disordered, and that
the state of the body inevitably
affected the action of the mind.
The study of the human body was
part of the historian's duty. The
accidents of health had more to
do with the march of great events
than was ordinarily suspected.
             Paris at High Noon.
       Atlantic Monthly, April 1941

John Fiske
[1842–1901]

[z] The United States—bounded
on the north by the Aurora Bore-
alis, on the south by the preces-
sion of the equinoxes, on the east
by the primeval chaos, and on the
west by the Day of Judgment.
      Bounding the United States

Edward FitzGerald
[1809–1883]

[a] Whether we wake or we sleep,
Whether we carol or weep,
The Sun with his Planets in
    chime,
Marketh the going of Time.
                    Chronomoros

[b] The King in a carriage may
    ride,
And the Beggar may crawl at his
    side;
But in the general race,
They are traveling all the same
    pace.   *Ibid.*

[c] I have heard tell of another
Poet's saying that he knew of no

human outlook so solemn as that
from an Infant's Eyes.
                      Euphranor

[*For translation of The Rubáiyát
see Omar Khayyám.*]

Francis Scott Fitzgerald
[1896–1940]

[d] The hangover became a part
of the day as well allowed-for as
the Spanish siesta.
             Echoes of the Jazz Age

[e] Show me a hero and I will
write you a tragedy. *Note-Books*
   [*In The Crack-up, edited by Ed-
   mund Wilson*]

[f] The worst things:
To be in bed and sleep not,
To want for one who comes not,
To try to please and please not.
   *"Egyptian Proverb," quoted in
                       Note-Books*

Robert Fitzsimmons
[1862–1917]

[g] The bigger they come, the
harder they fall.
   *Before Fitzsimmons' fight with
   James J. Jeffries, a heavier man,
   in San Francisco, July 25, 1902*

James Elroy Flecker
[1884–1915]

[h] I am emptied of all my
    dreams:
I only hear Earth turning, only
    see
Ether's long bankless streams,
And only know I should drown if
    you laid not your hand on me.
             Stillness. Stanza 3

[i] I who am dead a thousand
    years,
And wrote this sweet archaic
    song,
Send you my words for messengers
The way I shall not pass along.
       *To a Poet a Thousand Years
                    Hence. Stanza 1*

[j] Oh shall I never be home
    again?
Meadows of England shining in
    the rain
Spread wide your daisied lawns.
                        Brumana

[k] Yet is not death the great ad-
    venture still,
And is it all loss to set ship clean
    anew,
When heart is young and life an
    eagle poised?
             The Burial in England

[l] I have seen old ships sail like
swans asleep.   *The Old Ships*

[m] My brother and good friend,
the Sun.   *A Western Voyage*

Andrew Fletcher of Saltoun
[1655–1716]

[n] Give me the making of the songs of a nation, and I care not who makes its laws.
> *Conversation Concerning a Right Regulation of Government for the Common Good of Mankind* [1703]

Giles Fletcher
[1549–1611]

[o] He is a path, if any be misled;
He is a robe, if any naked be;
If any chance to hunger, he is bread;
If any be a bondman, he is free;
If any be but weak, how strong is he!
To dead men life is he, to sick men, health;
To blind men, sight, and to the needy, wealth;
A pleasure without loss, a treasure without stealth.
> *Excellency of Christ*

John Fletcher
[1579–1625]

[p] Our acts our angels are, or good or ill,
Our fatal shadows that walk by us still.
> *Upon an "Honest Man's Fortune"*

[q] Man is his own star; and that soul that can
Be honest is the only perfect man.
> *Ibid.*

[r] There's naught in this life sweet
But only melancholy.
> *Melancholy*

[s] O woman, perfect woman! what distraction
Was meant to mankind when thou wast made a devil!
> *Monsieur Thomas. Act. III, Sc. 1*

[t] Drink to-day, and drown all sorrow;
You shall perhaps not do 't to-morrow.
> *The Bloody Brother. Act. II, Sc. 2*

[u] And he that will to bed go sober
Falls with the leaf still in October.
> *Ibid.*

Annie Johnson Flint
[1862–1932]

[v] Have you come to the Red Sea place in your life,
Where, in spite of all you can do,
There is no way out, there is no way back,
There is no other way but through?
> *At the Place of the Sea. Stanza 1*

Ferdinand Foch
[1852–1929]

[w] A guest at a dinner given in honor of Marshal Foch in Denver, Colorado, said that there was nothing but wind in French politeness. Marshal Foch retorted: "Neither is there anything but wind in a pneumatic tire, yet it eases wonderfully the jolts along life's highway."

James William Foley
[1874–1939]

[x] It does a heap o' good sometimes, to go a little slow,
To say a word o' comfort to th' man that's stubbed his toe.
> *Stubbed His Toe. Stanza 2*

Eliza Lee Cabot Follen
[1787–1860]

[y] Dear mother, how pretty
The moon looks to-night!
She was never so cunning before:
Her two little horns
Are so sharp and so bright,
I hope she'll not grow any more.
> *The New Moon. Stanza 1*

Jean de la Fontaine
[1621–1695]

[z] It is a double pleasure to deceive the deceiver.
> *Book II. Fable 15, The Cock and the Fox*

[a] The sign brings customers.
> *Book VII. Fable 15, The Fortune-Tellers*

[b] Let ignorance talk as it will, learning has its value.
> *Book VIII. Fable 19, The Use of Knowledge*

[c] People who make no noise are dangerous.
> *Ibid. Fable 23, The Current and the Stream*

[d] No path of flowers leads to glory.
> *Book X. Fable 14*

Samuel Foote
[1720–1777]

[e] So she went into the garden to cut a cabbage leaf to make an apple pie; and at the same time a great she-bear, coming up the street, pops its head into the shop. "What! no soap?" So he died, and she very imprudently married the barber; and there were present the Picninnies, and the Joblillies, and the Garyulies, and the Grand Panjandrum himself, . . . and they all fell to playing the game of catch as catch can, till the gunpowder ran out at the heels of their boots.
> *Nonsense written to test the*

boasted memory of Charles Macklin, The Quarterly Review, London [September 1854], Page 516. Quoted in Harry and Lucy, Concluded, Volume II, by Maria Edgeworth

Esther Forbes
[1894?-   ]

[f] Women have almost a genius for anti-climaxes.
O Genteel Lady!

[g] Most American heroes of the Revolutionary period are by now two men, the actual man and the romantic image. Some are even three men—the actual man, the image, and the debunked remains.
Paul Revere

Ford Madox (Hueffer) Ford
[1873–1939]

[h] But we who remain shall grow old,
We shall know the cold
Of cheerless
Winter and the rain of Autumn . . .
And the long gamut of human fears—
But for you—it shall be forever Spring.   *One Day's List*

[i] Only two classes of books are of universal appeal: the very best and the very worst.
Joseph Conrad

[j] Goodness, how we'd like to know
Why the weather alters so.
Children's Song. Stanza 1

Henry Ford
[1863–1947]

[k] History is bunk.

Lena Guilbert Ford
[*Floruit* 1915]

[l] Keep the home fires burning,
While your hearts are yearning,
Though your lads are far away
They dream of home.
There's a silver lining
Through the dark clouds shining,
Turn the dark clouds inside out,
Till the boys come home.
Keep the Home Fires Burning

Howell M. Forgy
[1908-   ]

[m] Praise the Lord and pass the ammunition.
Pearl Harbor, December 7, 1941

[n] When enough people really praise the Lord, it will no longer be necessary to pass the ammunition. *"And Pass the Ammunition"* [closing words] [1944]

Edward Morgan Forster
[1879-   ]

[o] The historian must have some conception of how men who are not historians behave.
Abinger Harvest. Captain Edward Gibbon

[p] It is not that the Englishman can't feel—it is that he is afraid to feel. He has been taught at his public school that feeling is bad form. He must not express great joy or sorrow, or even open his mouth too wide when he talks—his pipe might fall out if he did.
Ibid. Notes on English Character

[q] Railway termini are our gates to the glorious and the unknown.   *Howards End. Chap. 2*

[r] Beethoven's Fifth Symphony is the most sublime noise that has ever penetrated into the ear of man.   *Ibid. Chap. 5*

Harry Emerson Fosdick
[1878-   ]

[s] The Sea of Galilee and the Dead Sea are made of the same water. . . . The Sea of Galilee makes beauty out of it, for the Sea of Galilee has an outlet. It gets to give. It gathers in its riches that it may pour them out again to fertilize the Jordan plain. But the Dead Sea with the same water makes horror. For the Dead Sea has no outlet. It gets to keep.
The Meaning of Service. Page 20

Sam Walter Foss
[1858–1911]

[t] The plain man is the basic clod
From which we grow the demigod;
And in the average man is curled
The hero stuff that rules the world.
In Memoriam. Stanza 2

[u] A hundred thousand men were led
By one calf near three centuries dead.
They followed still his crooked way,
And lost one hundred years a day;
For thus such reverence is lent
To well-established precedent.
The Calf-Path

[v] There are plenty of fish still
      left in the streams
For the angler who has no rod.
           The Bloodless Sportsman

[w] The paths that lead to a Loaf
      of Bread
And the Suit of Clothes are hard
      to tread.   *Paths. Stanza 1*

[x] Let me live in my house by
      the side of the road
Where the race of men go by;
They are good, they are bad, they
      are weak, they are strong,
Wise, foolish—so am I.
Then why should I sit in the
      scorner's seat,
Or hurl the cynic's ban?
Let me live in my house by the
      side of the road
And be a friend of man.
           *The House by the Side
             of the Road. Stanza 5*

Stephen Collins Foster
[1826–1864]

[y] The day goes by like a shadow
      o'er the heart,
With sorrow where all was de-
      light;
The time has come when the
      darkies have to part:
Then my old Kentucky home,
      good night!
  My Old Kentucky Home. Stanza 2

[z] Oh! darkies, how my heart
      grows weary,
Far from the old folks at home.
      The Old Folks at Home. Chorus

[a] 'Tis the song, the sigh of the
      weary,
Hard times, come again no more.
           *Hard Times Come Again
             No More*

[b] Where are the hearts once so
      happy and so free?
The children so dear that I held
      upon my knee?
Gone to the shore where my soul
      has longed to go,
I hear their gentle voices calling,
      "Old Black Joe!"
           Old Black Joe. Stanza 3

[c] O, Susanna! O, don't you cry
      for me,
I've come from Alabama, wid my
      banjo on my knee.
           O, Susanna. Chorus

[d] Gwine to run all night!
Gwine to run all day!
I'll bet my money on de bobtail
      nag—
Somebody bet on de bay.
           Camptown Races

[e] I dream of Jeanie with the
      light brown hair,
  Borne like a vapor on the sum-
      mer air;
I see her tripping where the bright
    streams play,

Happy as the daisies that dance
    on her way.   *Jeanie with the
          Light Brown Hair. Stanza 1*

[f] Beautiful dreamer, wake unto
      me,
Starlight and dewdrop are waiting
      for thee;
Sounds of the rude world heard in
      the day,
Lulled by the moonlight have all
      passed away.
      Beautiful Dreamer. Stanza 1

[g] He had no wool on the top of
      his head
In the place where the wool ought
      to grow.   *Uncle Ned*

Baron de la Motte Fouqué
[1777–1843]

[h] Death comes to set thee free;
Oh, meet him cheerily
      As thy true friend.
      *Sintram and His Companions
      (tr. Thomas Tracy). Pilgrim
      Song, Stanza 3*

Ellen Thorneycroft Fowler
[1875–1929]

[i] The inner half of every cloud
      Is bright and shining;
I therefore turn my clouds about,
And always wear them inside out
      To show the lining.
      The Wisdom of Folly. Stanza 3

H. W. Fowler
[1859–1933]
and
F. G. Fowler
[1871–1918]

[j] Prefer geniality to grammar.
      The King's English. Chap. 2

[k] The obvious is better than
obvious avoidance of it.
      Modern English Usage

George Fox
[1624–1691]

[l] When the Lord sent me forth
into the world, He forbade me to
put off my hat to any, high or low.
                  Journal

[m] Justice Bennet of Derby, was
the first that called us Quakers,
because I bid them tremble at the
word of the Lord. This was in the
year 1650.   *Ibid.*

[n] He [Oliver Cromwell] said: 'I
see there is a people risen, that I
cannot win either with gifts,
honours, offices or places; but all
other sects and people I can.'
                  Ibid. [1654]

Anatole France
[1844–1924]

[o] All the historical books which contain no lies are extremely tedious.
The Crime of Sylvestre Bonnard (tr. Lafcadio Hearn. Modern Library edition). The Log, December 24, 1849

[p] Lovers who love truly do not write down their happiness.
Ibid. November 30, 1859

[q] To know is nothing at all; to imagine is everything.
Ibid. Part II, Chap. 2

[r] The domestic hearth. There only is real happiness.
Ibid. Chap. 3

[s] He flattered himself on being a man without any prejudices; and this pretension itself is a very great prejudice.   *Ibid. Chap. 4*

[t] Those who have given themselves the most concern about the happiness of peoples have made their neighbours very miserable.
Ibid.

[u] People who have no weaknesses are terrible; there is no way of taking advantage of them.
Ibid.

[v] The faculty of doubting is rare among men. A few choice spirits carry the germ of it in them, but these do not develop without training.
Penguin Island. Book VI, Chap. 2

[w] We reproach people for talking about themselves; but it is the subject they treat best.
La Vie Littéraire. Journal des Goncourt

Francis I
[1494–1547]

[x] All is lost save honour and my life.   *Letter to his mother*

Benjamin Franklin
[1706–1790]

[y] They that can give up essential liberty to obtain a little temporary safety deserve neither liberty nor safety.   *Historical Review of Pennsylvania*

[z] God helps them that help themselves.   *Maxims prefixed to Poor Richard's Almanac [1757]*

[a] Dost thou love life? Then do not squander time, for that is the stuff life is made of.   *Ibid.*

[b] Early to bed and early to rise, Makes a man healthy, wealthy, and wise.   *Ibid.*

[c] Little strokes fell great oaks.
Ibid.

[d] A little neglect may breed mischief: for want of a nail the shoe was lost; for want of a shoe the horse was lost; and for want of a horse the rider was lost.
Ibid.

[e] He that goes a borrowing goes a sorrowing.   *Ibid.*

[f] Vessels large may venture more,
But little boats should keep near shore.   *Ibid.*

[g] Experience keeps a dear school, but fools will learn in no other.   *Ibid.*

[h] Idleness and pride tax with a heavier hand than kings and parliaments. If we can get rid of the former, we may easily bear the latter.   *Letter on the Stamp Act [July 11, 1765]*

[i] Here Skugg lies snug
As a bug in a rug.
Letter to Miss Georgiana Shipley [September 1772]

[j] There never was a good war or a bad peace.
Letter to Josiah Quincy [September 11, 1773]

[k] We must all hang together, or assuredly we shall all hang separately.   *At the signing of the Declaration of Independence [July 4, 1776]*

[l] Our Constitution is in actual operation; everything appears to promise that it will last; but in this world nothing is certain but death and taxes.
Letter to M. Leroy [1789]

[m] The next thing most like living one's life over again seems to be a recollection of that life, and to make that recollection as durable as possible by putting it down in writing.
Autobiography. Page 6 (Everyman edition)

[n] Persons of good sense, I have since observed, seldom fall into disputation, except lawyers, university men, and men of all sorts that have been bred at Edinborough.   *Ibid. Page 17*

[o'] An advantage itinerant preachers have over those who are stationary, the latter cannot well improve their delivery of a sermon by so many rehearsals.
Ibid. Page 129

[p'] 8th and lastly. They are so grateful!!   *Reasons for Preferring an Elderly Mistress [1745]*
[*Quoted by Dr. A. S. W. Rosenbach, owner of the original MS., in his The All-Embracing Doctor Franklin*]

] I wish the Bald Eagle had not
een chosen as the Representative
f our Country; he is a Bird of bad
oral Character; like those among
en who live by Sharping and
obbing, he is generally poor, and
ften very lousy.
The Turky is a much more re-
pectable Bird, and withal a true
riginal Native of America.
Letter to Sarah Bache
[January 26, 1784]

Sir James George Frazer
[1854–1941]

r] The wine-coloured amethyst
eceived its name, which means
not drunken," because it was
upposed to keep the wearer of it
ober.   *The Golden Bough*
(abridged one-volume edition,
Macmillan). Chap. 3

s] Dwellers by the sea cannot fail
o be impressed by the sight of its
easeless ebb and flow, and are
ot . . . to trace a subtle relation,
secret harmony, between its
des and the life of man. . . .
he belief that most deaths hap-
en at ebb tide is said to be held
long the east coast of England
rom Northumberland to Kent.
Ibid.

t] It is a common rule with
rimitive people not to waken a
.eeper, because his soul is away
nd might not have time to get
ack.   *Ibid. Chap. 18*

u] The awe and dread with
hich the untutored savage con-
emplates his mother-in-law are
mongst the most familiar facts
f anthropology.   *Ibid.*

John Freeman
[1881–1929]

v] Who may regret what was,
since it has made
imself himself? All that I was I
am,
nd the old childish joy now lives
in me
.t sight of a green field or a green
tree.   *All That I Was I Am*

w] Happy is England in the
brave that die
or wrongs not hers and wrongs
so sternly hers.
Happy Is England Now. Stanza 3

John Hookham Frere
[1769–1846]

x] And don't confound the lan-
guage of the nation
Vith long-tailed words in *osity*
and *ation*.
The Monks and the Giants.
Canto I, Line 6

[y] Despair in vain sits brooding
over the putrid eggs of hope.
The Rovers. Act I, Sc. 2

Charles Frohman
[1860–1915]

[z] Why fear death? Death is only
a beautiful adventure.
(Last words to a group of friends
as the Lusitania was sinking [May
7, 1915]. Report of conversation
with Rita Jolivet, a survivor, in a
letter from C. Haddon Chambers
to Alfred Hayman [May 18, 1915])

Jean Froissart
[1337–1410]

[a] Above all flowers, I find the
Daisy dear.   *Above All Flowers*
(tr. Grace Warwick)

Robert Frost
[1875–   ]

[b] Something there is that
doesn't love a wall.
Mending Wall

[c] My apple trees will never get
across
And eat the cones under his pines,
I tell him.
He only says, "Good fences make
good neighbors."   *Ibid.*

[d] Earth's the right place for
love:
I don't know where it's likely to go
better.   *Birches*

[e] No, from the time when one
is sick to death,
One is alone, and he dies more
alone.
Friends make pretence of following to the grave,
But before one is in it, their minds
are turned
And making the best of their way
back to life
And living people, and things they
understand.   *Home Burial*

[f] "Home is the place where,
when you have to go there
They have to take you in." "I
should have called it
Something you somehow haven't
to deserve."
The Death of the Hired Man

[g] As a child misses the unsaid
Good-night,
And falls asleep with heartache.
The Black Cottage

[h] Two roads diverged in a wood,
and I—
I took the one less travelled by,
And that has made all the difference.   *The Road Not Taken*

[i] I wonder about the trees:
Why do we wish to bear
Forever the noise of these

More than another noise
So close to our dwelling-place?
The Sound of Trees

[j] I met a Californian who would
Talk California—a state so
blessed,
He said, in climate none had ever
died there
A natural death.
New Hampshire. Stanza 3

[k] The Vermont mountains
stretch extending straight;
New Hampshire mountains curl
up in a coil. *Ibid. Stanza 19*

[l] The sun was warm but the
wind was chill.
You know how it is with an April
day:
When the sun is out and the wind
is still,
You're one month on in the
middle of May,
But if you so much as dare to
speak,
A cloud comes over the sunlit
arch,
A wind comes off a frozen peak,
And you're two months back in
the middle of March.
Two Tramps in Mud Time

[m] Keep cold, young orchard.
Good-bye and keep cold.
Dread fifty above more than fifty
below.
Good-bye and Keep Cold

[n] The woods are lovely, dark
and deep.
But I have promises to keep,
And miles to go before I sleep.
*Stopping by Woods
on a Snowy Evening*

[o] Nobody was ever meant
To remember or invent
What he did with every cent.
The Hardship of Accounting

[p] Some say the world will end
in fire,
Some say in ice.
From what I've tasted of desire
I hold with those who favor fire.
But if it had to perish twice,
I think I know enough of hate
To say that for destruction ice
Is also great
And would suffice. *Fire and Ice*

[q] Happiness makes up in height
for what it lacks in length.
Title of poem

[r] I never dared be radical when
young
For fear it would make me conservative when old.
Precaution

Ethel Romig Fuller

[s] If radio's slim fingers can
pluck a melody

From night, and toss it over a con-
tinent or sea . . .
Why should mortals wonder ?
God hears prayer? *Proc*

Henry Blake Fuller
[1857–1929]

[t] The martyrdom involved in
fortnight's entertainment of any
body whomsoever. *The Chevalie
of Pensieri-Vani. Chap. 1*

(Sarah) Margaret Fuller
(Ossoli)
[1810–1850]

[u] It does not follow becaus
many books are written by person
born in America that there exist
an American literature. Book
which imitate or represent th
thoughts and life of Europe d
not constitute an American litera
ture. Before such can exist, a
original idea must animate thi
nation and fresh currents of lif
must call into life fresh thought
along its shores.
In the New York Tribune [1833

[v] Truth is the nursing mothe
of genius. *Ibid*

[w] Beware of over-great pleasur
in being popular or even beloved
As far as an amiable dispositio
and powers of entertainmen
make you so, it is happiness, bu
if there is one grain of plausi
bility, it is a poison.
*Letter to her brother Arthu
[December 20, 1840*

[x] The golden-rod is one of th
fairy, magical flowers; it grows no
up to seek human love amid th
light of day, but to mark to th
discerning what wealth lies hid in
the secret caves of earth.
Journal. September 184

[y] This was one of the rye-brea
days, all dull and damp without.
*Diary. Quoted by Thoma
Wentworth Higginson: Lif
of Margaret Fuller Ossoli
Chap. 7*

[z] For precocity some grea
price is always demanded soone
or later in life. *Ibid. Chap. 1*

[a] Genius will live and thriv
without training, but it does no
the less reward the watering-po
and pruning-knife. *Ibid*

Richard Buckminster Fuller
[1895–   ]

[b] God is a verb,
Not a noun.
No More Secondhand God

Roy Fuller
[1912-   ]

[c] Tonight I'd like to bring
The poets from their safe and
    paper beds,
Show them my comrades and the
    silver pall
Over the airfield, ask them what
    they'd sing.
                A Wry Smile. Stanza 2

Thomas Fuller
[1608-1661]

[d] He was one of a lean body
and visage, as if his eager soul,
biting for anger at the clog of his
body, desired to fret a passage
through it.
        Life of the Duke of Alva

[e] She commandeth her husband, in any equal matter, by
constant obeying him.   *Holy and
    Profane State. The Good Wife*

[f] He knows little who will tell
his wife all he knows.
            Ibid. The Good Husband

[g] Who durst be so bold with a
few crooked boards nailed together, a stick standing upright,
and a rag tied to it, to adventure
into the ocean?
        Ibid. The Good Sea-Captain

[h] The Pyramids themselves,
doting with age, have forgotten
the names of their founders.
                Ibid. Of Tombs

[i] Learning hath gained most by
those books by which the printers
have lost.   *Ibid. Of Books*

[j] Deceive not thy self by over-
expecting happiness in the married estate. Remember the nightingales which sing only some
months in the spring, but commonly are silent when they have
hatched their eggs.
            Ibid. Of Marriage

[k] Anger is one of the sinews of
the soul; he that wants it hath a
maimed mind.   *Ibid. Of Anger*

[l] Light, God's eldest daughter,
is a principal beauty in a building.   *Ibid. Of Building*

Rose Fyleman
[1877-   ]

[m] Cheerfully   adorn   the
    proudest table,
Since yours it is to bear the glori-
    ous label—
"Richest in Vitamines!"
        To an Orange. Stanza 4

Frances Dana Gage
[1808-1884]

[n] Wife, mother, nurse, seam-
stress, cook, housekeeper,
chambermaid,   laundress,
dairy-woman, and scrub generally, doing the work of six,
For the sake of being supported.
        *The Housekeeper's Soliloquy.
                    Stanza 10*

Norman Gale
[1862-1942]

[o] God comes down in the rain,
    And the crop grows tall—
This is the country faith,
    And the best of all!
        The Country Faith. Stanza 3

[p] Write:—He had made a finer
    man
And left increased renown be-
    hind,
If he had only shut his books
    To read the chapters of man-
    kind!   *Last Words. Stanza 10*

John Galsworthy
[1867-1933]

[q] Justice is a machine that,
when some one has once given it
the starting push, rolls on of itself.   *Justice. Act II*

[r] There is nothing more tragic
in life than the utter impossibility
of changing what you have done.
                Ibid.

[s] You called me a damned Jew.
My race was old when you were all
savages. I am proud to be a Jew.
            Loyalties. Act II, Sc. 1

[t] Public opinion's always in advance of the Law.
                Windows. Act I

[u] Love is no hot-house flower,
but a wild plant, born of a wet
night, born of an hour of sunshine; sprung from wild seed,
blown along the road by a wild
wind. A wild plant that, when it
blooms by chance within the
hedge of our gardens, we call a
flower; and when it blooms outside we call a weed; but, flower or
weed, whose scent and colour are
always wild!   *The Man of
        Property. Part II, Chap. 4*

[v] If you do not think about the
future, you cannot have one.
        Swan Song. Part II, Chap. 6

[w] There's just one rule for politicians all over the world: Don't
say in Power what you say in Op-
position; if you do, you only have
to carry out what the other fellows have found impossible.
        Maid in Waiting. Chap. 7

[x] The beginnings and endings
of all human undertakings are
untidy, the building of a house,
the writing of a novel, the demo-
lition of a bridge, and, eminently,
the finish of a voyage.
            Over the River. Chap. 1

[y] Religion was nearly dead because there was no longer real belief in future life; but something was struggling to take its place—service—social service—the ants' creed, the bees' creed.
Ibid. Chap. 11

[z] Headlines twice the size of the events.   *Ibid. Chap. 27*

[a] How to save the old that's worth saving, whether in landscape, houses, manners, institutions, or human types, is one of our greatest problems, and the one that we bother least about.
Ibid. Chap. 39

[b] I've seen the moon, with lifted wing,
A white hawk, over cypress tree.
At Sunset. Stanza 1

William Channing Gannett
[1840–1923]

[c] The Christ sees white in Judas's heart
And loves His traitor well;
The God, to angel His new heaven,
Explores His lowest hell.
We See as We Are

James Abram Garfield
[1831–1881]

[d] I am not willing that this discussion should close without mention of the value of a true teacher. Give me a log hut, with only a simple bench, Mark Hopkins on one end and I on the other, and you may have all the buildings, apparatus and libraries without him.
Address to Williams College Alumni, New York [December 28, 1871]

Hamlin Garland
[1860–1940]

[e] Do you fear the force of the wind,
The slash of the rain?
Go face them and fight them,
Be savage again.
Do You Fear the Wind?

[f] The palms of your hands will thicken,
The skin of your cheek will tan,
You'll go ragged and weary and swarthy,
But you'll walk like a man!
Ibid.

Richard Garnett
[1835–1906]

[g] Man and Woman may only enter Paradise hand in hand. Together, the myth tells us, they

left it and together must they return.
De Flagello Myrteo. Preface, XII

[h] Have patience with the jealousies and petulances of actors, for their hour is their eternity.
Ibid. Preface, XV

[i] Evergreens are said to be associated with Death as emblems of immortality, and this is true. But there is another and perhaps a deeper symbol: that all seasons are alike to him, as to them.
Ibid. Preface, XXXI

[j] To become Love, Friendship needs what Morality needs to become Religion—the fire of emotion.   *Ibid. LV*

[k] Joy to forgive and joy to be forgiven
Hang level in the balances of Love.
Ibid. LXII

[l] Is life worth living? This if thou inquire,
'Tis probable that thou hast never lived,
And palpable that thou hast never loved.   *Ibid. CCVII*

[m] "Let the man that woos to win
Woo with an unhairy chin;"
Thus she said, and as she bid
Each devoted Vizier did.
The Fair Circassian. Stanza 3

David Garrick
[1716–1779]

[n] Heaven sends us good meat, but the Devil sends cooks.
Epigram on Goldsmith's Retaliation (in Murphy's Life of Garrick. Vol II)

Lloyd McKim Garrison
[1867–1900]

[o] Like misers, our usurious memories bring
Their coins each day of greedy reckoning—
Grieved, if they miss one as they count their store,
Or find one brass, long loved as gold before.
Souvenirs

Theodosia Garrison
[1874–1944]

[p] I sicken of men's company,
The crowded tavern's din,
Where all day long with oath and song
Sit they who entrance win,
So come I out from noise and rout
To rest in God's Green Inn.
The Green Inn. Stanza 1

[q] The kindliest thing God ever
made,
His hand of very healing laid
Upon a fevered world, is shade.
Shade. Stanza 1

[r] Just children on their way to
school again?
Nay, it is ours to watch a greater
thing.
These are the World's Rebuilders!
The Rebuilders. Stanza 3

William Lloyd Garrison
[1805–1879]

[s] My country is the world; my
countrymen are mankind.
*Prospectus of the Public
Liberator [1830]*

[t] I am in earnest. I will not
equivocate; I will not excuse; I
will not retreat a single inch; and
I will be heard!   *Salutatory of
the Liberator [January 1, 1831]*

[u] Since the creation of the
world there has been no tyrant
like Intemperance, and no slaves
so cruelly treated as his.
Life. Vol. I, Page 268

[v] Though woman never can be
man,
By change of sex and a' that,
To social rights, 'gainst class and
clan,
Her claim is just, and a' that,
For a' that, and a' that,
Her Eden slip, and a' that,
In all that makes a living soul
She matches man, for a' that.
An Autograph [January 3, 1875]

Elizabeth Cleghorn Gaskell
[1810–1865]

[w] A man is so in the way in the
house.   *Cranford. Chap. 1*

[x] Correspondence, which bears
much the same relation to personal intercourse that the books
of dried plants I sometimes see
("Hortus Siccus," I think they
call the thing) do to the living
and fresh flowers in the lanes and
meadows.   *Ibid. Chap. 3*

[y] A little credulity helps one on
through life very smoothly.
Ibid. Chap. 11

[z] I'll not listen to reason. . . .
Reason always means what some
one else has got to say.
Ibid. Chap. 14

Théophile Gautier
[1811–1872]

[a] All things return to dust
Save beauty fashioned well;
The bust
Outlasts the citadel.   *L'Art*

John Gay
[1688–1732]

[b] 'Tis woman that seduces all
mankind;
By her we first were taught the
wheedling arts.
The Beggar's Opera. Act I, Sc. 1

[c] Over the hills and far away.
Ibid.

[d] If the heart of a man is de-
press'd with cares,
The mist is dispell'd when a
woman appears.
Ibid. Act II, Sc. 1

[e] The fly that sips treacle is lost
in the sweets.   *Ibid. Sc. 2*

[f] How happy could I be with
either,
Were t'other dear charmer away!
Ibid.

[g] My lodging is on the cold
ground,
And hard, very hard, is my fare,
But that which grieves me more
Is the coldness of my dear.
*My Lodging is on the Cold
Ground. Stanza 1*

[h] Where yet was ever found a
mother
Who'd give her booby for another?
*The Mother, the Nurse, and
the Fairy*

[i] When we risk no contradiction,
It prompts the tongue to deal in
fiction.
The Elephant and the Bookseller

[j] From wine what sudden
friendship springs!
The Squire and His Cur

[k] Life is a jest, and all things
show it;
I thought so once, but now I know
it.   *My Own Epitaph*

Edward Gibbon
[1737–1794]

[l] The reign of Antoninus is
marked by the rare advantage of
furnishing very few materials for
history; which is indeed little
more than the register of the
crimes, follies, and misfortunes of
mankind.
*Decline and Fall of the Roman
Empire. Chap. 3. Modern Library Giant, Vol. I, Page 69*

[m] Our sympathy is cold to the
relation of distant misery.
Vol. II, Chap. 49, Page 597

[n] The winds and waves are always on the side of the ablest
navigators.   *Ibid. Chap. 68,
Page 1343*

[o] Vicissitudes of fortune, which
spares neither man nor the proudest of his works, which buries em-

pires and cities in a common grave.
Ibid. Chap. 71, Page 1438

[p] I was never less alone than when by myself.
Memoirs. Vol. I, Page 117

James Sloane Gibbons
[1810–1892]

[q] We are coming, Father Abraham, three hundred thousand more,
From Mississippi's winding stream and from New England's shore;
We leave our ploughs and workshops, our wives and children dear,
With hearts too full for utterance, with but a silent tear.
Three Hundred Thousand More [First printed in New York Evening Post, July 16, 1862]. Stanza 1

Thomas Gibbons
[1720–1785]

[r] That man may last, but never lives,
Who much receives, but nothing gives;
Whom none can love, whom none can thank,—
Creation's blot, creation's blank.
When Jesus Dwelt

Kahlil Gibran
[1883–1931]

[s] Let there be spaces in your togetherness.
The Prophet. On Marriage

[t] You are the bows from which your children as living arrows are sent forth.
Ibid. On Children

[u] Work is love made visible. And if you cannot work with love but only with distaste, it is better that you should leave your work and sit at the gate of the temple and take alms of those who work with joy.
Ibid. On Work

[v] The lust for comfort, that stealthy thing that enters the house a guest, and then becomes a host, and then a master.
Ibid. On Houses

[w] Beauty is eternity gazing at itself in a mirror.
Ibid. On Beauty

[x] He who wears his morality but as his best garment were better naked.
Ibid. On Religion

[y] An exaggeration is a truth that has lost its temper.
Sand and Foam

[z] Sadness is a wall between two gardens.
Ibid.

[a] We shall never understand one another until we reduce the language to seven words.
Ibid.

Wilfrid Wilson Gibson
[1878–   ]

[b] I did not write; and now I cannot write—
Or, rather, it were useless; no king's head
That pence or pounds might purchase may secure
Delivery in the region of the dead—
And all I meant to say remains unsaid.
The Unwritten Letter

[c] All life moving to one measure—
Daily bread.
All Life Moving to One Measure

[d] Just what it meant to smile and smile
And let my son go cheerily—
My son . . . and wondering all the while
What stranger would come back to me.
The Return. Stanza 2

André Paul Guillaume Gide
[1869–1951]

[e] What another would have done as well as you, do not do it. What another would have said as well as you, do not say it; written as well, do not write it. Be faithful to that which exists nowhere but in yourself—and thus make yourself indispensable.
Les Nourritures Terrestres. Envoi

[f] A unanimous chorus of praise is not an assurance of survival; authors who please everyone at once are quickly exhausted.
Pretexts

Fred Gilbert
[1850–1903]

[g] The Man Who Broke the Bank at Monte Carlo.
Title of song [1892]

William Schwenck Gilbert
[1836–1911]

[h] These passengers, by reason of their clinging to a mast,
Upon a desert island were eventually cast.
They hunted for their meals, as Alexander Selkirk used,
But they couldn't chat together—they had not been introduced.
Etiquette. Stanza 3

i] Oh, I am a cook and a captain bold
And the mate of the *Nancy* brig,
And a bo'sun tight, and a midshipmite,
And the crew of the captain's gig. *The Yarn of the "Nancy Bell." Stanza 3*

j] Roll on, thou ball, roll on
Through pathless realms of Space,
Roll on!
To the Terrestrial Globe. Stanza 1

k] It's true I've got no shirts to wear;
It's true my butcher's bill is due;
It's true my prospects all look blue,
But don't let that unsettle you!
Never *you* mind!
Roll on! (*It rolls on.*)
Ibid. Stanza 2

l] As innocent as a new-laid egg.
Engaged. Act I

m] Bad language or abuse,
never, never use,
Whatever the emergency;
Though "Bother it" I may
Occasionally say,
never never use a big, big D.
*H.M.S. Pinafore. Act I,
I Am the Captain*

n] Stick close to your desks and
never go to sea,
And you all may be Rulers of the
Queen's Navee!
Ibid. When I Was a Lad

o] Things are seldom what they seem,
Skim milk masquerades as cream.
*Ibid. Act II, Duet, Buttercup
and Captain*

p] He is an Englishman!
For he himself has said it,
And it's greatly to his credit,
That he is an Englishman!
For he might have been a Roosian,
A French or Turk or Proosian,
Or perhaps Itali-an.
But in spite of all temptations
To belong to other nations,
He remains an Englishman.
Ibid. Boatswain's Song

q] Ah, take one consideration with another—
A policeman's lot is not a happy one! *The Pirates of
Penzance. Act II, Sergeant's Song*

r] Let's vary piracee
With a little burglaree.
Ibid. Pirates' Chorus

s] I am not fond of uttering platitudes
In stained-glass attitudes.
Patience. Act I, Bunthorne's Song

t] If he's content with a vegetable love which would certainly not suit *me*,

Why, what a most particularly
pure young man this pure
young man must be! *Ibid.*

u] Thou the tree and I the flower—
Thou the idol; I the throng—
Thou the day and I the hour—
Thou the singer; I the song!
*Iolanthe. Act I, Duet, Strephon
and Phyllis*

v] The Law is the true embodiment
Of everything that's excellent.
It has no kind of fault or flaw,
And I, my Lords, embody the Law.
Ibid. Lord Chancellor's Song

w] Darwinian Man, though well-behaved,
At best is only a monkey shaved!
*Princess Ida. Act II,
Psyche's Song*

x] As some day it may happen
that a victim must be found,
I've got a little list—I've got a
little list.
Of society offenders who might
well be under ground,
And who never would be
missed—
Who never would be missed.
The Mikado. Act I, KoKo's Song

y] My object all sublime
I shall achieve in time—
To let the punishment fit the
crime. *Ibid. Mikado's Song*

z] He led his regiment from behind—
He found it less exciting.
*The Gondoliers. Act I,
Duke of Plaza-Toro*

a] No soldier in that gallant band
Hid half as well as he did.
He lay concealed throughout the war
And this preserved his gore, O!
Ibid.

b] Life's perhaps the only riddle
That we shrink from giving up.
Ibid. Life's Tangled Skein

c] Old wine is a true panacea
For ev'ry conceivable ill,
When you cherish the soothing idea
That somebody else pays the
bill! *The Grand Duke.
Act II, Baroness' Song*

d] Quixotic is his enterprise and
hopeless his adventure is,
Who seeks for jocularities that
haven't yet been said.
The world has joked incessantly
for over fifty centuries,
And every joke that's possible has
long ago been made.
*His Excellency. The Played-Out
Humorist*

e] Humour is a drug which it's
the fashion to abuse. *Ibid.*

Richard Watson Gilder
[1844–1909]

[f] Not from the whole wide
    world I chose thee,
Sweetheart, light of the land
    and the sea!
The wide, wide world could not
    enclose thee,
For thou art the whole wide
    world to me.   *Song*

[g] I am a woman—therefore I
    may not
Call to him, cry to him,
Fly to him,
Bid him delay not.
      A Woman's Thought

[h] What is a sonnet? 'Tis a
    pearly shell
That murmurs of the far-off
    murmuring sea;
A precious jewel carved most
    curiously:
It is a little picture painted well.
      The Sonnet

[i] I count my time by times that
    I meet thee;
These are my yesterdays, my mor-
    rows, noons
And nights; these my old moons
    and my new moons.
      The New Day. Book IV, 6

Mrs. C. Gildersleeve (Longstreet)
[*Floruit* 1885]

[j] Mrs. Lofty keeps a carriage,
    So do I;
She has dappled grays to draw it,
    None have I;
She's no prouder with her coach-
    man
    Than am I
With my blue-eyed, laughing baby
    Trundling by.
      Mrs. Lofty and I. Stanza 1

Robert Gilfillan
[1798–1850]

[k] In the days of langsyne we
    were happy and free,
Proud lords on the land, and kings
    on the sea!
To our foes we were fierce, to our
    friends we were kind,
And where battle raged loudest,
    you ever did find
The banner of Scotland float high
    in the wind!
In the Days o' Langsyne. Stanza 2

Strickland Gillilan
[1869–   ]

[l] Bilin' down 's repoort, wuz
    Finnigin!
An' he writed this here: *"Musther
    Flannigan—*
Off agin, on agin,

Gone agin.—FINNIGIN."
    Finnigin to Flannigan. Stanza

[m] Just stand aside and watch
    yourself go by;
Think of yourself as "he" instead
    of "I."
    Watch Yourself Go By. Stanza

[n] Folks need a lot of loving in
    the morning;
The day is all ahead with care
    beset—
The cares we know, and those that
    give no warning;
For love is God's own antidote
    for fret.   *Folks Need a Lot
    of Loving. Stanza*

[o] Although it's sternest duty
    Yet to me it seems a crime—
Giving folks the lovely present
    That I got last Christmas time.
The Last Year's Presents. Stanza

James Gillray
[1757–1815]

[p] The Old Lady of Thread-
needle Street. [The Bank of Eng-
land]   *Title of cartoon [1797*

Caroline Howard Gilman
[1794–1888]

[q] You must know I've resolved
    and agreed
My books from my room not to
    lend,
But you may sit by my fire and
    read.

My bellows I never will lend,
But you may sit at my fire and
    blow.
    *One Good Turn Deserves
    Another. Stanzas 2 and*

Charlotte Perkins Stetson Gilman
[1860–1935]

[r] Said the little Eohippus,
"I am going to be a horse!" . .

Cried all, "Before such things can
    come,
You idiotic child,
You must alter Human Nature!
And they all sat back and smiled.
      Similar Cases

[s] I ran against a Prejudice
    That quite cut off the view.
      An Obstacle. Stanza

[t] The people people work with
    best
Are sometimes very queer;
The people people own by birth
Quite shock your first idea.
The people people have for friends
Your common sense appal,
But the people people marry
Are the queerest folk of all.
      Queer People

[u] If fifty men did all the work,
And gave the price to five,
And let those five make all the
    rules—
You'd say the fifty men were fools,
Unfit to be alive.
    Five and Fifty. Stanza 1

[v] Human life consists in mutual
service. No grief, pain, misfortune,
or "broken heart," is excuse for
cutting off one's life while any
power of service remains. But
when all usefulness is over, when
one is assured of an unavoidable
and imminent death, it is the
simplest of human rights to
choose a quick and easy death in
place of a slow and horrible one.
    Note written before her suicide
    [August 17, 1935]

Louis Ginsberg
[1896-   ]

[w] Love that is hoarded moulds
    at last
Until we know some day
The only thing we ever have
Is what we give away.
    Song. Stanza 1

Henri-Honoré Giraud
[1879-1949]

[x] Men pass, but France is eternal.   *To his troops, on his re-*
    tirement as Commander-in-
    Chief of the Free French Army
    [June 1940]

George Gissing
[1857-1903]

[y] It is because nations tend to
stupidity and baseness that mankind moves so slowly; it is because
individuals have a capacity for
better things that it moves at all.
    The Private Papers of Henry
    Ryecroft. I, 16

[z] Education is a thing of which
only the few are capable; teach
as you will only a small percentage
will profit by your most zealous
energy.   *Ibid. 22*

[a] For the man sound in body
and serene of mind there is no
such thing as bad weather; every
sky has its beauty, and storms
which whip the blood do but
make it pulse more vigorously.
    Ibid. IV, 1

[b] In the days to come, as
through all time that is past, man
will lord it over his fellow, and
earth will be stained red from
veins of young and old. That sweet
and sounding name of *patria* becomes an illusion and a curse.
    By the Ionian Sea. XVIII

William Ewart Gladstone
[1809-1898]

[c] To be engaged in opposing
wrong affords, under the conditions of our mental constitution,
but a slender guarantee for being
right.   *Time and Place of*
    Homer. Introduction

[d] Decision by majorities is as
much an expedient as lighting by
gas.   *Speech, House of Com-*
    mons [1858]

[e] The disease of an evil conscience is beyond the practice of
all the physicians of all the countries in the world.
    Speech, Plumstead [1878]

[f] I have always regarded that
Constitution as the most remarkable work known to me in modern
times to have been produced by
the human intellect, at a single
stroke (so to speak), in its application to political affairs.
    Letter to the Committee in
    charge of the celebration of
    the Centennial Anniversary of
    the American Constitution
    [July 20, 1887]

Richard Butler Glaenzer
[1876-1937]

[g] Indian only in this:
Your sudden way
Of stealing on us—but to kiss
With peace, not slay!
    Indian Summer. Stanza 1

Ellen Glasgow
[1874-1945]

[h] No idea is so antiquated that
it was not once modern. No idea
is so modern that it will not some
day be antiquated. . . . To seize
the flying thought before it es-
capes us is our only touch with
reality.   *Address to the Modern*
    Language Association [1936]

[i] Tilling the fertile soil of man's
vanity.   *A Certain Measure*

Lady Pamela Wyndham Glenconner
[1871-1928]

[j] Bitter are the tears of a child:
    Sweeten them.
Deep are the thoughts of a child:
    Quiet them.
Sharp is the grief of a child:
    Take it from him.
Soft is the heart of a child:
    Do not harden it.   *A Child*

[k] Giving presents is a talent;
to know what a person wants, to
know when and how to get it, to
give it lovingly, and well. Unless

a character possesses this talent there is no moment more annihilating to ease than that in which a present is received and given.
Edward Wyndham Tennant: A Memoir. Chap. 5

Paul Joseph Goebbels
[1897–1945]

[1] We have made the Reich by propaganda.   *Address at Essen*
[*June 25, 1939*]

Hermann Goering
[1893–1946]

[m] I am in the habit of shooting from time to time, and if I sometimes make mistakes, at least I have shot.   *Address at Essen*
[*March 10, 1933*]

[n] Guns will make us powerful; butter will only make us fat.
Radio broadcast [summer of 1936]

Johann Wolfgang von Goethe
[1749–1832]

[o] The history of science is science itself; the history of the individual, the individual.
Mineralogy and Geology

[p] Three things are to be looked to in a building: that it stand on the right spot; that it be securely founded; that it be successfully executed.   *Elective Affinities*
(tr. James Anthony Froude).
Book I, Chap. 9

[q] The sum which two married people owe to one another defies calculation. It is an infinite debt, which can only be discharged through all eternity.   *Ibid.*

[r] A pretty foot is a great gift of nature.   *Ibid. Chap. 11*

[s] The fate of the architect is the strangest of all. How often he expends his whole soul, his whole heart and passion, to produce buildings into which he himself may never enter.
Ibid. Book II, Chap. 3

[t] A teacher who can arouse a feeling for one single good action, for one single good poem, accomplishes more than he who fills our memory with rows on rows of natural objects, classified with name and form.   *Ibid. Chap. 7*

[u] No one feels himself easy in a garden which does not look like the open country.   *Ibid. Chap. 8*

[v] We lay aside letters never to read them again, and at last we destroy them out of discretion, and so disappears the most beau-

tiful, the most immediate breath of life, irrecoverably for ourselves and for others.   *Ibid. Chap. 9*

[w] To know of some one here and there whom we accord with, who is living on with us, even in silence,—this makes our earthly ball a peopled garden.   *Wilhelm Meister's Apprenticeship. Book VII, Chap. 5*

[x] A king there was once reigning,
Who had a goodly flea,
Him loved he without feigning,
As his own son were he!
Faust. (tr. Anna Swanwick). Mephistopheles' Song of the Flea

[y] The Eternal Feminine draws us on.   *Ibid. (closing line)*

[z] Light,—more light!
Last words

Oliver St. John Gogarty
[1878–   ]

[a] O Boys, the times I've seen!
The things I've done and known!
If you knew where I have been
Or half the joys I've had,
You never would leave me alone;
But pester me to tell,
Swearing to keep it dark. . . .
No one believes in joys,
And Peace on Earth is a joke,
Which, anyhow, telling destroys;
So better go on with your work:
But Boys! O Boys! O Boys!
O Boys! O Boys!

[b] Only the Lion and the Cock,
As Galen says, withstand Love's shock.
So, Dearest, do not think me rude
If I yield now to lassitude,
But sympathize with me. I know
You would not have me roar, or crow.   *After Galen*

[c] And up the back-garden
The sound comes to me
Of the lapsing, unsoilable,
Whispering sea.   *Ringsend*

[d] What should we know,
For better or worse,
Of the Long Ago,
Were it not for Verse?   *Verse*

[e] A vitalized symbol
Of earth and of storm,
Of Chaos contracted
To intricate form.   *The Crab Tree*

Isaac Goldberg
[1887–1938]

[f] Diplomacy is to do and say
The nastiest thing in the nicest way.   *The Reflex*

Oliver Goldsmith
[1728–1774]

[g] Such is the patriot's boast, where'er we roam,

His first, best country ever is, at home.
The Traveller. Line 73

[h] Where wealth and freedom reign contentment fails,
And honour sinks where commerce long prevails.
Ibid. Line 91

[i] But winter lingering chills the lap of May. *Ibid. Line 172*

[j] Cheerful at morn, he wakes from short repose,
Breasts the keen air, and carols as he goes. *Ibid. Line 185*

[k] For just experience tells, in every soil,
That those that think must govern those that toil.
Ibid. Line 372

[l] Laws grind the poor, and rich men rule the law.
Ibid. Line 386

[m] Sweet Auburn! loveliest village of the plain.
The Deserted Village. Line 1

[n] The hawthorn bush, with seats beneath the shade,
For talking age and whispering lovers made. *Ibid. Line 13*

[o] The bashful virgin's sidelong looks of love. *Ibid. Line 29*

[p] Princes and lords may flourish or may fade;
A breath can make them, as a breath has made.
Ibid. Line 53

[q] A bold peasantry, their country's pride,
When once destroy'd, can never be supplied. *Ibid. Line 55*

[r] His best companions, innocence and health:
And his best riches, ignorance of wealth. *Ibid. Line 61*

[s] How blest is he who crowns in shades like these,
A youth of labour with an age of ease! *Ibid. Line 99*

[t] The loud laugh that spoke the vacant mind. *Ibid. Line 122*

[u] And even his failings lean'd to Virtue's side.
Ibid. Line 164

[v] As a bird each fond endearment tries
To tempt its new-fledg'd offspring to the skies. *Ibid. Line 167*

[w] Truth from his lips prevail'd with double sway,
And fools, who came to scoff, remain'd to pray.
Ibid. Line 179

[x] In arguing too, the parson own'd his skill,
For e'en though vanquished, he could argue still;

While words of learned length and thundering sound
Amaz'd the gazing rustics rang'd around,
And still they gaz'd, and still the wonder grew,
That one small head could carry all he knew. *Ibid. Line 209*

[y] Where village statesmen talk'd with looks profound,
And news much older than their ale went round.
Ibid. Line 223

[z] Her modest looks the cottage might adorn,
Sweet as the primrose peeps beneath the thorn.
Ibid. Line 329

[a] On the stage he was natural, simple, affecting;
'Twas only that when he was off he was acting.
Retaliation. Line 101

[b] He cast off his friends, as a huntsman his pack,
For he knew when he pleas'd he could whistle them back.
Ibid. Line 107

[c] Friendship is a disinterested commerce between equals; love, an abject intercourse between tyrants and slaves.
The Good-Natur'd Man. Act I

[d] The very pink of perfection.
She Stoops to Conquer. Act I

[e] Let school-masters puzzle their brain,
With grammar, and nonsense, and learning;
Good liquor, I stoutly maintain,
Gives *genus* a better discerning.
Ibid.

[f] The genteel thing is the genteel thing at any time. If so be that a gentleman bees in a concatenation accordingly. *Ibid.*

[g] A modest woman, dressed out in all her finery, is the most tremendous object of the whole creation. *Ibid. Act II*

[h'] This is Liberty Hall. *Ibid.*

[i'] They liked the book the better the more it made them cry.
Ibid.

[j'] Ask me no questions, and I'll tell you no fibs.
Ibid. Act III

[k'] I . . . chose my wife, as she did her wedding-gown, not for a fine glossy surface, but such qualities as would wear well.
The Vicar of Wakefield. Chap. 1

[l'] When lovely woman stoops to folly,
And finds too late that men betray,

What charm can soothe her melancholy?
What art can wash her guilt
  away?
   Ibid. Chap. 5, Song, Stanza 1

[m] Man wants but little here
  below,
Nor wants that little long.
   *Ibid. Chap. 8, The Hermit
  (Edwin and Angelina), Stanza 8*

[n] And in that town a dog was
  found,
As many dogs there be,
Both mongrel, puppy, whelp, and
  hound,
And curs of low degree.
   *Ibid. Chap. 17, An Elegy on the
  Death of a Mad Dog, Stanza 4*

[o] The dog, to gain some private
  ends,
Went mad, and bit the man.

The man recovered of the bite—
The dog it was that died.
   Ibid. Stanzas 5 and 8

[p] The true use of speech is not
so much to express our wants as
to conceal them.   *The Bee.
   No. 3, October 20, 1759*

[q] [To Dr. Johnson] If you were
to make little fishes talk, they
would talk like whales.
   *Boswell's Life of Dr. Johnson.
  Vol. I, Page 466, Everyman Edition*

[r] There is no arguing with
Johnson: for if his pistol misses
fire, he knocks you down with the
butt end of it.   *Quoted, Ibid.,
   Vol. II, Page 509*

Edmond de Goncourt
[1822–1896]
Jules de Goncourt
[1830–1870]

[s] We do believe that at that
particular stage of scientific development, the good Lord, with a
flowing white beard, will arrive on
Earth with his chain of keys and
will say to humanity, just like
they do at the Art Gallery at five
o'clock, "Gentlemen, it's closing
time." (*"Messieurs, on ferme."*)
   Journals, April 7, 1869

Orrin Goodrich
[*Floruit* 1855]

[t]   A two-hour sermon
On a theme I scarce can name.
'Twas all about some heathen,
  Thousands of miles afar,
Who lived in a land of darkness
  Called Borrioboola Gha.

Alas, for the cold and hungry
  That met me every day,
While all my tears were given
  To the suffering far away!
   *Borrioboola Gha.
  Stanzas 1 and 8*

John Cheever Goodwin
[1850–1912]

[u] For that elephant ate all
  night,
And that elephant ate all day;
Do what he could to furnish him
  food,
The cry was still *more hay.*
   *Wang: The Man with an Ele-
  phant on His Hands*

Adam Lindsay Gordon
[1833–1870]

[v] In a thousand years we shall
  all forget
The things that trouble us now.
   After the Quarrel

[w] On earth there's little worth
  a sigh,
  And nothing worth a tear!
   To My Sister. Stanza 8

[x] Lay me low, my work is done,
I am weary. Lay me low.
   Valedictory

Maxim Gorky
[1868–1936]

[y] It is quiet here and restful
and the air is delicious. There are
gardens everywhere, nightingales
sing in the gardens and police
spies lie in the bushes. There are
nightingales in every garden, but
police spies only in mine, I think.
They sit under my windows in the
darkness of the night and try to
get a glimpse of how I spread
sedition in Russia.
   Letter to Chekhov

[z] Lies—there you have the religion of slaves and taskmasters.
   The Lower Depths

Edmund Gosse
[1849–1928]

[a] The girls nowadays display a
shocking freedom; but they were
partly led into it by the relative
laxity of their mothers, who, in
their turn, gave great anxiety to a
still earlier generation.
   The Whole Duty of Woman

[b] There never, we suppose,
from the beginning of the world,
was a man-preacher who did not
warn the women of his congregation against the vanity of fair
raiment.   *Ibid.*

[c] The wizard silence of the
hours of dew.
   The White Throat

[d] The Past is like a funeral
  gone by,
The Future comes like an unwelcome guest.   *May-Day*

Frederic William Goudy
[1865–1947]

[e] I am the voice of today, the herald of tomorrow. . . . I coin for you the enchanting tale, the philosopher's moralizing, and the poet's visions. . . . I am the leaden army that conquers the world—I am TYPE.
The Type Speaks

John Ballantine Gough
[1817–1886]

[f] What is a minority? The chosen heroes of this earth have been in a minority. There is not a social, political, or religious privilege that you enjoy today that was not bought for you by the blood and tears and patient suffering of the minority. It is the minority that have . . . achieved all that is noble in the history of the world.
What Is a Minority?

[g] Everywhere water is a thing of beauty, gleaming in the dewdrop; singing in the summer rain; shining in the ice-gems till the leaves all seem to turn to living jewels; spreading a golden veil over the setting sun; or a white gauze around the midnight moon.
A Glass of Water

Hannah Flagg Gould
[1789–1865]

[h] "Now, just to set them a-thinking,
I'll bite this basket of fruit," said he,
"This costly pitcher I'll burst in three;
And the glass of water they've left for me
Shall 'tchick!' to tell them I'm drinking!"
The Frost. Stanza 4

[i] Wisdom, Power and Goodness meet
In the bounteous field of wheat.
The Wheatfield. Stanza 4

Remy de Gourmont
[1858–1915]

[j] Aesthetic emotion puts man in a state favorable to the reception of erotic emotion. Art is the accomplice of love. Take love away and there is no longer art.
Decadence (tr. W. A. Bradley)

[k] I do not believe it useful to generalize opinions, to teach admirations. It is for each man to procure himself the emotion he needs, and the morality which suits him.
Ibid.

Margaret Johnston Grafflin
[1849–1925]

[l] None other can pain me as you, dear, can do;
None other can please me or praise me as you.
To My Son. Stanza 1

[m] "Like mother, like son," is the saying so true,
The world will judge largely of "Mother" by you.
Ibid. Stanza 2

Richard Grafton
[?–1572]

[n] Thirty dayes hath Nouember, April, June, and September,
February hath xxviii alone,
And all the rest have xxxi.
Chronicles of England

Harry Graham
("Col. D. Streamer")
[1874–1936]

[o] Though the noblest disposition you inherit,
And your character with piety is pack'd,
All such qualities have very little merit,
Unaccompanied by Tact.
Tact. Stanza 1

[p] Little Willie, in the best of sashes
Fell in the fire and was burned to ashes.
By and by the room grew chilly,
But not one liked to poke up Willie.   *Ruthless Rhymes for Heartless Homes. Tender-Heartedness*

Robert Bontine Cunninghame Graham
[1852–1936]

[q] Success, which touches nothing that it does not vulgarize, should be its own reward . . . the odium of success is hard enough to bear, without the added ignominy of popular applause.
Success

[r] The ancient seat of pedantry [Oxford], where they manufacture prigs as fast as butchers in Chicago handle hogs.
With the North-West Wind

[s] Every American child should learn at school the history of the conquest of the West. The names of Kit Carson, of General Custer and of Colonel Cody should be as household words to them. These men as truly helped to form an empire as did the Spanish conquistadores. Nor should Sitting Bull, the Short Wolf, Crazy Horse,

and Rain-in-the-Face be forgotten. They too were Americans, and showed the same heroic qualities as did their conquerors.
Letter to Theodore Roosevelt
[1917]

[t] God forbid that I should go to any heaven in which there are no horses.   *Ibid.*

Kenneth Grahame
[1859-1932]

[u] As a rule, indeed, grown-up people are fairly correct on matters of fact; it is in the higher gift of imagination that they are so sadly to seek.   *The Golden Age. The Finding of the Princess*

[v] A man can stand very much in the cause of love: poverty, aunts, rivals, barriers of every sort,—all these only serve to fan the flame. But personal ridicule is a shaft that reaches the very vitals.
Ibid. "Young Adam Cupid"

[w] The year was in its yellowing time, and the face of Nature a study in old gold.
Ibid. A Harvesting

[x] Those who painfully and with bleeding feet have scaled the crags of mastery over musical instruments have yet their loss in this, —that the wild joy of strumming has become a vanished sense.
Ibid.

[y] Monkeys, who very sensibly refrain from speech, lest they should be set to earn their livings.
Ibid. "Lusisti Satis"

[z] There is nothing—absolutely nothing—half so much worth doing as simply messing about in boats, . . . or with boats. . . . In or out of 'em, it doesn't matter.
The Wind in the Willows. Chap. 1

Ulysses S. Grant
[1822-1885]

[a] I propose to fight it out on this line, if it takes all summer.
Dispatch to Washington, Before Spottsylvania Court House
[May 11, 1864]

[b] I know no method to secure the repeal of bad or obnoxious laws so effective as their stringent execution.   *Inaugural Address*
[March 4, 1869]

[c] Leave the matter of religion to the family altar, the church, and the private school, supported entirely by private contributions. Keep the church and the State for ever separate.   *Speech at Des Moines, Iowa [1875]*

[d] Labor disgraces no man; unfortunately you occasionally find men disgrace labor.   *Speech at Midland International Arbitration Union, Birmingham, England [1877]*

Helen Huntington Granville-Barker

[e] Night and the curtains drawn, The household still,
Fate, with appointed strength, Hath worked its will.

Dearest, the whole world ends, Ends well—in this—
Night—and the firelit dark, Your touch, your kiss.
Night and the Curtains Drawn

John Woodcock Graves
[*Circa* 1800]

[f] Do ye ken John Peel with his coat so gay?
Do ye ken John Peel at the break of day?
John Peel. Old Hunting Song

[g] 'Twas the sound of his horn brought me from my bed,
And the cry of his hounds, which he oft-times led,
For Peel's view-hallo would waken the dead,
Or the fox from his lair in the morning.   *Ibid. Refrain*

Robert Graves
[1895-   ]

[h] As you are woman, so be lovely:
As you are lovely, so be various,
Merciful as constant, constant as various,
So be mine, as I yours for ever.
Pygmalion to Galatea

[i] Look: the constant marigold Springs again from hidden roots.
Baffled gardener, you behold New beginnings and new shoots.
Marigolds

[j] Hate is a fear, and fear is rot That cankers root and fruit alike:
Fight cleanly then, hate not, fear not,
Strike with no madness when you strike.
Hate Not, Fear Not

[k] "How is your trade, Aquarius, This frosty night?"
"Complaints is many and various, And my feet are cold," says Aquarius.
Star Talk. Stanza 5

[l] I do not love the Sabbath, The soapsuds and the starch,

The troops of solemn people
Who to Salvation march. . . .
Resolved that church and Sabbath
Were never made for man.
The Boy Out of Church

[m] May the gift of heavenly
peace
And glory for all time
Keep the boy Tom who, tending
geese,
First made the nursery rhyme.
*A Ballad of Nursery Rhyme.
Stanza 6*

[n] A well-chosen anthology is a
complete dispensary of medicine
for the more common mental dis-
orders, and may be used as much
for prevention as cure.
On English Poetry. XXIX

Agnes Kendrick Gray
[1894-   ]

[o] Sure, 'tis God's ways is very
quare,
An' far beyont my ken,
How o' the selfsame clay he makes
Poets an' useful men. *The
Shepherd to the Poet. Stanza 4*

Thomas Gray
[1716–1771]

[p] What female heart can gold
despise?
What cat's averse to fish?
*On the Death of a Favourite Cat.
Stanza 4*

[q] A fav'rite has no friend!
Ibid. Stanza 6

[r] Daughter of Jove, relentless
power,
Thou tamer of the human
breast,
Whose iron scourge and torturing
hour
The bad affright, afflict the best!
Hymn to Adversity. Stanza 1

[s] Bright-eyed Fancy, hov'ring
o'er,
Scatters from her pictured urn
Thoughts that breathe and words
that burn. *The Progress of
Poesy. III, 3, Line 2*

[t] Fair laughs the morn, and
soft the zephyr blows,
While proudly riding o'er the
azure realm,
In gallant trim the gilded vessel
goes,
Youth on the prow, and Pleasure at the helm;
Regardless of the sweeping whirlwind's sway,
That, hush'd in grim repose, expects his evening prey.
The Bard. II, 2, Line 9

[u] While bright-eyed Science
watches round. *Ode for
Music. Chorus, Line 3*

[v] The still small voice of gratitude. *Ibid. V, Line 8*

[w] Iron sleet of arrowy shower
Hurtles in the darken'd air.
The Fatal Sisters. Line 3

[x] The curfew tolls the knell of
parting day,
The lowing herd wind slowly
o'er the lea,
The ploughman homeward plods
his weary way,
And leaves the world to darkness and to me. *Elegy in a
Country Churchyard. Stanza 1*

[y] Nor grandeur hear with a disdainful smile
The short and simple annals of
the poor. *Ibid. Stanza 8*

[z] The boast of heraldry, the
pomp of pow'r,
And all that beauty, all that
wealth e'er gave,
Await alike the inevitable hour:
The paths of glory lead but to
the grave. *Ibid. Stanza 9*

[a] Full many a gem of purest
ray serene
The dark unfathom'd caves of
ocean bear:
Full many a flower is born to
blush unseen,
And waste its sweetness on the
desert air. *Ibid. Stanza 14*

[b] Some village Hampden, that
with dauntless breast
The little tyrant of his fields
withstood,
Some mute inglorious Milton here
may rest,
Some Cromwell guiltless of his
country's blood. *Ibid. Stanza 15*

[c] Far from the madding crowd's
ignoble strife
Their sober wishes never learn'd
to stray;
Along the cool sequester'd vale of
life
They kept the noiseless tenor of
their way. *Ibid. Stanza 19*

[d] Here rests his head upon the
lap of earth,
A youth to fortune and to fame
unknown.

Large was his bounty, and his soul
sincere,
Heaven did a recompense as
largely send:
He gave to mis'ry (all he had) a
tear,
He gain'd from Heav'n ('twas
all he wish'd) a friend.
The Epitaph. Stanzas 1 and 2

[e] Too poor for a bribe, and too
proud to importune;
He had not the method of making
a fortune.
On His Own Character

Horace Greeley
[1811–1872]

[f] The illusion that times that were are better than those that are, has probably pervaded all ages. *The American Conflict*

[g] A widow of doubtful age will marry almost any sort of a white man. *Letter to Dr. Rufus Wilmot Griswold*

[h] And now, having fully expressed our conviction that the punishment of death is one which should sometimes be inflicted, we may add that we would have it resorted to as unfrequently as possible. Nothing, in our view, but cold-blooded, premeditated, unpalliated murder, can fully justify it. Let this continue to be visited with the sternest penalty. *The New Yorker [June 1836]*

[i] The best business you can go into you will find on your father's farm or in his workshop. If you have no family or friends to aid you, and no prospect opened to you there, turn your face to the great West, and there build up a home and fortune. *To Aspiring Young Men. (Life of Horace Greeley, by James Parton, Page 414)*

[j] 'Twas the voice of the Press— on the startled ear breaking In giant-born prowess, like Palla of old; 'Twas the flash of Intelligence, gloriously waking A glow on the cheek of the noble and bold. *Ode to the Press. Stanza 2*

John Richard Green
[1837–1883]

[k] The words of consecration, "Hoc est corpus," were travestied into a nickname for jugglery, as "Hocus-pocus." *A Short History of the English People. Chap. VII, Sect. 1*

Albert Gorton Greene
[1802–1868]

[l] Old Grimes is dead, that good old man We never shall see more; He used to wear a long black coat All buttoned down before. *Old Grimes. Stanza 1*

[m] He had no malice in his mind, No ruffles on his shirt. *Ibid. Stanza 8*

[n] Fill every beaker up, my men, pour forth the cheering wine: There's life and strength in every drop,—thanksgiving to the vine! *The Baron's Last Banquet. Stanza 7*

Robert Greene
[1560–1592]

[o] Sweet are the thoughts that savour of content; The quiet mind is richer than a crown.... A mind content both crown and kingdom is. *Farewell to Folly*

George Grenville
[1712–1770]

[p] A wise Government knows how to enforce with temper or to conciliate with dignity. *Speech against the Expulsion of John Wilkes, House of Parliament [1769]*

Walter J. Gresham
[1834–]

[q] I think, when I read of the poet's desire, That a house by the side of the road would be good; But Service is found in its tenderest form When we walk with the crowd in the road. *Where Cross the Crowded Ways*

Mrs. Greville
[Floruit 1753]

[r] Nor ease, nor peace, that heart can know, That like the needle true, Turns at the touch of joy or woe, But, turning, trembles too.

O! haste to shed the sovereign balm, My shatter'd nerves new-string; And for my guest, serenely calm, The nymph Indifference bring. *Prayer for Indifference. Stanzas 6 and 9*

Joseph Clark Grew
[1880–]

[s] This [sartorial convention] is a real problem with which I shall have to wrestle during the next few days, for of such stuff is diplomacy made. *Ten Years in Japan. July 20, 1932*

[t] We have a phrase in English "straight from the horse's mouth." I never knew why the particular animal chosen was a horse, expecially as most horses are generally not very communicative. *Ibid. October 19, 1939*

Edward, Viscount Grey of Fallodon
[1862–1933]

[u] The lamps are going out all over Europe; we shall not see them lit again in our lifetime.
Comment, August 4, 1914, standing at the windows of his room in the Foreign Office, London, as the lamplighters were turning off the lights in St. James's Park

Edmund L. Gruber
[1879–1941]

[v] Over hill, over dale, we have hit the dusty trail
And those caissons go rolling along.
Countermarch! Right about! hear those wagon soldiers shout
While the caissons go rolling along.
Oh, it's hi-hi-yee! for the field artilleree,
Shout out your numbers loud and strong,
And where'er we go, you will always know
That those caissons are rolling along.   *The Caisson Song*
[Major Gruber wrote this song when he was a lieutenant in the 5th Field Artillery in the Philippines. In April, 1908, the 1st Battalion came from the United States to relieve the 2nd Battalion, and Lt. Gruber was asked to write a song that would symbolize the spirit of the reunited regiment. More widely sung than any song in the Army, it has undergone some changes in words and music. This is the popular version.]

Philip Guedalla
[1889–1944]

[w] Biography, like big game hunting, is one of the recognized forms of sport, and it is as unfair as only sport can be.
Supers and Supermen

[x] An Englishman is a man who lives on an island in the North Sea governed by Scotsmen.   *Ibid.*

[y] The cheerful clatter of Sir James Barrie's cans as he went round with the milk of human kindness.   *Some Critics*

[z] The true history of the United States is the history of transportation . . . in which the names of railroad presidents are more significant than those of Presidents of the United States.
The Hundred Years

[a] The little ships, the unforgotten un-Homeric catalogue of

Mary Jane and Peggy IV, of Folkestone Belle, Boy Billy, and Ethel Maud, of Lady Haig and Skylark . . . the little ships of England brought the army home.
Ibid. [Evacuation of Dunkirk]

[b] Logically the operations on the Continent pointed to a German victory; and the French, always logical, succumbed. But the British mind, impervious to logic, entirely failed to follow this disastrous reasoning. They were helped to that conclusion by the cheerful voice of the Prime Minister; and no man ever rendered greater service to his people than their spokesman in those summer weeks of 1940.   *Ibid.*

Edgar Albert Guest
[1881–   ]

[c] Somebody said that it couldn't be done
But he with a chuckle replied
That "maybe it couldn't," but he would be one
Who wouldn't say so till he'd tried.   *It Couldn't Be Done*

[d] It takes a heap o' livin' in a house t' make it home,
A heap o' sun an' shadder, an' ye sometimes have t' roam
Afore ye really 'preciate the things ye lef' behind,
An' hunger fer 'em somehow, with 'em allus on yer mind.   *Home*

[e] Let me be a little kinder,
Let me be a little blinder
To the faults of those around me,
Let me praise a little more.
A Creed. Stanza 1

[f] I'd rather see a sermon than hear one any day;
I'd rather one should walk with me than merely tell the way.
Sermons We See

[g] In this bright little package, now isn't it odd?
You've a dime's worth of something known only to God!
The Package of Seeds

[h] Who shall sit at the table, then, when the terms of peace are made—
The wisest men of the troubled lands in their silver and gold brocade?
Yes, they shall gather in solemn state to speak for each living race,
But who shall speak for the unseen dead that shall come to the council place?
At the Peace Table. Stanza 1

Texas Guinan
[1884–1933]

[i] Hello, sucker!
Greeting to night-club patrons

[j] A big butter-and-egg man.
*Describing a lavish spender or
theatrical "angel"*

Louise Imogen Guiney
[1861–1920]

[k] Cowley said it engagingly:
. . . he lives well, that has lain
well hidden. The pleasantest condition of life is in incognito.
*Patrins. On the Delights of an
Incognito*

[l] "Isn't there heaven,"
(She was but seven)
"Isn't there" (sobbing), "for
dogs?" she said.
Davy. Stanza 1

[m] A passing salute to this world
and her pitiful beauty.
The Wild Ride. Stanza 5

[n] We spur to a land of no name,
outracing the stormwind;
We leap to the infinite dark like
sparks from the anvil.
Ibid. Stanza 7

[o] Quotations (such as have
point and lack triteness) from the
great old authors are an act of
filial reverence on the part of the
quoter, and a blessing to a public
grown superficial and external.
*In Scribner's Magazine,
January 1911*

Arthur Guiterman
[1871–1943]

[p] Bless the four corners of this
house,
And be the lintel blest;
And bless the hearth and bless the
board
And bless each place of rest.
House Blessing

[q] Hail Guest! We ask not what
thou art:
If Friend, we greet thee, hand and
heart;
If Stranger, such no longer be;
If Foe, our love shall conquer thee.
Door Verse

[r] The Antiseptic Baby and the
Prophylactic Pup
Were playing in the garden when
the Bunny gamboled up;
They looked upon the Creature
with a loathing undisguised;—
It wasn't Disinfected and it wasn't
Sterilized.
Strictly Germ-Proof. Stanza 1

[s] The Cat on your hearthstone
to this day presages,
By solemnly sneezing, the coming
of rain!
The First Cat. Stanza 7

[t] Oh, the saddest of sights in
a world of sin
Is a little lost pup with his tail
tucked in!
Little Lost Pup. Stanza 1

[u] The finest thing in London
is the Bobby;
Benignant information is his
hobby.
The Lyric Baedeker. London

[v] Drab is the town as a shawl-
hooded crone,
And dreary and cold with a chill
all its own.
You ask them for bread and they
give you a scone,
In Glasgow.
Ibid. Glasgow, Stanza 2

[w] Amoebas at the start
Were not complex;
They tore themselves apart
And started Sex.
Sex. Stanza 1

[x] The three-toed tree-toad
Sings his sweet ode
To the moon.
Nocturne

[y] I breathed a song into the
air;
That little song of beauty rare
Is flying still, for all I know,
Around the world by Radio.
Radiolatry

[z] Of all cold words of tongue
or pen
The worst are these: "I knew him
when—"
Prophets in Their Own Country

[a] Oh, the Brown Missouri Mule
has a copper-plated throat
And the welkin splits apart when
he hits an upper note.
Mule Song. Stanza 1

Dorothy Frances Blomfield
(Mrs. Gerald) Gurney
[?–1932]

[b] The kiss of the sun for par-
don,
The song of the birds for
mirth,—
One is nearer God's heart in a gar-
den
Than anywhere else on earth.
*The Lord God Planted a Garden.
Stanza 4*
(*Inscription at the Bok Singing
Tower, Lake Wales, Florida*)

Jeanne Guyon
[1648–1717]

[c] Well pleased a prisoner to be,
Because, my God, it pleases Thee.
*A Prisoner's Song, Castle of
Vincennes, France. Stanza 1*

[d] But though my wing is
closely bound,
My heart's at liberty;
My prison walls cannot control
The flight, the freedom of the
soul.
Ibid. Stanza 4

Emperor Hadrian
[A.D. 76–138]

[e] Dear fleeting, sweeting, little
soul,

My body's comrade and its guest,
What region now must be thy
goal,
Poor little wan, numb, naked soul,
Unable, as of old, to jest?
*Dying Farewell to His Soul, to
Honor the Tomb of His Friend,
Voconius*

[f] I've no mind to be a Florus,
Strolling round among the drink-
shops,
Skulking round among the cook-
shops,
Victim of fat-gorged mosquitoes.
Retort to Florus

Hermann Hagedorn
[1882–]

[g] Down the fair-chambered
corridor of years,
The quiet shutting, one by one,
of doors. *Doors*

[h] You'll find us kindly on the
whole, though queer;
Not ever quite so bad as we appear,
And at our maddest not without
our graces. *"A Traveler
from a Distant Land"*

[i] How like the stars are these
white, nameless faces—
These far innumerable burning
coals!
This pale procession out of stellar
spaces,
This Milky Way of souls!
Each in its own bright nebulae
enfurled,
Each face, dear God, a world!
Broadway

[j] And now you others who must
live
Shall do a harder thing than
dying is—
For you shall *think!* And ghosts
will drive you on.
The Boy in Armor

[k] The bomb that fell on Hiro-
shima fell on America too.
It fell on no city, no munition
plants, no docks.
It erased no church, vaporized no
public buildings, reduced no
man to his atomic elements.
But it fell, it fell.
It burst. It shook the land.
God, have mercy on our children.
God have mercy on America.
*The Bomb That Fell on
America* [1946]

Samuel Miller Hageman
[1848–1905]

[l] Slowly climb the moon-
touched mountains up their
stairway to the sky,
Slowly each white cloud ascending, seems a soul that passed
on high. *Silence. Stanza 1*

[m] Every sound shall end in
silence, but the silence never
dies. *Ibid. Stanza 10*

[n] Earth is but the frozen echo
of the silent voice of God.
Ibid. Stanza 19

[o] Faith is but an idle canvas,
flapping on an idle mast,
If it be not found within thee as
the work of life at last.
Ibid. Stanza 70

John Burdon Sanderson Haldane
[1892–]

[p] Science is vastly more stimu-
lating to the imagination than are
the classics. *Daedalus*

Edward Everett Hale
[1822–1909]

[q] Its pink and white are every-
where,
A ray of sun—and all the slope
Laughs with its white and red.
"It is the Mayflower of our hope;
The spring is come."
*The Finding of the First May-
flower. Stanza 3*

[r] Behind all these men you
have to do with, behind officers,
and government, and people even,
there is the Country Herself, your
Country, and . . . you belong to
Her as you belong to your own
mother. Stand by Her, boy, as you
would stand by your mother.
The Man Without a Country

[s] It is not necessary to finish
your sentences in a crowd, but by
a sort of mumble, omitting sibi-
lants and dentals. This, indeed, if
your words fail you, answers even
in public extempore speech, but
better where other talking is going on. *My Double and
How He Undid Me*

Sir Matthew Hale
[1609–1676]

[t] Be not biassed with compassion to the poor, or favour to the
rich, in point of justice.

[u] To be short, and sparing, at
meals, that I may be the fitter for
business.
*Things Necessary to be Con-
tinually Had in Remembrance*

Nathan Hale
[1755–1776]

[v] I only regret that I have but
one life to lose for my country.
*Before his execution, September
22, 1776*

Sarah Josepha Hale
[1790–1879]

[w] Mary had a little lamb,
  Its fleece was white as snow,
And everywhere that Mary went
  The lamb was sure to go;
He followed her to school one day,
  That was against the rule;
It made the children laugh and
  play
To see a lamb in school.
  *Mary's Lamb. In the Juvenile
  Miscellany [September 1830]*

[x] "It snows!" cries the school-
  boy, "Hurrah!" and his shout
Is ringing through parlor and
  hall,
While swift as the wing of a swallow, he's out,
And his playmates have answered his call.
  It Snows. Stanza 1

Molly Anderson
(Mrs. Frank LeRoy)
Haley
[1888–   ]

[y] Between the tonics and the
  beauty-creams,
This shabby slowly-turning shelf
  of dreams!   *Loan Library
  at the Corner Drug Store*

[z] Thy blessing, Lord, on all
  vacation days,
For weary ones who seek the quiet
  ways.   *Thy Blessing, Lord,
  On All Vacation Days*

Thomas Chandler Haliburton
("Sam Slick")
[1796–1865]

[a] We reckon hours and minutes
to be dollars and cents.
  The Clockmaker

[b] We can do without any article
of luxury we have never had; but
when once obtained, it is not in
human natur' to surrender it voluntarily.   *Ibid.*

Barclay Hall
[*Floruit* 1940]

[c] Just the little things that I
  forget
Would make a lesser love's whole
  dictionary.   *Sonnet*

Granville Stanley Hall
[1846–1924]

[d] The mother's face and voice
are the first conscious objects as
the infant soul unfolds, and she
soon comes to stand in the very
place of God to her child.
  *Article in Pedagogical Seminary,
  June 1891, Page 199*

Hattie Vose Hall
[1866–1942]

[e] Gone is the builder's temple,
  Crumbled into the dust; . . .
But the temple the mother
  builded
Will last while the ages roll,
For that beautiful unseen temple
Was a child's immortal soul.
  Two Temples. Stanza 3

James Norman Hall
[1887–1951]

[f] The thing that numbs the
  heart is this:
That men cannot devise
Some scheme of life to banish fear
  That lurks in most men's eyes.

Fear of the lack of shelter, food,
  And fire for winter's cold;
Fear of their children's lacking
  these,
This in a world so old.   *Fear*

[g] Nor grief nor bitterness gives
  life again
To ninety thousand drowned and
  butchered men.
  *In Memoriam: Third Ypres
  [July 31–Nov. 4, 1917]*

Joseph Hall, Bishop
of Norwich
[1574–1656]

[h] So little in his purse, so much
  upon his back.
  Portrait of a Poor Gallant

[i] Moderation is the silken string
running through the pearl chain
of all virtues.   *Christian Moderation. Introduction*

[j] Death borders upon our birth,
and our cradle stands in the grave.
  Epistles. Dec. III, Ep. 2

Marguerite Radclyffe Hall
[1886–1943]

[k] God, who took away my eyes,
That my soul might see.
  The Blind Plowman

Robert Hall
[1764–1831]

[l] Call things by their right
names. . . . Glass of brandy and
water! That is the current but
not the appropriate name: ask for
a glass of liquid fire and distilled
damnation.
  Gregory's Life of Hall

Cecily R. Hallack
[1898–1938]

[m] Lord of the pots and pipkins,
  since I have no time to be

A saint by doing lovely things and
    vigilling with Thee,
By watching in the twilight dawn,
    and storming Heaven's gates,
Make me a saint by getting meals
    and washing up the plates!
            The Divine Office of the
                Kitchen. Stanza 1

Fitz-Greene Halleck
[1790–1867]

[n] Come to the bridal chamber,
    Death!
Come to the mother, when she
    feels
For the first time her first-born's
    breath;
Come when the blessed seals
Which close the pestilence are
    broke,
And crowded cities wail its stroke;
Come in consumption's ghastly
    form,
The earthquake's shock, the ocean
    storm,
Come when the heart beats high
    and warm
    With banquet song, and dance,
    and wine,
And thou art terrible: the tear,
The groan, the knell, the pall, the
    bier,
And all we know, or dream, or fear
Of agony are thine.
            Marco Bozzaris. Stanza 5

[o] There is an evening twilight
    of the heart,
When its wild passion-waves are
    lulled to rest.   *Twilight*

[p] They love their land because
    it is their own,
And scorn to give aught other
    reason why;
Would shake hands with a king
    upon his throne,
And think it kindness to his
    Majesty.   *Connecticut*

[q] This bank-note world.
            Alnwick Castle. Stanza 7

James Orchard Halliwell
[1820–1889]

[r] A warke it ys as easie to be
    done
As tys to saye *Jacke robyson.*
            Archaeological Dictionary
            (cited from an old play)

Charles Graham Halpine
("Miles O'Reilly")
[1829–1868]

[s] Old pipe, now battered,
    bruised, and brown,
    With silver spliced and linked
    together,
With hopes high up and spirits
    down
I've puffed thee in all kinds of
    weather.   *My Broken*
            Meerschaum. Stanza 1

[t] If Christ again should visit
    earth,
    A man of toil and care,
Howe'er divine, whate'er his
    worth,
    How, think you, would he fare?
            A Dollar in His Pouch. Stanza 5

[u]   Brain and heart
            Alike depart
From him who worships gin or
    brandy.
            Holland Gin. Stanza 3

[v] There's never a bond, old
    friend, like this,—
We have drunk from the same
    canteen!
            The Canteen. Stanza 1

[w] Trace back the greatest deed
    —it springs
From trifles which no poet sings.
    A Little Rhyme of Little Things.
                Stanza 5

[x] The constellation of O'Ryan,
    ignorantly and falsely spelled
    Orion.   *Subtitle of poem,*
                Irish Astronomy

William Frederick Halsey, Jr.
[1882–   ]

[y] Hit hard, hit fast, hit often.
            Formula for waging war

[z] Our dirty trick department is
    working overtime.
    Reply to reporters when ques-
    tioned about future strategy be-
    ing planned against the enemy
    [September 1944]

[a] Our ships have been salvaged
    and are retiring at high speed
    toward the Japanese fleet.
    Radio message [October 1944]
    after Japanese claims that most
    of the U.S. Third Fleet had
    either been sunk or had retired

Anna E. Hamilton
[1843–1876]

[b] This learned I from the
    shadow of a tree,
    That to and fro did sway against
    a wall,
    Our shadow selves, our influ-
    ence, may fall
Where we ourselves can never be.
            Influence

Robert Browning Hamilton
[1880–1950]

[c] I walked a mile with Pleasure.
    She chattered all the way,
But left me none the wiser
    For all she had to say.

I walked a mile with Sorrow,
    And ne'er a word said she;
But, oh, the things I learned from
    her
    When Sorrow walked with me!
            Along the Road

James Henry Hammond
[1807–1864]

[d] The very mudsills of society.
. . . We call them slaves. . . . But I
will not characterize that class at
the North with that term; but you
have it. It is there, it is everywhere; it is eternal.   *Speech,*
U.S. Senate [*March* 1858]

Percy Hammond
[1873–1936]

[e] The female knee is a joint and
not an entertainment.
Dramatic Review

Thomas Chalmers Harbaugh
[1849–1924]

[f] I've sung the Psalms of David
for nearly eighty years,
They've been my staff and comfort
and calmed life's many fears;
I'm sorry I disturb the choir, per-
haps I'm doing wrong,
But when my heart is filled with
praise
I can't keep back a song.
Trouble in the "Amen Corner."
Stanza 15

The Rev. E. J. Hardy
[g] How To Be Happy Though
Married.   *Title of book.*
[*circa* 1910]

Thomas Hardy
[1840–1928]

[h] When false things are
brought low,
And swift things have grown
slow,
Feigning like froth shall go,
Faith be for aye.
Between Us Now

[i] My argument is that War
makes rattling good history; but
Peace is poor reading.
The Dynasts. Act. II, Sc. 5,
Spirit Sinister

[j] Like the British Constitution,
she owes her success in practice to
her inconsistencies in principle.
The Hand of Ethelberta

[k] A lover without indiscretion
is no lover at all.
Ibid.

[l] That cold accretion called the
world, which, so terrible in the
mass, is so unformidable, even
pitiable, in its units.   *Tess of*
the D'Urbervilles. Chap. 13

[m] That shabby corner of God's
allotment where He lets the
nettles grow, and where all unbap-
tized infants, notorious drunk-
ards, suicides, and others of the
conjecturally damned are laid
Ibid. Chap. 14

[n] Patience, that blending of
moral courage with physical
timidity.   *Ibid. Chap. 43*

[o] "Justice" was done, and the
President of the Immortals (in
Aeschylean phrase) had ended his
sport with Tess.   *Ibid. Chap. 59*

[p] And they shall see what is,
ere long,
Not through a glass, but face to
face;
And Right shall disestablish
Wrong.
"There Seemed a Strangeness,"
A Phantasy. Stanza 4

[q] That faiths by which my
comrades stand
Seem fantasies to me,
And mirage-mists their Shining
Land,
Is a strange destiny.
The Impercipient at a Cathe-
dral Service. Stanza 1

[r] To see stand weeping by
A woman once embraced, will try
The tension of a man the most
austere.   *The Contretemps.*
Stanza 6

[s] One pairing is as good as an-
other
Where all is venture!
Ibid. Stanza 10

[t] You have not known
Men's lives, deaths, toils, and
teens;
You are but a heap of stick and
stone:
A new house has no sense of the
have-beens.
.   *The Two Houses. Stanza 5*

[u] "Yes; quaint and curious war
is!
You shoot a fellow down
You'd treat if met where any bar
is,
Or help to half-a-crown."
The Man He Killed. Stanza 5

[v] A star looks down at me,
And says: "Here I and you
Stand, each in our degree:
What do you mean to do?"
Waiting Both. Stanza 1

[w] We two kept house, the Past
and I,
The Past and I;
I tended while it hovered nigh,
Leaving me never alone.
The Ghost of the Past. Stanza 1

[x] Do you think of me at all,
Wistful ones?
Do you think of me at all
As if nigh?

You may hear a jump or trot
On the stair or path or plat;
But I shall cause it not,
Be not there.
Dead "Wessex," the Dog, to the
Household. Stanzas 1 and 3

[y] Yes, yes; I am old. In me appears
The history of a hundred years.
Empires', kings', captives' births and deaths;
Strange faiths and fleeting shibboleths;
Tragedy, comedy, through my pages
Beyond all mummed on any stages;
Cold hearts beat hot, hot hearts beat cold,
And I beat on.
The Newspaper Soliloquizes: London Observer, March 14, 1926

Abu Mohammed Kasim Ben Ali Hariri
[1054–1122]

[z] We praise Thee, O God,
For whatever perspicuity of language
Thou hast taught us
And whatever eloquence Thou hast inspired us with. . . .
Guard us from error in narration,
And keep us from folly even in pleasantry,
So that we may be safe from the censure of sarcastic tongues.
Makamat. Prayer

Mrs. J. Borden Harriman
[1870–]

[a] Next to entertaining or impressive talk, a thoroughgoing silence manages to intrigue most people. *From Pinafores to Politics. Chap. 4*

Sir John Harrington
[1561–1612]

[b] Treason doth never prosper; what's the reason?
Why, if it prosper, none dare call it treason.
Epigrams. Of Treason

[c] Fortune, men say, doth give too much to many,
But yet she never gave enough to any. *Ibid. Of Fortune*

Joel Chandler Harris
[1848–1908]

[d] Brer Fox, he lay low.
Legends of the Old Plantation

[e] Ez soshubble ez a baskit er kittens. *Ibid.*
[f] Lazy fokes's stummucks don't git tired. *Plantation Proverbs*
[g] Licker talks mighty loud w'en it gits loose from de jug. *Ibid.*

[h] Watch out w'en youer gittin' all you want. Fattenin' hogs ain't in luck. *Ibid.*

[i] Hop light, ladies,
Oh, Miss Loo!
Oh, swing dat yaller gal!
Do, boys, do!
Plantation Play Song

[j] How many po' sinners'll be kotched out late
En fin' no latch ter de golden gate? . . .
Sin's ez sharp ez a bamboo-brier,—
O Lord! fetch de mo'ners up higher!
Negro Revival Hymn. Stanza 1

[k] When you've got a thing to say,
Say it! Don't take half a day. . . .
Life is short—a fleeting vapor—
Don't you fill the whole blamed paper
With a tale which, at a pinch,
Could be cornered in an inch!
Boil her down until she simmers,
Polish her until she glimmers.
Advice to Writers for the Daily Press

Jane Ellen Harrison
[1850–1928]

[l] Language is as much an art and as sure a refuge as painting or music or literature.
Reminiscences of a Student's Life. Chap. 2

[m] Old age, believe me, is a good and pleasant time. It is true that you are gently shouldered off the stage, but then you are given such a comfortable front stall as spectator, and, if you have really played your part, you are more content to sit down and watch.
Ibid. Conclusion

William Henry Harrison
[1773–1841]

[n] We admit of no government by divine right . . . the only legitimate right to govern is an express grant of power from the governed.
Inaugural Address [March 4, 1841]

[o] If parties in a republic are necessary to secure a degree of vigilance sufficient to keep the public functionaries within the bounds of law and duty, at that point their usefulness ends. *Ibid.*

Francis Bret Harte
[1839–1902]

[p] The patient stars
Lean from their lattices, content to wait.

All is illusion till the morning bars
Slip from the levels of the Eastern
    gate.
            Cadet Grey. Song, Not Yet

[q] Fades the light,
    And afar
Goeth day, cometh night;
    And a star
        Leadeth all,
        Speedeth all
            To their rest.
            Ibid. Bugle Song

[r] Never a lip is curved with
        pain
That can't be kissed into smiles
    again.   *The Lost Galleon*

[s] And the way to look for a
        thing is plain,
To go where you lost it, back
    again.   *Ibid.*

[t] Which I wish to remark,
    And my language is plain,
That for ways that are dark
    And for tricks that are vain,
The heathen Chinee is peculiar.
        *Plain Language from Truthful
            James. Stanza 1*

[u] What was it the Engines said,
Pilots touching,—head to head
Facing on the single track,
Half a world behind each back?
    *What the Engines Said (Open-
        ing of the Pacific Railroad)*

[v] I reside at Table Mountain,
    and my name is Truthful
    James;
I am not up to small deceit, or any
    sinful games.
    The Society upon the Stanislaus

[w] For there be women, fair as
        she,
Whose verbs and nouns do more
    agree.   *Mrs. Judge Jenkins*

[x] Oh, yer's yer good old
        whiskey,
    Drink it down.
    Two Men of Sandy Bar. Act. IV

[y] One big vice in a man is apt
to keep out a great many smaller
ones.   *Ibid.*

[z] Give me a man that is capable
of a devotion to anything, rather
than a cold, calculating average of
all the virtues!   *Ibid.*

Minnie Louise Haskins
[1875-   ]

[a] And I said to the man who
stood at the gate of the year:
"Give me a light that I may tread
safely into the unknown." And he
replied: "Go out into the darkness
and put your hand into the hand
of God. That shall be to you better than light and safer than a
known way." So I went forth, and
finding the Hand of God, trod
gladly into the night. And He led
me towards the hills and the
breaking of day in the lone East.
    [Quoted by King George VI in a
    radio broadcast to the Empire, De-
    cember 25, 1939. At that time the
    authorship was unknown.]
            God Knows. Proem.

Lady Flora Hastings
[1806-1839]

[b] Get up; for when all things
        are merry and glad,
Good children should never be
    lazy and sad;
For God gives us daylight, dear
        sister, that we
May rejoice like the lark and may
        work like the bee.
    Early Rising. A Spring Morning

Nathaniel Hawthorne
[1804-1864]

[c] Sleeping or waking, we hear
not the airy footsteps of the
strange things that almost happen.
        Twice-Told Tales. David Swan

[d] The sky, now gloomy as an
author's prospects.
        Ibid. Sights from a Steeple

[e] Our Creator would never have
made such lovely days, and have
given us the deep hearts to enjoy
them, above and beyond all
thought, unless we were meant to
be immortal.   *Mosses from an
        Old Manse. The Old Manse*

[f] That lack of energy that distinguishes the occupants of alms-
houses, and all other human beings who depend for subsistence
on charity, on monopolized labor,
or anything else, but their own independent exertions.
    *The Scarlet Letter. The Custom-
            House*

[g] It is a good lesson—though it
may often be a hard one—for a
man who has dreamed of literary
fame, and of making for himself
a rank among the world's digni-
taries by such means, to step aside
out of the narrow circle in which
his claims are recognized, and to
find how utterly devoid of significance, beyond that circle, is all
that he achieves, and all he aims
at.   *Ibid.*

[h] The black flower of civilized
society, a prison.   *Ibid. Chap. 1*

[i] On the breast of her gown, in
red cloth, surrounded with an
elaborate embroidery and fantastic flourishes of gold-thread, appeared the letter A.
            Ibid. Chap. 2

i] She named the infant "Pearl,"
as being of great price,—purchased with all she had. *Ibid.*
Chap. 6

k] Life is made up of marble and
mud. *The House of the Seven
Gables. Chap. 2*

l] Providence seldom vouchsafes
to mortals any more than just
that degree of encouragement
which suffices to keep them at a
reasonably full exertion of their
powers. *Ibid. Chap. 3*

m] A stale article, if you dip it
in a good, warm, sunny smile, will
go off better than a fresh one that
you've scowled upon.
Ibid. Chap. 4

n] Life, within doors, has few
pleasanter prospects than a neatly
arranged and well-provisioned
breakfast-table. *Ibid. Chap. 7*

o] There is no greater bugbear
than a strong-willed relative, in
the circle of his own connections.
Ibid. Chap. 11

p] Once in every half-century, at
longest, a family should be merged
into the great, obscure mass of
humanity, and forget all about its
ancestors. *Ibid. Chap. 12*

q] It is a token of healthy and
gentle characteristics, when wom-
en of high thoughts and accom-
plishments love to sew; especially
as they are never more at home
with their own hearts than while
so occupied.
The Marble Faun. Chap. 5

r] Rome? The city of all time,
and of all the world!
Ibid. Chap. 12

s] Every young sculptor seems to
think that he must give the world
some specimen of indecorous
womanhood, and call it Eve,
Venus, a Nymph, or any name that
may apologize for a lack of decent
clothing. *Ibid. Chap. 14*

t] Caskets!—a vile modern
phrase, which compels a person of
sense and good taste to shrink
more disgustfully than ever before
from the idea of being buried at
all.
Our Old Home. About Warwick

u] Mountains are earth's unde-
caying monuments.
*Sketches from Memory. The
Notch of the White Mountains*

John Hay
[1838–1905]

v] He trumped Death's ace for
me that day,
And I'm not goin' back on him!
Banty Tim

w] He was hard on women and
rough on his friends;
And he didn't have many, I'll
let you know. *Golyer*

x] Bring me to-night a lotus tied
With thread from a house where
none has died. . . .
There stands not by the Ganges'
side
A house where none hath ever
died. *The Law of Death*

y] Good Luck is the gayest of all
gay girls,
Long in one place she will not
stay,
Back from your brow she strokes
the curls,
Kisses you quick and flies away.
But Madame Bad Luck soberly
comes . . .
And sits by your bed, and brings
her knitting.
Good and Bad Luck (After Heine)

z] There are three species of
creatures who when they seem
coming are going,
When they seem going they come:
Diplomats, women, and crabs.
Distichs. II

a] When you break up housekeeping, you learn the extent
of your treasures. *Ibid. IX*

b] Who would succeed in the
world should be wise in the
use of his pronouns.
Utter the You twenty times, where
you once utter the I.
Ibid. XIII

c] True luck consists not in
holding the best of the cards
at the table:
Luckiest he who knows just when
to rise and go home.
Ibid. XV

Sara Henderson Hay
(Mrs. Raymond Holden)
[1906–   ]

d] He sees the people come and
go,
He feels Time's feathered wing
brush by,
Nods his head sagely, and says he,
"Indubitably . . . indubitably . . ."
Pigeon English

Joseph Hayden
[*Floruit* 1896]

e] There'll be a hot time in the
old town to-night.
*A Hot Time in the Old Town
[The favorite rallying song of
Theodore Roosevelt's Rough
Riders in Cuba, and later the
campaign song of Colonel
Roosevelt.]*

Paul Hamilton Hayne
[1830-1886]

[f] Know you why the robin's
breast
Gleameth of a dusky red,
Like the lustre 'mid the stars
Of the potent planet Mars?
'Tis—a monkish myth has said—
Owing to his cordial heart;
For, long since, he took the part
Of those hapless children, sent
Heavenward, for punishment;
And to quench the fierce desire
Bred in them by ruthless fire,
Brought on tiny bill and wing,
Water from some earthly spring.
Why the Robin's Breast Is Red

William Hazlitt
[1778-1830]

[g] One of the pleasantest things
in the world is going a journey;
but I like to go by myself.
On Going a Journey

[h] The soul of a journey is liberty, perfect liberty, to think, feel,
do just as one pleases.   *Ibid.*

[i] What I mean by living to one's
self is living in the world, as in it,
not of it. . . . It is to be a silent
spectator of the mighty scene of
things; . . . to take a thoughtful,
anxious interest or curiosity in
what is passing in the world, but
not to feel the slightest inclination to make or meddle with it.
On Living to One's Self

[j] There is not a more mean,
stupid, dastardly, pitiful, selfish,
spiteful, envious, ungrateful animal than the Public. It is the
greatest of cowards, for it is afraid
of itself.   *Ibid.*

[k] If our hours were all serene,
we might probably take almost as
little note of them, as the dial
does of those that are clouded.
On a Sun-Dial

[l] No young man believes he
shall ever die.   *The Feeling of
Immortality in Youth*

[m] As we advance in life, we acquire a keener sense of the value
of time. Nothing else, indeed,
seems of any consequence; and we
become misers in this respect.
Ibid.

[n] When I take up a work that I
have read before (the oftener the
better) I know what I have to expect. The satisfaction is not lessened by being anticipated.
On Reading Old Books

[o] It is better to be able neither
to read nor write than to be able
to do nothing else.
On the Ignorance of the Learned

[p] Men of genius do not excel in
any profession because they labour in it, but they labour in it
because they excel.
Characteristics

[q] We are not hypocrites in our
sleep.   *On Dreams*

[r] Takes up the meanest subjects with the same tenderness
that we do an insect's wing, and
would not kill a fly.
*Lectures on the Comic Writers.
Shakespeare*

Lafcadio Hearn
[1850-1904]

[s] My friends are much more
dangerous than my enemies. . . .
These latter help me so much by
their unconscious aid that I almost love them. They help me to
maintain the isolation indispensable to quiet regularity of work.
*Letter to Ernest Fenollosa, 1899.
Quoted by Vera McWilliams:
Lafcadio Hearn*

Clara B. Sawyer Heath
[1837-1911]

[t] Four-score! yet softly the
years have swept by thee,
Touching thee lightly with tenderest care;
Sorrow and death they have often
brought nigh thee,
Yet they have left thee but
beauty to wear,
Growing old gracefully, graceful
and fair.
Growing Old Gracefully

Rose Henniker Heaton

[u] She answered by return of
post
The invitation of her host.
She caught the train she said she
would,
And changed at junctions as she
should.
She brought a light and smallish
box
And keys belonging to the
locks. . . .
She left no little things behind
Excepting loving thoughts and
kind.   *The Perfect Guest*

Reginald Heber
[1783-1826]

[v] Brightest and best of the sons
of the morning,
Dawn on our darkness, and lend
us thine aid.
Epiphany. Stanza 1

[w] By cool Siloam's shady rill
How sweet the lily grows!
*First Sunday after Epiphany.
No. II*

[x] When Spring unlocks the
flowers to paint the laughing
soil.
Seventh Sunday after Trinity

[y] The Son of God goes forth to
war,
A kingly crown to gain;
His blood-red banner streams afar,
Who follows in His train?
*The Son of God Goes Forth to
War. Stanza 1*

[z] From Greenland's icy moun-
tains,
From India's coral strand,
Where Afric's sunny fountains
Roll down their golden sand.
Missionary Hymn. Stanza 1

[a] Though every prospect pleases,
And only man is vile.
Ibid. Stanza 2

Georg Wilhelm Friedrich Hegel
[1770–1831]

[b] Peoples and governments
never have learned anything from
history, or acted on principles de-
duced from it.
*Philosophy of History (tr. J.
Sibree). Introduction*

[c] The history of the world is
none other than the progress of
the consciousness of Freedom.
Ibid.

[d] We may affirm absolutely that
nothing great in the world has
been accomplished without passion. *Ibid.*

[e] When liberty is mentioned,
we must always be careful to observe whether it is not really the
assertion of private interests
which is thereby designated.
Ibid. Part IV, Sect. 3, Chap. 2

[f] The Few assume to be the
deputies, but they are often only
the *despoilers* of the Many.
Ibid. Chap. 3

Heinrich Heine
[1797–1856]
Translations by Louis Untermeyer

[g] Toward France there journeyed two grenadiers
Who had been captured in Russia;
And they hung their heads and
their eyes had tears
As they came to the border of
Prussia. *Nach Frankreich
zogen zwei Grenadier'. Stanza 1*

[h] Upon the wings of Song, love,
I would bear thee far, and go
Where the Ganges ripples along,
love—
There is a place I know.
*Auf Flügeln des Gesanges.
Stanza 1*

[i] A pine tree stands so lonely
In the North where the high
winds blow,
He sleeps; and the whitest blanket
Wraps him in ice and snow.
*Ein Fichtenbaum steht einsam.
Stanza 1*

[j] I do not know why this con-
fronts me,
This sadness, this echo of pain;
A curious legend still haunts me,
Still haunts and obsesses my
brain.
*Ich weiss nicht, was soll es be-
deuten (The Lorelei). Stanza 1*

[k] Child, you are like a flower,
So sweet and pure and fair.
Du bist wie eine Blume. Stanza 1

[l] He who, for the first time,
loves,
Even vainly, is a God.
But the man who loves again,
And still vainly, is a fool.
*Wer zum erstenmale liebt.
Stanza 1*

[m] Oh what lies there are in
kisses! *In den Küssen,
welche Lüge. Stanza 1*

[n] Death—it is but the long,
cool night;
And Life is but a sultry day.
*Der Tod, das ist die kühle Nacht.
Stanza 1*

[o] The deep, blue eyes of Spring-
time
Peer from the grass beneath;
They are the tender violets
That I will twine in a wreath.
*Die blauen Frühlingsaugen.
Stanza 1*

[p] This is America!
This is the new world!
Not the present European
Wasted and withering sphere.
*Vitzliputzli. Prelude, Dieses ist
Amerika! Stanza 1*

[q] For Sleep is good, but Death
is better still—
The best is never to be born at all.
*Gross ist die Ähnlichkeit der
beiden schönen*

Roy Helton
[1886-   ]

[r] I'd drunk lonesome water,
I knowed in a minute:
Never larnt nothing
From then till today:

Nothing worth larning
Nothing worth knowing,
I'm bound to the hills
And I can't get away.
        Lonesome Water. Stanza 4

[s] The power in these feet and
        hands
    Is adequate for me
And in this atom of myself
    Explodes what needs to be free.
        *Come Back to Earth. II
            Stanza 1 [1946]*

[t] Oaks are the true conserva-
        tives;
    They hold old leaves till summer
        gives
    A green exchange.   *Ibid. XLIX*

[u] Poplars anticipate the fall,
Grow yellow briefly in September
And then have little to remember.
On hope the poplar springs up
        fast.
But as a tree, it cannot last.
        Ibid.

Felicia Dorothea Hemans
[1793–1835]

[v] The stately homes of Eng-
        land!
    How beautiful they stand,
Amidst their tall ancestral trees,
    O'er all the pleasant land!
        The Homes of England. Stanza 1

[w] The breaking waves dashed
        high
    On a stern and rock-bound
        coast,
And the woods, against a stormy
        sky,
    Their giant branches tossed.
        *The Landing of the Pilgrim
            Fathers. Stanza 1*

[x] A band of exiles moored their
        bark
On a wild New England shore.
        Ibid. Stanza 2

[y] Ay, call it holy ground,
    The soil where first they trod!
They have left unstained what
        there they found—
    Freedom to worship God.
        Ibid. Stanza 10

[z] The boy stood on the burning
        deck,
Whence all but he had fled;
The flame that lit the battle's
        wreck
    Shone round him o'er the dead.
        Casabianca. Stanza 1

[a] Come to the sunset tree!
    The day is past and gone;
The woodman's axe lies free,
    And the reaper's work is done.
        Tyrolese Evening Song. Stanza 1

[b] Oh, call my brother back to
        me!
    I cannot play alone:

The summer comes with flower
        and bee,—
    Where is my brother gone?
        The Child's First Grief. Stanza 1

[c] I have looked o'er the hills of
        the stormy North,
And the larch has hung all his
        tassels forth.
        The Voice of Spring. Stanza 3

[d] Wave may not foam nor wild
        wind sweep
    Where rest not England's Dead.
        England's Dead

Ernest Hemingway
[1898–   ]

[e] A growing ecstasy of ordered,
formal, passionate, increasing dis-
regard for death. . . .
    It is impossible to believe the
emotional and spiritual intensity
and pure, classic beauty that can
be produced by a man, an animal,
and a piece of scarlet serge draped
over a stick.
        Death in the Afternoon. Chap. 18

[f] All modern American litera-
ture comes from one book by Mark
Twain called *Huckleberry Finn*.
. . . There was nothing before.
There has been nothing as good
since.
        The Green Hills of Africa. Chap. 1

[g] The first panacea for a mis-
managed nation is inflation of the
currency; the second is war. Both
bring a temporary prosperity;
both bring a permanent ruin. But
both are the refuge of political
and economic opportunists.
        *Notes on the Next War
            [Esquire, September 1935]*

[h] They wrote in the old days
that it is sweet and fitting to die
for one's country. But in modern
war there is nothing sweet nor
fitting in your dying. You will die
like a dog for no good reason.
        Ibid.

Graham Lee Hemminger
[1896–1949]

[i] Tobacco is a dirty weed. I like
        it.
It satisfies no normal need. I like
        it.
It makes you thin, it makes you
        lean,
It takes the hair right off your
        bean.
It's the worst darn stuff I've ever
        seen.
    I like it.
        *Tobacco [First published in
            Penn State Froth, November
            1915.]*

Burton J. Hendrick
[1871–1949]

[j] The dissenting opinions of one generation become the prevailing interpretation of the next.
Bulwark of the Republic. Page 417

William Ernest Henley
[1849–1903]

[k] The Hospital, grey, quiet, old,
Where Life and Death like friendly chafferers meet.
In Hospital. Enter Patient

[l] Far in the stillness a cat
Languishes loudly. *Ibid. Vigil*

[m] His wise, rare smile is sweet with certainties,
And seems in all his patients to compel
Such love and faith as failure cannot quell.
Ibid. "The Chief" (Lister)

[n] As dust that drives, as straws that blow,
Into the night go one and all.
Ballade of Dead Actors

[o] Let us break out, and taste the morning prime . . .
Let us be drunk.
To F. W.

[p] Out of the night that covers me,
Black as the Pit from pole to pole,
I thank whatever gods may be
For my unconquerable soul.
Echoes. IV, In Memoriam R. T. Hamilton Bruce ["Invictus"]

[q] Under the bludgeonings of chance
My head is bloody, but unbowed.
Ibid.

[r] It matters not how strait the gate,
How charged with punishments the scroll,
I am the master of my fate;
I am the captain of my soul.
Ibid.

[s] We'll go no more a-roving by the light of the moon.
November glooms are barren beside the dusk of June.
Ibid. VIII

[t] The nightingale has a lyre of gold,
The lark's is a clarion call,
And the blackbird plays but a boxwood flute,
But I love him best of all.
Ibid. XVIII, To A. D.

[u] Tired of experience, he turns
To the friendly and comforting breast
Of the old nurse, Death.
Ibid. XXIX, To R. L. S.

[v] Night with her train of stars
And her great gift of sleep.
Ibid.

[w] Or ever the knightly years were gone,
With the old world to the grave,
I was a King in Babylon
And you were a Christian Slave.
Ibid. XXXVII, To W. A.

[x] The Spirit of Wine
Sang in my glass, and I listened
With love to his odorous music,
His flushed and magnificent song.
Ibid. XLI, To R. A. M. S.

[y] With what a genius for administration
We rearrange the rumbling universe,
And map the course of man's regeneration
Over a pipe. *Inter Sodales*

Henry VI
[1421–1471]

[z] Kingdoms are but cares,
State is devoid of stay;
Riches are ready snares,
And hasten to decay.
From Sir John Harrington's Nugae Antiquae (Quoted in Edward Bulwer Lytton's novel, The Last of the Barons, Book III, Chap. 5)

Mathew Henry
[1662–1714]

[a] Many a dangerous temptation comes to us in fine gay colours that are but skin-deep.
Commentaries. Genesis, III

[b] They that die by famine die by inches. *Ibid. Psalm LIX*

[c] Hearkners, we say, seldom hear good of themselves.
Ibid. Ecclesiastes, VII

[d] It was a common saying among the Puritans, "Brown bread and the Gospel is good fare."
Ibid. Isaiah, XXX

[e] It is good news, worthy of all acceptation; and yet not too good to be true
Ibid Timothy. I

[f] It is not fit the public trusts should be lodged in the hands of any, till they are first proved and found fit for the business they are to be entrusted with.
Ibid. Timothy, III

"O. Henry"
(William Sydney Porter)
[1862–1910]

[g] No calamity so touches the common heart of humanity as does the straying of a little child.

Their feet are so uncertain and feeble; the ways are so steep and strange. *The Four Million. Between Rounds*

[h] If men knew how women pass the time when they are alone, they'd never marry.
Ibid. Memoirs of a Yellow Dog

[i] What a woman wants is what you're out of. She wants more of a thing when it's scarce.
Heart of the West. Cupid à la Carte

[j] Love and business and family and religion and art and patriotism are nothing but shadows of words when a man's starving. *Ibid.*

[k] It was beautiful and simple as all truly great swindles are.
The Gentle Grafter. The Octopus Marooned

[l] There are two times when you can never tell what is going to happen. One is when a man takes his first drink; and the other is when a woman takes her latest. *Ibid.*

[m] It brings up happy old days when I was only a farmer and not an agriculturist.
Ibid. Modern Rural Sports

[n] Busy as a one-armed man with the nettle-rash pasting on wall-paper.
Ibid. The Ethics of Pig

[o] Bagdad-on-the-Subway.
Roads of Destiny. The Discounters of Money

[p] You can't appreciate home till you've left it, money till it's spent, your wife till she's joined a woman's club, nor Old Glory till you see it hanging on a broomstick on the shanty of a consul in a foreign town.
Ibid. The Fourth in Salvador

[q] Men to whom life had appeared as a reversible coat—seamy on both sides.
Options. The Hiding of Black Bill

[r] A man asleep is certainly a sight to make angels weep. Now, a woman asleep you regard as different. No matter how she looks, you know it's better for all hands for her to be that way. *Ibid.*

[s] The big city is like a mother's knee to many who have strayed far and found the roads rough beneath their uncertain feet. At dusk they come home and sit upon the door-step.
Ibid. Supply and Demand

[t] She would have made a splendid wife, for crying only made her eyes more bright.
Ibid. No Story

[u] I was made by a Dago and presented to the American people on behalf of the French Government for the purpose of welcomin' Irish immigrants into the Dutch city of New York. *Sixes and Sevens. The Lady Higher Up*

[v] A straw vote only shows which way the hot air blows.
Rolling Stones. A Ruler of Men

[w] We may achieve climate, but weather is thrust upon us.
Ibid. A Fog in Santone

[x] Most wonderful of all are words, and how they make friends one with another, being oft associated, until not even obituary notices them do part.
Whirligigs. Calloway's Code

[y] When a poor man finds a long-hidden quarter-dollar that has slipped through a rip in his vest lining, he sounds the pleasure of life with a deeper plummet than any millionaire can hope to cast. *The Voice of the City. The Complete Life of John Hopkins*

[z] Ready to melt in the crucible of her ire a little more gold plating from the wrought steel chains of matrimony. *The Trimmed Lamp. The Pendulum*

[a] There is one day that is ours. There is one day when all we Americans who are not self-made go back to the old home to eat saleratus biscuits and marvel how much nearer to the porch the old pump looks than it used to. . . . Thanksgiving Day . . . is the one day that is purely American.
Ibid. Two Thanksgiving Day Gentlemen

[b] Perhaps there is no happiness in life so perfect as the martyr's. *Ibid.*

[c] Bohemia is nothing more than the little country in which you do not live.
Ibid. The Country of Elusion

[d] A story with a moral appended is like the bill of a mosquito. It bores you, and then injects a stinging drop to irritate your conscience. *Strictly Business. The Gold that Glittered*

[e] She plucked from my lapel the invisible strand of lint (the universal act of woman to proclaim ownership).
Ibid. A Ramble in Aphasia

[f] Californians are a race of people; they are not merely inhabitants of a State. *Ibid. A Municipal Report*

[g] Turn up the lights; I don't want to go home in the dark.
Last words (quoted in the biography by C. Alphonso Smith)

Patrick Henry
[1736–1799]

[h] Tarquin and Caesar each had his Brutus, Charles the First his Cromwell, and George the Third "'Treason!'" cried the Speaker]—may profit by their example. If this be treason, make the most of it. *Speech on the Stamp Act, House of Burgesses, Williamsburg, Virginia [May 29, 1765]*

[i] I am not a Virginian, but an American. *Speech in First Continental Congress, Philadelphia, [October 14, 1774]*

[j] Is life so dear, or peace so sweet, as to be purchased at the price of chains and slavery? Forbid it, Almighty God! I know not what course others may take, but as for me, give me liberty, or give me death! *Speech in Virginia Convention, St. John's Episcopal Church, Richmond, Virginia [March 23, 1775]*

Sir Alan Patrick Herbert
[1890–   ]

[k] When laughing Ann trips down the street
The sun comes out as well,
The town is at her twinkling feet,
The crier rings his bell,
The young men leap like little fish,
Policemen stand and purr,
While husbands look behind and wish
That they had married her.
Laughing Ann. Stanza 1

[l] I wish I hadn't broke that dish,
I wish I was a movie-star,
I wish a lot of things, I wish
That life was like the movies are. *It May Be Life, But Ain't It Slow? Stanza 1*

[m] If there's an end
On which I'd spend
My last remaining cash,
It's sausage, friend,
It's sausage, friend,
It's sausage, friend, and mash.

When Love is dead,
Ambition fled,
And Pleasure, lad, and Pash,
You'll still enjoy
A sausage, boy,
A sausage, boy, and mash.
Sausage and Mash. Stanzas 1 and 3

[n] Teetot'lers seem to die the same as others,
So what's the use of knocking off the beer?
The Ladies' Bar. Refrain

[o] I'm not a jealous woman, but I *can't* see what he sees in her,
I can't see *what* he sees in her, I can't see what he *sees* in her!
I Can't Think What He Sees in Her

[p] Putting paint on everything in sight
Is surely Art's most satisfying form.
Spring Cleaning. Stanza 6

[q] Don't take my boy to the Talkies!
It's puttin' ideas in 'is 'ead,
'E makes the most 'orrible faces,
And sleeps with a gun in 'is bed.
'E uses outlandish American words,
It's nothin' but "bootleggers," "babies," and "birds."
'E says I've an English accent
An' it's not that I mind the snub,
But I want my boy to be British,
So take 'im with you to the pub!
Dreadful Ballad of a Talkie-Ruined Home

[r] Holy Deadlock.
Title of novel, satirizing the paradoxes of British divorce law

[s] I regard the pub as a valuable institution. *Letter to the Electors of Oxford University [1935]*

[t] They tell us that capitalism is doomed: Karl Marx, I believe, made the same announcement 80 years ago. He may still be right: but the old clock ticks on.
Ibid.

[u] Great science nobly labored to increase the people's joys,
But every new invention seemed to add another noise.
Read in the House of Commons [November 1938]

[v] A new, unnatural cross between
A mystic, monster, and machine;
From every weakening force apart,
Untouched by alcohol—and heart.
A. H. An Epitaph [October 1939]

George Herbert
[1593–1632]

[w] Sweet day, so cool, so calm, so bright,
The bridal of the earth and sky.
Virtue. Stanza 1

[x] Sweet spring, full of sweet days and roses,
A box where sweets compacted lie.
Ibid. Stanza 3

[y] Only a sweet and virtuous soul,
Like seasoned timber, never gives.
Ibid. Stanza 4

[z] A verse may find him who a sermon flies,
And turn delight into a sacrifice.
The Church Porch. Stanza 1

[a] Drink not the third glass, which thou canst not tame, When once it is within thee.
Ibid. Stanza 5

[b] By no means run in debt: take thine own measure.
Who cannot live on twenty pound a year,
Cannot on forty.
Ibid. Stanza 30

[c] Wit's an unruly engine, wildly striking
Sometimes a friend, sometimes the engineer.
Ibid. Stanza 41

[d] Pleasing ware is half sold.
Jacula Prudentum

[e] Love, and a cough, cannot be hid.   *Ibid.*

[f] Deceive not thy physician, confessor, nor lawyer.   *Ibid.*

[g] A snow year, a rich year.
Ibid.

[h] Hell is full of good meanings and wishings.   *Ibid.*

[i] Whose house is of glass, must not throw stones at another.
Ibid.

[j] By suppers more have been killed than Galen ever cured.   *Ibid.*

[k] The best mirror is an old friend.   *Ibid.*

[l] Stay till the lame messenger come, if you will know the truth of the thing.   *Ibid.*

[m] The buyer needs a hundred eyes, the seller not one.   *Ibid.*

[n] My house, my house, though thou art small, thou art to me the Escurial.   *Ibid.*

[o] Thursday come, and the week is gone.   *Ibid.*

[p] Time is the rider that breaks youth.   *Ibid.*

[q] You may bring a horse to the river, but he will drink when and what he pleaseth.   *Ibid.*

[r] Before you make a friend, eat a bushel of salt with him.   *Ibid.*

[s] Show me a liar, and I will show thee a thief.   *Ibid.*

[t] One father is more than a hundred school-masters.   *Ibid.*

[u] Reason lies between the spur and the bridle.   *Ibid.*

[v] One sword keeps another in the sheath.   *Ibid.*

[w] He that lends, gives.   *Ibid.*

[x] Poverty is no sin.   *Ibid.*

[y] Words are women, deeds are men.   *Ibid.*

[z] One hour's sleep before midnight is worth three after.
Ibid.

[a'] He hath no leisure who useth it not.   *Ibid.*

[b'] Half the world knows not how the other half lives.   *Ibid.*

[c'] All are presumed good till they are found in a fault.   *Ibid.*

[d'] Every mile is two in winter.
Ibid.

[e'] He that steals an egg will steal an ox.
Ibid. [second edition, 1651]

[f'] There is an hour wherein a man might be happy all his life could he find it.   *Ibid.*

[g'] Woe be to him who reads but one book.   *Ibid.*

Oliver Herford
[1863–1935]

[h'] God made Man
   Frail as a bubble;
God made Love,
   Love made Trouble.
A Plea

[i'] God made the Vine,
   Was it a sin
That Man made Wine
   To drown Trouble in?
Ibid.

[j'] Children, behold the Chimpanzee:
He sits on the ancestral tree
From which we sprang in ages gone.   *The Chimpanzee*

[k'] Ermined and minked and Persian-lambed,
Be-puffed (be-painted, too, alas!)
Be-decked, be-diamonded—be-damned!
The women of the better class.
The Women of the Better Class. Stanza 4

[l'] It is not fair to visit all
The blame on Eve, for Adam's fall;
The most Eve did was to display
Contributory negligé.
Eve: Apropos de Rien

[m'] O Mongoose, where were you that day
When Mistress Eve was led astray?
If you'd but seen the serpent first,
Our parents would not have been cursed.   *Child's Natural History. The Mongoose*

Herodotus
[484–424 B.C.]
Translation by William Beloe

[n'] Call no man happy till you know the nature of his death; he is at best but fortunate.
Book I, Clio. Chap. 32

[o'] They [the Persians] are accustomed to deliberate on matters of the highest moment when

warm with wine. . . . Whatever also they discuss when sober, is always a second time examined after they have been drinking.
Ibid. Chap. 133

[p] You may have observed how the thunderbolt of Heaven chastises the insolence of the more enormous animals, whilst it passes over without injury the weak and insignificant: before these weapons of the gods you must have seen how the proudest palaces and the loftiest trees fall and perish.
Book VII, Polymnia. Chap. 10

[q] The Persian messengers travel with a velocity which nothing human can equal. . . . Neither snow, nor rain, nor heat, nor darkness, are permitted to obstruct their speed.   *Book VIII, Urania. Chap. 98*
[Neither snow, nor rain, nor heat, nor gloom of night stays these couriers from the swift completion of their appointed rounds.
—*Inscription on the Main Post Office, New York City.*]

Robert Herrick
[1591–1674]

[r] What is a kiss? Why this, as some approve:
The sure, sweet cement, glue, and lime of love.   *A Kiss*

[s] Cherry ripe, ripe, ripe, I cry,
Full and fair ones,—come and buy!
If so be you ask me where
They do grow, I answer, there,
Where my Julia's lips do smile.
Cherry Ripe

[t] A sweet disorder in the dress
Kindles in clothes a wantonness. . . .
A winning wave, deserving note,
In the tempestuous petticoat;
A careless shoe-string, in whose tie
I see a wild civility,—
Do more bewitch me than when art
Is too precise in every part.
Delight in Disorder

[u] Gather ye rosebuds while ye may,
Old Time is still a-flying,
And this same flower that smiles today
To-morrow will be dying.
To the Virgins to make much of Time

[v] Fair daffadills, we weep to see
You haste away so soon.
To Daffadills

[w] Thus woe succeeds a woe, as wave a wave.
Sorrows Succeed

[x] Her pretty feet, like snails, did creep
A little out, and then,
As if they played at bo-peep,
Did soon draw in again.
To Mistress Susanna Southwell

[y] Her legs were such Diana shows
When tuckt up she a-hunting goes
With Buskins shortned to descrie
The happy dawning of her thigh.
The Vision

[z] Get up, sweet Slug-a-bed, and see
The Dew bespangling Herbe and Tree.
Corinna's Going a-Maying

[a] Whenas in silks my Julia goes,
Then, then (methinks) how sweetly flowes
That liquefaction of her clothes.
Upon Julia's Clothes

William Herschell
[1873–1939]

[b] The Kid has gone to the Colors
And we don't know what to say;
The Kid we have loved and cuddled
Stepped out for the Flag to-day.
The Kid Has Gone to the Colors
[1917]. Stanza 1

[c] What do little girls talk about?
What is their mystic theme?
Those still too young for puppy love,
Yet old enough to dream.
What Do Little Girls Talk About? Stanza 1

Hesiod
[*Circa* 720 B.C.?]
Translation by J. Banks, M.A., with a few alterations. Bohn Classical Library

[d] We know to tell many fictions like to truths, and we know, when we will, to speak what is true.
The Theogony. Line 27

[e] Both potter is jealous of potter and craftsman of craftsman; and poor man has a grudge against poor man, and poet against poet.
Works and Days. Line 25

[f] For full indeed is earth of woes, and full the sea; and in the day as well as night diseases unbidden haunt mankind, silently bearing ills to men. . . . So utterly impossible is it to escape the will of Zeus.   *Ibid. Line 101*

[g] Oft hath even a whole city reaped the evil fruit of a bad man.
Ibid. Line 240

[h] For himself doth a man work evil in working evils for another.
Ibid. Line 265

[i] Badness, look you, you may choose easily in a heap: level is the path, and right near it dwells. But before Virtue the immortal gods have put the sweat of man's brow; and long and steep is the way to it, and rugged at the first.
Ibid. Line 287

[j] A bad neighbour is as great a misfortune as a good one is a great blessing. *Ibid. Line 346*

[k] Gain not base gains; base gains are the same as losses.
Ibid. Line 353

[l] If thou shouldst lay up even a little upon a little, and shouldst do this often, soon would even this become great.
Ibid. Line 360

DuBose Heyward
[1885–1940]

[m] Compassionate the mountains rise,
Dim with the wistful dimness of old eyes
That, having looked on life time out of mind,
Know that the simple gift of being kind
Is greater than all wisdom of the wise. *Sonnet. Evening in in the Great Smokies*

[n] You could not give me toys in those bleak days;
So when my playmates proudly boasted theirs,
You caught me to the shelter of your arms,
And taught me how to laugh away my tears. *Your Gifts*

John Heywood
[1497–1580]

[o] The loss of wealth is loss of dirt,
As sages in all times assert;
The happy man's without a shirt.
Be Merry Friends

[p] Let the world slide, let the world go;
A fig for care, and a fig for woe!
If I can't pay, why I can owe,
And death makes equal the high and low. *Ibid.*

[The *Proverbes* of John Heywood is the earliest collection of English colloquial sayings. It was first printed in 1546. The title of the edition of 1562 is *John Heywoodes Woorkes. A Dialogue conteyning the number in effect of all the proverbes in the English tounge, compact in a matter concernynge two maner of Maryages,*

etc. The selection following is from the edition of 1874 (a reprint of 1598), edited by Julian Sharman.]

[q] Haste maketh waste.
Proverbes. Part I, Chap. II

[r] Look ere ye leape. *Ibid.*

[s] The fat is in the fire. *Ibid.*

[t] When the sunne shineth, make hay. *Ibid.*

[u] When the iron is hot, strike. *Ibid.*

[v] The tide tarrieth no man. *Ibid.*

[w] And while I at length debate and beate the bush,
There shall steppe in other men and catch the burdes.
Ibid.

[x] While betweene two stooles my taile goe to the ground.
Ibid.

[y] Wedding is destiny,
And hanging likewise. *Ibid.*

[z] God never sends th' mouth but he sendeth meat.
Ibid. Chap. IV

[a] More frayd then hurt.
Ibid.

[b] Feare may force a man to cast beyond the moone.
Ibid.

[c] Nothing is impossible to a willing hart. *Ibid.*

[d] Rule the rost.
Ibid. Chap. V

[e] Hold their noses to grinstone.
Ibid.

[f] Better to give then to take.
Ibid.

[g] When all candles bee out, all cats be gray. *Ibid.*

[h'] No man ought to looke a given horse in the mouth.
Ibid.

[i'] Cut my cote after my cloth.
Ibid. Chap. VIII

[j'] The neer to the church, the further from God.
Ibid. Chap. IX

[k'] Now for good lucke, cast an old shooe after me. *Ibid.*

[l'] Better is to bow then breake.
Ibid.

[m'] Two heads are better then one. *Ibid.*

[n'] To tell tales out of schoole.
Ibid. Chap. X

[o'] To hold with the hare and run with the hound. *Ibid.*

[p'] She is neither fish nor flesh, nor good red herring. *Ibid.*

[q'] All is well that endes well.
Ibid.

[r] Better late than never.
Ibid.

[s] Ill weede growth fast.   *Ibid.*

[t] When the steede is stolne, shut the stable durre.   *Ibid.*

[u] Pryde will have a fall;
For pryde goeth before and shame commeth after.   *Ibid.*

[v] She looketh as butter would not melt in her mouth.   *Ibid.*

[w] Beggars should be no choosers.   *Ibid.*

[x] Every cocke is proud on his owne dunghill.
Ibid. Chap. XI

[y] The rolling stone never gathereth mosse.   *Ibid.*

[z] To robbe Peter and pay Poule.
Ibid.

[a] A man may well bring a horse to the water,
But he cannot make him drinke without he will.   *Ibid.*

[b] Rome was not built in one day.   *Ibid.*

[c] Yee have many strings to your bowe.   *Ibid.*

[d] Better is halfe a lofe than no bread.   *Ibid.*

[e] Who is worse shod than the shoemaker's wife?   *Ibid.*

[f] One good turne asketh another.   *Ibid.*

[g] By hooke or crooke.   *Ibid.*

[h] She frieth in her owne grease.
Ibid.

[i] Who waite for dead men shall goe long barefoote.   *Ibid.*

[j] I pray thee let me and my fellow have
A haire of the dog that bit us last night.   *Ibid.*

[k] But in deede,
A friend is never knowne till a man have neede.   *Ibid.*

[l] This wonder (as wonders last) lasted nine daies.
Ibid. Part II, Chap. I

[m] New brome swepth cleene.
Ibid.

[n] All thing is the woorse for the wearing.   *Ibid.*

[o] Burnt child fire dreadth.
Ibid. Chap. II

[p] Love me litle, love me long.
Ibid.

[q] A fooles bolt is soone shot.
Ibid. Chap. III

[r'] A woman hath nine lives like a cat.   *Ibid. Chap. IV*

[s'] A peny for your thought.
Ibid.

[t'] You stand in your owne light.   *Ibid.*

[u'] Small pitchers have wyde eares.   *Ibid. Chap. V*

[v'] Many hands make light warke.   *Ibid.*

[w'] There is no fire without some smoke.   *Ibid.*

[x'] One swallow maketh not summer.   *Ibid.*

[y'] Fieldes have eies and woods have eares.   *Ibid.*

[z'] A cat may looke on a King.
Ibid.

[a'] It is a foule byrd that fyleth his owne nest.   *Ibid.*

[b'] Mad as a march hare.   *Ibid.*

[c'] Much water goeth by the mill
That the miller knoweth not of.
Ibid.

[d'] He must needes goe whom the devill doth drive.
Ibid. Chap. VII

[e'] Set the cart before the horse.
Ibid.

[f'] The moe the merrier.   *Ibid.*

[g'] It is better to be
An old man's derling than a yong man's werling.   *Ibid.*

[h'] Be the day never so long,
Evermore at last they ring to evensong.   *Ibid.*

[i'] The moone is made of a greene cheese.   *Ibid.*

[j'] I know on which side my bread is buttred.   *Ibid.*

[k'] It will not out of the flesh that is bred in the bone.
Ibid. Chap. VIII

[l'] Who is so deafe or so blinde as is hee
That wilfully will neither heare nor see?   *Ibid. Chap. IX*

[m'] Went in at the tone eare and out at the tother.   *Ibid.*

[n'] Love me, love my dog.   *Ibid.*

[o'] An ill winde that bloweth no man to good.   *Ibid.*

[p'] For when I gave you an inch, you tooke an ell.   *Ibid.*

[q'] Would yee both eat your cake and have your cake?
Ibid.

[r''] Every man for himselfe and God for us all.   *Ibid.*

[s''] Though he love not to buy the pig in the poke.   *Ibid.*

[t''] This hitteth the naile on the hed.   *Ibid. Chap. XI*

[u''] Enough is as good as a feast.   *Ibid.*

Daniel Whitehead Hicky
[1902-   ]

[v] No friend like music when the
last word's spoken
And every pleading is a plea in
vain;
No friend like music when the
heart is broken,
To mend its wings and give it
flight again.
No Friend Like Music

Ella Higginson
[1862-1940]

[w] One leaf is for hope, and one
is for faith,
And one is for love, you know,
And God put another in for luck.
Four-Leaf Clover. Stanza 2

[x] The low brown hills, the bare
brown hills
Of San Francisco Bay.
The Low Brown Hills. Stanza 1

[y] Forgive you?—Oh, of course,
dear,
A dozen times a week!
We women were created
Forgiveness but to speak.
Wearing Out Love. Stanza 1

Thomas Wentworth Higginson
[1823-1911]

[z] The test of an author is not to
be found merely in the number of
his phrases that pass current in
the corner of newspapers . . . but
in the number of passages that
have really taken root in younger
minds.
Margaret Fuller Ossoli. Chap. 18

[a] When a thought takes one's
breath away, a lesson on grammar
seems an impertinence.
*Preface to Emily Dickinson's
Poems, First Series*

[b] Age, I make light of it,
Fear not the sight of it,
Time's but our playmate, whose
toys are divine.   *Sixty and
Six: A Fountain of Youth*

"Dr. Brewster Higley"

[c] Oh, give me a home where the
buffalo roam,
Where the deer and the antelope
play,
Where seldom is heard a discour-
aging word
And the skies are not cloudy all
day.
Home on the Range [1873]

Aaron Hill
[1685-1750]

[d] Tender-handed   stroke   a
nettle,
And it stings you for your pains;

Grasp it like a man of mettle,
And it soft as silk remains.

'Tis the same with common
natures:
Use 'em kindly, they rebel;
But be rough as nutmeg-graters,
And the rogues obey you well.
*Verses Written on a Window
in Scotland*

Rowland Hill
[1744-1833]

[e] Why should the Devil have all
the good tunes?

Sidney Hillman
[1887-1946]

[f] Politics is the science of how
who gets what, when and why.
*Political Primer for
All Americans*

Robert Hillyer
[1895-   ]

[g] As one who bears beneath his
neighbor's roof
Some thrust that staggers his un-
ready wit
And brooding through the night
on such reproof
Too late conceives the apt reply to
it,
So all our life is but an afterthought.
Sonnet: As One Who Bears

[h] Men lied to them, and so they
went to die.
Thermopylae and Golgotha. [1919]

[i] Each finger nail a crimson
petal, seen
Through a pale garnishing of
nicotine.
A Letter to the Editor

James Hilton
[1900-   ]

[j] Anno domini—that's the most
fatal complaint of all in the end.
Good-bye, Mr. Chips. Chap. 1

[k] The austere serenity of Shan-
gri-La. Its forsaken courts and
pale pavilions shimmered in repose from which all the fret of
existence had ebbed away, leaving
a hush as if moments hardly dared
to pass.
Lost Horizon. Chap. 5

Howard Lister Hindley
[1870-1943]

[l] There was an old man of Tar-
entum
Who gnashed his false teeth till he
bent 'em.
When asked for the cost
Of what he had lost,
He replied, "I don't know; I just
rent 'em."   *Limerick*

Katharine Tynan Hinkson
[1861–1931]

[m] All in the April evening,
    April airs were abroad,
I saw the sheep with their lambs,
    And thought on the Lamb of
        God.   *Sheep and Lambs.*
                        Stanza 6

[n] There's a lark in the noon
        sky, a thrush on the tree,
And a linnet sings wildly across
        the green lea,
And the finches are merry, the
        cuckoos still call,
But where is my Blackbird, the
        dearest of all?
        The Blackbird. Stanza 1

[o] Of all the birds from East to
        West
    That tuneful are and dear,
I love that farmyard bird the best,
    They call him Chanticleer.
        Chanticleer. Stanza 1

[p] God clad the country
    In a green gown.
        The Maker. Stanza 1

Hippocrates
[460–377 B.C.]
*Translation by William Henry
Rich Jones*

[q] I swear by Apollo Physician,
by Asclepius, by Health, by Panacea, and by all the gods and god-
desses, making them my witnesses,
that I will carry out, according to
my ability and judgment, this
oath and this indenture. To hold
my teacher in this art equal to my
own parents. . . . I will use treatment to help the sick according to
my ability and judgment, but
never with a view to injury and
wrong-doing. I will keep pure and
holy both my life and my art. In
whatsoever houses I enter, I will
enter to help the sick, and I will
abstain from all intentional wrong-
doing and harm. And whatsoever
I shall see or hear in the course of
my profession in my intercourse
with men, if it be what should
not be published abroad, I will
never divulge, holding such things
to be holy secrets. Now if I carry
out this oath, and break it not,
may I gain forever reputation
among all men for my life and for
my art; but if I transgress it and
forswear myself, may the opposite
befall me.
        The Physician's Oath

[r] Healing is a matter of time,
but it is sometimes also a matter
of opportunity.
        Precepts. Chap. 1

[s] Sometimes give your services
for nothing, calling to mind a
previous benefaction or present
satisfaction. . . . For where there
is love of man, there is also love of
the art. For some patients, though
conscious that their condition is
perilous, recover their health
simply through their contentment
with the goodness of the physician.   *Ibid. Chap. 6*

Adolf Hitler
[1889–1945]

[t] Then will come a National-
Socialist State tribunal; then will
November, 1918, be expiated; then
heads will roll!
        *Spoken in testimony at a trial
        of German army officers, in
        Leipzig [1930]*

[u] I know that one is able to win
people far more by the spoken
than by the written word, and
that every great movement on this
globe owes its rise to the great
speakers and not to the great
writers.   *Mein Kampf [Com-
        plete and Unabridged Edition,
        published by Reynal and Hitch-
        cock, 1940]. Preface*

[v] The one means that wins the
easiest victory over reason: terror
and force.   *Ibid. Vol. I, Chap. 2.
                        Page 53*

[w] From a feeble cosmopolite I
had turned into a fanatical anti-
Semite.   *Ibid. Page 83*

[x] A majority can never replace
the man. . . . Just as a hundred
fools do not make one wise man,
an heroic decision is not likely to
come from a hundred cowards.
        Ibid. Chap. 3. Page 105

[y] There is only one real "statesman" once in a blue moon in one
nation, and not a hundred or more
at a time.   *Ibid. Page 113*

[z] Every movement with great
aims has anxiously to watch that
it does not lose connection with
the great masses.   *Ibid. Page 137*

[a] The efficiency of the truly national leader consists primarily in
preventing the division of the attention of a people, and always in
concentrating it on a single
enemy.   *Ibid. Page 152*

[b] Mankind has grown strong
in eternal struggles and it will
only perish through eternal peace.
        Ibid. Chap. 4. Page 175

[c] If this earth really has room
enough for all to live in, then one
should give us the space that we
need for living.   *Ibid. Page 179*

[d] Strength lies not in defense
but in attack.   *Ibid. Page 191*

[e] One should guard against believing the great masses to be

more stupid than they actually
are.   *Ibid. Chap. 5. Page 224*

[f] All propaganda has to be popular and has to adapt its spiritual level to the perception of the
least intelligent of those towards
whom it intends to direct itself.
Ibid. Chap. 6. Page 232

[g] As soon as by one's own
propaganda even a glimpse of
right on the other side is ad-
mitted, the cause for doubting
one's own right is laid.
Ibid. Page 237

[h] All advertising, whether it
lies in the field of business or of
politics, will carry success by con-
tinuity and regular uniformity of
application.   *Ibid. Page 240*

[i] The great masses of the people
. . . will more easily fall victims
to a great lie than to a small one.
Ibid. Chap. 10. Page 313

[j] There is only one disgrace: to
be sick.   *Ibid. Vol. II, Chap. 2.
Page 608*

[k] In the morning and even during the day men's will power re-
volts with highest energy against
an attempt at being forced under
another's will and another's opinion. In the evening, however, they
succumb more easily to the domi-
nating force of a stronger will.
Ibid. Chap. 6. Page 710

[l] One makes alliances only for
fighting.   *Ibid. Chap. 14.
Page 959*

[m] After fifteen years of work I
have achieved, as a common German soldier and merely with my
fanatical will power, the unity of
the German nation, and have
freed it from the death sentence
of Versailles.   *Proclamation to
the Troops on taking over the
leadership of the German
armed forces [December 21,
1941]*

[n] This war no longer bears the
characteristics of former inter-
European conflicts. It is one of
those elemental conflicts which
usher in a new millennium and
which shake the world once in a
thousand years.
*Speech before the Reichstag
[April 26, 1942]*

[o] My possessions belong to the
party, or, if this no longer exists,
to the state. If the state, too, is
destroyed, there is no need for any
further instructions.
*Extract from Adolf Hitler's per-
sonal will, dated Berlin, 29 April,
1945. Released by the Allied authorities at Nuremberg, December 30, 1945*

Thomas Hobbes
[1588–1679]

[p] Words are wise men's coun-
ters,—they do but reckon by
them; but they are the money of
fools.
Leviathan. Part I, Chap. IV

[q] The privilege of absurdity; to
which no living creature is subject
but man only.   *Ibid. Chap. V*

[r] As the nature of foul weather
lieth not in a shower or two of
rain but in an inclination thereto
of many days together, so the nature of war consisteth not in actual fighting but in the known
disposition thereto during all the
time there is no assurance to the
contrary. All other time is peace.
Ibid. Chap. XIII

Ralph Hodgson
[1871-   ]

[s] 'Twould ring the bells of
Heaven
The wildest peal for years,
If Parson lost his senses
And people came to theirs,
And he and they together
Knelt down with angry prayers
For tamed and shabby tigers
And dancing dogs and bears,
And wretched, blind pit ponies,
And little hunted hares.
The Bells of Heaven

[t] God loves an idle rainbow
No less than labouring seas.
A Wood Song

[u] I saw with open eyes
Singing birds sweet
Sold in the shops
For the people to eat,
Sold in the shops of
Stupidity Street.
Stupidity Street. Stanza 1

[v] Time, you old gipsy man,
Will you not stay,
Put up your caravan
Just for one day?
*Time, You Old Gipsy Man.
Stanza 1*

Samuel Hoffenstein
[1890–1947]

[w] You buy some flowers for
your table;
You tend them tenderly as you're
able;
You fetch them water from hither
and thither—
What thanks do you get for it all?
They wither.
*Poems in Praise of Practically
Nothing. I*

[x] When the wind is in the tree,
It makes a noise just like the sea,
As if there were not noise enough
To bother one, without that stuff.
*A Garden of Verses for the
Little Ones. XIII, The Wind in
the Tree*

[y] Loyal be to loyal friends;
Make them pay you dividends;
Work, like the industrious bee,
Your friends and foes impartially.
*Ibid. XIX, For Little Boys
Destined for Big Business*

[z] The apple grows so bright and
high,
And ends its days in apple pie.
Songs about Life. XXXIII

[a] The muddy sparrow, mean
and small,
I like, by far, the best of all.
Ibid. LIII

[b] I play with the bulls and the
bears;
I'm the Bartlett of market quotations.   *Songs for an Old-
Fashioned Lute. VI*

[c] The stars, like measles, fade
at last.   *The Mimic Muse. V*

[d] Babies haven't any hair;
Old men's heads are just as
bare;—
Between the cradle and the grave
Lies a haircut and a shave.
*Songs of Faith in the Year after
Next. VIII*

[e] My soul is dark with stormy
riot,
Directly traceable to diet.
*Out of the Everywhere into the
Here. XIII*

[f] Little by little we subtract
Faith and Fallacy from Fact,
The Illusory from the True,
And starve upon the residue.
*Rag-Bag, II. Observation,
Stanza 1*

[g] To You, oh, Goddess of Efficiency,
Your happy vassals bend the reverent knee,
Save when arthritis, your benighted foe,
Sulks in the bones and sourly
mumbles "No!"
Hymn to Science

Charles Fenno Hoffman
[1806–1884]

[h] Sparkling and bright in liquid
light
Does the wine our goblets gleam
in;
With hue as red as the rosy bed
Which a bee would choose to
dream in.
Sparkling and Bright

Phoebe Hoffman
(Mrs. Spencer Bickerton)

[i] N. and W., the *Great Northern,
Lehigh Valley, B. and O.,*
Like a giant earth-worm twisting,
slowly 'round the curve they
flow.
Caravans of freight move westward, bearing eastern goods
away—
To come back with hogs and cattle, bales of sweet Kentucky
hay.
Brakemen walk along the
roof-tops, lingering for a moment's chat:
There an engineer, while smoking,
long and eloquently spat.
*The Freight Yards.
Stanza 2*

James Hogg
[1770–1835]

[j] She left this world of sorrow
and pain,
And returned to the Land of
Thought again.   *Kilmeny*

[k] Bird of the wilderness,
Blithesome and cumberless.
The Skylark

[l] Love is like a dizziness.
It winna let a poor body
Gang about his bizziness.
Love is Like a Dizziness. Stanza 1

Josiah Gilbert Holland
[1819–1881]

[m] Heaven is not reached at a
single bound;
But we build the ladder by
which we rise
From the lowly earth to the
vaulted skies,
And we mount to its summit
round by round.
Gradatim. Stanza 1

[n] Wings for the angels, but feet
for men.   *Ibid. Stanza 6*

[o] Who can tell what a baby
thinks?   *Cradle Song.
Stanza 2*

[p] My dear dumb friend, low
lying there,
A willing vassal at my feet—
Glad partner of my home and fare,
My shadow in the street.
To My Dog, Blanco. Stanza 1

[q] Where shall the baby's dimple
be,
Cheek, chin, knuckle or knee?
*Where Shall the Baby's
Dimple Be?*

[r] Hearts, like apples, are hard
and sour,
Till crushed by Pain's resistless
power.
Bitter-Sweet. First Episode

Norah Mary Holland
(Mrs. Lionel William Claxton)
[1876–1925]

[s] High up in the courts of
    Heaven to-day
A little dog-angel waits;
With the other angels he will not
    play,
But he sits alone at the gates.
        The Little Dog-Angel.

Robert Cortes Holliday
[1880–   ]

[t] The best, the most exquisite
automobile is a walking-stick; and
one of the finest things in life is
going a journey with it.
        Walking-Stick Papers

[u] They [women] are too personal for the high enjoyment of
going a journey. They must be
forever thinking about you or
about themselves.   *Ibid.*

[v] There is not in the press any
reading so improving as the
"obits" . . . I doubt very much
indeed whether any one could
read obituaries every day for a
year and remain a bad man or
woman.   *Ibid. The Deceased*

John Haynes Holmes
[1879–   ]

[w] I've been married eighteen
    years
And still adore my wife.
I have no hunger for other women,
I am content to be faithful,
I am resigned to decency.
I actually think I have found love
And life.
What's the matter with me?
    Lines on Reading D. H. Law-
    rence, Sherwood Anderson, et
    al. Stanza 5

[x] If Christians were Christians,
there would be no anti-Semitism.
Jesus was a Jew. There is nothing
that the ordinary Christian so dis-
likes to remember as this awkward historical fact. But it happens, none the less, to be true.
    Sensible Man's View of Religion

[y] Priests are no more necessary
to religion than politicians to
patriotism.   *Ibid.*

[z] The life of humanity upon
this planet may yet come to an
end, and a very terrible end. But
I would have you notice that this
end is threatened in our time not
by anything that the universe
may do to us, but only by what
man may do to himself.   *Ibid.*

Oliver Wendell Holmes
[1809–1894]

[a] Ay, tear her tattered ensign
    down!
Long has it waved on high,
And many an eye has danced to
    see
That banner in the sky.

Nail to the mast her holy flag,
Set every threadbare sail,
And give her to the god of storms,
The lightning and the gale!
    Old Ironsides. Stanzas 1 and 3

[b] I know it is a sin
For me to sit and grin
    At him here;
But the old three-cornered hat,
And the breeches, and all that,
    Are so queer!

And if I should live to be
The last leaf upon the tree
    In the spring,
Let them smile, as I do now,
At the old forsaken bough
    Where I cling.
    The Last Leaf. Stanzas 7 and 8

[c] Little I ask; my wants are
    few,
I only wish a hut of stone,
(A *very plain* brown stone will do,)
That I may call my own.
    Contentment. Stanza 1

[d] And when you stick on con-
    versation's burs,
Don't strew your pathway with
    those dreadful *urs.*
    A Rhymed Lesson. Urania

[e] Be sure your tailor is a man of
    sense.   *Ibid.*

[f] Wear seemly gloves; not black,
    nor yet too light,
And least of all the pair that once
    was white.   *Ibid.*

[g] Now when a doctor's patients
    are perplexed,
A consultation comes in order
    next—
You know what that is? In a cer-
    tain place
Meet certain doctors to discuss a
    case
And other matters, such as
    weather, crops,
Potatoes, pumpkins, lager-beer,
    and hops.
    Rip Van Winkle, M.D.

[h] Where go the poet's lines?
Answer, ye evening tapers!
Ye auburn locks, ye golden curls,
    Speak from your folded papers!
    The Poet's Lot. Stanza 3

[i] Old Time is a liar! We're
    twenty tonight!
    The Boys. Stanza 1

[j] Where the snow-flakes fall
    thickest there's nothing can
    freeze!   *Ibid. Stanza 2*

k] You hear that boy laughing?
—You think he's all fun;
But the angels laugh, too, at the
good he has done;
Ibid. Stanza 9

l] Build thee more stately man-
sions, O my soul,
As the swift seasons roll!
Leave thy low-vaulted past!
Let each new temple, nobler than
the last,
Shut thee from heaven with a
dome more vast,
Till thou at length art free,
Leaving thine outgrown shell by
life's unresting sea!
The Chambered Nautilus. Stanza 5

m] One unquestioned text we
read,
All doubt beyond, all fear above,—
Nor crackling pile nor cursing
creed
Can burn or blot it: God is love.
What We All Think. Stanza 10

n] Have you heard of the won-
derful one-hoss shay,
That was built in such a logical
way
It ran a hundred years to a day?
*The Deacon's Masterpiece.
Stanza 1*

o] A general flavor of mild decay.
Ibid. Stanza 10

p] It went to pieces all at once,—
All at once, and nothing first,
Just as bubbles do when they
burst.   *Ibid. Stanza 11*

q] Where we love is home,
Home that our feet may leave, but
not our hearts.
Homesick in Heaven. Stanza 5

r] The brightest blade grows dim
with rust,
The fairest meadow white with
snow.
Chanson Without Music. Stanza 3

s] Fame is the scentless sunflower, with gaudy crown of
gold;
But friendship is the breathing
rose, with sweets in every fold.
*No Time Like the Old Time.
Stanza 3*

t] I, who have never deemed it
sin to gladden
This vale of sorrows with a
wholesome laugh.
The Iron Gate. Stanza 16

u] Everybody likes and respects
self-made men. It is a great deal
better to be made in that way
than not to be made at all.
*The Autocrat of the Breakfast-
Table. I*

v] Insanity is often the logic of
an accurate mind overtaxed.
Ibid.

w] Put not your trust in money,
but put your money in trust.
Ibid. II

x] Sin has many tools, but a lie
is the handle which fits them all.
Ibid. VI

y] Boston State-house is the hub
of the solar system. You couldn't
pry that out of a Boston man, if
you had the tire of all creation
straightened out for a crow-bar.
Ibid.

z] Knowledge   and   timber
shouldn't be much used till they
are seasoned.   *Ibid.*

a] The hat is the *ultimum mori-
ens* of respectability. *Ibid. XIII*

b] I firmly believe that if the
whole *materia medica* as now used
could be sunk to the bottom of
the sea, it would be all the better
for mankind—and all the worse
for the fishes. *Address, Massachusetts Medical Society
[May 30, 1860]*

Oliver Wendell Holmes, Jr.
[1841–1935]

c] The Law, wherein, as in a
magic mirror, we see reflected not
only our own lives, but the lives
of all men that have been! When
I think on this majestic theme,
my eyes dazzle.   *To the Suffolk
Bar Association [1885]*

d] The riders in a race do not
stop short when they reach the
goal. There is a little finishing
canter before coming to a standstill. There is time to hear the
kind voice of friends and to say to
one's self: "The work is done."
But just as one says that, the answer comes: "The race is over, but
the work never is done while the
power to work remains." The canter that brings you to a standstill
need not be only coming to rest.
It cannot be, while you still live.
For to live is to function. That is
all there is in living.
*Radio address on his ninetieth
birthday [March 8, 1931]*

Homer
[*Circa* 850 B.C.]

(For other quotations from the
Iliad and *Odyssey* see Alexander
Pope)

e] These things surely lie on the
knees of the gods.   *Odyssey (tr
Butcher and Lang). Book I,
Line 267*

f] Few sons are like their father
many are worse,
Few, indeed, are better than the
father.
Ibid. Book II

Thomas Hood

[1798–1845]

[g] There is a silence where hath
        been no sound,
There is a silence where no sound
        may be,
In the cold grave—under the deep,
        deep sea,
Or in wide desert where no life is
        found.   *Sonnet, Silence*

[h] Our very hopes belied our
        fears,
Our fears our hopes belied;—
We thought her dying when she
        slept,
And sleeping when she died.
        The Death-Bed. Stanza 3

[i] Never go to France
        Unless you know the lingo,
If you do, like me,
        You will repent, by jingo.
        French and English. Stanza 1

[j] Never, from folly or urbanity,
Praise people thus profusely to
        their faces,
Till quite in love with their own
        graces,
They're eaten up by vanity!
        The Turtles. Moral

[k] I remember, I remember
The house where I was born,
The little window where the sun
Came peeping in at morn;
He never came a wink too soon
Nor brought too long a day.
        *I Remember, I Remember.
        Stanza 1*

[l] I remember, I remember
The fir-trees dark and high;
I used to think their slender tops
Were close against the sky:
It was a childish ignorance,
But now 'tis little joy
To know I'm farther off from
        heaven
Than when I was a boy.
        Ibid. Stanza 4

[m] When he's forsaken,
        Withered and shaken,
What can an old man do but die?
        Spring It is Cheery. Stanza 1

[n] And there is even a happiness
That makes the heart afraid.
        Ode to Melancholy

[o] Oh! would I were dead now,
Or up in my bed now,
To cover my head now,
        And have a good cry!
        A Table of Errata. Stanza 15

[p] No warmth, no cheerfulness,
        no healthful ease,
No comfortable feel in any
        member—
No shade, no shine, no butterflies,
        no bees,
No fruits, no flowers, no leaves,
        no birds,
        November!
                        No

[q] O bed! O bed! delicious bed!
That heaven upon earth to the
        weary head!
        *Miss Kilmansegg and Her Pre-
        cious Leg. Her Dream, Stanzas
        7, 8*

[r] He lies like a hedgehog rolled
        up the wrong way,
Tormenting himself with his
        prickles.   *Ibid. Stanza 14*

[s] There's a double beauty when-
        ever a swan
Swims on a lake, with her double
        thereon.   *Ibid. Her Honey-
        moon, Stanza 9*

[t] Home-made dishes that drive
        one from home.   *Ibid.
        Her Misery, Stanza 1*

[u] Gold! Gold! Gold! Gold!
Bright and yellow, hard and
        cold. . . .
How widely its agencies vary,—
To save—to ruin—to curse—to
        bless,—
As even its minted coins express,
Now stamped with the image of
        Good Queen Bess,
And now of a Bloody Mary.
        Ibid. Her Moral

[v] Another tumble!—that's his
        precious nose!   *Parental Ode
        to My Infant Son. Stanza 3*

[w] With fingers weary and worn,
        With eyelids heavy and red,
A woman sat in unwomanly rags
        Plying her needle and thread—
        Stitch! stitch! stitch!
        The Song of the Shirt. Stanza 1

[x] O men, with sisters dear!
O men, with mothers and wives!
It is not linen you're wearing out,
        But human creatures' lives!
        Ibid. Stanza 4

[y] Sewing at once with a double
        thread,
A shroud as well as a shirt.
        Ibid.

[z] O God! that bread should be
        so dear,
And flesh and blood so cheap!
        Ibid. Stanza 5

[a] No blessed leisure for love or
        hope,
But only time for grief.
        Ibid. Stanza 10

[b] I saw old Autumn in the
        misty morn
Stand shadowless like silence,
        listening
To silence.   *Ode, Autumn.
        Stanza 1*

[c] Ben Battle was a soldier bold,
        And used to war's alarms;
But a cannon-ball took off his
        legs,
So he laid down his arms!
        Faithless Nellie Gray. Stanza 1

d] One more unfortunate,
Weary of breath,
Rashly importunate,
Gone to her death!

Take her up tenderly,
Lift her with care;
Fashioned so slenderly,
Young, and so fair!
The Bridge of Sighs.
Stanzas 1 and 2

[e] Alas for the rarity
Of Christian charity
Under the sun!
Ibid. Stanza 9

James Hook
[1746–1827]

[f] A little farm well tilled,
A little barn well filled,
A little wife well willed,
Give me, give me.

I like the farm well tilled,
And I like the house well filled,
But no wife at all
Give me, give me.
The Soldier's Return.
Stanzas 1 and 3

Brian Hooker
[1880–1946]

[g] O youth foregone, foregoing!
O dream unseen, unsought!
God give you joy of knowing
What life your death has bought.
A. D. 1919. Stanza 5 [Inscription
on a tablet at Yale University
commemorating the Yale men
who died in the First World
War.]

Ellen Sturgis Hooper
[1816–1841]

[h] I slept and dreamed that life
was beauty.
I woke—and found that life was
duty;
Was my dream, then, a shadowy
lie?
Toil on, sad heart, courageously,
And thou shalt find thy dream
shall be
A noonday light and truth to thee.
Beauty and Duty

Earnest A. Hooton
[1887–   ]

[i] I taste the flavor of your
thumbs
While you massage my flabby
gums.
Ode to a Dental Hygienist

[j] If you had lived to breed your
kind
It would have had the sort of
mind

That feeds upon the comic strips
And reads with movements of the
lips.   *Lines to Homo*
Somejerktensis [The skull of a
baby pithecanthropus, found in
Java, 1936.]

Herbert Clark Hoover
[1874–   ]

[k] A great social and economic
experiment, noble in motive and
far-reaching in purpose.
[Of National Prohibition.] Let-
ter to Senator Borah [February
28, 1928]

[l] The American system of
rugged individualism.
Campaign speech, New York
[October 22, 1928]

[m] Absolute freedom of the press
to discuss public questions is a
foundation stone of American liberty.
Address, Annual Luncheon of
the Associated Press, New York
[April 22, 1929]

[n] No economic equality can
survive the working of biological
inequality.   *The Challenge to*
Liberty. Chap. 3

[o] Foreign relations are not sudden things created by books or
speeches or banquets. The history
of nations is more important than
their oratory.
Speech, Republican National
Convention, Chicago, Illinois
[June 27, 1944]

[p] Older men declare war. But it
is youth that must fight and die.
And it is youth who must inherit
the tribulation, the sorrow, and
the triumphs that are the after-
math of war.   *Ibid.*

"Laurence Hope"
(Adela Florence
Cory Nicolson)
[1865–1904]

[q] Less than the dust, beneath
thy Chariot wheel,
Less than the rust, that never
stained thy Sword.
Less Than the Dust. Stanza 1

[r] Pale hands I loved beside the
Shalimar,
Where are you now? Who lies
beneath your spell?
Whom do you lead on Rapture's
roadway, far,
Before you agonize them in
farewell?
Kashmiri Song. Stanza 1

[s] Often devotion to virtue arises
from sated desire
I Arise and Go Down to the River.
Stanza 6

Alphonso Alva Hopkins
[1843–1918]

[t] Flitting away, flitting away,
All that we cherished most dear;
There is nothing on earth that
　will stay,
Roses must die with the year.
　　　　　　　Flitting Away

Gerard Manley Hopkins
[1844–1889]

[u] Glory be to God for dappled
　things—
For skies as couple-colored as a
　brindled cow;
For rose-moles all in stipple upon
　trout that swim.
　　　　　　　Pied Beauty

[v] Elected Silence, sing to me
And beat upon my whorlèd ear,
Pipe me to pastures still and be
The music that I care to hear.
　　　The Habit of Perfection

[w] To lift up the hands in prayer
gives God glory, but a man with a
dungfork in his hand, a woman
with a slop-pail, give him glory
too. He is so great that all things
give him glory if you mean they
should. So then, my brethren, live.
　　An Address on St. Ignatius

Joseph Hopkinson
[1770–1842]

[x] Hail, Columbia! happy land!
Hail, ye heroes! heaven-born
　band!
Who fought and bled in Free-
　dom's cause,
And when the storm of war was
　gone,
Enjoyed the peace your valor won.
Let independence be our boast,
Ever mindful what it cost;
Ever grateful for the prize,
Let its altar reach the skies!
　　Hail, Columbia. Stanza 1

Ronald Arthur Hopwood
[1868–　　]

[y] The strength of the ship is
　the Service,
And the strength of the Service,
　the ship.
　The Laws of the Navy. Stanza 2

[z] If ye win through an African
　jungle,
Unmentioned at home in the
　press,
Heed it not; no man seeth the
　piston,
But it driveth the ship none the
　less.　　　　*Ibid. Stanza 12*

[a] They prosper who burn in
　the morning
The letters they wrote over night.
　　　　　　Ibid. Stanza 17

Horace
[65–8 B.C.]
Everyman Edition

[b] No task's too steep for human
　wit.　*Odes, Book I (tr. Dr.
John Marshall). III, To a Ship
Bearing Virgil Over Seas, Line 37*

[c] With equal foot Pluto knocks
　at hovels of the poor,
And at the tyrant's towers.
　　　Ibid. IV, Spring, Line 13

[d] To-night with wine drown
　care.
　Ibid. VII, To Plancus, Line 30

[e] Seize now and here the hour
　that is, nor trust some later
　day!
　Ibid. XI, Leuconoé, Last line

[f] Daughter, than lovely mother
　lovelier still.
　*Ibid. XVI, A Palinode or Song
of Apology, To a Beloved Girl,
Line 1*

[g] Brace thee, my friend, when
　times are hard, to show
A mind unmoved; nor less, when
　fair thy state,
A sober joy.　　*Ibid. Book II. III,
To Dellius, Line 1*

[h] Good 'tis and fine, for father-
　land to die!　*Ibid. Book III.
II, Of Roman Virtue, Line 13*

[i] Our fathers' age, than their
　sires' not so good,
Bred us ev'n worse than they; a
　brood
We'll leave that's viler still.
　*Ibid. VI, Of Rome's Degeneracy,
Line 46*

[j] Years with their whitening
　locks subdue the heart
Once keen for lawsuits and the
　reckless fray;
I had not taken thus the peaceful
　part
　　　In Plancus' day.
　*Ibid. XIV, Triumphal Ode to
Augustus, Line 25*

[k] As riches grow, care follows,
　and a thirst
For more and more.
　*Ibid. XVI, Of Riches and
Contentment, Line 17*

[l] No one lives content with his
condition, whether reason gave it
him, or chance threw it in his
way.　　*Satires (tr. Christopher
Smart) Book I. I, Line 1*

[m] This is a fault common to
all singers, that among their
friends they never are inclined to
sing when they are asked, unasked
they never desist.
　　　　　Ibid. III, Line 1

[n] There are many who recite
their writings in the middle of the
forum; and who do it while bath-

ing: the closeness of the place
gives melody to the voice.
Ibid. IV, Line 74

[o] Ridicule often decides matters of importance more effectually, and in a better manner, than severity.   *Ibid. X, Line 14*

[p] Carrying timber into a wood.
Ibid. Line 34

[q] Now learn what and how great benefits a temperate diet will bring along with it. In the first place you will enjoy good health.
Ibid. Book II. II, Line 70

[r] At Rome, you long for the country; when you are in the country, fickle, you extol the absent city to the skies.
Ibid. VII, Line 28

[s] He has half the deed done, who has made a beginning.
*Epistles, (tr. Christopher Smart)
Book I. II, To Lollius, Line 40*

[t] The covetous man is ever in want.   *Ibid. Line 56*

[u] Sicilian tyrants never invented a greater torment than envy.   *Ibid. Line 58*

[v] In the midst of hope and care, in the midst of fears and disquietudes, think every day that shines upon you is the last. Thus the hour, which shall not be expected, will come upon you an agreeable addition.   *Ibid. IV, To Albius Tibullus, Line 12*

[w] They change their climate, not their disposition, who run beyond the sea.   *Ibid. XI, To Bullatius, Line 27*

[x] That man is by no means poor, who has the use of everything he wants. If it is well with your belly, your back, and your feet, regal wealth can add nothing greater.   *Ibid. XII, To Iccius, Line 4*

[y] Joys are not the property of the rich alone: nor has he lived ill, who at his birth and at his death has passed unnoticed.
Ibid. XVII, To Scaeva, Line 9

Richard Henry Hengist Horne
[1803–1884]

[z] 'Tis always morning somewhere in the world.
Orion. Book III, Canto II

[a] The wisdom of mankind creeps slowly on,
Subject to every doubt that can retard
Or fling it back upon an earlier time.   *Ibid.*

Karen Horney, M.D.
[1885–   ]

[b] Fortunately [psycho-] analysis is not the only way to resolve inner conflicts. Life itself still remains a very effective therapist.
Our Inner Conflicts

Alfred Edward Housman
[1859–1936]

[c] Loveliest of trees, the cherry now
Is hung with bloom along the bough.
A Shropshire Lad. II

[d] Now, of my threescore years and ten,
Twenty will not come again,
And take from seventy springs a score,
It only leaves me fifty more.
Ibid.

[e] Up, lad: when the journey's over
There'll be time enough to sleep.
Ibid. IV, Reveille

[f] When I was one-and-twenty
I heard a wise man say,
"Give crowns and pounds and guineas
But not your heart away;
Give pearls away and rubies
But keep your fancy free."
But I was one-and-twenty,
No use to talk to me.

"The heart out of the bosom
Was never given in vain;
'Tis paid with sighs a-plenty
And sold for endless rue."
And I am two-and-twenty,
And Oh, 'tis true, 'tis true.
Ibid. XIII

[g] And silence sounds no worse than cheers
After earth has stopped the ears.
Ibid. XIX, To an Athlete Dying Young

[h] Oh, 'tis jesting, dancing, drinking
Spins the heavy world around.
If young hearts were not so clever,
Oh, they would be young for ever:
Think no more; 'tis only thinking
Lays lads underground.
Ibid. XLIX

[i] With rue my heart is laden
For golden friends I had,
For many a rose-lipt maiden
And many a lightfoot lad.
Ibid. LIV

[j] And cowards' funerals, when they come,
Are not wept so well at home,
Therefore, though the best is bad,
Stand and do the best, my lad.
Ibid. LVI, The Day of Battle

[k] Why, if 'tis dancing you
would be,
There's brisker pipes than poetry.
Ibid. LXII

[l] Ale, man, ale's the stuff to
drink
For fellows whom it hurts to
think. *Ibid.*

[m] Luck's a chance, but
trouble's sure,
I'd face it as a wise man would,
And train for ill and not for good.
Ibid.

[n] The troubles of our proud
and angry dust
Are from eternity, and shall not
fail.
Bear them we can, and if we can
we must.
Shoulder the sky, my lad, and
drink your ale.
Last Poems. IX

[o] Could man be drunk for ever
With liquor, love, or fights,
Lief should I rouse at morning
And lief lie down of nights.
Ibid. X

[p] The laws of God, the laws of
man,
He may keep that will and can;
Not I: let God and man decree
Laws for themselves and not for
me. *Ibid. XII*

[q] And how am I to face the
odds
Of man's bedevilment and God's?
I, a stranger and afraid
In a world I never made. *Ibid.*

[r] And then the clock collected
in the tower
Its strength, and struck.
Ibid. XV, Eight O'Clock

[s] Oh stay with company and
mirth
And daylight and the air;
Too full already is the grave
Of fellows that were good and
brave
And died because they were.
Ibid. XXXVIII

[t] The rainy Pleiads wester,
Orion plunges prone,
And midnight strikes and hastens,
And I lie down alone.
More Poems. XI

[u] Oh, the pearl seas are yonder,
The gold and amber shore;
Shires where the girls are fonder,
Towns where the pots hold
more. *Ibid. XXXIII*

[v] I was brought up in the
Church of England and in the
High Church party, which is much
the best religion I have ever come
across. But Lemprière's "Classical
Dictionary," read when I was
eight, made me prefer paganism
to Christianity; I abandoned

Christianity at thirteen, and became an atheist at twenty-one.
*Autobiographical note written
for a French translation of his
poems*

[w] My poetry, so far as I could
make out, sprang chiefly from
physical causes, such as a relaxed
sore throat during my most pro-
lific period, the first five months
of 1895. *Ibid.*

[x] Experience has taught me,
when I am shaving of a morning,
to keep watch over my thoughts,
because, if a line of poetry strays
into my memory, my skin bristles
so that the razor ceases to act.
. . . The seat of this sensation is
the pit of the stomach. *Ibid.*

Laurence Housman
[1865-   ]

[y] Minority is no disproof:
Wisdom is not so strong and fleet
As never to have known defeat.
Advocatus Diaboli.

Richard Hovey
[1864–1900]

[z] Eleazar Wheelock was a very
pious man;
He went into the wilderness to
teach the Indian,
With a *Gradus ad Parnassum*, a
Bible, and a drum,
And five hundred gallons of New
England rum. . . .
Eleazar was the faculty, and the
whole curriculum
Was five hundred gallons of New
England rum.
Dartmouth College Song

[a] For 'tis always fair weather
When good fellows get together
With a stein on the table and a
good song ringing clear.
A Stein Song. Stanza 1

[b] The guns that spoke at Lex-
ington
Knew not that God was plan-
ning then
The trumpet word of Jefferson
To bugle forth the rights of
men.
Unmanifest Destiny. Stanza 3

[c] Whose furthest footstep never
strayed
Beyond the village of his birth
Is but a lodger for the night
In this old wayside inn of earth.
*More Songs from Vagabondia.
Envoy, Stanza 1*

Rowland Howard
[*Floruit* 1876]

[d] You never miss the water till
the well runs dry.
You Never Miss the Water

Edgar Watson Howe
[1853-1937]

[e] A really busy person never
nows how much he weighs.
Country Town Sayings

[f] What people say behind your
ack is your standing in the com-
nunity.   *Ibid.*

Julia Ward Howe
[1819-1910]

[g] Mine eyes have seen the glory
of the coming of the Lord;
Ie is trampling out the vintage
where the grapes of wrath are
stored;
Ie hath loosed the fateful lightning of His terrible, swift
sword;
His truth is marching on.
Battle Hymn of the Republic.
Stanza 1

[h] In the beauty of the lilies
Christ was born across the sea,
With a glory in His bosom that
transfigures you and me;
As He died to make men holy, let
us die to make men free.
Ibid. Stanza 5

[i] Don't trouble more to celebrate this natal day of mine,
But keep the grasp of fellowship
which warms us more than
wine.   *Growing Old*

[j] I have made a voyage upon a
golden river.
Reminiscences. At the end

Marc Antony De Wolfe Howe
[1864-   ]

[k] Not for the star-crowned
heroes, the men that conquer
and slay,
But a song for those that bore
them, the mothers braver
than they!
With never a blare of trumpets,
with never a surge of cheers,
They march to the unseen hazard
—pale, patient volunteers.
The Valiant

Mildred Howells
[1872-   ]

[l] Within a garden once there
grew
A flower that seemed the very
pattern
Of all propriety; none knew
She was at heart a wandering
slattern.
A Very Wild Flower. Stanza 1

[m] And so it criticized each
flower,
This supercilious seed;

Until it woke one summer hour,
And found itself a weed.
The Difficult Seed. Stanza 5

William Dean Howells
[1837-1920]

[n] Though I move with leaden
feet,
Light itself is not so fleet;
And before you know me gone
Eternity and I are one.   *Time*

[o] I know his name, I know his
note,
That so with rapture takes my
soul;
Like flame the gold beneath his
throat,
His glossy cope is black as coal.
The Song the Oriole Sings

[p] He who sleeps in continual
noise is wakened by silence.
Pordenone. IV

[q] Yes, death is at the bottom
of the cup,
And every one that lives must
drink it up;
And yet between the sparkle at
the top
And the black lees where lurks
that bitter drop,
There swims enough good liquor,
Heaven knows,
To ease our hearts of all their
other woes.   *If*

[r] The first night, when at
night I went about
Locking the doors and windows
everywhere,
After she died, I seemed to lock
her out
In the starred silence and the
homeless air.   *Experience*

[s] Tossing his mane of snows in
wildest eddies and tangles,
Lion-like March cometh in,
hoarse, with tempestuous
breath.
Earliest Spring. Stanza 1

[t] The Bostonian who leaves
Boston ought to be condemned to
perpetual exile.   *The Rise
of Silas Lapham. Chap. 5*

[u] The book which you read
from a sense of duty, or because
for any reason you must, does not
commonly make friends with you.
My Literary Passions. Chap. 7

[v] Last night, after I got back
from my Balfour tailor, I expressed my surprise that B. should
go to such a simple shop. "Well,
I don't think, sir, Mr. Balfour
cares much for his clothes, sir.
Them distinguished men can't,
sir. Their thoughts soars to 'igher
things, sir."   *Letter to Mrs.
Howells [April 12, 1904], quoting
his London landlord (Life in
Letters, Vol. II, Page 191)*

Mary Howitt
[1799–1888]

[w] Old England is our home,
and Englishmen are we;
Our tongue is known in every
clime, our flag in every sea.
Old England Is Our Home

[x] "Will you walk into my parlour?" said the spider to the
fly;
" 'Tis the prettiest little parlour
that ever you did spy."
The Spider and the Fly

William Howitt
[1792–1879]

[y] The Wind one morning
sprang up from sleep,
Saying, "Now for a frolic, now for
a leap!
Now for a madcap galloping chase!
I'll make a commotion in every
place!"
The Wind in a Frolic

Edmond Hoyle
[1672–1769]

[z] When in doubt, win the trick.
*Twenty-four Rules for Learners.
Rule 12*

Elbert Hubbard
[1859–1915]

[a] It is not book learning young
men need, nor instruction about
this and that, but a stiffening of
the vertebrae which will cause
them to be loyal to a trust, to act
promptly, concentrate their energies, do a thing—"carry a message
to Garcia." [After the declaration
of the Spanish-American War,
Andrew Summers Rowan, then
Lieutenant, United States Bureau
of Military Intelligence, was sent
to communicate with General
Calixto Garcia. He landed in an
open boat near Turquino Peak,
April 24, 1898, executed the mission, and brought back information regarding the insurgent
army.] *A Message to Garcia*
[*The Philistine, March 1900.*]

[b] The final proof of greatness
lies in being able to endure contumely without resentment.
Get Out or Get in Line

Frank McKinney ("Kin") Hubbard
see "Abe Martin"

Edwin Powell Hubble
[1889–   ]

[c] On the grand scale, the Ob-
servable Region [of space] is very
much the same everywhere and in
all directions—in other words, it
is homogeneous.
The Exploration of Space [*1945*]

William Henry Hudson
[1841–1922]

[d] When I meet with a falsehood, I care not who the great
persons who proclaim it may be,
I do not try to like it or believe
it or mimic the fashionable
prattle of the world about it.
The Purple Land. Chap. 28

[e] When I hear people say they
have not found the world and life
so agreeable or interesting as to
be in love with it, or that they
look with equanimity to its end,
I am apt to think they have never
been properly alive nor seen with
clear vision the world they think
so meanly of, or anything in it—
not a blade of grass.   *Far Away
and Long Ago. Chap. 24*

Baron Ehrenfried Gunther von Huenefeld
[1893–1929]

[f] To-morrow, we shall start on
our great journey. After a trying
period of expectancy, we have entered upon the stage of certainty.
Now the last word lies with the
God of weathers and to confide in
Him is the duty of every sincere
sportsman.   *Interview, before
his transatlantic air flight in
the Bremen* [*April 12–13, 1928*]

[g] He who has glimpsed the awful face of Death
Can but confess Thy mercy and
Thy might.
*Song of Thanks in the Light-
house at Greenly, after the safe
landing of the Bremen*

Langston Hughes
[1902–   ]

[h] De railroad bridge's
A sad song in de air.
Ever' time de trains pass
I wants to go somewhere.
Homesick Blues. Stanza 1

[i] I swear to the Lord
I still can't see
Why Democracy means
Everybody but me.
The Black Man Speaks

[j] A bright bowl of brass is
beautiful to the Lord.
Bright polished brass like the
cymbals
Of King David's dancers,
Like the wine cups of Solomon.
Hey, boy!
A clean spittoon on the altar of
the Lord.

A clean bright spittoon all newly
polished,—
At least I can offer that.
Com'mere, boy!
Brass Spittoons

Richard Hughes
[1900–   ]

[k] Puddings should be
Full of currants, for me:
Boiled in a pail,
Tied in the tail
Of an old bleached shirt:
So hot that they hurt.
Poets, Painters, Puddings

Rupert Hughes
[1872–   ]

[l] Dear little child, this little
book
Is less a primer than a key
To sunder gates where wonder
waits
Your "Open Sesame!"
With a First Reader. Stanza 1

Thomas Hughes
[1822–1896]

[m] Life isn't all beer and
skittles; but beer and skittles, or
something better of the same sort,
must form a good part of every
Englishman's education.
Tom Brown's School-days.
Chap. 2

Victor Hugo
[1802–1885]

[n] The three problems of the
age—the degradation of man by
poverty, the ruin of woman by
starvation, and the dwarfing of
childhood by physical and spiritual night.   *Les Misérables* (tr.
Charles E. Wilbour). *Preface*

[o] Far be it from me to insult
the pun! I honor it in proportion
to its merits—no more.
Ibid. Fantine, Book III, Chap. 7

[p] Indigestion is charged by God
with enforcing morality on the
stomach.   *Ibid.*

[q] Mothers' arms are made of
tenderness, and sweet sleep
blesses the child who lies therein.
Ibid. Book IV, Chap. 1

[r] The supreme happiness of
life is the conviction that we are
loved.   *Ibid. Book V, Chap. 4*

[s] For prying into any human
affairs, none are equal to those
whom it does not concern.
Ibid. Chap. 8

[t] The malicious have a dark
happiness.   *Ibid. Chap. 9*

[u] Great grief is a divine and
terrible radiance which transfigures the wretched.
Ibid. Chap. 13

[v] No human feeling can ever
be so appalling as joy.
Ibid. Book VIII, Chap. 3

[w] Death has its own way of
embittering victory. . . . Typhus
is the successor of triumph.
Ibid. Cosette, Book I, Chap. 2

[x] The doll is one of the most
imperious necessities, and at the
same time one of the most charming instincts of female childhood.
Ibid. Book III, Chap. 8

[y] Great blunders are often
made, like large ropes, of a multitude of fibers.
Ibid. Book V, Chap. 10

[z] Upon the first goblet he read
this inscription: Monkey wine;
upon the second: lion wine; upon
the third: sheep wine; upon the
fourth: swine wine. These four
inscriptions expressed the four
descending degrees of drunkenness: the first, that which enliv-
ens; the second, that which irritates; the third, that which
stupefies; finally the last, that
which brutalizes.
Ibid. Book VI, Chap. 9

[a] No one ever keeps a secert so
well as a child.
Ibid. Book VIII, Chap. 8

[b] Life, misfortunes, isolation,
abandonment, poverty, are battlefields which have their heroes;
obscure heroes, sometimes greater
than the illustrious heroes.
Ibid. Marius. Book V, Chap. 1

[c] A creditor is worse than a
master; for a master owns only
your person, a creditor owns your
dignity, and can belabor that.
Ibid. Chap. 2

[d] Seeing that Mother Plutarch
had a gloomy and thoughtful air,
he tapped her on the shoulder
and said with a smile: "We have
the indigo."   *Ibid. Chap. 4*

[e] Where the telescope ends, the
microscope begins. Which of the
two has the grander view?
Ibid. Saint Denis, Book III,
Chap. 3

[f] A compliment is something
like a kiss through a veil.
Ibid. Book VIII, Chap. 1

[g] Situated in the moon, kingdom of dream, province of illusion, capital Soap-Bubble.
Ibid. Chap. 3

[h] When grace is joined with
wrinkles, it is adorable. There is

an unspeakable dawn in happy old age. *Ibid. Jean Valjean, Book V, Chap. 2*

[i] *Angel* is the only word in the language which cannot be worn out. No other word would resist the pitiless use which lovers make of it. *Ibid. Chap. 4*

[j] Nothing is more gentle than smoke, nothing more frightful. There is the smoke of peace, and the smoke of villainy. Smoke, the density and color of smoke, makes all the difference between peace and war, between brotherhood and hatred, between hospitality and the grave, between life and death. Smoke rising through the trees may signify the most charming thing in the world, the hearth; or the most terrible, a conflagration. *Ninety-Three. Part I, Book IV, Chap. 7*

[k] There is a sacred horror about everything grand. It is easy to admire mediocrity and hills; but whatever is too lofty, a genius as well as a mountain, an assembly as well as a masterpiece, seen too near, is appalling. *Ibid. Part II, Book III, Chap. 1*

[l] The sublimest song to be heard on earth is the lisping of the human soul on the lips of children. *Ibid. Part III, Book III, Chap. 1*

[m] Nothing is so like a soul as a bee. It goes from flower to flower as a soul from star to star, and it gathers honey as a soul gathers light. *Ibid. Chap. 3*

[n] Popularity? It is glory's small change. *Ruy Blas. Act III, Sc. 5*

[o] I represent a party which does not yet exist:
the party of revolution, civilization.
This party will make the twentieth century.
There will issue from it first
the United States of Europe, then
the United States of the World.
Prophecy in autograph on the wall of the room in which Hugo died, Place des Vosges, Paris

Leigh Hunt
[1784–1859]

[p] Abou Ben Adhem (may his tribe increase!)
Awoke one night from a deep dream of peace. *Abou Ben Adhem*

[q] An angel writing in a book of gold. *Ibid.*

[r] Write me as one who loves his fellowmen. *Ibid.*

[s] The world was all forgot, the struggle o'er,
Desperate the joy.—That day they read no more. *The Story of Rimini. Canto III, Line 607*

[t] Say I'm weary, say I'm sad,
Say that health and wealth have missed me,
Say I'm growing old, but add,
Jenny kissed me. *Rondeau*

[u] Coining words in the quick mint of joy. *A Rustic Walk and Dinner. Line 33*

[v] Those who have lost an infant are never, as it were, without an infant child. They are the only persons who, in one sense, retain it always. *Deaths of Little Children*

[w] The groundwork of all happiness is health. *Ibid.*

[x] A fireside is a great opiate. *A Few Thoughts on Sleep*

[y] It has been said of ladies when they write letters, that they put their minds in their postscripts—let out the real objects of their writing, as if it were a second thought, or a thing comparatively indifferent. *Anacreon*

[z] The only place a new hat can be carried into with safety is a church, for there is plenty of room there. *A Chapter on Hats*

Francis Hutcheson
[1694–1746]

[a] That action is best which procures the greatest happiness for the greatest numbers. *Inquiry Concerning Moral Good and Evil. Sect. 3*

Robert Maynard Hutchins
[1899–   ]

[b] A world community can exist only with world communication, which means something more than extensive shortwave facilities scattered about the globe. It means common understanding, a common tradition, common ideas, and common ideals. . . . The task is overwhelming, and the chance of success is slight. We must take the chance or die. *The Atomic Bomb versus Civilization, December 1945*

[c] We do not know what education could do for us, because we have never tried it. *Ibid.*

Jesse Hutchinson, Jr.
[1813–1853]

[d] Here's a general invitation To the people of the world.

Uncle Sam is rich enough
  To give us all a farm.
    *Uncle Sam's Farm. Stanza 1
        and Refrain*

[e] Then ho, brothers, ho,
To California go;
There's plenty of gold in the world
    we're told
On the banks of the Sacramento.
  Ho for California [1849]. Refrain

Aldous Leonard Huxley
[1894–   ]

[f] It is far easier to write ten
passably effective Sonnets, good
enough to take in the not too in-
quiring critic, than one effective
advertisement that will take in a
few thousand of the uncritical
buying public.   *On the Margin*

[g] There are not enough *bon
mots* in existence to provide any
industrious conversationalist with
a new stock for every social occasion.
     Point Counter Point. Chap. 7

[h] Seated   upon   the   convex
    mound
Of one vast kidney, Jonah prays
And   sings   his   canticles   and
    hymns,
Making the hollow vault resound
God's goodness and mysterious
    ways,
Till the great fish spouts music as
    he swims.   *Jonah*

[i] Life is their madness, life that
    all night long
Bids them to sing and sing, they
    know not why.
     The Cicadas. Stanza 5

[j] A poor degenerate from the
    ape,
Whose hands are four, whose tail's
    a limb,
I contemplate my flaccid shape
And know I may not rival him
Save with my mind.
     First Philosopher's Song

[k] A million million spermato-
    zoa,
  All of them alive:
Out of their cataclysm but one
    poor Noah
  Dare hope to survive.
And among that billion minus
    one
  Might have chanced to be
Shakespeare, another Newton, a
    new Donne—
  But the One was Me.
     Fifth Philosopher's Song

Thomas Henry Huxley
[1825–1895]

[1] I cannot but think that he
who finds a certain proportion of
pain and evil inseparably woven

up in the life of the very worms,
will bear his own share with more
courage and submission.
     *On the Educational Value of
        the National History Sciences*

[m] To a person uninstructed in
natural history, his country or
seaside stroll is a walk through a
gallery filled with wonderful
works of art, nine-tenths of which
have their faces turned to the
wall.   *Ibid.*

[n] The rung of a ladder was
never meant to rest upon, but only
to hold a man's foot long enough
to enable him to put the other
somewhat higher.
     On Medical Education

[o] There is the greatest practical
benefit in making a few failures
early in life.   *Ibid.*

[p] It is futile to expect a hungry
and squalid population to be anything but violent and gross.
     Joseph Priestley

[q] Size is not grandeur, and territory does not make a nation.
     On University Education

[r] The chess-board is the world,
the pieces are the phenomena of
the universe, the rules of the game
are what we call the laws of
Nature. The player on the other
side is hidden from us. We know
that his play is always fair, just,
and patient. But also we know, to
our cost, that he never overlooks a
mistake, or makes the smallest
allowance for ignorance.
     Lay Sermons

[s] Perhaps the most valuable result of all education is the ability
to make yourself do the thing you
have to do, when it ought to be
done, whether you like it or not
. . . however early a man's training
begins, it is probably the last lesson that he learns thoroughly.
     Technical Education

[t] The great end of life is not
knowledge but action.   *Ibid.*

[u] It is the customary fate of
new truths to begin as heresies
and to end as superstitions.
     *The Coming of Age of "The
        Origin of Species"*

[v] Logical consequences are the
scarecrows of fools and the
beacons of wise men.
     Animal Automatism

Joris Karl Huysmans
[1848–1907]

[w] The pleasure of travel, . . .
only exists as a matter of fact in
retrospect and seldom in the present, at the instant when it is being experienced.   *Against the
Grain (tr. John Howard). Chap 3*

[x] Is there a woman, whose form is more dazzling, more splendid than the two locomotives that pass over the Northern Railroad lines?   *Ibid.*

[y] The loveliest tune imaginable becomes vulgar and insupportable as soon as the public begins to hum it and the hurdy-gurdies make it their own.   *Ibid. Chap. 9*

[z] Perfumes, in fact, rarely come from the flowers whose names they bear . . . with the exception of the inimitable jasmine which it is impossible to counterfeit.
    Ibid. Chap. 10

[a] Art is the only clean thing on earth, except holiness.
    Les Foules de Lourdes

Henrik Ibsen
[1828–1906]

[b] A community is like a ship; every one ought to be prepared to take the helm.   *An Enemy of the People. Act. I*

[c] The most crying need in the humbler ranks of life is that they should be allowed some part in the direction of public affairs. That is what will develop their faculties and intelligence and self-respect.   *Ibid. Act II*

[d] Politics are the most important thing in life—for a newspaper.   *Ibid. Act III*

[e] The most dangerous enemy to truth and freedom amongst us is the compact majority.
    Ibid. Act IV

[f] You should never wear your best trousers when you go out to fight for freedom and truth.
    Ibid. Act V

[g] It is not only what we have inherited from our fathers that exists again in us, but all sorts of old dead ideas and all kinds of old dead beliefs. . . . They are not actually alive in us; but there they are dormant, all the same, and we can never be rid of them. Whenever I take up a newspaper and read it, I fancy I see ghosts creeping between the lines. There must be ghosts all over the world.
    Ghosts. Act II

[h] There can be no freedom or beauty about a home life that depends on borrowing and debt.
    A Doll's House. Act I

[i] Marriage is a thing you've got to give your whole mind to.
    The League of Youth. Act IV

[j] These heroes of finance are like beads on a string—when one slips off, all the rest follow.   *Ibid.*

[k] He has the luck to be unhampered by either character, or conviction, or social position; so that Liberalism is the easiest thing in the world for him.
    Ibid. Act V

[l] Rob the average man of his life-illusion, and you rob him of his happiness at the same stroke.
    The Wild Duck. Act V

[m] A lie, turned topsy-turvy, can be prinked and tinselled out, decked in plumage new and fine, till none knows its lean old carcass.   *Peer Gynt. Act I*

[n] I hold that man is in the right who is most closely in league with the future.   *Letter to Georg Brandes [January 3, 1882]*

Harold L. Ickes
[1874–1952]

[o] I am against government by crony.   *On resigning as Secretary of the Interior, February 1946*

Jeremy Ingalls
[1911–   ]

[p] There is much to learn.
But strictest thought and deepest sense pertain
To the honor of God. Do not shun His name.
Now the sun goes noonward. Whether you return
With two or three or singly, still you walk
Companioned, among brothers, going home.   *A Plain Poem*

John James Ingalls
[1833–1900]

[q] The purification of politics is an iridescent dream.   *Epigram*

[r] In the democracy of the dead, all men at last are equal. There is neither rank nor station nor prerogative in the republic of the grave.   *On the Death of Senator Barnes*

[s] Grass is the forgiveness of nature—her constant benediction. Fields trampled with battle, saturated with blood, torn with the ruts of the cannon, grow green again with grass, and carnage is forgotten. Forests decay, harvests perish, flowers vanish, but grass is immortal.   *Blue Grass*

[t] I knock unbidden once at every gate!
If sleeping, wake; if feasting, rise before
I turn away. It is the hour of fate.
    Opportunity

Jean Ingelow
[1820–1897]

[u] Man dwells apart, though not alone,
He walks among his peers unread;
The best of thoughts which he hath known
For lack of listeners are not said.
Afterthought. Stanza 1

[v] It is a comely fashion to be glad,—
Joy is the grace we say to God.
Dominion

[w] Like coral insects multitudinous
The minutes are whereof our life is made. *Work*

[x] I marked my love by candlelight
Sewing her long white seam.
The Long White Seam. Stanza 1

Robert Green Ingersoll
[1833–1899]

[y] These heroes are dead. They died for liberty—they died for us. They are at rest. They sleep in the land they made free, under the flag they rendered stainless, under the solemn pines, the sad hemlocks, the tearful willows, the embracing vines. They sleep beneath the shadows of the clouds, careless alike of sunshine or storm, each in the windowless palace of rest. Earth may run red with other wars—they are at peace. In the midst of battles, in the roar of conflict, they found the serenity of death.
Vision of War [Speech at Indianapolis, Indiana, September 21, 1876; repeated by request in the Metropolitan Opera House, New York, May 30, 1888]

[z] I am the inferior of any man whose rights I trample under foot. Men are not superior by reason of the accidents of race or color. They are superior who have the best heart—the best brain. . . . The superior man . . . stands erect by bending above the fallen. He rises by lifting others. *Liberty*

[a] Every cradle asks us, "Whence?" and every coffin, "Whither?" The poor barbarian, weeping above his dead, can answer these questions as intelligently as the robed priest of the most authentic creed.
Address at a Little Boy's Grave

[b] That imperial impersonation of force and murder known as Napoleon the Great.
At the Tomb of Napoleon

[c] We have our dream. The idea of immortality, that like a sea has ebbed and flowed in the human heart, beating with its countless waves against the sands and rocks of time and fate, was not born of any creed, nor of any book, nor of any religion. It was born of human affection, and it will continue to ebb and flow beneath the mists and clouds of doubt and darkness, as long as love kisses the lips of death.
At the Bier of a Friend

[d] An honest God is the noblest work of man. *Epigram*

[e] Happiness is the only good.
The time to be happy is now,
The place to be happy is here,
The way to be happy is to make others so. *Creed*

[f] Is there beyond the silent night
An endless day?
Is death a door that leads to light?
We cannot say.
Declaration of the Free. Stanza 16

Washington Irving
[1783–1859]

[g] How convenient it would be to many of our great men and great families of doubtful origin, could they have the privilege of the heroes of yore, who, whenever their origin was involved in obscurity, modestly announced themselves descended from a god.
Knickerbocker's History of New York. Book II, Chap. 3

[h] Who ever hears of fat men heading a riot, or herding together in turbulent mobs?—no—no, 'tis your lean, hungry men who are continually worrying society, and setting the whole community by the ears. *Ibid. Book III, Chap. 2*

[i] Your true dull minds are generally preferred for public employ, and especially promoted to city honors; your keen intellects, like razors, being considered too sharp for common service. *Ibid.*

[j] His wife "ruled the roast," and in governing the governor, governed the province, which might thus be said to be under petticoat government.
Ibid. Book IV, Chap. 4

[k] Whenever a man's friends begin to compliment him about looking young, he may be sure that they think he is growing old.
Bracebridge Hall. Bachelors

[l] The constant interchange of those thousand little courtesies which imperceptibly sweeten life,

has a happy effect upon the features, and spreads a mellow evening charm over the wrinkles of old age.   *Wolford's Roost.*
A Contented Man

[m] There is in every true woman's heart a spark of heavenly fire, which lies dormant in the broad daylight of prosperity; but which kindles up, and beams and blazes in the dark hour of adversity.
The Sketch-Book. The Wife

[n] Those men are most apt to be obsequious and conciliating abroad, who are under the discipline of shrews at home.
Ibid. Rip Van Winkle

[o] A sharp tongue is the only edge tool that grows keener with constant use.   *Ibid.*

[p] That happy age when a man can be idle with impunity. *Ibid.*

[q] The sorrow for the dead is the only sorrow from which we refuse to be divorced. Every other wound we seek to heal, every other affliction to forget; but this wound we consider it a duty to keep open; this affliction we cherish and brood over in solitude.
Ibid. Rural Funerals

[r] There is certainly something in angling . . . that tends to produce a gentleness of spirit, and a pure serenity of mind.
Ibid. The Angler

Wallace Irwin
[1876–   ]

[s] Of all the fish that swim or swish
In ocean's deep autocracy,
There's none possess such haughtiness
As the codfish aristocracy.
Codfish Aristocracy. Stanza 1

[t] "Suppose that this here vessel," says the skipper, with a groan,
"Should lose 'er bearin's, run away, and bump upon a stone;
Suppose she'd shiver and go down, when save ourselves we couldn't—"
The mate replies, "O, blow me eyes, suppose again she shouldn't."   *The Sorrows of a Skipper. Stanza 3*

[u] "Sayin' nothin'," says the goldsmith, "is a woman's rarest skill."
"Birds should sing," remarked the Doctor, "but a woman should be still."   *The Chamber of Tranquillity. Stanza 10*

Helen Hunt Jackson
("Saxe Holm")
[1831–1885]

[v] O suns and skies and clouds of June,
And flowers of June together,
Ye cannot rival for one hour
October's bright blue weather.
October's Bright Blue Weather.
Stanza 1

[w] On the king's gate the moss grew gray;
The king came not. They called him dead
And made his eldest son one day
Slave in his father's stead.
Coronation. Stanza 10

[x] Oh, write of me, not "Died in bitter pains,"
But "Emigrated to another star!"
Emigravit

[y] My body, eh. Friend Death, how now?
Why all this tedious pomp of writ?
Thou hast reclaimed it sure and slow
For half a century, bit by bit.
Habeas Corpus. Stanza 1

[z] There is nothing so skillful in its own defence as imperious pride.   *Ramona. Chap. 13*

[a] That indescribable expression peculiar to people who hope they have not been asleep, but know they have.   *Ibid. Chap. 14*

Robert Houghwout Jackson
[1892–   ]

[b] The first trial in history for crimes against the peace of the world imposes a grave responsibility. The wrongs which we seek to condemn and punish have been so calculated, so malignant and so devastating that civilization cannot tolerate their being ignored because it cannot survive their being repeated.
Opening Address before the International Military Tribunal [1945]

Joe Jacobs
[1896–1940]

[c] We wuz robbed!
After the fight between Max Schmeling and Jack Sharkey, June 21, 1932, when Sharkey had been awarded the decision and the heavyweight title, Jacobs, Schmeling's manager, shouted this protest into the radio microphone so that it was heard from coast to coast.

[d] I should of stood in bed.
Jacobs left a sick-bed to go to Detroit in October, 1935, to attend the World's Series baseball games. He bet on Chicago, and Detroit won the series. When he returned to New York he made this comment to the sports writers who came to interview him.

George Payne Rainsford James
[1799–1860]

[e] Thou'rt an ass, Robin, thou'rt an ass,
To think that great men be
More gay than I that lie on the grass
Under the greenwood tree.
I tell thee no, I tell thee no,
The Great are slaves to their gilded show.   *Richelieu.*
Chap. 3, Robber's Song, Stanza 1

[f] The best happiness a woman can boast is that of being most carefully deceived. *Ibid. Chap. 4*

[g] A great bad man is worse than one of less talents, for he has the extended capability of doing harm.   *Ibid. Chap. 6*

[h] Age is the most terrible misfortune that can happen to any man; other evils will mend, this is every day getting worse.
          Ibid. Chap. 14

Henry James
[1843–1916]

[i] There are few hours in life more agreeable than the hour dedicated to the ceremony known as afternoon tea.
          The Portrait of a Lady. I

[j] At moments she discovered she was grotesquely wrong, and then she treated herself to a week of passionate humility. *Ibid. VI*

[k] The time-honored breadsauce of the happy ending.
          Theatricals: Second Series

[l] It's a complex fate, being an American, and one of the responsibilities it entails is fighting against a superstitious valuation of Europe.
Letter, 1872. (Quoted by Van Wyck Brooks: The Pilgrimage of Henry James)

William James
[1842–1910]

[m] Habit is thus the enormous fly-wheel of society, its most precious conservative agent. It alone is what keeps us all within the bounds of ordinance.
          Psychology. Chap. 10

[n] It is well for the world that in most of us, by the age of thirty, the character has set like plaster, and will never soften again.
          Ibid.

[o] There is no more miserable human being than one in whom nothing is habitual but indecision.   *Ibid.*

[p] With mere good intentions, hell is proverbially paved. *Ibid.*

[q] We have an innate propensity to get ourselves noticed, and noticed favorably, by our kind. No more fiendish punishment could be devised, were such a thing physically possible, than that one should be turned loose in society and remain absolutely unnoticed by all the members thereof.   *Ibid. Chap. 12*

[r] Genius, in truth, means little more than the faculty of perceiving in an unhabitual way.
          Ibid. Chap. 20

[s] The great source of terror to infancy is solitude. *Ibid. Chap. 25*

[t] Be not afraid of life. Believe that life is worth living, and your belief will help create the fact.
          The Will to Believe

[u] The whole drift of my education goes to persuade me that the world of our present consciousness is only one out of many worlds of consciousness that exist.
          The Varieties of Religious Experience. Lecture XX

Margaret Thomson Janvier
("Margaret Vandegrift")
[1845–1913]

[v] You needn't be trying to comfort me—
I tell you my dolly is dead!
There's no use in saying she isn't, with a crack like that in her head.
          The Dead Doll. Stanza 1

Jarrett and Palmer
[*Floruit* 1866]

[w] Legs are staple articles and will never go out of fashion while the world lasts.
Of the original production [1866] of their Grand Magical Spectacular Drama, The Black Crook, by Charles M. Barras

Sir James Hopwood Jeans
[1877–1946]

[x] Taking a very gloomy view of the future of the human race, let us suppose that it can only expect to survive for two thousand mil-

lion years longer, a period about equal to the past age of the earth. Then, regarded as a being destined to live for threescore years and ten, humanity, although it has been born in a house seventy years old, is itself only three days old.
The Wider Aspects of Cosmogony

Richard Jefferies
[1848–1887]

[**y**] The most extraordinary spectacle is the vast expenditure of labor and time wasted in obtaining mere subsistence.   *The Story of My Heart. Chap. X*

[**z**] I hope succeeding generations will be able to be idle. I hope that nine-tenths of their time will be leisure time; that they may enjoy their days, and the earth, and the beauty of this beautiful world; that they may rest by the sea and dream; that they may dance and sing, and eat and drink.
Ibid. Chap. XI

Robinson Jeffers
[1887-   ]

[**a**] The gulls, the cloud-calligraphers of windy spirals before a storm.   *The Cycle*

[**b**] Four pelicans went over the house,
Sculled their worn oars over the courtyard;
I saw that ungainliness
Magnifies the idea of strength.
Pelicans

[**c**]   Corruption
Never has been compulsory, when the cities lie at the monster's feet there are left the mountains.   *Shine, Perishing Republic. Stanza 4*

[**d**] We take our mortal momentary hour
With too much gesture. . . .
Look up the night, starlight's a steadying draught
For nerves at angry tension.
The Truce and the Peace. 7 [1918]

[**e**] All the arts lose virtue
Against the essential reality
Of creatures going about their business among the equally
Earnest elements of nature.
Boats in a Fog

[**f**] Grass that is made each year equals the mountains in her past and future;
Fashionable and momentary things we need not see nor speak of.   *Point Joe*

[**g**] Lend me the stone strength of the past and I will lend you
The wings of the future, for I have them.   *To the Rock That Will Be a Cornerstone*

[**h**] The beauty of things was born before eyes and sufficient to itself; the heart-breaking beauty
Will remain when there is no heart to break for it.   *Credo*

[**i**] The heads of strong old age are beautiful
Beyond all grace of youth. They have strange quiet,
Integrity, health, soundness, to the full
They've dealt with life and been atempered by it.
Promise of Peace

[**j**] Humanity is the mold to break away from, the crust to break through, the coal to break into fire,
The atom to be split.
Roan Stallion

Joseph Jefferson
[1829–1905]

[**k**] Are we to blame for being caterpillars?
Will the same God that doomed us crawl the earth
A prey to every bird that's given birth,
Forgive our captor as he eats and sings,
And damn poor us because we have not wings?   *Immortality*
[The New York Tribune, 1905]

Thomas Jefferson
[1743–1826]

[**l**] A lively and lasting sense of filial duty is more effectually impressed on the mind of a son or daughter by reading King Lear, than by all the dry volumes of ethics, and divinity, that ever were written.   *Letter to Robert Skipwith [August 3, 1771]*

[**m**] The God who gave us life, gave us liberty at the same time.
Summary View of the Rights of British America

[**n**] When, in the course of human events, it becomes necessary for one people to dissolve the political bands which have connected them with another, and to assume among the powers of the earth the separate and equal station to which the laws of nature and of nature's God entitle them, a decent respect to the opinions of mankind requires that they should declare the causes which impel them to the separation.
Declaration of Independence

[**o**] We hold these truths to be self-evident,—that all men are created equal; that they are endowed by their Creator with cer-

tain unalienable rights; that among these are life, liberty, and the pursuit of happiness. *Ibid.*

[p] The tree of liberty must be refreshed from time to time with the blood of patriots and tyrants. It is its natural manure.
Letter to William Stevens Smith
[November 13, 1787]

[q] Error of opinion may be tolerated where reason is left free to combat it.   *First Inaugural*
Address [March 4, 1801]

[r] Of the various executive abilities, no one excited more anxious concern than that of placing the interests of our fellow-citizens in the hands of our honest men, with understanding sufficient for their stations.   *Letter to Elias Shipman and Others of New Haven*
[July 12, 1801]

[s] When a man assumes a public trust, he should consider himself as public property.   *Rayner's Life of Jefferson. Page 356*

Charles Jefferys
[1807–1865]

[t] Oh! if I were Queen of France, or still better, Pope of Rome,
I'd have no fighting men abroad, no weeping maids at home;
All should be at peace; or, if kings must show their might,
Why, let them who make the quarrel be the only men to fight.
Jeannette and Jeannot. Stanza 4

[u] Were only kings themselves to fight, there'd be an end of war.
Jeannot's Answer. Stanza 4

Francis Jeffrey
[1773–1850]

[v] This will never do.
Opening sentence of review of Wordsworth's "Excursion" in The Edinburgh Review, November 1814. Probably the most famous book review ever written

Edward Jenner
[1749–1823]

[w] The hollow winds begin to blow;
The clouds look black, the glass is low;
The soot falls down, the spaniels sleep,
And spiders from their cobwebs peep. . . .
'Twill surely rain; I see with sorrow
Our jaunt must be put off to-morrow.   *Forty Signs of Rain*

Soame Jenyns
[1704–1787]

[x] Let each fair maid, who fears to be disgraced,
Ever be sure to tie her garters fast,
Lest the loosed string, amidst the public hall,
A wished-for prize to some proud fop should fall.
The Art of Dancing

[y] Ever let my lovely pupils fear
To chill their mantling blood with cold small beer:
Destruction lurks within the poisonous dose,
A fatal fever or a pimpled nose.   *Ibid.*

Jerome Klapka Jerome
[1859–1927]

[z] Let your boat of life be light, packed with only what you need —a homely home and simple pleasures, one or two friends, worth the name, some one to love and some one to love you, a cat, a dog, and a pipe or two, enough to eat and enough to wear, and a little more than enough to drink; for thirst is a dangerous thing.
Three Men in a Boat. Chap. 3

[a] Fox-terriers are born with about four times as much original sin in them as other dogs.
Ibid. Chap. 13

[b] The love of the young for the young, that is the beginning of life. But the love of the old for the old, that is the beginning of—of things longer.   *The Passing of the Third Floor Back*

[c] Leave-takings are but wasted sadness. Let me pass out quietly.   *Ibid.*

St. Jerome
[A.D. 345–420]
Translation by F. A. Wright

[d] Avoid, as you would the plague, a clergyman who is also a man of business.
Letter 52, To Nepotian

[e] A fat paunch never breeds fine thoughts.   *Ibid.*

[f] Preferring to store her money in the stomachs of the needy rather than hide it in a purse.
Letter 127, To Principia

Douglas Jerrold
[1803–1857]

[g] He is one of those wise philanthropists who in a time of famine would vote for nothing but a supply of toothpicks.
Douglas Jerrold's Wit

[h] Dogmatism is puppyism come to its full growth.   *Ibid.*

[i] The surest way to hit a woman's heart is to take aim kneeling.   *Ibid.*

[j] Some people are so fond of ill-luck that they run half-way to meet it.
        Meeting Troubles Half-Way

[k] Earth is here [Australia] so kind, that just tickle her with a hoe and she laughs with a harvest.
        A Land of Plenty

[l] The ugliest of trades have their moments of pleasure. Now, if I were a grave-digger, or even a hangman, there are some people I could work for with a great deal of enjoyment.   *Ugly Trades*

[m] He was so good he would pour rosewater on a toad.
        A Charitable Man

Sarah Orne Jewett
[1849–1909]

[n] A harbor, even if it is a little harbor, is a good thing, since adventurers come into it as well as go out, and the life in it grows strong, because it takes something from the world and has something to give in return.   *Country By-Ways. River Driftwood*

[o] Look bravely up into the sky,
  And be content with knowing
That God wished for a buttercup
  Just here, where you are growing.   *Discontent. Stanza 9*

Orrick Johns
[1887–1946]

[p] There's nothing very beautiful and nothing very gay
About the rush of faces in the town by day,
But a light tan cow in a pale green mead,
That is very beautiful, beautiful indeed.   *Little Things*

[q] Love is a proud and gentle thing, a better thing to own
Than all of the wide impossible stars over the heavens blown.
        The Door

Alvin Saunders Johnson
[1874–   ]

[r] As in the bosom of the earth vestiges of all earlier life may still be found, so in the bosom of public opinion are to be found vestiges of the early dinosaurs of thought.
        On German Pacification

Burges Johnson
[1877–   ]

[s] Let not some well-groomed lap-cat e'er decry
The humble realm of that backyard obscure—
The battered gate, the clothes-line whence there fly
The short and simple flannels of the poor.   *Elegy in a City Backyard (with Gelett Burgess)*

Charles Frederick Johnson
[1836–1931]

[t] Surely, the ups and downs of this world are past calculation. . . .

Persian and Arab, and Greek, and Hun, and Roman, and Vandal,
Master the world in turn and then disappear in the darkness,
Leaving a remnant as hewers of wood and drawers of water.
        The Modern Romans

George Washington Johnson
[1838–1917]

[u] I wandered to-day to the hill, Maggie,
To watch the scene below,
The creek and the creaking old mill, Maggie,
As we used to, long ago.
        When You and I Were Young, Maggie. Stanza 1

[v] To me you're as fair as you were, Maggie,
When you and I were young.
        Ibid. Stanza 3

Gerald White Johnson
[1890–   ]

[w] A man who has tried to play Mozart, and failed, through that vain effort comes into position better to understand the man who tried to paint the Sistine Madonna, and did.
        A Little Night-Music

[x] Nothing changes more constantly than the past; for the past that influences our lives does not consist of what actually happened, but of what men believe happened.   *American Heroes and Hero-Worship. Chap. 1*

[y] Heroes are created by popular demand, sometimes out of the scantiest materials . . . such as the apple that William Tell never shot, the ride that Paul Revere never finished, the flag that Barbara Frietchie never waved.
        Ibid.

Hewlett Johnson
[1874–   ]

[z] Not so easily does a people liberate itself from its social past.

Many ideas, customs, intolerances,
and tolerances, too, cling on unperceived by those who think that
they live in days where all things
are new.
  *The Soviet Power: The Socialist
  Sixth of the World. Book II:2*

Hugh S. Johnson
[1882–1942]

[a] There was never a war at
arms that was not merely the ex-
tension of a preceding war of
commerce grown fiercer until the
weapons of commerce seemed no
longer sufficiently deadly.
  *Radio broadcast for "World
  Peaceways" [1935]*

James Weldon Johnson
[1871–1938]

[b] And God stepped out on
  space,
And He looked around and said,
"I'm lonely—
I'll make me a world."
  *The Creation: A Negro Sermon.
  Stanza 1*

[c] Weep not, weep not,
She is not dead;
She's resting in the bosom of
  Jesus.
Heart-broken husband—weep no
  more;
Grief-stricken son—weep no more;
Left-lonesome daughter—weep no
  more;
She's only just gone home.
  *Go Down Death: A Funeral
  Sermon. Stanza 1*

Philander Johnson
[1866–1939]

[d] Sometimes the new friends
Leave the heart aglow,
But it's when they're like the men
We cherished long ago.
  Old Friends. Stanza 2

[e] A tiny bit of Camembert!
What strange illusions linger
  there!
What visions direful and dis-
  tressed
Through hours that should be
  sweet with rest!
  A Fromage Fantasy. Stanza 1

[f] You'll find that any dog's a
  prize,
Provided he's Your Dog.
  Pride of Possession. Stanza 8

Rossiter Johnson
[1840–1931]

[g] O for a lodge in a garden of
  cucumbers!
O for an iceberg or two at control!

O for a vale which at mid-day the
  dew cumbers!
O for a pleasure trip up to the
  Pole!   *Ninety-nine in
          the Shade. Stanza 1*

Samuel Johnson
[1709–1784]

[h] Let observation with exten-
  sive view
Survey mankind, from China to
  Peru.   *Vanity of Human
          Wishes. Line 1*

[i] Deign on the passing world to
  turn thine eyes,
And pause a while from learning
  to be wise.   *Ibid. Line 157*

[j] This mournful truth is ev'ry-
  where confess'd,—
Slow rises worth, by poverty de-
  press'd.   *London. Line 176*

[k] And panting Time toil'd after
  him in vain.   *Prologue on the
  Opening of Drury Lane Theatre*

[l] Declamation roar'd, while Passion slept.   *Ibid.*

[m] The wild vicissitudes of
  taste.   *Ibid.*

[n] For we that live to please
  must please to live.   *Ibid.*

[o] Curiosity is one of the permanent and certain characteristics of a vigorous mind.
  The Rambler [March 12, 1751]

[p] No place affords a more striking conviction of the vanity of
  human hopes, than a public
  library. *Ibid. [March 23, 1751]*

[q] It is one of the maxims of the
  civil law, that definitions are
  hazardous. *Ibid. [May 28, 1751]*

[r] Praise like gold and diamonds
  owes its value only to its scarcity.
  Ibid. [June 6, 1751]

[s] Almost all absurdity of conduct arises from the imitation of
  those whom we can not resemble.
  Ibid. [July 2, 1751]

[t] Ingenious contrivances to fa-
  cilitate motion, and unite levity
  with strength.
  *Rasselas. Chap. VI, A Dissertation
  on the Art of Flying*

[u] A man used to vicissitudes is
  not easily dejected.
          Ibid. Chap. XII

[v] Few things are impossible to
  diligence and skill.   *Ibid.*

[w] Knowledge is more than
  equivalent to force.
          Ibid. Chap. XIII

[x] I live in the crowd of jollity,
  not so much to enjoy company as
  to shun myself.
          Ibid. Chap. XVI

[y] The endearing elegance of female friendship.
Ibid. Chap. XLVI

[z] I am not so lost in lexicography as to forget that *words are the daughters of earth, and that things are the sons of heaven.*
Preface to His Dictionary

[a] OATS—A grain which in England is generally given to horses, but in Scotland supports the people.
Definition in the Dictionary

[b] PENSION—An allowance made to any one without an equivalent. In England, it is generally understood to mean pay given to a state hireling for treason to his country.
Ibid.

[c] PIRATE—A sea robber, any robber; particularly a bookseller who seizes the copies of other men.
Ibid.

[d] To be of no church is dangerous. Religion, of which the rewards are distant, and which is animated only by faith and hope, will glide by degrees out of the mind unless it be invigorated and reimpressed by external ordinances, by stated calls to worship, and the salutary influence of example.
Life of Milton

[e] On clean-shirt-day he went abroad, and paid visits.
Boswell's Life of Dr. Johnson
[Everyman edition, 2 vols.]
Vol. I, Page 50

[f] Tom Birch is as brisk as a bee in conversation; but no sooner does he take a pen in his hand, than it becomes a torpedo to him, and benumbs all his faculties.
Ibid. Page 92

[g] I'll come no more behind your scenes, David; for the silk stockings and white bosoms of your actresses excite my amorous propensities.
Ibid. Page 117

[h] Wretched un-idea'd girls.
Ibid. Page 143

[i] If a man does not make new acquaintances as he advances through life, he will soon find himself left alone. A man, sir, should keep his friendship in a constant repair.
Ibid. Page 182

[j] Towering in the confidence of twenty-one.
Ibid. Page 197

[k] Being in a ship is being in a jail, with the chance of being drowned.
Ibid. Page 215

[l] A short letter to a distant friend is, in my opinion, an insult like that of a slight bow or cursory salutation.
Ibid. Page 223

[m] Nothing is little to him that feels it with great sensibility.
Ibid. Page 230

[n] Sir, I think all Christians whether Papists or Protestants agree in the essential articles, and that their differences are trivial and rather political than religious.
Ibid. Page 251

[o] The noblest prospect which a Scotchman ever sees, is the high-road that leads him to England.
Ibid. Page 264

[p] If he does really think that there is no distinction between virtue and vice, why, sir, when he leaves our house let us count our spoons.
Ibid. Page 268

[q] If I accustom a servant to tell a lie for *me*, have I not reason to apprehend that he will tell many lies for *himself?*
Ibid. Page 270

[r] Sir, your levellers wish to level *down* as far as themselves; but they cannot bear levelling *up* to themselves.
Ibid. Page 277

[s] [He] is dull, naturally dull; but it must have taken him a great deal of pains to become what we now see him. Such an excess of stupidity, sir, is not in Nature.
Ibid. Page 280

[t] This was a good dinner enough, to be sure, but it was not a dinner to *ask* a man to.
Ibid. Page 291

[u] Gloomy calm of idle vacancy.
Ibid. Page 294

[v] Life is not long, and too much of it must not pass in idle deliberation how it shall be spent.
Ibid. Page 325

[w] Were he not to marry again, it might be concluded that his first wife had given him a disgust to marriage; but by taking a second wife he pays the highest compliment to the first, by showing that she made him so happy as a married man, that he wishes to be so a second time.
Ibid. Page 360

[x] I do not know, sir, that the fellow is an infidel; but if he be an infidel, he is an infidel as a dog is an infidel; that is to say, he has never thought upon the subject.
Ibid. Page 370

[y'] That fellow seems to me to possess but one idea, and that is a wrong one.
Ibid. Page 393

[z'] A decent provision for the poor is the true test of civilization.
Ibid. Page 396

[a'] Nobody can write the life of a man, but those who have eat and drunk and lived in social intercourse with him.
Ibid. Page 422

[b'] A cow is a very good animal in the field; but we turn her out of a garden.
Ibid. Page 436

[c] Much may be made of a Scotchman if he be caught young.
Ibid. Page 440

[d] Patriotism is the last refuge of a scoundrel. *Ibid. Page 547*

[e] I never take a nap after dinner but when I have had a bad night; and then the nap takes me.
Ibid. Page 589

[f] There is now less flogging in our great schools than formerly, but then less is learned there; so that what the boys get at one end they lose at the other. *Ibid.*

[g] There is nothing which has yet been contrived by man by which so much happiness is produced as by a good tavern or inn.
Ibid. Page 620

[h] Questioning is not the mode of conversation among gentlemen.
Ibid. Page 635

[i] A man is very apt to complain of the ingratitude of those who have risen far above him.
Ibid. Vol. II, Page 5

[j] If a man could say nothing against a character but what he can prove, history could not be written. *Ibid. Page 13*

[k] No man but a blockhead ever wrote except for money.
Ibid. Page 16

[l] While grief is fresh, every attempt to divert only irritates.
Ibid. Page 21

[m] When a man is tired of London, he is tired of life; for there is in London all that life can afford.
Ibid. Page 131

[n] He was so generally civil, that nobody thanked him for it.
Ibid. Page 134

[o] As the Spanish proverb says, "He, who would bring home the wealth of the Indies, must carry the wealth of the Indies with him," so it is in travelling, a man must carry knowledge with him if he would bring home knowledge. *Ibid. Page 216*

[p] It is amazing how little literature there is in the world.
Ibid. Page 217

[q] It is better to live rich, than to die rich. *Ibid. Page 218*

[r] I would rather be attacked than unnoticed. For the worst thing you can do to an author is to be silent as to his works.
Ibid. Page 257

[s] Claret is the liquor for boys, port for men; but he who aspires to be a hero must drink brandy.
Ibid. Page 271

[t] Worth seeing? yes; but not worth going to see.
Ibid. Page 291

[u] He that outlives a wife whom he has long loved, sees himself disjoined from the only mind that has the same hopes, and fears, and interest; from the only companion with whom he has shared much good and evil; and with whom he could set his mind at liberty, to retrace the past or anticipate the future. *Ibid. Page 298*

[v] A Frenchman must be always talking, whether he knows anything of the matter or not; an Englishman is content to say nothing, when he has nothing to say. *Ibid. Page 326*

[w] A jest breaks no bones.
Ibid. Page 405

[x] To let friendship die away by negligence and silence, is certainly not wise. It is voluntarily to throw away one of the greatest comforts of this weary pilgrimage.
Ibid. Page 417

[y] Whatever you have, spend less. *Ibid. Page 427*

[z] He is not only dull himself, but the cause of dullness in others. *Ibid. Page 441*

[a] I have found you an argument; I am not obliged to find you an understanding.
Ibid. Page 536

[b] Don't *attitudenize.*
Ibid. Page 541

[c'] I look upon every day to be lost, in which I do not make a new acquaintance. *Ibid. Page 579*

[d'] Life is very short, and very uncertain; let us spend it as well as we can. *Ibid. Page 583*

[e'] He was a very good hater.
Johnsoniana. Piozzi, 39

[f'] The law is the last result of human wisdom acting upon human experience for the benefit of the public. *Ibid. 58*

[g'] The use of travelling is to regulate imagination by reality, and instead of thinking how things may be, to see them as they are. *Ibid. 154*

[h'] Dictionaries are like watches; the worst is better than none, and the best cannot be expected to go quite true. *Ibid. 178*

[i'] Round numbers are always false. *Ibid. Hawkins, 235*

[j'] Hunting was the labour of the savages of North America, but the amusement of the gentlemen of England. *Ibid. 606*

[k'] I am very fond of the company of ladies. I like their beauty,

I like their delicacy, I like their
vivacity, and I like their silence.
Ibid. Seward, 617

[l] Preserve me from unseasonable and immoderate sleep.
Prayers and Meditations. 1767

[m] Gratitude is a fruit of great
cultivation; you do not find it
among gross people.
Tour to the Hebrides

[n] A fellow that . . . has a mind
as narrow as the neck of a vine-
gar-cruet. *Ibid.*

Eric A. Johnston
[1896–   ]

[o] I am no Horatio Alger hero.
Although I did start out in prescribed style as a newsboy, I did
not end up as a multi-millionaire.
America Unlimited

[p] America and defeat cannot be
made to rhyme. *Ibid.*

Ernest Fenwick Johnstone
[1867–1933]

[q] I dreamed that I went to the
City of Gold,
To Heaven resplendent and fair,
And after I entered that beautiful
fold
By one in authority there I was
told
That not a Vermonter was there.

We give them the best the King-
dom provides;
They have everything here that
they want,
But not a Vermonter in Heaven
abides;
A very brief period here he resides,
Then hikes his way back to
Vermont.
No Vermonters in Heaven.
Stanzas 1 and 6

"Gordon Johnstone"
(Joseph Sweeney)
[1876–1926]

[r] Death's but an open door,
We move from room to room.
There is one life, no more,
No dying, and no tomb.
There Is No Death. Stanza 3

Howard Mumford Jones
[1892–   ]

[s] They say the forties are the
dangerous ages. *The Forties*

[t] But do not meet meanwhile
with your own ghost
Who died before the god, Success,
was born,
For he will greet you with such
wild surmise

Flushing his cheeks and startling
in his eyes
As will revive the ambition, the
pain, the lost
Sweet passion and the beautiful
young scorn. *Ibid.*

John Paul Jones
[1747–1792]

[u] I have not yet begun to fight.
Aboard the Bonhomme Richard,
September 23, 1779

Thomas Samuel Jones, Jr.
[1882–1932]

[v] Across the fields of yesterday
He sometimes comes to me,
A little lad just back from play—
The lad I used to be.

I wonder if he hopes to see
The man I might have been.
Sometimes. Stanzas 1 and 2

Ben Jonson
[1573?–1637]

[w] He despises me, I suppose,
because I live in an alley: tell him
his soul lives in an alley.
Of James I. Quoted in Leigh
Hunt's essay, Coaches

[x] The dignity of truth is lost
with much protesting.
Catiline's Conspiracy. Act III,
Sc. 2

[y] Hang sorrow! care'll kill a cat.
Every Man in his Humour. Act I,
Sc. 3

[z] As he brews, so shall he drink.
Ibid. Act II, Sc. 1

[a] Give me a look, give me a face,
That makes simplicity a grace;
Robes loosely flowing, hair as free,
Such sweet neglect more taketh
me
Than all the adulteries of art.
Epicœne; Or, the Silent Woman.
Act I, Sc. 1

[b] Truth is the trial of itself
And needs no other touch,
And purer than the purest gold,
Refine it ne'er so much.
On Truth. Stanza 1

[c] Follow a shadow, it still flies
you;
Seem to fly it, it will pursue:
So court a mistress, she denies
you;
Let her alone, she will court you.
Follow a Shadow. Stanza 1

[d] That old bald cheater, Time.
The Poetaster. Act I, Sc. 1

[e] Drink to me only with thine
eyes,
And I will pledge with mine;
Or leave a kiss but in the cup
And I'll not look for wine.
The Forest: To Celia, Stanza 1

[f] I sent thee late a rosy wreath,
Not so much honouring thee
As giving it a hope that there
   It could not wither'd be.
        Ibid. Stanza 2

[g] Have you seen but a bright
   lily grow,
   Before rude hands have touched
   it?
Have you marked but the fall o'
   the snow
Before the soil hath smutched
   it?   *Her Triumph. Stanza 3*

[h]   Soul of the age!
The applause, delight, the wonder
   of our stage!
My Shakespeare, rise!
  To the Memory of Shakespeare

[i] Small Latin and less Greek.
              Ibid.

[j] He was not of an age but for
   all time.   *Ibid.*

[k] Those that merely talk and
   never think,
That live in the wild anarchy of
   drink.
   *Underwoods. An Epistle, an-
   swering to One that asked to
   be sealed of the Tribe of Ben*

[l] In small proportions we just
   beauties see,
And in short measures life may
   perfect be.
   *Ibid. To the immortal Memory
   of Sir Lucius Cary and Sir
   Henry Morison, III*

[m] Greatness of name in the
father ofttimes overwhelms the
son; they stand too near one another. The shadow kills the
growth.   *Timber, or Discoveries
   Made Upon Men and Matter*

[n] Though the most be players,
some must be spectators. *Ibid.*

[o] Whom the disease of talking
once possesseth, he can never hold
his peace. Nay, rather than he will
not discourse he will hire men to
hear him.   *Ibid.*

Thomas Jordan
[1612–1685]

[p] Fish dinners will make a man
   spring like a flea.
   *Coronemus nos Rosis Antequam
   Marcescant. Stanza 2*

[q] Though now she be pleasant
   and sweet to the sense,
Will be damnable mouldy a
   hundred years hence.
         Ibid. Stanza 3

James Joyce
[1882–1941]

[r] Pity is the feeling which ar-
rests the mind in the presence of
whatsoever is grave and constant

in human sufferings and unites it
with the human sufferer.
   *A Portrait of the Artist as a
   Young Man. Chap. 5*

[s] A man of genius makes no
mistakes. His errors are volitional
and are the portals of discovery.
   *Ulysses. Page 188 [Random
   House edition]*

[t] Why, why, why! Weh, O weh!
I'se so silly to be flowing but I no
   canna stay!   *Song of the
   river, Finnegan's Wake [Viking
   Press edition]. Page 159*

[u] When thou hast heard his
   name upon
The bugles of the cherubim,
Begin thou softly to unzone
Thy girlish bosom unto him
And softly to undo the snood
That is the sign of maidenhood.
   *Bid Adieu to Maidenhood.
       Stanza 2*

John Alexander Joyce
[1842–1915]

[v] You must leave your many
   millions
And the gay and festive crowd;
Though you roll in royal billions,
There's no pocket in a shroud.
   *There's No Pocket in a
      Shroud. Stanza 1*

Andoche Junot,
Duc d'Abrantes
[1771–1813]

[w] I know nothing about it; I
am my own ancestor.
   When asked about his ancestry

Juvenal
[A.D. 47–138]

[x] Honesty is praised and starves.
       Satire I. Line 74

[y] No man ever became extremely wicked all at once.
       Satire II. Line 83

MacKinlay Kantor
[1904–   ]

[z] I was a dog at Gettysburg. I
   trotted near the train
And nosed among the officers who
   kicked me to my pain.
A man came by . . . I could not
   see. I howled. The light was
   dim,
But when I brushed against his
   legs, I liked the smell of him.
   *Abraham Lincoln at Gettysburg.
       Stanza 9*

John Keats
[1795–1821]

[a] There is not a fiercer hell
than the failure in a great object.
   Preface to Endymion

[b] A thing of beauty is a joy for-
ever:
Its loveliness increases; it will
never
Pass into nothingness.
Endymion. Book I, Line 1

[c] Time, that aged nurse,
Rock'd me to patience.
Ibid. Line 705

[d] To sorrow,
I bade good-morrow,
And thought to leave her far away
behind;
But cheerly, cheerly,
She loves me dearly;
She is so constant to me, and so
kind.
Ibid. Book IV, Line 173

[e] Love in a hut, with water and
a crust,
Is—Love, forgive us!—cinders,
ashes, dust.
Lamia. Part II, Line 1

[f] St. Agnes' Eve—Ah, bitter chill
it was!
The owl, for all his feathers, was
a-cold.
The Eve of St. Agnes. Stanza 1

[g] The silver, snarling trumpets
'gan to chide.
Ibid. Stanza 4

[h] Asleep in lap of legends old.
Ibid. Stanza 15

[i] Sudden a thought came like a
full-blown rose,
Flushing his brow.
Ibid. Stanza 16

[j] A poor, weak, palsy-stricken,
churchyard thing.
Ibid. Stanza 18

[k] O for a beaker full of the
warm South,
Full of the true, the blushful Hip-
pocrene,
With beaded bubbles winking at
the brim,
And purple-stained mouth.
Ode to a Nightingale. Stanza 2

[l] I have been half in love with
easeful Death,
Call'd him soft names in many a
mused rhyme.
Ibid. Stanza 6

[m] The self-same song that
found a path
Through the sad heart of Ruth,
when, sick for home,
She stood in tears amid the alien
corn;
The same that oft-times hath
Charm'd magic casements, open-
ing on the foam
Of perilous seas, in faery lands
forlorn.
Ibid. Stanza 7

[n] Thou foster-child of Silence
and slow Time.
Ode on a Grecian Urn. Stanza 1

[o] Heard melodies are sweet, but
those unheard
Are sweeter.
Ibid. Stanza 2

[p] Beauty is truth, truth beauty,
—that is all
Ye know on earth, and all ye
need to know.
Ibid.

[q] In a drear-nighted December
Too happy, happy tree
Thy branches ne'er remember
Their green felicity.
Stanzas

[r] To one who has been long in
city pent,
'Tis very sweet to look into the
fair
And open face of heaven.
*Sonnet, To One Who Has Been
Long in City Pent*

[s] Then felt I like some watcher
of the skies
When a new planet swims into
his ken;
Or like stout Cortez when with
eagle eyes
He stared at the Pacific and all
his men
Look'd at each other with a wild
surmise
Silent, upon a peak in Darien.
*Sonnet, On First Looking Into
Chapman's Homer*

[t] When I have fears that I may
cease to be.
Sonnet, When I Have Fears

[u] Life is but a day;
A fragile dewdrop on its perilous
way
From a tree's summit.
Sleep and Poetry. Line 85

[v] Life is the rose's hope while
yet unblown. *Ibid. Line 90*

[w] Too many tears for lovers
have been shed,
Too many sighs give we to them
in fee,
Too much of pity after they are
dead,
Too many doleful stories do we
see,
Whose matter in bright gold were
best be read. *Isabella
[The Pot of Basil]. Stanza 12*

[x] Where's the eye, however blue,
Doth not weary? Where's the face
One would meet in every place?
Where's the voice, however soft,
One would hear so very oft?
Fancy. Line 72

[y] Season of mists and mellow
fruitfulness,
Close bosom-friend of the ma-
turing sun;
Conspiring with him how to load
and bless
With fruit the vines.
To Autumn. Stanza 1

[z] Those green-robed senators of
mighty woods,

Tall oaks, branch-charmed by the
   earnest stars.
         Hyperion. Book I, Line 73

[a] Fame, like a wayward girl, will
   still be coy
To those who woo her with too
   slavish knees.
         Sonnet on Fame

[b] Disappointment, parent of
   Despair.
         To Hope. Stanza 3

[c] I stood tip-toe upon a little
   hill,
The air was cooling, and so very
   still.
         I Stood Tip-toe. Line 1

[d] Open afresh your round of
   starry folds,
Ye ardent marigolds!
         Ibid. Line 47

[e] The moon lifting her silver
   rim
Above a cloud, and with a gradual
   swim
Coming into the blue with all her
   light.   *Ibid. Line 113*

[f] And no birds sing.
         La Belle Dame Sans Merci.
              Stanza 1

[g] Bright star, would I were
   stedfast as thou art—
Not in lone splendour hung aloft
   the night
And watching, with eternal lids
   apart,
   Like nature's patient, sleepless
   Eremite.
The moving waters at their priest-
   like task
   Of pure ablution round earth's
   human shores.
         The Last Sonnet

[h] Blue! Gentle cousin of the
   forest-green,
Married to green in all the sweetest flowers,—
Forget-me-not,—the blue bell,—
   and, that Queen
Of secrecy, the violet.
         Sonnet, Blue

[i] I am certain of nothing but
of the holiness of the heart's affections, and the truth of Imagination.
         Letter [November 22, 1817]

[j] Poetry should surprise by a
fine excess, and not by singularity;
it should strike the reader as a
wording of his own highest
thoughts, and appear almost a remembrance.
         Letter [February 27, 1818]

[k] I have loved the principle of
beauty in all things, and if I had
had time I would have made myself remembered.   *Letter [1820]*

[l] Here lies one whose name was
writ in water.
         Epitaph for himself

Helen Keller
[1880-   ]

[m] Literature is my Utopia. Here
I am not disfranchised. No barrier of the senses shuts me out
from the sweet, gracious discourse
of my book-friends. They talk to
me without embarrassment or
awkwardness. [Helen Keller has
been blind and deaf since infancy.]   *The Story of My Life*

Frances Anne Kemble
[1809–1893]

[n] What shall I do with all the
   days and hours
That must be counted ere I see
   thy face?
How shall I charm the interval
   that lowers
Between this time and that
   sweet time of grace?
         Absence. Stanza 1

[o] Maids must be wives and
   mothers to fulfil
The entire and holiest end of
woman's being.
         Woman's Heart

John Philip Kemble
[1757–1823]

[p] Perhaps it was right to dis-
   semble your love,
But—why did you kick me down
   stairs?
         The Panel. Act I, Sc.1

Harry Kemp
[1883-   ]

[q] I pitied him in his blindness;
But can I boast, "I see"?
Perhaps there walks a spirit
Close by, who pities me.
         Blind. Stanza 2

[r] Where the vast cloudless sky
   was broken by one crow
I sat upon a hill—all alone—long
   ago;
But I never felt so lonely and so
   out of God's way
As here, where I brush elbows with
   a thousand every day.
         Kansas and London

Thomas à Kempis
[1380–1471]

[s] Be not angry that you cannot
make others as you wish them to
be, since you cannot make yourself as you wish to be.
         Imitation of Christ. Book I,
              Chap. 16

[t] Man proposes, but God disposes.   *Ibid. Chap. 19*

[u] It is easier not to speak a
word at all than to speak more
words than we should.   *Ibid.*

[v] No man ruleth safely but he that is willingly ruled.   *Ibid.*

Bishop Thomas Ken
[1637–1711]

[w] Teach me to live, that I may dread
The grave as little as my bed.
*Morning and Evening Hymn.
Stanza 3*

[x] Praise God, from whom all blessings flow!
Praise Him, all creatures here below!
Praise Him above, ye heavenly host!
Praise Father, Son, and Holy Ghost!   *Ibid. Stanza 10*

George Kennan
[1845–1924]

[y] Heroism, the Caucasian mountaineers say, is endurance for one moment more.   *Letter to Henry Munroe Rogers [July 25, 1921]*

Charles Rann Kennedy
[1871–1950]

[z] A peculiar kind of fear they call courage.   *The Terrible Meek*

[a] The meek, the terrible meek, the fierce agonizing meek, are about to enter into their inheritance.   *Ibid.*

Bernice Lesbia Kenyon
(Mrs. Walter Gilkyson)
[1897–   ]

[b] Never return in August to what you love;
Along the leaves will be rust
And over the hedges dust,
And in the air vague thunder and silence burning . . .
Choose some happier time for your returning.
Return. Stanza 1

Paul Kester
[1870–1933]

[c] I want to go home
To the dull old town,
With the shaded street
And the open square;
And the hill
And the flats
And the house I love,
And the paths I know—
I want to go home.   *Home*

Charles Francis Kettering
[1876–   ]

[d] A man must have a certain amount of intelligent ignorance to get anywhere.   *On his 70th birthday, August 29, 1946*

Thomas Kettle
[?–1916?]

[e] Know that we dead, now with the foolish dead,
Died not for flag nor king nor emperor,
But for a dream born in a herdsman's shed
And for the secret scripture of the poor.   *Sonnet*

Francis Scott Key
[1779–1843]

[f] And the star-spangled banner, oh long may it wave
O'er the land of the free and the home of the brave!
*The Star-Spangled Banner.
Stanza 2 [September 14, 1814]*

[g] O! thus be it ever when freemen shall stand
Between their loved homes and the foe's desolation.   *Ibid. Stanza 4*

[h] Then conquer we must, for our cause it is just,—
And this be our motto,—"In God is our trust!"   *Ibid.*

John Maynard Keynes
(Lord Keynes)
[1883–1946]

[i] He [Clemenceau] had one illusion—France; and one disillusion—mankind, including Frenchmen.   *Economic Consequences of the Peace. Chap. 3 [1919]*

[j] He [Woodrow Wilson] could write Notes from Sinai or Olympus; he could remain unapproachable in the White House or even in the Council of Ten and be safe. But if he once stepped down to the intimate quality of the Four, the game was evidently up.   *Ibid.*

[k] It is ideas, not vested interests, which are dangerous for good or evil.   *The Power of Ideas*

James Michael Kieran
[1863–1936]

[l] The Brain Trust.
Description of the professorial advisors chosen by President Franklin D. Roosevelt

John Kieran
[1892–   ]

[m] Who harbors in memory a wealth of valued verse has laid up unto himself treasures that moths will not corrupt nor thieves break in and steal. This is the conviction of one who . . . as a soldier in World War I, trudged the desolate

sector of the Somme and the ruined region of Arras with little limp volumes of Shakespeare in his pockets and miniature collections of Burns, Browning, Swinburne, and Tennyson wedged in his pack between the top of the blanket roll and the strapped-down flap that held his mess kit.
Foreword to Poems I Remember

Aline (Mrs. Joyce) Kilmer
[1888–1941]

[n] Deborah danced, when she was two,
As buttercups and daffodils do.
Experience

[o] I'm sorry you are wiser,
I'm sorry you are taller;
I liked you better foolish,
And I liked you better smaller.
*For the Birthday of a Middle-
Aged Child. Stanza 1*

[p] As shells remember the lost sea.
Prevision (To a Child). Stanza 4

[q] Things have a terrible permanence
When people die.
Things. Stanza 6

Joyce Kilmer
[1886–1918]

[r] The midnight train is slow and old,
But of it let this thing be told,
To its high honor be it said,
It carries people home to bed.
My cottage lamp shines white and clear.
God bless the train that brought me here.
The Twelve-Forty-Five

[s] I think that I shall never see
A poem lovely as a tree.
*Trees [First published in Poetry:
A Magazine of Verse, August
1913]*

[t] A tree that may in Summer wear
A nest of robins in her hair.
Ibid.

[u] Poems are made by fools like me,
But only God can make a tree.
Ibid.

[v] There is no peace to be taken
With poets who are young,
For they worry about the wars to be fought
And the songs that must be sung.   *Old Poets*

[w] Her lips' remark was: "Oh, you kid!"
Her soul spoke thus (I know it did):
"O king of realms of endless joy,
My own, my golden grocer's boy."
Servant Girl and Grocer's Boy

[x] Main Street bordered with autumn leaves, it was a pleasant thing.   *Main Street*

[y] But we who inherit the primal curse, and labour for our bread,
Have yet, thank God, the gift of Home, though Eden's gate is barred.
The Snowman in the Yard

[z] My shoulders ache beneath my pack
(Lie easier, Cross, upon His back).
Prayer of a Soldier in France

[a] When God's great voice assembles
The fleet on Judgment Day,
The ghosts of ruined ships will rise
In sea and strait and bay.
The White Ships and the Red

Benjamin Franklin King, Jr.
[1857–1894]

[b] Nothing to do but work,
Nothing to eat but food,
Nothing to wear but clothes
To keep one from going nude.
*The Pessimist (The Sum of
Life). Stanza 1*

[c] If I should die to-night
And you should come in deepest grief and woe—
And say: "Here's that ten dollars that I owe,"
I might arise in my large white cravat
And say, "What's that?"
If I Should Die. Stanza 1

Henry King, Bishop of Chichester
[1592–1669]

[d] And that tame Lover who unlocks his heart
Unto his mistress, teaching her an art
To plague himself, shows her the secret way
How she may tyrannize another day!   *The Steed
that Comes to Understand*

[e] Thou art the book,—
The library whereon I look.
*Exequy on the Death of a
Beloved Wife*

Stoddard King
[1889–1933]

[f] I like calm hats and I don't wear spats,
But I want my neckties wild!

Give me a wild tie, brother,
One with a cosmic urge!
A tie that will swear and rip and tear
When it sees my old blue serge.
The Tie That Blinds

[g] Of all the pestilences dire,
Including famine, flood, and fire,
By Satan and his imps rehearsed,
The neighbors' children are the
   worst.
   Philosophy for Parents. Stanza 1

[h] There's a long, long trail a-
   winding
Into the land of my dreams,
Where the nightingales are sing-
   ing
And a white moon beams;
There's a long, long night of wait-
   ing
Until my dreams all come true,
Till the day when I'll be going
   down
That long, long trail with you.
   The Long, Long Trail

[i] Let's sing a song of glory to
   Themistocles O'Shea,
Who ate a dozen oysters on the
   second day of May.
   The Man Who Dared

Charles Kingsley
[1819-1875]

[j] O Mary, go and call the cattle
   home,
And call the cattle home,
And call the cattle home,
Across the sands o' Dee!
   The Sands of Dee. Stanza 1

[k] The cruel crawling foam.
   Ibid. Stanza 4

[l] Men must work, and women
   must weep,
And there's little to earn and
   many to keep,
Though the harbor bar be moaning.
   The Three Fishers. Stanza 1

[m] Be good, sweet maid, and let
   who can be clever;
Do lovely things, not dream
   them, all day long;
And so make Life, Death, and that
   vast Forever
   One grand sweet song.
   A Farewell. Stanza 3

[n] Oh! that we two were Maying.   *The Saint's Tragedy.
                Act II, Sc. 9*

[o] Oh England is a pleasant
   place for them that's rich and
   high,
But England is a cruel place for
   such poor folks as I.
   The Last Buccaneer. Stanza 1

[p] I once had a sweet little doll,
   dears,
The prettiest doll in the world;
Her cheeks were so red and so
   white, dears,
And her hair was so charmingly
   curled.   *Water Babies.
                Song IV, Stanza 1*

[q] See in every hedgerow
   Marks of angels' feet,
Epics in each pebble
   Underneath our feet.
   The Invitation to Tom Hughes

[r] A lone man's companion, a
bachelor's friend, a hungry man's
food, a sad man's cordial, a wakeful man's sleep, and a chilly man's
fire . . . there's no herb like unto
it under the canopy of heaven.
[*Tobacco*] *Westward Ho, Chap. 7*

[s] Thank God every morning
when you get up that you have
something to do that day which
must be done, whether you like
it or not. Being forced to work,
and forced to do your best, will
breed in you temperance and self-
control, diligence and strength of
will, cheerfulness and content,
and a hundred virtues which the
idle never know.   *Letter*

[t] "What is the secret of your
life?" asked Mrs. Browning of
Charles Kingsley. "Tell me, that I
may make mine beautiful, too."
He replied: "I had a friend."
   *Related by William Channing
                Gannett*

Coates Kinney
[1826-1904]

[u] What a bliss to press the pil-
   low
Of a cottage-chamber bed
And to listen to the patter
Of the soft rain overhead!
   Rain on the Roof. Stanza 1

Rudyard Kipling
[1865-1936]

[v] I have eaten your bread and
   salt,
I have drunk your water and
   wine.
The deaths ye died I have watched
   beside
And the lives ye led were mine.
   *Departmental Ditties. Prelude,
                Stanza 1*

[w] Who shall doubt "the secret
   hid
Under Cheops' pyramid"
Was that the contractor did
   Cheops out of several millions?
   A General Summary. Stanza 4

[x] Little Tin Gods on Wheels.
   Public Waste. Stanza 4

[y] And a woman is only a
woman, but a good cigar is a
smoke.
   The Betrothed. Stanza 25

[z] Pleasant the snaffle of Courtship, improving the manners
and carriage;
But the colt who is wise will abstain from the terrible thorn-
bit of Marriage.
   Certain Maxims of Hafiz. XI

[a] My Son, if a maiden deny
thee and scufflingly bid thee
give o'er,
Yet lip meets with lip at the last-
ward. Get out! She has been
there before.
They are pecked on the ear and
the chin and the nose who are
lacking in lore.   *Ibid. XVI*

[b] How can I turn from any fire
On any man's hearthstone?
I know the wonder and desire
That went to build my own!
          The Fires. Stanza 7

[c] I am sick of endless sunshine,
sick of blossom-burdened
bough.
Give me back the leafless wood-
lands where the winds of
Springtime range—
Give me back one day in England,
for it's Spring in England
now!
          In Springtime. Stanza 1

[d] It's like a book, I think, this
bloomin' world,
Which you can read and care for
just so long,
But presently you feel that you
will die
Unless you get the page you're
readin' done,
An' turn another—likely not so
good;
But what you're after is to turn
'em all.   *Sestina of
the Tramp-Royal. Stanza 6*

[e] And the tunes that mean so
much to you alone—
Common tunes that make you
choke and blow your nose,
Vulgar tunes that bring the laugh
that brings the groan—
I can rip your very heartstrings
out with those.   *The Song
of the Banjo. Stanza 6*

[f] Who hath desired the Sea?—
the sight of salt water unbounded—
The heave and the halt and the
hurl and the crash of the
comber wind-hounded?
The Sea and the Hills. Stanza 1

[g] Lord, send a man like Robbie
Burns to sing the Song o'
Steam!   *M'Andrew's Hymn*

[h] The Liner she's a lady, and if
a war should come,
The Man-o'-War's 'er 'usband,
and 'e'd bid 'er stay at home;
But, oh, the little cargo-boats that
fill with every tide!
'E'd 'ave to up an' fight for them
for they are England's pride.
The Liner She's a Lady. Stanza 5

[i] There are triple ways to take,
of the eagle or the snake,
Or the way of a man with a
maid;

But the sweetest way to me is a
ship's upon the sea
In the heel of the North-East
Trade.
          The Long Trail. Stanza 4

[j] We have fed our sea for a
thousand years
And she calls us, still unfed,
Though there's never a wave of all
her waves
But marks our English dead.
          *The Song of the Dead. II,
Stanza 1*

[k] If blood be the price of ad-
miralty,
Lord God, we ha' paid in full!
          Ibid.

[l] Ever the wide world over, lass,
Ever the trail held true,
Over the world and under the
world,
And back at the last to you.
          The Gypsy Trail. Stanza 2

[m] The wild hawk to the wind-
swept sky,
The deer to the wholesome wold
And the heart of a man to the
heart of a maid,
As it was in the days of old.
          Ibid. Stanza 11

[n] Enslaved, illogical, elate,
He greets the embarrassed Gods,
nor fears
To shake the iron hand of Fate
Or match with Destiny for
beers.
          An American. Stanza 13

[o] Buy my English posies!
Kent and Surrey may—
Violets of the Undercliff
Wet with Channel spray;
Cowslips from a Devon combe—
Midland furze afire.
          The Flowers. Stanza 1

[p] For where there are Irish
there's loving and fighting,
And when we stop either, it's
Ireland no more!
          The Irish Guards. Stanza 4

[q] A fool there was and he made
his prayer
(Even as you and I!)
To a rag and a bone and a hank of
hair
(We called her the woman who did
not care)
But the fool he called her his lady
fair—
(Even as you and I!)
          The Vampire. Stanza 1

[r] And only the Master shall
praise us, and only the Master
shall blame;
And no one shall work for money,
and no one shall work for
fame;
But each for the joy of the working, and each, in his separate
star,

Shall draw the Thing as he sees
    It for the God of Things as
    They Are!   *When Earth's
Last Picture Is Painted. Stanza 3*

[s] Oh, East is East, and West is
    West, and never the twain
    shall meet,
Till Earth and Sky stand presently
    at God's great Judgment Seat.
But there is neither East nor
    West, Border, nor Breed, nor
    Birth,
When two strong men stand face
    to face, though they come
    from the ends of the earth!
        The Ballad of East and West

[t] Make ye no truce with Adam-
    zad—the Bear that walks like
    a Man!   *The Truce of the
        Bear. Stanza 2*

[u] Strictest judge of her own
    worth, gentlest of man's mind,
First to face the Truth and last
    to leave old Truths behind—
France, beloved of every soul that
    loves or serves its kind!
        France

[v] This is our lot if we live so
    long and labour unto the
    end—
That we outlive the impatient
    years and the much too pa-
    tient friend:
And because we know we have
    breath in our mouth and
    think we have thoughts in
    our head,
We shall assume that we are alive,
    whereas we are really dead.
        The Old Men. Stanza 1

[w] Take up the White Man's
    burden.   *The White
        Man's Burden. Stanza 1*

[x] The tumult and the shouting
    dies;
The Captains and the Kings de-
    part:
Still stands Thine ancient sacri-
    fice,
An humble and a contrite heart.
        Recessional. Stanza 2

[y] Lest we forget—lest we for-
    get!   *Ibid.*

[z] Lo, all our pomp of yesterday
Is one with Nineveh and Tyre!
        Ibid. Stanza 3

[a] You must hack through much
    deposit
Ere you know for sure who was
    it
Came to burial with such honour
    in the Files
(Only seven seasons back beneath
    the Files).
"Very great our loss and griev-
    ous—
So our best and brightest leave us,
And it ends the Age of Giants,"
    say the Files.   *The Files
    [of back copies of a newspaper]*

[b] When your Imp of Blind De-
    sire
Bids you set the Thames afire,
You'll remember men have done
    so—in the Files.   *Ibid.*

[c] The female of the species is
    more deadly than the male.
        *The Female of the Species
            Stanza 1*

[d] For as we come and as we go
    (and deadly-soon go we!)
The people, Lord, Thy people, are
    good enough for me!
        A Pilgrim's Way. Stanza 1

[e] And when they bore me over-
    much, I will not shake mine
    ears,
Recalling many thousand such
    whom I have bored to tears.
And when they labour to impress,
    I will not doubt nor scoff;
Since I myself have done no less
    and—sometimes pulled it off.
        Ibid. Stanza 3

[f] My son was killed while
    laughing at some jest. I would
    I knew
What it was, and it might serve
    me in a time when jests are
    few.
        Epitaphs of the War. A Son

[g] They've taken of his buttons
    off an' cut his stripes away,
An' they're hangin' Danny Deever
    in the mornin'.
        Danny Deever. Stanza 5

[h] We aren't no thin red 'eroes.
        Tommy. Stanza 4

[i] Single men in barricks don't
    grow into plaster saints.
        Ibid.

[j] It's Tommy this, an' Tommy
    that, an' "Chuck 'im out, the
    brute!"
But it's "Savior of 'is country,"
    when the guns begin to shoot.
        Ibid. Stanza 5

[k] So 'ere's *to* you, Fuzzy-
    Wuzzy, at your 'ome in the
    Soudan;
You're a pore benighted 'eathen
    but a first-class fightin' man.

'E's all 'ot sand an' ginger when
    alive,
An' 'e's generally shammin' when
    'e's dead.   *"Fuzzy-Wuzzy."
        Stanzas 1 and 4*

[l] Though I've belted you an'
    flayed you,
By the livin' Gawd that made you,
You're a better man than I am,
    Gunga Din!
        Gunga Din. Stanza 5

[m] 'Ave you 'eard o' the Widow
    at Windsor
With a hairy gold crown on 'er
    'ead?   *The Widow at
        Windsor. Stanza 1*

[n] Walk wide o' the Widow at
    Windsor,
For 'alf o' Creation she owns:
We 'ave bought 'er the same with
    the sword an' the flame,
An' we've salted it down with
    our bones!   *Ibid. Stanza 2*

[o] On the road to Mandalay,
Where the flyin'-fishes play,
An' the dawn comes up like thun-
    der outer China 'crost the
    Bay!   *Mandalay. Stanza 1*

[p] Ship me somewheres east of
    Suez, where the best is like
    the worst,
Where there aren't no Ten Com-
    mandments an' a man can
    raise a thirst.
                    Ibid. Stanza 6

[q] Back to the Army again, ser-
    geant,
Back to the Army again.
Out o' the cold an' the rain.
    "Back to the Army Again."
                    Refrain

[r] I've taken my fun where I've
    found it.
        The Ladies. Stanza 1

[s] An' I learned about women
    from 'er.   *Ibid. Refrain*

[t] For the Colonel's Lady an'
    Judy O'Grady
Are sisters under their skins!
                    Ibid. Stanza 8

[u] The backbone of the Army is
    the Noncommissioned Man!
        The 'Eathen. Stanza 18

[v] Boots—boots—boots—boots—
    movin' up and down again!
        Boots. Stanza 1

[w] The bachelor may risk 'is
    'ide
    To 'elp you when you're
        downed;
But the married man will wait
    beside
    Till the ambulance comes
        round.

The married man must sink or
    swim
An'—'e can't afford to sink!
The Married Man. Stanzas 5 and 7

[x] Ride with an idle whip, ride
    with an unused heel,
But, once in a way, there will
    come a day
When the colt must be taught to
    feel
The lash that falls, and the curb
    that galls, and the sting of the
    rowelled steel.   *The Con-
    version of Aurelian McGoggin*

[y] One man in a thousand,
    Solomon says,
Will stick more close than a
    brother.

But the Thousandth Man will
    stand by your side
To the gallows-foot—and after!
    *The Thousandth Man. Stanzas
                        1 and 4*

[z] The end of the fight is a
    tombstone white with the
    name of the late deceased,
And the epitaph drear: "A Fool
    lies here who tried to hustle
    the East."
        The Naulahka. Chap. 5

[a] Now these are the Laws of the
    Jungle, and many and mighty
    are they;
But the head and the hoof of the
    Law and the haunch and the
    hump is—Obey!   *The Law
        of the Jungle. Refrain*

[b] If you can meet with Tri-
    umph and Disaster
And treat those two impostors
    just the same.

If you can talk with crowds and
    keep your virtue,
    Or walk with Kings—nor lose
        the common touch. . . .
Yours is the Earth and everything
    that's in it,
    And—which is more—you'll be
        a Man, my son!
        If. Stanzas 2 and 4

[c] The arrows of our anguish
Fly farther than we guess.
    The Rabbi's Song. Stanza 3

[d] I keep six honest serving-men
    (They taught me all I knew);
Their names are What and Why
    and When
And How and Where and Who.
    The Elephant's Child. Stanza 1

[e] I'd love to roll to Rio
Some day before I'm old!
The Beginning of the Armadilloes.
                    Stanza 4

[f] When the ship goes *wop*
    (with a wiggle between)
And the steward falls into the
    soup-tureen.
    How the Whale Got His Throat

[g] If I were damned of body and
    soul,
I know whose prayers would make
    me whole,
    Mother o' mine.
                Mother o' Mine

[h] Them that asks no questions
    isn't told a lie.
    A Smuggler's Song. Stanza 6

[i] When Crew and Captain un-
    derstand each other to the
    core,
It takes a gale and more than a
    gale to put their ship ashore.
            Together. Stanza 2

[j] The snow lies thick on Valley
    Forge,
The ice on the Delaware,

But the poor dead soldiers of King
George
They neither know nor care.
*The American Rebellion.
II, After, Stanza 1*

[k] Our England is a garden, and
such gardens are not made
By singing:—"Oh, how beautiful!" and sitting in the shade.
The Glory of the Garden. Stanza 5

[l] Oh, Adam was a gardener, and
God who made him sees
That half a proper gardener's
work is done upon his knees.
Ibid. Stanza 8

[m] Our realm is diminished
With Great-Heart away.
*Great-Heart (Theodore
Roosevelt). Stanza 1*

[n] As I pass through my incar-
nations in every age and race,
I make my proper prostrations to
the gods of the Market Place;
Peering through reverent fingers,
I watch them flourish and fall,
And the Gods of the Copybook
Maxims, I notice, outlast them
all.   *The Gods of the
Copybook Maxims. Stanza 1*

[o] There rise her timeless capi-
tals of empires daily born,
Whose plinths are laid at midnight and whose streets are
packed at morn;
And here come tired youths and
maids that feign to love or sin
In tones like rusty razor blades to
tunes like smitten tin.
*Naaman's Song [interpreted as
a description of Hollywood]*

[p] After marriage arrives a reaction, sometimes a big, sometimes a little, one; but it comes
sooner or later, and must be tided
over by both parties if they desire
the rest of their lives to go with
the current.
Plain Tales. Three and—an Extra

[q] The silliest woman can manage a clever man; but it needs a
very clever woman to manage a
fool!   *Ibid.*

[r] Never praise a sister to a sister, in the hope of your compliments reaching the proper ears.
Ibid. False Dawn

[s] Many religious people are
deeply suspicious. They seem—for
purely religious purposes, of
course—to know more about iniquity than the Unregenerate.
Ibid. Watches of the Night

[t] She was as immutable as the
Hills. But not quite so green. . . .
Youth had been a habit of hers
for so long, that she could not
part with it.
Ibid. Venus Annodomini

[u] The first proof a man gives of
his interest in a woman is by talking to her about his own sweet
self. If the woman listens without
yawning, he begins to like her. If
she flatters the animal's vanity,
he ends by adoring her.
*Under the Deodars. The
Education of Otis Yeere*

[v] He wrapped himself in quotations—as a beggar would enfold
himself in the purple of Emperors.
*Many Inventions. The Finest
Story in the World*

[w] More men are killed by over-
work than the importance of the
world justifies.
The Phantom 'Rickshaw

[x] There aren't twelve hundred
people in the world who understand pictures. The others pretend
and don't care.
The Light That Failed. Chap. 7

[y] "What did the Governor of
North Carolina say to the Gov-
ernor of South Carolina?"
"Excellent notion. It *is* a long
time between drinks."
Ibid. Chap. 8

[z] A man may be festooned with
the whole haberdashery of success, and go to his grave a castaway.   *Independence*

[a] Enough work to do, and
strength enough to do the work.
A Doctor's Work

[b] That packet of assorted miseries which we call a Ship.
The First Sailor

[c] Never again will I spend another winter in this accursed
bucket-shop of a refrigerator
called England.
Letter to Sidney Colvin

[d] He became an officer *and* a
gentleman, which is an enviable
thing.   *Only a Subaltern*

[e] Tea fights.   *Ibid.*

[f] An imperfectly denatured
animal intermittently subject to
the unpredictable reactions of an
unlocated spiritual area.
*Surgeons and The Soul.
(Definition of man)*

[g] I taught Turkey all he ever
knew of French, and he tried to
make Stalky and me comprehend
a little Latin. There is much to be
said for this system, if you want
a boy to learn anything, because
he will remember what he gets
from an equal where his master's
words are forgotten.
*Something of Myself for My
Friends Known and Unknown.
Chap. 2 (Posthumous autobiography, 1937)*

Richard R. Kirk
[1877-   ]

[h] Thrice blessed are our friends: they come, they stay, And presently they go away.
Thrice Blessed

[i] A book's an Inn whose patrons' praise Depends on seasons and on days, On dispositions, and—in fine— Not wholly on the landlord's wine.
A Book's an Inn

Walter Kittredge
[1834-1905]

[j] We're tenting to-night on the old camp-ground, Give us a song to cheer Our weary hearts, a song of home And friends we love so dear.
Tenting on the Old Campground. Stanza 1

Grenville Kleiser
[1868-   ]

[k] She gleans how long you wish to stay; She lets you go without delay.
The Ideal Hostess

[l] She is not difficult to please; She can be silent as the trees. She shuns all ostentatious show; She knows exactly when to go.
The Ideal Guest

Henry Herbert Knibbs
[1874-   ]

[m] Along the sea, across the land, the birds are flying South, And you, my sweet Penelope, out there somewhere you wait for me, With buds of roses in your hair and kisses on your mouth.
Out There Somewhere

[n] Adventure was his coronal, And all his wealth was wandering.
The Journey

[o] After the coffee things ain't so bad.
That Inside Song

[p] The heart of a dog—and he love a man—may never forget or change.
The Dog-Star Pup

Herman W. Knickerbocker
[1868-1934]

[q] I believe that when you say one is a "dead game sport" you have reached the climax of human philosophy.
Eulogy at the funeral of Riley Grannan. Rawhide, Nevada [April 3, 1908]

Frederic Lawrence Knowles
[1869-1905]

[r] When navies are forgotten And fleets are useless things, When the dove shall warm her bosom Beneath the eagle's wings.
The New Age. Stanza 1

[s] Our crosses are hewn from different trees, But we all must have our Calvaries.
Golgotha

[t] Joy is a partnership, Grief weeps alone; Many guests had Cana, Gethsemane had one.
Grief and Joy

[u] In purple and fine linen My country farmhouse shines, The purple on the lilacs— The linen on the lines.
Royalty

[v] I have no other foe to fear save Fear.
Fear. Stanza 7

James Sheridan Knowles
[1784-1862]

[w] A sound so fine, there's nothing lives 'Twixt it and silence.
Virginius. Act V, Sc. 2

John Knox
[1505-1572]

[x] A man with God is always in the majority. (Un homme avec Dieu est toujours la majorité.)
Inscription on the Reformation Monument, Geneva, Switzerland

William Knox
[1789-1825]

[y] Oh why should the spirit of mortal be proud? Like a fast-flitting meteor, a fast-flying cloud, A flash of the lightning, a break of the wave, He passes from life to his rest in the grave.
Songs of Israel. Mortality, Stanza 1

[z] The fool hath said: There is no God! No God! Who lights the morning sun, And sends him on his heavenly road, A far and brilliant course to run?
The Atheist. Stanza 1

Jean de La Bruyère
see Bruyère

Jean de La Fontaine
see Fontaine

Fiorello H. LaGuardia
[1882–1948]

[a] Ticker tape ain't spaghetti.
*Speech to the United Nations
Relief and Rehabilitation Ad-
ministration, March 29, 1946*

Alphonse M. L. Lamartine
[1790–1869]

[b] What is our life but a succession of preludes to that unknown
song whose first solemn note is
sounded by Death?
*Méditations Poétiques.
Second Series, XV*

Arthur J. Lamb
[1870–1928]

[c] Her beauty was sold for an
old man's gold,
She's a bird in a gilded cage.
A Bird in a Gilded Cage [1900]

[d] "He don't know Nellie like I
do,"
Said the saucy little bird on
Nellie's hat.
The Bird on Nellie's Hat [1906]

Charles Lamb
[1775–1834]

[e] Credulity is the man's weakness, but the child's strength.
Witches, and Other Night Fears

[f] The human species, according
to the best theory I can form of
it, is composed of two distinct
races, the men who borrow, and
the men who lend.
The Two Races of Men

[g] Of all sound of all bells—
(bells, the music nighest border-
ing upon heaven)—most solemn
and touching is the peal which
rings out the Old Year.
New Year's Eve

[h] A clear fire, a clean hearth,
and the rigour of the game.
Mrs. Battle's Opinions on Whist

[i] Sentimentally I am disposed
to harmony; but organically I am
incapable of a tune.
A Chapter on Ears

[j] Not many sounds in life, and
I include all urban and all rural
sounds, exceed in interest a knock
at the door.
Valentine's Day

[k] A God-send, as our familiarly
pious ancestors termed a benefit
received where the benefactor was
unknown.   *Ibid.*

[l] The custom of saying grace at
meals had, probably, its origin in
the early times of the world, and
the hunter-state of man, when
dinners were precarious things,
and a full meal was something
more than a common blessing.
Grace Before Meat

[m] Nothing is to me more dis-
tasteful than that entire complacency and satisfaction which
beam in the countenances of a
new-married couple.
The Behaviour of Married People

[n] He has left off reading altogether, to the great improvement
of his originality.   *Detached
Thoughts on Books and Reading*

[o] Newspapers always excite curiosity. No one ever lays one down
without a feeling of disappointment.   *Ibid*

[p] If there be a regal solitude
it is a sick bed.
The Convalescent

[q] Your absence of mind we
have borne, till your presence of
body came to be called in question
by it.   *Amicus Redivivus*

[r] A pun is a pistol let off at the
ear; not a feather to tickle the
intellect.   *Popular Fallacies. IX
That the Worst Puns are the Best*

[s] The growing infirmities of age
manifest themselves in nothing
more strongly, than in an inveter-
ate dislike of interruption.
*Ibid. XII, That Home is Home
Though it is Never so Homely*

[t] Reputation said: "If once we
sever,
Our chance of future meeting is
but vain:
Who parts from me, must look to
part for ever,
For Reputation lost comes no
again."   *Love, Death, and
Reputation. Stanza 4*

[u] A bird appears a thoughtless
thing . . .
No doubt he has his little cares,
And very hard he often fares,
The which so patiently he bears.
Crumbs to the Birds

[v] For thy sake, tobacco, I
Would do anything but die.
A Farewell to Tobacco

[w] Who first invented work, and
bound the free
And   holiday-rejoicing   spirit
down . . .
To that dry drudgery at the desk's
dead wood?   *Work*

[x] The not unpeaceful evening
of a day
Made black by morning storms.
Poem-letter to Coleridge [1797]

[y] A good-natured woman, which
is as much as you can expect from
a friend's wife.
Letter to Hazlitt [1805]

[z] Anything awful makes me
laugh. I misbehaved once at a
funeral.
Letter to Southey [1815]

[a] Fanny Kelly's divine plain face.
Letter to Mrs. Wordsworth [1818]

[b] An archangel a little damaged.
His description of Coleridge

[c] I came home for ever!
Letter to Bernard Barton [1825], on leaving his "33 years' desk" at the East India House

Mary Lamb
[1765–1847]

[d] Thou straggler into loving arms,
Young climber-up of knees.
A Child. Stanza 3

William Lamb,
Viscount Melbourne
[1779–1848]

[e] I wish that I could be as cocksure of anything as Tom Macaulay is of everything.
Quoted

William James Lampton
[1859–1917]

[f] Same old slippers,
Same old rice,
Same old glimpse of Paradise.
June Weddings. Stanza 10

[g] Where the corn is full of kernels
And the colonels full of corn.
Kentucky

Letitia Elizabeth Landon
[1802–1838]

[h] As beautiful as woman's blush,—
As evanescent too.
Apple Blossoms

Walter Savage Landor
[1775–1864]

[i] Rose Aylmer, whom these wakeful eyes
May weep, but never see,
A night of memories and of sighs
I consecrate to thee.
Rose Aylmer

[j] But I have sinuous shells of pearly hue. . . .
Shake one, and it awakens; then apply
Its polished lips to your attentive ear,
And it remembers its august abodes,
And murmurs as the ocean murmurs there. *Gebir. Book I*

[k] Around the child bend all the three
Sweet Graces—Faith, Hope, Charity.
Around the man bend other faces—
Pride, Envy, Malice, are his Graces. *Around the Child*

[l] Children are what the mothers are.
No fondest father's fondest care
Can fashion so the infant heart.
Children

[m] When we play the fool, how wide
The theatre expands! beside,
How long the audience sits before us!
How many prompters! what a chorus! *Plays. Stanza 2*

[n] I strove with none, for none was worth my strife;
Nature I loved; and next to Nature, Art.
I warm'd both hands before the fire of life;
It sinks, and I am ready to depart. *Dying Speech of an Old Philosopher*

[o] Of all failures, to fail in a witticism is the worst, and the mishap is the more calamitous in a drawn out and detailed one.
Imaginary Conversations. Chesterfield and Chatham

[p] 'Tis verse that gives
Immortal youth to mortal maids.
Verse

George Martin Lane
[1823–1897]

[q] The waiter he to him doth call,
And gently whispers—"One Fish-ball."
The waiter roars it through the hall,
The guests they start at "One Fish-ball!"
The guest then says, quite ill at ease,
"A piece of bread, sir, if you please."
The waiter roars it through the hall:
"We don't give bread with one Fish-ball!" *One Fish-ball. Couplets 7–10 [The Drawer, Harper's Monthly, July 1855]*

Andrew Lang
[1844–1912]

[r] Such is the fate of borrowed books: they're lost,
Or not the book returneth, but its ghost! *From Colletet*

[s] One gift the fairies gave me: (three
They commonly bestowed of yore)

The love of books, the golden key
That opens the enchanted door.
          Ballade of the Bookworm.
          Stanza 2

[t] Prince, you may storm and
          ban—
Joe Millers *are* a pest,
Suppress me if you can!
I am a Merry Jest!   *Ballade of*
          the Primitive Jest. Envoy

[u] There's a joy without canker
          or cark,
There's a pleasure eternally
          new,
'Tis to gloat on the glaze and the
          mark
Of china that's ancient and
          blue.
Ballade of Blue China. Stanza 1

[v] We marvel, now we look be-
          hind:
Life's more amusing than we
          thought!
          Ballade of Middle Age. Stanza 1

[w] The windy lights of Autumn
          flare:
I watch the moonlit sails go by;
I marvel how men toil and fare,
The weary business that they
          ply!
Their voyaging is vanity,
And fairy gold is all their gain,
And all the winds of winter cry,
"My Love returns no more again."
          Ballade of Autumn. Stanza 2

[x] Sleep, that giv'st what Life
          denies,
Shadowy bounties and supreme,
Bring the dearest face that flies
Following darkness like a dream!
          Ballade of the Dream. Envoy

[y] The Angler hath a jolly life
Who by the rail runs down,
And leaves his business and his
          wife,
And all the din of town.
The wind down stream is blowing
          straight,
And nowhere cast can he:
Then lo, he doth but sit and wait
In kindly company.
          The Contented Angler. Stanza 1

[z] Why ladies read what they *do*
          read
Is a thing that no man may ex-
          plain.   *A Remonstrance with*
          the Fair. Stanza 1

[a] Had cigarettes no ashes,
          And roses ne'er a thorn,
The big trout would not ever
Escape into the river.
          A Highly Valuable Chain of
          Thoughts. Stanza 2

[b] We meet him first in Homer's
          verse,
The dog by the Aegean seas;
He barks at strangers, ay, and
          worse,

He bites! We learn, in languag
          terse,
That even Argos has the curse
          Of fleas!
          The Friend of Man. Stanza

[c] And, if one Rag of Characte
          they spare,
Comes the Biographer, and strip
          it bare!
          Letters to Dead Authors
          Epistle to Mr. Alexander Pop

[d] Perchance for poets dea
there is prepared a place mor
beautiful than their dreams.
          Ibid. To Theocritu

[e] The dusty and stony ways o
contemporary criticism.
          Ibid. To Edgar Allan Po

[f] The eye of each man sees bu
what it has the power of seeing.
          Ibid. To Home

Sidney Lanier
[1842–1881]

[g] Ye marshes, how candid an
          simple and nothing-with
          holding and free
Ye publish yourselves to the sk
          and offer yourselves to th
          sea!
          The Marshes of Glynn. IV,

[h] Death, thou'rt a cordial ol
          and rare:
Look how compounded, with wha
          care!
Time got his wrinkles reaping the
Sweet herbs from all antiquity.
          The Stirrup-Cup. Stanza

[i] The incalculable Up-and
          Down of Time.   *Clove*

[j] Life! thou sea-fugue, wri
          from east to west,
Love, Love alone can pore
On thy dissolving score
Of harsh half-phrasings,
          Blotted ere writ,
And double erasings
          Of chords most fit.
          The Symphon

[k] Music is Love in search of
          word.   *Ibid*

[l] A rainbow span of fifty year
Painted upon a cloud of tears,
In blue for hopes and red for fear
          Finds end in a golden hour to
          day.
          The Golden Wedding of Sterlin
          and Sarah Lanier. Stanza

[m] My soul is sailing throug
          the sea,
But the Past is heavy an
          hindereth me.
          Barnacles. Stanza

George Thomas Lanigan
[1845–1886]

[n] What, what, what,
What's the news from Swat?

Sad news,
Bad news,
Comes by cable led
Through the Indian Ocean's bed,
Through the Persian Gulf, the Red
Sea and the Med-
Iterranean—he's dead;
The Ahkoond is dead!
A Threnody. Stanza 1

Lucy Larcom
[1826–1893]

[o] If the world seems cold to
you,
Kindle fires to warm it!
Three Old Saws

[p] If the world's a wilderness,
Go, build houses in it! *Ibid.*

[q] If the world's a vale of tears,
Smile, till rainbows span it!
Ibid.

Ringgold ("Ring") Wilmer Lardner
[1885–1933]

[r] A good many young writers
make the mistake of enclosing a
stamped, self-addressed envelope,
big enough for the manuscript to
come back in. This is too much of
a temptation to the editor.
How to Write Short Stories

[s] Mother set facing the front
of the train, as it makes her giddy
to ride backwards. I set facing her,
which does not affect me.
The Golden Honeymoon

Harold Joseph Laski
[1893–1950]

[t] It would be madness to let the
purposes or the methods of private
enterprise set the habits of the
age of atomic energy.
Plan or Perish [1945]

Mary Artemisia Lathbury
[1841–1913]

[u] Children of yesterday,
Heirs of to-morrow,
What are you weaving?
Labor and sorrow?
Look to your looms again,
Faster and faster
Fly the great shuttles
Prepared by the Master.
Life's in the loom,
Room for it—room!
Song of Hope. Stanza 1

Frederick Palmer Latimer
[1875–1940]

[v] I wish I were a little rock,
A-sitting on a hill,
A-doing nothing, all day long,
But just a-sitting still;
I wouldn't eat, I wouldn't sleep,
I wouldn't even wash—

I'd sit and sit a thousand years,
And rest myself, b'Gosh!
The Weary Wisher

Hugh Latimer
[1485–1555]

[w] Play the man, Master Ridley;
we shall this day light such a
candle, by God's grace, in England, as I trust shall never be put
out.
*Addressed to Nicholas Ridley as
they were being burned alive at
Oxford, for heresy, October 16,
1555 (Quoted by J. R. Green: A
Short History of the English
People, Chap. 7)*

Sir Harry Lauder
[1870–1950]

[x] Oh, it's nice to get up in the
mornin',
But it's nicer to lie in bed. *Song*

[y] Just a wee doch-an'-dorris
Before we gang awa' . . .
If y' can say
It's a braw brecht moonlecht
necht,
Yer a' recht, that's a'. *Song*

[z] Roamin' in the gloamin'
By the bonny banks of Clyde.
Song

William L. Laurence
[1888–   ]

[a] The Atomic Age began at
exactly 5:30 Mountain War Time
on the morning of July 16, 1945,
on a stretch of semi-desert land
about fifty airline miles from Ala-
mogordo, New Mexico.
At that great moment in history,
ranking with the moment in the
long ago when man first put fire
to work for him and started on his
march to civilization, the vast
energy locked within the hearts
of the atoms of matter was released for the first time in a burst
of flame such as had never before
been seen on this planet. . . .
A great ball of fire about a mile
in diameter, changing colors as it
kept shooting upward, from deep
purple to orange, expanding,
growing bigger, rising as it was
expanding, an elemental force
freed from its bonds after being
chained for billions of years. . . .
*In The New York Times,
September 26, 1945*

[b] At first it was a giant column
that soon took the shape of a
supramundane mushroom. For a
fleeting instant it took the form
of the Statue of Liberty magnified
many times. *Ibid.*

Johann Kaspar Lavater
[1741–1801]

From the Aphorisms on Man [London, 1788] much admired and privately annotated by William Blake. See the one-volume edition of Blake's Poetry and Prose, edited by Geoffrey Keynes.

[c] Who has many wishes has generally but little will. Who has energy of will has few diverging wishes. Whose will is bent with energy on *one*, *must* renounce the wishes for *many* things.

[d] Say not you know another entirely, till you have divided an inheritance with him.

[e] He who, when called upon to speak a disagreeable truth, tells it boldly and has done is both bolder and milder than he who nibbles in a low voice and never ceases nibbling.

[f] The public seldom forgive twice.

[g] Trust not him with your secrets, who, when left alone in your room, turns over your papers.

David Herbert Lawrence
[1885–1930]

[h] I never saw a wild thing
Sorry for itself.   *Self-Pity*

[i] When I wish I was rich, then
I know I am ill.   *Riches*

[j] When I read Shakespeare I am struck with wonder
That such trivial people should muse and thunder
In such lovely language. *When I Read Shakespeare. Stanza 1*

[k] Men are free when they are in a living homeland, not when they are straying and breaking away. . . . The most unfree souls go west, and shout of freedom. Men are freest when they are most unconscious of freedom. The shout is a rattling of chains.
          Studies in Classic American Literature. Chap. 1

[l] Necessary, for ever necessary, to burn out false shames and smelt the heaviest ore of the body into purity.
          Lady Chatterley's Lover

[m] One realm we have never conquered—the pure present. One great mystery of time is terra incognita to us—the instant. The most superb mystery we have hardly recognized—the immediate, instant self. The quick of all time is the instant. The quick of all the universe, of all creation, is the incarnate, carnal self.
          New Poems. Preface

[n] The dead don't die. They look on and help.
          Quoted by Catherine Carswell in The Savage Pilgrimage, a biography

Edwin Gordon Lawrence
[1859–   ]

[o] Take these two messengers
With you o'er land or seas
To close and ope the doors:
"Thank you" and "If you please."
          Two Messengers. Stanza 1

Thomas Edward Lawrence
[1888–1935]

[p] I loved you, so I drew these tides of men into my hands and wrote my will across the sky in stars.   *Seven Pillars of Wisdom. Dedication*

[q] There could be no honour in a sure success, but much might be wrested from a sure defeat.
          Revolt in the Desert. Chap. 19

[r] It came upon me freshly how the secret of uniform was to make a crowd solid, dignified, impersonal: to give it the singleness and tautness of an upstanding man. This death's livery which walled its bearers from ordinary life, was sign that they had sold their wills and bodies to the State: and contracted themselves into a service not the less abject for that its beginning was voluntary.
          Ibid. Chap. 35

Henry Lawson
[1867–1922]

[s] When you wear a cloudy collar and a shirt that isn't white,
And you cannot sleep for thinking how you'll reach tomorrow night,
You may be a man of sorrows, and on speaking terms with Care,
And as yet be unacquainted with the Demon of Despair;
But I rather think that nothing heaps the trouble on your mind
Like the knowledge that your trousers badly need a patch behind.   *When Your Pants Begin to Go. Stanza 1*

[t] A man's an awful coward when his pants begin to go.
          Ibid.

Emma Lazarus
[1849–1887]

[u] Give me your tired, your poor,
Your huddled masses yearning to breathe free,

The wretched refuse of your teem-
ing shore,
Send these, the homeless, tem-
pest-tossed, to me:
I lift my lamp beside the golden
door.
*The New Colossus: Inscription
for the Statue of Liberty, New
York harbor*

Fanny Heaslip Lea
[1884–   ]

[v] It's odd to think we might
have been
Sun, moon and stars unto each
other—
Only, I turned down one little
street
As you went up another.
Fate. Stanza 5

Stephen Leacock
[1869–1944]

[w] If I were founding a university I would found first a smoking room; then when I had a little
more money in hand I would
found a dormitory; then after
that, or more probably with it, a
decent reading room and a library.
After that, if I still had more
money that I couldn't use, I would
hire a professor and get some text-
books.   *Oxford As I See It*

[x] He flung himself from the
room, flung himself upon his horse
and rode madly off in all directions.   *Gertrude the Governess*

[y] The average man goes to
church six times a year and has
attended Sunday School for two
afternoons and can sing half a
hymn.
Winnowed Wisdom. Preface

[z] The general idea, of course, in
any first class laundry, is to see
that no shirt or collar ever comes
back twice.   *Ibid. Chap. 6*

Edward Lear
[1812–1888]

[a] They went to sea in a sieve,
they did;
In a sieve they went to sea;
In spite of all their friends could
say.   *The Jumblies. Stanza 1*

[b] The Pobble who has no toes
Swam across the Bristol Chan-
nel;
But before he set out he wrapped
his nose
In a piece of scarlet flannel.
*The Pobble Who Has No Toes.
Stanza 2*

[c] On the top of the Crumpetty
Tree
The Quangle Wangle sat,

But his face you could not see,
On account of his Beaver Hat.
*The Quangle Wangle's Hat.
Stanza 1*

[d] The Owl and the Pussy-Cat
went to sea
In a beautiful pea-green boat.

They sailed away, for a year and a
day,
To the land where the bong-
tree grows.
*The Owl and the Pussy-Cat.
Stanzas 1 and 2*

[e] There was an Old Man with a
beard,
Who said: "It is just as I feared!
Two Owls and a Hen,
Four Larks and a Wren
Have all built their nests in my
Beard."   *Limerick*

Walter Learned
[1847–1915]

[f] Her lips were so near
That—what else could I do?
An Explanation

[g] This world is a difficult world,
indeed,
And people are hard to suit,
And the man who plays on the
violin
Is a bore to the man with the
flute.   *Consolation. Stanza 4*

Robert Keith Leavitt
[1895–   ]

[h] People don't ask for facts in
making up their minds. They
would rather have one good, soul-
satisfying emotion than a dozen
facts.   *Voyages and Discoveries*

William Edward Hartpole Lecky
[1838–1903]

[i] And while the great and wise
decay,
And all their trophies pass away,
Some sudden thought, some care-
less rhyme,
Still floats above the wrecks of
Time.   *On an Old Song*

Francis Ledwidge
[1891–1917]

[j] Had I a golden pound to
spend,
My love should mend and sew no
more.
Had I a Golden Pound. Stanza 1

[k] From its blue vase the rose
of evening drops;
Upon the streams its petals float
away.
An Evening in England

Agnes Lee
(Mrs. Otto Freer)
[?–1939]

[1] Then she gazed down some
    wilder, darker hour,
And said—when Mary questioned,
    knowing not,
"Who art thou, mother of so sweet
    a flower?"—
"I am the mother of Iscariot."
    Motherhood. Stanza 6

Henry Lee
[1756–1818]

[m] To the memory of the Man,
first in war, first in peace, and
first in the hearts of his countrymen.
    *Memoirs of Lee. Eulogy on Wash-
    ington [December 26, 1799]*

Eugene Lee-Hamilton
[1845–1907]

[n] Things bygone are the only
    things that last:
The present is mere grass, quick-
    mown away;
The past is stone, and stands for
    ever fast.   *Roman Baths*

Richard Le Gallienne
[1866–1947]

[o] There's too much beauty
    upon this earth
For lonely men to bear. *A Ballad
    of Too Much Beauty. Stanza 1*

[p] One asked of Regret,
    And I made reply:
To have held the bird,
    And let it fly.   *Regret*

[q] Shadow and sun—so too our
    lives are made—
Here learn how great the sun, how
    small the shade!
            For Sundials

[r] How many friends I loved are
    gone!
Death delicately takes the best:
O Death, be careful of the rest!
I cannot spare another one.
        How Many Friends

[s] May is building her house.
    With apple blooms
She is roofing over the glimmer-
    ing rooms.   *May Is Building
            Her House. Stanza 1*

[t] Behind the times I know I
    am,
But what is a tired man to do?
I light my pipe, and read Charles
    Lamb.   *Ballade of the
    Noisiness of the Times. Stanza 1*

[u] I would make a list against
    the evil days
Of lovely things to hold in
    memory.   *A Ballade-Cata-
    logue of Lovely Things. Stanza 1*

[v] "Name your favorite writer"
should be one of the first questions in the Engagement Catechism.   *The Quest of the Golden
            Girl. Book II, Chap. 6*

[w] Wild oats will get sown some
time, and one of the arts of life is
to sow them at the right time.
        Ibid. Book III, Chap. 9

Henry Sambrooke Leigh
[1837–1883]

[x] In form and feature, face and
    limb,
I grew so like my brother,
That folks got taking me for him
    And each for one another.

And when I died the neighbors
    came
    And buried brother John.
        The Twins. Stanzas 1 and 3

[y] My love she is a kitten,
And my heart's a ball of string.
    My Love and My Heart. Stanza 1

Robert Leighton
[1822–1869]

[z] With liberty and endless time
    to read
The libraries of Heaven!
        Books. Stanza 3

"W. Compton Leith"
(Ormonde Maddock Dalton)
[1866–   ]

[a] What song the Sirens sang?
. . . They sang of all that is above
fulfilment and beyond clear
vision; of the immeasurable, the
uncontained, the half-imagined;
of that which is touched but never
held, implored but unpossessed.
. . . They sang the vileness of all
who live contented upon an alms,
and are at ease in bonds, the
slaves whose servitude is made
sweet by habit.   *Sirenica*

Nikolai Lenin
[1870–1924]

[b] Political institutions are a
superstructure resting on an economic foundation.
    *The Three Sources and Three
    Constituent Parts of Marxism
    (tr. Max Eastman)*

[c] It is true that liberty is
precious—so precious that it must
be rationed.
    *Quoted by Sidney and Bea-
    trice Webb in Soviet Commu-
    nism: a New Civilization? Page
    1035*

[d] The most important thing in
illness is never to lose heart.
    *To his mother. Quoted by Hew-
    lett Johnson in The Secret of
    Soviet Strength. Page 111*

[e] International imperialism disposing of the might of capital cannot coexist with the Soviet Republic. Conflict is unavoidable, and here is the greatest difficulty of the Russian Revolution, its greatest historical task, that of provoking the International Revolution. *Collected Works. Vol. XXII, Page 37*

Pope Leo XIII
(Giacchino Pecci)
[1810–1903]

[f] Every man has by nature the right to possess property as his own.
Encyclical Letter on the Condition of Labor [May 15, 1891]

[g] It is one thing to have a right to the possession of money, and another to have a right to use money as one pleases. *Ibid.*

[h] Among the purposes of a society should be to try to arrange for a continuous supply of work at all times and seasons. *Ibid.*

Baird Leonard
(Mrs. Harry S. Clair Zogbaum)
[1888–1941]

[i] That nonchalant attempt of Eve's
To fashion garments out of leaves
Was not, as you have heard, inspired
By shame at being unattired.

Our mercantile statistics show
She started something here below.
As It Was in the Beginning. Stanza 1 and closing lines

Winifred Mary Letts
[1882–   ]

[j] I like the people who keep shops,
Busy and cheerful folk with friendly faces.
Shops. Stanza 1

[k] To serve us seems their only aim,
Asking our wishes, quick to crave our pardon,
And yet I know in each of these shop people
There dwells a soul withdrawn from us, elusive,
The shop can never know—a secret garden. *Ibid. Stanza 4*

[l] I laugh when I hear thim make it plain
That dogs and men never meet again.
For all their talk, who'd listen to thim,

With the soul in the shining eyes of him?
Would God be wasting a dog like Tim?   *Tim, an Irish Terrier. Stanza 4*

[m] A soft day, thank God!
A wind from the south
With a honeyed mouth;
A scent of drenching leaves,
Brier and beech and lime,
White elder-flower and thyme.
A Soft Day. Stanza 1

[n] Morning and noon are good, but night is best—
Maker of stars! Oh, give us back the night.
No Night in Heaven. Stanza 5

Richard Leveridge
[1670–1758]

[o] When mighty roast beef was the Englishman's food,
It ennobled our hearts, and enriched our blood,
Our soldiers were brave and our courtiers were good.
Oh! the roast beef of old England!   *The Roast Beef of Old England. Stanza 1*

Newman Levy
[1888–   ]

[p] No longer are her invitations sought and fought for eagerly,
Her parties once so popular are now attended meagerly.
A blunder unforgivable made life no longer livable,
For she served the sparkling burgundy in glasses made for port.
The Glass of Fashion. Stanza 3

[q] If a man builds a better mousetrap than his neighbor, the world will not only beat a path to his door, it will make newsreels of him and his wife in beach pajamas, it will discuss his diet and his health, it will publish heart-throb stories of his love life, it will publicize him, analyze him, photograph him, and make his life thoroughly miserable by feeding to the palpitant public intimate details of things that are none of its damned business.
The Right To Be Let Alone [American Mercury, June 1935]

Cecil Day Lewis
[1904–   ]

[r] There was laughter and loving in the lanes at evening;
Handsome were the boys then, and girls were gay.
But lost in Flanders by medalled commanders
The lads of the village are vanished away.   *A Time to Dance*

[s] Stake out your claim. Go
  downwards. Bore
Through the tough crust. Oh learn
  to feel
A way in darkness to good ore.
You are the magnet and the steel.
Out of that dark a new world
  flowers.
There in the womb, in the rich
  veins
Are tools, dynamos, bridges,
  towers,
Your tractors and your travelling-
  cranes.
  The Magnetic Mountain. 28

[t] Make us a wind
To shake the world out of this
  sleepy sickness
Where flesh has dwindled and
  brightness waned!
New life multiple in seed and cell
Mounts up to brace our slackness.
Oppression's passion, a full organ
  swell
Through our throats welling wild
Of angers in unison arise
And hunger haunted with a mil-
  lion sighs,
Make us a wind to shake the
  world!   *Ibid. 31*

[u] Sleep-walking on that silver
  wall, the furious
Sick shapes and pregnant fancies
  of your world.
  Newsreel. Stanza 3 [1941]

[v] See the big guns, rising,
  groping, erected
To plant death in your world's soft
  womb.
Fire-bud, smoke-blossom, iron
  seed projected—
Are these exotics? They will grow
  nearer home. *Ibid. Stanza 6*

[w] . . . Out of the dream-house
  stumbling
One night into a strangling air
  and the flung
Rags of children and thunder of
  stone niagaras tumbling,
You'll know you slept too long.
  Ibid. Stanza 7

Clive Staples Lewis
[1898-   ]

[x] The safest road to Hell is the
gradual one—the gentle slope,
soft underfoot, without sudden
turnings, without milestones,
without signposts.
  The Screwtape Letters. XII

[y] The Future is something
which everyone reaches at the rate
of sixty minutes an hour, whatever he does, whoever he is.
  Ibid. XXV

Sinclair Lewis
[1885-1951]

[z] Not only Gopher Prairie, but
ten thousand towns from Albany
to San Diego . . . not a dozen
buildings which suggested that, in
the fifty years of Gopher Prairie's
existence, the citizens had realized
that it was either desirable or
possible to make this, their common home, amusing or attractive.
  Main Street. Chap. 4

[a] A sensational event was
changing from the brown suit to
the gray the contents of his
pockets. He was earnest about
these objects. They were of eternal importance, like baseball or
the Republican Party.
  Babbitt. Chap. 1

[b] Pastoral visiting:
No partiality.
Don't neglect hired girls, be
  cordial.
Guard conversation, pleasing
  manner and laugh and maybe
  one funny story but no scandal or crit. of others.
Stay only 15-30 minutes.
Ask if like to pray with, not insist.
Rem gt opportunities during
  sickness, sorrow, marriage.
Ask jokingly why husband not
  oftener to church.
  *Elmer Gantry. Chap. 8, notes
  on Practical Theology lectures*

[c] To a true-blue professor of
literature in an American university, literature is not something that a plain human being,
living today, painfully sits down
to produce. No; . . . it is something
magically produced by super-
human beings who must, if they
are to be regarded as artists at all,
have died at least one hundred
years before the diabolical invention of the typewriter. . . .
Our American professors like
their literature clear and cold and
pure and very dead.
  *The American Fear of Litera-
  ture, address given at Stock-
  holm, on receiving the Nobel
  Prize for Literature* [Decem-
  ber 12, 1930]

Robert Ley
[1890-1945]

[d] Strength through Joy.
  *Instruction for the German
  Labor Front* [December 2, 1933]

George Leybourne
[?-1884]

[e] He'd fly through the air with
  the greatest of ease,
This handsome young man on the
  flying trapeze;
His movements were graceful, all
  girls he could please,
And my love he purloined away!
  The Man on the Flying Trapeze

Abraham Lincoln
[1809–1865]

[f] If the good people, in their wisdom, shall see fit to keep me in the background, I have been too familiar with disappointments to be very much chagrined.
Address, New Salem, Illinois
[March 9, 1832]

[g] I believe this government cannot endure permanently half slave and half free.
Speech, Republican State Convention, Springfield, Illinois
[June 16, 1858]

[h] As I would not be a slave, so I would not be a master. This expresses my idea of democracy. Whatever differs from this, to the extent of the difference, is no democracy.
Letter [August 1 (?), 1858]

[i] If we do not make common cause to save the good old ship of the Union on this voyage, nobody will have a chance to pilot her on another voyage.
Address, Cleveland, Ohio
[February 15, 1861]

[j] While the people retain their virtue and vigilance, no administration, by any extreme of wickedness or folly, can very seriously injure the government in the short space of four years.
First Inaugural Address
[March 4, 1861]

[k] Labor is prior to, and independent of, capital. Capital is only the fruit of labor, and could never have existed if labor had not first existed. *First Annual Message to Congress [December 3, 1861]*

[l] It is difficult to make a man miserable while he feels he is worthy of himself and claims kindred to the great God who made him.
Address on Colonization to a Deputation of Colored Men
[August 14, 1862]

[m] My paramount object in this struggle is to save the Union, and is not either to save or destroy slavery. If I could save the Union without freeing any slave, I would do it; and if I could do it by freeing all the slaves, I would do it; and if I could save it by freeing some and leaving others alone, I would also do that. *Letter to Horace Greeley [August 22, 1862]*

[n] In giving freedom to the slave we assure freedom to the free,—honorable alike in what we give and what we preserve
Second Annual Message to Congress [December 1, 1862]

[o] The Father of Waters again goes unvexed to the sea.
Letter to James C. Conkling
[August 26, 1863]

[p] Among freemen there can be no successful appeal from the ballot to the bullet, and .. they who take such appeal are sure to lose their case and pay the cost.
Ibid.

[q] But, in a larger sense, we cannot dedicate, we cannot consecrate, we cannot hallow this ground. The brave men, living and dead, who struggled here, have consecrated it, far above our poor power to add or to detract. The world will little note nor long remember what we say here, but it can never forget what they did here. *Address, Gettysburg*
[November 19, 1863]

[r] It is rather for us to be here dedicated to the great task remaining before us; that from these honored dead we take increased devotion to that cause for which they gave the last full measure of devotion. *Ibid.*

[s] That this nation, under God, shall have a new birth of freedom, and that government of the people, by the people, for the people, shall not perish from the earth. *Ibid.*

[t] I have not permitted myself, gentlemen, to conclude that I am the best man in the country; but I am reminded in this connection of a story of an old Dutch farmer, who remarked to a companion once that it was not best to swap horses when crossing a stream.
Reply to National Union League
[June 9, 1864]

[u] Human nature will not change. In any future great national trial, compared with the men of this, we shall have as weak and as strong, as silly and as wise, as bad and as good.
Response to a Serenade
[November 10, 1864]

[v] With malice toward none; with charity for all; with firmness in the right, as God gives us to see the right, let us strive on to finish the work we are in; to bind up the nation's wounds; to care for him who shall have borne the battle, and for his widow and his orphan —to do all which may achieve and cherish a just and lasting peace among ourselves and with all nations. *Second Inaugural Address*
[March 4, 1865]

[w] Men are not flattered by being shown that there has been a

difference of purpose between the Almighty and them.
Letter to Thurlow Weed
[March 15, 1865]

[x] Important principles may and must be flexible.
Last public address, Washington [April 11, 1865]

[y] If you once forfeit the confidence of your fellow citizens, you can never regain their respect and esteem. It is true that you may fool all the people some of the time; you can even fool some of the people all the time; but you can't fool all of the people all the time.
To a caller at the White House.
In Alexander K. McClure's Lincoln's Yarns and Stories.
Page 124

[z] One night he dreamed that he was in a crowd, when someone recognized him as the President, and exclaimed in surprise, "He is a very common-looking man." Whereupon he answered, "Friend, the Lord prefers common-looking people. That is the reason he makes so many of them."
James Morgan: Our Presidents.
Chap. 6

[a] I do the very best I know how —the very best I can; and I mean to keep doing so until the end. If the end brings me out all right, what is said against me won't amount to anything. If the end brings me out wrong, ten angels swearing I was right would make no difference.
Conversation at the White House, reported by Frank B. Carpenter

[b] As thin as the homœopathic soup that was made by boiling the shadow of a pigeon that had been starved to death.
Quoted by Alonzo Rothschild: Lincoln, Master of Men. Chap. 3

[c] I don't s'pose anybody on earth takes gingerbread better'n I do—and gets less'n I do.
Quoted by Carl Sandburg: Abraham Lincoln: The Prairie Years. II, 290

[d] If you call a tail a leg, how many legs has a dog? Five? No; calling a tail a leg don't *make* it a leg.   *Traditionally attributed to Lincoln*

Anne Morrow
(Mrs. Charles) Lindbergh
[1908-   ]

[e] [Radio] Living proof of that bond with the world. Touch of flesh and blood to the doubting. Sound, mind, spirit, cutting across

space, over water, through wind— unwavering, undeterred, like light through darkness.
"Listen! the Wind." Chap. 11

[f] That familiar indefinable lump in the chest . . . the going-away lump, that had been there when I was a child and was as uncontrollable now as then. Leaving the seaside after the summer was over . . . leaving houses . . . — any place that you had made with difficulty and affection your home. In fact, simply going away.
Ibid. Chap. 18

[g] The world has different owners at sunrise. Fields belong to hired men opening gates for cows; meadows, to old women with carpetbags, collecting mushrooms. Even your own garden does not belong to you. Rabbits and blackbirds have the lawns; a tortoiseshell cat who never appears in daytime patrols the brick walks, and a golden-tailed pheasant glints his way through the iris spears.   *Ibid. Chap. 19*

[h] The wave of the future is coming and there is no fighting it.
The Wave of the Future

[i] Lost time was like a run in a stocking. It always got worse.
The Steep Ascent. Chap. 3

Charles Augustus Lindbergh
[1902-   ]

[j] We (that's my ship and I) took off rather suddenly. We had a report somewhere around 4 o'clock in the afternoon before that the weather would be fine, so we thought we would try it. . . .

I saw a fleet of fishing boats. . . . I flew down almost touching the craft and yelled at them, asking if I was on the right road to Ireland.

They just stared. Maybe they didn't hear me. Maybe I didn't hear them. Or maybe they thought I was just a crazy fool. An hour later I saw land.
Lindbergh's Own Story [of his non-stop flight, Long Island to Paris], in The New York Times, May 23, 1927

Nicholas Vachel Lindsay
[1879–1931]

[k] They spoke, I think, of perils past.
They spoke, I think, of peace at last.
One thing I remember:
Spring came on forever,
Spring came on forever,
Said the Chinese nightingale.
The Chinese Nightingale

[l] The flower-fed buffaloes of the
   spring
In the days of long ago,
Ranged where the locomotives
   sing
And the prairie flowers lie low.
   The Flower-Fed Buffaloes

[m] Then you died on the prairie,
   and scorned all disgraces,
O broncho that would not be
   broken of dancing.
   *The Broncho That Would Not
   Be Broken. Stanza 5*

[n] A bronzed, lank man! His suit
   of ancient black,
A famous high top-hat and plain
   worn shawl
Make him the quaint great figure
   that men love,
The prairie-lawyer, master of us
   all.   *Abraham Lincoln
   Walks at Midnight. Stanza 3*

[o] I look on the specious elec-
   trical light
Blatant, mechanical, crawling and
   white,
Wickedly red or malignantly green
Like the beads of a young Sene-
   gambian queen.
   *A Rhyme About an Electrical
      Advertising Sign*

[p] See how the generations pass
Like sand through Heaven's blue
   hour-glass.   *Shantung*

[q] I want live things in their
   pride to remain.
I will not kill one grasshopper vain
Though he eats a hole in my shirt
   like a door.
I let him out, give him one chance
   more.
Perhaps, while he gnaws my hat
   in his whim,
Grasshopper lyrics occur to him.
   The Santa Fé Trail

[r] Fat black bucks in a wine-
   barrel room,
Barrel-house kings, with feet un-
   stable,
Sagged and reeled and pounded
   on the table,
Pounded on the table,
Beat an empty barrel with the
   handle of a broom,
Hard as they were able,
Boom, boom, Boom,
With a silk umbrella and the
   handle of a broom,
Boomlay, boomlay, boomlay, Boom.
   The Congo. Part I

[s] Then I saw the Congo, creeping through the black,
Cutting through the jungle with
   a golden track.   *Ibid.*

[t] Mumbo-Jumbo is dead in the
   jungle,
Never again will he hoo-doo you.
   Ibid. Part III

[u] Planting the trees that would
   march and train

On, in his name to the great
   Pacific,
Like Birnam Wood to Dunsinane,
Johnny Appleseed swept on.
   In Praise of Johnny Appleseed
      (1775–1847)

Carl Linnaeus
[1707–1778]

[v] To live by medicine is to live
horribly.
   Diaeta Naturalis. Introduction

[w] A professor can never better
distinguish himself in his work
than by encouraging a clever
pupil, for the true discoverers are
among them, as comets amongst
the stars.
   *Quoted in biography of Lin-
   naeus by Benjamin Daydon
   Jones, Chap. 9*

[x] If a tree dies, plant another
in its place.
   *Ibid. Chap. 15 (Inscribed over
   the door of Linneaus' bedchamber)*

William James Linton
[1812–1898]

[y] His blood hath run in peasant
   veins through many a noteless
   year;
Yet, search in every prince's court,
   you'll rarely find his peer.
For he's one of Nature's Gentlemen, the best of every time.
   Nature's Gentleman. Stanza 1

[z] Be patient, O be patient! Put
   your ear against the earth;
Listen there how noiselessly the
   germ o' the seed has birth;
How noiselessly and gently it up-
   heaves its little way
Till it parts the scarcely broken
   ground, and the blade stands
   up in day.   *Patience*

Walter Lippmann
[1889–   ]

[a] Copeland of Harvard once remarked when he was asked
whether he had enjoyed a tea
party, "if I had not been there I
should have been very much
bored."
   William Bolitho—A Memoir

[b] The final test of a leader is
that he leaves behind him in other
men the conviction and the will
to carry on. . . . The genius of a
good leader is to leave behind him
a situation which common sense,
without the grace of genius, can
deal with successfully.
   *Roosevelt Has Gone.
   [April 14, 1945]*

[c] The world state is inherent in the United Nations as an oak tree is in an acorn.
One World or None. Chap. 13, International Control of Atomic Energy

Joseph Rouget de Lisle
[1760–1836]

[d] Ye sons of France, awake to glory!
Hark! hark! what myriads bid you rise!
Your children, wives, and grandsires hoary,
Behold their tears and hear their cries!   *The Marseillaise*

[e] To arms! to arms! ye brave!
The avenging sword unsheathe!
March on! march on! all hearts resolved
On victory or death!   *Ibid.*

Lizzie M. Little
[*Floruit* 1905]

[f] There will be always one or two who hold
Earth's coin of less account than fairy gold;
Their treasure, not the spoil of crowds and kings,
But the dim beauty at the heart of things.   *Fairy Gold*

Maxim Maximovich Litvinov
[1876–   ]

[g] Peace is indivisible.
Said at Geneva

David Ross Locke
("Petroleum V. Nasby")
[1833–1888]

[h] The contract 'twixt Hannah, God and me,
Was not for one or twenty years, but for eternity.
Hannah Jane. [Harper's Monthly, October 1871]. Stanza 29

John Locke
[1847–1889]

[i] O Ireland, isn't it grand you look—
Like a bride in her rich adornin'?
And with all the pent-up love of my heart
I bid you the top o' the mornin'!
The Exile's Return (Dawn on the Irish Coast). Stanza 1

Frederick Locker-Lampson
[1821–1895]

[j] What an arm—what a waist
For an arm!
To My Grandmother

[k] The world's as ugly, ay, as Sin,—
And almost as delightful.
The Jester's Plea

[l] If you lift a guinea-pig up by the tail
His eyes drop out!   *A Garden Lyric. Stanza 5*

Henry Cabot Lodge
[1850–1924]

[m] New England has a harsh climate, a barren soil, a rough and stormy coast, and yet we love it, even with a passing that of dwellers in more favored regions.
Address, New England Society of New York [December 22, 1884]

[n] Of "Americanism" of the right sort we cannot have too much. Mere vaporing and boasting become a nation as little as a man. But honest, outspoken pride and faith in our country are infinitely better and more to be respected than the cultivated reserve which sets it down as ill-bred and in bad taste ever to refer to our country except by way of deprecation, criticism, or general negation.   *Ibid.*

John Logan
[1748–1788]

[o] Thou hast no sorrow in thy song,
No winter in thy year.
To the Cuckoo

[p] Oh could I fly, I'd fly with thee!
We'd make with joyful wing
Our annual visit o'er the globe,
Companions of the spring.   *Ibid.*

Russell Hillard Loines
[1874–1922]

[q] "Scorn not the sonnet," though its strength be sapped,
Nor say malignant its inventor blundered:
The corpse that here in fourteen lines is wrapped
Had otherwise been covered with a hundred.
On a Magazine Sonnet

Cesare Lombroso
[1836–1909]

[r] Not only is fame (and until recent years even liberty), denied to men of genius during their lives, but even the means of subsistence. After death they receive monuments and rhetoric by way of compensation.
The Man of Genius. Preface

[s] A patient one day presented himself to Abernethy; after careful

examination the celebrated practitioner said, "You need amusement; go and hear Grimaldi; he will make you laugh, and that will be better for you than any drugs." "My God," exclaimed the invalid, "but I *am* Grimaldi!"
Ibid. Part I, Chap. 2

[t] The appearance of a single great genius is more than equivalent to the birth of a hundred mediocrities.
Ibid. Part II, Chap. 2

[u] The ignorant man always adores what he cannot understand. *Ibid. Part III, Chap. 3.*

Henry Wadsworth Longfellow
[1807–1882]

[v] I heard the trailing garments of the Night
Sweep through her marble halls.
Hymn to Night. Stanza 1

[w] Tell me not, in mournful numbers,
Life is but an empty dream!
For the soul is dead that slumbers,
And things are not what they seem.
A Psalm of Life. Stanza 1

[x] Life is real! Life is earnest!
And the grave is not its goal;
Dust thou art, to dust returnest,
Was not spoken of the soul.
Ibid. Stanza 2

[y] Lives of great men all remind us
We can make our lives sublime,
And, departing, leave behind us
Footprints on the sands of time.
Ibid. Stanza 7

[z] Let us, then, be up and doing,
With a heart for any fate;
Still achieving, still pursuing,
Learn to labour and to wait.
Ibid. Stanza 9

[a] There is a Reaper whose name is Death,
And, with his sickle keen,
He reaps the bearded grain at a breath,
And the flowers that grow between.
The Reaper and the Flowers. Stanza 1

[b] He called the flowers, so blue and golden,
Stars, that in earth's firmament do shine.
Flowers. Stanza 1

[c] The hooded clouds, like friars,
Tell their beads in drops of rain.
Midnight Mass for the Dying Year. Stanza 4

[d] His brow is wet with honest sweat,
He earns whate'er he can,

And looks the whole world in the face,
For he owes not any man.
The Village Blacksmith. Stanza 2

[e] Into each life some rain must fall,
Some days must be dark and dreary.
The Rainy Day. Stanza 3

[f] I like that ancient Saxon phrase, which calls
The burial-ground God's-Acre!
God's-Acre. Stanza 1

[g] Standing with reluctant feet,
Where the brook and river meet,
Womanhood and childhood fleet!
Maidenhood. Stanza 3

[h] A banner with the strange device,
Excelsior!
Excelsior. Stanza 1

[i] Stars of the summer night!
Far in yon azure deeps,
Hide, hide your golden light!
She sleeps.
The Spanish Student. Act I, Sc. 3, Serenade

[j] Heaven gives almonds
To those who have no teeth.
Ibid. Act III, Sc. 5

[k] Between the dark and the daylight,
When the night is beginning to lower,
Comes a pause in the day's occupations,
That is known as the Children's Hour.
The Children's Hour. Stanza 1

[l] The day is done, and the darkness
Falls from the wings of Night,
As a feather is wafted downward
From an eagle in his flight.
The Day Is Done. Stanza 1

[m] A feeling of sadness and longing
That is not akin to pain,
And resembles sorrow only
As the mist resembles the rain.
Ibid. Stanza 3

[n] And the night shall be filled with music,
And the cares, that infest the day,
Shall fold their tents, like the Arabs,
And as silently steal away.
Ibid. Stanza 11

[o] I shot an arrow into the air,
It fell to earth, I knew not where.
The Arrow and the Song. Stanza 1

[p] Joy and Temperance and Repose
Slam the door on the doctor's nose. *The Best Medicines*

[q] This is the forest primeval.
Evangeline. Prelude

[r]   Alike were they free from
Fear, that reigns with the tyrant,
and envy, the vice of republics.
Ibid. Part I, 1

[s] When she had passed, it
seemed like the ceasing of exquisite music.   *Ibid.*

[t] Silently one by one, in the infinite meadows of heaven
Blossomed the lovely stars, the
forget-me-nots of the angels.
Ibid. 3

[u] Over the sea-like, pathless,
limitless waste of the desert.
Ibid. Part II, 4

[v]   Sail on, O Ship of State!
Sail on, O Union, strong and
great!
Humanity with all its fears,
With all the hopes of future years,
Is hanging breathless on thy fate!
The Building of the Ship

[w] There is no fireside, howsoe'er
defended,
But has one vacant chair!
Resignation. Stanza 1

[x] This life of mortal breath
Is but a suburb of the life elysian,
Whose portal we call Death.
Ibid. Stanza 5

[y] As unto the bow the cord is,
So unto the man is woman,
Though she bends him, she obeys
him,
Though she draws him, yet she
follows,
Useless each without the other!
The Song of Hiawatha. Part X

[z] Oh the long and dreary Win-
ter!
Oh the cold and cruel Winter!
Ibid. Part XX

[a] If I am not worth the wooing,
I surely am not worth the
winning.   *The Courtship of
Miles Standish. Part III*

[b] "Why don't you speak for
yourself, John?"   *Ibid.*

[c] He is a little chimney, and
heated hot in a moment.
Ibid. Part VI

[d] The long mysterious Exodus
of death.   *The Jewish
Cemetery at Newport. Stanza 1*

[e] Pride and humiliation hand
in hand
Walked with them through the
world where'er they went;
Trampled and beaten were they as
the sand,
And yet unshaken as the continent.   *Ibid. Stanza 12*

[f] A boy's will is the wind's will.
My Lost Youth. Stanza 1

[g] Listen, my children, and you
shall hear.   *Tales of a Wayside Inn. Paul Revere's Ride,
Stanza 1*

[h] The fate of a nation was riding that night.
Ibid. Stanza 8

[i] There never was so wise a man
before;
He seemed the incarnate "Well, I
told you so!"
*Ibid. The Birds of Killingworth,
Stanza 9*

[j] For after all, the best thing
one can do
When it is raining, is to let it rain.
Ibid. Stanza 26

[k] Ships that pass in the night,
and speak each other in passing,
Only a signal shown and a distant
voice in the darkness;
So on the ocean of life we pass and
speak one another,
Only a look and a voice; then
darkness again and a silence.
Ibid. Elizabeth, IV

[l] He speaketh not; and yet there
lies
A conversation in his eyes.
The Hanging of the Crane. III

[m] "O Caesar, we who are about
to die
Salute you!" was the gladiators'
cry
In the arena, standing face to face
With death and with the Roman
populace.
Morituri Salutamus. Stanza 1

[n] The love of learning, the
sequestered nooks,
And all the sweet serenity of
books.   *Ibid. Stanza 21*

[o]   Ah, nothing is too late,
Till the tired heart shall cease to
palpitate.
Cato learned Greek at eighty;
Sophocles
Wrote his grand Oedipus, and
Simonides
Bore off the prize of verse from his
compeers,
When each had numbered more
than fourscore years.
Ibid. Stanza 22

[p] The birds, God's poor who
cannot wait.
*The Sermon of St. Francis.
Stanza 3*

[q] Be not like a stream that
brawls
Loud with shallow waterfalls,
But in quiet self-control
Link together soul and soul.
Songo River. Stanza 11

[r'] Thine was the prophet's
vision, thine
The exaltation, the divine
Insanity of noble minds.
Kéramos

s] Turn, turn, my wheel! 'Tis
    nature's plan
The child should grow into the
    man.   *Ibid.*

t] She knew the life-long mar-
    tyrdom,
The weariness, the endless pain
Of waiting for some one to come
Who nevermore would come
    again.
        Vittoria Colonna. Stanza 6

u] Three Silences there are: the
    first of speech,
The second of desire, the third of
    thought.
    The Three Silences of Molinos

v] The holiest of all holidays are
    those
Kept by ourselves in silence and
    apart;
The secret anniversaries of the
    heart.   *Holidays*

w] Your silent tents of green
We deck with fragrant flowers;
Yours has the suffering been,
The memory shall be ours.
        Decoration Day. Stanza 6

x] Out of the shadows of night
The world rolls into light;
It is daybreak everywhere.
    The Bells of San Blas. Stanza 11

y] Who ne'er his bread in sorrow
    ate,
Who ne'er the mournful mid-
    night hours
Weeping upon his bed has sate,
He knows you not, ye Heavenly
    Powers.
        Hyperion. Book I, Motto

z] Alas! it is not till time, with
    reckless hand, has torn out half
the leaves from the Book of Human Life to light the fires of passion with from day to day, that
man begins to see that the leaves
which remain are few in number.
        Ibid. Book IV, Chap. 8

a] If we could read the secret
history of our enemies, we should
find in each man's life sorrow and
suffering enough to disarm all
hostility.   *Driftwood*

b]   There was a little girl
      Who had a little curl
Right in the middle of her fore-
    head;
    And when she was good
    She was very, very good,
But when she was bad she was
    horrid.
        There Was a Little Girl

Longus
[FIFTH CENTURY]

c] There was never any yet that
wholly could escape love, and
never shall there be any, never so

long as beauty shall be, never so
long as eyes can see.
        *Daphnis and Chloe. Proem,
                        Chap. 2*

d] He is so poor that he could
not keep a dog.   *Ibid. Chap. 15*

Anita Loos
[1893–   ]

e] Gentlemen always seem to remember blondes.
        *Gentlemen Prefer Blondes.
                        Chap. 1*

Louis XII of France
[1462–1515]

f] Let George do it, he is the
man of the time. [Referring to his
prime minister, Cardinal Georges
d'Amboise. George McManus,
American cartoonist, in his comic
series, *Let George Do It*, popular-
ized the saying in the early 1900s.]

Richard Lovelace
[1618–1658]

g] Oh, could you view the
    melody
    Of every grace
    And music of her face,
You'd drop a tear;
    Seeing more harmony
    In her bright eye
Than now you hear.
        Orpheus to Beasts

h] I could not love thee, dear, so
    much,
Lov'd I not honour more.
    *To Lucasta, on Going to the
                Wars. Stanza 3*

i] Stone walls do not a prison
    make,
    Nor iron bars a cage;
Minds innocent and quiet take
    That for an hermitage;
If I have freedom in my love,
    And in my soul am free,
Angels alone that soar above
    Enjoy such liberty.
    To Althea from Prison. Stanza 4

Robert Loveman
[1864–1923]

j] It is not raining rain to me,
    It's raining daffodils;
In every dimpled drop I see
    Wild flowers on the hills.
    *April Rain [Harper's Magazine,
            May 1901]. Stanza 1*

Samuel Lover
[1797–1868]

k] For dhrames always go by
    contrairies, my dear.
        Rory O'More. Stanza 2

[1] "That's eight times to-day
    that you've kissed me before."
"Then here goes another," says he,
    "to make sure,
For there's luck in odd numbers,"
    says Rory O'More.
                    Ibid. Stanza 3

[m] As she sat in the low-backed
        car
The man at the turn-pike bar
Never asked for the toll
But just rubbed his old poll
And looked after the low-backed
        car.
    The Low-Backed Car. Stanza 1

[n] And with my advice, faith I
    wish you'd take me.
                    Widow Machree

David Low
[1891–   ]

[o] I have never met anybody who
wasn't against War. Even Hitler
and Mussolini were, according to
themselves.
            *In The New York Times,
            February 10, 1946*

Amy Lowell
[1874–1925]

[p] A pattern called a war.
Christ! What are patterns for?
                    Patterns

[q] Heart-leaves of lilac all over
    New England,
Roots of lilac under all the soil
    of New England,
Lilac in me because I am New
    England.   *Lilacs*

[r] The sight of a white church
    above thin trees in a city
    square
Amazes my eyes as though it were
    the Parthenon.
                Meeting-House Hill

James Russell Lowell
[1819–1891]

[s] She doeth little kindnesses
Which most leave undone, or de-
    spise.   *My Love. Stanza 4*

[t] Great souls are portions of
    Eternity.   *Sonnet VI*

[u] To win the secrets of a weed's
    plain heart.   *Sonnet XXV*

[v] No man is born into the
    world whose work
Is not born with him; there is
    always work,
And tools to work withal, for those
    who will;
And blessèd are the horny hands
    of toil.
    A Glance Behind the Curtain

[w] They are slaves who fear to
    speak
For the fallen and the weak. . . .
They are slaves who dare not be
In the right with two or three.
            Stanzas on Freedom. IV

[x] The nurse of full-grown souls
    is solitude.   *Columbus*

[y] Truth forever on the scaffold,
Wrong forever on the throne.
        The Present Crisis. Stanza 8

[z]   The coward stands aside,
Doubting in his abject spirit, till
    his Lord is crucified.
                    Ibid. Stanza 11

[a] The birch, most shy and lady-
    like of trees.
            *An Indian-Summer Reverie.
                        Stanza 8*

[b] Dear common flower, that
    grow'st beside the way,
Fringing the dusty road with
    harmless gold.
        To the Dandelion. Stanza 1

[c] They came three thousand
    miles, and died,
To keep the Past upon its throne;
Unheard, beyond the ocean tide,
Their English mother made her
    moan.
    *Graves of Two English Soldiers
        On Concord Battle-ground.
                        Stanza 3*

[d] 'Tis heaven alone that is
    given away;
'Tis only God may be had for the
    asking.   *The Vision of Sir
            Launfal. Part I, Prelude,
                        Stanza 4*

[e] And what is so rare as a day
    in June?
Then, if ever, come perfect days;
Then Heaven tries the earth if it
    be in tune,
And over it softly her warm ear
    lays.   *Ibid. Stanza 5*

[f] The gift without the giver is
    bare;
Who gives himself with his alms
    feeds three,—
Himself, his hungering neighbor,
    and me.
            Ibid. Part II, Stanza 8

[g] A weed is no more than a
    flower in disguise.
                A Fable for Critics

[h] For reading new books is like
    eating new bread,
One can bear it at first, but by
    gradual steps he
Is brought to death's door of a
    mental dyspepsy.   *Ibid.*

[i] A reading-machine, always
    wound up and going,
He mastered whatever was not
    worth the knowing.   *Ibid.*

[j] And I honor the man who is
    willing to sink

Half his present repute for the
freedom to think,
And, when he has thought, be his
cause strong or weak,
Will risk t' other half for the freedom to speak.   *Ibid.*

[k] There comes Poe, with his
raven, like Barnaby Rudge,
Three fifths of him genius and two
fifths sheer fudge.   *Ibid.*

[l] Nature fits all her children
with something to do,
He who would write and can't
write, can surely review.
                            Ibid.

[m] Ez fer war, I call it murder,—
There you hev it plain an' flat;
I don't want to go no furder
Than my Testyment fer that. . . .
An' you've gut to git up airly
Ef you want to take in God.
    *The Biglow Papers. Series I,
                No. 1, Stanza 5*

[n] Gineral C. is a dreffle smart
man:
He's ben on all sides thet give
places or pelf;
But consistency still wuz a part of
his plan,—
He's true to *one* party,—an'
thet is himself.
    Ibid. No. 3, Stanza 3

[o] We kind o' thought Christ
went agin war an' pillage.
                Ibid. Stanza 5

[p] A marciful Providence fashioned us holler
O' purpose thet we might our
principles swaller.
        Ibid. No. 4, Stanza 2

[q] God makes sech nights, all
white and still,
Fur'z you can look or listen.
    *Ibid. Series II, The Courtin',
                    Stanza 1*

[r] His heart kep' goin' pity-pat,
But hern went pity-Zekle.
            Ibid. Stanza 15

[s] To say why gals acts so or so,
Or don't, 'ould be presumin';
Mebby to mean *yes* an' say *no*
Comes nateral to women.
            Ibid. Stanza 18

[t] My gran'ther's rule was safer
'n 'tis to crow:
Don't never prophesy—onless ye
know.   *Ibid. No. 2*

[u] It's 'most enough to make a
deacon swear.   *Ibid.*

[v] The one thet fust gits mad's
most ollers wrong.   *Ibid.*

[w] Folks never understand the
folks they hate.   *Ibid.*

[x] Ef you want peace, the thing
you've gut tu du
Is jes' to show you're up to
fightin', tu.   *Ibid.*

[y] Our lives in sleep are some
like streams that glide
'Twixt flesh an' sperrit boundin'
on each side,
Where both shores' shadders kind
o' mix an' mingle
In sunthin' thet ain't jes' like
either single.
    *Ibid. No. 6, Sunthin' in the
                Pastoral Line*

[z] Each year to ancient friendships adds a ring,
As to an oak.
        Under the Willows

[a] I thought of a mound in
sweet Auburn
Where a little headstone stood;
How the flakes were folding it
gently,
As did robins the babes in the
wood.
    The First Snowfall. Stanza 5

[b] Granting our wish one of
Fate's saddest jokes is!
    *Two Scenes from the Life of
        Blondel. Sc. II, Stanza 2*

[c] For somehow the poor old
Earth blunders along,
Each son of hers adding his mite
of unfitness,
And, choosing the sure way of
coming out wrong,
Gets to port as the next gener-
ation will witness.
                Ibid. Stanza 4

[d] The unmotived herd that only
sleep and feed.
    *Under the Old Elm. Part VII,
                    Stanza 3*

[e] And Death is beautiful as feet
of friend
Coming with welcome at our journey's end.
    *Epistle to George William Curtis,
                    Postscript*

[f] Like him who, in the desert's
awful frame,
Notches his cockney initials on
the Sphinx.
    *Sonnet on Being Asked for an
            Autograph in Venice*

[g] The Maple puts her corals on
in May.   *The Maple*

[h]   As brief
As a dragon-fly's repose.
            Scherzo. Stanza 3

[i] In vain we call old notions
fudge,
And bend our conscience to our
dealing;
The Ten Commandments will not
budge,
And stealing will continue stealing.
    *Motto of the American Copy-
    right League [November 20,
                        1885]*

[j] In the parliament of the present every man represents a constituency of the past.   *Keats*

[k] From the days of the first grandfather, everybody has remembered a golden age behind him!   *Carlyle*

[l] Truly there is a tide in the affairs of men, but there is no gulf-stream setting forever in one direction.
New England Two Centuries Ago

[m] There is no better ballast for keeping the mind steady on its keel, and saving it from all risk of crankiness, than business.   *Ibid.*

[n] Puritanism, believing itself quick with the seed of religious liberty, laid, without knowing it, the egg of democracy.   *Ibid.*

[o] It was in making education not only common to all, but in some sense compulsory on all, that the destiny of the free republics of America was practically settled.   *Ibid.*

[p] Talent is that which is in a man's power; genius is that in whose power a man is.
Rousseau and the Sentimentalists

[q] It is singular how impatient men are with over-praise of others, how patient with over-praise of themselves; and yet the one does them no injury, while the other may be their ruin.
Literary Remains of the Rev. Homer Wilbur

[r] There is nothing so desperately monotonous as the sea, and I no longer wonder at the cruelty of pirates.
Fireside Travels. At Sea

[s] Mishaps are like knives, that either serve us or cut us, as we grasp them by the blade or the handle.
Cambridge Thirty Years Ago

[t] No man, I suspect, ever lived long in the country without being bitten by these meteorological ambitions. He likes to be hotter and colder, to have been more deeply snowed up, to have more trees and larger blown down than his neighbors.
My Garden Acquaintance

[u] The pompous mediocrity of middle life!
A Good Word for Winter

[v] There is no good in arguing with the inevitable. The only argument available with an east wind is to put on your overcoat.
Democracy and Addresses

[w] There is no bore we dread being left alone with so much as our own minds.
A Moosehead Journal

Robert Traill Spence Lowell
[1816–1891]

[x] It was the pipes of the Highlanders,
And now they played "Auld Lang Syne."
It came to our men like the voice of God,
And they shouted along the line.
*The Relief of Lucknow,
September 25, 1857*

St. Ignatius Loyola
[1491–1556]

[y] Teach us, good Lord, to serve Thee as Thou deservest:
To give and not to count the cost . . .
To labour and not ask for any reward
Save that of knowing that we do Thy will.
Prayer for Generosity

Sir John Lubbock,
Lord Avebury
[1834–1913]

[z] As the sun colors flowers, so does art color life.   *The Pleasures of Life. Page 177*

[a] The idle man does not know what it is to enjoy rest. Hard work, moreover, not only tends to give us rest for the body, but, what is even more important, peace to the mind.
Ibid. Page 316

Lucan
[A.D. 39–65]
*Translation by J. D. Duff. Loeb
Classical Library*

[b] Poverty, the mother of manhood.   *The Civil War.
Book I, Line 165*

[c] Delay is ever fatal to those who are prepared.
Ibid. Line 281

[d] Boldness is a mask for fear, however great.
Ibid. Book IV, Line 702

Edward Verrall Lucas
[1868–1938]

[e] You ask me "why I like him." Nay,
I cannot; nay, I would not, say.
I think it vile to pigeonhole
The pros and cons of a kindred soul.   *Friends. Stanza 1*

[f] A stamp's a tiny, flimsy thing,
No thicker than a beetle's wing,

And yet 'twill roam the world for you
Exactly where you tell it to.
*The Three-Halfpenny Traveller.
Stanza 1*

[g] Americans are people who prefer the Continent to their own country, but refuse to learn its languages.
*Wanderings and Diversions:
The Continental Dictionary*

[h] Mosquitoes.—Flying insects with a damnably poisonous bite, which every one except hotel-managers has seen, heard, or suffered from. *Ibid.*

[i] Ticket Collector.—The man who never wants to see your ticket unless you are asleep. *Ibid.*

[j] He says one of the two things that men who have lasted for a hundred years always say—either that they have drunk whisky and smoked all their lives, or that neither tobacco nor spirits ever made the faintest appeal to them.
Ibid.: Secrets

[k] A genius is a man who does unique things of which nobody would expect him to be capable.
Reading, Writing and Remembering

[l] There can be no defence like elaborate courtesy. *Ibid.*

[m] The art of life is to keep down acquaintances. One's friends one can manage, but one's acquaintances can be the devil.
Over Bremerton's

[n] The noise from good toast should reverberate in the head like the thunder of July.
A Word on Toast

St. John Lucas
[1879–1934]

[o] The curate thinks you have no soul;
I know that he has none.
My Dog

[p] This prayer at least the gods fulfill:
That when I pass the flood and see
Old Charon by the Stygian coast
Take toll of all the shades who land,
Your little, faithful, barking ghost
May leap to lick my phantom hand. *Ibid.*

Lucretius
[95–55 B.C.]

[q] Continual dropping wears away a stone.
De Rerum Natura. I, 313

[r] What is food to one man may be fierce poison to others.
Ibid. IV, 637

[s] In the midst of the fountain of wit there arises something bitter, which stings in the very flowers. *Ibid. 1133*

Erich Friedrich Wilhelm Ludendorff
[1865–1937]

[t] I decline Christianity because it is Jewish, because it is international and because, in cowardly fashion, it preaches Peace on Earth. *Deutsche Gottesglaube*

Fitzhugh Ludlow
[1836–1870]

[u] While we wait for the napkin, the soup gets cold,
While the bonnet is trimming, the face grows old,
When we've matched our buttons, the pattern is sold,
And everything comes too late—too late. *Too Late. Stanza 2*

Charles Fletcher Lummis
[1859–1928]

[v] My cigarette! The amulet
That charms afar unrest and sorrow,
The magic wand that, far beyond
To-day, can conjure up to-morrow.
My Cigarette. Stanza 1

Martin Luther
[1483–1546]

[w] A mighty fortress is our God,
A bulwark never failing;
Our helper He amid the flood
Of mortal ills prevailing.
Psalm, Ein' Feste Burg (tr. Frederic H. Hedge)

[x] Here I stand; I can do no otherwise. God help me. Amen!
Speech at the Diet of Worms

[y] A faithful and good servant is a real godsend; but truly 'tis a rare bird in the land.
Table Talk. 156

Sir Alfred Comyn Lyall
[1835–1911]

[z] Is life, then, a dream and delusion, and where shall the dreamer awake?
Is the world seen like shadows on water, and what if the mirror break?
Shall it pass a camp that is struck, as a tent that is gathered and gone
From the sands that were lamplit at eve, and at morning are level and lone? *Meditations of a Hindu Prince and Sceptic*

John Lyly
[Circa 1553–1606]

[a] It seems to me (said she) that you are in some brown study.
Euphues (Arber's reprint).
Page 80

[b] The soft droppes of rain perce the hard marble; many strokes overthrow the tallest oaks.
Ibid. Page 81

[c] Maydens, be they never so foolyshe, yet beeing fayre they are commonly fortunate.
Euphues and his England.
Page 279

[d] Your eyes are so sharpe that you cannot onely looke through a Milstone, but cleane through the minde.   *Ibid. Page 289*

[e] I am glad that my Adonis hath a sweete tooth in his head.
Ibid. Page 308

[f] A Rose is sweeter in the budde than full blowne.   *Ibid. Page 314*

George Washington Lyon
[1879–1948]

[g] Worry, the interest paid by those who borrow trouble.
Epigram in Judge, March 1, 1924

James Gilborne Lyons
[1800–1868]

[h] For stronger far than hosts that march with battle-flags unfurled,
It goes with freedom, thought, and truth to rouse and rule the world.   *The Triumphs of the English Language*

George, Lord Lyttelton
[1709–1773]

[i] Women, like princes, find few real friends.
Advice to a Lady

[j] What is your sex's earliest, latest care,
Your heart's supreme ambition? To be fair.   *Ibid.*

[k] The lover in the husband may be lost.   *Ibid.*

[l] How much the wife is dearer than the bride.
An Irregular Ode

Edward Bulwer Lytton
[1805–1873]

[m] Love, like Death,
Levels all ranks, and lays the shepherd's crook
Beside the sceptre   *The Lady of Lyons. Act III, Sc. 2*

[n] Curse away!
And let me tell thee, Beauseant, a wise proverb
The Arabs have,—"Curses are like young chickens,
And still come home to roost."
Ibid. Act V, Sc. 2

[o] 'Tis at sixty man learns how to value home.
Walpole. Act II, Sc. 5

[p] The mate for beauty
Should be a man, and not a money-chest.
Richelieu. Act I, Sc. 2

[q] Great men gain doubly when they make foes their friends.
Ibid.

[r] Take away the sword;
States can be saved without it.
Ibid. Act II, Sc. 2

[s] In the lexicon of youth, which fate reserves
For a bright manhood, there is no such word
As "fail."   *Ibid.*

[t] What's affection, but the power we give another to torment us?   *Darnley. Act II, Sc. 1*

[u] A good cigar is as great a comfort to a man as a good cry to a woman.
Ibid. Act III, Sc. 2

[v] *Alone!*—that worn-out word,
So idly spoken, and so coldly heard;
Yet all that poets sing and grief hath known
Of hopes laid waste, knells in that word ALONE!
The New Timon. Part II

[w] When stars are in the quiet skies,
Then most I pine for thee;
Bend on me then thy tender eyes,
As stars look on the sea.
When Stars Are in the Quiet Skies

[x] The magic of the tongue is the most dangerous of all spells.
Eugene Aram. Book I, Chap. 7

[y] Fate laughs at probabilities.
Ibid. Chap. 10

[z] He who has little silver in his pouch must have the more silk on his tongue.   *The Last of the Barons. Book I, Chap. 3*

[a'] Happy is the man who hath never known what it is to taste of fame—to have it is a purgatory, to want it is a hell.
Ibid. Book V, Chap. 1

[b'] The man who smokes, thinks like a sage and acts like a Samaritan.
Night and Morning. Chap. 6

[c'] The worst part of an eminent man's conversation is, nine times out of ten, to be found in that part which he means to be clever.   *Caxtonia. Differences Between the Urban and Rural Temperament*

[d] In science, read, by preference, the newest works; in literature, the oldest. The classic literature is always modern.
Ibid. Hints on Mental Culture

Edward Robert Bulwer Lytton, Earl of Lytton ("Owen Meredith")
[1831–1891]

[e] Since we parted yester eve,
I do love thee, love, believe,
Twelve times dearer, twelve hours longer—
One dream deeper, one night stronger,
One sun surer—thus much more
Than I loved thee, love, before.
Since We Parted

[f] The heart of a man's like that delicate weed
Which requires to be trampled on, boldly indeed,
Ere it gives forth the fragrance you wish to extract.
Lucile. Part I, Canto 1, IV

[g] Let any man once show the world that he feels
Afraid of its bark, and 'twill fly at his heels:
Let him fearlessly face it, 'twill leave him alone:
But 'twill fawn at his feet if he flings it a bone.
Ibid. Canto 2, VII

[h] The Italians have voices like peacocks; the Spanish
Smell, I fancy, of garlic; the Swedish and Danish
Have something too Runic, too rough and unshod, in
Their accent for mouths not descended from Odin;
German gives me a cold in the head, sets me wheezing
And coughing; and Russian is nothing but sneezing.
Ibid. XII

[i] Whene'er I hear French spoken as I approve,
I feel myself quietly falling in love.   *Ibid.*

[j] We may live without friends; we may live without books;
But civilized man can not live without cooks.
He may live without books,—what is knowledge but grieving?
He may live without hope,—what is hope but deceiving?
He may live without love,—what is passion but pining?
But where is the man that can live without dining?
Ibid. XIX

[k] There's no weapon that slays Its victim so surely (if well aimed) as praise.
Ibid. Part II, Canto 1, XX

[l] A nun hath no nation.
Wherever man suffers or woman may soothe,
There her land! there her kindred!
Ibid. Canto 6, XII

[m] Love thou the rose, yet leave it on its stem.   *The Wanderer. Prologue, Part I, 19*

[n] Oh, moment of sweet peril, perilous sweet!
When woman joins herself to man.   *Ibid. 27*

[o] But I am sick of all the din That's made in praising Verdi,
Who only know a violin
Is not a hurdy-gurdy.
The Wanderer in France. "Prensus in Aegaeo"

[p] She will show us her shoulder, her bosom, her face;
But what the heart's like, we must guess.   *Ibid. Madame La Marquise, 12*

[q] My life is a torn book. But at the end
A little page, quite fair, is saved, my friend,
Where thou didst write thy name.
The Wanderer in Holland. Jacqueline

[r] Soon as the great tree falls, the rabble run
To strip him of his branches one by one.
Wallenstein's Death

Hamilton Wright Mabie
[1846–1916]

[s] The peculiarity of the New England hermit has not been his desire to get near to God, but his anxiety to get away from man.
Backgrounds of Literature. Emerson and Concord

[t] There will come another era when it shall be light and man will awaken from his lofty dreams, and find his dreams all there, and nothing is gone save his sleep.
The Awakening

Douglas MacArthur
[1880–   ]

[u] I shall return.
Message on leaving Corregidor for Australia, March 11, 1942

Thomas Babington, Lord Macaulay
[1800–1859]

[v] That is the best government which desires to make the people happy, and knows how to make

them happy.   *On Mitford's History of Greece* [*In Knight's Quarterly, November 1824*]

[**w**] Free trade, one of the greatest blessings which a government can confer on a people, is in almost every country unpopular.   *Ibid.*

[**x**] Perhaps no person can be a poet, or even can enjoy poetry, without a certain unsoundness of mind.   *On Milton* [*In Edinburgh Review, August 1825*]

[**y**] The English Bible,—a book which if everything else in our language should perish, would alone suffice to show the whole extent of its beauty and power.   *On John Dryden* [*In Edinburgh Review, January 1828*]

[**z**] His imagination resembled the wings of an ostrich. It enabled him to run, though not to soar.   *Ibid.*

[**a**] The gallery in which the reporters sit has become a fourth estate of the realm.   *On Hallam's Constitutional History* [*September 1828*]

[**b**] Men are never so likely to settle a question rightly as when they discuss it freely.   *Southey's Colloquies* [*January 1830*]

[**c**] Nothing is so galling to a people, not broken in from the birth, as a paternal or, in other words, a meddling government, a government which tells them what to read and say and eat and drink and wear.   *Ibid.*

[**d**] She [the Roman Catholic Church] may still exist in undiminished vigour when some traveller from New Zealand shall, in the midst of a vast solitude, take his stand on a broken arch of London Bridge to sketch the ruins of St. Paul's.   *On Ranke's History of the Popes* [*October 1840*]

[**e**] The chief-justice was rich, quiet, and infamous.   *On Warren Hastings* [*October 1841*]

[**f**] I shall not be satisfied unless I produce something which shall for a few days supersede the last fashionable novel on the tables of young ladies.   *Letter to Macvey Napier* [*November 5, 1841*]

[**g**] The highest proof of virtue is to possess boundless power without abusing it.   *Review of Aikin's Life of Addison* [*July 1843*]

[**h**] Your Constitution is all sail and no anchor.   *Letter to H. S. Randall, author of a Life of Thomas Jefferson* [*May 23, 1857*]

[**i**] Those who compare the age in which their lot has fallen with a golden age which exists only in imagination, may talk of degeneracy and decay; but no man who is correctly informed as to the past, will be disposed to take a morose or desponding view of the present.   *History of England. Vol. I, Chap. 1*

[**j**] The Puritan hated bear-baiting, not because it gave pain to the bear, but because it gave pleasure to the spectators.   *Ibid. Chap. 2*

[**k**] There were gentlemen and there were seamen in the navy of Charles II. But the seamen were not gentlemen, and the gentlemen were not seamen.   *Ibid. Chap. 3*

[**l**] The ambassador [of Russia] and the grandees who accompanied him were so gorgeous that all London crowded to stare at them, and so filthy that nobody dared to touch them. They came to the court balls dropping pearls and vermin.   *History of England. Vol. V, Chap. 23*

[**m**] I hate the notion of gregarious authors. The less we have to do with each other, the better.   *Quoted in George Otto Trevelyan's Life and Letters of Lord Macaulay. Vol. II, Page 245*

[**n**] April's ivory moonlight.   *The Prophecy of Capys. Stanza 18*

Joseph P. MacCarthy
[1863–1934]

[**o**] You must select the Puritans for your ancestors. You must have a sheltered youth and be a graduate of Harvard. . . . Eat beans on Saturday night and fish-balls on Sunday morning. . . . You must be a D.A.R., a Colonial Dame, an S.A.R. or belong to the Mayflower Society. . . . You must read the *Atlantic Monthly*. . . . You must make sure in advance that your obituary appears in the *Boston Transcript*. There is nothing else.   *To be Happy in New England, Letter to the Editor of The Christian Register*

George Macdonald
[1824–1905]

[**p**] Where did you come from, baby dear?
Out of the everywhere into the here.   *At the Back of the North Wind. Baby, Stanza 1*

[**q**] Where did you get those eyes so blue?
Out of the sky as I came through.   *Ibid. Stanza 2*

[r] They were all looking for a
    king
To slay their foes and lift them
    high;
Thou cam'st, a little baby thing
    That made a woman cry.
       That Holy Thing. Stanza 1

[s] Love is the part, and love is
    the whole;
Love is the robe, and love is the
    pall;
Ruler of heart and brain and soul,
Love is the lord and the slave of
    all!   *A Lover's Thought
        of Love. Stanza 1*

[t] Said the Wind to the Moon, "I
    will blow you out!"
    *The Wind and the Moon.
        Stanza 1*

Arthur Machen
[1863–1947]

[u] It was better, he thought, to
fail in attempting exquisite
things than to succeed in the department of the utterly contemptible.
    The Hill of Dreams. Chap. 5

Niccolò Machiavelli
[1469–1527]

[v] There is nothing more difficult to take in hand, more perilous
to conduct, or more uncertain in
its success, than to take the lead
in the introduction of a new order
of things.   *The Prince (tr.
W. K. Marriott). Chap. 6*

[w] The chief foundations of all
states, new as well as old or composite, are good laws and good
arms; and as there cannot be good
laws where the state is not well
armed, it follows that where they
are well armed they have good
laws.   *Ibid. Chap. 12*

[x] When neither their property
nor their honor is touched, the
majority of men live content.
    Ibid. Chap. 19

[y] God is not willing to do
everything, and thus take away
our free will and that share of
glory which belongs to us.
    Ibid. Chap. 26

Charles Mackay
[1814–1889]

[z] Some love to roam o'er the
    dark sea's foam,
Where the shrill winds whistle
    free.   *Some Love to Roam*

[a] There's a good time coming,
    boys!
    A good time coming.
The Good Time Coming. Stanza 1

[b] Cannon-balls may aid the
    truth,
But thought's a weapon
    stronger;
We'll win our battles by its aid;—
    Wait a little longer.   *Ibid.*

[c] Where the prairies, like seas
    where the billows have rolled,
Are broad as the kingdoms and
    empires of old.
        To the West. Stanza 2

[d] Make my coffee strong!
        The Quarrel

[e] The king can drink the best
    of wine—
    So can I;
And has enough when he would
    dine—
    So have I;
And can not order rain or shine—
    Nor can I.
Then where's the difference—let
    me see—
Betwixt my lord the king and
    me? . . .
If happy I and wretched he,
Perhaps the king would change
    with me.   *Differences*

Percy MacKaye
[1875–   ]

[f] Because he never wore his
    sentient heart
For crows and jays to peck, oft-
    times to such
He seemed a silent fellow.
        Uriel. Stanza 11

[g] A man went down to Panama
    Where many a man has died
To slit the sliding mountains
    And lift the eternal tide:
A man stood up in Panama,
    And the mountains stood aside.
        Goethals. Stanza 1

T. Maclagan
[*Floruit* 1870]

[h] I'm Captain Jinks of the
    Horse Marines,
I give my horse good corn and
    beans;
Of course 'tis quite beyond my
    means,
    Though a Captain in the army.
        Captain Jinks. Refrain

Archibald MacLeish
[1892–   ]

[i] Sometimes within the brain's
    old ghostly house,
I hear, far off, at some forgot-
    ten door,
A music and an eerie faint ca-
    rouse,
    And stir of echoes down the
    creaking floor.
    Chambers of Imagery. Stanza 1

[j] Beauty is that Medusa's head
Which men go armed to seek and
   sever.
It is most deadly when most dead,
And dead will stare and sting for-
   ever. *Beauty*

[k] The trumpet of
Time in our ears and the brazen
   and
Breaking shout of our days!
   Panic: Chorus

[l] A poem should not mean
But be. *Ars Poetica*

[m] There with vast wings across
   the canceled skies,
There in the sudden blackness,
   the black pall
Of nothing, nothing, nothing—
   nothing at all.
   The End of the World

[n] She's a tough land under the
   corn mister:
She has changed the bone in the
   cheeks of many races;
She has tried the fat from the
   round rumps of Italians:
Even the voice of the English has
   gone dry
And hard on the tongue and alive
   in the throat speaking.
   *Frescoes for Mr. Rockefeller's
   City. Background with Revolu-
   tionaries*

[o] America was promises. . . .
It was Man who had been promised. *America Was Promises*

[p] And Man turned into men in
   Philadelphia
Practising prudence on a long-
   term lease. *Ibid.*

[q] The scholar digs his ivory cellar in the ruins of the past and
lets the present sicken as it will.
   The Irresponsibles

[r] They were the first self-con-
stituted, self-declared, self-created
People in the history of the world.
And their manners were their own
business. And so were their politics. And so, but ten times so, were
their souls. [Americans]
   A Time to Act

Louis MacNeice
[1907–   ]

[s] Holidays should be like this,
Free from over-emphasis,
Time for soul to stretch and spit
Before the world comes back on it.
   Epilogue, for W. H. Auden

[t] But down the ladder in the
   engineroom
(Doom, doom, doom, doom)
The great cranks rise and fall, re-
   peat,
The great cranks plod with their
   Assyrian feet

To match the monotonous energy
   of the sea.
   Passage Steamer

[u] I have no liking to defer
To capitalist or bureaucrat;
As for your Social Register
You know what you can do with
   that!
   Ballade in a Bad Temper

Arthur Macy
[1842–1904]

[v] Cheers for the sailors that
   fought on the wave for it,
Cheers for the soldiers that always
   were brave for it,
Tears for the men that went down
   to the grave for it,
   Here comes the Flag!
   The Flag. Stanza 4

[w] A little cat played on a silver
   flute,
And a big cat sat and listened;
The little cat's strains gave the
   big cat pains,
And a tear on his eyelids glis-
   tened. *The Boston Cats*

Samuel Madden
[1686–1765]

[x] In an orchard there should
be enough to eat, enough to lay
up, enough to be stolen, and
enough to rot upon the ground.
   *Quoted by Samuel Johnson
   [Boswell's Life of Dr. Johnson,
   Vol. II, Page 457, Everyman
   edition]*

Sister Mary Madeleva
[1887–   ]

[y] Death is no foeman, we were
   born together;
He dwells between the places of
   my breath.
Night vigil at my heart he keeps
   and whether
I sleep or no, he never slumbereth.
   Knights-Errant

[z] It was a bird first spoke to me
   at Oxford
Through the white fog a single,
   tentative word.
   I Enter Oxford

[a] The day you do not write and
   silence follows, to be broken
   only by my life's end,
I shall know that you have not
   forgotten, that now you love
   me perfectly,
For I shall understand that you
   are dead.
   The Day No Letter Comes

Maurice Maeterlinck
[1864–1949]

[b] The future is a world limited
by ourselves; in it we discover
only what concerns us and, some-

imes, by chance, what interests
hose whom we love the most.
Joyzelle. Act I

c] Men's weaknesses are often
necessary to the purposes of life.
Ibid. Act II

d] I have never for one instant
seen clearly within myself; how
then would you have me judge the
deeds of others?
Pelleas and Melisande. Act I, Sc. 3

e] Old men have need to touch
sometimes with their lips the
brow of a woman or the cheek of
a child, that they may believe
again in the freshness of life.
Ibid. Act IV, Sc. 2

John Gillespie Magee, Jr.
[1922–1941]

f] Oh! I have slipped the surly
bonds of Earth
And danced the skies on laughter-
silvered wings;
Sunward I've climbed, and joined
the tumbling mirth
Of sun-split clouds.
Sonnet. High Flight

g] And, while with silent, lifting
mind I've trod
The high untrespassed sanctity of
space,
Put out my hand and touched the
face of God.   *Ibid.*

Francis Sylvester Mahony
("Father Prout")
[1804–1866]

h] The bells of Shandon
That sound so grand on
The pleasant waters
Of the river Lee.   *The Bells
of Shandon. Stanza 2*

Moses Ben Maimon
(Maimonides)
[1135–1204]

i] Anticipate charity by preventing poverty; assist the reduced
fellowman, either by a considerable gift, or a sum of money, or by
teaching him a trade, or by putting him in the way of business,
so that he may earn an honest
livelihood, and not be forced to
the dreadful alternative of holding out his hand for charity. This
is the highest step and the summit
of charity's golden ladder.
*Charity's Eight Degrees [New
York Sun, January 6, 1933.]*

Joseph Malins
[*Floruit* 1895]

j] Better put a strong fence
'round the top of the cliff,
Than an ambulance down in
the valley.   *A Fence or an
Ambulance. Stanza 7*

Douglas Malloch
[1877–1938]

k] If you can't be a pine on the
top of the hill,
Be a scrub in the valley—but be
The best little scrub by the side of
the rill;
Be a bush if you can't be a tree.
*Be the Best of Whatever You
Are. Stanza 1*

l] The river belongs to the Na-
tion,
The levee, they say, to the
State;
The Government runs navigation,
The Commonwealth, though,
pays the freight.
Now, here is the problem that's
heavy—
Please, which is the right or the
wrong—
When the water runs over the
levee,
To whom does the river belong?
Uncle Sam's River. Stanza 1

m] Courage is to feel
The daily daggers of relentless
steel
And keep on living.
Courage. Stanza 2

n] Ah, that's the reason a bird
can sing—
On his darkest day he believes in
Spring.
You Have to Believe

Walter Malone
[1866–1915]

o] They do me wrong who say I
come no more
When once I knock and fail to
find you in;
For every day I stand outside your
door,
And bid you wake, and rise to
fight and win.
Opportunity. Stanza 1

p] Lord, we are setting in this
chosen ground
These tender nurslings, trusting
in Thy grace
To cherish them in infancy, to
guide
Their tiny rootlets through the
darksome earth,
To lift their boughs to heaven,
and give them power
To yield their tribute unto grate-
ful men
In fruit, or flower, or shade.
Prayer Before Planting Trees

John Manifold

q] One morning in spring
We marched from Devizes
All shapes and all sizes
Like beads on a string,

But yet with a swing
We trod the bluemetal
And full of high fettle
We started to sing.
Fife Tune. Stanza 1

Horace Mann
[1796–1859]

[r] Lost, yesterday, somewhere between sunrise and sunset, two golden hours, each set with sixty diamond minutes. No reward is offered for they are gone forever.
Aphorism

Thomas Mann
[1875–   ]

[s] Space, like time, engenders forgetfulness; but it does so by setting us bodily free from our surroundings and giving us back our primitive, unattached state. . . . Time, we say, is Lethe; but change of air is a similar draught, and, if it works less thoroughly, does so more quickly.
The Magic Mountain (tr. H. T. Lowe-Porter. Modern Library edition). Chap. 1

[t] It gives me a most peculiar feeling, when somebody is so stupid, and then ill into the bargain. It must be the most melancholy thing in life. . . . One always has the idea of a stupid man as perfectly healthy and ordinary, and of illness as making one refined and clever and unusual.
Ibid. Chap. 4

[u] The solemn, discreet, almost over-awed bearing which the young German's respect for authority leads him to assume in the presence of pens, ink, and paper, or anything else which bears to his mind an official stamp.
Ibid.

[v] I have the feeling that once I am at home again I shall need to sleep three weeks on end to get rested from the rest I've had!
Ibid.

[w] The only religious way to think of death is as part and parcel of life; to regard it, with the understanding and the emotions, as the inviolable condition of life.
Ibid. Chap. 5

[x] Time has no divisions to mark its passage, there is never a thunder-storm or blare of trumpets to announce the beginning of a new month or year. Even when a new century begins it is only we mortals who ring bells and fire off pistols.
Ibid.

[y] Chop-fallen funeral processions, with their dignity curtailed by present-day traffic conditions.
Ibid. Chap. 6

[z] The invention of printing and the Reformation are and remain the two outstanding services of central Europe to the cause of humanity.
Ibid.

[a] Speech is civilization itself. The word, even the most contradictory word, preserves contact—it is silence which isolates.
Ibid.

[b] What we call mourning for our dead is perhaps not so much grief at not being able to call them back as it is grief at not being able to want to do so.
Ibid. Chap. 7

Katherine Mansfield
(Mrs. John Middleton Murry)
[1889–1923]

[c] Oh, flock of thoughts with their shepherd Fear
Shivering, desolate, out in the cold,
That entered into my heart to fold!
Two Nocturnes. II, Stanza 3

[d] I want, by understanding myself, to understand others. I want to be all that I am capable of becoming. . . . This all sounds very strenuous and serious. But now that I have wrestled with it, it's no longer so. I feel happy—deep down. *All is well.*
Journal, 1922
(end of her journal)

Marcus Aurelius Antoninus
[A.D. 121–180]
Translation by Morris Hickey Morgan

[e] This Being of mine, whatever it really is, consists of a little flesh, a little breath, and the part which governs.
Meditations. II, 2

[f] For a man can lose neither the past nor the future; for how can one take from him that which is not his? So remember these two points: first, that each thing is of like form from everlasting and comes round again in its cycle, and that it signifies not whether a man shall look upon the same things for a hundred years or two hundred, or for an infinity of time; second, that the longest lived and the shortest lived man, when they come to die, lose one and the same thing.
Ibid. 14

[g] A man should *be* upright, not be *kept* upright.
Ibid. III, 5

[h] Never esteem anything as of advantage to thee that shall make thee break thy word or lose thy self-respect.
Ibid. 7

[i] Think on this doctrine,—that reasoning beings were created for

one another's sake; that to be patient is a branch of justice, and that men sin without intending it. *Ibid. IV, 3*

[j] The universe is change; our life is what our thoughts make it. *Ibid.*

[k] Death, like generation, is a secret of Nature. *Ibid. 5*

[l] Whatever is in any way beautiful hath its source of beauty in itself, and is complete in itself; praise forms no part of it. So it is none the worse nor the better for being praised. *Ibid. 20*

[m] Everything is fruit to me that thy seasons bring, O Nature. All things come of thee, have their being in thee, and return to thee. *Ibid. 23*

[n] Get used to thinking that there is nothing Nature loves so well as to change existing forms and to make new ones like them. *Ibid. 36*

[o] Time is a sort of river of passing events, and strong is its current; no sooner is a thing brought to sight than it is swept by and another takes its place, and this too will be swept away. *Ibid. 43*

[p] Mark how fleeting and paltry is the estate of man,—yesterday in embryo, to-morrow a mummy or ashes. So for the hair's-breadth of time assigned to thee live rationally, and part with life cheerfully, as drops the ripe olive, extolling the season that bore it and the tree that matured it. *Ibid. 48*

[q] In the morning, when thou art sluggish at rousing thee, let this thought be present; "I am rising to a man's work." *Ibid. V, 1*

[r] A man makes no noise over a good deed, but passes on to another as a vine to bear grapes again in season. *Ibid. 6*

[s] If any man can convince me and bring home to me that I do not think or act aright, gladly will I change; for I search after truth, by which man never yet was harmed. *Ibid. VI, 21*

[t] What is not good for the swarm is not good for the bee. *Ibid. 54*

[u] Just as the sand-dunes, heaped one upon another, hide each the first, so in life the former deeds are quickly hidden by those that follow after. *Ibid. VII, 34*

[v] The art of living is more like wrestling than dancing, in so far as it stands ready against the ac-

cidental and the unforeseen, and is not apt to fall. *Ibid. 61*

[w] Remember this,—that very little is needed to make a happy life. *Ibid, 67*

[x] A wrong-doer is often a man that has left something undone, not always he that has done something. *Ibid. IX, 5*

[y] Be satisfied with success in even the smallest matter, and think that even such a result is no trifle. *Ibid. 29*

[z] Whatever may befall thee, it was preordained for thee from everlasting. *Ibid. X, 5*

[a] "The earth loveth the shower," and "the holy ether knoweth what love is." The Universe, too, loves to create whatsoever is destined to be made. *Ibid. 21*

Jacques Maritain
[1882–   ]

[b] In the modern social order, the *person* is sacrificed to the *individual*. The individual is given universal suffrage, equality of rights, freedom of opinion; while the person, isolated, naked, with no social armor to sustain and protect him, is left to the mercy of all the devouring forces which threaten the life of the soul, exposed to relentless actions and reactions of conflicting interests and appetites. . . . It is a homicidal civilization.
Trois Reformateurs. Page 29

Edwin Markham
[1852–1940]

[c] Bowed by the weight of centuries he leans
Upon his hoe and gazes on the ground,
The emptiness of ages in his face,
And on his back the burden of the world.
The Man with the Hoe. Stanza 1

[d] Here was a man to hold against the world,
A man to match the mountains and the sea. *Lincoln, the Man of the People. Stanza 1*

[e] And when he fell in whirlwind, he went down
As when a lordly cedar, green with boughs,
Goes down with a great shout upon the hills,
And leaves a lonesome place against the sky. *Ibid.*

[f] He drew a circle that shut me out—
Heretic, rebel, a thing to flout.

But Love and I had the wit to
win:
We drew a circle that took him
in.   *Outwitted*

Earl Marlatt
[1892-   ]

[g] Fancy the rapture
Of being there
When the world was made!
            May Morning. Stanza 1

Christopher Marlowe
[1564-1593]

[h] Comparisons are odious.
        Lust's Dominion. Act. III, Sc. 4

[i] I'm armed with more than
complete steel,—
The justice of my quarrel.   *Ibid.*

[j] Who ever loved that loved not
at first sight?
            Hero and Leander

[k] Come live with me, and be my
love;
And we will all the pleasures prove
That hills and valleys, dales and
fields,
Woods or steepy mountain yields.
            *The Passionate Shepherd
                to his Love*

[l] And I will make thee beds of
roses
And a thousand fragrant posies.
                            Ibid.

[m] Infinite riches in a little
room.
            The Jew of Malta. Act I

[n] Hell hath no limits, nor is
circumscribed
In one self-place; for where we
are is Hell,
And where Hell is, there must we
ever be.   *Faustus*

[o] Was   this   the   face   that
launch'd a thousand ships,
And burnt the topless towers of
Ilium?
Sweet Helen, make me immortal
with a kiss!   *Ibid.*

[p] Stand still, you ever moving
spheres of heaven,
That time may cease, and midnight never come.   *Ibid.*

[q] My men, like satyrs grazing
on the lawn,
Shall with their goat feet dance
the antic hay.
            Edward II. Act. 1, Sc. 1

John Phillips Marquand
[1893-   ]

[r] His   father   watched   him
across the gulf of years and pathos
which always must divide a
father from his son.
    The Late George Apley. Chap. 10

[s] There is a certain phase in the
life of the aged when the warmth
of the heart seems to increase in
direct proportion with the years.
This is a time of life when a so-
licitous family does well to watch
affectionately over the vagaries of
its unattached relatives, particularly of those who are comfortably
off.   *Ibid. Chap. 23*

Donald Robert Perry Marquis
[1878-1937]

[t] The saddest ones are those
that wear
The jester's motley garb.
            The Tavern of Despair

[u] For him who fain would teach
the world
The world holds hate in fee—
For Socrates, the hemlock cup;
For Christ, Gethsemane.
                    The Wages

[v] No doubt the cherubs earn
their wage
Who wind each ticking star.
                    The Rebel

[w] A little while with grief and
laughter,
And then the day will close;
The shadows gather . . . what
comes after
No man knows.   *Ibid.*

[x] Fill me with sassafras, nurse,
And juniper juice!
Let me see if I'm still any use!
For I want to be young and to sing
again,
Sing again, sing again!
Middle age is a curse!
                    Spring Ode

[y] For I want to hire out as the
Skipper
(Who dodges life's stress and its
strains)
Of the Trolley, the Toonerville
Trolley,
The Trolley that Meets all the
Trains.   *The Toonerville
            Trolley: To Fontaine Fox*

[z] Comet, shake out your locks
and let them flare
Across the startled heaven of my
soul!
Pluck out the hairpins, Sue, and
let her roll!
Don't be so stingy with your
blooming hair.   *Sonnets to a
                Red-Haired Lady. I*

[a] I love you as New Englanders
love pie!   *Ibid. XII*

[b] One boob may die, but death-
less is
The royal race of hicks—
When Ahab went to Ascalon
They sold him gilded bricks.
                    Boob Ballad

[c] How often when they find a
    sage
As sweet as Socrates or Plato
They hand him hemlock for his
    wage,
Or bake him like a sweet potato!
            Taking the Longer View

[d] "Oh, what the hell, it's Spring!
And just for the sake of argyment,
I'll show 'em who is king."
            David and Bathsheba
(As Interpreted by the Old Soak)

[e] Speed, I bid you, speed the
    earth
Onward with a shout of mirth,
Fill your eager eyes with light,
Put my face and memory
Out of mind and out of sight.
Nothing I have caused or done,
But this gravestone, meets the
    sun:
Friends, a great simplicity
Comes at last to you and me.
            Lines for a Gravestone

[f] There will be no beans in the
Almost Perfect State.
            The Almost Perfect State

[g] The human population of the
entire world should be kept well
under a hundred millions. . . . If
the world were not so full of
people, and most of them did not
have to work so hard, there would
be more time for them to get out
and lie on the grass, and there
would be more grass for them to
lie on.   *Ibid.*

[h] procrastination is the
art of keeping
up with yesterday
    *archy and mehitabel. certain
    maxims of archy.*

[i] dance mehitabel dance
caper and shake a leg
what little blood is left
will fizz like wine in a keg   *Ibid.*
    mehitabel dances with boreas

[j] toujours gai
    *archy's life of mehitabel: the
    life of mehitabel the cat*

[k] so unlucky
that he runs into accidents
which started out to happen
to somebody else
            Ibid. archy says

[l] a suicide is a person who has
considered his own case and decided
that he is worthless and who acts
as his own judge jury and execu-
tioner
and he probably knows better
than anyone else whether there is
justice
in the verdict   *archy does his
            part. now look at it*

[m] it is a cheering thought to
think

that god is on the side of the best
digestion
            Ibid. the big bad wolf. page 11

[n] there is bound to be a certain
    amount of
trouble running any country
if you are president the trouble
    happens to you
but if you are a tyrant you can
    arrange things so
that most of the trouble happens
    to other people
            Ibid. archy's newest deal. page 18

[o] the females of all species are
    most
dangerous when they appear to
    retreat
            Ibid. a farewell. page 252

[p] To stroke a platitude until it
purrs like an epigram.
            The Sun Dial

[q] Publishing a volume of verse
is like dropping a rose-petal down
the Grand Cañon and waiting for
the echo.   *Ibid.*

[r] Poetry is what Milton saw
when he went blind.   *Ibid.*

[s] If you make people think
they're thinking, they'll love you.
If you really make them think
they'll hate you.   *Ibid.*

[t] *Jehovah.* Did I ever mention
publicly how Hell got started? I
don't think I ever did. It was this
way: I thought I'd do something
nice for a lot of theologians who
had, after all, been doing the best
they could, according to their
lights; so I gave them an enormous tract of Heaven to do what
they pleased with—set it apart for
them to inhabit and administer. I
didn't pay any attention to it for
a few thousand years, and when I
looked at it again, they'd made it
into Hell.   *Chapters for the
            Orthodox. Chap. 7*

[u] All religion, all life, all art, all
expression come down to this: to the
effort of the human soul to break
through its barrier of loneliness, of
intolerable loneliness, and make some
contact with another seeking soul, or
with what all souls seek, which is (by
any name) God.   *Ibid. Chap. 11*

Frederick Marryat
[1792–1848]

[v] I haven't the gift of the gab,
my sons—because I'm bred to
the sea.
            The Old Navy. Stanza 1

Sir Edward Marsh
[1872–1944?]

[w] Yet pretermitted not the
strait Command,

Eternal, indispensable, to off-
cleanse
From their white elephantin
Teeth the stains
Left by those tastie Pulps that late
they chewd
At supper. First from a salubrious
Fount
Our general Mother, stooping, the
pure Lymph
Insorb'd, which, mingled with tart
juices prest
From pungent Herbs, on sprigs of
Myrtle smeared,
(Then were not brushes) scrub'd
gumms more impearl'd
Than when young *Telephus* with
Lydia strove
In mutual bite of Shoulder and
ruddy Lip.
This done (by *Adam* too no less)
the pair
[Straight side by side were
laid.] *Milton's Adam and Eve
Brush Their Teeth*
[*Prize-winning parody, in The
Week-End Review, 1931, "to re-
pair the regrettable omission of
any reference to tooth-brushing"
when Adam and Eve retire, as of
Paradise Lost, Book IV*]

George Catlett Marshall
[1880–   ]

[**x**] If man does find the solution
for world peace it will be the most
revolutionary reversal of his
record we have ever known.
*Biennial Report of the Chief of
Staff of the U.S. Army, September 1, 1945*

Thomas Riley Marshall
[1854–1925]

[**y**] What this country needs is a
good five-cent cigar.
*Remark to John Crockett, Chief
Clerk of the United States Senate*

Philip Bourke Marston
[1850–1887]

[**z**] A little time for laughter,
A little time to sing,
A little time to kiss and cling,
And no more kissing after.
After. Stanza 1

Martial
[A.D. 40–102]

[**a**] To yield to the stronger is
valor's second prize.
On the Spectacles. Epigram 32

[**b**] He does not write at all whose
poems no man reads.
Epigrams. Book III, 9

[**c**] The good man prolongs his

life; to be able to enjoy one's past
life is to live twice.
Ibid. Book X, 23

[**d**] There is no glory in outstrip-
ping donkeys. *Ibid. Book XII, 36*

"Abe Martin"
(Frank McKinney ["Kin"]
Hubbard)
[1868–1930]

[**e**] Miss Fawn Lippincut says
she wouldn' marry th' best man
on earth, but we supposed she wuz
much younger.
The Sayings of Abe Martin

[**f**] Miss Tawney Apple is confined t' her home by a swollen
dresser drawer. *Ibid.*

[**g**] It's no disgrace t' be poor, but
it might as well be. *Ibid.*

[**h**] He was a power politically fer
years, but he never got prominent
enough t' have his speeches
garbled. *Ibid.*

Edward Sandford Martin
[1856–1939]

[**i**] Within my earthly temple
there's a crowd.
There's one of us that's humble;
one that's proud.
There's one that's broken-hearted
for his sins,
And one who, unrepentant, sits
and grins.
There's one who loves his neigh-
bor as himself,
And one who cares for naught but
fame and pelf.
From much corroding care would
I be free
If once I could determine which
is Me. *Mixed*

"IK. Marvel"
see Donald Grant Mitchell

Andrew Marvell
[1620–1678]

[**j**] Had we but world enough, and
time,
This coyness, lady, were no crime.
To His Coy Mistress

[**k**] But at my back I always hear
Time's winged chariot hurrying
near;
And yonder all before us lie
Deserts of vast eternity. *Ibid.*

[**l**] Annihilating all that's made
To a green thought in a green
shade. *The Garden*

[**m**] The inglorious arts of peace.
*Upon Cromwell's return from
Ireland [1650]*

[n] As lines, so loves oblique, may
well
Themselves in every angle greet;
But ours, so truly parallel,
Though infinite, can never meet.
The Definition of Love

Karl Marx
[1818–1883]

[o] From each according to his
abilities, to each according to his
needs.   *The Criticism of the
Gotha Program*

[p] Nothing can have value without being an object of utility. If it
be useless, the labor contained in
it is useless, cannot be reckoned as
labor, and cannot therefore create
value.
*Capital (abridged edition pre-
pared by Julian Borchardt. Tr.
Stephen L. Trask, Modern Library edition). Part II, Chap. 3,
Page 33*

[q] The capitalist himself is a
practical man, who, it is true, does
not always reflect on what he says
outside his office, but who always
knows what he does inside the latter.   *Ibid. Chap. 5, Page 43*

[r] Constant labor of one uniform
kind destroys the intensity and
flow of a man's animal spirits,
which find recreation and delight
in mere change of activity.
Ibid. Chap. 9, Page 74

[s] The intellectual desolation,
artificially produced by converting
immature human beings into
mere machines.
Ibid. Chap. 10, Page 102

[t] The only part of the so-called
national wealth that actually
enters into the collective possessions of modern peoples is their
national debt.
Ibid. Chap. 14, Page 199

[u] The history of all hitherto
existing society is the history of
class struggles.
*Manifesto of the Communist
Party (written in collabora-
tion with Friedrich Engels,
tr. Samuel Moore). I*

[v] In proportion as the an-
tagonism between classes within
the nation vanishes, the hostility
of one nation to another will come
to an end.   *Ibid. II*

[w] The proletarians have nothing to lose but their chains. They
have a world to win. Workers of
the world, unite!   *Ibid. IV*

John Masefield
[1874–   ]

[x] Of the maimed, of the halt
and the blind in the rain and
the cold—

Of these shall my songs be fashioned, my tales be told.
A Consecration. Stanza 7

[y] I must go down to the seas
again, to the lonely sea and
the sky,
And all I ask is a tall ship and a
star to steer her by.
Sea-Fever. Stanza 1

[z] And all I ask is a merry yarn
from a laughing fellow-rover,
And quiet sleep and a sweet dream
when the long trick's over.
Ibid. Stanza 3

[a] Dunno about Life—it's jest a
tramp alone
From wakin'-time to doss.
Dunno about Death—it's jest a
quiet stone
All over-grey wi' moss.
Vagabond

[b] It's a warm wind, the west
wind, full of birds' cries.
The West Wind

[c] One road leads to London,
One road runs to Wales,
My road leads me seawards
To the white dipping sails.
Roadways

[d] And he who gives a child a
treat
Makes joy-bells ring in Heaven's
street,
And he who gives a child a home
Builds palaces in Kingdom come.
The Everlasting Mercy

[e] The rain that makes things
new,
The earth that hides things old.
Ibid.

[f] When I am buried, all my
thoughts and acts
Will be reduced to lists of dates
and facts,
And long before this wandering
flesh is rotten
The dates which made me will be
all forgotten   *Biography*

[g] The days that make us happy
make us wise.   *Ibid.*

[h] Man with his burning soul
Has but an hour of breath
To build a ship of Truth
In which his soul may sail,
Sail on the sea of death,
For death takes toll
Of beauty, courage, youth,
Of all but Truth. *Truth. Stanza 1*

[i] In the dark womb where I be-
gan
My mother's life made me a man.
Through all the months of human
birth
Her beauty fed my common earth.
I cannot see, nor breathe, nor
stir,
But through the death of some of
her.   *C. L. M. Stanza 1*

[j] Quinquireme of Nineveh from distant Ophir,
Rowing home to haven in sunny Palestine,
With a cargo of ivory,
And apes and peacocks,
Sandalwood, cedarwood, and sweet white wine.
                    Cargoes. Stanza 1

[k] But rum alone's the tipple, and the heart's delight
Of the old bold mate of Henry Morgan.   *Captain Stratton's Fancy. Stanza 1*

[l] So I'm for drinking honestly, and dying in my boots.
                    Ibid. Stanza 7

[m] Oh London Town's a fine town, and London sights are rare,
And London ale is right ale, and brisk's the London air.
                    London Town. Stanza 1

[n] All the great things of life are swiftly done,
Creation, death, and love the double gate.
However much we dawdle in the sun
We have to hurry at the touch of Fate;
When Life knocks at the door no one can wait,
When Death makes his arrest we have to go.   *The Widow in the Bye Street. Part 2*

[o] Love is a flame to burn out human wills,
Love is a flame to set the will on fire,
Love is a flame to cheat men into mire.
One of the three, we make Love what we choose.   *Ibid.*

[p] All through the windless night the clipper rolled
In a great swell with only gradual heaves
Which rolled her down until her timebells tolled,
Clang, and the weltering water moaned like beeves.
The thundering rattle of slatting shook the sheaves,
Startles of water made the swing ports gush.
The sea was moaning and sighing and saying "Hush!"
                    Dauber. Part 6

[q] Then in the sunset's flush they went aloft,
And unbent sails in that most lovely hour,
When the light gentles and the wind is soft,
And beauty in the heart breaks like a flower.   *Ibid. Part 7*

[r] What am I, Life? A thing of watery salt

Held in cohesion by unresting cells,
Which work they know not why, which never halt,
Myself unwitting where their Master dwells?   *Sonnets. 14*

[s] Is there a great green commonwealth of Thought
Which ranks the yearly pageant, and decides
How Summer's royal progress shall be wrought,
By secret stir which in each plant abides?   *Ibid. 28*

[t] Be with me Beauty for the fire is dying,
My dog and I are old, too old for roving,
Man, whose young passion sets the spindrift flying
Is soon too lame to march, too cold for loving.   *On Growing Old. Sonnet 1*

[u] Bitter it is, indeed, in human Fate
When Life's supreme temptation comes too late.
                    The Woman Speaks

[v] Go forth to seek: the quarry never found
It still a fever to the questing hound,
The skyline is a promise, not a bound.
                    The Wanderer of Liverpool

[w] I touch my country's mind, I come to grips
With half her purpose, thinking of these ships,
That art untouched by softness, all that line
Drawn ringing hard to stand the test of brine. . . .
That art of masts, sail crowded, fit to break,
Yet stayed to strength and backstayed into rake. . . .
They mark our passage as a race of men,
Earth will not see such ships as those again.   *Ships*

[x] May shipwreck and collision, fog and fire,
Rock, shoal and other evils of the sea
Be kept from you; and may the heart's desire
Of those who speed your launching come to be.
                    Launching of the "Queen Mary," September 26, 1934. Stanza 7

[y] Then the black-bright, smooth-running, clicking clean
Brushed, oiled and dainty typewriting machine,
With tins or ribbons waiting for the blows

Which soon will hammer them to
verse and prose.
Shopping in Oxford

[z] Commonplace people dislike
tragedy, because they dare not
suffer and cannot exult. The
truth and rapture of man are holy
things, not lightly to be scorned.
A carelessness of life and beauty
marks the glutton, the idler, and
the fool in their deadly path
across history.
The Tragedy of Nan. Preface

[a] Man consists of body, mind,
and imagination. His body is
faulty, his mind untrustworthy,
but his imagination has made him
remarkable. In some centuries, his
imagination has made life on this
planet an intense practice of all
the lovelier energies.
Shakespeare and Spiritual Life

[b] Wartime is a bad time for
writers, artists and thinking
people. No clear or beautiful
thought is possible in any country
in Europe because of the curse of
war, a more fatal disease than
cholera, typhoid fever and the rest
put together.   *Radio Broadcast
to America [November 3, 1941]*

Caroline Atherton
Briggs Mason
[1823–1890]

[c] Do they miss me at home—do
they miss me?
'Twould be an assurance most
dear,
To know that this moment some
loved one
Were saying, "I wish he were
here."   *Do They Miss Me
at Home? Stanza 1*

[d] Whichever way the wind doth
blow,
Some heart is glad to have it so;
Then, blow it east, or blow it west,
The wind that blows, that wind is
best.   *En Voyage. Stanza 1*

Daniel Gregory Mason
[1873–   ]

[e] The ideal of Independence requires resistance to the herd spirit
now so widespread, to our worship of quantity and indifference
to quality, to our unthinking devotion to organization, standard-
ization, propaganda, and advertising.   *Artistic Ideals. Page 3*

Donald Francis Mason
[1913–   ]

[f] Sighted sub, sank same.
*Radio message to U. S. Navy
Base, January 8, 1942*

Walt Mason
[1862–1939]

[g] The little green tents where
the soldiers sleep and the sun-
beams play and the women weep,
are covered with flowers to-day.
The Little Green Tents

[h] The statesman throws his
shoulders back, and straightens
out his tie,
And says, "My friends, unless it
rains, the weather will be
dry."
And when this thought into our
brains has percolated through,
We common people nod our heads
and loudly cry, "How true!"
The Statesman

[i] Little drops of water poured
into the milk, give the milkman's
daughter lovely gowns of silk.
Little grains of sugar mingled
with the sand, make the grocer's
assets swell to beat the band.
Little Things

Philip Massinger
[1583–1640]

[j] I in mine own house am an
emperor
And will defend what's mine.
The Roman Actor. Act I, Sc. 2

[k]   Whose wealth
Arithmetic cannot number.
Ibid. Sc. 3

[l] Good kings are mourned for
after life; but ill,
And such as governed only by
their will
And not their reason, unlamented
fall,—
No good man's tear shed at their
funeral.   *Ibid. Act V, Sc. 2*

Thomas L. Masson
[1866–1934]

[m] Obey that impulse.
*Subscription slogan for "Life," of
which he was editor, 1893–1922*

[n] A safe and sane Fourth.
Slogan

Edgar Lee Masters
[1869–1950]

[o] All, all are sleeping on the
hill.   *Spoon River
Anthology. The Hill*

[p] I am Anne Rutledge who
sleep beneath these weeds,
Beloved in life of Abraham Lin-
coln,
Wedded to him, not through
union,
But through separation.
Bloom forever, O Republic,
From the dust of my bosom!
Ibid. Anne Rutledge

[q] Hats may make divorces.
Ibid. Mrs. Williams

[r] And there is the silence of
age,
Too full of wisdom for the tongue
to utter it
In words intelligible to those who
have not lived
The great range of life.		*Silence*

Edward Powys Mathers
[1892–   ]

[s] A love-sick heart dies when
the heart is whole,
For all the heart's health is to be
sick with love.
*Fard. Translation from the
Hindustani of Miyan Jagnu,
Eighteenth Century*

[t] Before you love,
Learn to run through snow
Leaving no footprint.
Translation of a Turkish Proverb

Brewer Mattocks
[1841–1934]

[u] The parish priest
Of Austerity
Climbed up in a high church
steeple
To be nearer God,
So that he might hand
His word down to His people.

In his age God said—
"Come down and die!"
And he cried out from the steeple,
"Where art Thou, Lord?"
And the Lord replied,
"Down here among my people."
*The Preacher's Mistake.
Stranzas 1 and 5*

William Somerset Maugham
[1874–   ]

[v] Like all weak men he laid an
exaggerated stress on not changing one's mind.
Of Human Bondage. Chap. 39

[w] People ask you for criticism,
but they only want praise.
Ibid. Chap. 50

[x] There is nothing so degrading
as the constant anxiety about
one's means of livelihood. . . .
Money is like a sixth sense without which you cannot make a
complete use of the other five.
Ibid. Chap. 51

[y] I forget who it was that
recommended men for their soul's
good to do each day two things
they disliked: . . . it is a precept
that I have followed scrupulously;
for every day I have got up and I
have gone to bed.		*The Moon and
Sixpence. Chap. 2*

[z] A woman can forgive a man
for the harm he does her, but she
can never forgive him for the sacrifices he makes on her account.
Ibid. Chap. 41

[a] Do you know that conversation is one of the greatest pleasures in life? But it wants leisure.
The Trembling of a Leaf. Chap. 3

[b] I would sooner read a time-
table or a catalogue than nothing
at all. They are much more entertaining than half the novels that
are written.		*The Summing Up*

[c] If a nation values anything
more than freedom, it will lose its
freedom; and the irony of it is
that if it is comfort or money that
it values more, it will lose that too.
Strictly Personal. Chap. 31

[d] As deserted as a playwright
after the first night of an unsuccessful play.
The Razor's Edge. Chap. 3

William H. ("Bill") Mauldin
[1921–   ]

[e] Look at an infantryman's eyes
and you can tell how much war he
has seen.
Up Front. Caption for cartoon

[f] "He's right, Joe, when we
ain't fightin' we should ack like
sojers."		*Ibid.*

André Maurois
[1885–   ]

[g] Middle Age looked at Youth
with a kindly irony, and promised
himself to dominate it by the
strength of a more cultivated
mind. Middle Age forgot that the
minds of different generations are
as impenetrable one by the other
as are the monads of Leibniz.
Ariel (tr. Ella D'Arcy). Chap. 12

[h] If in the eyes of an Irishman
there is any one being more
ridiculous than an Englishman, it
is an Englishman who loves Ire-
land.		*Ibid. Chap. 13*

[i] Learning is nothing without
cultivated manners, but when the
two are combined in a woman you
have one of the most exquisite
products of civilization.
Ibid. Chap. 16

[j] Housekeeping in common is
for women the acid test.
Ibid. Chap. 35

Theodore Maynard
[1890–   ]

[k] I know a sheaf of splendid
songs by heart
Which stir the blood or move
the soul to tears,

Of death or honour or of love's
    sweet smart,
  The runes and legends of a
    thousand years;
And some of them go plaintively
    and slow,
  And some are jolly like the earth
    in May—
But this is *really* the best song I
    know:
I-tiddly-iddly-i-ti-iddly-ay.
  *Ballade of the Best Song in the
      World. Stanza 1*

Roy Larcom McCardell
[1870–   ]

[l] Keep me, I pray, unharmed
    this day
As I go forth where danger lies,
But if with harm or hurt I meet,
Let it be done, I pray, entreat,
  By those responsible, complete
    For damages and compromise.
      The Pedestrian's Prayer

David McCord
[1897–   ]

[m] A handful of sand is an anthology of the universe.
    Once and for All: Introduction

[n] Call home the child, whose
    credulous first hours
Burn at the heart of living, and
    surprise
The better reason with unbidden
    truth.   *A Bucket of Bees*

[o] March is outside the door
Flaming some old desire
As man turns uneasily from his
    fire.   *The Crows*

[p] The tiger lily is a panther,
Orange to black spot:
Her tongue is the velvet pretty
    anther,
And she's in the vacant lot.
      Tiger Lily

[q] By and by
God caught his eye.
      Epitaphs: The Waiter

[r] I recommend for plain dis-
    ease
A good post-operative sneeze;
You might as well be on the rack
When every stitch takes up its
    slack.   *And What's More:
        Convalescence: The Sneeze*

[s] I want to know not his earn-
  ing power but his yearning power.
      Epigram

John McCrae
[1872–1918]

[t] In Flanders fields the poppies
    blow
Between the crosses, row on row.
  *In Flanders Fields [London
    Punch, December 8, 1915].
        Stanza 1*

[u] O guns, fall silent till the
    dead men hear
  Above their heads the legions
    pressing on:
(These fought their fight in time
    of bitter fear,
  And died not knowing how the
    day had gone.)
      The Anxious Dead. Stanza 1

William McFee
[1881–   ]

[v] To those who live and toil
    and lowly die,
  Who pass beyond and leave no
    lasting trace,
To those from whom our queen
    Prosperity
  Has turned away her fair and
    fickle face.
    Casuals of the Sea. Dedication

[w] A trouble is a trouble, and
the general idea, in the country,
is to treat it as such, rather than
to snatch the knotted cords from
the hand of God and deal out
murderous blows.
      Ibid. Book I, 4

[x] It is extraordinary how many
emotional storms one may weather
in safety if one is ballasted with
ever so little gold.   *Ibid. 10*

[y] Terrible and sublime thought,
that every moment is supreme for
some man and woman, every hour
the apotheosis of some passion!
      Ibid. Book II, 4

[z] It's the people who're comfortable who have time to worry
over little trivial things.
      Ibid. 6

[a] Responsibility's like a string
we can only see the middle of.
Both ends are out of sight.
      Ibid.

[b] Steam engines are very human. Their very weaknesses are
understandable. Steam engines do
not flash back and blow your face
in. They do not short-circuit and
rive your heart with imponderable
electric force. They have arms and
legs and warm hearts and veins
full of warm vapour. Give us
steam every time. You know
where you are with steam.
      A Six-Hour Shift

Phyllis McGinley
[1905–   ]

[c] We never sit down to our pot-
    tage,
We never go calm to our rest,
But lo! at the door of our cottage,
The knock of the Guest.
  *Elegy from a Country Dooryard.
        Stanza 3*

[d] Meek-eyed parents hasten
    down the ramps
To greet their offspring, terrible
    from camps.
                    Ode to the End of Summer

Irene Rutherford McLeod
(Mrs. Aubrey de Selincourt)
[1891-   ]

[e] I'm a lean dog, a keen dog, a
    wild dog, and alone;
I'm a rough dog, a tough dog,
    hunting on my own;
I'm a bad dog, a mad dog, teasing
    silly sheep;
I love to sit and bay the moon, to
    keep fat souls from sleep.
                    Lone Dog. Stanza 1

[f] I've hated all that's mean and
    cold,
All that's dusty, tame, and old,
Comfortable lies in books,
Pallid Virtue's sidelong looks,
Saints who wash their hands too
    clean,
And walk where only saints have
    been.   *Rebel*

Guy Humphries McMaster
[1829-1887]

[g] In their ragged regimentals,
Stood the old Continentals,
    Yielding not,
While the grenadiers were lung-
    ing,
And like hail fell the plunging
    Cannon-shot.
                    Carmen Bellicosum. Stanza 1

Hughes Mearns
[1875-   ]

[h] As I was going up the stair
I met a man who wasn't there.
He wasn't there again to-day.
I wish, I wish he'd stay away.
                    The Psychoed. [Antigonish]

Herman Melville
[1819-1891]

[*May one cry of human distress
interpolate here? The editors of
BARTLETT confess the complete in-
adequacy of these few quotations
from Moby Dick. For that great
book there is no substitute; it
cannot be represented in excerpts.*

*Melville died the same year that
John Bartlett completed the Ninth
Edition of this work. Neither then,
nor in Dole's Tenth Edition (1914)
was Melville's name mentioned. It
was his centennial in 1919 . . .
that brought him alive for a new
generation. But ne is too dense
with intuition to be parcelled out
in clippings.*]

[i] Thou belongest to that hopeless, sallow tribe which no wine of

this world will ever warm; and for
whom even Pale Sherry would be
too rosy-strong; but with whom
one sometimes loves to sit, and
feel poor-devilish, too; and grow
convivial upon tears; and say to
them bluntly, with full eyes and
empty glasses, and in not altogether unpleasant sadness—Give
it up, Sub-Subs! For by how much
the more pains ye take to please
the world, by so much the more
shall ye for ever go thankless!
            Moby Dick: Preface, the Sub-
                        Sub-Librarian

[j] Thou great democratic God!
who didst not refuse to the swart
convict, Bunyan, the pale poetic
pearl; Thou who didst clothe with
doubly hammered leaves of finest
gold, the stumped and paupered
arm of old Cervantes; Thou who
didst pick up Andrew Jackson
from the pebbles; who didst hurl
him upon a warhorse; who didst
thunder him higher than a
throne!   *Ibid. Chap. 26*

[k] The starred and stately nights
seemed haughty dames in jewelled
velvets, nursing at home in lonely
pride the memory of their absent
conquering Earls, the golden hel-
meted suns!   *Ibid. Chap. 29*

[l] Give me a condor's quill! Give
me Vesuvius' crater for an ink-
stand! . . . To produce a mighty
book you must choose a mighty
theme.   *Ibid. Chap. 104*

Menander
[343-292 B.C.]
*Translation by Francis G. Allin-
son, Loeb Classical Library*

[m] You knew not how to live in
clover.
            The Girl from Samos. Act II, Sc. 4

[n] The man who first invented
the art of supporting beggars
made many wretched.
                The Fishermen. Fragment

[o] In many ways the saying,
"Know thyself" is not well said.
It were more practical to say
"Know other people."
                Thrasyleon. Fragment

[p] A woman is necessarily an
evil, but he that gets the most
tolerable one is lucky.
            Unidentified minor fragment

Henry Louis Mencken
[1880-   ]

See also George Jean Nathan

[q] Poverty is a soft pedal upon
all branches of human activity,
not excepting the spiritual.
            A Book of Prefaces. Chap. 4,
                            Sect. 3

[r] Time is a great legalizer, even in the field of morals.   *Ibid.*

[s] All successful newspapers are ceaselessly querulous and bellicose. They never defend anyone or anything if they can help it; if the job is forced upon them, they tackle it by denouncing someone or something else.
Prejudices, First Series. Chap. 13

[t] To be in love is merely to be in a state of perceptual anaesthesia—to mistake an ordinary young man for a Greek god or an ordinary young woman for a goddess.
Ibid.

[u] Philadelphia is the most pecksniffian of American cities, and thus probably leads the world.
The American Language

[v] Injustice is relatively easy to bear; what stings is justice.
Prejudices, Third Series

[w] Poetry is a comforting piece of fiction set to more or less lascivious music.   *Ibid.*

[x] Christian endeavor is notoriously hard on female pulchritude.
The Aesthetic Recoil

[y] The learned are seldom pretty fellows, and in many cases their appearance tends to discourage a love of study in the young.
The New Webster International Dictionary

[z] I've made it a rule never to drink by daylight and never to refuse a drink after dark.
Quoted in New York Post, September 18, 1945

Adah Isaacs Menken
[1835–1868]

[a] Where is the promise of my years,
Once written on my brow? . . .
Where sleeps that promise now?
El Suspiro (Infelix)

[b] I stand a wreck on Error's shore,
A spectre not within the door,
A houseless shadow evermore,
An exile lingering here.   *Ibid.*

George Meredith
[1828–1909]

[c] Bury thy sorrows, and they shall rise
As souls to the immortal skies,
And there look down like mothers' eyes.
Sorrows and Joys. Stanza 1

[d] Life is but the pebble sunk;
Deeds, the circle growing!
The Head of Bran the Blest. IV, Stanza 4

[e] Not till the fire is dying in the grate,
Look we for any kinship with the stars.
Oh, wisdom never comes when it is gold,
And the great price we pay for it full worth;
We have it only when we are half earth.
Little avails that coinage to the old!   *Modern Love. IV*

[f] The actors are, it seems, the usual three:
Husband, and wife, and lover.
Ibid. XXV

[g] Ah, what a dusty answer gets the soul
When hot for certainties in this our life!   *Ibid. L*

[h]   See ye not, Courtesy
Is the true Alchemy,
Turning to gold all it touches and tries?
The Song of Courtesy. IV

[i] The old hound wags his shaggy tail,
And I know what he would say:
It's over the hills we'll bound, old hound,
Over the hills, and away.
Over the Hills

[j] Women are such expensive things.
The Beggar's Soliloquy. I

[k] Earth knows no desolation.
She smells regeneration
In the moist breath of decay.
The Spirit of Earth in Autumn. Stanza 14

[l] Full lasting is the song, though he,
The singer, passes.
The Thrush in February. Stanza 17

[m] She whom I love is hard to catch and conquer,
Hard, but O the glory of the winning were she won!
Love in the Valley. Stanza 2

[n] Darker grows the valley, more and more forgetting:
So were it with me if forgetting could be willed.
Tell the grassy hollow that holds the bubbling well-spring,
Tell it to forget the source that keeps it filled.
Ibid. Stanza 5

[o] But O the truth, the truth! the many eyes
That look on it! the diverse things they see.
A Ballad of Fair Ladies in Revolt. Stanza 16

[p] When we have thrown off this old suit,
So much in need of mending,

To sink among the naked mute,
  Is that, think you, our ending?
  The Question Whither. Stanza 1

[q] Thence had he the laugh . . .
Broad as ten thousand beeves
At pasture.
  The Spirit of Shakespeare

[r] Civil limitation daunts
His utterance never; the nymphs
  blush, not he.
  An Orson of the Muse
  [*Walt Whitman*]

[s] Cannon his name,
  Cannon his voice, he came.
  Napoleon. I

[t]   Evermore shall tyrant Force
Beget the greater for its overthrow.   *Ibid. XIII*

[u] For iron Winter held her firm;
Across her sky he laid his hand;
And bird he starved, he stiffened
  worm;
A sightless heaven, a shaven
  land. . . .
Now the North wind ceases,
The warm South-west awakes,
The heavens are out in fleeces,
And earth's green banner shakes.
  Tardy Spring

[v] When the grasp on the bow
  was decision,
And arrow and hand and eye were
  one;
When the Pleasures, like waves to
  a swimmer,
Came heaving for rapture ahead!
  Ode to Youth in Memory

[w] A witty woman is a treasure;
a witty beauty is a power.
  Diana of the Crossways. Chap. 1

[x] The well of true wit is truth
itself.   *Ibid.*

[y] Woman is the last thing
which will be civilized by man.
  *The Ordeal of Richard Feverel.
  Chap. 1*

[z] Who rises from prayer a better
man, his prayer is answered.
  Ibid. Chap. 12

[a] The sun is coming down to
earth, and the fields and the
waters shout to him golden
shouts.   *Ibid. Chap. 19*

"Owen Meredith"
see Edward Robert Lytton, Earl of Lytton

Dixon Lanier Merritt
[1879–   ]

[b] A wonderful bird is the peli-
  can,
His bill will hold more than his
  belican.
  He can take in his beak
  Food enough for a week,
But I'm damned if I see how the
  helican.   *The Pelican*

Charlotte Mew
[1870–1928]

[c] What shall we do with this
  strange Summer, meant for
  you,—
Dear, if we see the Winter
  through
What shall be done with
  Spring—?
  To a Child in Death

Alice Meynell
[1850–1922]

[d] She walks—the lady of my de-
  light—
  A shepherdess of sheep.
Her flocks are thoughts. She keeps
  them white;
  She guards them from the steep.
  The Shepherdess. Stanza 1

[e] O heavenly colour, London
  town
  Has blurred it from her skies;
And, hooded in an earthly brown,
  Unheaven'd the city lies.
  November Blue. Stanza 1

[f] It is principally for the sake
of the leg that a change in the
dress of man is so much to be desired. . . . The leg is the best part
of the figure . . . and the best leg
is the man's. Man should no
longer disguise the long lines, the
strong forms, in those lengths of
piping or tubing that are of all
garments the most stupid.
  Essays. Unstable Equilibrium

Viola Meynell
(Mrs. John Dalleyn)

[g] His kisses touch her marvelling eyes
And wander searching through
  her thinking face;
  And though so loved and near
  she lies
He knows he travels in a distant
  place.
  A Girl Adoring. Prefatory verses

[h] The dust comes secretly day
  after day,
Lies on my ledge and dulls my
  shining things.
But O this dust that I shall drive
  away
  Is flowers and kings,
  Is Solomon's temple, poets, Nineveh.   *Dusting*

Michelangelo
[1474–1564]

[i] The more the marble wastes,
The more the statue grows.
  Sonnet

[j] If it be true that any beauteous thing
Raises the pure and just desire of
  man

From earth to God, the eternal
fount of all,
Such I believe my love.
Sonnet

William Julius Mickle
[1735–1788]

[k] The dews of summer nights
did fall,
The moon (sweet regent of the
sky)
Silvered the walls of Cumnor Hall
And many an oak that grew
thereby.
Cumnor Hall. Stanza 1

[l] For there's nae luck about the
house,
There's nae luck at a';
There's little pleasure in the
house
When our gudeman's awa.
The Mariner's Wife. Stanza 1

Thomas Middleton
[1570–1627]

[m] On his last legs.
The Old Law. Act V, Sc. 1

[n] A little too wise, they say, do
ne'er live long.
The Phœnix. Act I, Sc. 1

[o] Ground not upon dreams; you
know they are ever contrary.
The Family of Love. Act IV, Sc. 3

[p] Have you summoned your
wits from wool-gathering?
Ibid. Act V, Sc. 3

[q]   That disease
Of which all old men sicken,—
avarice.
The Roaring Girl. Act I, Sc. 1

[r] How many honest words have
suffered corruption since Chaucer's
days!
*No Wit, no Help, Like a
Woman's. Act II, Sc. 1*

John Stuart Mill
[1806–1873]

[s] To question all things;—never
to turn away from any difficulty;
to accept no doctrine either from
ourselves or from other people
without a rigid scrutiny by nega-
tive criticism; letting no fallacy,
or incoherence, or confusion of
thought, step by unperceived;
above all, to insist upon having
the meaning of a word clearly understood before using it, and the
meaning of a proposition before
assenting to it;—these are the lessons we learn from ancient dialec-
ticians.
*Inaugural Address as Rector,
University of St. Andrew
[February 1, 1867]*

Edna St. Vincent Millay
(Mrs. Eugen Jan Boissevain)
[1892–1950]

[t] I would I were alive again
To kiss the fingers of the rain,
To drink into my eyes the shine
Of every slanting silver line,
To catch the freshened, fragrant
breeze
From drenched and dripping
apple-trees.
Renascence. Line 119

[u] The world stands out on
either side
No wider than the heart is wide;
Above the world is stretched the
sky,—
No higher than the soul is high.
The heart can push the sea and
land
Farther away on either hand;
The soul can split the sky in two,
And let the face of God shine
through.
Renascence. Line 189

[v] The fabric of my faithful love
No power shall dim or ravel
Whilst I stay here,—but oh, my
dear,
If I should ever travel!
*To the Not Impossible Him.
Stanza 3*

[w] She that had no need of me,
Is a little lonely child
Lost in Hell. Persephone,
Take her head upon your knee,
Say to her: "My dear, my dear,
It is not so dreadful here."
A Prayer to Persephone

[x] I know I am but summer to
your heart,
And not the full four seasons of
the year.
Two Seasons. Sonnet 1

[y] I drank at every vine.
The last was like the first.
I came upon no wine
So wonderful as thirst.
Feast. Stanza 1

[z]   Euclid alone
Has looked on Beauty bare. Fortu-
nate they
Who, though once only and then
but far away,
Have heard her massive sandal set
on stone.
*Euclid Alone Has Looked on
Beauty Bare*

[a] My candle burns at both
ends;
It will not last the night;
But, ah, my foes, and, oh, my
friends—
It gives a lovely light.
Figs from Thistles. First Fig

[b] Music my rampart, and my
only one.
*On Hearing a Symphony of
Beethoven*

[c] Stranger, pause and look;
From the dust of ages
Lift this little book,
Turn the tattered pages,
Read me, do not let me die!
Search the fading letters, finding
Steadfast in the broken binding
All that once was I!
   The Poet and His Book. Stanza 6

[d] Weep him dead and mourn as
   you may,
Me, I sing as I must:
Blessed be death, that cuts in
   marble
What would have sunk in dust.
   Keen. Stanza 1

[e] Who builds her a house with
   love for timber,
Builds her a house of foam;
And I'd rather be bride to a lad
   gone down
Than widow to one safe home.
   Ibid. Stanza 5

[f] Spring rides no horses down
   the hill,
But comes on foot, a goose girl
   still.
And all the loveliest things there
   be
Come simply, so it seems to me.
If ever I said, in grief or pride,
I tired of honest things, I lied.
   The Goose Girl

[g] O world, I cannot hold thee
   close enough!
Thy winds, thy wide gray skies!
Thy mists, that roll and rise!
Thy woods, this autumn day, that
   ache and sag
And all but cry with color.
   God's World. Stanza 1

[h] I will be the gladdest thing
   under the sun!
I will touch a hundred flowers and
   not pick one.
   Afternoon on a Hill

[i] And if I loved you Wednesday,
   Well, what is that to you?
I do not love you Thursday—
   So much is true.
   Thursday. Stanza 1

[j] There's little kind and little
   fair
Is worth its weight in smoke
To me, that's grown so free from
   care
Since my heart broke!
   The Merry Maid. Stanza 2

[k] Life goes on forever like the
   gnawing of a mouse.
   Ibid. Stanza 3

[l] My heart is warm with the
   friends I make,
And better friends I'll not be
   knowing;
Yet there isn't a train I wouldn't
   take,
No matter where it's going.
   Travel. Stanza 3

[m] Men say the winter
   Was bad that year;
Fuel was scarce,
   And food was dear.

A wind with a wolf's head
Howled about our door.
   The Ballad of the Harp-Weaver.
   Stanzas 13 and 14

[n] Into the darkness they go,
   the wise and the lovely.
   Crowned
With lilies and with laurel they go.
   Dirge Without Music. Stanza 1

[o] I had a little Sorrow,
   Born of a little Sin.
   The Penitent. Stanza 1

[p] Love in the open hand, nothing but that,
Ungemmed, unhidden, wishing
   not to hurt,
As one should bring you cowslips
   in a hat
Swung from the hand, or apples in
   her skirt,
I bring you, calling out as children
   do:
"Look what I have!—And these are
   all for you."
   Fatal Interview. XI

[q] See how these masses mill and
   swarm
And troop and muster and assail:
God! we could keep this planet
   warm
By friction, if the sun should fail.
   Three Sonnets in Tetrameter.
   I [1938]

Alice Duer Miller
[1874–1942]

[r] O, agony infernal
   That lovers undergo!
O, secret trysts diurnal
   That nobody must know.
O, vigilance eternal
   The whole world for a foe.
   Forsaking All Others

[s] When a woman like that
   whom I've seen so much
All of a sudden drops out of touch,
Is always busy and never can
Spare you a moment, it means a
   Man.
   Ibid.

[t] Once I remember in London
   how I saw
Pale shabby people standing in a
   long
Line in the twilight and the misty
   rain
To pay their tax. I then saw England plain.
   The White Cliffs

[u] They make other nations
   seem pale and flighty,
But they do think England is God
   almighty,

And you must remind them now
and then
That other countries breed other
men.   *Ibid.*

[v] Bad news is not broken by
kind tactful word.
The message is spoken ere the
word can be heard.
The eye and the bearing, the
breath make it clear,
And the heart is despairing before
the ears hear.   *Ibid.*

Cincinnatus Heine ("Joaquin") Miller
[1841–1913]

[w] Is it worth while that we
jostle a brother
Bearing his load on the rough
road of life?
Is it worth while that we jeer at
each other
In blackness of heart?—that we
war to the knife?
God pity us all in our pitiful
strife.
Is It Worth While? Stanza 1

[x] That man who lives for self
alone
Lives for the meanest mortal
known.   *Walker in Nicaragua.
Chant I, Stanza 1*

[y] I do not question school nor
creed
Of Christian, Protestant, or
Priest;
I only know that creeds to me
Are but new names for mystery,
That good is good from east to
east,
And more I do not know nor need
To know, to love my neighbor well.
The Tale of the Tall Alcalde

[z] Lo! Christ himself chose only
twelve,
Yet one of these turned out a
thief.   *A Song of the South.
Part II, Canto 3*

[a] Who taught you tender Bible
tales
Of honey-lands, of milk and
wine?
Of happy, peaceful Palestine?
Of Jordan's holy harvest vales?
Who gave the patient Christ? I say
Who gave your Christian creed?
Yea, yea,
Who gave your very God to you?
Your Jew! Your Jew! Your hated
Jew!   *To Russia. Stanza 3*

[b] The bravest battle that ever
was fought;
Shall I tell you where and when?
On the maps of the world you will
find it not;
It was fought by the mothers
of men.
The Bravest Battle. Stanza 1

[c] Aye, wisest he is in this whole
wide land,
Of hoarding till bent and gray;
For all you can hold in your cold,
dead hand
Is what you have given away
*Peter Cooper, April, 1883.
Stanza 3*

[d] He gained a world; he gave
that world
Its grandest lesson: "On! sail on!"
Columbus. Stanza 5

[e] The Lightning reached a fiery
rod,
And on Death's fearful forehead
wrote
The autograph of God.
*With Love to You
and Yours. Part I, Canto III*

Emily Huntington Miller
[1833–1913]

[f] Hang up the baby's stocking;
Be sure you don't forget
The dear little dimpled darling!
She ne'er saw Christmas yet.
Hang Up the Baby's Stocking

J. Corson Miller
[1883–   ]

[g] Lo! he is gone—the Searcher
of the Skies!
No more the mountain breezes
stir his hair,
The while he marks, with genius-
flaming eyes,
The hills on Mars, or some
young comet's lair.
The Dead Astronomer. Stanza 2

Thomas Miller
[1808–1874]

[h] What though upon his hoary
head
Have fallen many a winter's snow?
His wreath is still as green and red
As 'twas a thousand years ago.
For what has he to do with care!
His wassail-bowl and old arm-
chair
Are ever standing ready there,
For Christmas comes but once a
year.   *Christmas Comes
but Once a Year*

William Miller
[1810–1872]

[i] Wee Willie Winkie rins
through the toun,
Upstairs and dounstairs, in his
nichtgoun,
Tirlin' at the window, cryin' at
the lock,
"Are the weans in their bed? for
it's nou ten o'clock."
Willie Winkie

Henry Hart Milman
[1791–1868]

[j] And the cold marble leapt to
life a god.
The Belvedere Apollo

[k] And more than wisdom, more
than wealth,—
A merry heart that laughs at care.
The Merry Heart. Stanza 1

Alan Alexander Milne
[1882–   ]

[l] Hush! Hush! Whisper who
dares!
Christopher Robin is saying his
prayers.   *Vespers*

[m] Could we have some butter
for
The Royal slice of Bread? . . .

"Nobody, my darling,
Could call me
A fussy man—
     BUT
I do like a little bit of butter to
my bread!"
The King's Breakfast

[n] It isn't really
Anywhere!
It's somewhere else
Instead! *Halfway Down. Stanza 2*

[o] Christopher Robin goes
Hoppity, hoppity,
Hoppity, hoppity, hop.
Whenever I tell him
Politely to stop it, he
Says he can't possibly stop.
Hoppity

[p] James James
     Morrison Morrison
     Weatherby George Dupree
     Took great
     Care of his Mother
     Though he was only three.
James James
Said to his Mother,
"Mother," he said, said he:
"You must never go down to the
end of the town, if you don't
go down with me."
Disobedience

[q] Old London's time-encrusted
walls
Are but the work of human
hands.
What man has fashioned for us
falls;
What God has breathed into us
stands.
London. Stanza 1 [during Blitz]

Richard Monckton Milnes
(Lord Houghton)
[1809–1885]

[r] But on and up, where
Nature's heart
Beats strong amid the hills.
*Tragedy of the Lac de Gaube.
Stanza 2*

[s] If what shone afar so grand
Turn to nothing in thy hand,
On again! the virtue lies
In the struggle, not the prize.
The World to the Soul

[t] A fair little girl sat under a
tree,
Sewing as long as her eyes could
see;
Then smoothed her work, and
folded it right,
And said, "Dear work, good-night,
good-night."   *Good-Night
and Good-Morning. Stanza 1*

[u] Heart of the people! Working-
men!
Marrow and nerve of human
powers;
Who on your sturdy backs sustain
Through streaming time this
world of ours.
Labor. Stanza 1

[v] They who have steeped their
souls in prayer
Can every anguish calmly bear.
The Sayings of Rabia. IV

[w] Lady Moon, Lady Moon,
where are you roving?
Over the sea.
Lady Moon, Lady Moon, whom are
you loving?
All that love me!
A Child's Song

[x] The sense of humour is the
just balance of all the faculties
of man, the best security against
the pride of knowledge and the
conceits of the imagination, the
strongest inducement to submit
with a wise and pious patience to
the vicissitudes of human existence. *Memoir of Thomas Hood*

John Milton
[1608–1674]

[y] Of Man's first disobedience,
and the fruit
Of that forbidden tree whose mortal taste
Brought death into the world, and
all our woe.
Paradise Lost. Book I, Line 1

[z] And justify the ways of God
to men.   *Ibid. Line 26*

[a]   To be weak is miserable,
Doing or suffering.
Ibid. Line 157

[b] And out of good still to find
means of evil.   *Ibid. Line 165*

[c] The mind is its own place, and
in itself
Can make a heaven of hell, a hell
of heaven.   *Ibid. Line 254*

[d] Better to reign in hell than
serve in heaven.
Ibid. Line 263

[e] When night
Darkens the streets, then wander
forth the sons
Of Belial, flown with insolence
and wine. *Ibid. Line 500*

[f] Th' imperial ensign, which,
full high advanc'd,
Shone like a meteor, streaming to
the wind. *Ibid. Line 536*

[g] Sonorous metal blowing martial sounds:
At which the universal host up
sent
A shout that tore hell's concave,
and beyond
Frighted the reign of Chaos and
old Night. *Ibid. Line 540*

[h] Who overcomes
By force hath overcome but half
his foe. *Ibid. Line 648*

[i] Mammon, the least erected
spirit that fell
From heaven; for ev'n in heaven
his looks and thoughts
Were always downward bent, admiring more
The riches of heaven's pavement,
trodden gold,
Than aught divine or holy else
enjoy'd
In vision beatific. *Ibid. Line 679*

[j] From morn
To noon he fell, from noon to
dewy eve,
A summer's day; and with the
setting sun
Dropp'd from the Zenith, like a
falling star. *Ibid. Line 742*

[k] Fairy elves,
Whose midnight revels, by a forest
side
Or fountain, some belated peasant
sees,
Or dreams he sees, while overhead
the moon
Sits arbitress. *Ibid. Line 781*

[l] The strongest and the fiercest
spirit
That fought in heaven, now fiercer
by despair.
Ibid. Book II, Line 44

[m] Rather than be less,
Car'd not to be at all.
Ibid. Line 47

[n] But all was false and hollow;
though his tongue
Dropp'd manna, and could make
the worse appear
The better reason, to perplex and
dash
Maturest counsels. *Ibid. Line 112*

[o] For who would lose,
Though full of pain, this intellectual being,
Those thoughts that wander
through eternity,
To perish rather, swallow'd up
and lost

In the wide womb of uncreated
night? *Ibid. Line 146*

[p] The never-ending flight
Of future days. *Ibid. Line 221*

[q] His look
Drew audience and attention still
as night
Or summer's noontide air.
Ibid. Line 307

[r] Their rising all at once was as
the sound
Of thunder heard remote.
Ibid. Line 476

[s] Arm th' obdur'd breast
With stubborn patience as with
triple steel. *Ibid. Line 568*

[t] Far off from these a slow and
silent stream,
Lethe the River of Oblivion.
Ibid. Line 582

[u] The parching air
Burns frore, and cold performs th'
effect of fire.
Thither by harpy-footed Furies
hail'd,
At certain revolutions all the
damn'd
Are brought: and feel by turns
the bitter change
Of fierce extremes,—extremes by
change more fierce;
From beds of raging fire to starve
in ice
Their soft ethereal warmth, and
there to pine
Immovable, infix'd, and frozen
round,
Periods of time; thence hurried
back to fire. *Ibid. Line 594*

[v] Black it stood as night,
Fierce as ten furies, terrible as
hell,
And shook a dreadful dart; what
seem'd his head
The likeness of a kingly crown
had on.
Satan was now at hand.
Ibid. Line 670

[w] Before mine eyes in oppo-
sition sits
Grim Death, my son and foe.
Ibid. Line 803

[x] With ruin upon ruin, rout on
rout,
Confusion worse confounded.
Ibid. Line 995

[y] And fast by, hanging in a
golden chain,
This pendent world, in bigness as
a star
Of smallest magnitude close by
the moon. *Ibid. Line 1051*

[z] Hail, holy light! offspring of
heav'n first-born.
Ibid. Book III, Line 1

[a] The rising world of waters
dark and deep. *Ibid. Line 11*

[b]   Now conscience wakes despair
That slumber'd,—wakes the bitter memory
Of what he was, what is, and what must be.
                    Ibid. Book IV, Line 23

[c]   Ease would recant
Vows made in pain, as violent and void.   *Ibid. Line 96*

[d] So farewell hope, and, with hope, farewell fear,
Farewell remorse; all good to me is lost.
Evil, be thou my good.
                    Ibid. Line 108

[e] For contemplation he and valour form'd,
For softness she and sweet attractive grace;
He for God only, she for God in him.   *Ibid. Line 297*

[f] Yielded with coy submission, modest pride,
And sweet, reluctant, amorous delay.   *Ibid. Line 309*

[g] Adam the goodliest man of men since born
His sons, the fairest of her daughters Eve.   *Ibid. Line 323*

[h]   And with necessity,
The tyrant's plea, excus'd his devilish deeds.   *Ibid. Line 393*

[i] Imparadis'd in one another's arms.   *Ibid. Line 506*

[j]   Twilight gray
Had in her sober livery all things clad   *Ibid. Line 598*

[k]   Now glow'd the firmament
With living sapphires; Hesperus, that led
The starry host, rode brightest, till the moon,
Rising in clouded majesty, at length
Apparent queen, unveil'd her peerless light,
And o'er the dark her silver mantle threw.   *Ibid. Line 604*

[l] The timely dew of sleep.
                    Ibid. Line 614

[m] Sweet is the breath of morn, her rising sweet,
With charm of earliest birds; pleasant the sun
When first on this delightful land he spreads
His orient beams on herb, tree, fruit, and flower,
Glist'ring with dew.
                    Ibid. Line 641

[n]   In naked beauty more adorn'd,
More lovely, than Pandora.
                    Ibid. Line 713

[o] Hail, wedded love, mysterious law, true source
Of human offspring.
                    Ibid. Line 750

[p]   Abash'd the devil stood,
And felt how awful goodness is, and saw
Virtue in her shape how lovely.
                    Line 846

[q] All hell broke loose.
                    Ibid. Line 918

[r] Now morn, her rosy steps in th' eastern clime
Advancing, sow'd the earth with orient pearl,
When Adam wak'd, so custom'd; for his sleep
Was aery light, from pure digestion bred.
                    Ibid. Book V, Line 1

[s] Hung over her enamour'd, and beheld
Beauty, which, whether waking or asleep,
Shot forth peculiar graces.
                    Ibid. Line 13

[t] So saying, with despatchful looks in haste
She turns, on hospitable thoughts intent.   *Ibid. Line 331*

[u]   Nor jealousy
Was understood, the injur'd lover's hell.   *Ibid. Line 449*

[v] Midnight brought on the dusky hour
Friendliest to sleep and silence.
                    Ibid. Line 667

[w] Innumerable as the stars of night,
Or stars of morning, dewdrops which the sun
Impearls on every leaf and every flower.   *Ibid. Line 745*

[x]   Morn,
Wak'd by the circling hours, with rosy hand
Unbarr'd the gates of light.
                    Ibid. Book VI, Line 2

[y] Let it profit thee to have heard,
By terrible example, the reward
Of disobedience.   *Ibid. Line 909*

[z]   God saw the Light was good;
And light from darkness by the hemisphere
Divided: Light the Day, and Darkness Night,
He named. Thus was the first Day even and morn.
                    Ibid. Book VII, Line 249

[a] A broad and ample road, whose dust is gold,
And pavement stars, as stars to thee appear
Seen in the galaxy, that milky way

Which nightly as a circling zone
thou seest
Powder'd with stars.
Ibid. Line 577

[b] Liquid lapse of murmuring
streams.
Ibid. Book VIII, Line 263

[c] And feel that I am happier
than I know.   *Ibid. Line 282*

[d] Among unequals what society
Can sort, what harmony or true
delight?   *Ibid. Line 383*

[e] To the nuptial bower
I led her blushing like the morn;
all heaven
And happy constellations, on that
hour
Shed their selectest influence.
Ibid. Line 510

[f] Accuse not Nature! she hath
done her part;
Do thou but thine!   *Ibid. Line 561*

[g]   Oft times nothing profits
more
Than self-esteem, grounded on
just and right.   *Ibid. Line 571*

[h]   Revenge, at first though
sweet,
Bitter ere long back on itself recoils.   *Ibid. Book IX, Line 171*

[i] For solitude sometimes is best
society,
And short retirement urges sweet
return.   *Ibid. Line 249*

[j] As one who long in populous
city pent,
Where houses thick and sewers
annoy the air.   *Ibid. Line 445*

[k] Led Eve, our credulous
mother, to the Tree
Of Prohibition, root of all our
woe.   *Ibid. Line 644*

[l]   His words, replete with
guile,
Into her heart too easy entrance
won.   *Ibid. Line 733*

[m] So dear I love him that with
him all deaths
I could endure, without him live
no life.   *Ibid. Line 832*

[n]   In her face excuse
Came prologue, and apology too
prompt.   *Ibid. Line 853*

[o] She gave me of the tree, and
I did eat.
Ibid. Book X, Line 143

[p] Dust thou art, and shalt to
dust return.   *Ibid. Line 208*

[q] A dismal universal hiss, the
sound
Of public scorn.   *Ibid. Line 508*

[r] Death . . . on his pale horse.
Ibid. Line 588

[s]   Whatever thing
The scythe of Time mows down.
Ibid. Line 606

[t]   How gladly would I meet
Mortality, my sentence, and be
earth
Insensible! how glad would lay
me down
As in my mother's lap!
Ibid. Line 775

[u]   Moping melancholy,
And moon-struck madness.
Ibid. Book XI, Line 485

[v] And over them triumphant
Death his dart
Shook, but delay'd to strike,
though oft invok'd.
Ibid. Line 491

[w] The rule of *Not too much.*
Ibid. Line 531

[x]   The evening star,
Love's harbinger.
Ibid. Line 588

[y] The brazen throat of war.
Ibid. Line 713

[z] The world was all before them,
where to choose
Their place of rest, and Providence
their guide.
They hand in hand, with wan-
d'ring steps and slow,
Through Eden took their solitary
way.
Ibid. Book XII, Line 646

[a]   Most men admire
Virtue who follow not her lore.
*Paradise Regained. Book I,
Line 482*

[b'] The childhood shows the
man,
As morning shows the day.
Ibid. Book IV, Line 220

[c'] Athens, the eye of Greece,
mother of arts
And eloquence.
Ibid. Line 240

[d'] O dark, dark, dark, amid the
blaze of noon,
Irrecoverably dark, total eclipse
Without all hope of day!
Samson Agonistes. Line 80

[e'] Just are the ways of God,
And justifiable to men;
Unless there be who think not God
at all.   *Ibid. Line 293*

[f'] In argument with men a
woman ever
Goes by the worse, whatever be
her cause.
For want of words, no doubt, or
lack of breath!
Ibid. Line 903

[g'] Fame, if not double-faced,
is double-mouthed,
And with contrary blast proclaims
most deeds;
On both his wings, one black, the
other white,
Bears greatest names in his wild
aery flight.   *Ibid. Line 971*

[h] For evil news rides post, while good news baits.
Ibid. Line 1538

[i] Suspense in news is torture.
Ibid. Line 1569

[j] Calm of mind, all passion spent.
Ibid. Line 1758

[k] Above the smoke and stir of this dim spot
Which men call earth.
Comus. Line 5

[l] Bacchus, that first from out the purple grape
Crush'd the sweet poison of mis-usèd wine.
Ibid. Line 46

[m] How sweetly did they float upon the wings
Of silence, through the empty-vaulted night.
Ibid. Line 249

[n] And Wisdom's self
Oft seeks to sweet retired solitude,
Where, with her best nurse Contemplation,
She plumes her feathers, and lets grow her wings.
Ibid. Line 375

[o]   The unsunn'd heaps
Of miser's treasure.
Ibid. Line 398

[p] Some say no evil thing that walks by night,
In fog or fire, by lake or moorish fen,
Blue meagre hag, or stubborn un-laid ghost,
That breaks his magic chains at curfew time,
No goblin, or swart faery of the mine,
Hath hurtful power o'er true virginity.
Ibid. Line 432

[q] How charming is divine philosophy!
Not harsh and crabbed, as dull fools suppose,
But musical as is Apollo's lute,
And a perpetual feast of nectar'd sweets
Where no crude surfeit reigns.
Ibid. Line 476

[s]   That power
Which erring men call Chance.
Ibid. Line 587

[t] It is for homely features to keep home,—
They had their name thence; coarse complexions
And cheeks of sorry grain will serve to ply
The sampler, and to tease the huswife's wool.
What need a vermeil-tinctur'd lip for that,
Love-darting eyes, or tresses like the morn?
Ibid. Line 748

[u] Under the glassy, cool, trans-lucent wave.   *Ibid. Line 861*

[v] Without the meed of some melodious tear.
Lycidas. Line 14

[w] To sport with Amaryllis in the shade,
Or with the tangles of Neæra's hair.
Ibid. Line 68

[x] Fame is the spur that the clear spirit doth raise
(That last infirmity of noble mind)
To scorn delights, and live laborious days;
But the fair guerdon when we hope to find,
And think to burst out into sudden blaze,
Comes the blind Fury with th' abhorred shears
And slits the thin-spun life.
Ibid. Line 70

[y] And purple all the ground with vernal flowers.
Bring the rathe primrose that forsaken dies,
The tufted crow-toe, and pale jessamine,
The white pink, and the pansy freaked with jet,
The glowing violet,
The musk-rose, and the well-attir'd woodbine,
With cowslips wan that hang the pensive head,
And every flower that sad embroidery wears.
Ibid. Line 141

[z] So sinks the day-star in the ocean bed,
And yet anon repairs his drooping head,
And tricks his beams, and with new-spangled ore
Flames in the forehead of the morning sky.   *Ibid. Line 168*

[a] Hence, loathed Melancholy,
Of Cerberus and blackest Midnight born.
L'Allegro. Line 1

[b] Haste thee, Nymph, and bring with thee
Jest, and youthful Jollity,
Quips and Cranks and wanton Wiles,
Nods and Becks and wreathèd Smiles. . . .
Sport, that wrinkled Care derides,
And Laughter holding both his sides.
Come, and trip it, as you go,
On the light fantastic toe.
Ibid. Line 25

[c] The mountain nymph, sweet Liberty.   *Ibid. Line 36*

[d] Then to the spicy nut-brown ale.   *Ibid. Line 100*

[e] Tower'd cities please us then,
And the busy hum of men.
Ibid. Line 117

[f] Ladies, whose bright eyes
Rain influence, and judge the
prize. *Ibid. Line* 121

[g] And ever, against eating cares,
Lap me in soft Lydian airs,
Married to immortal verse.
Such as the meeting soul may
pierce,
In notes with many a winding
bout
Of linkèd sweetness long drawn
out. *Ibid. Line* 135

[h] Vain deluding Joys,
The brood of Folly without father
bred! *Il Penseroso. Line* 1

[i] And add to these retired Leisure,
That in trim gardens takes his
pleasure. *Ibid. Line* 49

[j] The wandering moon,
Riding near her highest noon,
Like one that had been led astray
Through the heav'n's wide path-
less way,
And oft, as if her head she bow'd,
Stooping through a fleecy cloud.
Ibid. Line 67

[k] Or bid the soul of Orpheus
sing
Such notes as, warbled to the
string,
Drew iron tears down Pluto's
cheek. *Ibid. Line* 105

[l] And storied windows richly
dight,
Casting a dim religious light.
Ibid. Line 159

[m] Till old experience do attain
To something like prophetic
strain. *Ibid. Line* 173

[n] This is the month, and this
the happy morn,
Wherein the Son of Heaven's
eternal King,
Of wedded maid and virgin
mother born,
Our great redemption from above
did bring.
*On the Morning of Christ's
Nativity. Stanza* 1, *Line* 1

[o] The lazy leaden-stepping
Hours,
Whose speed is but the heavy
plummet's pace.
On Time

[p] All this earthy grossness quit,
Attired with stars we shall for ever
sit,
Triumphing over Death, and
Chance, and thee, O Time.
Ibid.

[q] What needs my Shakespeare
for his honour'd bones
The labour of an age in pilèd
stones?

Or that his hallow'd relics should
be hid
Under a star-ypointing pyramid?
Dear son of memory, great heir of
fame,
What need'st thou such weak wit-
ness of thy name?
On Shakespeare

[r] Thy liquid notes that close
the eye of day.
Sonnet: To the Nightingale

[s] Time, the subtle thief of
youth.
*On His Having Arrived at
the Age of Twenty-three*

[t] They also serve who only
stand and wait.
On his Blindness

[u] But oh! as to embrace me she
inclin'd,
I wak'd, she fled, and day brought
back my night.
On his Deceased Wife

[v] For such kind of borrowing
as this, if it be not bettered by the
borrower, among good authors is
accounted Plagiarè.
Iconoclastes, XXIII

[w] Truth is as impossible to be
soiled by any outward touch as the
sunbeam. *Doctrine and Discipline of Divorce*

[x] By labour and intent study
(which I take to be my portion in
this life), joined with the strong
propensity of nature, I might perhaps leave something so written to
after times as they should not
willingly let it die.
*The Reason of Church Govern-
ment. Book II, Introduction*

[y] His words, like so many nimble and airy servitors, trip about
him at command.
Apology for Smectymnuus

[z] In those vernal seasons of the
year, when the air is calm and
pleasant, it were an injury and
sullenness against Nature not to
go out and see her riches, and
partake in her rejoicing with
heaven and earth.
Tractate of Education

[a] As good almost kill a man as
kill a good book: who kills a man
kills a reasonable creature, God's
image ; but he who destroys a good
book kills reason itself.
Areopagitica

[b] I cannot praise a fugitive and
cloistered virtue, unexercised and
unbreathed, that never sallies out
and sees her adversary, but slinks
out of the race where that immortal garland is to be run for,
not without dust and heat.
Ibid.

[c] Methinks I see in my mind a
noble and puissant nation rousing

herself like a strong man after
sleep, and shaking her invincible
locks: methinks I see her as an
eagle mewing her mighty youth,
and kindling her undazzled eyes
at the full midday beam.
Ibid.

[d] Though all the winds of doctrine were let loose to play upon
the earth, so Truth be in the field,
we do ingloriously, by licensing
and prohibiting, to misdoubt her
strength. Let her and Falsehood
grapple: who ever knew Truth
put to the worse in a free and
open encounter? *Ibid.*

[e] Such bickerings to recount,
met often in these our writers,
what more worth is it than to
chronicle the wars of kites or
crows flocking and fighting in the
air?
The History of England. Book IV

Mimnermus
[*Floruit* 630–600 B. C.]

[f] We are all clever enough at
envying a famous man while he is
yet alive, and at praising him
when he is dead.
Fragment 1

Charles Miner
[1780–1865]

[g] When I see a merchant over-
polite to his customers, begging
them to taste a little brandy and
throwing half his goods on the
counter,—thinks I, that man has
an axe to grind.
Who'll Turn Grindstones

John Clair Minot
[1872–1941]

[h] May the God we trust as a
nation
Throw the light of His peace and
grace
On a flag with its stripes untarn-
ished,
And with every star in place.
*The Flag of Fort McHenry.
Stanza 10*

Agnes E. Mitchell
[*Floruit* 1880]

[i] Klingle, klangle, klingle,
Far down the dusky dingle,
The cows are coming home;
Now sweet and clear, and faint
and low,
The airy tinklings come and go,
Like chimings from the far-off
tower,

Or patterings of an April shower
That makes the daisies grow.
*When the Cows Come Home.
Stanza 1*

Donald Grant Mitchell
("IK. Marvel")
[1822–1908]

[j] Blessed be letters—they are
the monitors, they are also the
comforters, and they are the only
true heart-talkers.
*Reveries of a Bachelor. Second
Reverie*

[k] Coquetry whets the appetite;
flirtation depraves it. Coquetry is
the thorn that guards the rose—
easily trimmed off when once
plucked. Flirtation is like the
slime on water-plants, making
them hard to handle, and when
caught, only to be cherished in
slimy waters. *Ibid.*

[l] A man without some sort of
religion is at best, a poor repro-
bate, the football of destiny, with
no tie linking him to infinity, and
the wondrous eternity that is begun with him; but a woman without it is even worse—a flame without heat, a rainbow without color,
a flower without perfume!
Ibid.

Silas Weir Mitchell
[1829–1914]

[m] Up anchor! Up anchor!
Set sail and away!
The ventures of dreamland
Are thine for a day.
Dreamland

[n] When youth as lord of my
unchallenged fate,
And time seemed but the vassal of
my will,
I entertained certain guests of
state—
The great of older days.
*On a Boy's First Reading of
"King Henry V"*

[o] There is no dearer lover of
lost hours
Than I.
I can be idler than the idlest
flowers,
More idly lie.
Idleness

[p] Show me the books he loves
and I shall know
The man far better than through
mortal friends.
Books and the Man. Stanza 1

[q] The first thing to be done by
a biographer in estimating character is to examine the stubs of
the victim's cheque-books.
*Quoted in Cushing: Life of Sir
William Osler. Vol. I, Chap. 21,
Page 583*

Jean Baptiste Molière
[1622–1673]

[r] The world, dear Agnes, is a strange affair.
L'École des Femmes. Act II, Sc. 6

[s] He's a wonderful talker, who has the art of telling you nothing in a great harangue.
Le Misanthrope. Act II, Sc. 5

[t] He makes his cook his merit, and the world visits his dinners and not him. *Ibid.*

[u] The more we love our friends, the less we flatter them; it is by excusing nothing that pure love shows itself. *Ibid.*

[v] Doubts are more cruel than the worst of truths.
Ibid. Act III, Sc. 7

[w] If everyone were clothed with integrity, if every heart were just, frank, kindly, the other virtues would be well-nigh useless, since their chief purpose is to make us bear with patience the injustice of our fellows. *Ibid. Act V, Sc. 1*

[x] There is no rampart that will hold out against malice.
Tartuffe. Act I, Sc. 1

[y] Those whose conduct gives room for talk are always the first to attack their neighbours.
Ibid.

[z] She is laughing in her sleeve at you. *Ibid. Sc. 6*

[a] The beautiful eyes of my cash-box. *L'Avare. Act V, Sc. 3*

[b] What the devil did he want in that galley? *Les Fourberies de Scapin. Act II, Sc. 11*

[c] Grammar, which knows how to control even kings.
Les Femmes Savantes [1672]. Act II, Sc. 6

[d] Ah, there are no longer any children!
Le Malade Imaginaire. Act II, Sc. 11

[e] Nearly all men die of their remedies, and not of their illnesses. *Ibid. Act III, Sc. 3*

Cosmo Monkhouse
[1840–1901]

[f] So we must part, my body, you and I
Who've spent so many pleasant years together.
'Tis sorry work to lose your company
Who clove to me so close.
Any Soul to Any Body

Harold Monro
[1879–1932]

[g] She nestles over the shining rim,
Buries her chin in the creamy sea;
Her tail hangs loose; each drowsy paw
Is doubled under each bending knee. *Milk for the Cat*

[h] We are going *Out.* You know the pitch of the word,
Probing the tone of thought as it comes through fog
And reaches by devious means (half-smelt, half-heard)
The four-legged brain of a walk-ecstatic dog. *Dog*

James Monroe
[1758–1831]

[i] National honor is national property of the highest value.
First Inaugural Address [March 4, 1817]

[j] The American continents . . . are henceforth not to be considered as subjects for future colonization by any European powers.
Annual Message to Congress [December, 1823] (The Monroe Doctrine)

Lady Mary Wortley Montagu
[1690–1762]

[k] Be plain in dress, and sober in your diet;
In short, my deary, kiss me, and be quiet.
A Summary of Lord Lyttelton's Advice

[l] Satire should, like a polished razor keen,
Wound with a touch that's scarcely felt or seen.
To the Imitator of the First Satire of Horace. Book II

[m] But the fruit that can fall without shaking
Indeed is too mellow for me.
The Answer

Charles Edward Montague
[1867–1928]

[n] A gifted small girl has explained that pins are a great means of saving life, "by not swallowing them."
Dramatic Values

[o] Among the mind's powers is . . . the power of taking delight in a thing, or rather in anything, everything, not as a means to some other end, but just because it is what it is, as the lover dotes

on whatever may be the traits of the beloved object.
Disenchantment. Chap. 15

[p] A lie will easily get you out of a scrape, and yet, strangely and beautifully, rapture possesses you when you have taken the scrape and left out the lie.   *Ibid.*

[q] War hath no fury like a non-combatant.   *Ibid.*

[r] "I was born below par to th' extent of two whiskies."
Fiery Particles

[s] Burgundy was the winiest wine, the central, essential, and typical wine, the soul and greatest common measure of all the kindly wines of the earth.   *Judith*

James Jackson Montague
[1873–1941]

[t] But no one ever is allowed in Sleepytown, unless
He goes to bed in time to take the Sleepytown Express!
The Sleepytown Express. Stanza 1

[u] My sportsmen friends, alert and keen,
Have roamed this wide world through
But nutria, they've never seen
An animal like you.
To Some Unknown Animals. Stanza 2

Michel de Montaigne
[1533–1592]
Translation by Charles Cotton, revised by Hazlitt and Wight

[v] Man in sooth is a marvellous vain, fickle, and unstable subject.
Works. Book I, Chap. 1, That Men by Various Ways Arrive at the Same End

[w] It is not without good reason said, that he who has not a good memory should never take upon him the trade of lying.
Ibid. Chap. 9, Of Liars

[x] The laws of conscience, which we pretend to be derived from nature, proceed from custom.
Ibid. Chap. 22, Of Custom

[y] It can be of no importance to me of what religion my physician or my lawyer is; this consideration has nothing in common with the offices of friendship which they owe me.
Ibid. Chap. 27, Of Friendship

[z] Nothing is so firmly believed as what we least know.
Ibid. Chap. 31, Of Divine Ordinances

[a] A wise man never loses anything if he have himself.
Ibid. Chap. 38, Of Solitude

[b] The middle sort of historians (of which the most part are) spoil all; they will chew our meat for us.
Ibid. Book II, Chap. 10, Of Books

[c] She [virtue] requires a rough and stormy passage; she will have either outward difficulties to wrestle with, or internal difficulties.   *Ibid. Chap. 11, Of Cruelty*

[d] There is, nevertheless, a certain respect, and a general duty of humanity, that ties us, not only to beasts that have life and sense, but even to trees and plants.
Ibid.

[e] When I play with my cat, who knows whether I do not make her more sport than she makes me?
Ibid. Chap. 12, Apology for Raimond Sebond

[f] The souls of emperors and cobblers are cast in the same mold. . . . The same reason that makes us wrangle with a neighbour causes a war betwixt princes.
Ibid.

[g] Man is certainly stark mad; he cannot make a worm, and yet he will be making gods by dozens.
Ibid.

[h] Why may not a goose say thus: "All the parts of the universe I have an interest in: the earth serves me to walk upon; the sun to light me; the stars have their influence upon me; I have such an advantage by the winds and such by the waters; there is nothing that yon heavenly roof looks upon so favourably as me. I am the darling of Nature! Is it not man that keeps, lodges, and serves me?"   *Ibid.*

[i] Arts and sciences are not cast in a mould, but are formed and perfected by degrees, by often handling and polishing, as bears leisurely lick their cubs into form.
Ibid.

[j] The mariner of old said thus to Neptune in a great tempest, "O God! thou mayest save me if thou wilt, and if thou wilt, thou mayest destroy me; but whether or no, I will steer my rudder true."
Ibid. Chap. 16, Of Glory

[k] Nature has presented us with a large faculty of entertaining ourselves alone; and often calls us to it, to teach us that we owe ourselves partly to society, but chiefly and mostly to ourselves.
Ibid. Chap. 18, On Giving the Lie

[l] There never was in the world two opinions alike, no more than

two hairs or two grains; the most universal quality is diversity.
Ibid. Chap. 37, Of the Resemblance of Children to Their Fathers

[m] I will follow the right side even to the fire, but excluding the fire if I can. *Ibid. Book III, Chap. 1, Of Profit and Honesty*

[n] Does not he to whom you betray another, to whom you were as welcome as to himself, know that you will at another time do as much for him? *Ibid.*

[o] I speak truth, not so much as I would, but as much as I dare; and I dare a little the more, as I grow older. *Ibid. Chap. 2, Of Repentance*

[p] 'Tis so much to be a king, that he only is so by being so. The strange luster that surrounds him conceals and shrouds him from us; our sight is there broken and dissipated, being stopped and filled by the prevailing light.
Ibid. Chap. 7, Of the Inconvenience of Greatness

[q] There is no man so good, who, were he to submit all his thoughts and actions to the laws, would not deserve hanging ten times in his life. *Ibid. Chap. 9, Of Vanity*

[r] Saturninus said, "Comrades, you have lost a good captain to make him an ill general." *Ibid.*

[s] I am further of opinion that it would be better for us to have [no laws] at all than to have them in so prodigious numbers as we have. *Ibid. Chap. 13, Of Experience*

[t] What can we do with those people who will not believe anything unless it is in print? . . . I would as soon quote one of my friends as I would Aulus Gellius or Macrobius. *Ibid.*

[u] Let us a little permit Nature to take her own way; she better understands her own affairs than we. *Ibid.*

[v] I have ever loved to repose myself, whether sitting or lying, with my heels as high or higher than my head. *Ibid.*

[w] Que scais-je (What do I know)? *Motto on his seal*

[x] I do not understand; I pause; I examine. *Inscription for his library*

Sir Bernard Law Montgomery
(Viscount Montgomery of Alamein)
[1887–   ]

[y] I am not a bit anxious about my battles. If I am anxious I don't

fight them. I wait until I am ready.
Quoted in "British Commanders," published [1945] by British Information Services

James Montgomery
[1771–1854]

[z] To-morrow—oh, 'twill never be,
If we should live a thousand years!
Our time is all to-day, to-day,
The same, though changed; and while it flies
With still small voice the moments say:
"To-day, to-day, be wise, be wise." *To-day*

[a] The rose has but a summer reign,
The daisy never dies. *The Daisy. Stanza 10*

[b] "The Press!—What is the Press?" I cried;
When thus a wondrous voice replied:
"In me all human knowledge dwells;
The oracle of oracles,
Past, present, future, I reveal,
Or in oblivion's silence seal;
What I preserve can perish never,
What I forego is lost forever." *The Press. Stanza 1*

[c] Joys too exquisite to last,
And yet *more* exquisite when past. *The Little Cloud. Stanza 9*

[d] Bliss in possession will not last;
Remembered joys are never past;
At once the fountain, stream, and sea,
They were, they are, they yet shall be. *Ibid. Stanza 10*

[e] 'Tis not the whole of life to live,
Nor all of death to die. *The Issues of Life and Death. Stanza 2*

[f] Here in the body pent,
Absent from Him I roam,
Yet nightly pitch my moving tent
A day's march nearer home. *At Home in Heaven*

[g] Prayer is the soul's sincere desire,
Uttered or unexpressed;
The motion of a hidden fire
That trembles in the breast. *What is Prayer? Stanza 1*

Robert Montgomery
[1807–1855]

[h] And thou, vast ocean! on whose awful face

Time's iron feet can print no ruin-
trace.
*The Omnipresence of the Deity.
Part I*

Roselle Mercier Montgomery
[1874–1933]

[i] Companioned years have made
them comprehend
The comradeship that lies beyond a kiss.
The young ask much of life—
they ask but this,
To fare the road together to its
end.   *For a Wedding Anniversary*

[j] Oh, there are many things
that women know,
That no one tells them, no one
needs to tell;
And that they know, their
dearest never guess!
Because the woman heart is fashioned so,
I know that he has loved another well,
Still his remembering lips
know her caress.
Ulysses Returns: Penelope Speaks

[k] Never a ship sails out of the
bay
But carries my heart as a stowaway.   *The Stowaway*

Percy Montross

[l] In a cavern, in a canyon,
Excavating for a mine,
Dwelt a miner, Forty-niner,
And his daughter Clementine.
Oh, my darling, oh, my darling,
oh, my darling Clementine,
Thou art lost and gone for-
ever—
Dreadful sorry, Clementine.
*Clementine (College Song 1880).
Stanza 1*

William Vaughan Moody
[1869–1910]

[m] This earth is not the stead-
fast place
We landsmen build upon;
From deep to deep she varies pace,
And while she comes is gone.
Gloucester Moors. Stanza 4

[n] Then not to kneel, almost
Seemed like a vulgar boast.
Good Friday. Stanza 9

[o]   Gigantic, wilful, young,
Chicago sitteth at the northwest
gates,
With restless violent hands and
casual tongue
Moulding her mighty fates.
*An Ode in Time of Hesitation.
Stanza 3*

[p]   The wars we wage
Are noble, and our battles still are
won
By justice for us, ere we lift the
gage.
We have not sold our loftiest
heritage.
The proud republic hath not
stooped to cheat
And scramble in the market-place
of war.   *Ibid. Stanza 5*

[q] Our fluent men of place and
consequence
Fumble and fill their mouths with
hollow phrase,
Or for the end-all of deep argu-
ments
Intone their dull commercial lit-
urgies.   *Ibid. Stanza 7*

[r] Shrill and high, newsboys cry
The worst of the city's infamy.
In New York. Stanza 4

[s] The roaring street is hung for
miles
With fierce electric fire.
Ibid. Stanza 9

Charles Leonard Moore
[1854–1923]

[t] And now for what comes next
Thou waitest in thine invulner-
able West,
Blazoning more large thy living-
lettered text,
"Chance and the tools to those
who use them best."
To America

[u] Accept thy privilege to be
great.   *Ibid.*

[v] Poppy, therefore, and every
poisonous growth
Took he, that could transport his
soul away
From his wide prison;—for his
eyes were loth
And weary of the day.
Elegy on Edgar Allan Poe

[w] Gods walked the streets not
knowing they were gods;
The gaunt and weary watcher for
his race
Rode past our door and I, I looked
on Lincoln's face.
*Ode on the Impressions of
Boyhood*

Clement Clarke Moore
[1779–1863]

[x] 'Twas the night before
Christmas, when all through
the house
Not a creature was stirring,—not
even a mouse;
The stockings were hung by the
chimney with care,
In hopes that St. Nicholas soon
would be there. . . .

"Happy Christmas to all, and to
all a good-night!"
A Visit from St. Nicholas

Edward Moore
[1712-1757]

[y] Can't I another's face com-
mend,
And to her virtues be a friend,
But instantly your forehead
lowers,
As if *her* merit lessen'd *yours?*
*The Farmer, the Spaniel, and
The Cat*

[z] Time still, as he flies, brings
increase to her truth,
And gives to her mind what he
steals from her youth.
The Happy Marriage

Frank Frankfort Moore
[1855-1931]

[a] He knew that to offer a man
friendship when love is in his
heart is like giving a loaf of bread
to one who is dying of thirst.
The Jessamy Bride. Chap. 9

[b] Happy it is for mankind that
Heaven has laid on few men the
curse of being poets.
Ibid. Chap 18

[c] Destiny has more resources
than the most imaginative com-
poser of fiction.
Ibid. Chap. 22

George Moore
[1852-1933]

[d] After all there is but one race
—humanity.   *The Bending
of the Bough. Act III*

[e] The difficulty in life is the
choice.   *Ibid. Act IV*

[f] The wrong way always seems
the more reasonable.   *Ibid.*

[g] English, Scotchmen, Jews, do
well in Ireland—Irishmen never;
even the patriot has to leave Ireland to get a hearing.
Ave. Overture

[h] Within the oftentimes bom-
bastic and truculent appearance
that I present to the world,
trembles a heart shy as a wren
in the hedgerow or a mouse along
the wainscoting.
Ibid. Chap. 2

[i] My one claim to originality
among Irishmen is that I have
never made a speech.
Ibid. Chap. 4

[j] A man travels the world over
in search of what he needs and
returns home to find it.
The Brook Kerith. Chap. 11

John Trotwood Moore
[1858-1929]

[k] Only the game fish swims up
stream.   *The Unafraid*

[l] I sing softly to myse'f dat good
ole hymn, sung by Moses an' de
profets so long ergo:
"Baptis', Baptis' is my name,
I'm Baptis' till I die.
I've been baptized in de Baptis'
church,
Gwin' ter eat all de Baptis' pie!"
*Old Mistis. How the Bishop
Broke the Record*

Julia A. Moore
[1847-1920]

[m] "Lord Byron" was an Eng-
lishman
A poet I believe,
His first works in old England
Was poorly received.
Perhaps it was "Lord Byron's"
fault
And perhaps it was not.
His life was full of misfortunes,
Ah, strange was his lot.
*Sketch of Lord Byron's Life.
Stanza 1*

Marianne Moore
[1887-   ]

[n] Denunciations do not affect
the culprit; nor blows, but it
is torture to him to not be spoken
to.
Spenser's Ireland. Stanza 1

[o] They're fighting that I
may yet recover from the disease,
myself; some have it lightly, some
will die.
In Distrust of Merits. Stanza 3

[p] There never was a war that
was not inward; I must
fight till I have conquered in myself what
causes war, but I would not believe it.
I inwardly did nothing.
O Iscariotlike crime!
Beauty is everlasting
And dust is for a time.
Ibid. Stanza 8

Merrill Moore
[1903-   ]

[q] Talking about men who are
richer than they are
And telling how things that are
might be otherwise
And looking out of the corners of
their eyes
Are what old men inordinately
like to do,
Men not so old that they have lost
all care
For matters they used to pride
themselves about

But certainly long since past the finding out
Of whether these matters were or were not true.　　*Old Men*

[r] Water has sunk more griev-ances than wine
And will continue to. Turn the water on;
Stick your hand in the stream; water will run
And kiss it like a dog, or it will shake
It like a friend, or it will tremble there
Like a woman sobbing with her hair
Falling in her face.
　　Hymn for Water. Stanza 2

[s] The noise that Time makes.
　　M. 1000 Sonnets

[t] You can notice peculiarities
In the motions of the people's eyes
In and near to public libraries.
Men and women go there to sit and read
But they squirm and rove, survey each other
Not as sister, quite, and not as brother,
But more with nervous desire or anxious dread.
　　Anxious Eyes in Libraries

Thomas Moore
[1780–1852]

[u] I knew by the smoke, that so gracefully curl'd
Above the green elms, that a cottage was near;
And I said, "If there's peace to be found in the world,
A heart that was humble might hope for it here!"
　　Ballad Stanzas. 1

[v] They made her a grave, too cold and damp
For a soul so warm and true;
And she's gone to the Lake of the Dismal Swamp,
Where, all night long, by a firefly lamp,
She paddles her white canoe.
　　The Lake of the Dismal Swamp.
　　　　Stanza 1

[w] Faintly as tolls the evening chime,
Our voices keep tune and our oars keep time.
　　A Canadian Boat-Song. Stanza 1

[x] The minds of some of our statesmen, like the pupil of the human eye, contract themselves the more, the stronger light there is shed upon them.　　*Preface*
　　to Corruption and Intolerance

[y]　　Young Love may go,
　　　　For aught I care,
　　　　To Jericho!
　　When Love is Kind. Stanza 6

[z] Go where glory waits thee!
But while fame elates thee,
Oh, still remember me!
　　Go Where Glory Waits Thee.
　　　　Stanza 1

[a] And the tear that we shed, though in secret it rolls,
Shall long keep his memory green in our souls.　　*Oh Breathe*
　　Not His Name. Stanza 2

[b] The harp that once through Tara's halls
The soul of music shed,
Now hangs as mute on Tara's walls
As if that soul were fled.
So sleeps the pride of former days,
So glory's thrill is o'er;
And hearts that once beat high for praise
Now feel that pulse no more.
　　The Harp That Once Through
　　　　Tara's Halls. Stanza 1

[c] Whose wit in the combat, as gentle as bright,
Ne'er carried a heart-stain on its blade.　　*On the Death*
　　　　of Sheridan. Stanza 11

[d] Fly not yet,—'tis just the hour,
When pleasure, like the midnight flower
That scorns the eye of vulgar light,
Begins to bloom for sons of night,
And maids who love the moon.
　　Fly Not Yet. Stanza 1

[e] Come, send round the wine, and leave points of belief
To simpleton sages, and reason-ing fools.　　*Come, Send*
　　Round the Wine. Stanza 1

[f]　　Beauty lies
　　　　In many eyes,
But Love in yours, my Nora Creina.　　*Lesbia Hath a*
　　Beaming Eye. Stanza 1

[g] What though youth gave love and roses,
Age still leaves us friends and wine.
　　Spring and Autumn. Stanza 1

[h] No, the heart that has truly lov'd never forgets,
But as truly loves on to the close;
As the sunflower turns on her god, when he sets,
The same look which she turn'd when he rose.
　　Believe Me, if All Those Endear-
　　ing Young Charms. Stanza 2

[i]　　The moon looks
　　　　On many brooks,
"The brook can see no moon but this."　　*When Gazing on the*
　　Moon's Light. Stanza 2

[j] 'Tis sweet to think, that,
    where'er we rove,
We are sure to find something
    blissful and dear;
And that when we're far from the
    lips we love,
We've but to make love to the
    lips we are near.
    'Tis Sweet to Think. Stanza 1

[k] Give smiles to those who love
    you less,
But keep your tears for me.
    *When Midst the Gay I Meet.
    Stanza 1*

[l] 'Tis believ'd that this harp
    which I wake now for thee
Was a siren of old who sung under
    the sea.
    The Origin of the Harp

[m] 'Tis the last rose of summer.
Left blooming alone.
    *The Last Rose of Summer.
    Stanza 1*

[n]   And the best of all ways
        To lengthen our days
Is to steal a few hours from the
    night, my dear.   *The Young
    May Moon. Stanza 1*

[o] You may break, you may
    shatter the vase if you will,
But the scent of the roses will
    hang round it still.   *Ibid.*

[p] The light that lies
In woman's eyes.   *The Time
I've Lost in Wooing. Stanza 1*

[q]   My only books
        Were woman's looks,
And folly's all they've taught me.
    Ibid.

[r] Oft in the stilly night,
    Ere slumber's chain has bound
    me,
Fond memory brings the light
    Of other days around me;
        The smiles, the tears,
        Of boyhood's years,
The words of love then spoken;
    The eyes that shone
    Now dimmed and gone,
The cheerful hearts now broken.
    Oft in the Stilly Night. Stanza 1

[s] As half in shade and half in
    sun
    This world along its path ad-
    vances,
May that side the sun's upon
    Be all that e'er shall meet thy
    glances!   *Peace Be
        Around Thee. Stanza 2*

[t] If I speak to thee in friend-
    ship's name,
    Thou think'st I speak too
    coldly;
If I mention love's devoted flame,
    Thou say'st I speak too boldly.
    How Shall I Woo? Stanza 1

[u] This world is all a fleeting
    show,
    For man's illusion given;

The smiles of joy, the tears of woe,
    Deceitful shine, deceitful flow,—
    There's nothing true but
    Heaven.   *This World is All
        a Fleeting Show. Stanza 1*

[v] Who has not felt how sadly
    sweet
The dream of home, the dream
    of home,
Steals o'er the heart, too soon to
    fleet,
    When far o'er sea or land we
    roam?
    The Dream of Home. Stanza 1

[w] Ask a woman's advice, and,
    whate'er she advise,
Do the very reverse and you're
    sure to be wise.   *How to
Make a Good Politician. Stanza 1*

[x] How oft we sigh
When histories charm to think
    that histories lie!
    The Sceptic

[y] That best of fame, a rival's
    praise.
    Rhymes of the Road. XV

[z] If thou would'st have me sing
    and play
As once I play'd and sung,
First take this time-worn lute
    away,
    And bring one freshly strung.
    *If Thou Would'st Have Me Sing
        and Play. Stanza 1*

[a] And from the lips of Truth
    one mighty breath
Shall like a whirlwind scatter in
    its breeze
That whole dark pile of human
    mockeries:—
Then shall the reign of mind com-
    mence on earth,
And starting fresh as from a sec-
    ond birth,
Man in the sunshine of the
    world's new spring
Shall walk transparent like some
    holy thing!
    *Lalla Rookh. The Veiled Prophet
        of Khorassan, Part I*

[b] The heaven of each is but
    what each desires.   *Ibid.*

[c] This narrow isthmus 'twixt
    two boundless seas,
The past, the future,—two eter-
    nities!   *Ibid. Part II*

[d] Oh! ever thus, from child-
    hood's hour,
    I've seen my fondest hope de-
    cay;
I never loved a tree or flower,
    But 'twas the first to fade away.
I never nurs'd a dear gazelle
    To glad me with its soft black
    eye,
But when it came to know me well
    And love me it was sure to die.
    Ibid. Part V, the Fire-Worshippers

[e] Alas! how light a cause may
      move
Dissension between hearts that
      love!
Hearts that the world in vain had
      tried,
And sorrow but more closely tied;
That stood the storm when waves
      were rough
Yet in a sunny hour fall off,
Like ships that have gone down
      at sea
When heaven was all tranquillity.
    *Ibid. Part VIII, The Light of
                the Haram*

[f] Humility, that low, sweet root
From which all heavenly virtues
      shoot.   *The Loves of the
      Angels. Third Angel's Story*

Michael Moran
[1794–1846]

[g] In Egypt's land, contagious
      to the Nile,
King Pharaoh's daughter went to
      bathe in style.
She tuk her dip, then walked unto
      the land,
To dry her royal pelt she ran
      along the strand.
A bulrush tripped her, whereupon
      she saw
A smiling babby in a wad o' straw.
She tuk it up, and said with ac-
      cents mild,
"Tare-and-agers, girls, which av
      yez owns the child?"
    *His parody of his poem, Moses.
    Quoted by W. B. Yeats in his
    essay, The Last Gleeman*

Hannah More
[1745–1833]

[h] To those who know thee not,
      no words can paint!
And those who know thee, know
      all words are faint!
                    Sensibility

[i] In men this blunder still you
      find,—
All think their little set mankind.
              Florio and His Friend

[j] Small habits well pursued be-
      times
May reach the dignity of crimes.
                          Ibid.

[k] Some phrase that with the
      public took
Was all he read of any book.
                          Ibid.

Paul Elmer More
[1864–1937]

[l] Great music is a psychical
storm, agitating to fathomless
depths the mystery of the past
within us. Or we might say that
it is a prodigious incantation. . . .

Well may the influence of music
seem inexplicable to the man who
idly dreams that his life began
less than a hundred years ago! He
who has been initiated into the
truth knows that to every ripple
of melody, to every billow of harmony, there answers within him,
out of the Sea of Death and Birth,
some eddying immeasurable of
ancient pleasure and pain.
    Shelburne Essays. Lafcadio Hearn

[m] All things are fleeting; nothing is our own, not even this
spark of life which is owed to
Death; but Oh, grant that after
our going some interposition of
human memory come between us
and utter obliteration!
    Ibid. The Greek Anthology

Sir Thomas More
[1478–1535]

[n] The Utopians wonder how
any man should be so much taken
with the glaring doubtful lustre
of a jewel or stone, that can look
up to a star, or to the sun himself.
    Utopia: Of Jewels and Wealth

[o] They have no lawyers among
them, for they consider them as a
sort of people whose profession it
is to disguise matters.
    Ibid. Of Law and Magistrates

[p] Assist me up, and in coming
down I will shift for myself.
    *Said at the scaffold, on the way
                    to execution*

[q] Wait till I put aside my beard,
for that never committed treason.
    To the headsman on the scaffold

John Richard Moreland
[1880–   ]

[r] Remember April
With its swords of jade on a thou-
      sand hills.
                Ye Who Fear Death

Angela Morgan

[s] Work!
Thank God for the swing of it,
For the clamoring, hammering
      ring of it,
Passion of labor daily hurled
On the mighty anvils of the world.
    Work: A Song of Triumph

Charles Langbridge Morgan
[1894–   ]

[t] The art of living does not
consist in preserving and clinging
to a particular mood of happiness,
but in allowing happiness to
change its form without being disappointed by the change; for hap-

piness, like a child, must be allowed to grow up. *An English Retrospect [Menander's Mirror, Times Literary Supplement, London, May 20, 1944.]*

Christopher Morley
[1890–   ]

[**u**] And of all man's felicities
The very subtlest one, say I,
Is when for the first time he sees
His hearthfire smoke against the
sky. *A Hallowe'en Memory. Stanza 5*

[**v**] Heaven is not built of country seats,
But little queer suburban streets.
To the Little House. Stanza 4

[**w**] The man who never in his
life
Has washed the dishes with his
wife
Or polished up the silver plate—
He still is largely celibate.
Washing the Dishes. Stanza 4

[**x**] The greatest poem ever
known
Is one all poets have outgrown:
The poetry, innate, untold,
Of being only four years old.
To a Child

[**y**] Unhappy lovers always should
be Frenchmen,
So sweet a tongue for any kind of
pain! *Toulemonde. III*

[**z**] Women all
Raiment themselves most brightly
for the dark
Which is, on information and belief,
Their true dominion. *Ibid. VI*

[**a**] When you sell a man a book
you don't sell him just twelve
ounces of paper and ink and glue
—you sell him a whole new life.
Parnassus on Wheels. Chap. 4

[**b**] That faint but sensitive enteric expectancy which suggests
the desirability of a cocktail. . . .
A drink has been arranged and
will shortly take place. *Swiss Family Manhattan. Chap. 9*

[**c**] A human being: an ingenious
assembly of portable plumbing.
Human Being. Chap. 11

[**d**] He is too experienced a parent
ever to make positive promises.
Thunder on the Left. Chap. 5

[**e**] Life is a foreign language: all
men mispronounce it.
Ibid. Chap. 14

[**f**] Poetry comes with anger,
hunger and dismay; it does not
often visit groups of citizens sitting down to be literary together,
and would appal them if it did.
John Mistletoe. 7

[**g**] April prepares her green traffic light and the world thinks Go.
Ibid. 8

[**h**] Dancing is wonderful training for girls, it's the first way you
learn to guess what a man is going
to do before he does it.
Kitty Foyle. Chap. 11

[**i**] The evening papers print
what they do and get away with it
because by afternoon the human
mind is ruined anyhow.
Ibid. Chap. 25

[**j**] New York, the nation's thyroid gland. *Shore Leave*

[**k**] Truth, like milk, arrives in
the dark
But even so, wise dogs don't bark.
Only mongrels make it hard
For the milkman to come up the
yard. *Dogs Don't Bark at the Milkman*

[**l**] Since men learned print, no
night is wholly black.
The Watchman's Sonnet

[**m**] All joys I bless, but I confess
There is one greatest thrill:
What the dentist does when he
stops the buzz
And puts away the drill.
Song in a Dentist's Chair. Stanza 1

[**n**] Chattering voltage like a
broken wire
The wild cicada cried, Six weeks to
frost! *End of August*

[**o**] Why do they put the Gideon
Bibles only in the bedrooms,
where it's usually too late, and
not in the barroom downstairs?
Contribution to a Contribution

John, Viscount Morley
[1838–1923]

[**p**] Evolution is not a force but a
process; not a cause but a law.
On Compromise

[**q**] It is not enough to do good;
one must do it the right way.
Ibid.

[**r**] You have not converted a
man because you have silenced
him. *Ibid.*

[**s**] The great business of life is
to be, to do, to do without, and to
depart. *Address on Aphorisms*

[**t**] Those who would treat politics
and morality apart will never understand the one or the other.
Rousseau

[**u'**] The most frightful idea that
has ever corroded human nature
—the idea of eternal punishment.
Vauvenargues

[v] Where it is a duty to worship the sun it is pretty sure to be a crime to examine the laws of heat.
Voltaire

[w] Simplicity of character is no hindrance to subtlety of intellect.
Life of Gladstone

[x] The proper memory for a politician is one that knows what to remember and what to forget.
Recollections. Vol. II, Book 4, Chap. 2

[y] Success depends on three things: who says it, what he says, how he says it; and of these three things, what he says is the least important. *Ibid. Book 5, Chap. 4*

George Pope Morris
[1802–1864]

[z] Woodman, spare that tree!
Touch not a single bough!
In youth it sheltered me,
And I'll protect it now.
Woodman, Spare that Tree. Stanza 1 [1830] [The tree for which Morris pleaded stood just about where is now the crossing of 98th Street and West End Avenue, New York City]

[a] The union of lakes, the union of lands,
The union of States none can sever,
The union of hearts, the union of hands,
And the flag of our Union forever!
The Flag of Our Union. Refrain

[b] The land of the heart is the land of the West.
The West. Stanza 1 (In Littell's Magazine, April 5, 1851)

[c] In other countries, when I heard
The language of my own,
How fondly each familiar word
Awoke an answering tone.
I'm With You Once Again. Stanza 3

[d] 'Tis ever thus, when in life's storm
Hope's star to man grows dim,
An angel kneels, in woman's form,
And breathes a prayer for him.
Pocahontas. Stanza 3

William Morris
[1834–1896]

[e] Dreamer of dreams, born out of my due time,
Why should I strive to set the crooked straight?
The Earthly Paradise. An Apology, Stanza 4

[f] Love is enough, though the world be a-waning.
Love Is Enough

M. T. Morrison
[*Circa* 1840– ?]

[g] A foolish little maiden bought a foolish little bonnet,
With a ribbon and a feather and a bit of lace upon it;
And that all the other maidens in the little town might know it,
She thought she'd go to meeting the next Sunday, just to show it.

"Alleluia, Alleluia!" sang the choir above her head;
"Hardly knew you, hardly knew you!" were the words she thought they said.
What the Choir Sang about the New Bonnet. Stanzas 1 and 3

Elizabeth Cutter (Mrs. Dwight Whitney) Morrow
[1873–]

[h] My friend and I have built a wall
Between us thick and wide:
The stones of it are laid in scorn
And plastered high with pride.
Wall. Stanza 1

[i] He who has given
A hostage knows
All ways of dying
Terror shows.
Hostage

David Morton
[1886–]

[j] Corridors, like windy tulip beds,
Of swaying girls and lifted, tossing heads. *In a Girls' School*

[k] Who walks with Beauty has no need of fear.
Who Walks With Beauty

[l] My faith is all a doubtful thing,
Wove on a doubtful loom,—
Until there comes, each showery spring,
A cherry-tree in bloom.
Symbol

[m] They are remembering forests where they grew—
The midnight quiet and the giant dance;
And all the murmuring summers that they knew
Are haunting still their altered circumstance.
Sonnet. Wooden Ships

Henry Vollam Morton
[1892–]

[n] One drink of wine, and you act like a monkey; two drinks, and you strut like a peacock; three

drinks, and you roar like a lion; and four drinks—you behave like a pig. *In the Steps of St. Paul. Chap. 1*

[o] A nobleman of . . . Parara in Asia Minor had lost all his money, and did not know how he could endow his three beautiful daughters, St. Nicholas, hearing of his trouble, went by night and flung through the window three bags of gold with which the nobleman was able to provide handsome dowries. These three bags are shown in all early ikons as three gold apples, and the gold apples of St. Nicholas are the origin of the pawnbroker's sign. *Ibid. Chap. 7*

Thomas Morton
[1764–1838]

[p] What will Mrs. Grundy say? What will Mrs. Grundy think? *Speed the Plough. Act I, Sc. 1*

Louise Chandler Moulton
[1835–1908]

[q] I hied me off to Arcady
The month it was the month of May,
And all along the pleasant way,
The morning birds were mad with glee,
And all the flowers sprang up to see,
As I went on to Arcady.
The Secret of Arcady

James Hilary Mulligan
[1844–1916]

[r] Songbirds are sweetest, in Kentucky,
Thoroughbreds the fleetest, in Kentucky;
The mountains tower proudest,
Thunder peals the loudest,
The landscape is the grandest,
And politics the damnedest,
In Kentucky.
In Kentucky. Stanza 7

Helene Mullins
[1899–   ]

[s] Only the stern self-confident can hold
Their peace amidst the clamor, nor betray
Their capabilities; can sit unmoved,
With all around them trembling to have told
The utmost of their merits; only they
Can bear to leave their strength unguessed, unproved.
Only the Self-Confident

Lewis Mumford
[1895–   ]

[t] People have hesitated to call Whitman's poems poetry; it is useless to deny that they belong to sacred literature.
The Golden Day. V

[u] The jolly and comfortable bourgeois tradition of the Victorian age, a state of mind composed of felt slippers and warm bellywash. *Ibid. VIII*

Arthur Joseph Munby
[1828–1910]

[v] Thou art my own, my darling, and my wife;
And when we pass into another life,
Still thou art mine. All this which now we see
Is but the childhood of Eternity.
Marriage

Hector Hugh Munro ("Saki")
[1870–1916]

[w] She took to telling the truth; she said she was forty-two and five months. It may have been pleasing to the angels, but her elder sister was not gratified.
Reginald. Reginald on Besetting Sins

[x] The cook was a good cook, as cooks go; and as cooks go she went. *Ibid.*

[y] The sacrifices of friendship were beautiful in her eyes as long as she was not asked to make them.
Beasts and Super-Beasts. Fur

[z] In baiting a mouse-trap with cheese, always leave room for the mouse. *The Square Egg. The Infernal Parliament*

[a] Confront a child, a puppy, and a kitten with a sudden danger; the child will turn instinctively for assistance, the puppy will grovel in abject submission, the kitten will brace its tiny body for a frantic resistance.
Ibid. The Achievement of the Cat

[b] A little inaccuracy sometimes saves tons of explanation. *Ibid. The Comments of Moung Ka*

[c] "It was their Silver Wedding; such lots of silver presents, quite a show."
"We must not grudge them their show of presents after twenty-five years of married life; it is the silver lining to their cloud."
The Unbearable Bassington

Axel Munthe
[1857–1949]

[d] It will be lonely to be dead, but it cannot be much more lonely than to be alive. *The Story of San Michele: Instead of a Preface*

Gilbert Murray
[1866–]

[e] Romantic plays with happy endings are almost of necessity inferior in artistic value to true tragedies. Not, one would hope, simply because they end happily; happiness in itself is certainly not less beautiful than grief; but because a tragedy in its great moments can generally afford to be sincere, while romantic plays live in an atmosphere of ingenuity and make-believe. *Preface to The Iphigenia in Tauris of Euripides*

[f] The life and liberty and property and happiness of the common man throughout the world are at the absolute mercy of a few persons whom he has never seen, involved in complicated quarrels that he has never heard of. *The League of Nations and the Democratic Idea.* [1921]

William Henry Harrison ("Adirondack") Murray
[1840–1904]

[g] Strong hands to weak, old hands to young, around the Christmas board, touch hands.
The false forget, the foe forgive, for every guest will go and every fire burn low and cabin empty stand.
Forget, forgive, for who may say that Christmas day may ever come to host or guest again.
Touch hands!
John Norton's Vagabond

Alfred de Musset
[1810–1857]

[h] How glorious it is—and also how painful—to be an exception. *The White Blackbird. I*

[i] Things they don't understand always cause a sensation among the English. *Ibid. VIII*

Benito Mussolini
[1883–1945]

[j] Italians, love bread, heart of the home, savor of the repast, joy of health;
Respect bread, sweat of the brow, pride of labor, poem of sacrifice;

Honor bread, glory of the fields, fragrance of the earth, feast of life;
Do not waste bread, richness of the fatherland, sweetest gift of God, most holy reward of human toil.
Proclamation [*April 14–15, 1928*]

[k] Three cheers for war in general! *Speech* [*Quoted in George Seldes's Sawdust Caesar*].

[l] Have you ever seen a lamb become a wolf? The Italian race is a race of sheep. Eighteen years are not enough to change them. It takes a hundred and eighty, and maybe a hundred and eighty centuries.
Quoted in The Ciano Diaries [*January 29, 1940*]. *Page 202*

[m] It is humiliating to remain with our hands folded while others write history. It matters little who wins. To make a people great it is necessary to send them to battle even if you have to kick them in the pants. This is what I shall do.
Ibid. [*April 11, 1940*]. *Page 236*

Mutsuhito, Emperor of Japan
[1852–1912]

[n] Be ever careful in your choice of friends,
And let your special love be given to those
Whose strength of character may prove the whip
That drives you ever to fair Wisdom's goal.
Wisdom's Goal (*tr. Arthur Lloyd*)

Frederic William Henry Myers
[1843–1901]

[o] But though the blast is frantic,
And though the tempest raves,
The deep immense Atlantic
It still beneath the waves.
Wind, Moon, and Tides

[p] Coldly sublime, intolerably just. *Saint Paul*

q] In no single act or passion can salvation stand; far hence, beyond Orion and Andromeda, the cosmic process works and shall work forever through unbegotten souls. *Human Personality. Chap. 10*

Gustave Nadaud
[1820–1893]

[r] I'm growing old, I've sixty years;
I've labored all my life in vain.

In all that time of hopes and
fears,
I've failed my dearest wish to
gain.
I see full well that here below
Bliss unalloyed there is for
none,
My prayer would else fulfilment
know—
Never have I seen Carcassonne!
　　*Carcassonne (tr. John R.
　　Thompson). Stanza 1*

[s] They tell me every day is there
Not more nor less than Sunday
gay.　　*Ibid. Stanza 3*

Lord Nancy

[t] To have a thing is nothing, if
you've not the chance to
show it,
And to know a thing is nothing,
unless others know you know
it.　　*Source unknown*

Napoleon I
see Bonaparte, Napoleon

Ogden Nash
[1902-   ]

[u] They have such refined and
delicate palates
That they can discover no one
worthy of their ballots,
And then when some one terrible
gets elected
They say, There, that's just what I
expected!
　　Election Day Is a Holiday

[v] I think that I shall never see
A billboard lovely as a tree.
Perhaps, unless the billboards
fall,
I'll never see a tree at all.
　　Song of the Open Road

[w] The season when ordinarily
kindhearted business men fill
up their pockets with car-
tridges
And go prowling around the woods
in search of caribous and
partridges.
　　Ode to the N.W. by W. Wind

[x] In the phalanx of hy-
Phenated names!
(Have you ever observed
That the name of Smith
Is the oftenest hy-
Phenated with?)
　　Pride Goeth Before a Raise

[y] There are some people who
are very resourceful
At being remorseful,
And who apparently feel that the
best way to make friends
Is to do something terrible and
then make amends.
　　Hearts of Gold

[z] Candy is dandy
But liquor is quicker.
　　Reflection on Ice-Breaking

[a] Some one invented the tele-
phone,
And interrupted a nation's slumbers,
Ringing wrong but similar numbers.
　　Look What You Did, Christopher

[b] One would be in less danger
From the wiles of the stranger
If one's own kin and kith
Were more fun to be with.
　　Family Court

[c] O money, money, money, I
am not necessarily one of
those who think thee holy,
But I often stop to wonder how
thou canst go out so fast when
thou comest in so slowly.
　　*Hymn to the Thing That
　　Makes the Wolf Go*

[d] There is only one way to
achieve happiness on this terrestrial ball,
And that is to have either a clear
conscience, or none at all.
　　Inter-Office Memorandum

[e] The old men know when an
old man dies.　　*Old Men*

[f] God rest you, merry Inno-
cents,
While innocence endures.
A sweeter Christmas than we to
ours
May you bequeath to yours.
　　A Carol for Children. Stanza 9

[g] I love the Baby Giant Panda;
I'd welcome one to my veranda.
　　The Panda

[h] Thanksgiving, like ambassadors, cabinet-officers and
others smeared with political
ointment,
Depends for its existence on
Presidential appointment.
　　A Short Outline of Thanksgiving

[i] Sleep is perverse as human
nature,
Sleep is perverse as a legisla-
ture. . . .
So people who go to bed to sleep
Must count French premiers or
sheep,
And people who ought to arise
from bed
Yawn and go back to sleep in-
stead.
　　Read This Vibrant Exposé

[j] Home is heaven and orgies are
vile,
But I like an orgy, once in a while.
　　Home, 99 44/100% Sweet Home

[k] So Columbus said, somebody
show me the sunset and somebody did and he set sail for it,
And he discovered America and
they put him in jail for it,

And the fetters gave him welts,
And they named America after
somebody else. *Columbus*

[l] Dogs display reluctance and
wrath
If you try to give them a bath.
They bury bones in hideaways
And half the time they trot side-
ways. *An Introduction
to Dogs. Stanza 4*

[m] There are two kinds of people
who blow through life like a
breeze,
And one kind is gossipers, and the
other kind is gossipees.
I Have It On Good Authority

[n] There is something about a
Martini,
A tingle remarkably pleasant;
A yellow, a mellow Martini;
I wish that I had one at present.
There is something about a Mar-
tini,
Ere the dining and dancing begin,
And to tell you the truth,
It is not the vermouth—
I think that perhaps it's the Gin.
*A Drink With Something
In It. Stanza 1*

Thomas Nash
[1567–1601]

[o] Spring, the sweet spring, is
the year's pleasant king;
Then blooms each thing, then
maids dance in a ring,
Cold doth not sting, the pretty
birds do sing. *Spring*

George Jean Nathan
(Mencken and Nathan)
[1882–]

[p] That all one has to do to
gather a large crowd in New York
is to stand on the curb a few moments and gaze intently at the
sky. *American Credo [1920]*

[q] That the postmasters in
small towns read all the postcards.
Ibid.

[r] That, when shaving on a railway train, a man invariably cuts
himself. *Ibid.*

[s] That the quality of the cham-
pagne may be judged by the
amount of noise the cork makes
when it is popped. *Ibid.*

[t] That all French women are
very passionate, and will sacrifice
everything to love. *Ibid.*

[u] That beer is very fattening.
Ibid.

Robert Nathan
[1894–]

[v] Love hath no physic for a
grief too deep.
A Cedar Box. Sonnet V

[w] True sorrow makes a silence
in the heart
Joy has its friends, but grief
its loneliness.
Ibid. Sonnet VII

[x] Bells in the country,
They sing the heart to rest
When night is on the high road
And day is in the west.
Bells in the Country

[y] Toward men and toward God,
she maintained a respectful atti-
tude, lightened by the belief that
in a crisis she could deal ade-
quately with either of them.
The Road of Ages. Chap. 2

James Ball Naylor
[1860–1945]

[z] King David and King Solomon
Led merry, merry lives,
With many, many lady friends
And many, many wives;
But when old age crept over
them—
With many, many qualms,
King Solomon wrote the Proverbs
And King David wrote the
Psalms. *Ancient Authors*

John Mason Neale
[1818–1866]

[a] Good King Wenceslas looked
out
On the Feast of Stephen,
When the snow lay round about,
Deep and crisp and even.
Good King Wenceslas

[b] Bring me flesh and bring me
wine,
Bring me pine-logs hither.
Ibid.

[c] Jerusalem the golden, with
milk and honey blest,
Beneath thy contemplation sink
heart and voice oppressed.
*Hymn (paraphrased from the
Latin of Bernard de Cluny)*

Meir Ben Isaac Neherai
[*Circa* 1050]

[d] Could we with ink the ocean
fill,
Were every blade of grass a quill,
Were the world of parchment
made,
And every man a scribe by trade,
To write the love
Of God above
Would drain the ocean dry;
Nor would the scroll
Contain the whole,
Though stretched from sky to sky.
*A Book of Jewish Thoughts
Selected for the Sailors and
Soldiers of England*

John Gneisenau Neihardt .
[1881–   ]

[e] Let me live out my years in
   heat of blood!
Let me die drunken with the
   dreamer's wine!
Let me not see this soul-house
   built of mud
Go toppling to the dust—a vacant
   shrine! . . .
Give me high noon—and let it
   then be night!
       Let Me Live Out My Years

[f] Glowing through the gray
   rack
Breaks the Day—
Like a burning haystack
Twenty farms away!
       Break of Day. Stanza 13

Horatio Nelson
[1758–1805]

[g] England expects every man
to do his duty.
       Southey's Life of Nelson.
       Vol. II, Page 131

[h] May the great God, whom I
worship, grant to my country and
for the benefit of Europe in general, a great and glorious victory,
and may no misconduct in anyone tarnish it, and may humanity
after the victory be the predomi-
nant feature in the British fleet.
       Prayer written in his diary
       [October 21, 1805]

Cornelius Nepos
[*Floruit* 75 B.C.]

[i] More brawn than brain.
   Epaminondas. Chap. V, Line 21

Wilbur Dick Nesbit
[1871–1927]

[j] The little children who grieve
   on Christmas Day
Are not in huts and hovels a thousand miles away—
They are so near they hear us, our
   laughter and our song,
And all the joys we have to-day
   serve to make great the wrong.
   The Unseen Tragedy. Stanza 3

[k] Who waits upon the when
   and how
Remains forever in the rear.
   A Plea for the Friendless
       Present. Stanza 4

[l] Who hath a book
   Has friends at hand,
And gold and gear
   At his command;
And rich estates,
   If he but look,
Are held by him
   Who hath a book.
   Who Hath a Book. Stanza 1

[m] Each page of them Quotations that this Bartlett man
   got out
Is sure to have old Ibid's prose or
   poems strung about;
There isn't any subject an' there
   isn't any style
That Ibid isn't good in; he can
   make you sigh or smile.
I'm gettin' so, when I read things
   particularly fine,
I know that Ibid's name will be
   below the endin' line.
       "Old Ibid." Stanza 2

Richard Lewis Nettleship
[1846–1892]

[n] It is literally true that this
world *is* everything to us, if only
we choose to make it so, if only we
"live in the present" *because* it is
eternity.
       Lectures and Memories. I, 72

Herman Neuman
[1806–1875]

[o] Two chambers has the heart,
Wherein dwell Joy and Sorrow;
When Joy awakes in one,
Then slumbers Sorrow in the
   other.
O Joy, take care!
Speak softly,
Lest you awaken Sorrow.
       The Heart

Sir Henry Newbolt
[1862–1938]

[p] To set the cause above re-
   nown,
To love the game beyond the
   prize,
To honor, while you strike him
   down,
The foe that comes with fearless
   eyes;
To count the life of battle good
   And dear the land that gave you
   birth,
And dearer yet the brotherhood
   That binds the brave of all the
   earth.
       Clifton Chapel. Stanza 2

[q]   When the strong command
Obedience is best.
       A Ballad of John Nicholson

[r] Like a sun bewitched in alien
   realms of night,
Mellow and yellow and rounded
   hangs the moon.   *Moonset*

[s] April's anger is swift to fall,
April's wonder is worth it all.
       The Adventurers. Stanza 8

[t] Beyond the book his teaching
   sped,
He left on whom he taught the
   trace

Of kinship with the deathless
dead. *Ionicus*

[u] He's sailed in a hundred
builds o' boat,
He's fought in a thousand kinds o'
coat,
He's the senior flag of all that
float,
And his name's Admiral Death.
Admiral Death

John Henry, Cardinal
Newman
[1801–1890]

[v] Time hath a taming hand.
Persecution. Stanza 3

[w] Lead, kindly Light, amid the
encircling gloom;
Lead thou me on!
The night is dark, and I am far
from home;
Lead thou me on!
Keep thou my feet: I do not ask to
see
The distant scene; one step
enough for me.
*The Pillar of the Cloud.
Stanza 1*

[x] Who lets his feelings run
In soft luxurious flow,
Shrinks when hard service must
be done,
And faints at every woe.
Flowers Without Fruit

[y] Living Nature, not dull Art
Shall plan my ways and rule my
heart.
Nature and Art. Stanza 12

[z] Growth is the only evidence
of life. *Dr. Scott, cited by
Cardinal Newman*

[a] It is almost a definition of a
gentleman to say he is one who
never inflicts pain. *Idea of a
University. The Man of the World*

[b] A great memory does not
make a philosopher, any more
than a dictionary can be called a
grammar. *Ibid. Knowledge in
Relation to Learning*

[c] Ex Umbris et Imaginibus in
Veritatem! (From shadows and
symbols into the truth.)
*Epitaph at Edgbaston, composed
by himself*

A. Edward Newton
[1864–1940]

[d] Young man, get a hobby;
preferably get two, one for indoors
and one for out; get a pair of
hobby-horses that can safely be
ridden in opposite directions.
*Amenities of Book-Collecting.
Chap. 1*

[e] Only when a man is safely
ensconced under six feet of earth,

with several tons of enlauding
granite upon his chest, is he in a
position to give advice with any
certainty, and then he is silent.
Ibid. Chap. 4

[f] I wish that some one would
give a course in how to live. It
can't be taught in the colleges:
that's perfectly obvious, for college professors don't know any
better than the rest of us.
*This Book-Collecting Game.
Chap. 10*

[g] Gilbert White discovered the
formula for complete happiness,
but he died before making the announcement, leaving it for me to
do so. It is to be very busy with the
unimportant. *Ibid.*

[h] I am by no means sure that
I've ever thought, and I'm not certain that I wish to; looking about
me, I see thinkers, and it does not
appear that they are any wiser or
better or happier than I.
A Magnificent Farce. Chap. 7

[i] I read for pleasure, mark you.
In general I like wedding bells at
the end of novels. "They married
and lived happily ever after"—
why not? it has been done.
A Great Victorian

Byron Rufus Newton
[1861–1938]

[j] Vulgar of manner, overfed,
Overdressed and underbred;
Heartless, Godless, hell's delight,
Rude by day and lewd by
night. . . .
Crazed with avarice, lust, and
rum,
New York, thy name's Delirium.
Owed to New York

Eddie Newton
and
T. Laurence Seiberg

[k] Casey Jones! Orders in his
hand.
Casey Jones! Mounted to the
cabin,
Took his farewell journey to that
promised land.
*Casey Jones [1900] (Adapted
from verses and melody by
Wallace Saunders)*

Sir Isaac Newton
[1642–1727]

[l] I do not know what I may appear to the world; but to myself I
seem to have been only like a boy
playing on the seashore, and di-
verting myself in now and then
finding a smoother pebble or a
prettier shell than ordinary, whilst

the great ocean of truth lay all undiscovered before me.
Brewster's Memoirs of Newton, Vol. II, Chap. 27

Friedrich Wilhelm Nietzsche
[1844–1900]

[m] Our destiny exercises its influence over us even when, as yet, we have not learned its nature: it is our future that lays down the law of our to-day.
Human, All Too Human (tr. Alexander Harvey).7

[n] Much more happiness is to be found in the world than gloomy eyes discover. *Ibid. 49*

[o] One must have a good memory to be able to keep the promises one makes. *Ibid. 59*

[p] How poor the human mind would be without vanity! It resembles a well stocked and ever renewed ware-emporium that attracts buyers of every class: they can find almost everything, have almost everything, provided they bring with them the right kind of money—admiration. *Ibid. 74*

[q] Man is a rope stretched between the animal and the Superman—a rope over an abyss.
Thus Spake Zarathustra (tr. Thomas Common). Prologue, Chap. 4

[r] No small art is it to sleep: it is necessary for that purpose to keep awake all day.
Ibid. Part I, Chap. 2

[s] This is hardest of all: to close the open hand out of love, and keep modest as a giver.
Ibid. Part II, Chap. 23

[t] Distrust all in whom the impulse to punish is powerful.
Ibid. Chap. 29

[u] Thoughts that come with doves' footsteps guide the world.
Ibid. Chap. 44

[v] Winter, a bad guest, sitteth with me at home; blue are my hands with his friendly handshaking.
Ibid. Part III, Chap. 50

[w] We ought to learn from the kine one thing: ruminating.
Ibid. Part IV, Chap. 68

[x] If ye would go up high, then use your own legs! Do not get yourselves *carried* aloft; do not seat yourselves on other people's backs and heads!
Ibid. Chap. 73, 10

[y] No one is such a liar as the indignant man. *Beyond Good and Evil (tr. Helen Zimmern). II, 26*

[z] In revenge and in love woman is more barbarous than man.
Ibid. IV, 139

[a] The thought of suicide is a great consolation: by means of it one gets successfully through many a bad night. *Ibid. 157*

[b] There are few pains so grievous as to have seen, divined, or experienced how an exceptional man has missed his way and deteriorated. *Ibid. V, 203*

[c] Blessed are the forgetful: for they get the better even of their blunders. *Ibid. VII, 217*

[d] Is not life a hundred times too short for us to bore ourselves? *Ibid. 227*

[e] The melancholia of everything completed! *Ibid. IX, 277*

[f] The broad effects which can be obtained by punishment in man and beast, are the increase of fear, the sharpening of the sense of cunning, the mastery of the desires; so it is that punishment tames man, but does not make him "better." *Genealogy of Morals (tr. Horace B. Samuel). Second Essay, Aphorism 15*

[g] The sick are the greatest danger for the healthy; it is not from the strongest that harm comes to the strong, but from the weakest.
Ibid. Third Essay, Aphorism 14

(The following translations by Anthony M. Ludovici)

[h] Contentment preserves one even from catching cold. Has a woman who knew that she was well dressed ever caught cold?— No, not even when she had scarcely a rag to her back.
The Twilight of the Idols. Maxims and Missiles, 25

[i] Without music life would be a mistake. *Ibid. 33*

[j] He who laughs best to-day, will also laugh last. *Ibid. 43*

[k] Two great European narcotics, alcohol and Christianity.
Ibid. Things the Germans Lack, 2

[l] Dancing in all its forms cannot be excluded from the curriculum of all noble education: dancing with the feet, with ideas, with words, and, need I add that one must also be able to dance with the pen? *Ibid. 7*

[m'] In the architectural structure, man's pride, man's triumph over gravitation, man's will to power, assume a visible form. Architecture is a sort of oratory of power by means of forms.
Ibid. Skirmishes in a War with the Age, 11

[n] If a man have a strong faith he can indulge in the luxury of scepticism. *Ibid. 12*

[o] The sick man is a parasite of society. In certain cases it is indecent to go on living. To continue to vegetate in a state of cowardly dependence upon doctors and special treatments, once the meaning of life, the right to life, has been lost, ought to be regarded with the greatest contempt by society. *Ibid. 36*

[p] God created woman. And boredom did indeed cease from that moment—but many other things ceased as well! Woman was God's *second* mistake.
The Antichrist. Aphorism 48

[q] I call Christianity the one great curse, the one enormous and innermost perversion, the one great instinct of revenge, for which no means are too venomous, too underhand, too underground and too petty,—I call it the one immortal blemish of mankind. *Ibid. Aphorism 62*

[r] Nothing on earth consumes a man more quickly than the passion of resentment. *Ecce Homo*

[s] Where one despises, one cannot wage war. Where one commands, where one sees something beneath one, one ought not to wage war. *Ibid.*

[t] No one can draw more out of things, books included, than he already knows. A man has no ears for that to which experience has given him no access. *Ibid.*

[u] I am not successful at being pompous, the most I can do is to appear embarrassed. *Ibid.*

[v] The Germans are like women, you can scarcely ever fathom their depths—they haven't any. *Ibid.*

[w] After coming in contact with a religious man, I always feel that I must wash my hands. *Ibid.*

[x] All prejudices may be traced back to the intestines. A sedentary life is the real sin against the Holy Ghost. *Ecce Homo (tr. Clifton P. Fadiman, Modern Library Edition).*

Chester William Nimitz
[1885–   ]

[y] A ship is always referred to as "she" because it costs so much to keep one in paint and powder.
Talk before the Society of Sponsors of the United States Navy [February 13, 1940]

Albert Jay Nock
[1873–1945]

[z] The mere vagrant lust of seeing things and going places.
A Journey Into Rabelais's France. Chap. 10

[a] Money does not pay for anything, never has, never will. It is an economic axiom as old as the hills that goods and services can be paid for only with goods and services; but twenty years ago this axiom vanished from everyone's reckoning, and has never reappeared. No one has seemed in the least aware that everything which is paid for must be paid for out of production, for there is no other source of payment.
Memoirs of a Superfluous Man. III, Chap. 13

[b] As sheer casual reading-matter, I still find the English dictionary the most interesting book in our language.
Ibid. IV, Chap. 1

Roden Berkeley Wriothesley Noel
[1834–1894]

[c] Ah! what if some unshamed iconoclast
Crumbling old fetish raiments of the past,
Rises from dead cerements the Christ at last?
What if men take to following where He leads,
Weary of mumbling Athanasian creeds? *The Red Flag*

Thomas Noel
[1799–1861]

[d] Let him push at the door,—in the chimney roar,
And rattle the window-pane;
Let him in at us spy with his icicle eye,
But he shall not entrance gain.
Old Winter. Stanza 5

Frank Norris
[1870–1902]

[e] He's the kind of man that gets up a reputation for being clever and artistic by running down the very one particular thing that every one likes, and cracking up some book or picture or play that no one has ever heard of. *The Pit. Chap. 2*

John Norris
[1657–1711]

[f] When after some delays, some dying strife,
The soul stands shivering on the ridge of life;

With what a dreadful curiosity
Does she launch out into the sea
  of vast eternity.
                    The Meditation

Caroline Elizabeth Sheridan Norton, Lady Maxwell
[1808–1877]

[g] I am listening for the voices
Which I heard in days of old.
                    The Lonely Harp

[h] A soldier of the Legion lay
    dying in Algiers;
There was lack of woman's nurs-
    ing, there was dearth of
    woman's tears.
  Bingen on the Rhine. Stanza 1

[i] O Twilight! Spirit that dost
    render birth
To dim enchantments; melting
    heaven with earth,
Leaving on craggy hills and run-
    ning streams
A softness like the atmosphere of
    dreams.   *The Winter's Walk*

Charles Eliot Norton
[1827–1908]

[j] It is perhaps the highest distinction of the Greeks that they
recognized the indissoluble connection of beauty and goodness.
  Fifth Annual Report [1883–84]
  of the Executive Committee of
  the Archaeological Institute of
  America. Page 28

[k] Is there a moral advance at
all in proportion to the material?
There is a wider diffusion of virtue, morality has become democratic, more men and women are
controlled by right principles, but
better men and even women than
there were two thousand years ago
are not easy to find.
  Letter to Samuel G. Ward
            [August 8, 1900]

[l] Whatever your occupation
may be and however crowded your
hours with affairs, do not fail to
secure at least a few minutes every
day for refreshment of your inner
life with a bit of poetry.
  Used by a Boston newspaper as
  a heading for a column of re-
  printed poems

Grace Fallow Norton
[1876–   ]

[m] O what shall give the land its
    men
If children fight its wars,
If youth to the market-place they
    bring,
And man his manhood mars
To give some king a golden ring,
Or his lords their gilded stars?
    Little Gray Songs from
          St. Joseph's. IX

Alfred Noyes
[1880–   ]

[n] There's a magic in the dis-
    tance, where the sea-line
    meets the sky.
  Forty Singing Seamen. Stanza 9

[o] Go down to Kew in lilac-time,
    in lilac-time, in lilac-time;
Go down to Kew in lilac-time
    (it isn't far from London!)
And you shall wander hand in
    hand with love in summer's
    wonderland;
Go down to Kew in lilac-time
    (it isn't far from London!)
                    Ibid. Stanza 5

[p] The red laugh of war.
    Love Will Find Out the Way

[q] England, my mother,
    Lift to my Western Sweet-
    heart
One full cup of English mead,
    breathing of the May!
Pledge the may-flower in her face
    that you and ah, none other,
    Sent her from the mother-
    land
    Across the dashing spray.
  America, My Sweetheart. Stanza
  1 (prologue to the American
  edition of Drake)

[r] The wind was a torrent of
    darkness among the gusty
    trees,
The moon was a ghostly galleon
    tossed upon cloudy seas,
The road was a ribbon of moon-
    light over the purple moor,
And the highwayman came riding
    —Riding—riding—
The highwayman came riding, up
    to the old inn-door.
  The Highwayman. I, Stanza 1

[s] God how the dead men
    Grin by the wall,
Watching the fun
    Of the Victory Ball.
    A Victory Dance. Stanza 9

[t] What will you say when the
    world is dying?
What, when the last wild mid-
    night falls
Dark, too dark for the bat to be
    flying
    Round the ruins of old St.
    Paul's?
  Tales of the Mermaid Tavern:
          The Little Red Ring

[u]   Each new grain of truth
Is packed, like radium, with whole
    worlds of light.
    The Torch-Bearers: Epilogue

[v] So the world shall sing of
    them—the white cliffs of Eng-
    land,
White, the glory of her sails, the
    banner of her pride.
    The White Cliffs. Stanza 4

Fitz-James O'Brien
[1828–1862]

[w] I know a lake where the cool
  waves break
  And softly fall on the silver
  sand. *Loch Ine. Stanza 1*

[x] And so the crew went one by
  one,
  Some with gladness, and few
  with fear—
Cold and hardship such work had
  done
  That few seemed frightened
  when death was near
Thus every soul on board went
  down—
  Sailor and passenger, little and
  great;
The last that sank was a man of
  my town,
  A capital swimmer—the second
  mate.
  The Second Mate. Stanza 9

Lucius O'Brien
[? –1841]

[y] To our old Alma Mater, our
  rockbound Highland home,
We'll cast back many a fond regret, as o'er life's sea we roam,
Until on our last battlefield the
  lights of heaven shall glow,
We'll never fail to drink to her
  and Benny Havens, oh!
  West Point Song [1838]

Adolph S. Ochs
[1858–1935]

[z] All the news that's fit to
print.
  Motto of The New York Times

Basil O'Connor
[1892–   ]

[a] The world cannot continue to
wage war like physical giants and
to seek peace like intellectual
pygmies.
  *Address at National Conference
  of Christians and Jews* [1945]

Charles Leo O'Donnell
[1884–1934]

[b] I have never been able to
  school my eyes
Against young April's blue surprise. *Wonder*

William Henry Ogilvie
[1869–   ]

[c] When the last fence looms
  up, I am ready
  And I hope when the rails of it
  crack,

There'll be nothing in front but
  the master,
  The huntsman, the fox and the
  pack.
  The Last Fence. Stanza 1

Patrick F. O'Keefe
[1872–1934]

[d] Say it with flowers.
  *Slogan for the Society of
  American Florists* [1917]

John O'Keeffe
[1747–1833]

[e] A glass is good, and a lass is
  good,
  And a pipe to smoke in cold
  weather;
The world is good, and the people
  are good,
  And we're all good fellows together.
  Sprigs of Laurel. Act II, Sc. 1

[f] And why I'm so plump the
  reason I tell,—
Who leads a good life is sure to
  live well. *Merry Sherwood.*
  A Friar of Orders Gray, Stanza 1

William Oldys
[1696–1761]

[g] Busy, curious, thirsty fly,
Drink with me, and drink as I.
  *On a Fly Drinking out of a
  Cup of Ale. Stanza 1*

[h] Three-score summers, when
  they're gone,
Will appear as short as one.
  Ibid. Stanza 2

Carolina Oliphant, Lady Nairne
[1766–1845]

[i] Would you be young again?
  So would not I—
One tear to memory given,
  Onward I'd hie.
  *Would You Be Young Again?
  [Looking Backward]. Stanza 1*

[j] Gude nicht, and joy be wi'
  you a'. *Gude Nicht*

[k] Oh, we're a' noddin', nid, nid,
  noddin';
Oh, we're a' noddin' at our house
  at hame. *We're a' Noddin'*

Ted Olson

[l] And a truth that has lasted a
  million years
  Is good for a million more.
  Things That Endure. Stanza 3

Frank Ward O'Malley
[1876–1932]

[m] Life is just one damned
thing after another. [Also attrib-

uted to Elbert Hubbard; probably precedes them both.]
Quoted in The Literary Digest, November 5, 1932

Omar Khayyám
[1070–1123]
Translation by Edward Fitzgerald

[n] Come, fill the Cup, and in the fire of Spring
Your Winter-garment of Repentance fling:
  The Bird of Time has but a little way
To flutter—and the Bird is on the Wing.
Rubáiyát (5th edition). Stanza 7

[o] Each Morn a thousand Roses brings, you say:
Yes, but where leaves the Rose of Yesterday?   *Ibid. Stanza 9*

[p] A Book of Verses underneath the Bough,
A Jug of Wine, a Loaf of Bread—and Thou
  Beside me singing in the Wilderness—
Oh, Wilderness were Paradise enow!   *Ibid. Stanza 12*

[q] Ah, take the Cash, and let the Credit go,
Nor heed the rumble of a distant Drum!   *Ibid. Stanza 13*

[r] The Worldly Hope men set their Hearts upon
Turns Ashes—or it prospers; and anon,
  Like Snow upon the Desert's dusty Face,
Lighting a little hour or two—is gone.   *Ibid. Stanza 16*

[s] I sometimes think that never blows so red
The Rose as where some buried Caesar bled;
  That every Hyacinth the Garden wears
Dropt in her Lap from some once lovely Head.
    Ibid. Stanza 19

[t] *To-morrow!*—Why, To-morrow I may be
Myself with Yesterday's Sev'n thousand Years.
    Ibid. Stanza 21

[u] Myself when young did eagerly frequent
Doctor and Saint, and heard great argument
  About it and about: but evermore
Came out by the same door where in I went.   *Ibid. Stanza 27*

[v] "While you live,
Drink!—for, once dead, you never shall return."
    Ibid. Stanza 35

[w] And fear not lest Existence closing your
Account, and mine, should know the like no more;
  The Eternal Sáki from that Bowl has pour'd
Millions of Bubbles like us, and will pour.   *Ibid. Stanza 46*

[x] A Hair perhaps divides the False and True.
    Ibid. Stanza 49

[y] Striking from the Calendar Unborn To-morrow and dead Yesterday.   *Ibid. Stanza 57*

[z] The Grape that can with Logic absolute
The Two-and-Seventy jarring Sects confute.
    Ibid. Stanza 59

[a] Strange, is it not? that of the myriads who
Before us pass'd the door of Darkness through,
  Not one returns to tell us of the Road,
Which to discover we must travel too.   *Ibid. Stanza 64*

[b] We are no other than a moving row
Of Magic Shadow-shapes that come and go.
    Ibid. Stanza 68

[c] This Chequer-board of Nights and Days.   *Ibid. Stanza 69*

[d] The Moving Finger writes; and, having writ,
Moves on: nor all your Piety nor Wit
Shall lure it back to cancel half a Line,
Nor all your Tears wash out a Word of it.
    Ibid. Stanza 71

[e] That inverted Bowl they call the Sky,
Whereunder crawling coop'd we live and die.
    Ibid. Stanza 72

[f] "And He that with his hand the Vessel made
Will surely not in after Wrath destroy."   *Ibid. Stanza 85*

[g] "Some there are who tell
Of one who threatens he will toss to Hell
  The luckless Pots he marr'd in making—Pish!
He's a Good Fellow, and 'twill all be well."   *Ibid. Stanza 88*

[h] I wonder often what the Vintners buy
One half so precious as the stuff they sell.   *Ibid. Stanza 95*

[i] Ah Love! could you and I with Him conspire
To grasp this Sorry Scheme of Things entire,
  Would not we shatter it to bits—and then

Re-mould it nearer to the Heart's
Desire!
Ibid. Stanza 99

[j] Yon rising Moon that looks
for us again—
How oft hereafter will she wax
and wane;
How oft hereafter rising look
for us
Through this same Garden—and
for *one* in vain!

And when like her, O Sákí, you
shall pass
Among the Guests Star-scatter'd
on the Grass,
And in your joyous errand reach
the spot
Where I made One—turn down an
empty Glass!
Ibid. Stanzas 100 and 101

Onasander
[*Floruit* A.D. 49]
*Translation by Illinois Greek
Club. Loeb Classical Library*

[k] Envy is a pain of mind that
successful men cause their neighbors. *The General.*
Chap. 42, Paragraph 25

Eugene O'Neill
[1888-]

[l] Dat ole davil, sea.
Anna Christie. Act I

[m] For de little stealin' dey gits
you in jail soon or late. For de big
stealin' dey makes you emperor
and puts you in de Hall o' Fame
when you croaks. If dey's one
thing I learns in ten years on de
Pullman cars listenin' to de white
quality talk, it's dat same fact.
The Emperor Jones. Sc. 1

[n] He couldn't design a cathe-
dral without it looking like the
First Supernatural Bank!
The Great God Brown

[o] *Yank.* Sure! Lock me up! Put
me in a cage! Dat's de on'y answer yuh know. G'wan, lock me
up!
Policeman. What you been
doin'?
Yank. Enough to gimme life
for! I was born, see? Sure, dat's de
charge. *The Hairy Ape*

[p] Our lives are merely strange
dark interludes in the electrical
display of God the Father!
Strange Interlude

Moira O'Neill
(Mrs. N. H. Skrine)

[q] Youth's for an hour,
Beauty's a flower,
But love is the jewel that wins the
world.
*Songs of the Glens of Antrim.
Beauty's a Flower*

John Boyle O'Reilly
[1844–1890]

[r] Like a mighty thought in a
mighty mind
In the clear cold depths he
swims;
Whilst above him the pettiest
form of his kind
With a dash o'er the surface
skims.
Prelude to the Amber Whale

[s] Doubt is brother-devil to Despair. *Prometheus*

[t] The world is large when weary
leagues two loving hearts divide
But the world is small when your
enemy is loose on the other
side. *Distance*

[u] You gave me the key to your
heart, my love;
Then why do you make me
knock?
"Oh, that was yesterday; Saints
above,
Last night I changed the lock!"
Constancy

[v] First across the gulf we cast
Kite-borne threads, till lines are
passed,
And habit builds the bridge at
last!
A Builder's Lesson. Stanza 3

[w] This truth keep in sight,—
every man on the planet
Has just as much right as yourself
to the road.
Rules of the Road

[x] The organized charity,
scrimped and iced,
In the name of a cautious, statis-
tical Christ.
In Bohemia. Stanza 5

[y] The anchor of a love is death.
Forever. Stanza 3

"Miles O'Reilly"
see Charles Graham Halpine

George Orwell
[1903–1950]

[z] All animals are equal, but
some animals are more equal than
others. *Animal Farm. Chap. 10*

Selleck Osborn
[1783–1826]

[a] "My father's trade!—why,
blockhead, art thou mad?
My father, sir, did never stoop so
low;
He was a Gentleman, I'd have you
know."
"Excuse the liberty I take,"
Modestus said, with archness
on his brow—

"Pray, why did not your father make
A Gentleman of you?"
The Modest Retort

Frances Sargent Osgood
[1812–1850]

[b] A whisper woke the air—
A soft, light tone, and low,
Yet barbed with shame and woe.

From ear to lip, from lip to ear,
Until it reached a gentle heart
That throbbed from all the world apart
And that—it broke!
Calumny. Stanzas 1 and 2

Arthur William Edgar O'Shaughnessy
[1844–1881]

[c] We are the music-makers,
And we are the dreamers of dreams . . .
World-losers and world-forsakers,
On whom the pale moon gleams:
Yet we are the movers and shakers
Of the world forever, it seems.

One man with a dream, at pleasure,
Shall go forth and conquer a crown;
And three with a new song's measure
Can trample an empire down.
Ode. Stanzas 1 and 2

[d] For each age is a dream that is dying,
Or one that is coming to birth.
Ibid. Stanza 3

Shaemas O'Sheel
[1886–   ]

[e] He whom a dream hath possessed knoweth no more of doubting . . .
And never comes darkness down, but he greeteth a million morns.
He Whom a Dream Hath Possessed. Stanza 1

[f] The ruin of worlds that fall he views from eternal arches,
And rides God's battlefield in a flashing and golden car.
Ibid. Stanza 4

Sir William Osler
[1849–1919]

[g] Speck in cornea, 50¢.
Entry in his account-book, first fee as a practicing physician. From Life of Sir William Osler by Harvey Cushing, Vol. I, Chap. 6

[h] The desire to take medicine is perhaps the greatest feature which distinguishes man from animals. *Ibid. Chap. 14*

[i] This is yet the childhood of the world, and a supine credulity is still the most charming characteristic of man. *Ibid.*

[j] Humanity has but three great enemies: fever, famine and war; of these by far the greatest, by far the most terrible, is fever. *Ibid. Chap. 16*

[k] Though a little one, the master-word [Work] looms large in meaning. It is the open sesame to every portal, the great equalizer in the world, the true philosopher's stone which transmutes all the base metal of humanity into gold. *Ibid. Chap. 22*

[l] Learn to . . . cultivate the gift of taciturnity and consume your own smoke with an extra draught of hard work, so that those about you may not be annoyed with the dust and soot of your complaints. *Ibid.*

[m] Take the sum of human achievement in action, in science, in art, in literature. . . . The effective, moving, vitalizing work of the world is done between the ages of twenty-five and forty. *Ibid. Chap. 24*

[n] In that charming novel, "The Fixed Period," [by] Anthony Trollope . . . the plot hinges upon the admirable scheme of a college into which at sixty men retired for a year of contemplation before a peaceful departure by chloroform. That incalculable benefits might follow such a scheme is apparent to anyone who, like myself, is nearing the limit, and who has made a careful study of the calamities which may befall men during the seventh and eighth decades. *Ibid.*

[o] Throw all the beer and spirits into the Irish Channel, the English Channel, and the North Sea for a year, and people in England would be infinitely better. It would certainly solve all the problems with which the philanthropists, the physicians, and the politicians have to deal.
Ibid. Vol. II, Chap. 26

[p] Nothing in life is more wonderful than faith—the one great moving force which we can neither weigh in the balance nor test in the crucible.
Ibid. Chap. 30

[q] In the life of a young man the most essential thing for happiness is the gift of friendship.
Ibid. Chap. 31

[r] No bubble is so iridescent or floats longer than that blown by the successful teacher. *Ibid.*

[s] It is one of the greatest blessings that so many women are so full of tact. The calamity happens when a woman who has all the other riches of life just lacks that one thing. *Ibid. Chap. 33*

[t] It is the prime duty of a woman of this terrestrial world to look well. Neatness is the asepsis of clothes. *Ibid.*

Martha Ostenso
[1900–   ]

[u] Pity the Unicorn,
Pity the Hippogriff,
Souls that were never born
Out of the land of If!
*The Unicorn and the Hippogriff.
Stanza 1*

James Otis
[1725–1783]

[v] Taxation without representation is tyranny.
Watchword of the American Revolution, attributed to him.

[w] Cradle of Liberty.
Referring to Faneuil Hall, Boston, meetingplace of American patriots during the Revolutionary period

Thomas Otway
[1651–1685]

[x] O woman! lovely woman! Nature made thee
To temper man: we had been brutes without you.
Venice Preserved. Act I, Sc. 1

[y] What mighty ills have not been done by woman! . . .
Who lost Mark Antony the world?
—A woman! . . .
And laid at last old Troy in ashes?
—Woman!
Destructive, damnable, deceitful woman!
The Orphan. Act III, Sc. 1

Clarence Ousley
[1863–1948]

[z] When the South was in the glory of a never-ending June,
The strings were on the banjo and the fiddle was in tune,
And we reveled in the plenty that we thought could never pass
And lingered at the julep in the ever-brimming glass.
*When the Mint Is in the Liquor.
Stanza 1*

Sir Thomas Overbury
[1581–1613]

[a] Give me, next good, an understanding wife,
By nature wise, not learnèd much by art;
Some knowledge on her part will, all her life,
More scope of conversation impart. *The Wife*

Ovid
[43 B.C.–A.D. 18]

[b] They come to see; they come that they themselves may be seen.
The Art of Love. I, 99

[c] I see the right, and I approve it, too,
Condemn the wrong and yet the wrong pursue.
Metamorphoses. VII, 17

[d] Poetry comes fine spun from a mind at peace. *Tristia.
Book I, Chap. 1, Line 39*

[e] Grateful must we be that the heart may go whithersoever it will.
Epistolae ex Ponto. Book III, Chap. 5, Line 48

[f] How little you know about the age you live in if you fancy that honey is sweeter than cash in hand.
Fasti. Book I, Line 191

Moses Owen
[1838–1878]

[g] Nothing but flags! but simple flags,
Tattered and torn and hanging in rags;
And we walk beneath them with careless tread,
Nor think of the hosts of the mighty dead
Who have marched beneath them in days gone by.
The Returned Maine Battle Flags. Stanza 1

Robert Owen
[1771–1858]

[h] All the world is queer save thee and me, and even thou art a little queer. *On severing business relations with his partner, William Allen* [1828]

Wilfred Owen
[1893–1918]

[i] What passing-bells for these who died as cattle?
Only the monstrous anger of the guns.
Only the stuttering rifles' rapid rattle
Can patter out their hasty orisons.
The Anthem for Doomed Youth

Vilda Sauvage (Mrs. Robert Elliott) Owens
[1875–1950]

[j] A land
Where kings may be beloved, and
Monarchy
Can teach Republics how they
may be free.
"What Has England Done?"

"John Oxenham" (William Arthur Dunkerley)
[? –1941]

[k] Art thou lonely, O my
brother?
Share thy little with another!
Stretch a hand to one unfriended,
And thy loneliness is ended.
Lonely Brother

[l] Kneel always when you light
a fire!
The Sacrament of Fire

[m] Thank God for sleep!
And, when you cannot sleep,
Still thank Him that you live
To lie awake.
The Sacrament of Sleep

[n] The High Soul climbs the
High Way,
The Low Soul gropes the Low,
And in between, on the misty
flats,
The rest drift to and fro.
The Ways

Walter Hines Page
[1855–1918]

[o] There is one thing better than
good government, and that is government in which all the people
have a part. *Life and Letters.*
Vol. 3, Page 31

William Tyler Page
[1868–1942]

[p] I believe in the United States
of America as a Government of the
people, by the people, for the
people; whose just powers are derived from the consent of the governed; a democracy in a republic,
a sovereign Nation of many sovereign States; a perfect Union one
and inseparable; established upon
those principles of freedom,
equality, justice and humanity for
which American patriots sacrificed their lives and fortunes. I
therefore believe it is my duty to
my country to love it, to support
its Constitution, to obey its laws,
to respect its flag, and to defend
it against all enemies.
The American's Creed
[*Adopted by the House of Repre-*
sentatives April 3, 1918]

Albert Bigelow Paine
[1861–1937]

[q] The Great White Way.
Title of a novel (1901) [adopted
as a name for Broadway and the
theatrical district of New York]

Thomas Paine
[1737–1809]

[r] These are the times that try
men's souls.
The American Crisis. No. 1. In
Pennsylvania Journal [Decem-
ber 19, 1776]

[s] Not a place upon earth might
be so happy as America. Her situation is remote from all the
wrangling world, and she has
nothing to do but to trade with
them. *Ibid.*

[t] In a chariot of light from the
region of day
The Goddess of Liberty came.
. . .
She brought in her hand as a
pledge of her love,
. . . the plant she named Liberty
Tree.
The Liberty Tree. Stanza 1. In
Pennsylvania Magazine [July,
1775]

[u] War involves in its progress
such a train of unforeseen and
unsupposed circumstances that no
human wisdom can calculate the
end. It has but one thing certain,
and that is to increase taxes.
Prospects on the Rubicon

[v] The world is my country,
All mankind are my brethren,
To do good is my religion,
I believe in one God and no more.
The Rights of Man. Chap. 5

[w] The sublime and the ridiculous are often so nearly related,
that it is difficult to class them
separately. One step above the
sublime makes the ridiculous, and
one step above the ridiculous
makes the sublime again.
Age of Reason. Part II, Note

William Paley
[1743–1805]

[x] Who can refute a sneer?
Moral Philosophy. Vol. II,
Book V, Chap. 9

Francis Turner Palgrave
[1825–1897]

[y] Their little language the
children
Have, on the knee as they sit;
And only those who love them
Can find the key to it.
Love's Language. Stanza 1

[z] Time's corrosive dewdrop.
A Danish Barrow

Edward E. Paramore, Jr.
[1895–   ]

[a] Oh, the North Countree is a
hard countree
That mothers a bloody brood;
And its icy arms hold hidden
charms
For the greedy, the sinful and
lewd.
The Ballad of Yukon Jake

[b] Oh, tough as a steak was
Yukon Jake—
Hard-boiled as a picnic egg.
Ibid.

Vilfredo Pareto
[1848–1923]

[c] Give me a fruitful error any
time, full of seeds, bursting with
its own corrections. You can keep
your sterile truth for yourself.
Comment on Kepler

Dorothy Parker
[1893–   ]

[d] Where's the man could ease a
heart
Like a satin gown?
The Satin Dress. Stanza 1

[e] Four be the things I am wiser
to know:
Idleness, sorrow, a friend, and a
foe. . . .
Four be the things I'd been better
without:
Love, curiosity, freckles, and
doubt.   *Inventory*

[f] And this is the sum of a last-
ing lore:
Scratch a lover, and find a foe.
*Ballade of a Great Weariness.
Stanza 1*

[g] Men seldom make passes
At girls who wear glasses.
News Item

[h] You are brief and frail and
blue—
Little sisters, I am, too.
You are heaven's masterpieces—
Little loves, the likeness ceases.
Sweet Violets

[i] Razors pain you;
Rivers are damp;
Acids stain you;
And drugs cause cramp.
Guns aren't lawful;
Nooses give;
Gas smells awful;
You might as well live.   *Résumé*

[j] Why is it no one ever sent me
yet
One perfect limousine, do you
suppose?

Ah no, it's always just my luck to
get
One perfect rose.
One Perfect Rose. Stanza 3

[k] He lies below, correct in
cypress wood,
And entertains the most exclusive worms.
Epitaph for a Very Rich Man

[l] The man she had was kind
and clean
And well enough for every day,
But, oh, dear friends, you should
have seen
The one that got away!
The Fisherwoman

[m] The affair between Margot
Asquith and Margot Asquith will
live as one of the prettiest love
stories in all literature.
*Review in The New Yorker of
the Autobiography of Margot
Asquith*

John Parker
[1729–1775]

[n] Stand your ground. Don't fire
unless fired upon; but if they
mean to have a war, let it begin
here!   *To his Minute Men at
Lexington, April 19, 1775*

Ross Parker
[1914–   ]
and
Hughie Charles
[1907–   ]

[o] There'll always be an England
While there's a country lane,
Wherever there's a cottage small
Beside a field of grain.
There'll always be an England
While there's a busy street,
Wherever there's a turning wheel,
A million marching feet.
*There'll Always Be an England
[Popular song of World War II.
Copyright 1939.]*

Theodore Parker
[1810–1860]

[p] Truth never yet fell dead in
the streets; it has such affinity
with the soul of man, the seed
however broadcast will catch
somewhere and produce its hun-
dredfold. . . .
Truth stood on one side and
Ease on the other; it has often
been so.   *A Discourse of Matters
Pertaining to Religion*

[q] A democracy,—that is a government of all the people, by all
the people, for all the people; of
course, a government of the principles of eternal justice, the unchanging law of God; for short-

ness' sake I will call it the idea of Freedom.   *The American Idea*

Thomas Parnell
[1679–1718]

[r] My days have been so wondrous free
The little birds that fly
With careless ease from tree to tree,
Were but as bless'd as I.
        Song [set to music by Francis Hopkins; one of the earliest American songs]. Stanza 1

[s] Let those love now who never loved before;
Let those who always loved, now love the more.   *Translation of the Pervigilium Veneris*

Blaise Pascal
[1623–1662]
Translation by O. W. Wight

[t] Man is but a reed, the weakest in nature, but he is a thinking reed.   *Thoughts. Chap. 2, 10*

[u] If the nose of Cleopatra had been shorter, the whole face of the earth would have been changed.
        Ibid. Chap. 8, 29

[v] Rivers are highways that move on, and bear us whither we wish to go.   *Ibid. Chap. 9, 38*

[w] What a chimera, then, is man! what a novelty, what a monster, what a chaos, what a subject of contradiction, what a prodigy! A judge of all things, feeble worm of the earth, depositary of the truth, cloaca of uncertainty and error, the glory and the shame of the universe!
        Ibid. Chap. 10, 1

[x] We know the truth, not only by the reason, but also by the heart.   *Ibid.*

Walter Pater
[1839–1894]

[y] That sweet look of devotion which men have never been able altogether to love, and which still makes the born saint an object almost of suspicion to his earthly brethren.
        The Renaissance. Botticelli

[z] The sunless pleasures of weary people, whose care for external things is slackening.
        Ibid. Michelangelo

[a] Hers is the head upon which all "the ends of the world are come," and the eyelids are a little weary. It is a beauty wrought out from within upon the flesh, the deposit, little cell by cell, of

strange thoughts and fantastic reveries and exquisite passions.
        Ibid. Leonardo da Vinci.
        [Mona Lisa]

[b] Religions, as they grow by natural laws out of man's life, are modified by whatever modifies his life.   *Ibid. Winckelmann*

[c] What we have to do is to be for ever curiously testing new opinions and courting new impressions.   *Ibid. Conclusion*

[d] Art comes to you proposing frankly to give nothing but the highest quality to your moments as they pass.   *Ibid.*

[e] A book, like a person, has its fortunes with one; is lucky or unlucky in the precise moment of its falling in our way, and often by some happy accident counts with us for something more than its independent value.
        Marius the Epicurean. Chap. 6

[f] To know when one's self is interested, is the first condition of interesting other people.   *Ibid.*

[g] We need some imaginative stimulus, some not impossible ideal such as may shape vague hope, and transform it into effective desire, to carry us year after year, without disgust, through the routine-work which is so large a part of life.   *Ibid. Chap. 25*

[h] Through the survival of their children, happy parents are able to think calmly, and with a very practical affection, of a world in which they are to have no direct share.   *Ibid.*

Andrew Barton ("Banjo") Paterson
[1864–1941]

[i] Once a jolly swagman camped by a billy-bong,
Under the shade of a kulibar tree,
And he sang as he sat and waited for his billy-boil,
"You'll come a-waltzing, Matilda, with me."
        Waltzing Matilda. Australian Soldiers' Marching Song

Coventry Kersey Dighton Patmore
[1823–1896]

[j] Life is not life at all without delight.   *Victory in Defeat*

[k] To have nought
Is to have all things without care or thought!
        Legem Tuam Dilexi

[l] Ah, wasteful woman! she who may
On her sweet self set her own price,
Knowing he cannot choose but pay,
How has she cheapened Paradise!
How given for nought her priceless gift,
How spoiled the bread and spilled the wine,
Which, spent with due respective thrift,
Had made brutes men and men divine!   *The Angel in the House. Preludes, Unthrift*

[m] Love wakes men, once a lifetime each;
They lift their heavy lids, and look;
And, lo, what one sweet page can teach
They read with joy, then shut the book.   *Ibid. Canto 8
Prelude 2, The Revelation*

[n] Angels may be familiar; those Who err each other must respect.   *Thoughts. V, Courtesy*

[o] Some who do not consider that Christianity has proved a failure, do, nevertheless, hold that it is open to question whether the race, as a race, has been much affected by it, and whether the external and visible evil and good which have come of it do not pretty nearly balance one another.   *Christianity and Progress*

[p] A Woman is a foreign land,
Of which, though there he settle young,
A man will ne'er quite understand
The customs, politics, and tongue.   *Woman*

Angelo Patri
[1877–   ]

[q] In one sense there is no death. The life of a soul on earth lasts beyond his departure. You will always feel that life touching yours, that voice speaking to you. . . . He lives on in your life and in the lives of all others that knew him.
          Keep Children from Funerals

Elliot Paul
[1891–   ]

[r] She had a complete ignorance of everything a woman does not need to know.   *The Life and Death of a Spanish Town. Chap. 1*

[s] Patience makes women beautiful in middle age.   *Ibid. Chap. 2*

[t] The last time I see Paris will be on the day I die. The city was

inexhaustible, and so is its memory.   *The Last Time I Saw Paris
Part II, 23*

James Payn
[1830–1898]

[u] I never had a piece of toast
Particularly long and wide
But fell upon the sanded floor,
And always on the buttered side.   *In Chambers's Journal, 1884*

John Howard Payne
[1792–1852]

[v] 'Mid pleasures and palaces though we may roam,
Be it ever so humble, there's no place like home;
A charm from the skies seems to hallow us there,
Which sought through the world is ne'er met with elsewhere.

An exile from home splendour dazzles in vain,
Oh give me my lowly thatched cottage again;
The birds singing gayly, that came at my call,
Give me them, and that peace of mind dearer than all.
          Home, Sweet Home. (From the opera Clari, the Maid of Milan)

Josephine Preston Peabody
(Mrs. Lionel Marks)
[1874–1922]

[w] Truly, one thing is sweet
Of things beneath the Sun;
This, that a man should earn his bread and eat
Rejoicing in his work which he hath done.   *The Singing Man*

[x] The little Road says, Go;
The little House says, Stay;
And oh, it's bonny here at home,
But I must go away.   *The House and the Road. Stanza 1*

Arthur Wallace Peach
[1886–   ]

[y] They light with joy the wintry scenes—
The candles of the evergreens!   *Candles*

[z] The home where happiness securely dwells
Was never wrought by charms or magic spells.
A mother made it beautiful, but knew
No magic save what toiling hands can do.   *The Reasons*

Sir Eustace Peachtree
[Floruit 1640]

[a] Among the notionable dictes of antique Rome was the fancy that when men heard thunder on the left the gods had somewhat of special advertisement to impart. Then did the prudent pause and lay down their affaire to study what omen Jove intended.
The Dangers of This Mortall Life

Thomas Love Peacock
[1785–1866]

[b] Seamen three! what men be ye?
Gotham's three Wise Men we be.
Whither in your bowl so free?
To rake the moon from out the sea.
The bowl goes trim. The moon doth shine,
And our ballast is old wine.
Three Men of Gotham. Stanza 1

[c] How troublesome is day!
It calls us from our sleep away;
It bids us from our pleasant dreams awake,
And sends us forth to keep or break
Our promises to pay.
How Troublesome Is Day

[d] Not drunk is he who from the floor
Can rise alone and still drink more;
But drunk is he, who prostrate lies,
Without the power to drink or rise.
The Misfortunes of Elphin. Heading, Chap. 3, translated from the Welsh

Edmund Lester Pearson
[1880–1937]

[e] No agreement about books can make us look upon another man with so friendly an eye as the discovery that he belonged to our period, and shared our special enthusiasms about reading, in the years that stretched between the sixth birthday and the sixteenth.
Books in Black or Red

James Larkin Pearson
[1879–   ]

[f] I've never been to London,
I've never been to Rome;
But on my Fifty Acres
I travel here at home.
Fifty Acres. Stanza 1

[g] A little land of Egypt
My meadow plot shall be,
With pyramids of hay stacks
Along its sheltered lee.
Ibid. Stanza 3

Robert Edwin Peary
[1856–1920]

[h] We returned from the Pole to Cape Columbia in only sixteen days . . . the exhilaration of success lent wings to our sorely battered feet. But Ootah, the Eskimo, had his own explanation. Said he: "The devil is asleep or having trouble with his wife, or we should never have come back so easily."
The North Pole

Donald Culross Peattie
[1898–   ]

[i] It is natural that women should like the birds whose domestic affairs can be observed under the eaves; they love the sweetest singers, the brightest plumage, the species not too shy to be seen at close range. For them the waders and swimmers, the awkward of leg, the harsh of cry, the wild of soul, have seldom the same appeal. But that which flees from men, that will men have. Women of all people ought to understand this, but they do not, quite.
An Almanac for Moderns. November 9

[j] Life is adventure in experience, and when you are no longer greedy for the last drop of it, it means no more than that you have set your face, whether you know it or not, to the day when you shall depart without a backward look.
Ibid. March 18

[k] The time to hear bird music is between four and six in the morning. Seven o'clock is not too late, but by eight the fine rapture is over, due, I suspect, to the contentment of the inner man that comes with breakfast; a poet should always be hungry or have a lost love.
Ibid. April 22

George Peele
[1558–1597]

[l] My merry, merry, merry roundelay
Concludes with Cupid's curse:
They that do change old love for new,
Pray gods, they change for worse!
Cupid's Curse

Westbrook Pegler
[1894–   ]

[m] For the fifth year in succession I have pored over the cata-

logue of dogs in the show at Madison Square Garden without finding a dog named Rover, Towser, Sport, Spot, or Fido.

Who is the man who can call from his back door at night: "Here, Champion Alexander of Clane o' Wind-Holme! Here, Champion Alexander of Clane o' Wind-Holme"?   *Here, Rover!*

[n] The thing we all love most about the glorious old United States of A.

Is that everybody, irregardless of creed or color, is entitled to have their say.   *Fair Enough*

William Penn
[1644–1718]

[o] The receipts of cookery are swelled to a volume; but a good stomach excels them all.
    Fruits of Solitude

[p] Men are generally more careful of the breed of their horses and dogs than of their children.
    Ibid.

[q] The public must and will be served.   *Ibid.*

[r] Much reading is an oppression of the mind, and extinguishes the natural candle, which is the reason of so many senseless scholars in the world.
    Advice to His Children

Samuel Pepys
[1633–1703]

[s] I pray God to keep me from being proud.
    Diary. March 22, 1660

[t] This morning came home my fine camlet cloak, with gold buttons, and a silk suit, which cost me much money, and I pray God to make me able to pay for it.
    Ibid. July 1, 1660

[u] And so to bed.
    Ibid. July 22, 1660; December 7, 1660; May 19, 1662; etc.

[v] But, good God! what an age is this, and what a world is this! that a man cannot live without playing the knave and dissimulation.
    Ibid. September 1, 1661

[w] My wife, poor wretch.
    Ibid. September 18, 1661; December 19, 1662; etc.

[x] Thanks be to God, since my leaving drinking of wine, I do find myself much better, and do mind my business better, and do spend less money, and less time lost in idle company.
    Ibid. January 26, 1662

[y] As happy a man as any in the world, for the whole world seems to smile upon me.
    Ibid. October 31, 1662

[z] Great talk among people how some of the Fanatiques do say that the end of the world is at hand, and that next Tuesday is to be the day. Against which, whenever it shall be, good God fit us all!
    Ibid. November 25, 1662

[a] Find myself £43 worse than I was the last month . . . chiefly arisen from my layings-out in clothes for myself and wife; viz., for her about £12, and for myself £55.   *Ibid. October 31, 1663*

[b] I am at a loss to know whether it be my hare's foot which is my preservative, or my taking of a pill of turpentine every morning.   *Ibid. March 26, 1665*

[c] Thus I ended this month with the greatest joy that ever I did any in my life, because I have spent the greatest part of it with abundance of joy, and honour, and pleasant journeys, and brave entertainments, and without cost of money.   *Ibid. July 31, 1665*

[d] Saw a wedding in the church; and strange to see what delight we married people have to see these poor fools decoyed into our condition.
    Ibid. December 25, 1665

[e] Musick and women I cannot but give way to, whatever my business is.   *Ibid. March 9, 1666*

[f] The truth is, I do indulge myself a little the more in pleasure, knowing that this is the proper age of my life to do it; and, out of my observation that most men that do thrive in the world do forget to take pleasure during the time that they are getting their estate, but reserve that till they have got one, and then it is too late for them to enjoy it.
    Ibid. March 10, 1666

[g] Home, and, being washingday, dined upon cold meat.
    Ibid. April 4, 1666

[h] But to think of the clatter they make with his coach, and their own fine cloathes, and yet how meanly they live within doors, and nastily, and borrowing everything of neighbours.
    Ibid. April 1, 1667

[i] Whose red nose makes me ashamed to be seen with him.
    Ibid. May 3, 1667

[j] I staid talking below, while my wife dressed herself, which vexed me that she was so long about it.   *Ibid. July 14, 1667*

[k] Gives me some kind of content to remember how painful it is sometimes to keep money, as well as to get it.
Ibid. October 11, 1667

[l] Not to make any more speech, which, while my fame is good, I will avoid, for fear of losing it.
Ibid. March 13, 1668

[m] I by little words find that she hath heard of my going to plays, and carrying people abroad every day, in her absence; and that I cannot but help the storm will break out in a little time.
Ibid. June 18, 1668

[n] In appearance, at least, he being on all occasions glad to be at friendship with me, though we hate one another, and know it on both sides.
Ibid. September 22, 1668

[o] And so I betake myself to that course, which is almost as much as to see myself go into my grave; for which, and all the discomforts that will accompany my being blind, the good God prepare me!
Ibid. May 31, 1669 (final entry)

Thomas Percy
[1728–1811]
Though only an indifferent poet himself, Bishop Percy is immortal for the "Reliques of Ancient English Poetry," which collected many of the old ballads and songs. This work has been a feeding-place for poets ever since.

[p] Everye white will have its blacke,
And everye sweete its sowre.
Reliques of Ancient English Poetry. Sir Cauline, Part II, Stanza 1

[q] Late, late yestreen I saw the new moone
Wi' the auld moone in hir arme.
Ibid. Sir Patrick Spence (Spens), Stanza 7

[r] Where gripinge grefes the hart would wounde
And dolefulle dumps the mynde oppresse,
There musicke with her silver sound
With spede is wont to send redresse.   *Ibid. A Song to the Lute in Musicke. Stanza 1*

[s] A poore soule sat sighing under a sicamore tree;
O willow, willow, willow!
With his hand on his bosom, his head on his knee.
Ibid. Willow, Willow, Willow, Stanza 1

[t] And how should I know your true love
From many another one?

Oh, by his cockle hat, and staff,
And by his sandal shoone.
Ibid. The Friar of Orders Gray, Stanza 3

[u] O Lady, he is dead and gone!
Lady, he's dead and gone!
And at his head a green grass turfe,
And at his heels a stone.
Ibid. Stanza 5

[v] Weep no more, lady, weep no more,
Thy sorrowe is in vaine;
For violets pluckt, the sweetest showers
Will ne'er make grow againe.
Ibid. Stanza 12

[w] Sigh no more, ladies, sigh no more!
Men were deceivers ever;
One foot in sea and one on shore,
To one thing constant never.
Ibid. Stanza 17

[x] And when with envy Time, transported,
Shall think to rob us of our joys,
You'll in your girls again be courted,
And I'll go wooing in my boys.
Ibid. Winifreda, Stanza 8

[y] When captaines couragious, whom death cold not daunte,
Ibid. Mary Ambree, Stanza 1

[z] "I'll rest," sayd hee, "but thou shalt walke";
So doth this wandring Jew
From place to place, but cannot rest
For seeing countries newe.
Ibid. The Wandering Jew, Stanza 9

[a] In Scarlet towne, where I was borne,
There was a fair maid dwellin,
Made every youth crye, Welawaye!
Her name was Barbara Allen.
Ibid. Barbara Allen's Cruelty, Stanza 1

[b] No burial this pretty pair
Of any man receives,
Till Robin Red-breast piously
Did cover them with leaves.
Ibid. The Children in the Wood, Stanza 16

[c] Under floods that are deepest,
Which Neptune obey;
Over rocks that are steepest,
Love will find out the way.
Ibid. Love Will Find Out the Way, Stanza 1

[d] For without money, George,
A man is but a beast:
But bringing money, thou shalt be
Always my welcome guest.
Ibid. George Barnwell, Part II, Stanza 25

William Alexander Percy
[1885–1942]

[e] I heard a bird at break of day
Sing from the autumn trees
A song so mystical and calm,
So full of certainties.
Overtones

[f] Enchanted ports we, too, shall
touch,
Cadiz or Cameroon;
Nor other pilot need beside
A magic wisp of moon.
March Magic

Bliss Perry
[1860–   ]

[g] The fact is, we are not a
book-reading people. The vast
majority of our ninety-odd millions of population have no literary appetites which cannot be
supplied by the newspapers, the
magazines, and an occasional
"best-seller" novel.
*The Praise of Folly. Criticism in
American Periodicals*

Lilla Cabot Perry
[1848–1933]

[h] Forgive me not! Hate me and
I shall know
Some of Love's fire still burns in
your breast!
Forgiveness finds its home in
hearts at rest,
On dead volcanoes only lies the
snow.   *Forgive Me Not*

[i] Though your cloak
Be threadbare, half of it is mine.
You are my friend.
A Friend. Stanza 2

Nora Perry
[1832–1896]

[j] Tying her bonnet under her
chin,
She tied her raven ringlets in;
But not alone in the silken snare
Did she catch her lovely floating
hair,
For, tying her bonnet under her
chin,
She tied a young man's heart
within.
The Love-Knot. Stanza 1

[k] What silences we keep, year
after year,
With those who are most near to
us, and dear!
Too Late. Stanza 1

[l] Who knows the thoughts of a
child?
Who Knows? Stanza 1

[m] The mad, merry music, that
set us a-dancing
Till over the midnight came stealing the morn.   *That Waltz of
von Weber's. Stanza 1*

Oliver Hazard Perry
[1785–1819]

[n] We have met the enemy, and
they are ours.
*Letter to General Harrison
[dated "United States Brig
Niagara. Off the Western Sisters. Sept. 10, 1813, 4 P.M."]*

John Tyler Pettee
[1822–1907]

[o] Pray for peace and grace and
spiritual food,
For wisdom and guidance, for all
these are good,
But don't forget the potatoes.
Prayer and Potatoes

Phaedrus
[*Circa* A.D. 8]
*Translation by Henry Thomas
Riley. Bohn Classic Library*

[p] Submit to the present evil,
lest a greater one befall you.
Book I. Fable 2, 31

[q] He who covets what belongs
to another deservedly loses his
own.   *Ibid. Fable 4, 1*

[r] Jupiter has loaded us with a
couple of wallets: the one, filled
with our own vices, he has placed
at our backs; the other, heavy
with those of others, he has hung
before.   *Book IV. Fable 10, 1*

[s] "I knew that before you were
born." Let him who would instruct a wiser man consider this as
said to himself. *Book V. Fable 9, 4*

Edward John Phelps
[1822–1900]

[t] Waiting for that delusive
train
That, always coming, never comes,
Till weary and worn, cold and for-
lorn,
And paralyzed in every function,
I hope in hell
Their souls may dwell
Who first invented Essex Junc-
tion.
Essex Junction. Stanza 1

Charles Phillips
[1789–1859]

[u] Grand, gloomy, and peculiar,
he sat upon the throne a sceptred
hermit, wrapped in the solitude of
his own originality.
The Character of Napoleon

Harry Irving ("H.I.") Phillips
[1887–   ]

[v] A Vermont Yankee in
King Ballyhoo's Court!
Calvin Coolidge

[w] Three dots . . . across the
        sea's expanse—
His signal, shore to shore!
And perils of the centuries
    Would haunt men's minds no
        more.   *Marconi. Stanza 5*

[x] When heat waves come to
        scorch the streets
And humid is the long-drawn
        day . . .
Then editors in huddles go
And to the cameramen declare:
"Quick! To the zoo, for we must
        show
Some pictures of a polar bear!"
    The Old Reliables. Stanza 1

[y] "One if by land and two if by
        sea—
And I will be loaded with Vitamin
        B,
Ready to ride and spread the
        alarm;
Wheaties will see that I'm kept
        from harm."
    *What a Modern Radio Sponsor
        Would Have Done to Paul Revere*

[z] "Courage," the Old Year whis-
        pers as it ends,
"Weary's the world, and peni-
        tent and sad,
'Waiting the touch to make all
        mankind friends—
Yours be the luck and strength
        to do it, lad!"
    Exit and Entrance: L'Envoi

Stephen Phillips
[1864–1915]

[a]   The moment deep
When we are conscious of the
        secret dawn,
Amid the darkness that we feel is
        green.   *Marpessa*

[b] Thy face remembered is from
        other worlds,
It has been died for, though I
        know not when,
It has been sung of, though I
        know not where.   *Ibid.*

[c] The half of music, I have
        heard men say,
Is to have grieved.   *Ibid.*

[d] O to recall!
What to recall?
Not the star in waters red,
    Not this:
Laughter of a girl that's dead,
    O this!   *Lyrics. I Stanza 4*

[e] Who shall set a shore to love?
When hath it ever swerved from
        death, or when
Hath it not burned away all bar-
        riers,
Even dearest ties of mother and of
        son,
Even of brothers?
    Paolo and Francesca. Act II, Sc. 1

Wendell Phillips
[1811–1884]

[f] Revolutions are not made;
they come.
    Speech [January 28, 1852]

[g] One on God's side is a
majority.
    Speech [November 1, 1859]

[h] Aristocracy is always cruel.
    *Address on Toussaint
        L'Ouverture [1861]*

Sarah Morgan Bryant Piatt
[1836–1919]

[i] My mother says I must not
        pass
Too near that glass;
She is afraid that I will see
A little witch that looks like me,
With a red mouth to whisper low
The very thing I should not know.
    The Witch in the Glass

[j] You did not sing to Shelley
        such a song
As Shelley sang to you.
    A Word with a Skylark

John Pierpont
[1785–1866]

[k] A weapon that comes down as
        still
    As snowflakes fall upon the sod;
But executes a freeman's will,
    As lightning does the will of
        God;
And from its force nor doors nor
        locks
Can shield you,—'tis the ballot-
        box.
    A Word from a Petitioner

[l] The Yankee boy, before he's
        sent to school,
Well knows the mystery of that
        magic tool,
The pocket-knife.   *Whittling,
    A Yankee Portrait. Stanza 1*

Albert Pike
[1809–1891]

[m] The spring has less of
        brightness,
        Every year;
And the snow a ghastlier white-
        ness,
        Every year;
Nor do summer flowers quicken,
Nor the autumn fruitage thicken,
As they once did, for they sicken,
        Every year.
    Every Year. Stanza 1

Pilpay or Bidpai
[*Circa* 326 B.C.?]

[n] We ought to do our neighbour all the good we can. If you
do good, good will be done to you;

but if you do evil, the same will be
measured back to you again.
Chap. 1. Dabschelim and Pilpay

[o] It has been the providence of
Nature to give this creature [the
cat] nine lives instead of one.
*Ibid. Fable 3, The Greedy
and Ambitious Cat*

[p] Wise men say that there are
three sorts of persons who are
wholly deprived of judgment,—
they who are ambitious of pre-
ferments in the courts of princes;
they who make use of poison to
show their skill in curing it; and
they who intrust women with
their secrets.   *Chap. 2. Fable 6,
The Two Travellers*

[q] Whoever . . . prefers the
service of princes before his duty
to his Creator, will be sure, early
or late, to repent in vain.
*Chap. 3. Fable 3, The Prince
and His Minister*

[r] Honest men esteem and
value nothing so much in this
world as a real friend. Such a one
is as it were another self, to whom
we impart our most secret
thoughts, who partakes of our
joy, and comforts us in our affliction; add to this, that his company is an everlasting pleasure to
us.   *Chap. 4. Choice of Friends*

[s] Wild elephants are caught by
tame;
With money it is just the same.
*The Panchatantra. Book I
(Translation adapted from
Arthur W. Ryder)*

Charles Cotesworth Pinckney
[1746–1825]

[t] Millions for defence, but not
one cent for tribute.
[Inscribed on the cenotaph in
his memory in St. Michael's
Church, Charleston, South Carolina. What Pinckney really said
was more forcible,—"not *a
damned penny* for tribute."]
*When Minister to the French
Republic [1797]*

Pindar
[518–438 B.C.]
*Translation by Sir J. E. Sandys.
Loeb Classic Library*

[u] The best of healers is good
cheer.   *Nemean Ode 4*

[v] Longer than deeds liveth the
word.   *Ibid.*

[w] The word that is overbearing
is a spur unto strife.
Fragment from Hymns

[x] To foolish men belongeth a
love for things afar.   *Paean 4*

Sir Arthur Wing Pinero
[1855–1934]

[y] From forty to fifty a man is
at heart either a stoic or a satyr.
*The Second Mrs. Tanqueray.
Act I*

[z] There are two sorts of affection—the love of a woman you respect, and the love for the woman
you love.   *Ibid. Act II*

[a] I believe the future is only
the past again, entered through
another gate.   *Ibid. Act IV*

[b] I've heard what doctors' con-
sultations consist of. After looking
at the pictures you talk about
whist.   *The Notorious Mrs.
Ebbsmith. Act I*

[c] There's only one hour in a
woman's life. . . . One supreme
hour. Her poor life is like the arch
of a crescent; so many years lead
up to that hour, so many weary
years decline from it.
Ibid. Act III

William Pitt, Earl of Chatham
[1708–1778]

[d] Where laws end, tyranny begins.   *Case of Wilkes. Speech
[January 9, 1770]*

[e] You cannot conquer America.
Speech [November 18, 1777]

[f] The poorest man may in his
cottage bid defiance to all the
force of the Crown. It may be
frail; its roof may shake; the wind
may blow through it; the storms
may enter, the rain may enter,—
but the King of England cannot
enter; all his forces dare not cross
the threshold of the ruined tenement!
Speech on the Excise Bill

William Pitt
[? –1840]

[g] One night came on a hurri-
cane,
The sea was mountains rolling,
When Barney Buntline turned
his quid,
And said to Billy Bowling:
"A strong nor'-wester's blowing,
Bill;
Hark! don't ye hear it roar,
now?
Lord help 'em, how I pities all
Unhappy folks on shore now!"
The Sailor's Consolation. Stanza 1

Ruth Pitter
[1897–   ]

[h] Towns and noblemen are
made
By silly fortune's dole,

But birds, and they who wield
the spade,
They are green England's singing
soul.   *The Realm. Stanza 4*

[i] When we have buried her,
made her unseen,
We will lie down and weep;
Our part is done; we have found
her a green
Quiet place wherein to sleep.
The Burial. Stanza 1

[j] Though our world burn, the
small dim words
Stand here in steadfast grace,
And sing, like the indifferent
birds
About a ruined place.
On an Old Poem. Stanza 2

Pope Pius XII
(Eugenio Pacelli)
[1876-   ]

[k] Whoever dared raise a hand
against Rome would be guilty of
matricide in the eyes of the civilized world and in the eternal
judgments of God.
*Address to the College of Cardi-
nals, Rome [June 2, 1944]*

[l] Private property is a natural
fruit of labor, a product of intense activity of man, acquired
through his energetic determina-
tion to ensure and develop with
his own strength his own existence and that of his family, and
to create for himself and his own
an existence of just freedom, not
only economic, but also political,
cultural and religious.
*Radio broadcast
[September 1, 1944]*

[m] The American people have a
genius for splendid and unselfish
action, and into the hands of
America God has placed the
destinies of afflicted humanity.
*Wisdom—Not Weapons of War
[Collier's, January 5, 1946]*

Plato
[427-347 B.C.]
*Translation by Benjamin Jowett.
Oxford University Press*

[n] He who is of a calm and
happy nature will hardly feel the
pressure of age, but to him who
is of an opposite disposition
youth and age are equally a burden.   *The Republic. Book I,
329-D*

[o] No physician, in so far as he
is a physician, considers his own
good in what he prescribes, but
the good of his patient; for the
true physician is also a ruler having the human body as a subject,
and is not a mere money-maker.
Ibid. 342-D

[p] When there is an income-tax,
the just man will pay more and
the unjust less on the same
amount of income.   *Ibid. 343-D*

[q] Mankind censure injustice,
fearing that they may be the victims of it and not because they
shrink from committing it.
Ibid. 344-C

[r] Necessity, who is the mother
of invention.
Ibid., Book II, 369-C

[s] Musical training is a more
potent instrument than any
other, because rhythm and harmony find their way into the inward places of the soul.
Ibid. Book III, 401-D

[t] The judge should not be
young; he should have learned to
know evil, not from his own soul,
but from late and long observation of the nature of evil in
others: knowledge should be his
guide, not personal experience.
Ibid. 409-B

[u] Everything that deceives may
be said to enchant.
Ibid. 413-C

[v] Under the influence either of
poverty or of wealth, workmen
and their work are equally liable
to degenerate.
Ibid. Book IV, 421-E

[w] Astronomy compels the soul
to look upwards and leads us from
this world to another.
Ibid. Book VII, 529

[x] I have hardly ever known a
mathematician who was capable
of reasoning.   *Ibid. 531-E*

[y] Solon was under a delusion
when he said that a man when he
grows old may learn many things
—for he can no more learn much
than he can run much; youth is
the time for any extraordinary
toil.   *Ibid. 536-D*

[z] Let early education be a sort
of amusement; you will then be
better able to find out the natural
bent.   *Ibid. 537*

[a] Democracy, which is a charming form of government, full of
variety and disorder, and dispens-
ing a sort of equality to equals
and unequals alike.
Ibid. Book VIII, 558-C

[b] The people have always some
champion whom they set over
them and nurse into greatness.
. . . This and no other is the root
from which a tyrant springs;
when he first appears he is a pro-
tector. . . .
    When the tyrant has disposed
of foreign enemies by conquest or
treaty, and there is nothing to
fear from them, then he is always

stirring up some war or other, in order that the people may require a leader.
Ibid. 565-C and 566-E

[c] The soul of man is immortal and imperishable.
Ibid. Book X, 608-D

[d] These are the Fates, daughters of Necessity . . . Lachesis singing of the past, Clotho of the present, Atropos of the future.
Ibid. 617-C

[e] Not one of them who took up in his youth with this opinion that there are no gods, ever continued until old age faithful to his conviction. *Laws. 888*

Plautus
[254-184 B.C.]
Translation by Henry Thomas Riley. Ritschl's second edition, Bohn Classical Library

[f] Not by years but by disposition is wisdom acquired.
Trinummus. Act II, Sc. 2, Line 88 (367)

[g] He whom the gods favor dies in youth. *Bacchides. Act IV, Sc. 7, Line 18 (816)*

[h] Patience is the best remedy for every trouble.
Rudens. Act II, Sc. 5, Line 71

[i] Consider the little mouse, how sagacious an animal it is which never entrusts its life to one hole only. *Truculentus. Act IV, Sc. 4, Line 15 (868)*

[j] Nothing is there more friendly to a man than a friend in need.
Epidicus. Act III, Sc. 3, Line 44 (425)

[k] Things which you do not hope happen more frequently than things which you do hope.
Mostellaria. Act I, Sc. 3, Line 40 (197)

Pliny the Elder
[A.D. 23-79]
With some alterations, from translations by John Bostock, M.D., and Henry Thomas Riley. Bohn Classical Library

[l] The world, and whatever that be which we call the heavens, by the vault of which all things are enclosed, we must conceive to be a deity, to be eternal, without bounds, neither created nor subject at any time to destruction. To inquire what is beyond it is no concern of man; nor can the human mind form any conjecture concerning it. *Natural History. Book II, Sect. 1*

[m] It is ridiculous to suppose that the great head of things,

whatever it be, pays any regard to human affairs. *Ibid. Sect. 20*

[n] Man is the only one that knows nothing, that can learn nothing without being taught. He can neither speak nor walk nor eat, and in short he can do nothing at the prompting of nature only, but weep.
Ibid. Book VII, Sect. 4

[o] The human features and countenance, although composed of but some ten parts or little more, are so fashioned that among so many thousands of men there are no two in existence who cannot be distinguished from one another. *Ibid. Sect. 8*

[p] It has been observed that the height of a man from the crown of the head to the sole of the foot is equal to the distance between the tips of the middle fingers of the two hands when extended in a straight line. *Ibid. Sect. 77*

[q] When a building is about to fall down, all the mice desert it.
Ibid. Book VIII, Sect. 103

[r] It has become quite a common proverb that in wine there is truth. *Ibid. Book XIV, Sect. 141*

[s] The agricultural population, says Cato, produces the bravest men, the most valiant soldiers, and a class of citizens the least given of all to evil designs.
Ibid. Book XVIII, Sect. 26

[t] They say that he [Apelles, the artist] was censured by a shoemaker for having represented the shoes with one latchet too few. The next day, the shoemaker, quite proud at seeing the former error corrected, thanks to his advice, began to criticize the leg; upon which Apelles, full of indignation, popped his head out and reminded him that a shoemaker should give no opinion beyond the shoes,—a piece of advice which has equally passed into a proverbial saying.
Ibid. Book XXXV, Sect. 84

Pliny the Younger
[A.D. 61-105]
Translation [1746] by William Melmoth. Bohn Classical Library

[u] Modestus said of Regulus that he was "the biggest rascal that walks upon two legs."
Letters. Book I, Letter 5, 14

[v] There is nothing to write about, you say. Well, then, write and let me know just this,—that there *is* nothing to write about; or tell me in the good old style if you are well. That's right. I am quite well. *Ibid. Letter 11, 1*

[w] That indolent but agreeable condition of doing nothing.
Ibid. Book VIII, Letter 9, 3

[x] His only fault is that he has no fault.
Ibid. Book IX, Letter 26, 1

Plutarch
[A.D. 46–120]

[y] Anacharsis, coming to Athens, knocked at Solon's door, and told him that he, being a stranger, was come to be his guest, and contract a friendship with him; and Solon replying, "It is better to make friends at home," Anacharsis replied, "Then you that are at home make friendship with me."
Lives (tr. John Dryden, revised by Arthur Hugh Clough, Modern Library Giant edition).
Solon, Page 99

[z] Of two who made love to his daughter, he preferred the man of worth to the one who was rich, saying he desired a man without riches, rather than riches without a man.
Ibid. Themistocles, Page 145

[a] Themistocles replied that a man's discourse was like to a rich Persian carpet, the beautiful figures and patterns of which can be shown only by spreading and extending it out; when it is contracted and folded up, they are obscure and lost. *Ibid. Page 152*

[b] Moderation is best, and to avoid all extremes.
Ibid. Camillus, Page 159

[c] Caesar once, seeing some wealthy strangers at Rome, carrying up and down with them in their arms and bosoms young puppy-dogs and monkeys, embracing and making much of them, took occasion not unnaturally to ask whether the women in in their country were not used to bear children.
Ibid. Pericles, Page 182

[d] So very difficult a matter is it to trace and find out the truth of anything by history.
Ibid. Page 194

[e] Be ruled by time, the wisest counsellor of all. *Ibid. Page 198*

[f] Old women should not seek to be perfumed. *Ibid. Page 203*

[g] Trees, when they are lopped and cut, grow up again in a short time, but men, being once lost, cannot easily be recovered.
Ibid. Page 207

[h] You know, Hannibal, how to gain a victory, but not how to use it. *Ibid Fabius, Page 224*

[i] A Roman divorced from his wife, being highly blamed by his friends, who demanded, "Was she not chaste? Was she not fair? Was she not fruitful?" holding out his shoe, asked them whether it was not new and well made. "Yet," added he, "none of you can tell where it pinches me."
Ibid. Aemilius Paulus, Page 322

[j] Petty repeated annoyances, arising from unpleasantness or incongruity of character, have been the occasion of such estrangement as to make it impossible for man and wife to live together with any content. *Ibid.*

[k] Archimedes had stated, that given the force, any given weight might be moved; and even boasted . . . that if there were another earth, by going into it he could remove this.
Ibid. Marcellus, Page 367

[l] They named it Ovation, from the Latin *ovis* (a sheep).
Ibid. Page 382

[m] It is a difficult task, O citizens, to make speeches to the belly, which has no ears.
Ibid. Marcus Cato, Page 416

[n] Cato used to assert that wise men profited more by fools, than fools by wise men; for that wise men avoided the faults of fools, but that fools would not imitate the good examples of wise men.
Ibid. Page 417

[o] Marius said that the law spoke too softly to be heard in such a noise of war.
Ibid. Caius Marius, Page 511

[p] It is no great wonder if in long process of time, while fortune takes her course hither and thither, numerous coincidences should spontaneously occur. If the number and variety of subjects to be wrought upon be infinite, it is all the more easy for fortune, with such an abundance of material, to effect this similarity of results.
Ibid. Sertorius, Page 678

[q] Perseverance is more prevailing than violence; and many things which cannot be overcome when they are together, yield themselves up when taken little by little. *Ibid. Page 688*

[r] Good fortune will elevate even petty minds, and give them the appearance of a certain greatness and stateliness, as from their high place they look down upon the world; but the truly noble and resolved spirit raises itself, and becomes more conspicuous

in times of disaster and ill fortune. *Ibid. Eumenes, Page 703*

[s] Agesilaus being invited once to hear a man who admirably imitated the nightingale, he declined, saying he had heard the nightingale itself.

Ibid. Agesilaus, Page 726

[t] If all the world were just, there would be no need of valour.

Ibid. Page 727

[u] A dead man cannot bite.

Ibid. Pompey, Page 795

[v] When asked why he parted with his wife, Caesar replied, "I wished my wife to be not so much as suspected."

Ibid. Caesar, Page 860

[w] He who reflects on another man's want of breeding, shows he wants it as much himself.

Ibid. Page 865

[x] Using the proverb frequently in their mouths who enter upon dangerous and bold attempts, "The die is cast," he took the river. *Ibid. Page 874*

[y] Men, steered by popular applause, though they bear the name of governors, are in reality the mere underlings of the multitude. The man who is completely wise and virtuous has no need at all of glory, except so far as it disposes and eases his way of action by the greater trust that it procures him. *Ibid. Agis, Page 960*

[z] Demosthenes overcame and rendered more distinct his inarticulate and stammering pronunciation by speaking with pebbles in his mouth.

Ibid. Demosthenes, Page 1028

[a] Medicine, to produce health, has to examine disease, and music, to create harmony, must investigate discord.

Ibid. Demetrius, Page 1073

[b] Once Antigonus was told his son was ill, and went to see him. At the door he met some young beauty. Going in, he sat down by the bed and took his pulse. "The fever," said Demetrius, "has just left me." "Oh, yes," replied the father, "I met it going out at the door." *Ibid. Page 1083*

[c] "It is not," said Caesar, "these well-fed, long-haired men that I fear, but the pale and the hungry-looking"; meaning Brutus and Cassius, by whose conspiracy he afterwards fell.

Ibid. Antony, Page 1111

[d] It is a true proverb, that if you live with a lame man you will learn to halt.

Of the Training of Children

[e] The very spring and root of honesty and virtue lie in the felicity of lighting on good education. *Ibid.*

[f] It is indeed a desirable thing to be well descended, but the glory belongs to our ancestors.

Ibid.

[g] The whole life of man is but a point of time; let us enjoy it, therefore, while it lasts, and not spend it to no purpose. *Ibid.*

[h] Knavery is the best defence against a knave.

Of Bashfulness

[i] Alexander wept when he heard from Anaxarchus that there was an infinite number of worlds; and his friends asking him if any accident had befallen him, he returns this answer: "Do you not think it a matter worthy of lamentation that when there is such a vast multitude of them, we have not yet conquered one?"

On the Tranquillity of the Mind

[j] Like the man who threw a stone at a bitch, but hit his stepmother, on which he exclaimed, "Not so bad!" *Ibid.*

[k] Pittacus said, "Every one of you hath his particular plague, and my wife is mine; and he is very happy who hath this only."

Ibid.

[l] All men whilst they are awake are in one common world; but each of them, when he is asleep, is in a world of his own.

Of Superstition

[m] I, for my own part, had much rather people should say of me that there neither is nor ever was such a man as Plutarch, than that they should say, "Plutarch is an unsteady, fickle, forward, vindictive, and touchy fellow."

Ibid.

[n] Dionysius the Elder, being asked whether he was at leisure, he replied, "God forbid that it should ever befall me!"

Apophthegms of Kings and Great Commanders. Dionysius

[o] A prating barber asked Archelaus how he would be trimmed. He answered, "In silence."

Ibid. Archelaus

[p] When Philip had news brought him of divers and eminent successes in one day, "O Fortune!" said he, "for all these so great kindnesses do me some small mischief." *Ibid. Philip*

[q] He made one of Antipater's recommendation a judge; and perceiving afterwards that his hair and beard were dyed, he re-

moved him, saying, "I could not think one that was faithless in his hair could be trusty in his deeds." *Ibid.*

[**r**] Themistocles being asked whether he would rather be Achilles or Homer, said, "Which would you rather be,—a conqueror in the Olympic games, or the crier that proclaims who are conquerors?"
Ibid. Themistocles

[**s**] To Harmodius, descended from the ancient Harmodius, when he reviled Iphicrates [a shoemaker's son] for his mean birth, "My nobility," said he, "begins with me, but yours ends in you." *Ibid. Iphicrates*

[**t**] Phocion compared the speeches of Leosthenes to cypress-trees. "They are tall," said he, "and comely, but bear no fruit."
Ibid. Phocion

[**u**] Cato requested old men not to add the disgrace of wickedness to old age, which was accompanied with many other evils.
Roman Apophthegms. Cato the Elder

[**v**] He said they that were serious in ridiculous matters would be ridiculous in serious affairs. *Ibid.*

[**w**] Cicero said loud-bawling orators were driven by their weakness to noise, as lame men to take horse. *Ibid. Cicero*

[**x**] After he routed Pharnaces Ponticus at the first assault, he wrote thus to his friends: "I came, I saw, I conquered."
Ibid. Caesar

[**y**] As Caesar was at supper the discourse was of death,—which sort was the best. "That," said he, "which is unexpected." *Ibid.*

[**z**] Whenever you are angry . . . say or do nothing before you have repeated the four-and-twenty letters to yourself.
Ibid. Caesar Augustus

[**a**] Socrates thought that if all our misfortunes were laid in one common heap, whence every one must take an equal portion, most persons would be contented to take their own and depart.
Consolation to Apollonius

[**b**] Diogenes the Cynic, when a little before his death he fell into a slumber, and his physician rousing him out of it asked him whether anything ailed him, wisely answered, "Nothing, sir; only one brother anticipates another,—Sleep before Death." *Ibid.*

[**c**] When one told Plistarchus that a notorious railer spoke well

of him, "I'll lay my life," said he, "somebody hath told him I am dead, for he can speak well of no man living."
Laconic Apophthegms. Of Plistarchus

[**d**] Socrates said, "Bad men live that they may eat and drink, whereas good men eat and drink that they may live."
How a Young Man Ought to Hear Poems. 4

[**e**] Archimedes, as he was washing, thought of a manner of computing the proportion of gold in King Hiero's crown by seeing the water flowing over the bathing-stool. He leaped up as one possessed or inspired, crying, "I have found it! Eureka!"
Pleasure Not Attainable, According to Epicurus. 11

[**f**] It is a thing of no great difficulty to raise objections against another man's oration,—nay, it is a very easy matter; but to produce a better in its place is a work extremely troublesome.
Of Hearing. 6

[**g**] Antiphanes said merrily, that in a certain city the cold was so intense that words were congealed as soon as spoken, but that after some time they thawed and became audible; so that the words spoken in winter were articulated next summer.
Of Man's Progress in Virtue

[**h**] What is bigger than an elephant? But this also is become man's plaything, and a spectacle at public solemnities; and it learns to skip, dance, and kneel. *Of Fortune*

[**i**] No man ever wetted clay and then left it, as if there would be bricks by chance and fortune. *Ibid.*

[**j**] When the candles are out all women are fair. *Conjugal Precepts*

[**k**] When Demosthenes was asked what was the first part of oratory, he answered, "Action"; and which was the second, he replied, "Action"; and which was the third, he still answered, "Action." *Lives of the Ten Orators*

[**l**] Xenophon says that there is no sound more pleasing than one's own praises.
Whether an Aged Man Ought to Meddle in State Affairs

[**m**] Statesmen are not only liable to give an account of what they say or do in public, but there is a busy inquiry made into their very

meals, beds, marriages, and every other sportive or serious action.
Political Precepts

[n] Though the boys throw stones at frogs in sport, yet the frogs do not die in sport but in earnest.
Which Are the Most Crafty, Water or Land Animals? 7

[o] For to err in opinion, though it be not the part of wise men, is at least human.
Against Colotes

[p] Simonides calls painting silent poetry, and poetry, speaking painting.
Whether the Athenians Were More Warlike or Learned. 3

[q] Pythagoras, when he was asked what time was, answered that it was the soul of this world.
Platonic Questions

Edgar Allan Poe
[1809–1849]

[r] *All* that we see or seem
Is but a dream within a dream.
A Dream within a Dream. Stanza 1

[s] Sound loves to revel in a summer night.
Al Aaraaf. Part II

[t] Years of love have been forgot
In the hatred of a minute.
To ——

[u] The play is the tragedy, "Man,"
And its Hero the Conqueror Worm.
Ligeia. The Conqueror Worm. Stanza 5

[v] Unthought-like thoughts that are the souls of thought.
To Marie Louise

[w] I was a child and she was a child,
In this kingdom by the sea,
But we loved with a love that was more than love—
I and my Annabel Lee—
With a love that the winged seraphs of heaven
Coveted her and me.
Annabel Lee. Stanza 2

[x] Keeping time, time, time,
In a sort of Runic rhyme,
To the tintinnabulation that so musically wells
From the bells.
The Bells. Stanza 1

[y] Hear the mellow wedding bells,
Golden bells!
What a world of happiness their harmony foretells!
Through the balmy air of night
How they ring out their delight!
Ibid. Stanza 2

[z] I feel that, in the Heavens above,
The angels, whispering to one another,
Can find, among their burning terms of love,
None so devotional as that of "Mother."
To My Mother [Mrs. Clemm]

[a] The fever called "Living"
Is conquered at last.
For Annie. Stanza 1

[b] A dirge for her, the doubly dead in that she died so young.
Lenore. Stanza 1

[c] Once upon a midnight dreary, while I pondered, weak and weary,
Over many a quaint and curious volume of forgotten lore—
While I nodded, nearly napping, suddenly there came a tapping,
As of some one gently rapping.
The Raven. Stanza 1

[d] Ah, distinctly I remember, it was in the bleak December,
And each separate dying ember wrought its ghost upon the floor.
Ibid. Stanza 2

[e] Whom unmerciful Disaster
Followed fast and followed faster.
Ibid. Stanza 11

[f] Take thy beak from out my heart, and take thy form from off my door!
Quoth the Raven, "Nevermore."
And my soul from out that shadow that lies floating on the floor
Shall be lifted—Nevermore!
Ibid. Stanzas 17 and 18

[g] To the glory that was Greece,
And the grandeur that was Rome.
To Helen. Stanza 2

[h] The skies they were ashen and sober;
The leaves they were crispèd and sere—
The leaves they were withering and sere;
It was night in the lonesome October
Of my most immemorial year.
Ulalume. Stanza 1

[i] With me poetry has been not a purpose, but a passion; and the passions should be held in reverence: they must not—they can not at will be excited, with an eye to the paltry compensations, or the more paltry commendations, of mankind.
Poems [1845], Preface

[j] I would define, in brief, the Poetry of words as the Rhythmical Creation of Beauty. Its sole arbiter is Taste.
The Poetic Principle

[k] Can it be fancied that Deity
       ever vindictively
Made in his image a mannikin
       merely to madden it?
                The Rationale of Verse

[l] There is something in the unselfish and self-sacrificing love of
a brute, which goes directly to the
heart of him who has had frequent occasion to test the paltry
friendship and gossamer fidelity
of mere Man.   *The Black Cat*

[m] The question is not yet
settled, whether madness is or is
not the loftiest intelligence—
whether much that is glorious—
whether all that is profound—
does not spring from disease of
thought—from moods of mind exalted at the expense of the general
intellect.   *Eleonora*

[n] Those who dream by day are
cognizant of many things which
escape those who dream only by
night.   *Ibid.*

Edward Pollock
[1823–1858]

[o] There's something in the
       parting hour
Will chill the warmest heart,
Yet kindred, comrades, lovers,
       friends,
Are fated all to part. . . .
The one who goes is happier
Than those he leaves behind.
                The Parting Hour

Robert Pollok
[1798–1827]

[p] Sorrows remembered sweeten
       present joy.
       *The Course of Time. Book I,
                        Line 464*

[q] Most wondrous book! bright
       candle of the Lord!
Star of Eternity! The only star
By which the bark of man could
       navigate
The sea of life, and gain the coast
       of bliss
Securely.
       Ibid. Book II, Line 270

Madame Jeanne de
Pompadour
[1721–1764]

[r] After us the deluge.
       *Reply to Louis XV [November
       5, 1757] after the defeat of the
       French and Austrian armies by
       Frederick the Great in the battle
       of Rossbach. Quoted by Madame
       de Hausset in Memoirs, Page 19
       [Sometimes credited to Louis
       XV]*

Alexander Pope
[1688–1744]

[s] Let us, since life can little
       more supply
Than just to look about us, and
       to die,
Expatiate free o'er all this scene
       of man;
A mighty maze! but not without
       a plan.   *Essay on Man.
                        Epistle I, Line 1*

[t] Eye Nature's walks, shoot folly
       as it flies,
And catch the manners living as
       they rise;
Laugh where we must, be candid
       where we can,
But vindicate the ways of God to
       man.   *Ibid. Line 13*

[u] Heaven from all creatures
       hides the book of Fate,
All but the page prescrib'd, their
       present state.   *Ibid. Line 77*

[v] Who sees with equal eye, as
       God of all,
A hero perish or a sparrow fall,
Atoms or systems into ruin hurl'd,
And now a bubble burst, and now
       a world.   *Ibid. Line 87*

[w] Hope springs eternal in the
       human breast:
Man never is, but always to be,
       blest.   *Ibid. Line 95*

[x] Lo, the poor Indian! whose
       untutor'd mind
Sees God in clouds, or hears him
       in the wind.   *Ibid. Line 99*

[y] Die of a rose in aromatic
       pain.   *Ibid. Line 200*

[z] The spider's touch, how ex-
       quisitely fine,
Feels at each thread, and lives
       along the line.
                Ibid. Line 217

[a] All are but parts of one stu-
       pendous whole,
Whose body Nature is, and God
       the soul.   *Ibid. Line 267*

[b] One truth is clear, Whatever
       is, is right.   *Ibid. Line 294*

[c] Know then thyself, presume
       not God to scan;
The proper study of mankind is
       man.
       Ibid. Epistle II, Line 1

[d] Vice is a monster of so fright-
       ful mien,
As to be hated needs but to be
       seen;
Yet seen too oft, familiar with
       her face,
We first endure, then pity, then
       embrace.
       Ibid. Epistle II, Line 217

[e] Behold the child, by Nature's
       kindly law,
Pleased with a rattle, tickled with
       a straw:

Some livelier plaything gives his
   youth delight,
A little louder, but as empty
   quite:
Scarfs, garters, gold, amuse his
   riper stage,
And beads and prayer-books are
   the toys of age.
Pleased with this bauble still, as
   that before,
Till tired he sleeps, and life's poor
   play is o'er.
                    Ibid. Line 274

[f] In faith and hope the world
   will disagree,
But all mankind's concern is
   charity.
         Ibid. Epistle III, Line 307

[g] O happiness! our being's end
   and aim!
Good, pleasure, ease, content!
   whate'er thy name:
That something still which
   prompts the eternal sigh,
For which we bear to live, or dare
   to die.
         Ibid. Epistle IV, Line 1

[h] A wit's a feather, and a chief
   a rod;
An honest man's the noblest work
   of God.   *Ibid. Line 247*

[i] One self-approving hour
   whole years outweighs
Of stupid starers and of loud huz-
   zas.   *Ibid. Line 255*

[j] 'Tis education forms the common mind:
Just as the twig is bent the tree's
   inclined.   *Moral Essays.*
                    Epistle I, Line 149

[k] Most women have no charac-
   ters at all.
            Ibid. Epistle II, Line 2

[l] Whether the charmer sinner
   it or saint it,
If folly grow romantic, I must
   paint it.   *Ibid. Line 15*

[m] Men, some to business, some
   to pleasure take;
But every woman is at heart a
   rake.   *Ibid. Line 215*

[n] And mistress of herself
   though china fall.
                    Ibid. Line 268

[o] Woman's at best a contradiction still.   *Ibid. Line 270*

[p] Who shall decide when doctors disagree?
            Ibid. Epistle III, Line 1

[q] Blest paper-credit! last and
   best supply!
That lends corruption lighter
   wings to fly!   *Ibid. Line 39*

[r] Who builds a church to God,
   and not to fame,
Will never mark the marble with
   his name.   *Ibid. Line 285*

[s] 'Tis with our judgments as
   our watches, none
Go just alike, yet each believes
   his own.
   Essay on Criticism. Part I, Line 9

[t] Music resembles poetry; in
   each
Are nameless graces which no
   methods teach,
And which a master-hand alone
   can reach.   *Ibid. Line 143*

[u] Of all the causes which conspire to blind
Man's erring judgment, and mis-
   guide the mind,
What the weak head with strongest bias rules,
Is pride, the never-failing vice of
   fools.   *Ibid. Part II, Line 1*

[v] A little learning is a danger-
   ous thing;
Drink deep, or taste not the
   Pierian spring:
There shallow draughts intoxicate
   the brain,
And drinking largely sobers us
   again.   *Ibid. Line 15*

[w] Words are like leaves; and
   where they most abound,
Much fruit of sense beneath is
   rarely found.   *Ibid. Line 109*

[x] In words, as fashions, the
   same rule will hold,
Alike fantastic if too new or old:
Be not the first by whom the new
   are tried,
Nor yet the last to lay the old
   aside.   *Ibid. Line 133*

[y] Some to church repair,
Not for the doctrine, but the
   music there.   *Ibid. Line 142*

[z] At ev'ry trifle scorn to take
   offence.   *Ibid. Line 186*

[a] Yet let not each gay turn thy
   rapture move;
For fools admire, but men of
   sense approve.
                    Ibid. Line 190

[b] Some judge of authors'
   names, not works, and then
Nor praise nor blame the writings,
   but the men.   *Ibid. Line 212*

[c] Some praise at morning what
   they blame at night,
But always think the last opinion
   right.   *Ibid. Line 230*

[d] Envy will merit as its shade
   pursue,
But like a shadow proves the substance true.   *Ibid. Line 266*

[e] To err is human, to forgive
   divine.   *Ibid. Line 325*

[f'] All seems infected that th'
   infected spy,
As all looks yellow to the jaun-
   dic'd eye.   *Ibid. Line 358*

[g'] The bookful blockhead, ig-
   norantly read,

With loads of learned lumber in
his head.
Ibid. Part III, Line 53

[h] For fools rush in where angels fear to tread.
Ibid. Line 66

[i] What dire offence from amorous causes springs!
What mighty contests rise from
trivial things! *The Rape
of the Lock. Canto I, Line 1*

[j] If to her share some female
errors fall,
Look on her face, and you'll forget 'em all.
Ibid. Canto II, Line 17

[k] Fair tresses man's imperial
race ensnare,
And beauty draws us with a single
hair. *Ibid. Line 27*

[l] At every word a reputation
dies. *Ibid. Canto III, Line 16*

[m] The hungry judges soon the
sentence sign,
And wretches hang that jurymen
may dine. *Ibid. Line 21*

[n] Coffee, which makes the politician wise. *Ibid. Line 117*

[o] Steel could the labour of the
gods destroy,
And strike to dust th' imperial
towers of Troy;
Steel could the works of mortal
pride confound
And hew triumphal arches to the
ground. *Ibid. Line 173*

[p] Charms strike the sight, but
merit wins the soul.
Ibid. Canto V, Line 34

[q] No creature smarts so little as
a fool.
*Epistle to Dr. Arbuthnot, Pro-
logue to the Satires, Line 84*

[r] This long disease, my life.
Ibid. Line 132

[s] Damn with faint praise, as-
sent with civil leer,
And without sneering teach the
rest to sneer;
Willing to wound, and yet afraid
to strike,
Just hint a fault, and hesitate
dislike. *Ibid. Line 201*

[t] Eternal smiles his emptiness
betray,
As shallow streams run dimpling
all the way. *Ibid. Line 315*

[u] Unlearn'd, he knew no
schoolman's subtle art,
No language but the language of
the heart. *Ibid. Line 398*

[v] I cannot sleep a wink.
*Satires, Epistles, and Odes of
Horace. Satire I, Book II, Line 12*

[w] Satire's my weapon, but I'm
too discreet
To run amuck, and tilt at all I
meet. *Ibid. Line 69*

[x] For I, who hold sage Homer's
rule the best,
Welcome the coming, speed the
going guest. *Ibid. Satire
II, Book II, Line 159*

[y] A patriot is a fool in ev'ry age.
*Epilogue to the Satires. Dia-
logue I, Line 41*

[z] Laugh then at any but at
fools or foes;
These you but anger, and you
mend not those.
Laugh at your friends, and if your
friends are sore,
So much the better, you may
laugh the more.
Ibid. Line 53

[a] When the brisk minor pants
for twenty-one. *Epistle I.
Book I, Line 38*

[b] Not to go back is somewhat
to advance. *Ibid. Line 53*

[c] He's armed without that's
innocent within.
Ibid. Line 94

[d] One simile that solitary
shines
In the dry desert of a thousand
lines.
Ibid. Book II, Line 111

[e] What will a child learn sooner
than a song? *Ibid. Line 205*

[f] The last and greatest art—
the art to blot.
Ibid. Line 281

[g] We poets are (upon a poet's
word)
Of all mankind the creatures
most absurd:
The season when to come, and
when to go,
To sing, or cease to sing, we never
know. *Ibid. Line 358*

[h'] Call, if you will, bad rhym-
ing a disease,
It gives men happiness, or leaves
them ease. *Epistle II.
Book II, Line 182*

[i'] The worst of madmen is a
saint run mad. *Epistle VI.
Book I, Line 27*

[j'] Vain was the chief's, the
sage's pride!
They had no poet, and they died.
Odes. Book IV, Ode 9, Stanza 4

[k'] Nature and Nature's laws
lay hid in night:
God said, Let Newton be! and all
was light. *Epitaph In-
tended for Sir Isaac Newton*

[l'] Poetic Justice, with her lifted
scale,

Where in nice balance truth with
  gold she weighs,
And solid pudding against empty
  praise.   *The Dunciad.*
               Book I, Line 52

[**m**] Next o'er his books his eyes
  begin to roll,
In pleasing memory of all he
  stole.   *Ibid. Line 127*

[**n**] The right divine of kings to
  govern wrong.
    Ibid. Book IV, Line 188

[**o**] To happy convents, bosom'd
  deep in vines,
Where slumber abbots purple as
  their wines.   *Ibid. Line 301*

[**p**] How vast a memory has Love!
    Sappho to Phaon. Line 52

[**q**] Curse on all laws but those
  which love has made!
Love, free as air at sight of human
  ties,
Spreads his light wings, and in a
  moment flies.
    Eloisa to Abelard. Line 74

[**r**] How happy is the blameless
  vestal's lot!
The world forgetting, by the world
  forgot.   *Ibid. Line 207*

[**s**] Unblemish'd let me live or
  die unknown;
Oh, grant an honest fame or grant
  me none!
    The Temple of Fame.
    Line 523 (last lines)

[**t**] Father of all! in every age,
In every clime adored,
By saint, by savage, and by sage,
Jehovah, Jove, or Lord!
  The Universal Prayer. Stanza 1

[**u**] Teach me to feel another's
  woe,
To hide the fault I see;
That mercy I to others show,
  That mercy show to me.
    Ibid. Stanza 10

[**v**] Vital spark of heavenly flame,
Quit, Oh quit, this mortal frame!
  The Dying Christian to His
    Soul. Stanza 1

[**w**] Is there no bright reversion
  in the sky
For those who greatly think, or
  bravely die?
  To the Memory of an Unfortu-
    nate Lady. Line 9

[**x**] How lov'd, how honour'd
  once, avails thee not,
To whom related, or by whom begot;
A heap of dust alone remains of
  thee:
'Tis all thou art, and all the proud
  shall be!   *Ibid. Line 71*

[**y**] You beat your pate, and fancy
  wit will come;

Knock as you please, there's nobody at home.
    Epigram: An Empty House

[**z**] For he lives twice who can at
  once employ
The present well, and ev'n the
  past enjoy.
    Imitation of Martial

[**a**] Party is the madness of many
  for the gain of a few.
  Thoughts on Various Subjects

[**b**] I never knew any man in my
life who could not bear another's
misfortunes perfectly like a
Christian.   *Ibid.*

[**c**] It is with narrow-souled
people as with narrow-necked
bottles; the less they have in
them the more noise they make in
pouring out.   *Ibid.*

[**d**] When men grow virtuous in
their old age, they only make a
sacrifice to God of the devil's
leavings.   *Ibid.*

[**e**] True disputants are like true
sportsmen, their whole delight is
in the pursuit.   *Ibid.*

[**f**] No literal Translation can be
just to an excellent Original: but
it is a great Mistake to imagine
that a rash Paraphrase can make
amends for this general Defect.
[Of Pope's translation Richard
Bentley, great classical scholar,
said, "A very pretty poem, Mr.
Pope, but it's not Homer."]
    Preface to the Iliad

[**g**] Words sweet as honey from
  his lips distill'd.   *The Iliad*
  of Homer. Book I, Line 332

[**h**] And unextinguish'd laughter
  shakes the skies.
    Ibid. Line 771

[**i**] The man who acts the least,
  upbraids the most.
    Ibid. Book II, Line 311

[**j**] But when he speaks, what
  elocution flows!
Soft as the fleeces of descending
  snows
The copious accents fall, with
  easy art;
Melting they fall, and sink into
  the heart.
    Ibid. Book III, Line 283

[**k**] Wrapt in the cold embraces
  of the tomb.
    Ibid. Line 312

[**l**] Plough the watery deep.
    Ibid. Line 357

[**m'**] The day shall come, the
  great avenging day,
Which Troy's proud glories in the
  dust shall lay,
When Priam's powers and Priam's
  self shall fall,
And one prodigious ruin swallow
  all.   *Ibid. Book IV, Line 196*

[n] The first in banquets, but the last in fight.
Ibid. Line 401

[o] Gods! How the son degenerates from the sire!
Ibid. Line 451

[p] A friend to human race.
Fast by the road, his ever-open door
Obliged the wealthy, and reliev'd the poor.
Ibid. Book VI, Line 18

[q] Like leaves on trees the race of man is found,
Now green in youth, now withering on the ground:
Another race the following spring supplies:
They fall successive, and successive rise.   *Ibid. Line 181*

[r] Inflaming wine, pernicious to mankind.   *Ibid. Line 330*

[s] Without a sign, his sword the brave man draws,
And asks no omen but his country's cause.
Ibid. Book XII, Line 283

[t] And seem to walk on wings, and tread in air.
Ibid. Book XIII, Line 106

[u] Not vain the weakest, if their force unite.   *Ibid. Line 311*

[v] The best of things, beyond their measure, cloy.
Ibid. Line 795

[w] And for our country 'tis a bliss to die.
Ibid. Book XV, Line 583

[x] It is not strength, but art, obtains the prize,
And to be swift is less than to be wise.
'Tis more by art, than force of num'rous strokes.
Ibid. Book XXIII, Line 383

[y] An honest business never blush to tell. *The Odyssey of Homer. Book III, Line 20*

[z] When now Aurora, daughter of the dawn,
With rosy lustre purpled o'er the lawn.   *Ibid. Line 516*

[a] His native home deep imag'd in his soul.
Ibid. Book XIII, Line 38

[b] The sex is ever to a soldier kind.
Ibid. Book XIV, Line 246

[c] For too much rest itself becomes a pain.
Ibid. Book XV, Line 429

[d] He knew his lord; he knew, and strove to meet;
In vain he strove to crawl and kiss his feet;
Yet (all he could) his tail, his ears, his eyes

Salute his master, and confess his joys. . . .
The dog, whom Fate had granted to behold
His lord, when twenty tedious years had roll'd,
Takes a last look, and, having seen him, dies:
So closed forever faithful Argus' eyes!
Ibid. Book XVII, Line 359

[e] Blessed is he who expects nothing, for he shall never be disappointed.
Letter to Gay [October 6, 1727]

Walter Pope
[1630?–1714]

[f] May I govern my passions with absolute sway,
And grow wiser and better, as strength wears away,
Without gout or stone, by a gentle decay.   *The Old Man's Wish*

Alan Porter
[1899–1942]

[g] Every countenance
That warms and lights the heart of the beholder
Shews, clear and true, the signature of pain.
The Signature of Pain

[h] "Good men have bags of money
And blazoned shields.
I wonder how much money
My new play yields?"
This is what Shakespeare said,
Wagging his wicked head,
Walking from Aldermanbury
To Bunhill Fields.
The Poet's Journey

[i] There should between true lovers be
An excellent immodesty.
A Plea That Shame Be Forgotten

[j] Were death forgotten, days were white
Circles of unimpaired delight.
Death. Stanza 4

William Sydney Porter
see "O. Henry"

Beilby Porteus
[1731–1808]

[k] One murder made a villain,
Millions, a hero. Princes were privileged
To kill, and numbers sanctified the crime.   *Death. Line 154*

[l] Love is something so divine,
Description would but make it less;

'Tis what I feel, but can't define,
'Tis what I know, but can't express.   *On Love*

Henry Codman Potter
[1835–1908]

[m] If there be no nobility of
descent, all the more indispensable is it that there should be
nobility of ascent,—a character
in them that bear rule so fine and
high and pure that as men come
within the circle of its influence
they involuntarily pay homage to
that which is the one pre-eminent
distinction, the royalty of virtue.
*Address at the Washington
Centennial Service in St. Paul's
Chapel, New York* [*April 30,
1889*]

Ezra Pound
[1885–   ]

[n] Sing we for love and idleness,
Naught else is worth the having.
                An Immortality

[o] And I would rather have my
sweet,
Though rose-leaves die of griev-
ing,
Than do high deeds in Hungary
To pass all men's believing.
                         Ibid.

[p] For God, our God, is a gallant
foe that playeth behind the
veil.
Whom God deigns not to overthrow hath need of triple
mail.
      Ballad for Gloom. Stanza 7

[q] They will come no more,
The old men with beautiful manners.   *I Vecchii*

[r] You can spot the bad critic
when he starts by discussing the
poet and not the poem.
    A, B, C of Reading. Page 71

[s] There is no reason why the
same man should like the same
book at 18 and at 48.
            Ibid. Page 72

Horatio Nelson Powers
[1826–1890]

[t] A flower unblown; a book un-
read;
A tree with fruit unharvested;
A path untrod; a house whose
rooms
Lack yet the heart's divine per-
fumes;
A landscape whose wide border
lies
In silent shade 'neath silent skies;
A wondrous fountain yet un-
sealed;
A casket with its gifts concealed—

This is the Year that for you waits
Beyond to-morrow's mystic gates.
                The New Year

Winthrop Mackworth Praed
[1802–1839]

[u] And oh! I shall find how, day
by day,
All thoughts and things look
older;
How the laugh of pleasure grows
less gay,
And the heart of friendship
colder.
    Twenty-eight and Twenty-nine

[v] I think that life is not too
long,
And therefore I determine
That many people read a song
Who will not read a sermon.
    *The Chant of the Brazen Head.
                    Stanza 1*

[w] His talk was like a stream
which runs
With rapid change from rocks
to roses,
It slipped from politics to puns;
It passed from Mahomet to
Moses.
        The Vicar. Stanza 5

[x] Events are writ by History's
pen:
Though causes are too much to
care for:—
Fame talks about the where and
when,
While folly asks the why and
wherefore.
    *Epitaph on the Late King of
the Sandwich Islands. Stanza 4*

[y] His partners at the whist-
club said
That he was faultless in his
dealings.

And cut the fiercest quarrel short
With "Patience, gentlemen, and
shuffle."
    Quince. Stanzas 3 and 5

[z] Dame Fortune is a fickle
gipsy,
And always blind, and often tipsy;
Sometimes for years and years together,
She'll bless you with the sunniest
weather . . .
Then in a moment—Presto,
pass!—
Your joys are withered like the
grass.   *The Haunted Tree*

Edwin John Pratt
[1883–   ]

[a] The great syllabic storm of
the age.
    *The Radio in the Ivory Tower
[September 1939]*

[b] Cold half-foundered bellies
  steam again
Under the red authority of rum.
    *The "Roosevelt" and the
          "Antinoe"*

[c] When he had lost his pipe, he
  swore,
Just a mild damn, and nothing
  more;
And once he cursed
The government; but then he
  reckoned
The Lord forgave him for the first,
And justified the second.
    The History of John Jones

William Prescott
[1726–1795]

[d] Don't fire until you see the
whites of their eyes.
    At Bunker Hill, June 17, 1775

William Hickling Prescott
[1796–1859]

[e] The surest test of the civilization of a people—at least, as sure
as any—afforded by mechanical
art is to be found in their architecture, which presents so noble a
field for the display of the grand
and the beautiful, and which, at
the same time, is so intimately
connected with the essential comforts of life.   *The Conquest of
      Peru. Book I, Chap. 5*

[f] Where there is no free agency,
there can be no morality. Where
there is no temptation, there can
be little claim to virtue. Where
the routine is rigorously pro-
scribed by law, the law, and not
the man, must have the credit of
the conduct.   *Ibid.*

Keith Preston
[1884–1927]

[g] The great god Ra whose
  shrine once covered acres
Is filler now for cross-word puzzle
  makers.   *The Destiny That
        Shapes Our Ends*

[h] Love, lay thy phobias to rest,
  Inhibit thy taboo!
We twain shall share, forever
  blest,
  A complex built for two.
    Love Song, Freudian

[i] He must not laugh at his own
  wheeze:
A snuff box has no right to sneeze.
    The Humorist

[j] I am the captain of my soul;
  I rule it with stern joy;
And yet I think I had more fun
  When I was a cabin boy.
    An Awful Responsibility

Margaret Junkin Preston
[1820–1897]

[k] If from his home the lad that
  day
  His five small loaves had failed
  to take,
Would Christ have wrought—can
  any say—
This miracle beside the lake?
    A Store of Loaves. Stanza 7

[l] And therefore, I, William
  Bradford (by the grace of
  God to-day,
And the franchise of this good
  people), governor of Plym-
  outh, say—
Through virtue of vested power—
  ye shall gather with one ac-
  cord,
And hold in the month of Novem-
  ber, thanksgiving unto the
  Lord.   *The First Thanks-
      giving Day, 1622. Stanza 2*

[m] What worth is eulogy's
  blandest breath,
When whispered in ears that are
  hushed in death?
    What Use?

Archibald Philip Primrose, Earl of Rosebery
[1847–1929]

[n] Few speeches which have produced an electrical effect on an
audience can bear the colorless
photography of a printed record.
    Life of Pitt

Matthew Prior
[1664–1721]

[o] Odds life! must one swear to
  the truth of a song?
    A Better Answer

[p] Be to her virtues very kind;
Be to her faults a little blind.
    An English Padlock

[q] That if weak women went
  astray,
Their stars were more in fault
  than they.   *Hans Carvel*

[r] They never taste who always
  drink;
They always talk who never
  think.   *Upon a Passage
      in the Scaligerana*

[s] Nobles and heralds, by your
  leave,
Here lies what once was Matthew Prior;
The son of Adam and of Eve:
  Can Stuart or Nassau claim
  higher?
    Epitaph. Extempore

[t] Lays the rough paths of peevish Nature even,
And opens in each heart a little
  heaven.   *Charity*

[u] Till their own dreams at
length deceive 'em,
And oft repeating, they believe
'em.
Alma. Canto III, Line 13

[v] Who breathes must suffer,
and who thinks must mourn;
And he alone is bless'd who ne'er
was born. *Solomon on the
Vanity of the World. Book III,
Line 240*

Adelaide Anne Procter
[1825–1864]

[w] Seated one day at the organ,
I was weary and ill at ease,
And my fingers wandered idly
Over the noisy keys.

It seemed the harmonious echo
From our discordant life.
A Lost Chord. Stanzas 1 and 4

[x] I will not let you say a
woman's part
Must be to give exclusive love
alone;
Dearest, although I love you so,
my heart
Answers a thousand claims besides your own.
A Woman's Answer. Stanza 1

Bryan Waller Procter
("Barry Cornwall")
[1787–1874]

[y] We know not alway who are
kings by day,
But the king of the night is the
bold brown owl.
The Owl. Stanza 3

[z] I'm on the sea! I'm on the
sea!
I am where I would ever be,
With the blue above and the blue
below,
And silence wheresoe'er I go.

I never was on the dull, tame
shore,
But I loved the great sea more
and more.
The Sea. Stanzas 2 and 4

[a] Touch us gently, Time!
Let us glide adown thy stream
Gently,—as we sometimes glide
Through a quiet dream.
A Petition to Time. Stanza 1

Edna Dean Proctor
[1838–1923]

[b] The rose may bloom for Eng-
land,
The lily for France unfold;
Ireland may honor the shamrock,
Scotland her thistle bold;

But the shield of the great Re-
public,
The glory of the West,
Shall bear a stalk of the tasselled
corn—
The sun's supreme bequest!
Columbia's Emblem

Propertius
[54 B.C.–A.D. 2]

[c] Never change when love has
found its home.
Book I. Elegy 1, Line 36

[d] Scandal has ever been the
doom of beauty.
Book II. Elegy 32, Line 26

David Law Proudfit
("Peleg Arkwright")
[1842–1897]

[e] A man sat on a rock and
sought
Refreshment from his thumb;
A dinotherium wandered by
And scared him some.
His name was Smith. The kind
of rock
He sat upon was shale.
One feature quite distinguished
him—
He had a tail. . . .
Nature abhors imperfect work
And on it lays her ban;
And all creation must despise
A tailless man.
Prehistoric Smith

Marcel Proust
[1871–1922]
*From A la Recherche du temps
perdu, Remembrance of Things
Past, Random House edition,
translated by C. K. Scott Mon-
crieff, except the last section, The
Past Recaptured, which was
translated by Frederick A. Blossom.*

[f] In his younger days a man
dreams of possessing the heart of
the woman whom he loves; later,
the feeling that he possesses the
heart of a woman may be enough
to make him fall in love with her.
Swann's Way. Page 253

[g] The time which we have at
our disposal every day is elastic;
the passions that we feel expand
it, those that we inspire contract it; and habit fills up what
remains. *Within a Budding
Grove. Part I, Page 264*

[h] Untruthfulness and dishonesty were with me, as with
most people, called into being in
so immediate, so contingent a
fashion, and in self-defence, by
some particular interest, that my
mind, fixed on some lofty ideal,

allowed my character, in the darkness below, to set about those urgent, sordid tasks, and did not look down to observe them.
The Guermantes Way.
Part I, Page 82

[i] Like everybody who is not in love, he imagined that one chose the person whom one loved after endless deliberations and on the strength of various qualities and advantages. *Cities of the Plain.*
Part I, Page 132

[j] The bonds that unite another person to ourself exist only in our mind. . . . Man is the creature that cannot emerge from himself, that knows his fellows only in himself; when he asserts the contrary, he is lying.
The Sweet Cheat Gone. Page 47

[k] We believe that according to our desire we are able to change the things round about us, we believe this because otherwise we can see no favourable solution. We forget the solution that generally comes to pass and is also favourable: we do not succeed in changing things according to our desire, but gradually our desire changes. . . . We have not managed to surmount the obstacle, as we were absolutely determined to do, but life has taken us round it, led us past it, and then if we turn round to gaze at the remote past, we can barely catch sight of it, so imperceptible has it become. *Ibid. Page 48*

[l] We are healed of a suffering only by experiencing it to the full.
Ibid. Page 165

[m] Happiness is beneficial for the body but it is grief that develops the powers of the mind.
The Past Recaptured. Page 237

Publilius Syrus

[Circa 42 B.C.]
Translation by Darius Lyman. The numbers are those of the translator.

[n] As men, we are all equal in the presence of death.   *Maxim 1*

[o] To do two things at once is to do neither.   *Maxim 7*

[p] Every one excels in something in which another fails.
Maxim 17

[q] A god could hardly love and be wise.   *Maxim 25*

[r] He sleeps well who knows not that he sleeps ill.   *Maxim 77*

[s] An agreeable companion on a journey is as good as a carriage.
Maxim 143

[t] While we stop to think, we often miss our opportunity.
Maxim 185

[u] Whatever you can lose, you should reckon of no account.
Maxim 191

[v] We may with advantage at times forget what we know.
Maxim 234

[w] The end justifies the means.
Maxim 244

[x] A fair exterior is a silent recommendation.   *Maxim 267*

[y] Fortune is like glass,—the brighter the glitter, the more easily broken.   *Maxim 280*

[z] His own character is the arbiter of every one's fortune.
Maxim 283

[a] Powerful indeed is the empire of habit.   *Maxim 305*

[b] It is easy for men to talk one thing and think another.
Maxim 322

[c] When two do the same thing, it is not the same thing after all.
Maxim 338

[d] The bow too tensely strung is easily broken.   *Maxim 388*

[e] Treat your friend as if he might become an enemy.
Maxim 402

[f] No pleasure endures unseasoned by variety.   *Maxim 406*

[g] The judge is condemned when the criminal is absolved.
Maxim 407

[h] Practice is the best of all instructors.   *Maxim 439*

[i'] It is better to have a little than nothing.   *Maxim 484*

[j'] It is an unhappy lot which finds no enemies.   *Maxim 499*

[k'] Necessity knows no law except to conquer.   *Maxim 553*

[l'] Nothing can be done at once hastily and prudently.
Maxim 557

[m'] We desire nothing so much as what we ought not to have.
Maxim 559

[n'] It is only the ignorant who despise education.   *Maxim 571*

[o'] It is not every question that deserves an answer.   *Maxim 581*

[p'] No man is happy who does not think himself so.
Maxim 584

[q'] You cannot put the same shoe on every foot.   *Maxim 596*

[r'] He bids fair to grow wise who has discovered that he is not so.
Maxim 598

[s] Money alone sets all the world in motion. *Maxim 656*

[t] It is a very hard undertaking to seek to please everybody. *Maxim 675*

[u] How happy the life unembarrassed by the cares of business! *Maxim 725*

[v] They who plough the sea do not carry the winds in their hands. *Maxim 759*

[w] It takes a long time to bring excellence to maturity. *Maxim 780*

[x] No one knows what he can do till he tries. *Maxim 786*

[y] The next day is never so good as the day before. *Maxim 815*

[z] He is truly wise who gains wisdom from another's mishap. *Maxim 825*

[a] Good health and good sense are two of life's greatest blessings. *Maxim 827*

[b] Everything is worth what its purchaser will pay for it. *Maxim 847*

[c] Better use medicines at the outset than at the last moment. *Maxim 866*

[d] Prosperity makes friends, adversity tries them. *Maxim 872*

[e] Let a fool hold his tongue and he will pass for a sage. *Maxim 914*

[f] Confession of our faults is the next thing to innocency. *Maxim 1060*

[g] Speech is a mirror of the soul: as a man speaks, so is he. *Maxim 1073*

Sir William Pulteney
[1684–1764]

[h] For twelve honest men have decided the cause,
Who are judges alike of the facts and the laws. *The Honest Jury*

Amelia Earhart Putnam
[1898–1937]

[i] Courage is the price that life exacts for granting peace.
The soul that knows it not, knows no release
From little things;
Knows not the livid loneliness of fear,
Nor mountain heights where bitter joy can hear
The sound of wings. *Courage*

Ernie Pyle
[1900–1945]

[j] If you go long enough without a bath even the fleas will let you alone. *Here is Your War*

[k] I walked around what seemed to be a couple of pieces of driftwood sticking out of the sand. But they weren't driftwood. They were a soldier's two feet. He was completely covered except for his feet; the toes of his G. I. shoes pointed toward the land he had come so far to see, and which he saw so briefly. [Description of the Normandy beachhead, June 1944.] *Brave Men*

[l] Then darkness enveloped the whole American armada. Not a pinpoint of light showed from those hundreds of ships as they surged on through the night toward their destiny, carrying across the ageless and indifferent sea tens of thousands of young men, fighting for . . . for . . . well, at least for each other. *Ibid.*

Francis Quarles
[1592–1644]

[m] Death aims with fouler spite
At fairer marks. *Divine Poems*

[n] Sweet Phosphor, bring the day!
Light will repay
The wrongs of night;
Sweet Phosphor, bring the day! *Emblems. Book I, Emblem 14*

[o] Be wisely worldly, be not worldly wise. *Ibid. Book II, Emblem 2*

[p] Let all thy joys be as the month of May,
And all thy days be as a marriage day:
Let sorrow, sickness, and a troubled mind
Be stranger to thee, let them never find
Thy heart at home. *To a Bride*

Sir Arthur Thomas Quiller-Couch
[1863–1944]

[q] Literature is not an abstract science, to which exact definitions can be applied. It is an art, the success of which depends on personal persuasiveness, on the author's skill to give as on ours to receive. *Inaugural Lecture at Cambridge University* [1913]

Josiah Quincy
[1744–1775]

[r] Blandishments will not fascinate us, nor will threats of a

"halter" intimidate. For, under God, we are determined that wheresoever, whensoever, or howsoever we shall be called to make our exit, we shall die free men.
Observations on the Boston Port Bill [1774]

Quintilian
[A.D. 42–118]

[s] We give to necessity the praise of virtue. *Institutiones Oratoriae. Book I, 8, 14*

[t] A liar should have a good memory. *Ibid. Book IV, 2, 91*

François Rabelais
[1495–1553]

[u] He left a paper sealed up, wherein were found three articles as his last will: "I owe much; I have nothing; I give the rest to the poor." *Peter Anthony Motteux: Life of Rabelais*

[v] One inch of joy surmounts of grief a span,
Because to laugh is proper to the man. *Works. To the Readers*

[w] I drink no more than a sponge. *Ibid. Book I, Chap. 5*

[x] He laid him squat as a flounder. *Ibid. Chap. 27*

[y] Send them home as merry as crickets. *Ibid. Chap. 29*

[z] War begun without good provision of money beforehand for going through with it is but as a breathing of strength and blast that will quickly pass away. Coin is the sinews of war. *Ibid. Chap. 46*

[a] How shall I be able to rule over others, that have not full power and command of myself? *Ibid. Chap. 52*

[b] Subject to a kind of disease, which at that time they called lack of money. *Ibid. Book II, Chap. 16*

[c] So much is a man worth as he esteems himself. *Ibid. Chap. 29*

[d] Then I began to think that it is very true which is commonly said, that the one half of the world knoweth not how the other half liveth. *Ibid. Chap. 32*

[e] The Devil was sick,—the Devil a monk would be;
The Devil was well,—the Devil a monk was he. *Ibid. Book IV, Chap. 24*

[f] Do not believe what I tell you here any more than if it were some tale of a tub. *Ibid. Chap. 38*

[g] He that has patience may compass anything. *Ibid. Chap. 48*

[h] We will take the good will for the deed. *Ibid. Chap. 49*

[i] You are Christians of the best edition, all picked and culled. *Ibid. Chap. 50*

[j] Scampering as if the Devil drove them. *Ibid. Chap. 62*

[k] He freshly and cheerfully asked him how a man should kill time. *Ibid.*

[l] Whose cockloft is unfurnished. *Ibid. Book V, Author's Prologue*

[m] Speak the truth and shame the Devil. *Ibid.*

[n] What cannot be cured must be endured. *Ibid. Chap. 15*

[o] Thought I to myself, we shall never come off scot-free. *Ibid.*

[p] It is enough to fright you out of your seven senses. *Ibid.*

[q] We saw a knot of others, about a baker's dozen. *Ibid. Chap. 23*

Jean Baptiste Racine
[1639–1699]

[r] Crime like virtue has its degrees. *Phèdre. Act IV, Sc. 2*

[s'] To repair the irreparable ravages of time. *Athalie. Act II, Sc. 5*

Ann Radcliffe
[1764–1823]

[t'] Fate sits on these dark battlements and frowns,
And as the portal opens to receive me,
A voice in hollow murmurs through the courts
Tells of a nameless deed.
Motto of her novel, The Mysteries of Udolpho, and presumably of her own composition

Thomas Rainborough
[?–1648]

[u'] The poorest he that is in England hath a life to live as the greatest he.
In the Army debates at Putney, October 29, 1647

Sir Walter Raleigh
[1552–1618]

[v'] If all the world and love were young,
And truth in every shepherd's tongue,
These pretty pleasures might me move

To live with thee, and be thy
love.
The Nymph's Reply to the Passionate Shepherd. [*An answer
to Christopher Marlowe's poem,
The Passionate Shepherd to His
Love*]. *Stanza 1*

[w] Passions are likened best to
floods and streams:
The shallow murmur, but the
deep are dumb.
The Silent Lover, Prelude

[x] Silence in love bewrays more
woe
Than words, though ne'er so
witty:
A beggar that is dumb, you know,
May challenge double pity.
Ibid. Stanza 7

[y] Cowards [may] fear to die;
but courage stout,
Rather than live in snuff, will be
put out.
Remains, Page 258 [*ed. 1661*].
*On the snuff of a candle the
night before he died.*

[z] Even such is time, that takes
in trust
Our youth, our joys, our all we
have,
And pays us but with age and
dust;
Who in the dark and silent grave,
When we have wandered all our
ways,
Shuts up the story of our days.
But from this earth, this grave,
this dust,
My God shall raise me up, I trust!
*Written the night before his
death; found in his Bible in the
Gate-house at Westminster*

[a] If she seem not chaste to me,
What care I how chaste she be?
Poem

[b] [History] hath triumphed
over time, which besides it nothing but eternity hath triumphed
over.
Historie of the World, Preface

[c] O eloquent, just, and mightie
Death! whom none could advise,
thou hast perswaded; what none
hath dared, thou hast done; and
whom all the world hath flattered, thou only hast cast out of
the world and despised. Thou hast
drawne together all the farre
stretchèd greatnesse, all the
pride, crueltie, and ambition of
man, and covered it all over with
these two narrow words, *Hic
jacet!*   *Ibid. Book V, Part I*

Sir Walter Raleigh
[1861–1922]

[d] I wish I loved the Human
Race;
I wish I loved its silly face;

I wish I liked the way it walks;
I wish I liked the way it talks;
And when I'm introduced to one
I wish I thought *What Jolly Fun!*
*Wishes of an Elderly Man
(Wished at a Garden-Party, June, 1914)*

[e] Listen; you may be allowed
To hear my laughter from a
cloud.   *My Last Will*

W. S. Ralph
[*Floruit* 1880]

[f] Unless there's a boy there
a-whistling,
Its music will not be complete.
Whistling in Heaven. Stanza 1

James Ryder Randall
[1839–1908]

[g] Hark to an exiled son's appeal,
Maryland, my Maryland!
My Mother State, to thee I kneel.
*Maryland, My Maryland.
Stanza 2*

[h] Teach me, my God, to bear
my cross
As Thine was borne;
Teach me to make of every loss
A crown of thorn.   *Resurgam*

[i] The Robin wears his silver
vest
In panoplies of red.
Why the Robin's Breast Is Red

Innes Randolph
[1837–1887]

[j] I am a good old rebel—
Yes; that's just what I am—
And for this land of freedom
I do not give a dam'.
I'm glad I fit agin 'em,
And I only wish we'd won;
And I don't ax no pardon
For anything I've done.
A Good Old Rebel (Unreconstructed). Stanza 1

[k] I cotch the rheumatism
A-campin' in the snow,
But I killed a chance of Yankees,
I'd like to kill some mo'.
Ibid. Stanza 4

John Randolph
[1773–1833]

[l] The surest way to prevent war
is not to fear it.
*Speech before Committee of
Whole, U. S. House of Representatives* [*March 5, 1806*]

[m] He is a man of splendid
abilities, but utterly corrupt. He
shines and stinks like rotten
mackerel by moonlight.
Of Edward Livingston

William Brighty Rands
("Matthew Browne")
[1823-1880]

[n] Never do to-day what you can
Put off till to-morrow.
Lilliput Levee

[o] Great wide, beautiful, wonderful world,
With the wonderful waters round you curled,
And the wonderful grass upon your breast,
World, you are beautifully drest.
The Child's World. Stanza 1

Jeremiah Eames Rankin
[1828-1904]

[p] God be with you, till we meet again,
  By His counsels guide, uphold you,
  With His sheep securely fold you:
God be with you, till we meet again.   *God Be With You*

John Crowe Ransom
[1888-   ]

[q] Up once I rose, in a fury of heard-of things,
  To travel the splendid sphere and see its fame;
But the wars and ships and towns and the roaring kings
  But flashed with the image of her I and back I came.
Sonnet of a Sure Heart

[r] And in the wood the furious winter blowing.
Winter Remembered

[s] Hands hold much of heat in little storage.
They Hail the Sunrise

[t] The lazy geese, like a snow cloud
Dripping their snow on the green grass,
Tricking and stopping, sleepy and proud,
Who cried in goose, Alas.   *Bells for John Whitesides' Daughter*

[u] Here lies a lady of beauty and high degree.
Of chills and fever she died, of fever and chills,
The delight of her husband, her aunts, an infant of three,
And of medicos marvelling sweetly on her ills.
Here Lies a Lady

[v] In Heaven you have heard no marriage is,
No white flesh tinder to your lecheries,
Your male and female tissue sweetly shaped.

Sublimed away, and furious blood escaped.   *The Equilibrists*

[w] God have mercy on the sinner
Who must write with no dinner,
No gravy and no grub,
No pewter and no pub,
No belly and no bowels,
Only consonants and vowels.
Survey of Literature

[x] Athens, a fragile kingdom by the foam,
Assumed the stranger's yoke; but then behold how meek
Those unbred Caesars grew, who spent their fruits of Rome
Forever after, trying to be Greek.
Triumph

Rudolf Erich Raspe
[1737-1794]

[y] What in the dark I had taken to be a stump of a little tree appearing above the snow, to which I had tied my horse, proved to have been the weathercock of the church steeple.   *Travels of Baron Munchausen. Chap. 2*

[z] His tunes were frozen up in the horn, and came out now by thawing.   *Ibid. Chap. 6*

[a] Upon this island of cheese grows great plenty of corn, the ears of which produce loaves of bread, ready made.
Ibid. Chap. 20

[b] A traveller has a right to relate and embellish his adventures as he pleases, and it is very unpolite to refuse that deference and applause they deserve.
Ibid. Chap. 21

[c] There is a right and wrong handle to everything.
Ibid. Chap. 30

John Revelstoke Rathom
[1868-1923]

[d] The "unknown" dead? Not so: we know him well . . .
He is all brothers dead, all lovers lost,
All sons and comrades resting there.   *The "Unknown" Dead*

Thomas Ravenscroft
[1592-1635]

[e] Nose, nose, nose, nose!
And who gave thee that jolly red nose?
Sinament and Ginger, Nutmegs and Cloves,
And that gave me my jolly red nose.
Deuteromelia. Song No. 7

Rossiter Worthington Raymond
[1840–1918]

[£] Life is eternal; and love is immortal; and death is only a horizon; and a horizon is nothing save the limit of our sight.
A Commendatory Prayer

[g] Beside the dead I knelt in prayer,
And felt a presence as I prayed,
Lo! It was Jesus standing there.
He smiled: "Be not afraid!"
Christus Consolator. Stanza 1

Herbert Read
[1893–   ]

[h] Poetry can never again become a popular art until the poet gives himself wholly to "the cadence of consenting feet."
Phases of English Poetry

[i] The no-man's-years between the wars. [1919–1939]   *Annals of Innocence and Experience*

Thomas Buchanan Read
[1822–1872]

[j] Within his sober realm of leafless trees,
The russet year inhaled the dreamy air;
Like some tanned reaper in his hour of ease,
When all the fields are lying brown and bare.
The Closing Scene. Stanza 1

[k] The old, old sea, as one in tears,
Comes murmuring with its foamy lips,
And knocking at the vacant piers,
Calls for its long-lost multitude of ships.
Come, Gentle Trembler, Stanza 5

[l]   Now begins
The housewife's happiest season of the year.
The ground, already broken by the spade—
The beds, made level by the passing rake.
The New Pastoral. Book V

[m] The terrible grumble, and rumble, and roar,
Telling the battle was on once more,
And Sheridan twenty miles away.
Sheridan's Ride. Stanza 1

[n] I hate the sin, but I love the sinner.
What a Word May Do. Stanza 1

Richard Realf
[1834–1878]

[o] Into the statue that breathes, the soul of the sculptor is bidden.
Indirection. Stanza 3

[p] Harms of the world have come unto us,
Cups of sorrow we yet shall drain;
But we have a secret that doth show us
Wonderful rainbows in the rain.
An Old Man's Idyl. Stanza 7

[q] Here, gathered from all places and all time,
The waifs of wisdom and of folly meet.   *In a Scrap-Book*

William Marion Reedy
[1862–1920]

[r] Force is good and fire is good and fancy is good in a poet, but if he have not Love then he is as sounding brass and tinkling cymbal. Love is best of all. There is not, nor ever shall be, true song without it.
A Nest of Singing Birds

[s] Where are they all—the conquerors?
How dim the din of all their wars!
Call to them and you call in vain.
Sesostris! Caesar! Charlemagne!
Napoleon! Alexander! Tamerlane!
No answer from the silence.
The Conquerors

Lizette Woodworth Reese
[1856–1935]

[t] Life and its few years—
A wisp of fog betwixt us and the sun.   *Tears*

[u] The burst of music down an unlistening street.   *Ibid.*

[v] Creeds grow so thick along the way,
Their boughs hide God.   *Doubt*

[w] An apple orchard smells like wine;
A succory flower is blue;
Until Grief touched these eyes of mine,
Such things I never knew.
Wise. Stanza 1

Dorothy E. Reid

[x] A goosegirl ermined is a goosegirl still
And geese will gabble everywhere she goes.   *Not in Andersen*

[y] There was a sunrise falling like red blood. . . .
And men and women creeping through the red
Of the marvellous city, could not quite deny
All day the life that startled them: they said
Beautiful things, and wept, and wondered why.
Poem Carried as a Banner

Erich Maria Remarque
[1897-   ]

[z] The army report confined itself to the single sentence: All quiet on the Western Front.
All Quiet on the Western Front (tr. A. W. Wheen)

[a] He had fallen forward and lay on the earth as though sleeping. His face had an expression of calm, as though almost glad the end had come.   *Ibid.*

[b] My father, a good man, told me "Never lose your ignorance; you cannot replace it."
Interview in The New York Times, January 27, 1946

Pierre Auguste Renoir
[1841-1919]

[c] I have a predilection for painting that lends joyousness to a wall.   *Quoted by Royal Cortissoz in The Painter's Craft*

Emery Reves
[1904-   ]

[d] The Golden Calf to which the most devoted and mystic adoration of the masses goes in our days is: Sovereignty. No symbol carrying the pretension of a deity caused so much misery, hatred, starvation and mass execution as the notion "Sovereignty of the Nation."
A Democratic Manifesto. Chap. 6

Eben Eugene Rexford
[1848-1916]

[e] Love can never more grow old,
Locks may lose their brown and gold,
Cheeks may fade and hollow grow,
But the hearts that love will know
Never winter's frost and chill,
Summer's warmth is in them still.
Silver Threads Among the Gold

Cecil John Rhodes
[1853-1902]

[f] Educational relations make the strongest tie.
Will, establishing the Rhodes Scholarships

[g] So little done—so much to do.   *Last words*

William Barnes Rhodes
[1772-1826]

[h] *Bombastes.* So have I heard on Afric's burning shore

A hungry lion give a grievous roar;
The grievous roar echoed along the shore.
Artaxaminous. So have I heard on Afric's burning shore
Another lion give a grievous roar;
And the first lion thought the last a bore.
Bombastes Furioso. Act 1, Sc. 4

Joachim von Ribbentrop
[1893-1946]

[i] The Führer is always right.
Königsberg address, August 24, 1939

[j] Dear Ciano, I cannot tell you anything as yet because every decision is locked in the impenetrable bosom of the Führer. However, one thing is certain: if we attack, the Russia of Stalin will be erased from the map within eight weeks.   *Quoted in The Ciano Diaries [June 15, 1941]*

Cale Young Rice
[1872-1943]

[k] Spring has come up from the South again,
With soft mists in her hair,
And a warm wind in her mouth again,
And budding everywhere.
The Immortal. Stanza 1

[l] You who are old,
And have fought the fight,
And have won or lost or left the fight,
Weight us not down
With fears of the world, as we run!   *The Young to the Old*

Grantland Rice
[1880-   ]

[m] When the One Great Scorer comes to write against your name—
He marks—not that you won or lost—but how you played the game.   *Alumnus Football*

[n] All wars are planned by old men
In council rooms apart,
Who plan for greater armament
And map the battle chart.

But where their sightless eyes stare out
Beyond life's vanished joys,
I've noticed nearly all the dead
Were hardly more than boys.
Two Sides of War. Stanzas 1 and 4

Ruth Mason Rice
[1884-1927]

[o] A curve for the shore,
A line for the lea,

A tint for the sky—
    Where the sunrise will be;
A stroke for a gull,
    A sweep for the main;
The skill to do more,
    With the will to refrain.
                    A Japanese Print

Paul Richard
[1874–   ]

[p] The vagabond, when rich, is
called a tourist.   *The Scourge of
                    Christ. Page 40*

[q] When the rich assemble to
concern themselves with the business of the poor it is called
charity. When the poor assemble
to concern themselves with the
business of the rich it is called
anarchy.   *Ibid. Page 63*

[r] Hunting—the least honourable form of war on the weak.
                    Ibid. Page 142

Edward Hersey Richards
[1874–   ]

[s] A wise old owl sat on an oak,
The more he saw the less he
    spoke;
The less he spoke the more he
    heard;
Why aren't we like that wise old
    bird?   *A Wise Old Owl*

[t] And if to-morrow shall be sad,
Or never come at all, I've had
At least
    To-day!   *Today. Stanza 3*

Laura Elizabeth Richards
[1850–1943]

[u] Every little wave had its
nightcap on.   *A Song for Hal*

[v] The branches of the pencil-
tree
Are pointed every one.
*Song of the Mother whose Chil-
dren Are Fond of Drawing.
Stanza 2*

[w] The fairest spot to me,
On the land or on the sea,
Is the charming little cupboard
    where the jam-pots grow.
                Master Jack's Song

[x] Baby said
When she smelt the rose,
"Oh! what a pity
I've only one nose!"
            The Difference. Stanza 1

Robert Richardson
[1850–1901]

[y] Warm summer sun, shine
    friendly here;
Warm western wind, blow kindly
    here;

Green sod above, rest light, rest
    light—
Good-night, Annette! Sweetheart,
    good-night.   *To Annette*

Felix Riesenberg
[1879–1939]

[z] City, lyric city. . . .

City of uncomfortable comfort
stations. City of clanging radi-
ators, of supine superintendents.
City wherein there is no room to
die. . . .

Fairy city in those magic hours
of the passing night; the pause
before the dawn. . . .

City that breathes of things too
large for books, that is too beautiful for poets, too terrible for
drama, too true for testimony.

City worth visiting, if only for
a week.   *East Side, West Side.
                        1919–1929*

[a] The sea has always been a
seducer, a careless lying fellow,
not feminine, as many writers
imagine, but strongly masculine
in its allurement. The king of the
sea, with his whiskers of weed
and his trident and dolphins,
truly represents the main and
gives it character. The sea, like a
great sultan, supports thousands
of ships, his lawful wives. These
he caresses and chastises as the
case may be. This explains the
feminine gender of all proper
vessels.   *Vignettes of the Sea*

James Whitcomb Riley
[1849–1916]

[b] O'er folded blooms
    On swirls of musk,
The beetle booms adown the
    glooms
And bumps along the dusk.
            The Beetle. Stanza 7

[c] The ripest peach is highest
on the tree.   *The Ripest Peach.
                        Stanza 1*

[d] An' the Gobble-uns'll git you
Ef you don't watch out.
    Little Orphant Annie. Stanza 2

[e] I can see the pink sunbonnet
    and the little checkered dress
She wore when first I kissed her
    and she answered the caress
With the written declaration that,
    "as surely as the vine
Grew 'round the stump," she
    loved me—that old sweetheart
    of mine.   *An Old Sweetheart
                of Mine. Stanza 12*

[f] How the grand band-wagon
    shone with a splendor all its
    own,

And glittered with a glory that
   our dreams had never known!
The Circus-Day Parade. Stanza 2

[g] Forget not that no fellow-
      being yet
May fall so low but love may
   lift his head.   *Let Some-
      thing Good Be Said. Stanza 2*

[h] Fer the world is full of roses,
      and the roses full of dew,
And the dew is full of heavenly
   love that drips fer me and you.
*Thoughts fer the Discuraged
         Farmer. Stanza 5*

[i] 'Long about knee-deep in
      June,
'Bout the time strawberries melts
On the vine.
   Knee-deep in June. Stanza 1

[j] Oh! the old swimmin'-hole!
      When I last saw the place,
The scene was all changed, like
   the change in my face.
The Old Swimmin'-Hole. Stanza 5

[k] Work is the least o' my idees
When the green, you know, gits
   back in the trees!
   *When the Green Gits Back in
      the Trees. Stanza 1*

[l] O, the Raggedy Man he works
      fer Pa,
An' he's the goodest man ever you
   saw!   *The Raggedy Man.
            Stanza 1*

[m] A pictur' that no painter has
      the colorin' to mock—
When the frost is on the pumpkin
   and the fodder's in the shock.
   *When the Frost Is on the
      Pumpkin. Stanza 2*

Rainer Maria Rilke
[1875–1926]

[n] Her smile was not meant to
be seen by anyone and served its
whole purpose in being smiled.
*The Journal of My Other Self
   (tr. John Linton)*

[o] Love consists in this, that
two solitudes protect and touch
and greet each other.
*Letters to a Young Poet (tr.
   M. D. Herter Norton)*

[p] The future enters into us, in
order to transform itself in us,
long before it happens.   *Ibid.*

Arthur Rimbaud
[1854–1891]

[q] A, black; E, white; I, red; O,
blue; U, green.   *Sonnet, Vowels*

Robert Leroy Ripley
[1893–1949]

[r] Believe it or not.
      *Title of syndicated
         newspaper feature*

Jessie Belle Rittenhouse
(Mrs. Clinton Scollard)
[1869–1948]

[s] My debt to you, Belovèd,
   Is one I cannot pay
In any coin of any realm
   On any reckoning day.   *Debt*

[t] I worked for a menial's hire,
   Only to learn, dismayed,
That any wage I had asked of Life,
   Life would have paid.
            My Wage

Leonard H. Robbins
[1877–1947]

[u] Who keeps the Truth from
   the people stands in the way
   of God!   *The Truth and
      John Billington. Stanza 8*

Charles George
Douglas Roberts
[1860–1943]

[v] Comes the lure of green things
   growing,
Comes the call of waters flowing—
   And the wayfarer desire
Moves and wakes and would be
   going.   *Afoot. Stanza 1*

Elizabeth Madox Roberts
[1886–1941]

[w] I used to think when I was a
young-one, Jasper, that all the
things you read about or hear
came to pass in some country, all
in one country somewhere. "Oh,
Mary go and call the cattle home,"
and "Lady Nancy died like it
might be today," all in one country. . . . A country a far piece off.
Off past Tennessee somewheres.
But now I know better and know
how the world is, a little.
The Time of Man

Kenneth Roberts
[1885–   ]

[x] On every side of us are men
who hunt perpetually for their
personal Northwest Passage, too
often sacrificing health, strength
and life itself to the search; and
who shall say they are not happier
in their vain but hopeful quest
than wiser, duller folks who sit at
home, venturing nothing and,
with sour laughs, deriding the
seekers for that fabled thoroughfare?   *Northwest Passage.
            Foreword*

Theodore Goodridge Roberts
[1877–   ]

[y] The wide seas and the mountains called to him

And gray dawn saw his campfires
     in the rain.
          A Vagrant's Epitaph. Stanza 1

[z] Change   was   his   mistress,
     Chance his counselor.
          Ibid. Stanza 4

[a] The tides go out; the tides
     come flooding in;
Still the old years die and the new
     begin;
          But Youth?—
Somewhere we lost each other,
     last year or yesterday.
          The Lost Shipmate. Stanza 1

Agnes Mary Frances Robinson

[1857–   ]

[b] To think the face we love
     shall ever die,
And be the indifferent earth,
     and know us not!
To think that one of us shall live
     to cry
On one long buried in a distant
     spot!   *Etruscan Tombs. I*

[c] You hail from Dream-land,
     Dragon-fly?
A stranger hither? So am I,
And (sooth to say) I wonder why
     We either of us came!
          To a Dragon-fly

Edwin Arlington Robinson

[1869–1935]

[d] I would have rid the earth of
     him
     Once, in my pride. . . .
I never knew the worth of him
     Until he died.   *An Old Story*

[e] Life is the game that must be
     played:
This truth at least, good friends,
     we know;
So live and laugh, nor be dis-
     mayed
As one by one the phantoms go.
          Ballade by the Fire. Envoy

[f] Like dead, remembered foot-
     steps on old floors.
          The Pity of the Leaves

[g] Still searching, like poor old
     astronomers
Who totter off to bed and go to
     sleep
To dream of untriangulated stars.
          Octaves. XI

[h] Two kinds of gratitude: the
     sudden kind
We feel for what we take, the
     larger kind
We feel for what we give.
          Captain Craig. Part I

[i]   Friends
To borrow my books and set wet
     glasses on them.
          Ibid. Part II

[j] Wearing upon his forehead,
     with no fear,
The laurel of approved iniquity.
          Uncle Ananias

[k] Miniver loved the Medici,
     Albeit he had never seen one;
He would have sinned incessantly
     Could he have been one.
          Miniver Cheevy

[l] I shall have more to say when
     I am dead.   *John Brown*

[m] Like a physician who can
     do no good,
But knows how soon another
     would have his fee
Were he to tell the truth.
          Avon's Harvest

[n]   Love that's wise
Will not say all it means.
          Tristram. Part VII

[o] For when a woman is left too
     much alone,
Sooner or later she begins to
     think;
And no man knows what then she
     may discover.   *Ibid.*

[p]   I like rivers
Better than oceans, for we see
     both sides.
An ocean is forever asking ques-
     tions
And writing them aloud along the
     shore.
          Roman Bartholow. Part III

[q] Of all small things
That have the most infernal
     power to grow,
Few may be larger than a few
     small words
That may not say themselves and
     be forgotten.
          Genevieve and Alexandra

[r] Here where the wind is al-
     ways north-north-east
And children learn to walk on
     frozen toes.   *New England*

Edwin Meade ("Ted") Robinson

[1878–1946]

[s] Some day I'll pass by the
     Great Gates of Gold,
And see a man pass through un-
     questioned and bold.
"A Saint?" I'll ask, and old Peter'll
     reply:
"No, he carries a pass—he's a
     newspaper guy."
          The Newspaper Guy. Stanza 4

[t] Write me a verse, my old ma-
     chine—
     I lack for an inspiration;
The skies are blue and the trees
     are green,
     And I long for a long vacation.
          The Typewriter's Song. Stanza 1

[u] Dying and letting die, they
     call "living and letting live";

They do not even make mistakes
  for live ones to forgive;
Wouldst thou be Nothing? Then,
  my son, be a Conservative!
                Conservatives

[v] Black-gowned upon the dear
    old steps he stands,
His brain with mingled junk
    and knowledge stored;
He carries on his head the
    mortar-board,
A roll of learned sheepskin in his
    hands.
                Sonnet. The Graduate

[w] Blest be the power to sweeten
    and pasteurize
Bygone mistakes.
                Glamour. Stanza 1

[x] Over that love affair, scrappy
    and clamorous,
Time throws a veil iridescent and
    glamorous.   *Ibid. Stanza 2*

James Harvey Robinson
[1863–1935]

[y] Political campaigns are de-
signedly made into emotional
orgies which endeavor to distract
attention from the real issues involved, and they actually paralyze
what slight powers of cerebration
man can normally muster.
                The Human Comedy. Chap. 9

Joshua Davenport Robinson
[1829–1866]

[z] I shall see his toys and his
    empty chair,
And the horse he used to ride,
And they will speak with a silent
    speech
Of the little boy that died.
                The Little Boy that Died.
                Stanza 3

James Jeffrey Roche
[1847–1908]

[a] The love of man and woman
    is as fire
To warm, to light, but surely to
    consume
And self-consuming die . . .
But comrade-love is as a welding
    blast
Of candid flame and ardent
    temperature:
Glowing more fervent, it doth
    bind more fast.
                My Comrade

[b] What careth the burden-
    bearer that Liberty packed his
    load,
If Hunger presseth behind him
    with a sharp and ready goad?
                For the People. Stanza 6

[c] The slaves of Pilate have
    washed his hands
As white as a king's might be.

Barabbas with wrists unfettered
    stands,
For the world has made him
    free.
But Thy palms toil-worn by nails
    are torn,
O Christ, on Calvary.
                The Way of the World. Stanza 2

[d] "No enemies! Can such a
    grace
To any erring mortal fall?"
A smile lit up the grim old face:
"None, padre, none; I slew them
    all."
                Carvajal the Thorough

[e] I'd rather be handsome than
    homely;
I'd rather be youthful than old;
If I can't have a bushel of silver
I'll do with a barrel of gold.
                Contentment

[f] All loved Art in a seemly way
With an earnest soul and a capital
    A.   *The V-A-S-E*

[g] Baby's brain is tired of think-
    ing
On the Wherefore and the
    Whence;
Baby's precious eyes are blinking
With incipient somnolence.
                A Boston Lullaby. Stanza 1

François, Duc de la Rochefoucauld
[1613–1680]
Reflections, or Sentences and Moral Maxims

[h] Our virtues are most frequently but vices disguised.
    [At the head of *Reflections,* 4th
edition.]

[i] We have all sufficient strength
to endure the misfortunes of
others.   *Maxim 19*

[j] Neither the sun nor death
can be looked at with a steady eye.
                    Maxim 26

[k] If we were without faults,
we should not take so much
pleasure in remarking them in
others.   *Maxim 31*

[l] True love is like ghosts, which
everybody talks about and few
have seen.   *Maxim 76*

[m] The love of justice is simply,
in the majority of men, the fear
of suffering injustice.
                    Maxim 78

[n] Friendship is only a reciprocal conciliation of interests, and
an exchange of good offices; it is a
species of commerce out of which
self-love always expects to gain
something.   *Maxim 83*

[o] Everyone complains of his
memory, and no one complains of
his judgment.   *Maxim 89*

[p] A man who is ungrateful is often less to blame than his benefactor. *Maxim 96*

[q] Our repentance is not so much regret for the ill we have done as fear of the ill that may happen to us in consequence.
Maxim 180

[r] Too great haste to repay an obligation is a kind of ingratitude.
Maxim 226

[s] There is great ability in knowing how to conceal one's ability. *Maxim 245*

[t] The pleasure of love is in loving. We are happier in the passion we feel than in that we inspire. *Maxim 259*

[u] We pardon in the degree that we love. *Maxim 330*

[v] We hardly find any persons of good sense save those who agree with us. *Maxim 347*

[w] The veracity which increases with old age is not far from folly.
Maxim 416

[x] Nothing prevents our being natural so much as the desire to appear so. *Maxim 431*

[y] Quarrels would not last long if the fault was only on one side.
Maxim 496

[z] To win that wonder of the world,
A smile from her bright eyes,
I fought my King, and would have hurled
The gods out of their skies.
To Madame de Longueville

John Wilmot, Earl of Rochester
[1647–1680]

[a] He never says a foolish thing,
Nor ever does a wise one.
Written on the Bedchamber Door of Charles II

[b] The world appears like a great family,
Whose lord, oppressed with pride and poverty,
(That to the few great bounty he may show)
Is fain to starve the numerous train below.
Like a Great Family

[c] There's not a thing on earth that I can name,
So foolish, and so false, as common fame.
Did E'er This Saucy World

[d] Reason, which fifty times to one does err,
Reason, an ignis fatuus of the mind.
Then Old Age and Experience

[e] Books bear him up a while, and make him try
To swim with bladders of philosophy. *Ibid.*

[f] Dead, we become the lumber of the world. *After Death*

W. R. Rodgers

[g] The dead diplomat, inseparable
On his finger-end the skeleton-keys
Of compromise and ambiguity.
End of a World [1941]

[h] There too floated the drowned scholar, his hand
Holding his pat reference and apt tag,
Index and document, his subscription
To Authority. *Ibid.*

[i] The record-keepers of record-breakers,
The lackers and onlookers of greatness,
Eunuch students of love and peeping Toms. *Ibid.*

[j] Today walk down the two-way street of words . . .
Often you'll see the window-dressing man
Emerging to admire his own effect . . .
Observe his dummy topics draped with speech. *Words*

[k] Your doubts are the private detectives
Employed by your dislike, to make a case
Against change or choice. *Ibid.*

Emily Bruce Roelofson
[1841–1921]

[l] When to the flowers so beautiful
The Father gave a name,
Back came a little blue-eyed one
(All timidly it came);
And standing at its Father's feet
And gazing in His face,
It said, in low and trembling tone,
"Dear God, the name Thou gavest me,
Alas! I have forgot!"
Kindly the Father looked Him down
And said: "Forget-me-not."
The Origin of the Forget-me-not

Robert Cameron Rogers
[1862–1912]

[m] The hours I spent with thee, dear heart,
Are as a string of pearls to me;
I count them over, every one apart,
My rosary, my rosary. . . .

Oh memories that bless—and
      burn!
  Oh barren gain—and bitter loss!
                        My Rosary

[n] Sage-brush to kindle with,
      Quaking-asp to glow,
Pine-roots to last until the dawn-
      winds blow.
      A Ballad of Dead Camp-Fires

[o] I cannot fawn and leap and
      be thy dog,
Thy dog of old—I cannot show
      the love
That I have kept so long for one
      caress,—
But, master, I have not forgotten
      thee.   *The Death of Argus*

[p] Visions I no longer see,
And smoke is only smoke to me,
      Now I am old.
                    The Old Smoker

Robert Emmons Rogers
[1888–1941]

[q] Marry the boss's daughter.
      *Advice to the Class of 1929,
      Massachusetts Institute of
      Technology*

Samuel Rogers
[1763–1855]

[r] Sweet Memory! wafted by
      thy gentle gale,
Oft up the stream of Time I turn
      my sail.   *The Pleasures of
                  Memory. Part II, I*

[s] She was good as she was fair,
None—none on earth above her!
As pure in thought as angels are:
To know her was to love her.
                  Jacqueline. Stanza 1

[t] A guardian angel o'er his life
      presiding,
Doubling his pleasures, and his
      cares dividing.   *Human Life*

[u] Mine be a cot beside the hill;
      A beehive's hum shall soothe
      my ear;
A willowy brook that turns a mill,
With many a fall shall linger
      near.   *A Wish. Stanza 1*

[v] That very law which moulds
      a tear
And bids it trickle from its
      source,—
That law preserves the earth a
      sphere,
And guides the planets in their
      course.   *On a Tear. Stanza 6*

[w] Go! you may call it madness,
      folly;
You shall not chase my gloom
      away!
There's such a charm in melan-
      choly
I would not if I could be gay.
                        To ——. Stanza 1

[x] Ward has no heart, they say,
      but I deny it:
He has a heart, and gets his
      speeches by it.   *Epigram*

Will Rogers
[1879–1935]

[y] All I know is just what I read
in the papers.
                  Prefatory remark

[z] I never met a man I didn't
like.   *Address, Tremont Temple,
                  Boston [June 1930]*

[a] A comedian can only last till
he either takes himself serious or
his audience takes him serious.
            *Syndicated newspaper article,
                        June 28, 1931*

[b] Politics has got so expensive
that it takes lots of money to even
get beat with.   *Ibid.*

Madame Roland
[1754–1793]

[c] O Liberty! Liberty! how many
crimes are committed in thy
name!   *Quoted by Macaulay in
            his Essay on Mirabeau*

Harry Romaine
[*Floruit* 1895]

[d] The one great God looked
      down and smiled,
And counted each His loving
      child;
For Turk and Brahmin, monk
      and Jew,
Had reached Him through the
      gods they knew.   *Ad Coelum*

[e] The little lonely souls go by,
Seeking their God who lives on
      high,
With conscious step and hat and
      all,
As if on Him they meant to call
In some sad ceremonial.
                  The Sabbath. Stanza 1

[f] The man who idly sits and
      thinks,
      May sow a nobler crop than
      corn,
For thoughts are seeds of future
      deeds,
      And when God thought—the
      world was born!   *Inaction*

Franklin Delano Roosevelt
[1882–1945]

[g] The forgotten man at the bottom of the economic pyramid.
      Radio address [April 7, 1932]

[h] A new deal for the American
people.   *Speech accepting the
      nomination for the Presidency,
      Democratic National Conven-
      tion, Chicago [July 2, 1932]*

[i] There is no indispensable man.   *Campaign speech*
[*November 3, 1932*]

[j] The only thing we have to fear is fear itself.
First Inaugural Address
[*March 4, 1933*]

[k] Continued dependence upon relief induces a spiritual and moral disintegration fundamentally destructive to the national fibre. To dole out relief in this way is to administer a narcotic, a subtle destroyer of the human spirit.   *Message to Congress*
[*January 4, 1935*]

[l] This generation of Americans has a rendezvous with destiny.
Speech accepting renomination
[*June 27, 1936*]

[m] We have always known that heedless self-interest was bad morals; we know now that it is bad economics.
Second Inaugural Address
[*January 20, 1937*]

[n] The test of our progress is not whether we add more to the abundance of those who have much; it is whether we provide enough for those who have too little.   *Ibid.*

[o] War is a contagion.
Speech at Chicago
[*October 5, 1937*]

[p] Quarantine the aggressors.
Ibid.

[q] We must be the great arsenal of democracy.
Message to Congress
[*January 6, 1941*]

[r] Four freedoms: The first is freedom of speech and expression —everywhere in the world. The second is freedom of every person to worship God in his own way, everywhere in the world. The third is freedom from want . . . everywhere in the world. The fourth is freedom from fear . . . anywhere in the world.   *Ibid.*

[s] Men with a passion for anonymity.   *Qualification for advisors and assistants*

[t] Yesterday, December 7, 1941— a date which will live in infamy— the United States of America was suddenly and deliberately attacked by naval and air forces of the Empire of Japan.
War Message to Congress
[*December 8, 1941*]

[u] Books cannot be killed by fire. People die, but books never die. No man and no force can abolish memory. . . . In this war, we know, books are weapons.
Message to the American Book-sellers Association [*April 23, 1942*]

[v] All of our people—except full-blooded Indians—are immigrants, or descendants of immigrants, including even those who came here on the Mayflower.
Campaign speech in Boston
[*November 4, 1944*]

[w] We have learned that we cannot live alone, in peace; that our own well-being is dependent on the well-being of other nations, far away. We have learned that we must live as men, and not as ostriches, nor as dogs in the manger. We have learned to be citizens of the world, members of the human community.
Fourth Term Inaugural Address
[*January 20, 1945*]

[x] There are a great many prima donnas in the world. All of them wish to be heard. There may be a little delay while we listen to more prima donnas.
Report of Crimea Conference to Congress [*March 1, 1945*]

[y] More than an end to war, we want an end to the beginnings of all wars.   *Address written for Jefferson Day Dinners broadcast, April 13, 1945* [*President Roosevelt died suddenly, April 12, at Warm Springs, Georgia*]

Franklin Delano Roosevelt and Winston Spencer Churchill

For other quotations from the latter, see Churchill

[z] The President of the United States and the Prime Minister, Mr. Churchill, representing His Majesty's Government in the United Kingdom, have met at sea. . . . They have agreed upon the following joint declaration.
FIRST, their countries seek no aggrandizement, territorial or other.
SECOND, they desire to see no territorial changes that do not accord with the freely expressed wishes of the peoples concerned. . . .
SIXTH, after the final destruction of the Nazi tyranny, they hope to see established a peace which will afford to all nations the means of dwelling in safety within their own boundaries, and which will afford assurance that all the men in all the lands may live out their lives in freedom from fear and want. . . .

EIGHTH, they believe that all of the nations of the world, for realistic as well as spiritual reasons, must come to the abandonment of the use of force. . . .
The Atlantic Charter, drawn up aboard U.S.S. Augusta, off the coast of Maine. Issued in Washington, August 14, 1941

Theodore Roosevelt
[1858–1919]

[a] I wish to preach, not the doctrine of ignoble ease, but the doctrine of the strenuous life.
Speech before the Hamilton Club, Chicago [April 10, 1899]

[b] We must remember not to judge any public servant by any one act, and especially should we beware of attacking the men who are merely the occasions and not the causes of disaster.   *Ibid.*

[c] I am as strong as a bull moose.
Letter to Mark Hanna, 1900

[d] There is a homely adage which runs, "Speak softly and carry a big stick; you will go far."
Speech at Minnesota State Fair [September 2, 1901]

[e] Men with the muck-rake are often indispensable to the well-being of society, but only if they know when to stop raking the muck.   *Address, Laying of the Corner Stone, Office Building of House of Representatives, Washington [April 14, 1906]*

[f] Malefactors of great wealth.
Speech at Provincetown [August 20, 1907]

[g] The lunatic fringe in all reform movements.
Autobiography. Chap. 7

E. Merrill Root
[1895–   ]

[h] Quietly I rise again
Over violence or chicane—
Defying from the deeper granite
The skin-diseases of the planet.

Build on waste and desolation
Your green towers of affirmation.
Scrub Oak. Stanzas 5 and 6

George Frederick Root
[1820–1895]

[i] Rally round the flag, boys,
Rally once again,
Shouting the battle-cry of Freedom   *The Battle-cry of Freedom. Stanza 1*

Abraham S. Wolf Rosenbach
[1876–1952]

[j] After love, book collecting is the most exhilarating sport of all.
A Book Hunter's Holiday. Page 106

[k] Lives of great men all remind us
As their pages o'er we turn,
That we're apt to leave behind us
Letters that we ought to burn.
Ibid. Page 36. Quoted by Dr. Rosenbach, authorship unknown

Christina Georgina Rossetti
[1830–1894]

[l] Hope is like a harebell trembling from its birth,
Love is like a rose the joy of all the earth,
Faith is like a lily lifted high and white,
Love is like a lovely rose the world's delight.
Harebells and sweet lilies show a thornless growth,
But the rose with all its thorns excels them both.
Hope Is Like a Harebell

[m] My heart is like a singing bird.   *A Birthday. Stanza 1*

[n] When I am dead, my dearest,
Sing no sad songs for me;
Plant thou no roses at my head,
Nor shady cypress tree.
Song. Stanza 1

[o] Better by far you should forget and smile
Than that you should remember and be sad.   *Remember*

[p] Does the road wind up-hill all the way?
Yes, to the very end.
Up-Hill. Stanza 1

[q] One day in the country
Is worth a month in town.
Summer

[r] Silence more musical than any song.   *Rest*

Dante Gabriel Rossetti
[1828–1882]

[s] The blessed damozel leaned out
From the gold bar of Heaven:
Her eyes were deeper than the depth
Of waters stilled at even;
She had three lilies in her hand,
And the stars in her hair were seven.
The Blessed Damozel. Stanza 1

[t] And the souls mounting up to God
Went by her like thin flames.
Ibid. Stanza 7

[u] I have been here before,
But when or how I can not tell;
I know the grass beyond the door,
The sweet keen smell,
The sighing sound, the lights
around the shore.
Sudden Light. Stanza 1

[v] Gather a shell from the
strown beach
And listen at its lips: they sigh
The same desire and mystery,
The echo of the whole sea's
speech.
The Sea Limits. Stanza 4

[w] A Sonnet is a moment's
monument,—
Memorial from the Soul's eternity
To one dead deathless hour.
The House of Life. Proem

[x] Look in my face: my name is
Might-have-been;
I am also called No-more, Too-
late, Farewell.
Ibid. 97, A Superscription

Edmond Rostand
[1868–1918]

[y] A great nose indicates a great
man—
Genial, courteous, intellectual,
Virile, courageous.
*Cyrano de Bergerac (tr.
Brian Hooker). Act I*

[z] What would you have me do?
Seek for the patronage of some
great man,
And like a creeping vine on a tall
tree
Crawl upward, where I cannot
stand alone?
No, thank you.   *Ibid. Act II*

[a] And what is a kiss, when all
is done?
A promise given under seal—a vow
Taken before the shrine of mem-
ory—
A signature acknowledged—a rosy
dot
Over the i of Loving.
Ibid. Act III

[b] How do you know I am a diplomat?
By the skilful way you hide your
claws.   *L'Aiglon (tr. Louis
N. Parker). Act IV*

[c] I fall back dazzled at behold-
ing myself all rosy red,
At having, I, myself, caused the
sun to rise.
Chantecler. Act II, Sc. 3

Jean Jacques Rousseau
[1712–1778]

[d] Man is born free, and everywhere he is in irons.
*The Social Contract (Everyman
ed., tr. G. D. H. Cole). Book I,
Chap. 1*

[e] The right of conquest has no
foundation other than the right
of the strongest.   *Ibid. Chap. 4*

[f] As soon as public service
ceases to be the chief business of
the citizens, and they would
rather serve with their money
than with their persons, the State
is not far from its fall.
Ibid. Book III, Chap. 15

[g] Good laws lead to the making
of better ones; bad ones bring
about worse. As soon as any man
says of the affairs of the State,
"What does it matter to me?" the
State may be given up for lost.
Ibid.

[h] Money is the seed of money,
and the first guinea is sometimes
more difficult to acquire than the
second million.
A Discourse on Political Economy

[i] God makes all things good;
man meddles with them and they
become evil.   *Émile, or Education (Everyman ed., tr. Barbara
Foxley). Book I*

[j] Medicine is all the fashion in
these days, and very naturally. It
is the amusement of the idle and
unemployed, who do not know
what to do with their time in taking care of themselves. . . . Such
men must have doctors to
threaten and flatter them, to give
them the only pleasure they can
enjoy, the pleasure of not being
dead.   *Ibid.*

[k] Temperance and industry
are man's true remedies; work
sharpens his appetite and temperance teaches him to control it.
Ibid.

[l] What wisdom can you find
that is greater than kindness?
Ibid. Book II

[m] Provided a man is not mad,
he can be cured of every folly but
vanity.   *Ibid. Book IV*

[n] A man says what he knows, a
woman says what will please.
Ibid. Book V

[o] I propose to show my fellow-
mortals a man in all the integrity
of nature; and this man shall be
myself.
Confessions. Opening words

[p] Hatred, as well as love, renders its votaries credulous.
Ibid. Book V

[q] To appear the friend of a
man, when in reality we are no
longer so, is to reserve to ourselves
the means of doing him an injury
by surprising honest men into an
error.   *Ibid. Book X*

"Red" Rowley

[r] Mademoiselle from Armen-
teers,
Hasn't been kissed in forty years,
Hinky dinky, parley-voo.
Mademoiselle from Armentières
[Soldier song of World War I,
with many versions]

[s] Mademoiselle from St. Na-
zaire,
She never heard of underwear.
Ibid.

Kenneth Claiborne Royall
[1894–   ]

[t] A "brass hat" is an officer of
at least one rank higher than you
whom you don't like and who
doesn't like you. *Speech,*
Chamber of Commerce, Wilson,
N.C. [February 15, 1946]

Muriel Rukeyser
[1897–   ]

[u] Women and poets see the
truth arrive,
Then it is acted out,
The lives are lost, and all the
newsboys shout. *Beast in*
View: Letter to the Front

[v] The world of man's selection
May widen more and more.
Women in drudgery knew
They must be one of four:
Whores, artists, saints, and wives.
There are composite lives
That women always live
Whose greatness is to give
Weakness its reasons
And strength its reassurance;
To kiss away the waste
Places and start them well.
Ibid. Wreath of Women

Richard Rumbold
[1622–1685]

[w] I never could believe that
Providence had sent a few men
into the world, ready booted and
spurred to ride, and millions
ready saddled and bridled to be
ridden. *On the scaffold [1685],*
(Macaulay's History of England,
Chapter 1)

Beardsley Ruml
[1894–   ]

[x] It takes only a period of
about a dozen years to implant a
basic culture in the mind of man
—the period between the age of
two and the age of fourteen. In a
psycho-biological sense, history,
tradition and custom are only
about twelve years old.
World Trade and Peace. Ad-
dress, National Foreign Trade
Convention [November 14, 1945]

John Ruskin
[1819–1900]

[y] He is the greatest artist who
has embodied, in the sum of his
works, the greatest number of the
greatest ideas.
Modern Painters. Vol. I,
Part I, Chap. 2, Sect. 9

[z] In order that people may be
happy in their work, these three
things are needed: They must be
for it: They must not do too
much of it: And they must have a
sense of success in it.
Pre-Raphaelitism

[a] *No great intellectual thing*
was ever done by great effort; a
great thing can only be done by
a great man, and he does it with-
out effort. *Ibid.*

[b] Blue colour is everlastingly
appointed by the Deity to be a
source of delight. *Lectures on*
Architecture and Painting. I

[c] The greatest efforts of the
race have always been traceable
to the love of praise, as its greatest catastrophes to the love of
pleasure. *Sesame and Lilies.*
Of Kings' Treasuries, Sect. 3

[d] No book is . . . serviceable,
until it has been read, and re-
read, and loved, and loved again;
and marked, so that you can refer to the passages you want in it.
Ibid. Sect. 32

[e] When men are rightly occupied, their amusement grows out
of their work, as the colour-petals
out of a fruitful flower.
Ibid. Sect. 39

[f] This is the true nature of
home—it is the place of Peace;
the shelter, not only from all injury, but from all terror, doubt,
and division. *Ibid. Of Queens'*
Gardens, Sect. 68

[g] Borrowers are nearly always
ill-spenders, and it is with lent
money that all evil is mainly
done, and all unjust war pro-
tracted. *The Crown of Wild*
Olive. Work, Sect. 34

[h] Give a little love to a child,
and you get a great deal back.
Ibid. Sect. 49

[i] There's no music in a "rest,"
Katie, that I know of: but there's
the making of music in it. And
people are always missing that
part of the life-melody.
Ethics of the Dust. Lecture 4,
The Crystal Orders

[j] That treacherous phantom
which men call Liberty. *Seven*
Lamps of Architecture. Chap. 7,
The Lamp of Obedience, Sect. 1

[k] Life without industry is guilt, industry without art is brutality.   *Lectures on Art. III, The Relation of Art to Morals*

[l] There is no Wealth but Life.   *Unto This Last. Sect. 77*

Bertrand Arthur William Russell
[1872–   ]

[m] It is preoccupation with possession, more than anything else, that prevents men from living freely and nobly.   *Principles of Social Reconstruction*

[n] Mathematics possesses not only truth, but supreme beauty—a beauty cold and austere, like that of sculpture, without appeal to any part of our weaker nature, sublimely pure, and capable of a stern perfection such as only the greatest art can show.   *The Study of Mathematics*

George W. Russell
("AE")
[1867–1935]

[o] Our hearts were drunk with a beauty
Our eyes could never see.   *The Unknown God*

[p] Twilight, a timid fawn, went glimmering by,
And Night, the dark-blue hunter, followed fast.   *Refuge*

[q] That blazing galleon the sun.   *Mutiny. Stanza 1*

[r] With these heaven-assailing spires
All that was in clay or stone
Fabled of rich Babylon
By these children is outdone.   *New York. Stanza 1*

Irwin Russell
[1853–1879]

[s] You mus' reason with a mule.   *Nebuchadnezzar. Stanza 3*

[t] You bless us, please sah, eben ef we's doin' wrong to-night,
Kase den we'll need de blessin' more'n ef we's doin' right;   *Christmas Night in the Quarters. Blessing the Dance*

[u] "Dar's gwine to be a overflow," said Noah, lookin' solemn—
Fur Noah tuk de *Herald,* an' he read de ribber column.   *De Fust Banjo. Stanza 2*

Abram Joseph Ryan
[1834–1886]

[v] When falls the soldier brave,
Dead at the feet of wrong,

The poet sings and guards his grave
With sentinels of song.   *Sentinel Songs. Stanza 1*

[w] A land without ruins is a land without memories—a land without memories is a land without history.   *A Land Without Ruins. Foreword*

[x] Crowns of roses fade—crowns of thorns endure. Calvaries and crucifixions take deepest hold of humanity.   *Ibid.*

Rafael Sabatini
[1875–1950]

[y] Born with the gift of laughter and the sense that the world was mad, and that was his only patrimony. [The quotation up to the comma was inscribed on one of the new buildings at Yale University under the misapprehension that it was a translation of some ancient classic]   *Scaramouche. Chap. 1*

George Saintsbury
[1845–1933]

[z] It must be remembered that the point of honour which decrees that a man must not under any circumstances accept money from a woman with whom he is on certain terms, is of very modern growth, and is still tempered by the proviso that he may take as much as he likes or can get from his wife.   *Preface to Fielding's Tom Jones*

[a] It is the first duty of the novelist to let himself be read—anything else that he gives you is a bonus, a trimming, a dessert.   *History of the English Novel*

[b] When they [wines] were good they pleased my sense, cheered my spirits, improved my moral and intellectual powers, besides enabling me to confer the same benefits on other people.   *Notes on a Cellar Book. Preface*

"Saki"
see Hector Hugh Munro

Leverett Saltonstall
[1892–   ]

[c] The real New England Yankee is a person who takes the midnight train home from New York.   *Press conference [May 4, 1939]*

Leon Samson

[d] Money is the power of impotence.   *The New Humanism. Page 206 [1930]*

[e] The Diplomat sits in silence, watching the world with his ears.
Ibid. Page 291

[f] Property is the pivot of civilization.
Ibid. Page 316

Carl Sandburg
[1878–   ]

[g] Pile the bodies high at Austerlitz and Waterloo,
Shovel them under and let me work—
I am the grass; I cover all.
Grass

[h] The fog comes on little cat feet.
Fog

[i] The peace of great churches be for you,
Where the players of lofty pipe organs
Practice old lovely fragments, alone.
For You

[j] For the laughter of children who tumble barefooted and bareheaded in the summer grass.
Our Prayer of Thanks

[k] The republic is a dream.
Nothing happens unless first a dream.
Washington Monument by Night

[l] That sergeant at Belleau Woods,
Walking into the drumfires, calling his men,
"Come on, you . . . Do you want to live forever?"
Losers

[m] The marvellous rebellion of man at all signs reading "Keep Off."
Who Am I?

[n] Take any streetful of people buying clothes and groceries, cheering a hero or throwing confetti and blowing tin horns . . . tell me if the lovers are losers . . . tell me if any get more than the lovers . . . in the dust . . . in the cool tombs.
Cool Tombs.

[o] I won't take my religion from any man who never works except with his mouth and never cherishes any memory except the face of the woman on the American silver dollar.
To a Contemporary Bunkshooter

[p] Time is a sandpile we run our fingers in.
Hotel Girl

[q] Hog Butcher for the World,
Tool Maker, Stacker of Wheat,
Player with Railroads and the Nation's Freight Handler
Stormy, husky, brawling,
City of the Big Shoulders.
Chicago

[r] I know a Jew fish crier down on Maxwell Street, with a voice like a north wind blowing over corn stubble in January.
Fish Crier

Margaret E. Sangster
(Mrs. Gerrit Van Deth)
[1894–   ]

[s] Oh, cakes and friends we should choose with care,
Not always the fanciest cake that's there
Is the best to eat! And the plainest friend
Is sometimes the finest one in the end!
French Pastry. Stanza 3

[t] I think that folk should carry bright umbrellas in the rain,
To smile into the sullen sky and make it glad again.
On a Rainy Day. Stanza 4

Margaret Elizabeth Sangster
[1838–1912]

[u] I know—yet my arms are empty,
That fondly folded seven,
And the mother heart within me
Is almost starved for heaven
Are the Children at Home?

[v] Never yet was a springtime
When the buds forgot to blow
Awakening

[w] There's nothing half so pleasant
As coming home again.
The Joy of Coming Home. Stanza 3

[x] The tender word forgotten,
The letter you did not write,
The flower you might have sent, dear,
Are your haunting ghosts to-night.
At Sunset (The Sin of Omission) Stanza 1

George Santayana
[1863–1952]

[y] He carries his English weather in his heart wherever he goes, and it becomes a cool spot in the desert, and a steady and sane oracle amongst all the delirium of mankind.
Soliloquies in England. The British Character

[z] The world is a perpetual caricature of itself; at every moment it is the mockery and the contradiction of what it is pretending to be.
Ibid. Dickens

[a] There is no cure for birth and death save to enjoy the interval.
Ibid. War Shrines

[b] I like to walk about amidst the beautiful things that adorn the world; but private wealth I should decline, or any sort of personal possessions, because they would take away my liberty.
Ibid. The Irony of Liberalism

[c] My atheism, like that of Spinoza, is true piety towards the universe and denies only gods fashioned by men in their own image, to be servants of their human interests.   *Ibid.*
On My Friendly Critics

[d] American life is a powerful solvent. It seems to neutralise every intellectual element, however tough and alien it may be, and to fuse it in the native goodwill, complacency, thoughtlessness, and optimism.   *Character and Opinion in the United States*

[e] All his life he [the American] jumps into the train after it has started and jumps out before it has stopped; and he never once gets left behind, or breaks a leg.
Ibid.

[f] The young man who has not wept is a savage, and the old man who will not laugh is a fool.
Dialogues in Limbo. III

[g] Beauty as we feel it is something indescribable: what it is or what it means can never be said.
The Sense of Beauty.
On Expression

[h] Perhaps the only true dignity of man is his capacity to despise himself.   *Introduction to*
The Ethics of Spinoza

[i] The Bible is literature, not dogma.   *Ibid.*

[j] Columbus found a world, and had no chart,
Save one that faith deciphered in the skies;
To trust the soul's invincible surmise
Was all his science and his only art.
O World, Thou Choosest Not

[k] Old age, on tiptoe, lays her jeweled hand
Lightly in mine. Come, tread a stately measure,
Most gracious partner, nobly poised and bland.
A Minuet on Reaching the Age of Fifty

Sappho of Lesbos
[Circa 610 B.C.]

[l] I loved thee, Atthis, once—long, long ago;
Long, long ago—the memory still is dear.
Stand face to face, friend, and unveil thine eyes,

Look deep in mine and keep the dead past clear
Of all regret.   *To Atthis,*
paraphrase by Anne Bunner

[m] For to whomsoever I do good they harm me most.
Fragments (tr. Mary Mills Patrick). 11

[n] Evening, thou that bringest all, whatever the light-giving dawn scattered; thou bringest the sheep, thou bringest the goat, thou bringest the child to its mother.   *Ibid. 93*

Lew Sarett
[1888-   ]

[o] Walk softly, March, forbear the bitter blow;
Her feet within a trap, her blood upon the snow,
The four little foxes saw their mother go—
Walk softly.
Four Little Foxes. Stanza 2

[p] In yonder room he lies
With pennies on his eyes.
Requiem for a Croesus

Epes Sargent
[1813-1881]

[q] A life on the ocean wave,
A home on the rolling deep;
Where the scattered waters rave,
And the winds their revels keep!
Like an eagle caged I pine
On this dull, unchanging shore:
Oh, give me the flashing brine,
The spray and the tempest's roar!   *A Life on the Ocean Wave. Stanza 1*

William Saroyan
[1908-   ]

[r] What they do, boys, is creep up on you.
And I don't mean Indians.
I mean Americans, over the radio,
Over the waves, from platform, pulpit, press and curb.
The Propagandists

[s] If you give to a thief he cannot steal from you, and he is then no longer a thief.
The Human Comedy. Chap. 4

Siegfried Sassoon
[1886-   ]

[t] Soldiers are citizens of death's grey land,
Drawing no dividend from time's tomorrows. . . .
Soldiers are dreamers; when the guns begin
They think of firelit homes, clean beds, and wives.   *Dreamers*

[u] Guest of those infinitely priv-
ileged ones
Whose lives are padded, petrified,
and pleasant.
*On Reading the War Diary of a
Defunct Ambassador. Stanza 3*

[v] Religion beats me. I'm
amazed at folk
Drinking the gospels in and never
scratching
Their heads for questions.
The Old Huntsman

[w] Who will remember, passing
through this Gate,
The unheroic Dead who fed the
guns?
Who shall absolve the foulness of
their fate,—
Those doomed, conscripted, un-
victorious ones?
On Passing the New Menin Gate

[x] How can they use such names
and be not humble?
Grandeur of Ghosts. Stanza 3

Minot Judson Savage
[1841–1918]

[y] Oh, where is the sea? the
fishes cried,
As they swam its crystal clearness
through.
Where Is God? Stanza 1

[z] A man's truest monument
must be a man.
*The Song of a Man
(Phillips Brooks). Stanza 8*

Sir George Savile,
Marquis of Halifax
[1633–1695]

[a] Popularity is a crime from
the moment it is sought; it is only
a virtue where men have it
whether they will or no.
Moral Thoughts and Reflections

[b] Children and fools want
everything because they want wit
to distinguish; there is no
stronger evidence of a crazy understanding than the making too
large a catalogue of things necessary.   *Advice to a Daughter*

John Godfrey Saxe
[1816–1887]

[c] There's a castle in Spain, very
charming to see,
Though built without money or
toil;
Of this handsome estate I am
owner in fee,
And paramount lord of the soil.
My Castle in Spain. Stanza 1

[d] For though we may think we
are specially blest,
We are certain to pay for the
favors we get!   *The Gifts
of the Gods. Stanza 1*

[e] Of all amusements for the
mind,
From logic down to fishing,
There isn't one that you can find
So very cheap as "wishing."
Wishing. Stanza 1

[f] I'm growing fonder of my
staff;
I'm growing dimmer in the eyes;
I'm growing fainter in my laugh;
I'm growing deeper in my sighs;
I'm growing careless of my dress;
I'm growing frugal of my gold;
I'm growing wise; I'm growing—
yes,—
I'm growing old!
I'm Growing Old. Stanza 3

[g] Of all the notable things on
earth,
The queerest one is pride of birth.
*The Proud Miss MacBride.
Stanza 13*

[h] Bless me! this is pleasant
Riding on the Rail.
Rhyme of the Rail. Stanza 1

[i] The victor is he who can go it
alone!
The Game of Life. Stanza 7

[j] I like the lad, who when his
father thought
To clip his morning nap by hack-
neyed phrase
Of vagrant worm by early song-
ster caught,
Cried, "Served him right! It's not
at all surprising;
The worm was punished, Sir, for
early rising!"
Early Rising. Stanza 8

[k] It was six men of Indostan
To learning much inclined,
Who went to see the Elephant
(Though all of them were
blind),
That each by observation
Might satisfy his mind.
*The Blind Men and the Elephant.
Stanza 1*

[l] I asked of Echo, 't other day
(Whose words are few and often
funny),
What to a novice she could say
Of courtship, love, and matri-
mony?
Quoth Echo, plainly:—"Matter-
o'-money."   *Echo. Stanza 1*

Dorothy Leigh Sayers
[1893-   ]

[m] To that still center where
the spinning world
Sleeps on its axis, to the heart of
rest.   *Gaudy Night.
Chap. 18, Sonnet*

[n] Death seems to provide the
minds of the Anglo-Saxon race

with a greater fund of innocent amusement than any other single subject . . . the tale must be about dead bodies or very wicked people, preferably both, before the Tired Business Man can feel really happy.   *The Third Omnibus of Crime. Introduction*

[o] Do you promise that your Detectives shall well and truly detect the Crimes presented to them, using those Wits which it shall please you to bestow upon them and not placing reliance upon, nor making use of, Divine Revelation, Feminine Intuition, Mumbo-Jumbo, Jiggery-Pokery, Coincidence or the Act of God? *Ibid. . Chap. XI. [Membership oath of the Detection Club, London, quoted by Miss Sayers]*

[p] . . . dangerous dreams of wishful men
Whose homes are safe, who never feel
The flying death that swoops and stuns,
The kisses of the curtseying guns
Slavering their streets with steel.
    The English War. Stanza 11

[q] If it were not for the war,
This war
Would suit me down to the ground. . . .
I have always detested travelling,
And now there is no travelling to do.   *London Calling: Lord, I Thank Thee*

[r] I need not shiver in silk stockings:—
I had a hunch about wool before it was rationed;
Now I have knitted myself woollen stockings
That come a long way up. . . .
As it happens, I like knitting
And nothing gratifies one more
Than to be admired for doing what one likes.   *Ibid.*

Henry J. Sayers
[?–1932]

[s] A sweet Tuxedo girl you see,
Queen of swell society,
Fond of fun as fond can be
When it's on the strict Q. T.
I'm not too young, I'm not too old,
Not too timid, not too bold,
Just the kind you'd like to hold—
Just the kind for sport I'm told—
Ta-ra-ra-boom-de-ay.
    Ta-ra-ra-boom-de-ay! [Minstrel show number (1891), made famous by Lottie Collins in 1892]. Stanza 1 of original version

Marshall Schacht
[1905–   ]

[t] Where God had walked,
The goldenrod
Sprang like fire
From the burning sod.
    The First Autumn. Stanza 1

Robert Haven Schauffler
[1879–   ]

[u] Newcomers all from the eastern seas,
Help us incarnate dreams like these.
Forget, and forgive, that we did you wrong,
Help us to father a nation strong
In the comradeship of an equal birth,
In the wealth of the richest bloods of earth.
    Scum o' the Earth

Johann Christoph Friedrich von Schiller
[1759–1805]

[v] Against stupidity the very gods
Themselves contend in vain.
    The Maid of Orleans. Act III, Sc. 6

[w] When the wine goes in, strange things come out.
    The Piccolomini. Act II, Sc. 12

[x] This feat of Tell, the archer, will be told
While yonder mountains stand upon their base.
By Heaven! the apple's cleft right through the core.
    William Tell. Act III, Sc. 3

Benjamin Schmolke
[1672–1737]

[y] The heavier cross, the heartier prayer;
The bruisèd herbs most fragrant are;
If wind and sky were always fair
The sailor would not watch the star,
And David's Psalms had ne'er been sung
If grief his heart had never wrung.
    Bearing the Burden. Stanza 4

Max Schneckenburger
[1819–1849]

[z] So long as blood shall warm our veins,
While for the sword one hand remains,
One arm to bear a gun,—no more
Shall foot of foeman tread thy shore!

Dear Fatherland, no fear be thine,
Firm stands thy guard along the
  Rhine.
    The Watch on the Rhine [Written in 1840, when France was threatening the left bank of the Rhine, set to music by Carl Wilhelm in 1854]. Stanza 4

Arthur Schopenhauer
[1788–1860]

[a] A certain amount of care or pain or trouble is necessary for every man at all times. A ship without ballast is unstable and will not go straight.
    Studies in Pessimism (tr. T. Bailey Saunders). On the Sufferings of the World

[b] Suicide thwarts the attainment of the highest moral aim by the fact that, for a real release from this world of misery, it substitutes one that is merely apparent.   *Ibid. On Suicide*

[c] Hatred comes from the heart; contempt from the head; and neither feeling is quite within our control.
    Ibid. Psychological Observations

[d] Every man takes the limits of his own field of vision for the limits of the world.   *Ibid.*

[e] Not to go to the theater is like making one's toilet without a mirror.   *Ibid.*

[f] Every parting gives a foretaste of death; every coming together again a foretaste of the resurrection.   *Ibid.*

[g] There is no absurdity so palpable but that it may be firmly planted in the human head if you only begin to inculcate it before the age of five, by constantly repeating it with an air of great solemnity.   *Ibid.*

[h] The fundamental fault of the female character is that it has no sense of justice.
    Ibid. On Women

[i] Noise is the most impertinent of all forms of interruption. It is not only an interruption, but also a disruption of thought.
    Ibid. On Noise

[j] Pride is an established conviction of one's own paramount worth in some particular respect; while vanity is the desire of rousing such a conviction in others. Pride works from within; it is the direct appreciation of oneself. Vanity is the desire to arrive at this appreciation indirectly, from without.
    Essays. Pride

[k] There is no more mistaken path to happiness than worldliness, revelry, high life.   *Ibid. Our Relation to Ourselves, Sect. 24*

[l] Rascals are always sociable, and the chief sign that a man has any nobility in his character is the little pleasure he takes in others' company.
    Counsels and Maxims. Chap. 2

[m] Do not shorten the morning by getting up late; look upon it as the quintessence of life, as to a certain extent sacred.   *Ibid.*

Olive Schreiner
("Ralph Iron")
[1855–1920]

[n] At last they come to where Reflection sits,—that strange old woman, who had always one elbow on her knee, and her chin in her hand, and who steals light out of the past to shed it on the future.   *Dreams. The Lost Joy*

[o] There's something so beautiful in coming on one's very own inmost thoughts in another. In one way it's one of the greatest pleasures one has.   *Letter to Havelock Ellis [March 2, 1885]*

[p] She had said she was twenty-eight years old when she came, and she was twenty-eight still; and they sometimes speculated as to when she would have another birthday.
    From Man to Man. Chap. 6

[q] Man individually and as a race is possible on earth only because . . . love and the guardianship of the strong over the weak has existed.   *Ibid. Chap. 7*

[r] The higher the flame has leaped, the colder and deader the ashes.   *Ibid. Chap. 8*

Carl Schurz
[1829–1906]

[s] Ideals are like stars; you will not succeed in touching them with your hands. But like the seafaring man on the desert of waters, you choose them as your guides, and following them you will reach your destiny.
    Address, Faneuil Hall, Boston [April 18, 1859]

[t] He [Lincoln] possesses to a remarkable degree the characteristic, God-given trait of this people, sound common sense.
    Letter to Theodore Petrasch [October 1864]

[u] Our country, right or wrong. When right, to be kept right; when wrong, to be put right.
    Address in Congress [1872]

Delmore Schwartz
[1914–   ]

[v] Save postage stamps or photographs,
But save your soul! Only the past is immortal.
The Repetitive Heart

Clinton Scollard
[1860–1932]

[w] Don't you hear the flutes of April calling clear and calling cool
From the crests that front the morning, from the hidden valley pool,
Runes of rapture half forgotten, tunes wherein old passions rule?
The Flutes of April. Stanza 1

Duncan Campbell Scott
[1862–1947]

[x] When wild the head-winds beat,
Thy sovereign Will commanding
Bring them who dare to fly
To a safe landing.
*Hymn for Those in the Air
(To the Royal Canadian Air Force). Stanza 2*

Fred Newton Scott
[1860–1931]

[y] Scarce did a lover e'er do as I did,
When his best girl to eternity slided;
I took cold poison and I suicided.
I'm Romeo, Romeo.

I am the heroine of this tale of woe.
I'm Juliet, I'm Juliet.
I am the darling that mashed Romeo.
I'm Juliet, I'm Juliet.
Locked in a tomb with no pick-axe to force it,
Gloomy old hole without room to stand or sit,
I up and stabbed myself right in the corset.
I'm Juliet, I'm Juliet.
*Glee Club Song.
Stanzas 2 and 3*

Geoffrey Scott
[1885–1929]

[z] In my garden goes a fiend
Dark and wild, whose name is Wind.
Wind

John Scott
[1730–1783]

[a] I hate the drum's discordant sound,

Parading round, and round, and round:
To me it talks of ravaged plains,
And burning towns, and ruined swains,
And mangled limbs, and dying groans,
And widows' tears, and orphans' moans;
And all that Misery's hand bestows
To fill the catalogue of human woes.   *I Hate the Drum's Discordant Sound. Stanza 2*

Robert Falcon Scott
[1868–1912]

[b] Make the boy interested in natural history if you can; it is better than games; they encourage it at some schools.
Last Message to His Wife

[c] Had we lived, I should have had a tale to tell of the hardihood, endurance, and courage of my companions which would have stirred the heart of every Englishman. These rough notes and our dead bodies must tell the tale.
Journal. Message to the Public

Sir Walter Scott
[1771–1832]

[d] His withered cheek, and tresses gray,
Seem'd to have known a better day.   *The Lay of the Last Minstrel. Introduction*

[e] If thou would'st view fair Melrose aright,
Go visit it by the pale moonlight.
Ibid. Canto II, Stanza 1

[f] I cannot tell how the truth may be;
I say the tale as 'twas said to me.
Ibid. Stanza 22

[g] In peace, Love tunes the shepherd's reed!
In war, he mounts the warrior's steed . . .
Love rules the court, the camp, the grove,
And men below, and saints above;
For love is heaven, and heaven is love.
Ibid. Canto III, Stanza 2

[h] When the poet dies,
Mute Nature mourns her worshipper,
And celebrates his obsequies.
Ibid. Canto V, Stanza 1

[i] Breathes there the man, with soul so dead,
Who never to himself hath said,
This is my own, my native land!
Whose heart hath ne'er within him burn'd

As home his footsteps he hath turn'd,
From wandering on a foreign strand?
Ibid. Canto VI, Stanza 1

[j] O Caledonia! stern and wild,
Meet nurse for a poetic child!
Land of brown heath and shaggy wood;
Land of the mountain and the flood! *Ibid. Stanza 2*

[k] Just at the age 'twixt boy and youth,
When thought is speech, and speech is truth.
Marmion. Introduction to Canto II, Stanza 4

[l] When, musing on companions gone,
We doubly feel ourselves alone.
Ibid. Stanza 5

[m] Lightly from fair to fair he flew,
And loved to plead, lament, and sue; *Ibid. Canto V, Stanza 9*

[n] Young Lochinvar is come out of the West. . . .
So faithful in love, and so dauntless in war,
There never was knight like the young Lochinvar. *Ibid. Stanza 12 [Lochinvar. Stanza 1]*

[o] Heap on more wood!—the wind is chill;
But let it whistle as it will,
We'll keep our Christmas merry still. *Ibid. Introduction to Canto VI, Stanza 1*

[p] And dar'st thou, then
To beard the lion in his den?
Ibid. Canto VI, Stanza 14

[q] Oh, what a tangled web we weave,
When first we practise to deceive!
Ibid. Stanza 17

[r] O woman! in our hours of ease,
Uncertain, coy, and hard to please,
And variable as the shade
By the light quivering aspen made;
When pain and anguish wring the brow,
A ministering angel thou!
Ibid. Stanza 30

[s] On his bold visage middle age
Had slightly press'd its signet sage,
Yet had not quench'd the open truth
And fiery vehemence of youth.
The Lady of the Lake. Canto I, Stanza 21

[t] Like the dew on the mountain,
Like the foam on the river,

Like the bubble on the fountain,
Thou are gone, and forever!
Ibid. Canto III, Stanza 16
[Coronach. Stanza 3]

[u] Come one, come all! this rock shall fly
From its firm base as soon as I.
Ibid. Canto V, Stanza 10

[v] And the stern joy which warriors feel
In foemen worthy of their steel.
Ibid.

[w] Who o'er the herd would wish to reign,
Fantastic, fickle, fierce, and vain!
Vain as the leaf upon the stream,
And fickle as a changeful dream;
Fantastic as a woman's mood,
And fierce as Frenzy's fever'd blood.
Thou many-headed monster thing,
Oh who would wish to be thy king! *Stanza 30*

[x] Oh, many a shaft at random sent
Finds mark the archer little meant!
And many a word, at random spoken,
May soothe or wound a heart that's broken! *The Lord of the Isles. Canto V, Stanza 18*

[y] Where lives the man that has not tried
How mirth can into folly glide,
And folly into sin!
The Bridal of Triermain. Canto I, Stanza 21

[z] Long loved, long woo'd, and lately won,
My life's best hope, and now mine own. *Ibid. Introduction to Canto II, Stanza 1*

[a] Two sisters by the goal are set,
Cold Disappointment and Regret;
One disenchants the winner's eyes,
And strips of all its worth the prize,
While one augments its gaudy show,
More to enhance the loser's woe.
Rokeby. Canto I, Stanza 31

[b] The tear down childhood's cheek that flows,
Is like the dewdrop on the rose;
When next the summer breeze comes by,
And waves the bush, the flower is dry.
Ibid. Canto IV, Stanza 11

[c] Thus aged men, full loth and slow,
The vanities of life forego,

And count their youthful follies
  o'er,
Till Memory lends her light no
  more.
          Ibid. Canto V, Stanza 1

[d] Time will rust the sharpest
  sword,
Time will consume the strongest
  cord;
That which moulders hemp and
  steel,
Mortal arm and nerve must feel.
          *Harold the Dauntless.
          Canto I, Stanza 4*

[e] Cursed war and racking tax
Have left us scarcely raiment to
  our backs.   *The Search
          after Happiness. Stanza 16*

[f] A lawyer without history or
literature is a mechanic, a mere
working mason; if he possesses
some knowledge of these, he may
venture to call himself an architect.   *Guy Mannering. Chap. 37*

[g] When Israel, of the Lord be-
  lov'd,
  Out of the land of bondage
    came,
Her fathers' God before her
    mov'd,
An awful guide, in smoking and
    flame.   *Ivanhoe. Chap. 39*
  [*Rebecca's Song. Stanza 1*]

[h] Sea of upturned faces.
          Rob Roy. Chap. 20

[i] The happy combination of
  fortuitous circumstances.
  *The Monastery. Answer of the
  Author of Waverley to the
  Letter of Captain Clutterbuck*

[j] Within that awful volume lies
The mystery of mysteries! . . .
And better had they ne'er been
  born,
Who read to doubt, or read to
  scorn. [Of the Bible]
          The Monastery. Chap. 12

[k] Spur not an unbroken horse;
put not your ploughshare too deep
into new land   *Ibid Chap 25*

[l] Meat eaten without either
mirth or music is ill of digestion.
          Ibid.

[m] Too much rest is rust.
          The Betrothed. Chap. 13

[n] If you keep a thing seven
years, you are sure to find a use
for it.   *Woodstock. Chap. 28*

[o] Recollect that the Almighty,
who gave the dog to be companion
of our pleasures and our toils,
hath invested him with a nature
noble and incapable of deceit.
          The Talisman. Chap. 24

[p] One hour of life, crowded to
the full with glorious action, and
filled with noble risks, is worth

whole years of those mean ob-
servances of paltry decorum.
          Count Robert of Paris. Chap. 25

[q] Good wine needs neither
bush nor preface
To make it welcome.
          Peveril of the Peak. Chap. 4

[r] When I hae a saxpence under
  my thumb,
Then I get credit in ilka town;
But when I am poor, they bid me
  gae by,
O, poverty parts good company.
          The Abbot. Chap. 7

[s] Tell that to the marines—the
sailors won't believe it.
          Redgauntlet. Vol. II, Chap. 7

[t] Although too much of a soldier among sovereigns, no one
could claim with better right to
be a sovereign among soldiers.
          Life of Napoleon

William Scott, Lord Stowell
[1745–1836]

[u] A dinner lubricates business.
  *Quoted in Boswell's Life of
  Dr. Johnson, London edition
  [1835], Vol. VIII, Page 67,
  Note*

Anderson M. Scruggs
[1897–   ]

[v] Only the dream will last.
  Some distant day
The wheels will falter, and the
  silent sun
Will see the last beam leveled to
  decay,
And all men's futile clangor spent
  and done.
Yet after brick and steel and
  stone are gone,
And flesh and blood are dust, the
  dream lives on.
  Sonnet. Only the Dream is Real

Edmund Hamilton Sears
[1810–1876]

[w] It came upon the midnight
  clear,
That glorious song of old.
          The Angels' Song

[x] When Peace shall over all the
  earth
Its ancient splendors fling
And the whole world send back
  the song
Which now the angels sing.
          Ibid.

Sir Charles Sedley
[1639–1701]

[y] When change itself can give
  no more,
'Tis easy to be true.   *Reasons for
          Constancy. Stanza 4*

Alan Seeger
[1888–1916]

[z] Whether I am on the winning or losing side is not the point with me: it is being on the side where my sympathies lie that matters, and I am ready to see it through to the end. Success in life means doing that thing than which nothing else conceivable seems more noble or satisfying or remunerative. *Letter to his Mother. [July 3, 1915]*

[a] I have a rendezvous with Death
At some disputed barricade,
When Spring comes back with rustling shade
And apple-blossoms fill the air.
I Have a Rendezvous with Death

John Selden
[1584–1654]

[b] Old friends are best. King James used to call for his old shoes; they were easiest for his feet. *Table Talk. Friends*

[c] Humility is a virtue all preach, none practise; and yet everybody is content to hear. *Ibid. Humility*

[d] 'Tis not the drinking that is to be blamed, but the excess. *Ibid.*

[e] Ignorance of the law excuses no man; not that all men know the law, but because 'tis an excuse every man will plead, and no man can tell how to refute him. *Ibid. Law*

[f] Take a straw and throw it up into the air,—you may see by that which way the wind is. *Ibid. Libels*

[g] Marriage is a desperate thing. *Ibid. Marriage*

[h] They that govern the most make the least noise. *Ibid. Power*

[i] Pleasures are all alike, simply considered in themselves. He that takes pleasure to hear sermons enjoys himself as much as he that hears plays. *Ibid. Pleasure*

[j] A King is a thing men have made for their own sakes, for quietness' sake. Just as in a Family one man is appointed to buy the meat. *Ibid. Of a King*

George Seldes
[1890–]

[k] Sawdust Caesar. [Mussolini] *Title of book*

Seneca
[8 B.C.–A.D. 65]

Translation by W. H. D. Rouse, Loeb Classical Library

[l] What fools these mortals be. *Epistles. 1, 3*

[m] It is not the man who has too little, but the man who craves more, that is poor. *Ibid. 2, 2*

[n] Love of bustle is not industry. *Ibid. 3, 5*

[o] Live among men as if God beheld you; speak to God as if men were listening. *Ibid. 10, 5*

[p] A great pilot can sail even when his canvas is rent. *Ibid. 30, 3*

[q] Man is a reasoning animal. *Ibid. 41, 8*

[r] That most knowing of persons,—gossip. *Ibid. 43, 1*

[s] All art is but imitation of nature. *Ibid. 65, 3*

[t] It is a rough road that leads to the heights of greatness. *Ibid. 84, 13*

[u] We are mad, not only individually, but nationally. We check manslaughter and isolated murders; but what of war and the much vaunted crime of slaughtering whole peoples? *Ibid. 95, 30*

[v] A great step towards independence is a good-humored stomach. *Ibid. 123, 3*

[w] There is no great genius without some touch of madness. *Moral Essays. On Tranquillity of the Mind, 17, 10*

[x] A great fortune is a great slavery. *Ibid. To Polybius on Consolation, 6, 5*

[y] He who receives a benefit with gratitude, repays the first instalment on his debt. *On Benefits. Book 2, 22, 1*

[z'] You roll my log, and I will roll yours. *Apocolocyntosis. Chap. 9*

[a'] Successful and fortunate crime is called virtue. *Hercules Furens. 1, 1, 255*

Robert William Service
[1874–]

[b'] This is the Law of the Yukon, that only the Strong shall thrive;
That surely the Weak shall perish, and only the Fit survive.
The Law of the Yukon

[c'] Not by my sins wilt Thou judge me, but by the work of my hands.

Master, I've done Thy bidding,
and the light is low in the
west,
And the long, long shift is over
    . . .
Master, I've earned it—Rest.
    The Song of the Wage-Slave

[d] Back of the bar, in a solo
game, sat Dangerous Dan Mc-
Grew,
And watching his luck was his
light-o'-love, the lady that's
known as Lou.   *The Shooting
    of Dan McGrew. Stanza 1*

[e] The Northern Lights have
seen queer sights,
But the queerest they ever did
see
Was that night on the marge of
Lake Lebarge
I cremated Sam McGee.
    *The Cremation of Sam McGee.
        Stanza 1*

[f] A promise made is a debt un-
paid.   *Ibid. Stanza 8*

[g] There's a race of men that
don't fit in,
A race that can't stay still;
So they break the hearts of kith
and kin,
And they roam the world at
will.   *The Men That Don't
    Fit In. Stanza 1*

[h] A million stars are in the sky;
A million planets plunge and die;
A million million men are sped;
A million million wait ahead.
Each plays his part and has his
day—
What ho! the World's all right, I
say.   *The World's All Right.
        Stanza 3*

[i] Ah! the clock is always slow;
It is later than you think.
    It Is Later than You Think

[j] When we, the Workers, all de-
mand:
"What are we fighting for?" . . .
Then, then we'll end that stupid
crime, that devil's madness—
War.   *Michael*

"Dr. Seuss"
(Theodor Seuss Geisel)
[1904–   ]

[k] When I leave home to walk
to school,
Dad always says to me,
"Marco, keep your eyelids up
And see what you can see."
    *And to Think that I Saw It on
        Mulberry Street*

William Shakespeare
[1564–1616]
*From the text of W. J. Craig,
M.A. (The Complete Works of
Shakespeare. Oxford University
Press.)*

[l] Now would I give a thousand
furlongs of sea for an acre of
barren ground.   *The Tempest.
    Act I, Sc. 1, Line 70*

[m] I would fain die a dry death.
    Ibid. Line 73

[n]   By telling of it,
Made such a sinner of his
memory,
To credit his own lie.
    Ibid. Sc. 2, Line 99

[o]   My library
Was dukedom large enough.
    Ibid. Line 109

[p]   The very rats
Instinctively have quit it.
    Ibid. Line 147

[q] Full fathom five thy father
lies;
Of his bones are coral made;
Those are pearls that were his
eyes:
Nothing of him that doth fade
But doth suffer a sea-change
Into something rich and strange.
    Ibid. Line 394

[r]   Lest too light winning
Make the prize light.
    Ibid. Line 448

[s] He receives comfort like cold
porridge.
    Ibid. Act II, Sc. 1, Line 10

[t] *Gonzalo.* Here is everything
advantageous to life.
Antonio. True; save means to live.
    Ibid. Line 52

[u] Misery acquaints a man with
strange bedfellows.
    Ibid. Sc. 2, Line 42

[v] He that dies pays all debts.
    Ibid. Act III, Sc. 2, Line 143

[w]   We are such stuff
As dreams are made on, and our
little life
Is rounded with a sleep.
    Ibid. Act IV, Sc. 1, Line 156

[x] With foreheads villanous low.
    Ibid. Line 252

[y] Where the bee sucks, there
suck I;
In a cowslip's bell I lie.
    Ibid. Act V, Sc. 1, Line 88

[z] O brave new world,
That has such people in't!
    Ibid. Line 183

[a] Let us not burden our re-
membrances
With a heaviness that's gone.
    Ibid. Line 199

[b] I have been in such a pickle
since I saw you last.
    Ibid. Line 282

[c] I have no other but a
woman's reason:
I think him so, because I think
him so.   *The Two Gentlemen
    of Verona. Act I, Sc. 2, Line 23*

[d] They do not love that do not show their love.
Ibid. Line 31

[e] Since maids, in modesty, say "No" to that
Which they would have the profferer construe "Ay."
Ibid. Line 53

[f] O! how this spring of love resembleth
The uncertain glory of an April day!
Ibid. Sc. 3, Line 84

[g] That man that hath a tongue, I say, is no man,
If with his tongue he cannot win a woman.
Ibid. Act III, Sc. 1, Line 104

[h] Who is Sylvia? what is she?
That all our swains commend her?
Ibid. Act IV, Sc. 2, Line 40

[i] How use doth breed a habit in a man!
Ibid. Act V, Sc. 4, Line 1

[j] If there be no great love in the beginning, yet heaven may decrease it upon better acquaintance, when we are married and have more occasion to know one another; I hope, upon familiarity will grow more contempt.
The Merry Wives of Windsor. Act I, Sc. 1, Line 255

[k] "Convey," the wise it call. "Steal!" foh! a fico for the phrase!
Ibid. Sc. 3, Line 30

[l] Here will be an old abusing of God's patience and the king's English.
Ibid. Sc. 4, Line 5

[m] Thereby hangs a tale.
Ibid. Line 155

[n] Why, then the world's mine oyster,
Which I with sword will open.
Ibid. Act II, Sc. 2, Line 2

[o] Better three hours too soon than a minute too late.
Ibid. Line 332

[p] We have some salt of our youth in us.
Ibid. Sc. 3, Line 50

[q] O, what a world of vile ill-favour'd faults
Looks handsome in three hundred pounds a year!
Ibid. Act III, Sc. 4, Line 32

[r] A woman would run through fire and water for such a kind heart. *Ibid. Line 106*

[s] The rankest compound of villanous smell that ever offended nostril. *Ibid. Sc. 5, Line 95*

[t] So curses all Eve's daughters, of what complexion soever.
Ibid. Act IV, Sc. 2, Line 24

[u] Wives may be merry, and yet honest too. *Ibid. Line 110*

[v] This is the third time; I hope good luck lies in odd numbers. . . . There is divinity in odd numbers, either in nativity, chance, or death.
Ibid. Act V, Sc. 1, Line 2

[w] Life is a shuttle.
Ibid. Line 25

[x] Nature never lends
The smallest scruple of her excellence
But, like a thrifty goddess, she determines
Herself the glory of a creditor,
Both thanks and use. *Measure for Measure. Act I, Sc. 1, Line 36*

[y] He was ever precise in promise-keeping.
Ibid. Sc. 2, Line 80

[z] A man whose blood
Is very snow-broth; one who never feels
The wanton stings and motions of the sense.
Ibid. Sc. 4, Line 57

[a] Our doubts are traitors,
And make us lose the good we oft might win
By fearing to attempt.
Ibid. Line 78

[b] The jury, passing on the prisoner's life,
May in the sworn twelve have a thief or two
Guiltier than him they try.
Ibid. Act II, Sc. 1, Line 19

[c] Some rise by sin, and some by virtue fall. *Ibid. Line 38*

[d'] Great with child, and longing for stewed prunes.
Ibid. Line 94

[e'] His face is the worst thing about him. *Ibid. Line 167*

[f'] The law hath not been dead, though it hath slept.
Ibid. Sc. 2, Line 90

[g'] O, it is excellent
To have a giant's strength; but it is tyrannous
To use it like a giant.
Ibid. Line 107

[h'] But man, proud man,
Drest in a little brief authority,
Most ignorant of what he's most assured,
His glassy essence, like an angry ape,
Plays such fantastic tricks before high heaven
As make the angels weep.
Ibid. Line 117

[i'] That in the captain's but a choleric word
Which in the soldier is flat blasphemy. *Ibid. Line 130*

[j] The miserable have no other
medicine,
But only hope.
Ibid. Act III, Sc. 1, Line 2

[k]   A breath thou art,
Servile to all the skyey influences.
Ibid. Line 8

[l] Ay, but to die, and go we know
not where;
To lie in cold obstruction and to
rot;
This sensible warm motion to be-
come
A kneaded clod; and the de-
lighted spirit
To bathe in fiery floods, or to re-
side
In thrilling region of thick-ribbed
ice;
To be imprison'd in the viewless
winds,
And blown with restless violence
round about
The pendent world. . . .
The weariest and most loathed
worldly life
That age, ache, penury, and im-
prisonment
Can lay on nature, is a paradise
To what we fear of death.
Ibid. Line 116

[m] O, what may man within
him hide,
Though angel on the outward
side!   *Ibid. Line 293*

[n] Take, O take those lips away,
That so sweetly were forsworn;
And those eyes, the break of day,
Lights that do mislead the
morn:
But my kisses bring again, bring
again;
Seals of love, but sealed in vain,
sealed in vain.
Ibid. Act IV, Sc. 1, Line 1

[o]   Truth is truth
To the end of reckoning.
Ibid. Act V, Sc. 1, Line 45

[p] Neither maid, widow, nor
wife.   *Ibid. Line 173*

[q] They say best men are
moulded out of faults.
And, for the most, become much
more the better
For being a little bad.
Ibid. Line 440

[r] What's mine is yours, and
what is yours is mine.
Ibid. Line 539

[s] The pleasing punishment that
women bear.   *The Comedy
of Errors. Act I, Sc. 1, Line 46*

[t] Every why hath a wherefore.
Ibid. Act II, Sc. 2, Line 45

[u] Neither rhyme nor reason.
Ibid. Line 49

[v] There's no time for a man to
recover his hair that grows bald
by nature. ◦ ◦ ◦

What he [Time] hath scanted
men in hair, he hath given them
in wit. . . .

Time himself is bald, and therefore to the world's end will have
bald followers.
Ibid. Lines 74, 83, 109

[w] Small cheer and great welcome makes a merry feast.
Ibid. Act III, Sc. 1, Line 26

[x] For slander lives upon succession,
For ever housed where it gets possession.   *Ibid. Line 105*

[y] A back-friend, a shoulder-
clapper.
Ibid. Act IV, Sc. 2, Line 37

[z] One Pinch, a hungry lean-
faced villain,
A mere anatomy.   *Ibid. Act V,
Sc. 1, Line 238*

[a] How much better is it to weep
at joy than to joy at weeping.
*Much Ado about Nothing. Act I,
Sc. 1, Line 28*

[b] A very valiant trencher-man.
Ibid. Line 52

[c] There's a skirmish of wit between them.   *Ibid. Line 64*

[d] He wears his faith but as the
fashion of his hat.
Ibid. Line 76

[e] I would my horse had the
speed of your tongue, and so good
a continuer.   *Ibid. Line 151*

[f] I could not endure a husband
with a beard on his face: I had
rather lie in the woollen.
Ibid. Act II, Sc. 1, Line 31

[g] Speak low, if you speak love.
Ibid. Line 104

[h] Friendship is constant in all
other things
Save in the office and affairs of
love:
Therefore, all hearts in love use
their own tongues;
Let every eye negotiate for itself,
And trust no agent.
Ibid. Line 184

[i] Silence is the perfectest herald
of joy: I were but little happy, if
I could say how much.
Ibid. Line 319

[j'] There was a star danced, and
under that was I born.
Ibid. Line 351

[k'] Sigh no more, ladies, sigh no
more,
Men were deceivers ever;
One foot in sea and one on shore;
To one thing constant never.
Ibid. Sc. 3, Line 65

[l'] The pleasant'st angling is to
see the fish
Cut with her golden oars the silver stream,

And greedily devour the treacherous bait.
Ibid. Act III, Sc. 1, Line 26

[m] From the crown of his head to the sole of his foot, he is all mirth. *Ibid. Sc. 2, Line 9*

[n] He hath a heart as sound as a bell. *Ibid. Line 12*

[o] Every one can master a grief but he that has it. *Ibid. Line 28*

[p] They that touch pitch will be defiled. *Ibid. Sc. 3, Line 61*

[q] The fashion wears out more apparel than the man. *Ibid. Line 147*

[r] I thank God, I am as honest as any man living, that is an old man and no honester than I. *Ibid. Sc. 5, Line 15*

[s] Comparisons are odorous. *Ibid. Line 18*

[t] O! what authority and show of truth
Can cunning sin cover itself withal! *Ibid. Act IV, Sc. 1, Line 35*

[u] I have mark'd
A thousand blushing apparitions
To start into her face; a thousand innocent shames
In angel whiteness beat away those blushes.
Ibid. Line 160

[v] For it so falls out
That what we have we prize not to the worth
Whiles we enjoy it, but being lack'd and lost,
Why, then we rack the value; then we find
The virtue that possession would not show us
Whiles it was ours.
Ibid. Line 219

[w] The idea of her life shall sweetly creep
Into his study of imagination,
And every lovely organ of her life,
Shall come apparell'd in more precious habit,
More moving-delicate, and full of life
Into the eye and prospect of his soul. *Ibid. Line 226*

[x] Patch grief with proverbs.
Ibid. Act V, Sc. 1, Line 17

[y] For there was never yet philosopher
That could endure the toothache patiently. *Ibid. Line 35*

[z] What though care killed a cat. *Ibid. Line 135*

[a] The huge army of the world's desires. *Love's Labour's Lost. Act I, Sc. 1, Line 10*

[b] At Christmas I no more desire a rose
Than wish a snow in May's new-fangled mirth;
But like of each thing that in season grows. *Ibid. Line 105*

[c] A man . . .
That hath a mint of phrases in his brain. *Ibid. Line 163*

[d] A child of our grandmother Eve, a female; or, for thy more sweet understanding, a woman.
Ibid. Line 263

[e] Affliction may one day smile again; and till then, sit thee down, sorrow! *Ibid. Line 312*

[f] Delivers in such apt and gracious words
That aged ears play truant at his tales,
And younger hearings are quite ravished;
So sweet and voluble is his discourse.
Ibid. Act II, Sc. 1, Line 73

[g] Remuneration! O! that's the Latin word for three farthings.
Ibid. Act III, Sc. 1, Line 143

[h] This senior-junior, giant-dwarf, Dan Cupid;
Regent of love-rhymes, lord of folded arms,
The anointed sovereign of sighs and groans,
Liege of all loiterers and malcontents. *Ibid. Line 190*

[i] He hath not fed of the dainties that are bred in a book; he hath not eat paper, as it were; he hath not drunk ink.
Ibid. Act IV, Sc. 2, Line 25

[j] As upright as the cedar.
Ibid. Sc. 3, Line 89

[k] And when Love speaks, the voice of all the gods
Makes heaven drowsy with the harmony. *Ibid. Line 344*

[l] From women's eyes this doctrine I derive:
They sparkle still the right Promethean fire;
They are the books, the arts, the academes,
That show, contain, and nourish all the world. *Ibid. Line 350*

[m'] He draweth out the thread of his verbosity finer than the staple of his argument.
Ibid. Act V, Sc. 1, Line 18

[n'] The naked truth.
Ibid. Sc. 2, Line 715

[o'] A jest's prosperity lies in the ear
Of him that hears it, never in the tongue
Of him that makes it.
Ibid. Line 869

[p] When daisies pied and violets
blue,
And lady-smocks all silver-
white,
And cuckoo-buds of yellow hue
Do paint the meadows with de-
light,
The cuckoo then, on every tree,
Mocks married men.
Ibid. Line 902

[q]   The moon, like to a silver
bow
New-bent in heaven.
*A Midsummer-Night's Dream.
Act I, Sc. 1, Line 9*

[r] But earthlier happy is the rose
distill'd
Than that which withering on the
virgin thorn
Grows, lives, and dies in single
blessedness.   *Ibid. Line 76*

[s] The course of true love never
did run smooth.
Ibid. Line 134

[t] Swift as a shadow, short as
any dream,
Brief as the lightning in the
collied night,
That, in a spleen, unfolds both
heaven and earth,
And ere a man hath power to say,
"Behold!"
The jaws of darkness do devour it
up:
So quick bright things come to
confusion.   *Ibid. Line 144*

[u] I will roar you as gently as
any sucking dove; I will roar you,
as 'twere any nightingale.
Ibid. Sc. 2, Line 85

[v] It is not night when I do see
your face. . . .
For you in my respect are all the
world:
Then how can it be said that I am
alone.
Ibid. Act II, Sc. 1, Line 221

[w] We cannot fight for love, as
men may do;
We should be woo'd and were not
made to woo.
Ibid. Line 241

[x] I know a bank whereon the
wild thyme blows.
Ibid. Line 249

[y] As a surfeit of the sweetest
things
The deepest loathing to the
stomach brings
Ibid. Sc. 2, Line 137

[z] Lord, what fools these mortals
be!
Ibid. Act III, Sc. 2, Line 115

[a] I have had a dream, past the
wit of man to say what dream it
was. *Ibid. Act IV, Sc. 1, Line 211*

[b] Eat no onions nor garlic, for
we are to utter sweet breath.
Ibid. Sc. 2, Line 44

[c] The lunatic, the lover, and
the poet
Are of imagination all compact:
One sees more devils than vast
hell can hold,
That is, the madman: the lover,
all as frantic,
Sees Helen's beauty in a brow of
Egypt:
The poet's eye, in a fine frenzy
rolling,
Doth glance from heaven to earth,
from earth to heaven;
And as imagination bodies forth
The forms of things unknown, the
poet's pen
Turns them to shapes, and gives
to airy nothing
A local habitation and a name.
Such tricks hath strong imagina-
tion,
That if it would but apprehend
some joy,
It comprehends some bringer of
that joy;
Or in the night, imagining some
fear,
How easy is a bush supposed a
bear!
Ibid. Act V, Sc. 1, Line 7

[d] The iron tongue of midnight
hath told twelve.
Ibid. Line 372

[e] Why should a man, whose
blood is warm within,
Sit like his grandsire cut in alabaster?   *The Merchant of
Venice. Act I, Sc. 1, Line 83*

[f] Gratiano speaks an infinite
deal of nothing, more than any
man in all Venice. His reasons are
as two grains of wheat hid in two
bushels of chaff: you shall seek
all day ere you find them, and
when you have them, they are not
worth the search.
Ibid. Line 114

[g] They are as sick that surfeit with too much, as they that
starve with nothing.
Ibid. Sc. 2, Line 5

[h] If to do were as easy as to
know what were good to do,
chapels had been churches, and
poor men's cottages princes'
palaces.   *Ibid. Line 13*

[i] The brain may devise laws for
the blood, but a hot temper leaps
o'er a cold decree.   *Ibid. Line 19*

[j] The devil can cite Scripture
for his purpose.
Ibid. Sc. 3, Line 99

[k] A goodly apple rotten at the
heart:
O, what a goodly outside falsehood hath!   *Ibid. Line 102*

[l] For sufferance is the badge of
all our tribe.   *Ibid. Line 110*

[m] O father Abram! what these Christians are,
Whose own hard dealings teaches them suspect
The thoughts of others!
Ibid. Line 161

[n] Mislike me not for my complexion,
The shadow'd livery of the burnish'd sun.
Ibid. Act II, Sc. 1, Line 1

[o] It is a wise father that knows his own child.
Ibid. Sc. 2, Line 83

[p] Who risest from a feast
With that keen appetite that he sits down?
Ibid. Sc. 6, Line 8

[q] All things that are,
Are with more spirit chased than enjoy'd. *Ibid. Line 12*

[r] But love is blind, and lovers cannot see
The pretty follies that themselves commit. *Ibid. Line 36*

[s] Hanging and wiving goes by destiny.
Ibid. Sc. 9, Line 83

[t] I am a Jew. Hath not a Jew eyes? Hath not a Jew hands, organs, dimensions, senses, affections, passions?
Ibid. Act III, Sc. 1, Line 62

[u] Tell me where is fancy bred,
Or in the heart or in the head?
How begot, how nourished?
Reply, reply.
Ibid. Sc. 2, Line 63

[v] In law, what plea so tainted and corrupt
But being season'd with a gracious voice,
Obscures the show of evil?
Ibid. Line 75

[w] The weakest kind of fruit
Drops earliest to the ground.
Ibid. Act IV, Sc. 1, Line 115

[x] I never knew so young a body with so old a head.
Ibid. Line 163

[y] The quality of mercy is not strain'd,
It droppeth as the gentle rain from heaven
Upon the place beneath. It is twice bless'd:
It blesseth him that gives and him that takes.
'T is mightiest in the mightiest: it becomes
The throned monarch better than his crown;
His sceptre shows the force of temporal power
But mercy is above this sceptred sway.
It is enthroned in the hearts of kings,

It is an attribute to God himself;
And earthly power doth then show likest God's,
When mercy seasons justice.
Ibid. Line 184

[z] To do a great right, do a little wrong.
Ibid. Line 216

[a] A Daniel come to judgment! yea, a Daniel!
Ibid. Line 223

[b] You take my life,
When you do take the means whereby I live.
Ibid. Line 377

[c] He is well paid that is well satisfied. *Ibid. Line 416*

[d] How sweet the moonlight sleeps upon this bank!
Here we will sit and let the sounds of music
Creep in our ears: soft stillness and the night
Become the touches of sweet harmony.
Sit, Jessica. Look how the floor of heaven
Is thick inlaid with patines of bright gold:
There's not the smallest orb which thou behold'st
But in his motion like an angel sings,
Still quiring to the young-eyed cherubins.
Such harmony is in immortal souls;
But whilst this muddy vesture of decay
Doth grossly close it in, we cannot hear it.
Ibid. Act V, Sc. 1, Line 54

[e] The man that hath no music in himself,
Nor is not moved with concord of sweet sounds,
Is fit for treasons, stratagems, and spoils . . .
Let no such man be trusted.
Ibid. Line 83

[f] How far that little candle throws his beams!
So shines a good deed in a naughty world.
Ibid. Line 90

[g] This night, methinks, is but the daylight sick.
Ibid. Line 124

[h] A light wife doth make a heavy husband.
Ibid. Line 130

[i] These blessed candles of the night. *Ibid. Line 220*

[j] Fleet the time carelessly, as they did in the golden world
As You Like It Act I, Sc. 1, Line 126

[k] Always the dulness of the fool
is the whetstone of the wits.
Ibid. Sc. 2, Line 59

[l] *Celia.* Not a word?
Rosalind. Not one to throw at a
dog. *Ibid. Sc. 3, Line 2*

[m] O, how full of briers is this
working-day world!
Ibid. Line 12

[n] Beauty provoketh thieves
sooner than gold.
Ibid. Line 113

[o] We'll have a swashing and a
martial outside,
As many other mannish cowards
have. *Ibid. Line 123*

[p] Sweet are the uses of adversity;
Which, like the toad, ugly and
venomous,
Wears yet a precious jewel in his
head;
And this our life, exempt from
public haunt,
Finds tongues in trees, books in
the running brooks,
Sermons in stones, and good in
every thing.
Ibid. Act II, Sc. 1, Line 12

[q] The big round tears
Coursed one another down his
innocent nose
In piteous chase. *Ibid. Line 38*

[r] "Poor deer," quoth he, "thou
mak'st a testament
As worldlings do, giving thy sum
of more
To that which had too much."
Ibid. Line 47

[s] For in my youth I never did
apply
Hot and rebellious liquors in my
blood.
Ibid. Sc. 3, Line 48

[t] Therefore my age is as a lusty
winter.
Frosty, but kindly.
Ibid. Line 52

[u] The fashion of these
times,
Where none will sweat but for
promotion. *Ibid. Line 59*

[v] Ay, now am I in Arden: the
more fool I. When I was at home I
was in a better place; but travellers must be content.
Ibid. Sc. 4, Line 16

[w] If you remember'st not the
slightest folly
That ever love did make thee run
into,
Thou hast not lov'd.
Ibid. Line 34

[x] Under the greenwood tree
Who loves to lie with me.
Ibid. Sc. 5, Line 1

[y] I met a fool i' the forest,
A motley fool.
Ibid. Sc. 7, Line 12

[z] And then he drew a dial from
his poke,
And looking on it with lack-lustre
eye,
Says, very wisely, "It is ten
o'clock:
Thus we may see," quoth he,
"how the world wags. . . .
And so from hour to hour we ripe
and ripe,
And then from hour to hour we
rot and rot."
Ibid. Line 20

[a] Motley's the only wear.
Ibid. Line 34

[b] I must have liberty
Withal, as large a charter as the
wind,
To blow on whom I please.
Ibid. Line 47

[c] All the world's a stage,
And all the men and women
merely players.
They have their exits and their
entrances;
And one man in his time plays
many parts,
His acts being seven ages. At first
the infant,
Mewling and puking in the
nurse's arms.
And then the whining school-
boy, with his satchel
And shining morning face, creep-
ing like snail
Unwillingly to school. And then
the lover,
Sighing like furnace, with a woful
ballad
Made to his mistress' eyebrow.
Then a soldier,
Full of strange oaths, and bearded
like the pard;
Jealous in honour, sudden and
quick in quarrel,
Seeking the bubble reputation
Even in the cannon's mouth. And
then the justice,
In fair round belly with good
capon lined,
With eyes severe and beard of
formal cut,
Full of wise saws and modern in-
stances;
And so he plays his part. The
sixth age shifts
Into the lean and slipper'd panta-
loon,
With spectacles on nose and
pouch on side;
His youthful hose, well saved, a
world too wide
For his shrunk shank; and his
big manly voice,
Turning again toward childish
treble, pipes
And whistles in his sound. Last
scene of all,

That ends this strange eventful
    history,
Is second childishness, and mere
    oblivion,
Sans teeth, sans eyes, sans taste,
    sans everything.
                    Ibid. Line 139

[d] Blow, blow, thou winter
    wind!
Thou art not so unkind
As man's ingratitude.
                    Ibid. Line 174

[e] These trees shall be my books.
            Ibid. Act III, Sc. 2, Line 5

[f] I am a true labourer: I earn
that I eat, get that I wear, owe no
man hate, envy no man's happiness, glad of other men's good.
                    Ibid. Line 78

[g] Do you not know I am a
woman? when I think, I must
speak.   *Ibid. Line 265*

[h] I do desire we may be better
strangers.   *Ibid. Line 276*

[i] *Jacques.* What stature is she
of?
Orlando. Just as high as my heart.
                    Ibid. Line 286

[j]   Down on your knees,
And thank Heaven, fasting, for a
good man's love.
                Ibid. Sc. 5, Line 57

[k] I am falser than vows made
in wine.   *Ibid. Line 73*

[l] It is a melancholy of mine
own, compounded of many sim-
ples, extracted from many objects, and indeed the sundry contemplation of my travels, in which
my often rumination wraps me in
a most humorous sadness.
            Ibid. Act IV, Sc. 1, Line 16

[m] I had rather have a fool to
make me merry than experience
to make me sad.   *Ibid. Line 28*

[n] Men have died from time to
time, and worms have eaten them,
but not for love. *Ibid. Line 110*

[o] Men are April when they woo,
December when they wed: maids
are May when they are maids, but
the sky changes when they are
wives.   *Ibid. Line 153*

[p] Chewing the food of sweet
and bitter fancy.
                Ibid. Sc. 3, Line 103

[q] "So so" is good, very good,
very excellent good; and yet it is
not; it is but so so.
            Ibid. Act V, Sc. 1, Line 30

[r] The fool doth think he is
wise, but the wise man knows
himself to be a fool.
                    Ibid. Line 35

[s] No sooner met but they
looked; no sooner looked but they
loved; no sooner loved but they
sighed; no sooner sighed but they
asked one another the reason; no
sooner knew the reason but they
sought the remedy.
                Ibid. Sc. 2, Line 37

[t] An ill-favoured thing, sir, but
mine own.
                Ibid. Sc. 4, Line 60

[u]   A woman's gift
To rain a shower of commanded
tears.   *The Taming of the
        Shrew. Induc. Sc. 1, Line 124*

[v] Let the world slip: we shall
ne'er be younger.
                Ibid. Sc. 2, Line 147

[w] No profit grows where is no
pleasure ta'en;
In brief, sir, study what you most
affect.
            Ibid. Act I, Sc. 1, Line 39

[x] There's small choice in rotten
apples.   *Ibid. Line 137*

[y] Who wooed in haste and
means to wed at leisure.
            Ibid. Act III, Sc. 2, Line 11

[z] Kindness in women, not their
beauteous looks,
Shall win my love.
            Ibid. Act IV, Sc. 2, Line 41

[a] Our purses shall be proud,
our garments poor:
For 'tis the mind that makes the
body rich.
                Ibid. Sc. 3, Line 173

[b] And as the sun breaks
through the darkest clouds,
So honour peereth in the meanest
habit.   *Ibid. Line 175*

[c] He that is giddy thinks the
world turns round.
            Ibid. Act V, Sc. 2, Line 20

[d'] A woman moved is like a
fountain troubled,
Muddy, ill-seeming, thick, bereft
of beauty.   *Ibid. Line 143*

[e'] Such duty as the subject
owes the prince,
Even such a woman oweth to her
husband.   *Ibid. Line 156*

[f'] The hind that would be
mated by the lion
Must die for love.   *All's Well
    that Ends Well. Act I, Sc. 1,
                        Line 103*

[g'] Our remedies oft in ourselves do lie,
Which we ascribe to Heaven.
                    Ibid. Line 235

[h'] Oft expectation fails, and
most oft there
Where most it promises.
            Ibid. Act II, Sc. 1, Line 145

[i'] A young man married is a
man that's marr'd.
                Ibid. Sc. 3, Line 315

[j] Make the coming hour o'er-
flow with joy,
And pleasure drown the brim.
Ibid. Sc. 4, Line 48

[k] No legacy is so rich as honesty.
Ibid. Act III, Sc. 5, Line 13

[l] The web of our life is of a
mingled yarn, good and ill together.
Ibid. Act IV, Sc. 3, Line 83

[m] I am a man whom Fortune
hath cruelly scratched.
Ibid. Act V, Sc. 2, Line 28

[n] The inaudible and noiseless
foot of Time.
Ibid. Sc. 3, Line 41

[o]   Love that comes too late,
Like a remorseful pardon slowly
carried.   *Ibid. Line 57*

[p] If music be the food of love,
play on.   *Twelfth-Night.*
Act I, Sc. 1, Line 1

[q] I am a great eater of beef, and
I believe that does harm to my
wit.   *Ibid. Sc. 3, Line 92*

[r] 'Tis beauty truly blent, whose
red and white
Nature's own sweet and cunning
hand laid on:
Lady, you are the cruell'st she
alive
If you will lead these graces to the
grave
And leave the world no copy.
Ibid. Sc. 5, Line 259

[s] Holla your name to the reverberate hills,
And make the babbling gossip of
the air
Cry out.   *Ibid. Line 293*

[t] Journeys end in lovers meet-
ing,
Every wise man's son doth know.
Ibid. Act II, Sc. 3, Line 46

[u] Then come kiss me, sweet
and twenty,
Youth's a stuff will not endure.
Ibid. Line 54

[v] He does it with a better grace,
but I do it more natural.
Ibid. Line 91

[w] *Sir Toby.* Dost thou think,
because thou art virtuous, there
shall be no more cakes and ale?
Clown. Yes, by Saint Anne, and
ginger shall be hot i' the mouth
too.   *Ibid. Line 124*

[x] These most brisk and giddy-
paced times.
Ibid. Sc. 4, Line 6

[y]   Let still the woman take
An elder than herself: so wears
she to him,
So sways she level in her husband's heart:

For, boy, however we do praise
ourselves,
Our fancies are more giddy and
unfirm,
More longing, wavering, sooner
lost and worn,
Than women's are.
Ibid. Line 29

[z]   She never
told her love,
But let concealment, like a worm
i' the bud,
Feed on her damask cheek: she
pined in thought,
And with a green and yellow
melancholy
She sat like patience on a monument,
Smiling at grief.   *Ibid. Line 113*

[a] Some are born great, some
achieve greatness, and some have
greatness thrust upon them.
Ibid. Sc. 5, Line 159

[b] Foolery, sir, does walk about
the orb like the sun; it shines
everywhere.
Ibid. Act III, Sc. 1, Line 44

[c] Oh, what a deal of scorn looks
beautiful
In the contempt and anger of his
lip!   *Ibid. Line 159*

[d] Love sought is good, but
given unsought, is better.
Ibid. Line 170

[e] Laugh yourself into stitches.
Ibid. Sc. 2, Line 75

[f] I can no other answer make
but thanks,
And thanks, and ever thanks.
Ibid. Sc. 3, Line 14

[g] This is very midsummer madness.   *Ibid. Sc. 4, Line 62*

[h] If this were played upon a
stage now, I could condemn it as
an improbable fiction.
Ibid. Line 142

[i] I hate ingratitude more in a
man
Than lying, vainness, babbling
drunkenness,
Or any taint of vice whose strong
corruption
Inhabits our frail blood.
Ibid. Line 390

[j'] Out of the jaws of death.
Ibid. Line 396

[k'] Thus the whirligig of time
brings in his revenges.
Ibid. Act V, Sc. 1, Line 388

[l'] For the rain it raineth every
day.   *Ibid. Line 404*

[m'] You pay a great deal too
dear for what's given freely.
The Winter's Tale. Act I, Sc. 1,
Line 18

[n]   Black brows, they say,
Become some women best, so that
there be not
Too much hair there, but in a
semi-circle,
Or a half-moon made with a pen.
          Ibid. Act II, Sc. 1, Line 8

[o] A sad tale's best for winter.
          Ibid. Line 24

[p] There's some ill planet reigns:
I must be patient till the heavens
look
With an aspect more favourable.
          Ibid. Line 104

[q] The silence often of pure innocence
Persuades when speaking fails.
          Ibid. Sc. 2, Line 41

[r] What's gone and what's past
help
Should be past grief.
          Ibid. Act III, Sc. 2, Line 223

[s] I am gone for ever. [*exit, pursued by a bear.*]
          Ibid. Sc. 3, Line 57

[t] A merry heart goes all the
day,
Your sad tires in a mile-a.
          Ibid. Act IV, Sc. 2, Line 135

[u]   Daffodils,
That come before the swallow
dares, and take
The winds of March with beauty.
          Ibid. Sc. 3, Line 118

[v]   When you do dance, I
wish you
A wave o' the sea, that you might
ever do
Nothing but that.
          Ibid. Line 140

[w] The self-same sun that
shines upon his court
Hides not his visage from our
cottage, but
Looks on alike.   *Ibid. Line 457*

[x] Let me have no lying; it becomes none but tradesmen.
          Ibid. Line 747

[y] And if his name be George,
I'll call him Peter;
For new-made honour doth forget
men's names.   *King John.
          Act. I, Sc. 1, Line 186*

[z] A hazard of new fortunes.
          Ibid. Act II, Sc. 1, Line 71

[a] For courage mounteth with
occasion.   *Ibid. Line 82*

[b] He is the half part of a
blessed man,
Left to be finished by such a she;
And she a fair divided excellence,
Whose fulness of perfection lies
in him.   *Ibid. Line 437*

[c] Talks as familiarly of roaring
lions
As maids of thirteen do of puppy-
dogs!   *Ibid. Line 459*

[d] I will instruct my sorrows to
be proud;
For grief is proud, and makes his
owner stoop.
          Ibid. Act III, Sc. 1, Line 68

[e] What hath this day deserved?
what hath it done
That it in golden letters should be
set
Among the high tides in the calendar?   *Ibid. Line 84*

[f] Thou ever strong upon the
stronger side!
Thou Fortune's champion that
dost never fight
But when her humorous ladyship
is by
To teach thee safety.
          Ibid. Line 117

[g] O, amiable lovely death!
          Ibid. Sc. 4, Line 25

[h] Grief fills the room up of my
absent child,
Lies in his bed, walks up and
down with me,
Puts on his pretty looks, repeats
his words,
Remembers me of all his gracious
parts,
Stuffs out his vacant garments
with his form.
          Ibid. Line 93

[i] Life is as tedious as a twice-
told tale,
Vexing the dull ear of a drowsy
man.   *Ibid. Line 108*

[j] To gild refined gold, to paint
the lily,
To throw a perfume on the violet,
To smooth the ice, or add another
hue
Unto the rainbow, or with taper-
light
To seek the beauteous eye of
heaven to garnish,
Is wasteful and ridiculous excess.
          Ibid. Act IV, Sc. 2, Line 11

[k] And oftentimes excusing of a
fault
Doth make the fault the worse by
the excuse.   *Ibid. Line 30*

[l] We cannot hold mortality's
strong hand.   *Ibid. Line 82*

[m] How oft the sight of means
to do ill deeds
Makes ill deeds done!
          Ibid. Line 219

[n'] The day shall not be up so
soon as I,
To try the fair adventure of to-
morrow.
          Ibid. Act V, Sc. 5, Line 21

[o'] This pale faint swan,
Who chants a doleful hymn to his
own death,
And from the organ-pipe of
frailty sings
His soul and body to their lasting
rest.   *Ibid. Sc. 7, Line 21*

[p] Now my soul hath elbow-room. *Ibid. Line 28*

[q] This England never did, nor never shall,
Lie at the proud foot of a conqueror. *Ibid. Line 112*

[r] Mine honour is my life; both grow in one;
Take honour from me, and my life is done. *King Richard II, Act I, Sc. 1, Line 182*

[s] Truth hath a quiet breast. *Ibid. Sc. 3, Line 96*

[t] How long a time lies in one little word! *Ibid. Line 213*

[u] O, who can hold a fire in his hand
By thinking on the frosty Caucasus?
Or cloy the hungry edge of appetite
By bare imagination of a feast?
Or wallow naked in December snow
By thinking on fantastic summer's heat?
O, no! the apprehension of the good
Gives but the greater feeling to the worse. *Ibid. Line 294*

[v] The tongues of dying men
Enforce attention like deep harmony. *Ibid. Act II, Sc. 1, Line 5*

[w] This other Eden, demi-paradise,
This fortress built by Nature for herself
Against infection and the hand of war,
This happy breed of men, this little world,
This precious stone set in the silver sea,
Which serves it in the office of a wall
Or as a moat defensive to a house,
Against the envy of less happier lands,
This blessed plot, this earth, this realm, this England. *Ibid. Line 42*

[x] I count myself in nothing else so happy
As in a soul remembering my good friends. *Ibid. Sc. 3, Line 46*

[y] I see thy glory like a shooting star
Fall to the base earth from the firmament. *Ibid. Sc. 4, Line 19*

[z] Eating the bitter bread of banishment. *Ibid. Act III, Sc. 1, Line 21*

[a] O, call back yesterday, bid time return! *Ibid. Sc. 2, Line 69*

[b] And nothing can we call our own but death;
And that small model of the barren earth,
Which serves as paste and cover to our bones.
For God's sake, let us sit upon the ground,
And tell sad stories of the death of kings. *Ibid. Line 152*

[c] Men judge by the complexion of the sky
The state and inclination of the day. *Ibid. Line 194*

[d] He is come to open
The purple testament of bleeding war. *Ibid. Sc. 3, Line 93*

[e] And my large kingdom for a little grave,
A little little grave, an obscure grave. *Ibid. Line 153*

[f] The noisome weeds, that without profit suck
The soil's fertility from wholesome flowers. *Ibid. Sc. 4, Line 38*

[g] So Judas did to Christ: but he, in twelve,
Found truth in all but one; I, in twelve thousand, none. *Ibid. Act IV, Sc. 1, Line 170*

[h] Some of you with Pilate wash your hands
Showing an outward pity. *Ibid. Line 239*

[i] As in a theatre, the eyes of men,
After a well-graced actor leaves the stage,
Are idly bent on him that enters next,
Thinking his prattle to be tedious. *Ibid. Act V, Sc. 2, Line 23*

[j] As hard to come as for a camel
To thread the postern of a small needle's eye. *Ibid. Sc. 5, Line 16*

[k] How sour sweet music is
When time is broke and no proportion kept!
So is it in the music of men's lives. *Ibid. Line 42*

[l] In those holy fields
Over whose acres walked those blessed feet
Which fourteen hundred years ago were nail'd
For our advantage on the bitter cross. *King Henry IV, Part I. Act I, Sc. 1, Line 24*

[m] I would to God thou and I knew where a commodity of good names were to be bought. *Ibid. Sc. 2, Line 92*

[n] If all the year were playing holidays,
To sport would be as tedious as to work. *Ibid. Line 226*

[o] You tread upon my patience.
Ibid. Sc. 3, Line 4

[p] Fresh as a bridegroom; and
his chin new reap'd,
Showed like a stubble-land at
harvest-home;
He was perfumed like a milliner.
Ibid. Line 34

[q] And as the soldiers bore dead
bodies by,
He called them untaught knaves,
unmannerly,
To bring a slovenly unhandsome
corse
Betwixt the wind and his nobility.
Ibid. Line 42

[r] By heaven, methinks it were
an easy leap
To pluck bright honour from the
pale-faced moon,
Or dive into the bottom of the
deep,
Where fathom-line could never
touch the ground,
And pluck up drowned honour by
the locks. *Ibid. Line 201*

[s] Falstaff sweats to death,
And lards the lean earth as he
walks along.
Ibid. Act II, Sc. 2, Line 119

[t] Out of this nettle, danger, we
pluck this flower, safety.
Ibid. Sc. 3, Line 11

[u] I have peppered two of them:
two I am sure I have paid, two
rogues in buckram suits. I tell
thee what, Hal, if I tell thee a lie,
spit in my face; call me horse.
Thou knowest my old ward;—here
I lay, and thus I bore my point.
Four rogues in buckram let drive
at me— *Ibid. Sc. 4, Line 215*

[v] Give you a reason on compulsion! If reasons were as plentiful
as blackberries, I would give no
man a reason upon compulsion, I.
Ibid. Line 267

[w] A plague of sighing and
grief! It blows a man up like a
bladder. *Ibid. Line 370*

[x] You may buy land now as
cheap as stinking mackerel.
Ibid. Line 399

[y] Diseased Nature oftentimes
breaks forth
In strange eruptions.
Ibid. Act III, Sc. 1, Line 27

[z] I had rather be a kitten and
cry mew,
Than one of these same metre
ballad-mongers.
Ibid. Line 128

[a] But in the way of bargain,
mark ye me,
I'll cavil on the ninth part of a
hair *Ibid. Line 138*

[b] A good mouth-filling oath.
Ibid. Line 258

[c] Company, villanous company,
hath been the spoil of me.
Ibid. Sc. 3, Line 10

[d] How has he the leisure to be
sick
In such a justling time?
Ibid. Act IV, Sc. 1, Line 17

[e] As full of spirit as the month
of May. *Ibid. Line 100*

[f] The cankers of a calm world
and a long peace.
Ibid. Sc. 2, Line 32

[g] I could be well content
To entertain the lag-end of my
life
With quiet hours.
Ibid. Act V, Sc. 1, Line 23

[h] Honour pricks me on. Yea,
but how if honour prick me off
when I come on,—how then? Can
honour set to a leg? no: or an
arm? no: or take away the grief
of a wound? no. . . . What is
honour? a word. What is in that
word honour; what is that honour? air. . . . Who hath it? he
that died o' Wednesday. Doth he
feel it? no. Doth he hear it? no. It
is insensible, then? yea, to the
dead. But will it not live with the
living? no. Why? detraction will
not suffer it. Therefore I'll none
of it. Honour is a mere scutcheon.
And so ends my catechism.
Ibid. Line 131

[i] The time of life is short;
To spend that shortness basely
were too long.
Ibid. Sc. 2, Line 81

[j] I could have better spared a
better man.
Ibid. Sc. 4, Line 104

[k] The better part of valour is
discretion. *Ibid. Line 120*

[l] I'll purge, and leave sack, and
live cleanly. *Ibid. Line 168*

[m] Yet the first bringer of un-
welcome news
Hath but a losing office, and his
tongue
Sounds ever after as a sullen bell,
Remember'd knolling a departing
friend. *Ibid.*
Part II. Act I, Sc. 1, Line 100

[n] I am not only witty in myself,
but the cause that wit is in other
men. *Ibid. Sc. 2, Line 10*

[o'] You lie in your throat if you
say I am any other than an honest
man. *Ibid. Line 97*

[p'] Some smack of age in you,
some relish of the saltness of
time. *Ibid. Line 112*

[q'] It is the disease of not listening, the malady of not marking, that I am troubled withal.
Ibid. Line 139

[r] Pray that our armies join not in a hot day; for, by the Lord, I take but two shirts out with me, and I mean not to sweat extraordinarily. *Ibid. Line 237*

[s] It was always yet the trick of our English nation, if they have a good thing, to make it too common. *Ibid. Line 244*

[t] Past and to come seem best; things present worst.
Ibid. Sc. 3, Line 108

[u] He hath eaten me out of house and home.
Ibid. Act II, Sc. 1, Line 82

[v] Thou didst swear to me upon a parcel-gilt goblet, sitting in my Dolphin-chamber, at the round table, by a sea-coal fire, upon Wednesday in Wheeson week.
Ibid. Line 96

[w] Thus we play the fools with the time, and the spirits of the wise sit in the clouds and mock us. *Ibid. Sc. 2, Line 155*

[x] He was indeed the glass Wherein the noble youth did dress themselves.
Ibid. Sc. 3, Line 21

[y] Is it not strange that desire should so many years outlive performance? *Ibid. Sc. 4, Line 283*

[z] O sleep, O gentle sleep,
Nature's soft nurse! how have I frighted thee,
That thou no more wilt weigh my eyelids down
And steep my senses in forgetfulness?
Ibid. Act III, Sc. 1, Line 5

[a] Uneasy lies the head that wears a crown.
Ibid. Line 31

[b] There is a history in all men's lives. *Ibid. Line 80*

[c] How many of mine old acquaintance are dead!
Ibid. Sc. 2, Line 37

[d] If I had a thousand sons, the first human principle I would teach them should be, to forswear thin potations and to addict themselves to sack.
Ibid. Act IV, Sc. 3, Line 133

[e] Will Fortune never come with both hands full
But write her fair words still in foulest letters?
She either gives a stomach and no food;
Such are the poor, in health; or else a feast
And takes away the stomach.
Ibid. Sc. 4, Line 103

[f] Golden care!
That keep'st the ports of slumber open wide
To many a watchful night!
Ibid. Sc. 5, Line 22

[g] Thy wish was father, Harry, to that thought.
Ibid. Line 91

[h] Commit The oldest sins the newest kind of ways. *Ibid. Line 124*

[i] *Falstaff.* What wind blew you hither, Pistol?
Pistol. Not the ill wind which blows no man to good.
Ibid. Act V, Sc. 3, Line 87

[j] *Falstaff.* What! is the old king dead?
Pistol. As nail in door.
Ibid. Line 123

[k] How ill white hairs become a fool and jester.
Ibid. Sc. 4, Line 53

[l] 'Tis ever common That men are merriest when they are from home. *King Henry V. Act I, Sc. 2, Line 271*

[m] O England! . . .
Like little body with a mighty heart.
Ibid. Act II, Prologue, Line 16

[n] His nose was as sharp as a pen, and a' babbled of green fields.
Ibid. Act II, Sc. 3, Line 17

[o] Once more unto the breach, dear friends, once more;
Or close the wall up with our English dead!
In peace there's nothing so becomes a man
As modest stillness and humility;
But when the blast of war blows in our ears,
Then imitate the action of the tiger;
Stiffen the sinews, summon up the blood.
Ibid. Act III, Sc. 1, Line 1

[p] I would give all my fame for a pot of ale and safety.
Ibid. Sc. 2, Line 14

[q] Men of few words are the best men. *Ibid. Line 40*

[r'] Impious war Array'd in flames like to the prince of fiends,
Do, with his smirch'd complexion, all fell feats
Enlink'd to waste and desolation.
Ibid. Sc. 3, Line 15

[s'] Giddy Fortune's furious fickle wheel,
That goddess blind,
That stands upon the rolling restless stone.
Ibid. Sc. 6, Line 28

[t] That island of England breeds very valiant creatures: their mastiffs are of unmatchable courage.
Ibid. Sc. 7, Line 155

[u] You may as well say that's a valiant flea that dare eat his breakfast on the lip of a lion.
Ibid. Line 160

[v] There is some soul of goodness in things evil,
Would men observingly distil it out.
Ibid. Act IV, Sc. 1, Line 4

[w] We few, we happy few, we band of brothers.
Ibid. Sc. 3, Line 60

[x] Those that leave their valiant bones in France,
Dying like men, . . .
They shall be fam'd; for there the sun shall greet them,
And draw their honours reeking up to heaven.
Ibid. Line 98

[y] By this leek, I will most horribly revenge. I eat and eat, I swear.
Ibid. Act V, Sc. 1, Line 49

[z] A fellow of plain and uncoined constancy.
Ibid. Sc. 2, Line 160

[a] Hung be the heavens with black, yield day to night!
King Henry VI, Part I. Act I, Sc. 1, Line 1

[b] Halcyon days.
Ibid. Sc. 2, Line 131

[c] Glory is like a circle in the water,
Which never ceaseth to enlarge itself,
Till by broad spreading it disperse to nought.   *Ibid. Line 133*

[d] The sun with one eye vieweth all the world.
Ibid. Sc. 4, Line 84

[e] Between two blades, which bears the better temper;
Between two horses, which doth bear him best;
Between two girls, which hath the merriest eye;
I have perhaps, some shallow spirit of judgment;
But in these nice sharp quillets of the law,
Good faith, I am no wiser than a daw.
Ibid. Act II, Sc. 4, Line 14

[f] Just death, kind umpire of men's miseries.
Ibid. Sc. 5, Line 29

[g] Chok'd with ambition of the meaner sort.
Ibid. Line 123

[h] Of all base passions, fear is most accurs'd.
Ibid. Act V, Sc. 2, Line 18

[i] She's beautiful and therefore to be wooed,
She is a woman, therefore to be won.   *Ibid. Sc. 3, Line 78*

[j] For what is wedlock forced, but a hell,
An age of discord and continual strife?
Whereas the contrary bringeth bliss,
And is a pattern of celestial peace.
Ibid. Sc. 5, Line 62

[k] O Lord! that lends me life,
Lend me a heart replete with thankfulness!
Ibid. Part II. Act I, Sc. 1, Line 19

[l]   Whose large style
Agrees not with the leanness of his purse.   *Ibid. Line 112*

[m] And after summer evermore succeeds
Barren winter, with his wrathful nipping cold:
So cares and joys abound, as seasons fleet.
Ibid. Act II, Sc. 4, Line 2

[n] Now 'tis the spring, and weeds are shallow-rooted;
Suffer them now and they'll o'ergrow the garden.
Ibid. Act III, Sc. 1, Line 31

[o] What stronger breastplate than a heart untainted!
Thrice is he armed that hath his quarrel just,
And he but naked, though locked up in steel,
Whose conscience with injustice is corrupted.
Ibid. Sc. 2, Line 232

[p] The gaudy, blabbing, and remorseful day
Is crept into the bosom of the sea.
Ibid. Act IV, Sc. 1, Line 1

[q] The first thing we do, let's kill all the lawyers.
Ibid. Sc. 3, Line 86

[r] Is not this a lamentable thing, that of the skin of an innocent lamb should be made parchment? that parchment, being scribbled o'er, should undo a man?   *Ibid. Line 88*

[s] Thou hast most traitorously corrupted the youth of the realm in erecting a grammar-school; and whereas, before, our forefathers had no other books but the score and the tally, thou hast caused printing to be used; and, contrary to the king, his crown, and dignity, thou hast built a paper-mill.   *Ibid. Sc. 7, Line 35*

[t'] Beggars mounted run their horse to death.   *Ibid.*
Part III. Act I, Sc. 4, Line 127

[u] O tiger's heart wrapp'd in a woman's hide!
Ibid. Line 137

[v] And many strokes, though with a little axe,
Hew down and fell the hardest-timbered oak.
Ibid. Act II, Sc. 1, Line 54

[w] To weep is to make less the depth of grief.
Ibid. Line 85

[x] The smallest worm will turn, being trodden on.
Ibid. Sc. 2, Line 17

[y] Didst thou never hear
That things ill got had ever bad success? *Ibid. Line 45*

[z] And what makes robbers bold but too much lenity?
Ibid. Sc. 6, Line 22

[a] My crown is in my heart, not on my head;
Not deck'd with diamonds and Indian stones,
Nor to be seen: my crown is call'd content;
A crown it is that seldom kings enjoy.
Ibid. Act III, Sc. 1, Line 62

[b] 'Tis a happy thing
To be the father unto many sons.
Ibid. Sc. 2, Line 104

[c] *Gloucester.* That would be ten days' wonder at the least.
Clarence. That's a day longer than a wonder lasts.
Ibid. Line 113

[d] Like one that stands upon a promontory,
And spies a far-off shore where he would tread,
Wishing his foot were equal with his eye. *Ibid. Line 135*

[e] What fates impose, that men must needs abide;
It boots not to resist both wind and tide.
Ibid. Act IV, Sc. 3, Line 57

[f] A little fire is quickly trodden out;
Which, being suffered, rivers cannot quench.
Ibid. Sc. 8, Line 7

[g] When the lion fawns upon the lamb,
The lamb will never cease to follow him. *Ibid. Line 49*

[h] What is pomp, rule, reign, but earth and dust?
And, live we how we can, yet die we must.
Ibid. Act V, Sc. 2, Line 27

[i] We are advertis'd by our loving friends.
Ibid. Sc. 3, Line 18

[j] Suspicion always haunts the guilty mind;
The thief doth fear each bush an officer. *Ibid. Sc. 6, Line 11*

[k] Now is the winter of our discontent
Made glorious summer by this sun of York. *King Richard III. Act I, Sc. 1, Line 1*

[l] Grim-visaged war hath smoothed his wrinkled front.
Ibid. Line 9

[m] Look, how my ring encompasseth thy finger,
Even so thy breast encloseth my poor heart;
Wear both of them, for both of them are thine.
Ibid. Sc. 2, Line 204

[n] They that stand high have many blasts to shake them.
Ibid. Sc. 3, Line 259

[o] And thus I clothe my naked villany
With odd old ends stolen forth of holy writ,
And seem a saint when most I play the devil.
Ibid. Line 336

[p] O, I have passed a miserable night,
So full of ugly sights, of ghastly dreams,
That, as I am a Christian faithful man,
I would not spend another such a night,
Though 'twere to buy a world of happy days.
Ibid. Sc. 4, Line 2

[q] Lord, Lord! methought, what pain it was to drown!
What dreadful noise of waters in mine ears!
What ugly sights of death within mine eyes! *Ibid. Line 21*

[r] So wise so young, they say, do never live long.
Ibid. Act III, Sc. 1, Line 79

[s] Lives like a drunken sailor on a mast,
Ready with every nod to tumble down. *Ibid. Line 98*

[t] True hope is swift, and flies with swallow's wings;
Kings it makes gods, and meaner creatures kings.
Ibid. Act V, Sc. 2, Line 23

[u'] My conscience hath a thousand several tongues,
And every tongue brings in a several tale,
And every tale condemns me for a villain.
Ibid. Sc. 3, Line 194

[v'] The early village cock
Hath twice done salutation to the morn. *Ibid. Line 210*

[w] By the apostle Paul, shadows to-night
Have struck more terror to the soul of Richard
Than can the substance of ten thousand soldiers.
Ibid. Line 217

[x] A horse! a horse! my kingdom for a horse!
Ibid. Sc. 4, Line 7

[y] I have set my life upon a cast,
And I will stand the hazard of the die.
Ibid. Line 9

[z] Anger is like
A full-hot horse, who being allow'd his way,
Self-mettle tires him.
King Henry VIII. Act I, Sc. 1, Line 132

[a] Heat not a furnace for your foe so hot
That it do singe yourself.
Ibid. Line 140

[b] New customs,
Though they be never so ridiculous,
Nay, let 'em be unmanly, yet are follow'd.
Ibid. Sc. 3, Line 2

[c] The mirror of all courtesy.
Ibid. Act II, Sc. 1, Line 53

[d] 'Tis better to be lowly born,
And range with humble livers in content,
Than to be perked up in a glistering grief
And wear a golden sorrow.
Ibid. Sc. 3, Line 19

[e] Orpheus with his lute made trees,
And the mountain-tops that freeze,
Bow themselves when he did sing.
Ibid. Act III, Sc. 1, Line 3

[f] Heaven is above all yet; there sits a judge
That no king can corrupt.
Ibid. Line 99

[g] I have touched the highest point of all my greatness;
And from that full meridian of my glory,
I haste now to my setting: I shall fall
Like a bright exhalation in the evening,
And no man see me more.
Ibid. Sc. 2, Line 224

[h] I have ventured,
Like little wanton boys that swim on bladders,
This many summers in a sea of glory,
But far beyond my depth: my high-blown pride
At length broke under me, and now has left me,
Weary and old with service, to the mercy

Of a rude stream, that must forever hide me.
Vain pomp and glory of this world, I hate ye.
Ibid. Line 359

[i] A peace above all earthly dignities,
A still and quiet conscience.
Ibid. Line 380

[j] I charge thee, fling away ambition:
By that sin fell the angels.
Ibid. Line 441

[k] Had I but served my God with half the zeal
I served my king, he would not in mine age
Have left me naked to mine enemies.
Ibid. Line 456

[l] He gave his honours to the world again,
His blessed part to heaven, and slept in peace.
So may he rest; his faults lie gently on him!
Ibid. Act IV, Sc. 2, Line 29

[m] He was a man
Of an unbounded stomach.
Ibid. Line 33

[n] Men's evil manners live in brass; their virtues
We write in water.
Ibid. Line 45

[o] Appetite, a universal wolf.
Troilus and Cressida. Act I, Sc. 3, Line 121

[p] The baby figure of the giant mass
Of things to come.
Ibid. Line 345

[q] 'Tis mad idolatry
To make the service greater than the god.
Ibid. Act II, Sc. 2, Line 56

[r] The elephant hath joints, but none for courtesy: his legs are legs for necessity, not for flexure.
Ibid. Sc. 3, Line 114

[s] He that is proud eats up himself; pride is his own glass, his own trumpet, his own chronicle.
Ibid. Line 165

[t] Words pay no debts.
Ibid. Act III, Sc. 2, Line 56

[u] To fear the worst oft cures the worse.
Ibid. Line 77

[v] All lovers swear more performance than they are able, and yet reserve an ability that they never perform; vowing more than the perfection of ten, and discharging less than the tenth part of one.
Ibid. Line 89

[w'] Time hath, my lord, a wallet at his back,
Wherein he puts alms for oblivion.
Ibid. Sc. 3, Line 145

[x]   Welcome ever smiles,
And farewell goes out sighing.
Ibid. Line 168

[y] One touch of nature makes
the whole world kin.
Ibid. Line 175

[z] My mind is troubled, like a
fountain stirr'd;
And I myself see not the bottom
of it.   *Ibid. Line 314*

[a] The kiss you take is better
than you give.
Ibid. Act IV, Sc. 5, Line 38

[b] There's language in her eye,
her cheek, her lip.
Ibid. Line 55

[c]   The gods sent not
Corn for the rich men only.
Coriolanus. Act I, Sc. 1, Line 213

[d] Had I dozen sons, each in my
love alike . . . I had rather eleven
die nobly for their country than
one voluptuously surfeit out of
action.   *Ibid. Sc. 3, Line 24*

[e] Nature teaches beasts to know
their friends.
Ibid. Act II, Sc. 1, Line 6

[f] A cup of hot wine with not a
drop of allaying Tiber in't.
Ibid. Line 52

[g] Bid them wash their faces,
And keep their teeth clean.
Ibid. Sc. 3, Line 65

[h] I thank you for your voices:
thank you,
Your most sweet voices.
Ibid. Line 179

[i] The mutable, rank-scented
many.
Ibid. Act III, Sc. 1, Line 65

[j] His nature is too noble for the
world:
He would not flatter Neptune for
his trident,
Or Jove for 's power to thunder.
Ibid. Line 254

[k]   I do love
My country's good with a respect
more tender,
More holy, more profound, than
mine own life.
Ibid. Sc. 3, Line 109

[l]   Chaste as the icicle
That's curdied by the frost from
purest snow
And hangs on Dian's temple.
Ibid. Act V, Sc. 3, Line 65

[m] Sweet mercy is nobility's
true badge.
*Titus Andronicus. Act I, Sc. 1,
Line 119*

[n] These words are razors to my
wounded heart.
Ibid. Line 314

[o] What you cannot as you would
achieve,
You must perforce accomplish as
you may.
Ibid. Act II, Sc. 1, Line 106

[p] How easily murder is discovered!
Ibid. Sc. 3, Line 287

[q] Poor harmless fly.
Ibid. Act III, Sc. 2, Line 63

[r] A pair of star-cross'd lovers.
*Romeo and Juliet. Act I, Pro-
logue, Line 6*

[s] An hour before the worshipp'd
sun
Peered forth the golden window
of the east.
Ibid. Act I, Sc. 1, Line 124

[t] As is the bud bit with an en-
vious worm,
Ere he can spread his sweet leaves
to the air,
Or dedicate his beauty to the sun.
Ibid. Line 156

[u] Saint-seducing gold.
Ibid. Line 220

[v] He that is strucken blind cannot forget
The precious treasure of his eye-
sight lost.   *Ibid. Line 238*

[w] One fairer than my love! the
all-seeing sun
Ne'er saw her match since first
the world begun.
Ibid. Sc. 2, Line 97

[x'] She [Queen Mab] is the
fairies' midwife, and she
comes
In shape no bigger than an agate-
stone
On the fore-finger of an alderman,
Drawn with a team of little
atomies
Athwart men's noses as they lie
asleep.   *Ibid. Sc. 4, Line 54*

[y'] Toes unplagu'd with corns.
Ibid. Sc. 5, Line 21

[z'] For you and I are past our
dancing days.   *Ibid. Line 35*

[a'] Her beauty hangs upon the
cheek of night
Like a rich jewel in an Ethiop's
ear.   *Ibid. Line 49*

[b'] But, soft! what light through
yonder window breaks?
It is the east, and Juliet is the sun.
Ibid. Act II, Sc. 2, Line 2

[c'] See, how she leans her cheek
upon her hand.
O! that I were a glove upon that
hand,
That I might touch that cheek.
Ibid. Line 23

[d'] O Romeo, Romeo! wherefore
art thou Romeo?
Ibid. Line 33

[e] What's in a name? That which we call a rose
By any other name would smell as sweet. *Ibid. Line 43*

[f] Alack! there lies more peril in thine eye
Than twenty of their swords. *Ibid. Line 71*

[g] *Romeo.* Lady, by yonder blessed moon I swear,
That tips with silver all these fruit-tree tops,—
Juliet. O! swear not by the moon, the inconstant moon,
That monthly changes in her circled orb,
Lest that thy love prove likewise variable. *Ibid. Line 107*

[h] This bud of love, by summer's ripening breath,
May prove a beauteous flower when next we meet. *Ibid. Line 121*

[i] Love goes toward love, as schoolboys from their books;
But love from love, toward school with heavy looks. *Ibid. Line 156*

[j] How silver-sweet sound lovers' tongues by night,
Like softest music to attending ears! *Ibid. Line 165*

[k] Good night, good night! parting is such sweet sorrow,
That I shall say good night till it be morrow. *Ibid. Line 184*

[l] Virtue itself turns vice, being misapplied;
And vice sometime's by action dignified. *Ibid. Sc. 3, Line 21*

[m] Wisely and slow; they stumble that run fast. *Ibid. Line 94*

[n] Stabbed with a white wench's black eye. *Ibid. Sc. 4, Line 14*

[o] Love's heralds should be thoughts,
Which ten times faster glide than the sun's beams. *Ibid. Sc. 5, Line 4*

[p] The excuse that thou dost make in this delay
Is longer than the tale thou dost excuse. *Ibid. Line 33*

[q] Here comes the lady: O! so light a foot
Will ne'er wear out the everlasting flint. *Ibid. Sc. 6, Line 16*

[r] Thy head is as full of quarrels as an egg is full of meat.
Ibid. Act III, Sc. 1, Line 23

[s] A plague o' both your houses! *Ibid. Line 96*

[t] *Romeo.* Courage, man; the hurt cannot be much.

Mercutio. No, 'tis not so deep as a well, nor so wide as a church-door; but 'tis enough, 'twill serve. *Ibid. Line 100*

[u] When he shall die,
Take him and cut him out in little stars,
And he will make the face of heaven so fine
That all the world will be in love with night,
And pay no worship to the garish sun. *Ibid. Sc. 2, Line 21*

[v] O! that deceit should dwell In such a gorgeous palace. *Ibid. Line 84*

[w] Adversity's sweet milk, philosophy. *Ibid. Sc. 3, Line 54*

[x] The lark, the herald of the morn. *Ibid. Sc. 5, Line 6*

[y] Night's candles are burnt out, and jocund day
Stands tiptoe on the misty mountain-tops. *Ibid. Line 9*

[z] All these woes shall serve For sweet discourses in our time to come. *Ibid. Line 52*

[a] Meagre were his looks,
Sharp misery had worn him to the bones. *Ibid. Act V, Sc. 1, Line 40*

[b] How oft when men are at the point of death
Have they been merry! *Ibid. Line 88*

[c] Beauty's ensign yet Is crimson in thy lips and in thy cheeks,
And death's pale flag is not advanced there. *Ibid. Sc. 3, Line 94*

[d] Eyes, look at your last! Arms, take your last embrace! *Ibid. Line 112*

[e'] 'Tis not enough to help the feeble up,
But to support him after.
Timon of Athens. Act I, Sc. 1, Line 108

[f'] Ceremony was but devis'd at first
To set a gloss on faint deeds, hollow welcomes . . .
But where there is true friendship, there needs none.
Ibid. Sc. 2, Line 15

[g'] Here's that which is too weak to be a sinner,
Honest water, which ne'er left man i' the mire. *Ibid. Line 60*

[h'] Every man has his fault, and honesty is his.
Ibid. Act III, Sc. 1, Line 30

[i'] I'll example you with thievery:
The sun's a thief, and with his great attraction

Rob's the vast sea; the moon's an
arrant thief,
And her pale fire she snatches
from the sun;
The sea's a thief, whose liquid
surge resolves
The moon into salt tears; the
earth's a thief,
That feeds and breeds by a com-
posture stolen
From general excrement, each
thing's a thief.
Ibid. Act IV, Sc. 3, Line 441

[j] A mender of bad soles . . . a
surgeon to old shoes.
Julius Caesar. Act I, Sc. 1, Line 15

[k] Beware the ides of March.
Ibid. Sc. 2, Line 18

[l] I had as lief not be as live to
be
In awe of such a thing as I myself.
Ibid. Line 95

[m] Why, man, he doth bestride
the narrow world
Like a Colossus; and we petty men
Walk under his huge legs, and
peep about
To find ourselves dishonourable
graves.
Men at some time are masters of
their fates:
The fault, dear Brutus, is not in
our stars,
But in ourselves, that we are underlings. *Ibid. Line 134*

[n] Upon what meat doth this
our Caesar feed,
That he is grown so great?
Ibid. Line 148

[o] Let me have men about me
that are fat;
Sleek-headed men, and such as
sleep o' nights.
Yond Cassius has a lean and hungry look;
He thinks too much: such men
are dangerous.
Ibid. Line 191

[p] Seldom he smiles, and smiles
in such a sort
As if he mock'd himself, and
scorn'd his spirit
That could be moved to smile at
anything. *Ibid. Line 204*

[q] But, for my own part, it was
Greek to me. *Ibid. Line 288*

[r] 'Tis a common proof,
That lowliness is young ambi-
tion's ladder,
Whereto the climber-upward
turns his face;
But when he once attains the
upmost round,
He then unto the ladder turns his
back,
Looks in the clouds, scorning the
base degrees
By which he did ascend.
Ibid. Act II, Sc. 1, Line 21

[s] A dish fit for the gods.
Ibid. Line 173

[t] But when I tell him he hates
flatterers,
He says he does, being then most
flattered. *Ibid. Line 207*

[u] Enjoy the honey-heavy dew
of slumber:
Thou hast no figures nor no fan-
tasies
Which busy care draws in the
brains of men;
Therefore thou sleep'st so sound.
Ibid. Line 230

[v] You are my true and honour-
able wife,
As dear to me as are the ruddy
drops
That visit my sad heart.
Ibid. Line 288

[w] Cowards die many times be-
fore their deaths;
The valiant never taste of death
but once.
Of all the wonders that I yet have
heard,
It seems to me most strange that
men should fear;
Seeing that death, a necessary
end,
Will come when it will come.
Ibid. Sc. 2, Line 32

[x] But I am constant as the
northern star,
Of whose true-fix'd and resting
quality
There is no fellow in the firmament.
Ibid. Act III, Sc. 1, Line 60

[y] Et tu, Brute! *Ibid. Line 77*

[z] Cry "Havoc!" and let slip the
dogs of war. *Ibid. Line 273*

[a] Not that I loved Caesar less,
but that I loved Rome more.
Ibid. Sc. 2, Line 22

[b] Friends, Romans, countrymen, lend me your ears;
I come to bury Caesar, not to
praise him.
The evil that men do lives after
them,
The good is oft interred with their
bones. *Ibid. Line 79*

[c] For Brutus is an honourable
man;
So are they all, all honourable
men. *Ibid. Line 88*

[d] But yesterday the word of
Caesar might
Have stood against the world; now
lies he there,
And none so poor to do him rever-
ence. *Ibid. Line 124*

[e] If you have tears, prepare to
shed them now.
Ibid. Line 174

[f] This was the most unkindest
cut of all. *Ibid. Line 188*

[g] When love begins to sicken and decay,
It useth an enforced ceremony.
There are no tricks in plain and simple faith.
Ibid. Act IV, Sc. 2, Line 20

[h] You yourself
Are much condemn'd to have an itching palm.
Ibid. Sc. 3, Line 9

[i] There is no terror, Cassius, in your threats;
For I am arm'd so strong in honesty
That they pass by me as the idle wind,
Which I respect not.
Ibid. Line 66

[j] There is a tide in the affairs of men,
Which, taken at the flood, leads on to fortune;
Omitted, all the voyage of their life
Is bound in shallows and in miseries. *Ibid. Line 217*

[k] This was the noblest Roman of them all.
Ibid. Act V, Sc. 5, Line 68

[l] His life was gentle, and the elements
So mix'd in him that Nature might stand up
And say to all the world, "This was a man!"
Ibid. Line 73

[m] Sleep shall neither night nor day
Hang upon his pent-house lid.
Macbeth. Act I, Sc. 3, Line 19

[n] If you can look into the seeds of time,
And say which grain will grow and which will not.
Ibid. Line 58

[o] The insane root
That takes the reason prisoner.
Ibid. Line 84

[p] Come what come may,
Time and the hour runs through the roughest day.
Ibid. Line 146

[q] Nothing in his life
Became him like the leaving it; he died
As one that had been studied in his death
To throw away the dearest thing he owed,
As 'twere a careless trifle.
Ibid. Sc. 4, Line 7

[r] Yet do I fear thy nature;
It is too full o' the milk of human kindness.
Ibid. Sc. 5, Line 17

[s] Look like the innocent flower,
But be the serpent under 't.
Ibid. Line 66

[t] This castle hath a pleasant seat; the air
Nimbly and sweetly recommends itself
Unto our gentle senses.
Ibid. Sc. 6, Line 1

[u] Where they [birds] most breed and haunt, I have observed
The air is delicate.
Ibid. Line 9

[v] If it were done when 'tis done, then 'twere well
It were done quickly; if the assassination
Could trammel up the consequence, and catch
With his surcease success; that but this blow
Might be the be-all and the end-all here,
But here, upon this bank and shoal of time,
We'd jump the life to come. But in these cases
We still have judgment here; that we but teach
Bloody instructions, which, being taught, return
To plague the inventor; this even-handed justice
Commends the ingredients of our poison'd chalice
To our own lips. *Ibid. Sc. 7, Line 1*

[w] His virtues
Will plead like angels, trumpet-tongued against
The deep damnation of his taking-off;
And pity, like a naked new-born babe,
Striding the blast, or heaven's cherubim, horsed
Upon the sightless couriers of the air,
Shall blow the horrid deed in every eye,
That tears shall drown the wind.
Ibid. Line 1

[x] Vaulting ambition, which o'erleaps itself
And falls on the other.
Ibid. Line 27

[y] But screw your courage to the sticking-place,
And we'll not fail.
Ibid. Line 60

[z] Memory, the warder of the brain. *Ibid. Line 65*

[a] There's husbandry in heaven; Their candles are all out.
Ibid. Act II, Sc. 1, Line 4

[b] Is this a dagger which I see before me,
The handle toward my hand? Come, let me clutch thee:
I have thee not, and yet I see thee still.

Art thou not, fatal vision, sensible
To feeling as to sight? or art thou but
A dagger of the mind, a false creation,
Proceeding from the heat-oppressed brain?
Ibid. Line 33

[c] It was the owl that shriek'd, the fatal bellman,
Which gives the stern'st goodnight.
Ibid. Sc. 2, Line 4

[d] Methought I heard a voice cry, "Sleep no more!
Macbeth does murder sleep!" the innocent sleep,
Sleep that knits up the ravell'd sleave of care,
The death of each day's life, sore labour's bath,
Balm of hurt minds, great nature's second course,
Chief nourisher in life's feast.
Ibid. Line 36

[e] Will all great Neptune's ocean wash this blood
Clean from my hand? No, this my hand will rather
The multitudinous seas incarnadine,
Making the green one red.
Ibid. Line 61

[f] It [drink] provokes the desire, but it takes away the performance.
Ibid. Sc. 3, Line 34

[g] The labour we delight in physics pain.
Ibid. Line 56

[h] The wine of life is drawn, and the mere lees
Is left this vault to brag of.
Ibid. Line 102

[i] I am one, my liege,
Whom the vile blows and buffets of the world
Have so incensed that I am reckless what
I do to spite the world.
Ibid. Act III, Sc. 1, Line 108

[j] Things without all remedy
Should be without regard; what's done is done.
Ibid. Sc. 2, Line 11

[k] We have scotch'd the snake, not kill'd it. *Ibid. Line 13*

[l] Duncan is in his grave;
After life's fitful fever he sleeps well. *Ibid. Line 22*

[m] But now I am cabin'd, cribb'd, confined, bound in
To saucy doubts and fears.
Ibid. Sc. 4, Line 24

[n] Now, good digestion wait on appetite,
And health on both! *Ibid. Line 38*

[o] I drink to the general joy of the whole table. *Ibid. Line 89*

[p] Thou hast no speculation in those eyes
Which thou dost glare with! *Ibid. Line 95*

[q] Stand not upon the order of your going,
But go at once. *Ibid. Line 119*

[r] *Macbeth.* What is the night?
Lady Macbeth. Almost at odds with morning, which is which.
Ibid. Line 126

[s] Double, double toil and trouble;
Fire burn and cauldron bubble.
Ibid. Act IV, Sc. 1, Line 10

[t] By the pricking of my thumbs,
Something wicked this way comes.
Ibid. Line 44

[u] I'll make assurance double sure,
And take a bond of fate.
Ibid. Line 83

[v] The weird sisters.
Ibid. Line 136

[w] When our actions do not,
Our fears do make us traitors.
Ibid. Sc. 2, Line 3

[x] Give sorrow words; the grief that does not speak
Whispers the o'er-fraught heart and bids it break.
Ibid. Sc. 3, Line 209

[y] Out, damned spot! out, I say!
Ibid. Act V, Sc. 1, Line 38

[z] Yet who would have thought the old man to have had so much blood in him? *Ibid. Line 42*

[a] All the perfumes of Arabia will not sweeten this little hand.
Ibid. Line 56

[b] My way of life
Is fall'n into the sere, the yellow leaf;
And that which should accompany old age,
As honour, love, obedience, troops of friends,
I must not look to have.
Ibid. Sc. 3, Line 22

[c'] *Macbeth.* Cure her of that:
Canst thou not minister to a mind diseas'd,
Pluck from the memory a rooted sorrow,
Raze out the written troubles of the brain,
And with some sweet oblivious antidote
Cleanse the stuff'd bosom of that perilous stuff
Which weighs upon the heart?

Doctor. Therein the patient Must minister to himself.
Macbeth. Throw physic to the dogs: I'll none of it.
Ibid. Line 39

[d] I would applaud thee to the very echo,
That should applaud again.
Ibid. Line 53

[e] My fell of hair
Would at a dismal treatise rouse and stir
As life were in 't. I have supp'd full with horrors.
Ibid. Sc. 5, Line 11

[f] To-morrow, and to-morrow, and to-morrow,
Creeps in this petty pace from day to day,
To the last syllable of recorded time;
And all our yesterdays have lighted fools
The way to dusty death. Out, out, brief candle!
Life's but a walking shadow, a poor player
That struts and frets his hour upon the stage
And then is heard no more: it is a tale
Told by an idiot, full of sound and fury,
Signifying nothing.
Ibid. Line 19

[g] Blow, wind! come, wrack!
At least we'll die with harness on our back. *Ibid. Line 51*

[h] Lay on, Macduff,
And damn'd be him that first cries,
"Hold, enough!"
Ibid. Sc. 7, Line 62

[i] Not a mouse stirring.
Hamlet. Act I, Sc. 1, Line 10

[j] Whose sore task
Does not divide the Sunday from the week. *Ibid. Line 75*

[k] The cock, that is the trumpet of the morn. *Ibid. Line 150*

[l] Some say that ever 'gainst that season comes
Wherein our Saviour's birth is celebrated,
The bird of dawning singeth all night long:
And then, they say, no spirit can walk abroad;
The nights are wholesome; then no planets strike,
No fairy takes, nor witch hath power to charm,
So hallow'd and so gracious is the time. *Ibid. Line 158*

[m] But, look, the morn in russet mantle clad,
Walks o'er the dew of yon high eastern hill.
Ibid. Line 166

[n] A little more than kin, and less than kind.
Ibid. Sc. 2, Line 65

[o] 'Tis not alone my inky cloak, good mother,
Nor customary suits of solemn black. . . .
But I have that within which passeth show;
These but the trappings and the suits of woe. *Ibid. Line 77*

[p] O! that this too too solid flesh would melt,
Thaw and resolve itself into a dew;
Or that the Everlasting had not fix'd
His canon 'gainst self-slaughter!
O God! O God!
How weary, stale, flat, and unprofitable
Seem to me all the uses of this world. *Ibid. Line 129*

[q] Frailty, thy name is woman!
Ibid. Line 146

[r] Like Niobe, all tears.
Ibid. Line 149

[s] Thrift, thrift, Horatio! the funeral baked meats
Did coldly furnish forth the marriage tables. *Ibid. Line 180*

[t] In my mind's eye, Horatio.
Ibid. Line 185

[u] He was a man, take him for all in all,
I shall not look upon his like again. *Ibid. Line 187*

[v] In the dead vast and middle of the night. *Ibid. Line 198*

[w] Distill'd
Almost to jelly with the act of fear. *Ibid. Line 204*

[x] A countenance more in sorrow than in anger.
Ibid. Line 231

[y] *Hamlet.* His beard was grizzled, no?
Horatio. It was, as I have seen it in his life,
A sable silver'd. *Ibid. Line 239*

[z] Do not, as some ungracious pastors do,
Show me the steep and thorny way to heaven,
Whiles, like a puff'd and reckless libertine,
Himself the primrose path of dalliance treads,
And recks not his own rede.
Ibid. Sc. 3, Line 47

[a] Those friends thou hast, and their adoption tried,
Grapple them to thy soul with hoops of steel. *Ibid. Line 62*

[b]   Beware
Of entrance to a quarrel, but, be-
    ing in,
Bear 't that the opposed may be-
    ware of thee.   *Ibid. Line 65*

[c] Costly thy habit as thy purse
    can buy,
But not express'd in fancy; rich,
    not gaudy;
For the apparel oft proclaims the
    man.   *Ibid. Line 70*

[d] Neither a borrower, nor a
    lender be;
For loan oft loses both itself and
    friend.   *Ibid. Line 75*

[e] This above all: to thine own
    self be true,
And it must follow, as the night
    the day,
Thou canst not then be false to
    any man.   *Ibid. Line 78*

[f] When the blood burns, how
    prodigal the soul
Lends the tongue vows.
                Ibid. Line 116

[g] *Hamlet.* The air bites shrewd-
    ly; it is very cold.
Horatio. It is a nipping and an
    eager air.
            Ibid. Sc. 4, Line 1

[h]   It is a cus-
    tom
More honoured in the breach than
    the observance.
                Ibid. Line 15

[i]   What may this mean,
That thou, dead corse, again in
    complete steel
Revisit'st thus the glimpses of the
    moon,
Making night hideous, and we
    fools of nature
So horridly to shake our disposi-
    tion
With thoughts beyond the reaches
    of our souls?   *Ibid. Line 51*

[j] I do not set my life at a pin's
    fee.   *Ibid. Line 65*

[k]   Unhand me, gentlemen,
By heaven! I'll make a ghost of
    him that lets me!
                Ibid. Line 84

[l] Something is rotten in the
    state of Denmark.
                Ibid. Line 90

[m] I could a tale unfold whose
    lightest word
Would harrow up thy soul, freeze
    thy young blood,
Make thy two eyes, like stars,
    start from their spheres,
Thy knotted and combined locks
    to part,
And each particular hair to stand
    on end,
Like quills upon the fretful por-
    pentine.   *Ibid. Sc. 5, Line 15*

[n] And duller shouldst thou be
    than the fat weed
That rots itself in ease on Lethe
    wharf.   *Ibid. Line 32*

[o]   Leave her to heaven
And to those thorns that in her
    bosom lodge,
To prick and sting her.
                Ibid. Line 86

[p] The glow-worm shows the
    matin to be near,
And 'gins to pale his uneffectual
    fire.   *Ibid. Line 89*

[q]   While memory holds a seat
In this distracted globe. Remem-
    ber thee!
Yea, from the table of my memory
I'll wipe away all trivial fond
    records. . . .
Within the book and volume of
    my brain.   *Ibid. Line 96*

[r] O villain, villain, smiling,
    damned villain! . . .
That one may smile, and smile,
    and be a villain.
                Ibid. Line 106

[s] There are more things in
    heaven and earth, Horatio,
Than are dreamt of in your phi-
    losophy.   *Ibid. Line 166*

[t] The time is out of joint; O
    cursed spite,
That ever I was born to set it
    right!   *Ibid. Line 188*

[u] Brevity is the soul of wit.
        Ibid. Act II, Sc. 2, Line 90

[v] That he is mad, 'tis true; 'tis
    true 'tis pity;
And pity 'tis 'tis true.
                Ibid. Line 97

[w] Doubt thou the stars are fire;
    Doubt that the sun doth move;
Doubt truth to be a liar;
    But never doubt I love.
                Ibid. Line 115

[x] To be honest, as this world
goes, is to be one man picked out
of ten thousand.   *Ibid. Line 179*

[y] *Polonius.* What do you read,
    my lord?
Hamlet. Words, words, words.
                Ibid. Line 195

[z] Though this be madness, yet
there is method in 't.
                Ibid. Line 211

[a]   There is nothing either good
or bad, but thinking makes it so.
                Ibid. Line 259

[b'] This goodly frame, the earth,
seems to me a sterile promontory;
this most excellent canopy, the
air, this brave o'erhanging firmament, this majestical roof fretted
with golden fire, why, it appears
no other thing to me than a foul
and pestilent congregation of
vapours.
                Ibid. Line 317

[c] Man delights not me; no, nor woman neither. *Ibid. Line 330*

[d] There is something in this more than natural, if philosophy could find it out. *Ibid. Line 392*

[e] I know a hawk from a handsaw. *Ibid. Line 406*

[f] They say an old man is twice a child. *Ibid. Line 413*

[g] The play, I remember, pleased not the million; 'twas caviare to the general. *Ibid. Line 465*

[h] What's Hecuba to him or he to Hecuba,
That he should weep for her? *Ibid. Line 593*

[i]   The play's the thing
Wherein I'll catch the conscience of the king. *Ibid. Line 641*

[j] To be, or not to be: that is the question:
Whether 'tis nobler in the mind to suffer
The slings and arrows of outrageous fortune,
Or to take arms against a sea of troubles,
And by opposing end them? To die: to sleep:
No more; and by a sleep to say we end
The heartache and the thousand natural shocks
That flesh is heir to, 'tis a consummation
Devoutly to be wish'd. To die, to sleep;
To sleep: perchance to dream: ay, there's the rub:
For in that sleep of death what dreams may come,
When we have shuffled off this mortal coil,
Must give us pause. There's the respect
That makes calamity of so long life;
For who would bear the whips and scorns of time,
The oppressor's wrong, the proud man's contumely,
The pangs of dispriz'd love, the law's delay,
The insolence of office and the spurns
That patient merit of the unworthy takes,
When he himself might his quietus make
With a bare bodkin? who would fardels bear,
To grunt and sweat under a weary life,
But that the dread of something after death,
The undiscover'd country from whose bourn
No traveller returns, puzzles the will

And makes us rather bear those ills we have
Than fly to others that we know not of?
Thus conscience does make cowards of us all;
And thus the native hue of resolution
Is sicklied o'er with the pale cast of thought.
Hamlet. Act III, Sc. 1, Line 56

[k] Rich gifts wax poor when givers prove unkind. *Ibid. Line 101*

[l] Be thou as chaste as ice, as pure as snow, thou shalt not escape calumny. Get thee to a nunnery, go. *Ibid. Line 142*

[m] I have heard of your paintings too, well enough; God has given you one face, and you make yourselves another. *Ibid. Line 150*

[n] The glass of fashion and the mould of form,
The observed of all observers! *Ibid. Line 162*

[o] Now see that noble and most sovereign reason,
Like sweet bells jangled, out of tune and harsh. *Ibid. Line 166*

[p] Nor do not saw the air too much with your hand, thus; but use all gently: for in the very . . . whirlwind of passion, you must acquire and beget a temperance, that may give it smoothness. Oh, it offends me to the soul to hear a robustious periwig-pated fellow tear a passion to tatters, to very rags, to split the ears of the groundlings. . . . I would have such a fellow whipped for o'erdoing Termagant; it out-herods Herod. *Ibid. Sc. 2, Line 4*

[q] Suit the action to the word, the word to the action. *Ibid. Line 20*

[r] To hold, as 'twere, the mirror up to nature. *Ibid. Line 25*

[s] They are not a pipe for fortune's finger
To sound what stop she please. Give me that man
That is not passion's slave, and I will wear him
In my heart's core, ay, in my heart of heart. *Ibid. Line 75*

[t] And my imaginations are as foul
As Vulcan's stithy. *Ibid. Line 88*

[u] The lady doth protest too much, methinks. *Ibid. Line 242*

[v] For some must watch, while some must sleep:
So runs the world away.
Ibid. Line 289

[w] By and by is easily said.
Ibid. Line 411

[x] 'Tis now the very witching time of night,
When churchyards yawn and hell itself breathes out
Contagion to this world.
Ibid. Line 413

[y] With all his crimes broad blown, as flush as May.
Ibid. Sc. 3, *Line* 81

[z] My words fly up, my thoughts remain below:
Words without thoughts never to heaven go.   *Ibid. Line* 97

[a] False as dicers' oaths.
Ibid. Sc. 4, *Line* 45

[b] A rhapsody of words.
Ibid. Line 48

[c] A combination and a form indeed,
Where every god did seem to set his seal,
To give the world assurance of a man.   *Ibid. Line* 60

[d] To flaming youth let virtue be as wax,
And melt in her own fire: proclaim no shame
When the compulsive ardour gives the charge.   *Ibid. Line* 84

[e] This is the very coinage of your brain:
This bodiless creation ecstasy
Is very cunning in.
Ibid. Line 136

[f]   Refrain to-night,
And that shall lend a kind of easiness
To the next abstinence: the next more easy;
For use almost can change the stamp of nature.
Ibid. Line 165

[g] I must be cruel, only to be kind.   *Ibid. Line* 178

[h] For 'tis the sport to have the enginer
Hoist with his own petar.
Ibid. Line 206

[i] A man may fish with the worm that hath eat of a king, and eat of the fish that hath fed of that worm.
Ibid. Act IV, *Sc.* 3, *Line* 29

[j] Sure, he that made us with such large discourse,
Looking before and after, gave us not
That capability and godlike reason
To fust in us unused.
Ibid. Sc. 4, *Line* 36

[k] When sorrows come, they come not single spies,
But in battalions.
Ibid. Sc. 5, *Line* 78

[l] There's rosemary, that's for remembrance; . . . and there is pansies, that's for thoughts.
Ibid. Line 174

[m] There is no ancient gentlemen but gardeners . . . they hold up Adam's profession.
Ibid. Act V, *Sc.* 1, *Line* 32

[n] Cudgel thy brains no more about it.   *Ibid. Line* 61

[o] But age, with his stealing steps,
Hath claw'd me in his clutch.
Ibid. Line 77

[p] A politician, . . . one that would circumvent God.
Ibid. Line 84

[q] Why may not that be the skull of a lawyer? Where be his quiddities now, his quillets, his cases, his tenures, and his tricks?
Ibid. Line 104

[r] Alas, poor Yorick! I knew him, Horatio: a fellow of infinite jest, of most excellent fancy; he hath borne me on his back a thousand times; and now, how abhorred in my imagination it is! my gorge rises at it. Here hung those lips that I have kissed I know not how oft. Where be your gibes now? your gambols? your songs? your flashes of merriment, that were wont to set the table on a roar? Not one now, to mock your own grinning? quite chapfallen? Now get you to my lady's chamber, and tell her, let her paint an inch thick, to this favour she must come.   *Ibid. Line* 201

[s] Imperious Caesar, dead and turn'd to clay,
Might stop a hole to keep the wind away.   *Ibid. Line* 235

[t]   Lay her i' the earth;
And from her fair and unpolluted flesh
May violets spring!
Ibid. Line 260

[u] Sweets to the sweet: farewell!   *Ibid. Line* 265

[v'] Let Hercules himself do what he may,
The cat will mew and dog will have his day.   *Ibid. Line* 313

[w'] There's a divinity that shapes our ends,
Rough-hew them how we will.
Ibid. Sc. 2, *Line* 10

[x'] There's a special providence in the fall of a sparrow. If it be now, 'tis not to come; if it be not to come, it will be now; if it be not now, yet it will come: the

readiness is all. Since no man has
aught of what he leaves, what is
't to leave betimes?
Ibid. Line 232

[y] A hit, a very palpable hit.
Ibid. Line 295

[z] This fell sergeant, death,
Is strict in his arrest.
Ibid. Line 350

[a] The rest is silence.
Ibid. Line 372

[b] Now cracks a noble heart.
Ibid. Line 373

[c] My love's
More richer than my tongue.
King Lear. Act. I, Sc. 1, Line 79

[d] Nothing will come of nothing. *Ibid. Line 92*

[e] I want that glib and oily art,
To speak and purpose not.
Ibid. Line 227

[f] Ingratitude, thou marble-
hearted fiend!
Ibid. Sc. 4, Line 283

[g] How sharper than a serpent's
tooth it is
To have a thankless child!
Ibid. Line 312

[h] Striving to better, oft we
mar what's well.
Ibid. Line 371

[i] That sir which serves and
seeks for gain,
And follows but for form,
Will pack when it begins to rain,
And leave thee in the storm.
Ibid. Act. II, Sc. 4, Line 79

[j] Necessity's sharp pinch!
Ibid. Line 214

[k] Let not women's weapons,
waterdrops,
Stain my man's cheeks!
Ibid. Line 280

[l] Blow, winds, and crack your
cheeks! rage! blow!
Ibid. Act III, Sc. 2, Line 1

[m] There was never yet fair
woman but she made mouths in
a glass. *Ibid. Line 35*

[n] I am a man
More sinn'd against than sin-
ning. *Ibid. Line 59*

[o] Oh! that way madness lies;
let me shun that.
Ibid. Sc. 4, Line 21

[p] Poor naked wretches, where-
soe'er you are,
That bide the pelting of this
pitiless storm,
How shall your houseless heads
and unfed sides,
Your looped and windowed rag-
gedness, defend you
From seasons such as these? . . .
Take physic, pomp;
Expose thyself to feel what
wretches feel. *Ibid. Line 28*

[q] The prince of darkness is a
gentleman. *Ibid. Line 147*

[r] Child Rowland to the dark
tower came.
His word was still, Fie, foh, and
fum,
I smell the blood of a British man.
Ibid. Line 185

[s] The little dogs and all,
Tray, Blanch, and Sweetheart,
see, they bark at me.
Ibid. Sc. 6, Line 65

[t] The worst is not
So long as we can say, "This is the
worst."
Ibid. Act. IV, Sc. 1, Line 27

[u] Sunshine and rain at once;
her smiles and tears.
Ibid. Sc. 3, Line 20

[v] It is the stars,
The stars above us, govern our
conditions. *Ibid. Line 34*

[w] Our foster-nurse of nature
is repose. *Ibid. Sc. 4, Line 12*

[x] Ay, every inch a king.
Ibid. Sc. 6, Line 110

[y'] A man may see how this
world goes with no eyes. Look
with thine ears: see how yon'
justice rails upon yon' simple
thief. Hark, in thine ear: change
places; and, handy-dandy, which
is the justice, which is the thief?
Ibid. Line 154

[z'] Through tatter'd clothes
small vices do appear;
Robes and furr'd gowns hide all.
Ibid. Line 169

[a'] Pray you now, forget and forgive. *Ibid. Sc. 7, Line 84*

[b'] Men must endure
Their going hence, even as their
coming hither.
Ibid. Act V, Sc. 2, Line 9

[c'] Upon such sacrifices, my Cor-
delia,
The gods themselves throw incense. *Ibid. Sc. 3, Line 20*

[d'] The gods are just, and of our
pleasant vices
Make instruments to plague us.
Ibid. Line 172

[e'] Her voice was ever soft,
Gentle, and low, an excellent
thing in woman.
Ibid. Line 274

[f'] Vex not his ghost: O! let him
pass! he hates him
That would upon the rack of this
tough world
Stretch him out longer.
Ibid. Line 315

[g'] 'Tis the curse of service,
Preferment goes by letter and
affection,

And not by old gradation, where
each second
Stood heir to the first.
Othello. Act I, Sc. 1, Line 35

[h]   Rude am I in my speech,
And little bless'd with the soft
phrase of peace.
Ibid. Sc. 3, Line 81

[i] I will a round unvarnish'd
tale deliver
Of my whole course of love.
Ibid. Line 90

[j] Wherein I spake of most disastrous chances,
Of moving accidents by flood and
field,
Of hair-breadth 'scapes i' the imminent deadly breach.
Ibid. Line 134

[k] Hills whose heads touch
heaven.   *Ibid. Line 141*

[l]   My story being done,
She gave me for my pains a world
of sighs:
She swore, in faith, 'twas strange,
'twas passing strange,
'Twas pitiful, 'twas wondrous
pitiful . . .
She loved me for the dangers I
had pass'd,
And I loved her that she did pity
them.
This only is the witchcraft I have
used.   *Ibid. Line 158*

[m] The robb'd that smiles,
steals something from the
thief.   *Ibid. Line 208*

[n] Our bodies are our gardens,
to the which our wills are gardeners; . . . either to have it
sterile with idleness or manured
with industry.   *Ibid. Line 324*

[o] For I am nothing if not critical.
Ibid. Act II, Sc. 1, Line 119

[p] I am not merry; but I do be-
guile
The thing I am, by seeming
otherwise.   *Ibid. Line 122*

[q] Base men being in love have
then a nobility in their natures
more than is native to them.
Ibid. Line 218

[r] Egregiously an ass.
Ibid. Line 321

[s] I have very poor and unhappy
brains for drinking.
Ibid. Sc. 3, Line 34

[t] King Stephen was a worthy
peer,
His breeches cost him but a
crown;
He held them sixpence all too
dear,
With that he called the tailor
lown [rascal].   *Ibid. Line 93*

[u] Reputation is an idle and
most false imposition; oft got

without merit, and lost without
deserving.   *Ibid. Line 270*

[v] O thou invisible spirit of
wine! if thou hast no name to be
known by, let us call thee devil!
. . .
O God! that men should put an
enemy in their mouths to steal
away their brains! *Ibid. Line 285*

[w] Good wine is a good familiar
creature if it be well used.
Ibid. Line 315

[x] How poor are they that have
not patience! *Ibid. Line 379*

[y] Good name in man and
woman, dear my lord,
Is the immediate jewel of their
souls:
Who steals my purse steals trash;
'tis something, nothing;
'Twas mine, 'tis his, and has been
slave to thousands;
But he that filches from me my
good name
Robs me of that which not en-
riches him,
And makes me poor indeed.
Ibid. Act III, Sc. 3, Line 155

[z] O! beware, my lord, of jeal-
ousy;
It is the green-eyed monster
which doth mock
The meat it feeds on.
Ibid. Line 165

[a] Poor and content is rich, and
rich enough.   *Ibid. Line 172*

[b]   I am declined
Into the vale of years.
Ibid. Line 265

[c]   O curse of marriage!
That we can call these delicate
creatures ours,
And not their appetites. I had
rather be a toad,
And live upon the vapour of a
dungeon,
Than keep a corner in the thing
I love
For others' uses.   *Ibid. Line 268*

[d]   Trifles light as air
Are to the jealous confirmations
strong
As proofs of holy writ.
Ibid. Line 323

[e] Not poppy, nor mandragora,
Nor all the drowsy syrups of the
world,
Shall ever medicine thee to that
sweet sleep
Which thou ow'dst yesterday.
Ibid. Line 331

[f] The neighing steed, and the
shrill trump,
The spirit-stirring drum, the ear-
piercing fife,
The royal banner, and all quality,
Pride, pomp, and circumstance of
glorious war!   *Ibid. Line 352*

[g] Be sure of it; give me the ocular proof. *Ibid. Line 361*

[h] No hinge nor loop To hang a doubt on. *Ibid. Line 366*

[i] On horror's head horrors accumulate. *Ibid. Line 371*

[j] Take note, take note, O world! To be direct and honest is not safe. *Ibid. Line 378*

[k] Even so my bloody thoughts, with violent pace, Shall ne'er look back, ne'er ebb to humble love, Till that a capable and wide revenge Swallow them up. *Ibid. Line 458*

[l] But, alas! to make me A fixed figure for the time of scorn To point his slow and moving finger at! *Ibid. Act IV, Sc. 2, Line 52*

[m] And put in every honest hand a whip To lash the rascals naked through the world. *Ibid. Line 142*

[n] He hath a daily beauty in his life. *Ibid. Act V, Sc. 1, Line 19*

[o] This is the night That either makes me or fordoes me quite. *Ibid. Line 128*

[p] But once put out thy light, Thou cunning'st pattern of excelling nature, I know not where is that Promethean heat That can thy light relume. *Ibid. Sc. 2, Line 10*

[q] Curse his better angel from his side, And fall to reprobation. *Ibid. Line 206*

[r] Then, must you speak Of one that loved not wisely but too well; Of one not easily jealous, but, being wrought, Perplex'd in the extreme; of one whose hand, Like the base Indian, threw a pearl away Richer than all his tribe. *Ibid. Line 342*

[s] There's beggary in the love that can be reckon'd. *Antony and Cleopatra. Act I, Sc. 1, Line 15*

[t] My salad days, When I was green in judgment. *Ibid. Sc. 5, Line 73*

[u] We, ignorant of ourselves, Beg often our own harms, which the wise powers

Deny us for our good; so find we profit By losing of our prayers. *Ibid. Act II, Sc. 1, Line 5*

[v] The barge she sat in, like a burnish'd throne, Burn'd on the water; the poop was beaten gold, Purple the sails, and so perfumed that The winds were love-sick with them; the oars were silver, Which to the tune of flutes kept stroke, and made The water which they beat to follow faster, As amorous of their strokes. For her own person, It beggar'd all description. *Ibid. Sc. 2, Line 199*

[w] Age cannot wither her, nor custom stale Her infinite variety. *Ibid. Line 243*

[x] Though it be honest, it is never good To bring bad news. *Ibid. Sc. 5, Line 85*

[y] Come, thou monarch of the vine, Plumpy Bacchus with pink eyne! *Ibid. Sc. 7, Line 120*

[z] Who does i' the wars more than his captain can Becomes his captain's captain. *Ibid. Act III, Sc. 1, Line 21*

[a] Celerity is never more admir'd Than by the negligent. *Ibid. Sc. 7, Line 7*

[b] He wears the rose Of youth upon him. *Ibid. Sc. 11, Line 20*

[c] To business that we love we rise betime, And go to 't with delight. *Ibid. Act IV, Sc. 4, Line 20*

[d] Sometimes we see a cloud that's dragonish; A vapour sometime like a bear or lion, A tower'd citadel, a pendant rock, A forked mountain, or blue promontory With trees upon 't. *Ibid. Sc. 12, Line 2*

[e] I am dying, Egypt, dying. *Ibid. Sc. 13, Line 18*

[f] For his bounty, There was no winter in 't; an autumn 'twas That grew the more by reaping. *Ibid. Act V, Sc. 2, Line 86*

[g'] The bright day is done, And we are for the dark. *Ibid. Line 192*

[h] Mechanic slaves
With greasy aprons, rules, and
hammers. *Ibid. Line 208*

[i] A woman is a dish for the
gods. *Ibid. Line 274*

[j] Lest the bargain should catch
cold and starve.
Cymbeline. Act I, Sc. 4, Line 186

[k] Hath his bellyful of fighting.
Ibid. Act II, Sc. 1, Line 24

[l] The most patient man in loss,
the most coldest that ever turned
up ace. *Ibid. Sc. 3, Line 1*

[m] Hark! hark! the lark at
heaven's gate sings,
And Phœbus 'gins arise,
His steeds to water at those
springs
On chaliced flowers that lies;
And winking Mary-buds begin
To ope their golden eyes:
With everything that pretty is,
My lady sweet, arise.
Ibid. Line 22

[n] As chaste as unsunn'd
snow. *Ibid. Sc. 5, Line 13*

[o] Some griefs are med'cinable.
Ibid. Act III, Sc. 2, Line 33

[p] Prouder than rustling in un-
paid-for silk.
Ibid. Sc. 3, Line 24

[q] So slippery that
The fear's as bad as falling.
Ibid. Line 48

[r] The game is up.
Ibid. Line 107

[s] Slander,
Whose edge is sharper than the
sword, whose tongue
Outvenoms all the worms of Nile,
whose breath
Rides on the posting winds and
doth belie
All corners of the world.
Ibid. Sc. 4, Line 35

[t] Weariness
Can snore upon the flint when
resty sloth
Finds the down pillow hard.
Ibid. Sc. 6, Line 33

[u] Society is no comfort
To one not sociable.
Ibid. Act IV, Sc. 2, Line 12

[v] Fear no more the heat o' the
sun,
Nor the furious winter's rages;
Thou thy worldly task hast done,
Home art gone, and ta'en thy
wages. *Ibid. Line 258*

[w] Golden lads and girls all
must,
As chimney-sweepers, come to
dust. *Ibid. Line 262*

[x] Fortune brings in some boats
that are not steer'd.
Ibid. Sc. 3, Line 46

[y] By medicine life may be pro-
long'd, yet death
Will seize the doctor too.
Ibid. Act V, Sc. 5, Line 29

[z] 3 *Fisherman.* Master, I marvel how the fishes live in the sea.
1 *Fisherman.* Why, as men do
aland; the great ones eat up the
little ones.
Pericles. Act II, Sc. 1, Line 29

[a] My good will is great, though
the gift small.
Ibid. Act III, Sc. 4, Line 18

[b] A red morn, that ever yet
betoken'd
Wrack to the seaman, tempest to
the field.
Venus and Adonis. Line 453

[c] The owl, night's herald.
Ibid. Line 531

[d] The path is smooth that
leadeth on to danger.
Ibid. Line 788

[e] Love comforteth like sunshine after rain.
Ibid. Line 799

[f] Lo! here the gentle lark,
weary of rest,
From his moist cabinet mounts
up on high,
And wakes the morning.
Ibid. Line 853

[g] The grass stoops not, she
treads on it so light.
Ibid. Line 1028

[h'] Beauty itself doth of itself
persuade
The eyes of men without an orator.
The Rape of Lucrece. Line 29

[i'] Those that much covet are
with gain so fond,
For what they have not, that
which they possess
They scatter and unloose it from
their bond,
And so, by hoping more, they have
but less. *Ibid. Line 134*

[j'] For men have marble, women
waxen minds. *Ibid. Line 1240*

[k'] To see sad sights moves
more than hear them told.
Ibid. Line 1324

[l'] Lucrece swears he did her
wrong. *Ibid. Line 1462*

[m'] Thou art thy mother's glass,
and she in thee
Calls back the lovely April of her
prime. *Sonnet 3*

[n'] The painful warrior fa-
moused for fight,
After a thousand victories, once
foil'd,
Is from the books of honour razed
quite,
And all the rest forgot for which
he toil'd. *Sonnet 25*

[o] When in disgrace with fortune and men's eyes
I all alone beweep my outcast state. *Sonnet 29*

[p] For thy sweet love remember'd such wealth brings
That then I scorn to change my state with kings. *Ibid.*

[q] When to the sessions of sweet silent thought
I summon up remembrance of things past,
I sigh the lack of many a thing I sought. *Sonnet 30*

[r] Nimble thought can jump both sea and land. *Sonnet 44*

[s] The rose looks fair, but fairer we it deem
For that sweet odour which doth in it live. *Sonnet 54*

[t] Like as the waves make towards the pebbled shore,
So do our minutes hasten to their end. *Sonnet 60*

[u] That time of year thou may'st in me behold
When yellow leaves, or none, or few, do hang
Upon those boughs which shake against the cold,
Bare ruin'd choirs, where late the sweet birds sang. *Sonnet 73*

[v] Your monument shall be my gentle verse,
Which eyes not yet created shall o'er-read;
You still shall live—such virtue hath my pen—
Where breath most breathes,—even in the mouths of men. *Sonnet 81*

[w] Which can say more
Than this rich praise,—that you alone are you? *Sonnet 84*

[x] Do not, when my heart hath 'scap'd this sorrow,
Come in the rearward of a conquer'd woe;
Give not a windy night a rainy morrow. *Sonnet 90*

[y] The summer's flower is to the summer sweet,
Though to itself it only live and die. *Sonnet 94*

[z] The hardest knife ill-used doth lose his edge. *Sonnet 95*

[a] When proud-pied April, dress'd in all his trim,
Hath put a spirit of youth in everything. *Sonnet 98*

[b] To me, fair friend, you never can be old,
For as you were when first your eye I ey'd
Such seems your beauty still. *Sonnet 104*

[c] That is my home of love; if I have ranged,
Like him that travels, I return again. *Sonnet 109*

[d] Love is not love
Which alters when it alteration finds. *Sonnet 116*

[e] No, I am that I am, and they that level
At my abuses reckon up their own. *Sonnet 121*

[f] O father! what a hell of witchcraft lies
In the small orb of one particular tear. *A Lover's Complaint. Line 288*

[g] When my love swears that she is made of truth,
I do believe her, though I know she lies. *The Passionate Pilgrim, I*

[h] Crabbed age and youth cannot live together.
Youth is full of pleasure, age is full of care. *Ibid. XII*

[i] Have you not heard it said full oft,
A woman's nay doth stand for naught? *Sonnets to Sundry Notes of Music. IV*

[j] Cursed be he that moves my bones.
Shakespeare's Epitaph

Edward Shanks
[1892–   ]

[k] Out they came, the little boats, from all the Channel shores:
Free men were these who hauled the ropes and sweated at the oars.
From Itchenor and Shoreham, from Deal and Winchelsea,
They put out into the Channel to keep their country free.

Men from Itchenor and Shoreham, men from Deal and Winchelsea,
Looked out happily from Heaven and cheered to see the work
Of their grandsons' grandsons' grandsons on the beaches of Dunkirk. *The Other Little Boats. Stanzas 1 and 3*

Karl Jay Shapiro
[1913–   ]

[l] Leaning and laughing, my warm-hearted beauty, you ride, you ride,
You tack on the curves with parabola speed. . . .
You leap, you intelligence, essence of wheelness with silvery nose,

And your platinum clocks of excitement stir like the hairs of
a fern.   *Buick*

[m] He cast his vote,
Distrusting all the elected but not
the law.
    Elegy for a Dead Soldier. VII

William Sharp
("Fiona Macleod")
[1855–1905]

[n] My heart is a lonely hunter
that hunts on a lonely hill.
    The Lonely Hunter. Stanza 6

[o] But sometimes, through the
Soul of Man,
Slow moving o'er his pain,
The moonlight of a perfect peace
Floods heart and brain.
    The White Peace. Stanza 2

George Sharswood
[1810–1883]

[p] It is not uncommon to hear
the expression, "The law is a
jealous mistress." It is true that
this profession, like all others, demands of those who would succeed in it an earnest and entire
devotion.
    *Memoir of William Blackstone,
    Blackstone's Commentaries*

Frances Shaw
[1872–1937]

[q] Who loves the rain
And loves his home,
And looks on life with quiet eyes,
Him will I follow through the
storm,
And at his hearth-fire keep me
warm.   *Who Loves the Rain*

George Bernard Shaw
[1856–1950]

[r] My method is to take the
utmost trouble to find the right
thing to say, and then to say it
with the utmost levity.
    Answers to Nine Questions

[s] We have no more right to
consume happiness without producing it than to consume wealth
without producing it.
    Candida. Act I

[t] We don't bother much about
dress and manners in England,
because, as a nation we don't
dress well and we've no manners.
    You Never Can Tell. Act I

[u] The fickleness of women I
love is only equaled by the infernal constancy of the women
who love me.
    The Philanderer. Act II

[v] The test of a man or woman's
breeding is how they behave in
a quarrel.   *Ibid. Act IV*

[w] The people who get on in
this world are the people who get
up and look for the circumstances
they want, and, if they can't find
them, make them.
    Mrs. Warren's Profession. Act II

[x] This is the true joy in life,
the being used for a purpose
recognized by yourself as a
mighty one; the being thoroughly
worn out before you are thrown
on the scrap heap; the being a
force of Nature instead of a fever-
ish selfish little clod of ailments
and grievances complaining that
the world will not devote itself to
making you happy.   *Man and
    Superman. Epistle Dedicatory*

[y] A lifetime of happiness! No
man alive could bear it: it would
be hell on earth.
    Man and Superman. Act I

[z] The more things a man is
ashamed of, the more respectable
he is.   *Ibid.*

[a] Home life as we understand
it is no more natural to us than a
cage is natural to a cockatoo.
    Getting Married. Preface

[b] When two people are under
the influence of the most violent,
most insane, most delusive, and
most transient of passions, they
are required to swear that they
will remain in that excited, ab-
normal, and exhausting condition
continuously until death do them
part.   *Ibid.*

[c] A man is like a phonograph
with half-a-dozen records. You
soon get tired of them all; and yet
you have to sit at table whilst he
reels them off to every new visitor.
    Ibid. (The Play)

[d] I like a bit of a mongrel myself, whether it's a man or a dog;
they're the best for every day.
    Misalliance. Episode I

[e] If parents would only realize
how they bore their children!
    Ibid.

[f] Women upset everything.
When you let them into your life,
you find that the woman is driving at one thing and you're driving at another.
    Pygmalion. Act II

[g] The great secret, Eliza, is not
having bad manners or good manners or any other particular sort
of manners, but having the same
manner for all human souls: in
short, behaving as if you were in
Heaven, where there are no third-
class carriages, and one soul is as
good as another.   *Ibid. Act V*

[h] Independence? That's middle class blasphemy. We are all dependent on one another, every soul of us on earth. *Ibid.*

[i] The nauseous sham goodfellowship our democratic public men get up for shop use.
Back to Methuselah. Gospel of the Brothers Barnabas

[j] Life is a disease; and the only difference between one man and another is the stage of the disease at which he lives. *Ibid.*

[k] A nap, my friend, is a brief period of sleep which overtakes superannuated persons when they endeavor to entertain unwelcome visitors or to listen to scientific lectures. *Ibid. Tragedy of an Elderly Gentleman*

[l] Silence is the most perfect expression of scorn. *Ibid.*

[m] The Jews generally give value. They make you pay; but they deliver the goods. In my experience the men who want something for nothing are invariably Christians.
Saint Joan. Scene IV

[n] Kings are not born: they are made by universal hallucination.
The Revolutionist's Handbook

[o] At last I went to Ireland,
'Twas raining cats and dogs:
I found no music in the glens,
Nor purple in the bogs.
And as far as angels' laughter in the smelly Liffy's tide—
Well, my Irish daddy said it, but the dear old humbug lied.
Envoi added to a song, My Irish Daddy, by Miss Maisie Hurl

[p] You in America should trust to that volcanic political instinct which I have divined in you.
Speech Metropolitan Opera House, New York [April 11, 1933]

Henry Wheeler Shaw
see "Josh Billings"

Irwin Shaw
[1913-   ]

[q] What do I care for the colored pins on a General's map? . . . It's not a fair bargain—this exchange of my life for a small part of a colored pin.
Bury the Dead. Page 74

[r] I got a religion that wants to take heaven out of the clouds and plant it right here on the earth where most of us can get a slice of it. *Ibid. Page 82*

Fulton John Sheen
[1895-   ]

[s] Baloney is flattery so thick it cannot be true, and blarney is flattery so thin we like it.
Address before the Ancient Order of Hibernians, Boston [December 3, 1938]

Arthur Frederick Sheldon
[1868–1935]

[t] He profits most who serves best.
Motto for Rotary International

Mary Wollstonecraft Shelley
[1797–1851]

[u] I beheld the wretch—the miserable monster whom I had created. *Frankenstein. Chap. 5*

Percy Bysshe Shelley
[1792–1822]

[v] With hue like that when some great painter dips
His pencil in the gloom of earthquake and eclipse.
The Revolt of Islam. Canto V, Stanza 23

[w]   I would give
All that I am to be as thou now art!
But I am chained to Time, and can not thence depart!
Adonais. XXVI

[x] A pard-like spirit, beautiful and swift. *Ibid. XXXII*

[y] In mockery of monumental stone. *Ibid. XXXV*

[z] Peace, peace! he is not dead, he doth not sleep—
He hath awakened from the dream of life. *Ibid. XXXIX*

[a] From the contagion of the world's slow stain
He is secure, and now can never mourn
A heart grown cold, a head grown gray in vain. *Ibid. XL*

[b] He is made one with Nature: there is heard
His voice in all her music, from the moan
Of thunder to the song of night's sweet bird. *Ibid. XLII*

[c] And many more, whose names on Earth are dark,
But whose transmitted effluence can not die
So long as fire outlives the parent spark,
Rose, robed in dazzling immortality. *Ibid. XLVI*

[d] Life, like a dome of many-coloured glass,
Stains the white radiance of eternity. *Ibid. LII*

[e] Some say that gleams of a remoter world
Visit the soul in sleep.
Mont Blanc. III

[f] O, wind,
If Winter comes, can Spring be far behind?
Ode to the West Wind. V

[g] Poets' food is love and fame.
An Exhortation. Stanza 1

[h] I bring fresh showers for the thirsting flowers,
From the seas and the streams.
The Cloud. Stanza 1

[i] That orbèd maiden with white fire laden,
Whom mortals call the moon.
Ibid. Stanza 4

[j] I am the daughter of Earth and Water,
And the nursling of the Sky;
I pass through the pores of the ocean and shores,
I change, but I cannot die.
Ibid. Stanza 6

[k] Hail to thee, blithe spirit!
Bird thou never wert.
To a Skylark. Stanza 1

[l] Our sweetest songs are those that tell of saddest thought.
Ibid. Stanza 18

[m] Teach me half the gladness
That thy brain must know,
Such harmonious madness
From my lips would flow,
The world should listen then, as I am listening now.
Ibid. Stanza 21

[n] Kings are like stars—they rise and set, they have
The worship of the world, but no repose.
Hellas. Line 195

[o] All love is sweet,
Given or returned. Common as light is love,
And its familiar voice wearies not ever. . . .
They who inspire it most are fortunate,
As I am now; but those who feel it most
Are happier still. *Prometheus Unbound. Act II, Sc. 5*

[p] Jealousy's eyes are green.
Swellfoot the Tyrant. Act II, Sc. 1

[q] Hell is a city much like London—
A populous and smoky city.
Peter Bell the Third. Part III, Stanza 1

[r] Teas,
Where small talk dies in agonies.
Ibid. Stanza 12

[s] He had as much imagination
As a pint-pot.
Ibid. Part IV, Stanza 8

[t] Music, when soft voices die,
Vibrates in the memory—
Odours, when sweet violets sicken,
Live within the sense they quicken.
To—: Music, When Soft Voices Die. Stanza 1

[u] The desire of the moth for the star,
Of the night for the morrow,
The devotion to something afar
From the sphere of our sorrow.
To—: One Word Is Too Often Profaned. Stanza 2

[v] The seed ye sow, another reaps;
The wealth ye find, another keeps;
The robes ye weave, another wears;
The arms ye forge, another bears.
Song to the Men of England. Stanza 5

[w] I arise from dreams of thee
In the first sweet sleep of night,
When the winds are breathing low,
And the stars are shining bright.
The Indian Serenade. Stanza 1

[x] A Sensitive Plant in a garden grew,
And the young winds fed it with silver dew. *The Sensitive Plant. I, Stanza 1*

[y] Man's yesterday may ne'er be like his morrow;
Naught may endure but Mutability. *Mutability. I, Stanza 4*

[z] What is this world's delight?
Lightning that mocks the night,
Brief even as bright.
Ibid. II, Stanza 1

[a] There is no sport in hate when all the rage
Is on one side.
Lines to a Reviewer

[b] The weary Day turned to his rest,
Lingering like an unloved guest.
To Night. Stanza 3

[c] When the lamp is shattered
The light in the dust lies dead.
When the Lamp Is Shattered. Stanza 1

[d] Once, early in the morning, Beelzebub arose,
With care his sweet person adorning,
He put on his Sunday clothes.
The Devil's Walk, A Ballad. Stanza 1

[e'] Power, like a desolating pestilence,
Pollutes whate'er it touches; and obedience,
Bane of all genius, virtue, freedom, truth,

Makes slaves of men, and, of the
human frame,
A mechanized automaton.
Queen Mab. III

[f]   Heaven's ebon vault,
Studded with stars unutterably
bright,
Through which the moon's un-
clouded grandeur rolls,
Seems like a canopy which love
had spread
To curtain her sleeping world.
Ibid. IV

[g] Poetry is the record of the
best and happiest moments of the
happiest and best minds.
A Defence of Poetry

[h] Poets are the unacknowl-
edged legislators of the world.
Ibid.

William Shenstone
[1714–1763]

[i] Whoe'er has travell'd life's
dull round,
Where'er his stages may have
been,
May sigh to think he still has
found
The warmest welcome at an inn.
*Written on a Window of an Inn
at Henley. Stanza 5*

Morgan Shepard
("John Martin")
[1865–1947]

[j] Perhaps I ain't relijus,
But when I say a prayer,
I sort er feel inside er me
That God is always there.
Relijus, Stanza 1

Odell Shepard
[1884–   ]

[k] October in New England,
And I not there to see
The glamour of the goldenrod,
The flame of the maple tree!
Home Thoughts. Stanza 1

Robert Lowe, Viscount
Sherbrooke
[1811–1892]

[l] They ran, but never betted on
the race;
Content with harmless sport and
simple food,
Boundless in faith and love and
gratitude;
Happy the man, if there be any
such—
Of whom his epitaph can say as
much.   *A Horse's Epitaph*

Helen Selina Sheridan,
Lady Dufferin
[1807–1867]

[m] I'm very lonely now, Mary,
For the poor make no new
friends;
But, oh! they love the better still
The few our Father sends!
*Lament of the Irish Emigrant.
Stanza 4*

Philip Henry Sheridan
[1831–1888]

[n] The only good Indians I ever
saw were dead.   *Remark at Fort
Cobb, Indian Territory
[January 1869]*

Richard Brinsley Sheridan
[1751–1816]

[o] *Mrs. Malaprop.* Illiterate him,
I say, quite from your memory.
The Rivals. Act I, Sc. 2

[p] 'Tis safest in matrimony to
begin with a little aversion.
Ibid.

[q] A circulating library in a
town is as an evergreen tree of
diabolical knowledge.   *Ibid.*

[r] Too civil by half.
Ibid. Act III, Sc. 4

[s] Our ancestors are very good
kind of folks; but they are the last
people I should choose to have a
visiting acquaintance with.
Ibid. Act IV, Sc. 1

[t] The quarrel is a very pretty
quarrel as it stands; we should
only spoil it by trying to explain
it.   *Ibid. Sc. 3*

[u] My valour is certainly going!
it is sneaking off! I feel it oozing
out, as it were, at the palm of my
hands!   *Ibid. Act V, Sc. 3*

[v] Love gilds the scene, and
women guide the plot.
Ibid. Epilogue

[w] A fluent tongue is the only
thing a mother don't like her
daughter to resemble her in.
St. Patrick's Day. Act I, Sc. 2

[x] Death's a debt; his mandamus
binds all alike—no bail, no de-
murrer.   *Ibid. Act II, Sc. 4*

[y] There is not a passion so
strongly rooted in the human
heart as envy.
The Critic. Act I, Sc. 1

[z] The newspapers! Sir, they are
the most villainous, licentious,
abominable, infernal— Not that I
ever read them! No, I make it a
rule never to look into a newspaper.   *Ibid.*

[a] The number of those who undergo the fatigue of judging for themselves is very small indeed. *Ibid. Sc. 2*

[b] Certainly nothing is unnatural that is not physically impossible. *Ibid. Act II, Sc. 1*

[c] Though hopeless love finds comfort in despair,
It never can endure a rival's bliss! *Ibid. Act III, Sc. 1*

[d] An oyster may be crossed in love. *Ibid.*

[e] I ne'er saw nectar on a lip
But where my own did hope to sip. *The Duenna. Act I, Sc. 2*

[f] I was struck all of a heap. *Ibid. Act II, Sc. 2*

[g] A bumper of good liquor
Will end a contest quicker
Than justice, judge, or vicar. *Ibid. Sc. 3*

[h] Conscience has no more to do with gallantry than it has with politics. *Ibid. Sc. 4*

[i] Tale-bearers are as bad as the tale-makers *The School for Scandal. Act I, Sc. 1*

[j] You had no taste when you married me. *Ibid. Sc. 2*

[k] Here's to the maiden of bashful fifteen;
Here's to the widow of fifty;
Here's to the flaunting, extravagant quean,
And here's to the housewife that's thrifty!
  Let the toast pass;
  Drink to the lass;
I'll warrant she'll prove an excuse for the glass. *Ibid. Act III, Sc. 3*

[l] An unforgiving eye, and a damned disinheriting countenance. *Ibid. Act IV, Sc. 1*

[m] Be just before you're generous. *Ibid.*

Frank Dempster Sherman
[1860–1916]

[n] Out of the scabbard of the night,
By God's hand drawn,
Flashes his shining sword of light,
And lo,—the dawn! *Dawn*

[o] Here in their bright metropolis of flowers
The banker bees are busy with their gold. *In a Garden*

[p] Hark to the noisy caravans of brown,
Intrepid Sparrows,—Arabs of the air! *City Sparrows*

[q] . . . Such be the library; and take
This motto of a Latin make

To grace the door through which I pass:
Hic habitat Felicitas!
  The Library

Colonel Sidney Sherman
[1805–1873]

[r] Remember the Alamo!
  Battle-cry, San Jacinto
  [April 21, 1836]

Stuart Pratt Sherman
[1881–1926]

[s] The delectable form which intelligence takes in its moments of surplus power—the form of wit.
  Introduction [1923] to American Prose Masters by W. C. Brownell

William Tecumseh Sherman
[1820–1891]

[t] War is cruel and you cannot refine it. *Reply to the protest of the Atlanta, Georgia, city government on invasion [1864]*

[u] I am tired and sick of war. Its glory is all moonshine. It is only those who have neither fired a shot nor heard the shrieks and groans of the wounded who cry aloud for blood, more vengeance, more desolation. War is hell.
  Attributed to an address before the graduating class, Michigan Military Academy [June 19, 1879], in a letter published in The National Tribune, Washington, D. C., November 26, 1914

Herbert Shipman
[1869–1930]

[v] Across the gateway of my heart
I wrote "No Thoroughfare,"
But love came laughing by, and cried:
"I enter everywhere."
  No Thoroughfare. Stanza 1

Lee Shippey
[1884–   ]

[w] I love to think her like a blessed candle
Burning through life's long night,
Quietly useful, simple, gentle, tender,
And always giving light.
  Mother. Stanza 1

Martha ("Mother") Shipton
[1488–1561]

[x] Carriages without horses shall go,
And accidents fill the world with woe. *Prophecy*

[y] Around the world thoughts
shall fly
In the twinkling of an eye.
Ibid.

[z] Under water men shall walk,
Shall ride, shall sleep, and talk.
Ibid.

[a] In the air men shall be seen
In white, in black, and in green.
Ibid.

Charles P. Shiras
[1824–1854]

[b] Oh, the debtor is but a shame-
faced dog
With the creditor's name on his
collar;
While I am king and you are
queen,
For we owe no man a dollar!
I Owe No Man a Dollar. Stanza 1

James Shirley
[1596–1666]

[c] The glories of our blood and
state
Are shadows, not substantial
things;
There is no armour against fate:
Death lays his icy hand on
kings. *Contention of Ajax
and Ulysses. Scene 3*

[d] Only the actions of the just
Smell sweet and blossom in their
dust. *Ibid.*

Sir Philip Sidney
[1554–1586]

[e] Sweet food of sweetly uttered
knowledge.
Defence of Poesy

[f] He cometh unto you with a
tale which holdeth children from
play, and old men from the chim-
ney-corner. *Ibid.*

[g] They are never alone that are
accompanied with noble thoughts.
Arcadia. Book I

[h] My dear, my better half.
Ibid. Book III

[i] With how sad steps, O Moon,
thou climb'st the skies!
Astrophel and Stella

Eli Siegel
[j] Hot afternoons have been in
Montana. *Title of a prize-
winning poem published
in The Nation, 1925*

Henryk Sienkiewicz
[1846–1916]

[k] The greater philosopher a
man is, the more difficult it is for
him to answer the foolish questions of common people.
*Quo Vadis (tr. Jeremiah
Curtin). Chap. 19*

[l] A man who leaves memoirs,
whether well or badly written,
provided they be sincere, renders
a service to future psychologists
and writers. *Without Dogma.
(tr. Iza Young). Page 1*

Dora Sigerson
(Mrs. Clement Shorter)
[1866–1918]

[m] All night the small feet of
the rain
Within my garden ran,
And gentle fingers tapped the
pane
Until the dawn began.
April. Stanza 1

Lydia Huntley Sigourney
[1791–1865]

[n] Toll for the queenly boat,
wrecked on rocky shore!
Sea-weed is in her palace halls;
she rides the surge no more.
*The Bell of the Atlantic. [The
Atlantic was wrecked on an island near New London, Connecticut, in 1846. The bell, on a
portion of the wreck, tolled for
many days until salvaged.]*

[o] Ye say that all have passed
away—
That noble race and brave . . .
But their name is on your
waters—
Ye may not wash it out.
Indian Names. Stanza 1

[p] Through the open window's
space
Behold, a camel thrust his face.
"My nose is cold," he meekly cried,
"Oh, let me warm it by thy side."
The Camel's Nose. Stanza 1

[q] To evil habit's earliest wile
Lend neither ear, nor glance, nor
smile—
Choke the dark fountain ere it
flows,
Nor e'en admit the camel's nose.
Ibid. Stanza 4

Edward Rowland Sill
[1841–1887]

[r] At the punch-bowl's brink
Let the thirsty think
What they say in Japan:
"First the man takes a drink,
Then the drink takes a drink,
Then the drink takes the
man!"
An Adage from the Orient

[s] 'Tis by our follies that so long
We hold the earth from heaven
away. *The Fool's Prayer*

[t] Earth bears no balsam for
mistakes. *Ibid.*

[u] What may we take into the
vast forever?
That marble door
Admits no fruit of all our long
endeavor,
No fame-wreathed crown we
wore,
No garnered lore.
The Future

[v] And what if then, while the
still morning brightened,
And freshened in the elm the
Summer's breath,
Should gravely smile on me the
gentle angel
And take my hand and say, "My
name is Death."
A Morning Thought

[w] You need not think to palm
yourself off as a freakish young
zephyr, just born of yonder snow-
streak and the sun-warmed rock;
you have been roaming this
planet ever since its birth. You
have whirled in cyclones and
danced with the streamers of the
aurora; it was you that breathed
Job's curses, and the love vows
of the first lover that was ever
forsworn.   *The Mountain Wind,*
Sierra Nevadas

José Asunción Silva
[1865–1896]

[x] Verse is a chalice; place with-
in it only
A stainless thought;
From out whose deeps the smoul-
dering radiance sparkles
Like bubbles in a golden vin-
tage caught.   *Art* (tr.
Thomas Walsh). *Stanza 1*

Sime Silverman
[1873–1933]

[y] Wall Street Lays An Egg.
*Headline announcing the stock
market collapse of October, 1929
[Silverman founded and edited
the famous theatrical trade
paper Variety]*

Laura Simmons
[1877–1949]

[z] How each man knows a dif-
ferent God!
Each for himself shall see
A shape of doom; a vengeful
Judge—
A dreaded mystery;
Or, blessed hope! a strength, a
Friend
Beloved utterly.
Ultimate. Stanza 1

[a] What though you hide it in
your trunk—
Ere sailing hour has set?
Jammed down beneath your old
blue serge? . . .

The face within that passport
book
Will rise to haunt you yet.
Your Passport Picture

Simonides of Ceos
[556–469 B.C.]

[b] There's no joy even in beautiful Wisdom, unless one have
holy Health.   *Sextus Empiricus:*
Against the Mathematicians

[c] Whereas gold is the kindest of
all hosts when it shines in the
sky,
It comes an evil guest unto those
that receive it in their hand.
Plutarch: The Malignity of
Herodotus

[d] Go tell the Spartans, thou
that passeth by,
That here, obedient to their laws,
we lie.
*Thermopylae [Inscribed on the
general monument to the
Greeks who fell there]*

Simplicius
[Early Sixth Century]

[e] They [atoms] move in the
void and catching each other up
jostle together, and some recoil in
any direction that may chance,
and others become entangled
with one another in various degrees according to the symmetry
of their shapes and sizes and
positions and order, and they remain together and thus the coming into being of composite
things is effected.
*De Caelo. 242, 15 [Quoted by
Cyril Bailey: The Greek Atom-
ists and Epicurus]*

Frank Simpson

[f] When every pool in Eden was
a mirror
That unto Eve her dainty
charms proclaimed,
She went undraped without a
single fear, or
Thought that she had need to
be ashamed.

'Twas only when she'd eaten of
the apple
That she became inclined to be
a prude. . . .

The snake should pass the apples
'round again.
*Needed Apples. Stanzas 1, 3
and 4 (Printed in Philip
Hale's column, As the World
Wags, Boston Herald, June 30,
1924)*

George Robert Sims
[1847–1922]

[g] Lor', but women's rum cattle
to deal with, the first man
found that to his cost,
And I reckon it's just through a
woman the last man on
earth'll be lost.
Moll Jarvis o' Morley

Edith Sitwell
[1887–   ]

[h] Down the horn
Of her ear-trumpet I convey
The news that: "It is Judgment
Day!"
"Speak louder; I don't catch, my
dear."
I roared: *"It is the Trump we
hear!"*
"The *What?"*—"The TRUMP!" ...
"I shall complain—
Those boy-scouts practising
again!"
Solo for Ear-Trumpet

[i] Still falls the Rain—
Dark as the world of man, black
as our loss—
Blind as the nineteen hundred
and forty nails
Upon the Cross.
Still Falls the Rain

Sir Osbert Sitwell
[1892–   ]

[j] Nothing exists which the
British bourgeoisie
Does not understand;
Therefore there is no death
—And, of course, no life.
At the House of Mrs. Kinfoot

John Skelton
[Circa 1460–1529]

[k] There is nothynge that more
dyspleaseth God,
Than from theyr children to
spare the rod.
Magnyfycence. Line 1954

Eleanor Slater
[1903–   ]

[l] I do not mind that gold is
often tinsel,
And if you please, I'd rather
not be told.
It's thinking it is gold that
makes it precious
And thinking it is precious
makes it gold.   *Substance*

Joseph Bert Smiley
[1864–1903]

[m] Thirty years with that
tongue so sharp?
Ho! Angel Gabriel! Give him a
Harp!

See that on finest ambrosia he
feeds,
He's had about all the Hades he
needs;
It isn't just hardly the thing to
do
To roast him on earth and the
future, too.   *St. Peter at the
Gate (Thirty Years with a
Shrew). Stanzas 13 and 14*

Alexander Smith
[1830–1867]

[n] In winter, when the dismal
rain
Comes down in slanting lines,
And Wind, that grand old harper,
smote
His thunder-harp of pines.
A Life Drama. Sc. 2

[o] A poem round and perfect as
a star.   *Ibid.*

[p] The saddest thing that can
befall a soul
Is when it loses faith in God and
woman.   *Ibid. Sc. 12*

[q] The soul of man is like the
rolling world,
One half in day, the other dipt in
night;
The one has music and the flying
cloud,
The other, silence and the wakeful stars.   *Horton*

[r] Each time we love,
We turn a nearer and a broader
mark
To that keen archer, Sorrow, and
he strikes.   *A Boy's Dream*

[s] Time has fallen asleep in the
afternoon sunshine.
Dreamthorp. First Essay

[t] The world is not so much in
need of new thoughts as that
when thought grows old and worn
with usage it should, like current
coin, be called in, and, from the
mint of genius, reissued fresh and
new.
Ibid. On the Writing of Essays

[u] Death is the ugly fact which
Nature has to hide, and she hides
it well.   *Ibid. Of Death and
the Fear of Dying*

[v] Everything is sweetened by
risk.   *Ibid.*

[w] In life there is nothing more
unexpected and surprising than
the arrivals and departures of
pleasure. If we find it in one place
to-day, it is vain to seek it there
to-morrow. You can not lay a trap
for it.   *Ibid.*

[x] A man's real possession is his
memory. In nothing else is he
rich, in nothing else is he poor.
Ibid.

[y] To be occasionally quoted is the only fame I care for.
Ibid. Men of Letters

[z] A man gazing on the stars is proverbially at the mercy of the puddles on the road.   *Ibid.*

[a] The skin of the man of letters is peculiarly sensitive to the bite of the critical mosquito; and he lives in a climate in which such mosquitoes swarm. He is seldom stabbed to the heart—he is often killed by pin-pricks.
Ibid.

[b] If you do your fair day's work, you are certain to get your fair day's wage—in praise or pudding, whichever happens to suit your taste.   *Ibid. On the Importance of a Man to Himself*

[c] The great man is the man who does a thing for the first time.   *Ibid.*

[d] How deeply seated in the human heart is the liking for gardens and gardening.
Ibid. Books and Gardens

[e] If you have once planted a tree . . . you have always in it a peculiar interest. You care more for it than you care for all the forests of Norway or America. You have planted it, and that is sufficient to make it peculiar amongst the trees of the world.
Ibid.

[f] It is high time, it seems to me, that a moral game-law were passed for the preservation of the wild and vagrant feelings of human nature.
Ibid. On Vagabonds

Alfred Emanuel Smith
[1873–1944]

[g] The kiss of death.
Alluding to W. R. Hearst's support of Ogden Mills, in the 1926 campaign for Governor of New York State. Smith was re-elected, and Mills defeated.

[h] Nobody shoots at Santa Claus.
Campaign Speeches, 1936

[i] No matter how thin you slice it, it's still boloney.   *Ibid.*

Arabella Eugenia Smith
[1845–1916]

[j] Keep not your kisses for my dead, cold brow;
The way is lonely, let me feel them now. . . .
When dreamless rest is mine, I shall not need
The tenderness for which I long to-night.   *If I Should Die To-night. Stanza 4*

Cecily Fox Smith
[1882–   ]

[k] As I went down by Hastings Mill I lingered in my going
To smell the smell of piled-up deals and feel the salt wind blowing.
Hastings Mill. Stanza 1

[l] "When a ship's no more than a ship to me,
An' there's nowheres left as I want to see:
When the fun's all flat, an' the jokes all stale,
An' there ain't no taste in the cakes an' ale,
You can stitch me up as soon as you like
In a corner o'. wore-out sail," said Mike,
"With 'olystones at my 'eels an' 'ead,
An' dollop me overboard. . . . I'll be dead!"   *The Wine of Life*

Edgar Smith
[1857–1938]

[m] You may tempt the upper classes
With your villainous demi-tasses,
But Heaven will protect the Working Girl.
Heaven Will Protect the Working Girl [Sung by Marie Dressler in Tillie's Nightmare]

Langdon Smith
[1858–1908]

[n] When you were a tadpole and I was a fish,
In the Paleozoic time.

And that was a million years ago,
In a time that no man knows;
Yet here to-night in the mellow light,
We sit at Delmonico's.
Evolution. Stanzas 1 and 11

Logan Pearsall Smith
[1865–1946]

[o] What a bore it is, waking up in the morning always the same person. I wish I were unflinching and emphatic, and had big, bushy eyebrows and a Message for the Age. I wish I were a deep Thinker, or a great Ventriloquist.
Trivia. Green Ivory

[p] There are two things to aim at in life: first, to get what you want; and, after that, to enjoy it. Only the wisest of mankind achieve the second.
Afterthoughts

[q] How awful to reflect that what people say of us is true!
Ibid.

[r] Solvency is entirely a matter of temperament and not of income. *Ibid.*

[s] It is almost always worth while to be cheated; people's little frauds have an interest which more than repays what they cost us. *Ibid.*

[t] When they come downstairs from their Ivory Towers, Idealists are apt to walk straight into the gutter. *Ibid.*

[u] The indefatigable pursuit of an unattainable Perfection, even though it consist in nothing more than in the pounding of an old piano, is what alone gives a meaning to our life on this unavailing star. *Ibid.*

[v] Eat with the Rich, but go to the play with the Poor, who are capable of Joy. *Ibid.*

[w] We need new friends; some of us are cannibals who have eaten their old friends up: others must have ever-renewed audiences before whom to re-enact an ideal version of their lives. *Ibid.*

[x] What I like in a good author is not what he says, but what he whispers. *Ibid.*

[y] Most of all I envy the octogenarian poet [Edmund Waller] who joined three words—
"Go, lovely Rose"—
so happily together, that he left his name to float down through Time on the wings of a phrase and a flower. *Ibid.*

[z] Thank heavens, the sun has gone in, and I don't have to go out and enjoy it. *Ibid.*

[a] What with its crude awakenings can youth know of the rich returns of awareness to elderly people from their afternoon naps; of their ironic thoughts and long retrospections, and the sweetness they taste of not being dead? *Ibid.*

Marion Couthouy Smith
[1853–1931]

[b] Go, then, and plant a tree,
lovely in sun and shadow,
Gracious in every kind—maple and oak and pine.
Peace of the forest glade, wealth of the fruitful meadow,
Blessings of dew and shade, hereafter shall be thine.
The Planting of a Tree. Stanza 4

Nora Archibald Smith
[1859–1934]

[c] They'd knock on a tree and would timidly say

To the Spirit who might be within in there that day:
"Fairy fair, Fairy fair, wish thou me well;
'Gainst evil witcheries weave me a spell!"

An e'en to this day is the practice made good
When, to ward off disaster, we knock upon wood. *Knocking on Wood. Stanzas 3 and 4*

Samuel Francis Smith
[1808–1895]

[d] My country, 'tis of thee,
Sweet land of liberty,
Of thee I sing:
Land where my fathers died,
Land of the pilgrims' pride,
From every mountain-side
Let freedom ring. *America*

[e] Our glorious land to-day,
'Neath Education's sway,
Soars upward still.
Its halls of learning fair,
Whose bounties all may share,
Behold them everywhere,
On vale and hill.
Ibid. (Discarded stanza)

Sydney Smith
[1771–1845]

[f] It requires a surgical operation to get a joke well into a Scotch understanding.
Lady Holland's Memoir. Vol. I, Chap. 2

[g] Preaching has become a byword for long and dull conversation of any kind; and whoever wishes to imply, in any piece of writing, the absence of everything agreeable and inviting, calls it a sermon. *Ibid. Chap. 3*

[h] The sense of sight is indeed the highest bodily privilege, the purest physical pleasure, which man has derived from his Creator. *Ibid.*

[i] Avoid shame, but do not seek glory,—nothing so expensive as glory. *Ibid. Chap. 4*

[j] What would have become of us had it pleased Providence to make the weather unchangeable? Think of the state of destitution of the morning callers. *Ibid.*

[k] Looked as if she had walked straight out of the ark. *Ibid. Chap. 7*

[l] Great men hallow a whole people, and lift up all who live in their time. *Ibid.*

[m] Madam, I have been looking for a person who disliked gravy all my life; let us swear eternal friendship. *Ibid. Chap. 9*

[n] Not body enough to cover his mind decently with; his intellect is improperly exposed.   *Ibid.*

[o] Ah, you flavour everything; you are the vanilla of society.
Ibid.

[p] As the French say, there are three sexes,—men, women, and clergymen.   *Ibid.*

[q] "Heat, ma'am!" I said; "it was so dreadful here, that I found there was nothing left for it but to take off my flesh and sit in my bones."   *Ibid.*

[r] Marriage resembles a pair of shears, so joined that they can not be separated; often moving in opposite directions, yet always punishing anyone who comes between them.   *Ibid. Chap. 11*

[s] Let onion atoms lurk within the bowl
And, half suspected, animate the whole.
Ibid. Recipe for Salad

[t] Serenely full, the epicure would say,
Fate cannot harm me,—I have dined to-day.   *Ibid.*

[u] Don't tell me of facts, I never believe facts; you know Canning said nothing was so fallacious as facts, except figures.
Ibid.

[v] Thank God for tea! What would the world do without tea? —how did it exist? I am glad I was not born before tea.   *Ibid.*

[w] That sign of old age, extolling the past at the expense of the present.   *Ibid.*

[x] Light, dust, contradiction, an absurd remark, the sight of a Dissenter—anything, sets me sneezing; and if I begin sneezing at twelve, I don't leave off till two o'clock, and am heard distinctly in Taunton, when the wind sets that way—a distance of six miles. Turn your mind to this little curse.   *To Dr. Holland, about Hay Fever [June 1835]*

[y] Correspondences are like smallclothes before the invention of suspenders; it is impossible to keep them up.   *Letter to Mrs. Crowe [January 31, 1841]*

[z] If you choose to represent the various parts in life by holes upon a table, of different shapes,— some circular, some triangular, some square, some oblong,—and the persons acting these parts by bits of wood of similar shapes, we shall generally find that the triangular person has got into the square hole, the oblong into the triangular, and a square person has squeezed himself into the round hole.
Sketches of Moral Philosophy

[a] Magnificent spectacle of human happiness.   *America. In Edinburgh Review, July, 1824*

Tobias Smollett
[1721–1771]

[b] Thy spirit, Independence, let me share,
Lord of the lion-heart and eagle-eye,
Thy steps I follow, with my bosom bare,
Nor heed the storm that howls along the sky.
Ode to Independence. Strophe 1

Jan Christiaan Smuts
[1870–1950]

[c] We the peoples of the United Nations, determined to save succeeding generations from the scourge of war, which twice in our lifetime has brought untold sorrow to mankind, and to reaffirm faith in fundamental human rights, in the dignity and worth of the human person, in the equal rights of men and women and of nations large and small . . .
And for these ends to practise tolerance and live together in peace with one another as good neighbors . . .
Have resolved to combine our efforts to accomplish these aims.
Preamble of the Charter of the United Nations. (The drafting of this preamble is generally attributed to Premier Smuts.)

Socrates
[470–399 B.C.]
Translation by Benjamin Jowett

[d] No evil can happen to a good man, either in life or after death.
Apology

[e] Man is a prisoner who has no right to open the door of his prison and run away. . . . A man should wait, and not take his own life until God summons him.
Dialogues of Plato. Phaedo

[f] The partisan, when he is engaged in a dispute, cares nothing about the rights of the question, but is anxious only to convince his hearers of his own assertions.
Ibid.

[g] I think that I had better bathe before I drink the poison, and not give the women the trouble of washing my dead body.
Ibid.

William Somerville
[1675-1742]

[h] How humble, and how com-
plaisant
Is the proud man reduced to
want!
With what a silly, hanging face
He bears his unforeseen dis-
grace! . . .
Let all the learned say what they
can,
'Tis ready money makes the man.
Ready Money

[i] For what is virtue, courage,
wit,
In all men, but a lucky hit?
The Lucky Hit

Sophocles
[496-406 B.C.]

*The Fragments are from pages
311-377 of the Everyman edition
of The Dramas of Sophocles.*

[j] Lady, cheer up; most of our
ills, blowing loudly
In dreams by night, grow milder
when 'tis day.
Acrisius. Fragment 63

[k] No man loves life like him
that's growing old.
Ibid. Fragment 64

[l] Truly, to tell lies is not honourable;
But when the truth entails tremendous ruin,
To speak dishonourably is par-
donable.
Creusa. Fragment 323

[m] Sons are the anchors of a
mother's life.
Phaedra. Fragment 612

[n] A wise gamester ought to
take the dice
Even as they fall, and pay down
quietly,
Rather than grumble at his luck.
Unknown Dramas. Fragment 686

[o] A woman's vows I write upon
the wave. *Ibid. Fragment 694*

*(The following translations by
Sir George Young)*

[p] The ship of state—the gods
once more,
After much rocking on a stormy
surge,
Set her on even keel. *Antigone*

[q] For money you would sell
your soul. *Ibid.*

[r] A man of worth
In his own household will appear
upright
In the state also. *Ibid.*

[s] There lives no greater fiend
than Anarchy;
She ruins states, turns houses out
of doors,

Breaks up in rout the embattled
soldiery. *Ibid.*

[t] Though a man be wise,
It is no shame for him to live and
learn. *Ibid.*

[u] A woman should be seen,
not heard. *Ajax*

[v] I would not take the fellow at
a gift
Who warms himself with unsub-
stantial hopes;
But bravely to live on, or bravely
end,
Is due to gentle breeding. *Ibid.*

[w] In the ills of men
There is none sorer than Necessity. *Ibid.*

[x] The happiest life consists in
ignorance,
Before you learn to grieve and to
rejoice. *Ibid.*

[y] Sleep, the universal van-
quisher. *Ibid.*

[z] Mortals most
Find friendship an unstable
anchorage. *Ibid.*

[a] 'Tis a long road knows no
turning. *Ibid.*

[b] The flower
Of our young manhood.
Oedipus Tyrannus

[c] Towers and ships are nothingness,
Void of our fellow men to inhabit
them. *Ibid.*

[d] The Sphinx
With her enigma. *Ibid.*

[e] Pride, when puffed up, vainly,
with many things
Unseasonable, unfitting, mounts
the wall,
Only to hurry to that fatal fall.
Ibid.

[f] One must learn
By doing the thing; for though
you think you know it
You have no certainty, until you
try. *Trachiniae*

[g] If any
Count on two days, or any more,
to come,
He is a fool; for a man has no
morrow,
Till with good luck he has got
through to-day. *Ibid.*

[h′] War never slays a bad man
in its course,
But the good always! *Philoctetes*

[i′] Who does not befriend him-
self
By doing good?
Oedipus Coloneus

[j′] To the gods alone
Belongs it never to be old or die,
But all things else melt with all-
powerful Time. *Ibid.*

[k] It is the merit of a general
To impart good news, and to conceal the bad.   *Ibid.*

John Babson Lane Soule
[1815–1891]

[l] Go west, young man.
   *Article in the Terre Haute,
   Indiana, Express, 1851*
   [*Horace Greeley was attracted
   by the expression, and used it in
   an editorial in The New York
   Tribune. As the saying, "Go west,
   young man, and grow up with
   the country," gained popularity,
   Greeley printed Soule's article, to
   show the source of his inspira-
   tion.*]

Caroline Anne Bowles
Southey
[1786–1854]

[m] All day the low-hung clouds
   have dropped
   Their garnered fullness down;
All day that soft gray mist hath
   wrapped
   Hill, valley, grove, and town.
      An April Day. Stanza 1

[n] Come not in terrors clad, to
   claim
An unresisting prey.   *To Death*

Robert Southey
[1774–1843]

[o] "You are old, Father William," the young man cried,
   "The few locks which are left
   you are gray;
You are hale, Father William, a
   hearty old man,
   Now tell me the reason I pray."
   *The Old Man's Comforts, and
   How He Gained Them. Stanza 1*
   [*Of several parodies of this
   poem, the one by "Lewis Carroll" is probably better known
   than the original.*]

[p] Who is yonder poor maniac,
   whose wildly fixed eyes
   Seem a heart overcharged to express?
She weeps not, yet often and
   deeply she sighs;
She never complains, but her
   silence implies
   The composure of settled distress.   *Mary, the Maid
      of the Inn. Stanza 1*

[q] Where Washington hath left
   His awful memory
A light for after times!
   *Ode Written during the War
   with America* [*1814*]

[r] Agreed to differ.
      Life of Wesley

[s] My days among the dead are
   passed;
   Around me I behold,
Where'er these casual eyes are
   cast,
   The mighty minds of old;
My never-failing friends are they,
   With whom I converse night and
   day.
      Occasional Pieces. The Library

[t]   Helter-skelter,
             Hurry-scurry.
      The Cataract of Lodore

[u] From his brimstone bed, at
   break of day,
A-walking the Devil is gone,
To look at his little snug farm of
   the World,
And see how his stock went on.

How then was the Devil dressed?
O, he was in his Sunday's best;
His coat was red, and his breeches
   were blue,
And there was a hole where his
   tail came through.
   The Devil's Walk. Stanzas 1 and 3

[v] He passed a cottage with a
   double coach-house,—
   A cottage of gentility;
      And he owned with a grin,
      That his favourite sin
   Is pride that apes humility.
      Ibid. Stanza 8

[w]   He was always found
Among your ten and twenty
   pound subscribers,
Your benefactors in the news-
   papers.
His alms were money put to in-
   terest
In the other world.
      The Alderman's Funeral

[x] As frozen as charity.
      The Soldier's Wife, Stanza 4

[y] "But what good came of it at
   last?"
Quoth little Peterkin.
"Why, that I cannot tell," said
   he;
"But 'twas a famous victory."
      *The Battle of Blenheim.
         Stanza 11*

[z] Blue, darkly, deeply, beautifully blue.
      Madoc in Wales. Part I, 5

[a] What will not woman, gentle
   woman dare,
When strong affection stirs her
   spirit up?   *Ibid. Part II, 2*

[b]   And last of all an Admiral
   came,
A terrible man with a terrible
   name,—
A name which you all know by
   sight very well,
But which no one can speak, and
   no one can spell.
   The March to Moscow. Stanza 8

[c] They sin who tell us love can
die;
With life all other passions fly,
  All others are but vanity. . . .
    Love is indestructible.
        *The Curse of Kehama.
        Canto X, Stanza 10*

[d] Oh, when a mother meets on
high
  The babe she lost in infancy,
Hath she not then for pains and
fears,
  The day of woe, the watchful
  night,
For all her sorrow, all her tears,
An over-payment of delight?
        Ibid. Stanza 11

[e] Snips and snails and puppy
dog tails
And such are little boys made of.
    What All the World is Made of

[f] Sugar and spice and all
things nice,
And such are young women made
of. *Ibid.*

Robert Southwell
[1561–1595]

[g] What thought can think, another thought can mend.
        Look Home

[h] He that high growth on
cedars did bestow,
Gave also lowly mushrumps leave
to grow. *Scorn Not the Least*

[i] May never was the month of
love,
For May is full of flowers;
But rather April, wet by kind,
For love is full of showers.
        Love's Servile Lot

[j] When Fortune smiles, I smile
to think
How quickly she will frown.
        I Envy Not Their Hap

[k] As I in hoary winter night
stood shivering in the snow,
Surprised was I with sudden heat
  which made my heart to glow;
And lifting up a fearful eye to
  view what fire was near
A pretty Babe all burning bright
did in the air appear.
        The Burning Babe

Francis Joseph,
Cardinal Spellman
[1889–   ]

[l] Somewhere—the place it matters not—somewhere
I saw a child, hungry and thin of
face—
Eyes in whose pools life's joys no
longer stirred,
Lips that were dead to laughter's
eager kiss,
Yet parted fiercely to a crust of
bread.
        Prayer for Children [1944]

Herbert Spencer
[1829–1903]

[m] The fact disclosed by a survey of the past that majorities have been wrong must not
blind us to the complementary
fact that majorities have usually
not been entirely wrong.
        First Principles

[n] Volumes might be written
upon the impiety of the pious.
        Ibid.

[o] Survival of the fittest. *Ibid.*

[p] With a higher moral nature
will come a restriction on the
multiplication of the inferior.
        Ibid.

[q] The tyranny of Mrs. Grundy
is worse than any other tyranny
we suffer under.
        *Essays on Education. On Prog-
        ress: On Manners and Fashion*

[r] Old forms of government
finally grow so oppressive that
they must be thrown off even at
the risk of reigns of terror.
        Ibid.

[s] Morality knows nothing of
geographical boundaries or distinctions of race.
        The Evanescence of Evil

[t] The Republican form of government is the highest form of
government: but because of this
it requires the highest type of
human nature—a type nowhere
at present existing.
        The Americans

[u] The ultimate result of shield-
ing men from the effects of folly
is to fill the world with fools.
        *State Tamperings with
        Money Banks*

[v] If a single cell, under appropriate conditions, becomes a
man in the space of a few years,
there can surely be no difficulty in
understanding how, under appropriate conditions, a cell may,
in the course of untold millions
of years, give origin to the human
race. *Principles of Biology*

Hiram Ladd Spencer
[1829–1915]

[w] O where will be the birds
that sing,
  A hundred years to come?

But other men our lands will till,
And others then our streets will
fill,
While other birds will sing as
gay,
As bright the sunshine as to-day.
        *A Hundred Years to Come.
        Stanzas 1 and 3*

Theodore Spencer
[1902–1949]

[x] Eunuchs, abortive Platonists
and priests
Speak always very wisely about
love.	*An Act of Life*

William Robert Spencer
[1770–1834]

[y] Too late I stayed,—forgive the
crime!
Unheeded flew the hours;
How noiseless falls the foot of
time
That only treads on flowers.
Lines to Lady Anne Hamilton.

[z] At the long string of ills a
kind goddess relented,
And slipped in three blessings—
wife, children, and friends.
Wife, Children, and Friends.

Stephen Spender
[1909–	]

[a] Central 'I' is surrounded by
'I eating,'
'I loving,' 'I angry,' 'I excreting,'
And the 'great I' planted in him
Has nothing to do with all these,
It can never claim its true place
Resting in the forehead, and se-
cure in his gaze.
The 'great I' is an unfortunate in-
truder
Quarrelling with 'I tiring' and 'I
sleeping'
And all those other 'I's who long
for 'We dying.'	*Poem. 9*

[b] After the first powerful plain
manifesto
The black statement of pistons,
without more fuss
But gliding like a queen, she
leaves the station. . . .
Beyond the town there lies the
open country
Where, gathering speed, she acquires mystery,
The luminous self-possession of
ships on ocean.
Poems. 34, The Express

[c] I think continually of those
who were truly great . . .
Born of the sun they traveled a
short while towards the sun,
And left the vivid air signed with
their honor.
I Think Continually of Those

Edmund Spenser
[1553?–1599]
*From the text of J. C. Smith and
E. De Selincourt. Oxford University Press [1932].*

[d] Ay me, how many perils doe
enfold
The righteous man, to make him
daily fall.
*The Faerie Queene. Book I,
Canto 8, Stanza 1*

[e] As great a noyse, as when in
Cymbrian plaine
An heard of Bulles, whom kindly
rage doth sting,
Do for the milkie mothers want
complaine,
And fill the fields with troublous
bellowing.	*Ibid. Stanza 11*

[f] All for love, and nothing for
reward.
Ibid. Book II, Canto 8, Stanza 2

[g] Roses red and violets blew,
And all the sweetest flowres, that
in the forrest grew.
Ibid. Book III, Canto 6, Stanza 6

[h] Me seemes the world is runne
quite out of square,
From the first point of his ap-
pointed sourse,
And being once amisse growes
daily wourse and wourse.
*Ibid. Book V, Introduction,
Stanza 1*

[i] Who will not mercie unto
others shew,
How can he mercy ever hope to
have?
Ibid. Book VI, Canto 1, Stanza 42

[j] The gentle minde by gentle
deeds is knowne.
For a man by nothing is so well
bewrayed,
As by his manners.
Ibid. Canto 3, Stanza 1

[k] The ever-whirling wheele
Of *Change*, the which all mortall
things doth sway.
Ibid. Book VII, Canto 6, Stanza 1

[l] But of all burdens, that a man
can beare,
Moste is, a fooles talke to beare
and to heare.
*The Shepheardes Calender.
Maye, Line 140*

[m] I hate the day, because it
lendeth light
To see all things, and not my love
to see.	*Daphnaida. Line 407*

[n] Death slue not him, but he
made death his ladder to the
skies.
*An Epitaph upon Sir Philip
Sidney. Line 20*

[o] Tell her the joyous time wil
not be staid
Unlesse she doe him by the fore-
lock take.
Amoretti. Sonnet 70

[p] For of the soule the bodie
forme doth take:
For soule is forme, and doth the
bodie make.	*An Hymne in
Honour of Beautie. Line 132*

[q] It was the time when rest the
gift of Gods
Sweetely sliding into the eyes of
men,

Doth drowne in the forgetfulnesse
    of slepe,
The carefull travailes of the
    painefull day.   *Sonnet 1*

[r] I was promised on a time
To have reason for my rhyme;
From that time unto this season,
I received nor rhyme nor reason.
    *Lines on his Promised Pension
    (Quoted by Thomas Fuller in
    Worthies of England, Vol. 2,
    Page 379)*

Leonora Speyer
[1872–   ]

[s] Out of my sorrow
I'll build a stair,
And every to-morrow
Will climb to me there
With ashes of yesterday
In its hair.
    Duet: I Sing with Myself.

Anne Higginson Spicer
[1871–1935]

[t] A Bible entry: "Born, a girl."
A knitted shoe, a golden curl,
A woolly lamb, gay-colored blocks,
Some wee worn garments in a box.

A rain of rice along the hall—
Tears on my cheeks—and that is
    all.   *Her Patteran. Stanzas
                1 and 3*

Benedict (Baruch) Spinoza
[1632–1677]

[u] Nature abhors a vacuum.
    *Ethics (Everyman edition,
    translated by Andrew Boyle,
    M.A.). Part I, Prop. XV,
    Note*

[v] God and all the attributes of
God are eternal.
    Ibid. Prop. XIX

[w] He who would distinguish
the true from the false must have
an adequate idea of what is true
and false.   *Ibid. Part II, Prop.
                XLII, Proof*

[x] Will and Intellect are one and
the same thing.   *Ibid. Prop.
                XLIX, Corollary*

[y] Surely human affairs would
be far happier if the power in
men to be silent were the same as
that to speak. But experience
more than sufficiently teaches
that men govern nothing with
more difficulty than their tongues.
    Ibid. Part III, Prop. II, Note

[z] Pride is therefore pleasure
arising from a man's thinking too
highly of himself.   *Ibid. Prop.
                XXVI, Note*

[a] It therefore comes to pass
that every one is fond of relating
his own exploits and displaying
the strength both of his body and
his mind, and that men are on
this account a nuisance one to
the other.   *Ibid. Prop. LIV, Note*

[b] So long as a man imagines
that he cannot do this or that, so
long is he determined not to do it:
and consequently, so long it is
impossible to him that he should
do it.   *Ibid. Definition XXVIII,
                Explanation*

[c] Those who are believed to be
most abject and humble are usually most ambitious and envious.
    *Ibid. Definition XXIX,
                Explanation*

[d] One and the same thing can
at the same time be good, bad,
and indifferent, e.g., music is good
to the melancholy, bad to those
who mourn, and neither good nor
bad to the deaf.
    Ibid. Part IV, Preface

[e] Those who commit suicide
are powerless souls, and allow
themselves to be conquered by external causes repugnant to their
nature.   *Ibid. Prop. XVIII, Note*

[f] Man is a social animal.
    Ibid. Prop. XXXV, Note

[g] Avarice, ambition, lust, etc.,
are nothing but species of madness, although not enumerated
among diseases.   *Ibid. Prop.
                XLIV, Note*

[h] It is the part of a wise man to
feed himself with moderate pleasant food and drink, and to take
pleasure with perfumes, with the
beauty of growing plants, dress,
music, sports, and theatres.
    Ibid. Prop. XLV, Note 2

[i] He whose honour depends on
the opinion of the mob must day
by day strive with the greatest
anxiety, act and scheme in order
to retain his reputation. For the
mob is varied and inconstant, and
therefore if a reputation is not
carefully preserved it dies quickly.
    Ibid. Prop. LVIII, Note

[j] All excellent things are as
difficult as they are rare.
    Ibid. Part V, Prop. XLII, Note

Harriet Prescott Spofford
[1835–1921]

[k] Dear the people coming home,
Dear glad faces long away,
Dear the merry cries, and dear
All the glad and happy play
Dear the thanks, too, that we give
For all of this, Thanksgiving
Day.   *Every Day Thanks-
                giving Day. Stanza 3*

Allen C. Spooner
[*Floruit* 1846]

[l] I mused upon the Pilgrim
flock
  Whose luck it was to land
Upon almost the only rock
  Among the Plymouth sand.
    Old Times and New. Stanza 2
    (Written for the New England
    Society Festival, New York, De-
    cember 22, 1846)

William Archibald Spooner
[1844–1930]

[m] Kinquering Congs their titles
take.
  Announcing the hymn in col-
  lege chapel [Canon Spooner, for
  many years warden of New Col-
  lege, Oxford, was famous for in-
  nocent confusions of word and
  thought. This form of metath-
  esis became known as a "spoon-
  erism"]

You have deliberately tasted
two worms and you can leave Oxford by the town drain.
    Dismissing a student

This audience of beery wenches.
    At a woman's college

I remember your name perfectly,
but I just can't think of your face.
    A greeting

Charles Sprague
[1791–1875]

[n] Gay, guiltless pair,
What seek ye from the fields of
heaven?
Ye have no need of prayer,
Ye have no sins to be forgiven.
  The Winged Worshippers. Stanza
  1 [Of two swallows that flew into
  church during service]

[o] Yes, social friend, I love thee
well,
  In learned doctors' spite;
Thy clouds all other clouds dispel,
  And lap me in delight.
    To My Cigar

[p] Through life's dark road his
sordid way he wends,
An incarnation of fat dividends.
  Phi Beta Kappa Ode, Curiosity

Nancy Dennis Sproat
[1766–1826]

[q] How pleasant is Saturday
night,
When I've tried all the week to
be good,
And not spoke a word that was
bad,
  And obliged every one that I
  could. *Lullabies for Chil-*
  dren. Saturday Night, Stanza 1

[r] To-morrow our holy da
comes,
  Which our merciful Father ha
  given,
That we may rest from our wor
  And prepare for His beautifu
  heaven. *Ibid. Stanza*

Sir John Collings Squire
[1884–   ]

[s] And stared, and saw, and di
not understand,
Columbus's doom-burdened cara
vels
Slant to the shore, and all thei
  seamen land. *Sonne*

Madame de Staël
[1766–1817]

[t] The sight of such a monu
ment is like a continuous an
stationary music.
  Corinne. Book IV, Chap.

[u] To understand all makes u
very indulgent.
  Ibid. Book XVIII, Chap.

Wendell Phillips Stafford
[1861–   ]

[v] My heart is where the hills
fling up
  Green garlands to the day.
'Tis where the blue lake brims her
cup,
  The sparkling rivers play.
My heart is on the mountain still
  Where'er my steps may be,
Vermont, O maiden of the hills,
  My heart is there with thee!
    Vermont: A Song. Stanza

Joseph Stalin
[1879–   ]

[w] The victory of socialism in
Russia is not complete because
the danger of intervention from
capitalist countries continues.
The problem can be solved only by
uniting the serious efforts of the
international proletariat with the
still more serious efforts of the
entire Soviet people.
  Letter to Comrade Ivanov,
  February 14, 1938

[x] History shows that there are
no invincible armies.
  Address broadcast July 3, 1941.
  Declaration of War. (Germany
  invaded Russia June 22, 1941)

[y] Socialism can succeed only on
the basis of a high productivity of
labour, higher than under capitalism, on the basis of an abundance
of products and of articles of consumption of all kinds, on the basis

of a prosperous and cultured life for all members of society.
Quoted by Hewlett Johnson in The Soviet Power. The Socialist Sixth of the World, Book III, 8

[z] Mr. Willkie, you know I grew up a Georgian peasant. I am unschooled in pretty talk. All I can say is I like you very much.
Quoted by Wendell Willkie in One World, Chap. 4

[a] In the U.S.S.R. work is the duty of every able-bodied citizen, according to the principle: "He who does not work, neither shall he eat."
In the U.S.S.R. the principle of socialism is realised: "From each according to his ability, to each according to his work."
Constitution of the Union of Soviet Socialist Republics [1936]. Article 12

[b] Citizens of the U.S.S.R. have the right to rest.
Ibid. Article 119

[c] Citizens of the U.S.S.R. have the right to education.
Ibid. Article 121

Philip Henry Stanhope, Lord Mahon
[1805–1875]

[d] The island of Sardinia, consisting chiefly of marshes and mountains, has from the earliest period to the present been cursed with a noxious air. . . . The convulsions produced by its poisonous plants gave rise to the expression of sardonic smile, which is as old as Homer (Odyssey, xx. 302).
History of England. Vol. I, Page 287

[There is no evidence that Sardinia was known to . . . Homer. It looks as though the word was to be connected with the verb (which means) "show the teeth."
—*Morris Hickey Morgan*]

Bessie Anderson (Mrs. Arthur J.) Stanley
[1879–   ]

[e] He has achieved success who has lived well, laughed often, and loved much.
Success (prize-winning definition in a contest conducted by the Brown Book Magazine, Boston, 1904)

Sir Henry M. Stanley
[1841–1904]

[f] Dr. Livingstone, I presume?
On meeting Livingstone in Ujiji, Central Africa [November 10, 1871]

Charles E. Stanton
[1859–1933]

[g] America has joined forces with the Allied Powers, and what we have of blood and treasure are yours. . . . And here and now in the presence of the illustrious dead we pledge our hearts and our honor in carrying this war to a successful issue. Lafayette, we are here.   *Address at the Tomb of Lafayette, Picpus Cemetery, Paris [July 4, 1917]*

Edwin M. Stanton
[1814–1869]

[h] Now he belongs to the ages.
At the deathbed of President Lincoln

Frank Lebby Stanton
[1857–1927]

[i] Jest a-wearyin' fer you—
All the time a-feelin' blue;
Wishin' fer you—wonderin' when
You'll be comin' home again.
Wearyin' for You. Stanza 1

[j] Sweetes' li'l' feller—
Everybody knows;
Dunno what ter call 'im,
But he mighty lak' a rose!
Sweetes' Li'l' Feller. Stanza 1

Henry Thompson Stanton
[1834–1898]

[k] Ah, search the wide world wherever you can,
There is no open door for the moneyless man!
The Moneyless Man. Stanza 1

John Stark
[1728–1822]

[l] We beat them today or Molly Stark's a widow.   *Before the Battle of Bennington, August 16, 1777*

Vincent Starrett
[1886–   ]

[m] Suicide . . . to the many is the final proof of insanity, and, therefore, in a writing man (or a painting man) of genius.
Buried Caesars. Two Suicides

[n] Time colors history as it does a meerschaum pipe.
Ibid. Robert Neilson Stephens and The Costume Novel

[o] Here dwell together still two men of note
Who never lived and so can never die.   *221-B [Sonnet on Sherlock Holmes and Dr. Watson]*

Edmund Clarence Stedman
[1833–1908]

[p] Prison-mate and dock-yard
fellow,
Blades to Meg and Molly dear,
Off to capture Porto Bello
Sailed with Morgan the Bucca-
neer!   *Morgan. Stanza 1*

[q] "Oh, anywhere! Forward! 'Tis
all the same, Colonel:
You'll find lovely fighting along
the whole line!"
*Kearny at Seven Pines.
Stanza 3*

[r] Look on this cast, and know
the hand
That bore a nation in its hold:
From this mute witness under-
stand
What Lincoln was,—how large
of mould.
The Hand of Lincoln. Stanza 1

Sir Richard Steele
[1672–1729]

[s] Every rich man has usually
some sly way of jesting, which
would make no great figure were
he not a rich man.
*The Spectator. No. 2,
March 2, 1711*

[t] When you fall into a man's
conversation, the first thing you
should consider is, whether he has
a greater inclination to hear you,
or that you should hear him.
Ibid. No. 49, April 26, 1711

[u] Of all the affections which
attend human life, the love of
glory is the most ardent.
Ibid. No. 139, August 9, 1711

[v] Age in a virtuous person, of
either sex, carries in it an authority which makes it preferable
to all the pleasures of youth.
Ibid. No. 153, August 25, 1711

[w] Will Honeycomb calls these
over-offended ladies the outra-
geously virtuous.
Ibid. No. 266, January 4, 1712

*From the Letters to His Wife
(Selected and collated by R. Brim-
ley Johnson)*

[x] I have partly succeeded in
my business today, and enclose
two guineas. Dear Prue, I can't
come home to dinner.
January 3, 1708

[y] I was going home two hours
ago, but was met by Mr. Griffith,
who has kept me ever since. I will
come within a pint of wine.
Eleven at Night, January 5, 1708

[z] A little in drink, but at all
times yr. faithfull husband.
September 27, 1708

[a] The finest woman in nature
should not detain me an hour
from you; but you must sometimes suffer the rivalship of the
wisest men.   *September 17, 1712*

Gertrude Stein
[1874–1946]

[b] Rose is a rose is a rose is a
rose.   *Sacred Emily*

[c] Pigeons in the grass alas.
Four Saints in Three Acts

[d] In the United States there is
more space where nobody is than
where anybody is.
This is what makes America
what it is.   *The Geographical
History of America*

John Ernst Steinbeck
[1902–]

[e] Man, unlike any other thing
organic or inorganic in the universe, grows beyond his work,
walks up the stairs of his con-
cepts, emerges ahead of his ac-
complishments.
The Grapes of Wrath. Chap. 14

[f] "Okie use' ta mean you was
from Oklahoma. Now it means
you're scum. Don't mean nothing
itself, it's the way they say it."
Ibid. Chap. 18

"Stendhal"
(Henri Beyle)
[1783–1842]

[g] One can acquire everything
in solitude—except character.
Fragments. I

[h] Prudery is a kind of avarice,
the worst of all.   *Ibid. V*

[i] A wise woman never yields by
appointment. It should always be
an unforeseen happiness.
De l'Amour. Chap. 60

James Kenneth Stephen
[1859–1892]

[j] If all the harm that women
have done
Were put in a bundle and rolled
into one,
Earth would not hold it,
The sky could not enfold it,
It could not be lighted nor
warmed by the sun.
*Lapsus Calami. A Thought,
Stanza 1*

[k] No cat so sweet a mistress
owned;
No mistress owned so sweet a cat.
*Ibid. Elegy on De Marsay,
Stanza 9*

James Stephens
[1882–1951]

[l] I saw God! Do you doubt it?
Do you dare to doubt it?
I saw the Almighty Man! His hand
Was resting on a mountain! And
He looked upon the World, and
all about it.
*What Tomas Said in a Pub.
Stanza 1*

[m] Forgive us all our trespasses,
Little creatures, everywhere!
Little Things. Stanza 5

[n] Let the man who has and
doesn't give
Break his neck, and cease to live!
Let him who gives without a care
Gather rubies from the air!
In the Imperative Mood

[o] I heard a bird at dawn
Singing sweetly on a tree,
That the dew was on the lawn,
And the wind was on the lea.
The Rivals. Stanza 1

[p] Women are wiser than men
because they know less and understand more.
The Crock of Gold. Chap. 2

[q] Virtue is the performance of
pleasant actions. *Ibid. Chap. 10*

[r] Women and birds are able to
see without turning their heads,
and that is indeed a necessary
provision, for they are both surrounded by enemies.
The Demi-Gods. Chap. 2

George Sterling
[1869–1926]

[s] Into a crystal cup the dusky
wine
I pour, and, musing at so rich a
shrine,
I watch the star that haunts its
ruddy gloom.
A Wine of Wizardry

[t] Let us be just with life. Although it bear
A thousand thorns for every perfect rose,
And though the happy day have
mournful close,
Slumber awaits to house the mind
from care. *The Balance*

Laurence Sterne
[1713–1768]

[u] For every ten jokes, thou hast
got an hundred enemies.
*Tristram Shandy. Book I,
Chap. 12*

[v] 'Tis known by the name of
perseverance in a good cause,—
and of obstinacy in a bad one.
Ibid. Chap. 17

[w] The history of a soldier's
wound beguiles the pain of it.
Ibid. Chap. 25

[x] Writing, when properly managed (as you may be sure I think
mine is) is but a different name
for conversation.
Ibid. Book II, Chap. 11

[y] Go, poor devil, get thee gone!
Why should I hurt thee? This
world surely is wide enough to
hold both thee and me. [Uncle
Toby to the fly] *Ibid. Chap. 12*

[z] The sweat of a man's brows,
and the exudations of a man's
brains, are as much a man's own
property as the breeches upon his
backside.
Ibid. Book III, Chap. 34

[a] As certainly as you can make
a velvet cap out of a sow's ear.
*Ibid. Book IV, Slawkenbergius's
Tale*

[b] One of the two horns of my
dilemma. *Ibid. Chap. 26*

[c] The Accusing Spirit, which
flew up to heaven's chancery with
the oath, blushed as he gave it in;
and the Recording Angel, as he
wrote it down, dropped a tear
upon the word and blotted it out
forever. *Ibid. Book VI, Chap. 8*

[d] I am as sick as a horse.
Ibid. Book VII, Chap. 2

[e] Hail, ye small, sweet courtesies of life! for smooth do ye make
the road of it. *A Sentimental
Journey. The Pulse, Paris*

[f] "Disguise thyself as thou
wilt, still, Slavery," said I, "still
thou are a bitter draught."
*Ibid. The Passport, The Hotel
at Paris*

Stesichorus
[630–550 B.C.]
*Loeb Classical Library, Lyra
Graeca, Vol. 2*

[g] 'Tis a vain and impotent
thing to bewail the dead.
Stobaeus: Anthology

Burton Egbert Stevenson
[1872–   ]

[h] "Baloney" and "bonehead"
and "stuffed shirt" deserve a place
no less than "magic casements."
*Preface to The Home Book
of Quotations (Second Edition, 1935)*

Robert Louis Stevenson
[1850–1894]

[1] In winter I get up at night
And dress by yellow candle-light.
In summer, quite the other way,
I have to go to bed by day.
Bed in Summer. Stanza 1

[j] A child should always say what's true
And speak when he is spoken to,
And behave mannerly at table;
At least as far as he is able.
Whole Duty of Children

[k] Dark brown is the river,
Golden is the sand.
It flows along for ever,
With trees on either hand.
Where Go the Boats? Stanza 1

[l] The pleasant land of counterpane.
The Land of Counterpane. Stanza 4

[m] I have a little shadow that goes in and out with me,
And what can be the use of him is more than I can see.
My Shadow. Stanza 1

[n] The world is so full of a number of things,
I'm sure we should all be as happy as kings. *Happy Thought*

[o] There are men and classes of men that stand above the common herd: the soldier, the sailor, and the shepherd not infrequently; the artist rarely; rarelier still, the clergyman; the physician almost as a rule. He is the flower (such as it is) of our civilization. *Underwoods. Dedication*

[p] Thanks, when they are expressed, are often more embarrassing than welcome. *Ibid.*

[q] Under the wide and starry sky,
Dig the grave and let me lie,
Glad did I live and gladly die,
And I laid me down with a will.

This be the verse you grave for me:
*Here he lies where he longed to be;
Home is the sailor, home from sea,
And the hunter home from the hill. Ibid. Requiem.
Stanzas 1 and 2*

[r] April came to bloom and never dim December
Breathed its killing chills upon the head or heart.
Ibid. In Memoriam F. A. Sitwell [who died at age 18]

[s] Let first the onion flourish there,
Rose among roots, the maiden-fair
Wine-scented and poetic soul
Of the capacious salad bowl.
Ibid. To a Gardener

[t] In the highlands, in the country places,
Where the old plain men have rosy faces,
And the young fair maidens
Quiet eyes. *Ibid. XVI*

[u] But the nearest friends are the auldest friends
And the grave's the place to seek them.
Ibid. In Scots, XVI, Stanza 3

[v] For all the story-books you read:
For all the pains you comforted:
For all you pitied, all you bore,
In sad and happy days of yore ...
Take, nurse, the little book you hold! *To Alison Cunningham from Her Boy*

[w] Be it granted me to behold you again in dying,
Hills of home!
Songs of Travel. XLIII, To S. R. Crockett

[x] Trusty, dusky, vivid, true,
With eyes of gold and bramble-dew,
Steel-true and blade-straight
The great artificer made my mate.
To My Wife. Stanza 1

[y] Mankind was never so happily inspired as when it made a cathedral. *An Inland Voyage. Noyon Cathedral*

[z] To love is the great Amulet that makes this world a garden.
Travels with a Donkey. The Heart of the Country

[a] The cruellest lies are often told in silence.
Virginibus Puerisque. IV, Truth of Intercourse

[b] Give me the young man who has brains enough to make a fool of himself.
Ibid. Crabbed Age and Youth

[c] Perpetual devotion to what a man calls his business, is only to be sustained by perpetual neglect of many other things.
Ibid. An Apology for Idlers

[d] There is no duty we underrate so much as the duty of being happy. *Ibid.*

[e] To travel hopefully is a better thing than to arrive.
Ibid. El Dorado

[f] Science carries us into zones of speculation, where there is no habitable city for the mind of man. *Pulvis et Umbra*

[g] You cannot run away from a weakness; you must some time fight it out or perish; and if that be so, why not now, and where you stand?
The Amateur Emigrant

[h] Youth is wholly experimental. *A Letter to a Young Gentleman*

[i] Fifteen men on the Dead Man's Chest—
Yo-ho-ho, and a bottle of rum!

Drink and the devil had done for
the rest—
Yo-ho-ho, and a bottle of rum!
Treasure Island

[j] There's no music like a little
river's. It plays the same tune
(and that's the favourite) over
and over again, and yet does not
weary of it like men fiddlers.
Prince Otto. Chap. 2

[k] I feel very strongly about
putting questions; it partakes too
much of the style of the day of
judgment. You start a question,
and it's like starting a stone. You
sit quietly on the top of a hill;
and away the stone goes, starting
others. *The Strange Case of
Dr. Jekyll and Mr. Hyde*

[l] Not every man is so great a
coward as he thinks he is—nor yet
so good a Christian.
*The Master of Ballantrae. Mr.
Mackellar's Journey*

[m] The kingdom of heaven is of
the childlike, of those who are
easy to please, who love and give
pleasure. *Across the Plains. A
Christmas Sermon*

[n] No man is useless while he
has a friend. *Lay Morals*

[o] When a road is once built, it
is a strange thing how it collects
traffic, how every year as it goes
on, more and more people are
found to walk thereon, and others
are raised up to repair and per-
petuate it, and keep it alive.
*Vailima Letters. Address to the
Chiefs on the Opening of the
Road of Gratitude, October 1894*

William Leroy Stidger
[1885–1949]

[p] I saw God wash the world
last night.
Ah, would He had washed me
As clean of all my dust and dirt
As that old white birch tree.
*I Saw God Wash the World.
Stanza 5*

Bishop John Still
[1543–1608]

[q] I cannot eat but little meat,
My stomach is not good;
But sure I think that I can drink
With him that wears a hood.

Back and side go bare, go bare,
Both foot and hand go cold;
But, belly, God send thee good ale
enough,
Whether it be new or old.
*Gammer Gurton's Needle.
Drinking Song, Act V*

Henry Lewis Stimson
[1867–1950]

[r] The only way to make a man
trustworthy is to trust him; and
the surest way to make him untrustworthy is to distrust him and
show your distrust.
*The Bomb and the Opportunity.
[Harper's Magazine, March 1946]*

Frank Richard Stockton
[1834–1902]

[s] He could open either door he
pleased. . . . If he opened the one,
there came out of it a hungry
tiger, the fiercest and most cruel
that could be procured, which immediately sprang upon him, and
tore him to pieces, as a punishment for his guilt. . . . But if the
accused person opened the other
door, there came forth from it a
lady, the most suitable to his years
and station that his Majesty could
select among his fair subjects.
. . . So I leave it with all of you:
Which came out of the opened
door—the lady or the tiger?
The Lady or the Tiger?

Richard Henry Stoddard
[1825–1903]

[t] Pale in her fading bowers the
Summer stands,
Like a new Niobe with claspèd
hands,
Silent above the flowers, her chil-
dren lost,
Slain by the arrows of the early
Frost. *Ode*

[u] Joy may be a miser,
But Sorrow's purse is free.
Persian Song

[v] Not what we would, but what
we must,
Makes up the sum of living;
Heaven is both more and less than
just
In taking and in giving.
The Country Life. Stanza 1

Rose Pastor Stokes
[1879–1933]

[w] Some pray to marry the man
they love,
My prayer will somewhat vary:
I humbly pray to Heaven above
That I love the man I marry.
My Prayer

Violet Alleyn Storey
[1900–]

[x] I have a small-town soul.
It makes me want to know
Wee, unimportant things
About the folks that go
Past on swift journeyings.
Ironical

Joseph Story
[1779–1845]

[y] Whene'er you speak, remember every cause
Stands not on eloquence, but stands on laws.
*Advice to Young Lawyers.
Stanza 1*

[z] Here shall the Press the People's right maintain,
Unaw'd by influence and unbrib'd by gain;
Here patriot Truth her glorious precepts draw,
Pledg'd to Religion, Liberty, and Law.
Motto of the Salem Register (In Life of Story, Vol. I, Page 127)

William Wetmore Story
[1819–1895]

[a] I sing the hymn of the conquered, who fell in the Battle of Life,—
The hymn of the wounded, the beaten, who died overwhelmed in the strife. . . .
Speak, History! Who are life's victors? Unroll thy long annals and say;
Are they those whom the world calls the victors, who won the success of a day?
The martyrs, or Nero? The Spartans who fell at Thermopylae's tryst,
Or the Persians and Xerxes? Pilate, or Christ?
A Poet's Portfolio. Io Victis

[b] Mosquito critics with a poisonous sting.
*Girolamo,
Detto il Fiorentino*

[c] Man is content to know that he is loved,
And tires the constant phrase "I love" to hear;
But woman doubts the instrument is broke
Unless she daily hear the sweet refrain. *Ginevra da Siena*

William Stoughton
[1631–1701]

[d] God sifted a whole nation that he might send choice grain over into this wilderness.
*Election Sermon at Boston
[April 29, 1669]*

Harriet Beecher Stowe
[1811–1896]

[e] It lies around us like a cloud,
A world we do not see;
Yet the sweet closing of an eye
May bring us there to be.
The Other World. Stanza 1

[f] I 'spect I growed. Don't think nobody never made me.
Uncle Tom's Cabin. Chap. 20

[g] I's wicked—I is. I's mighty wicked, anyhow. I can't help it.
Ibid.

[h] Whipping and abuse are like laudanum: you have to double the dose as the sensibilities decline. *Ibid.*

[i] Legree, taking up a cow-hide, and striking Tom a heavy blow across the cheek, and following up the infliction by a shower of blows. *Ibid. Chap. 33*

Leland Stowe
[1899–   ]

[j] An American will tinker with anything he can put his hands on. But how rarely can he be persuaded to tinker with an abstract idea.
They Shall Not Sleep [1944]

Giles Lytton Strachey
[1880–1932]

[k] In women's hearts he [Disraeli] had always read as in an open book. . . . He realised everything—the interacting complexities of circumstance and character, the pride of place mingled so inextricably with personal arrogance, the super-abundant emotionalism, the ingenuousness of outlook, the solid, the laborious respectability, shot through so incongruously by temperamental cravings for the coloured and the strange, the singular intellectual limitations, and the mysteriously essential female elements impregnating every particle of the whole. A smile hovered over his impassive features, and he dubbed Victoria "the Faery."
Queen Victoria. Chap. 8

[l] Perhaps of all the creations of man language is the most astonishing. *Words and Poetry*

Arthur Stringer
[1874–1950]

[m] Beauty is not immortal. In a day
Blossom and June and rapture pass away. *A Fragile
Thing Is Beauty. Stanza 2*

Simeon Strunsky
[1879–1948]

[n] The milkman alone is enough to redeem the night from its undeserved evil reputation. A cartload of pasteurized milk for nurslings at four o'clock in the

morning represents more service to civilization than a cartful of bullion on its way from the Sub-treasury to the vaults of a national bank five hours later.
Belshazzar Court. Night Life

[o] People who want to understand democracy should spend less time in the library with Aristotle and more time on the buses and in the subway.
No Mean City. Chap. 2

[p] The people whom the sons and daughters find it hardest to understand are the fathers and mothers, but young people can get on very well with the grandfathers and grandmothers.
Ibid. Chap. 18

[q] The years by themselves do not make a place historic. It is men who give the color of history to a place by their deeds there or by merely having lived there.
Ibid. Chap. 27

[r] No man is really depraved who can spend half an hour by himself on the floor playing with his little boy's electric train.
Ibid. Chap. 28

[s] Famous remarks are very seldom quoted correctly.
Ibid. Chap. 38

Jan Struther
(Joyce Anstruther)
[1901–   ]

[t] One day my life will end; and lest
Some whim should prompt you to review it,
Let her who knows the subject best
Tell you the shortest way to do it:

Then say, "Here lies one doubly blest."
Say "She was happy." Say "She knew it." *Betsinda Dances*

[u] She saw every personal relationship as a pair of intersecting circles. . . . Probably perfection is reached when the area of the two outer crescents, added together, is exactly equal to that of the leaf-shaped piece in the middle. On paper there must be some neat mathematical formula for arriving at this; in life, none.
Mrs. Miniver

[v] I think, "London's burning, London's burning,"
I think, "London Bridge is falling down."
Then something wiser than thought says, "Heart, take comfort:
Buildings and bridges do not make a town.

A city is greater than its bricks and mortar;
It is greater than tower or palace, church or hall:
A city's as great as the little people that live there.
You know those people. How can London fall?"
A Londoner in New England, 1941

Mary Stuart, Queen of Scots
[1542–1587]

[w] O Master and Maker! my hope is in thee.
My Jesus, dear Saviour! now set my soul free.
From this my hard prison, my spirit uprisen,
Soars upward to thee.
Thus moaning and groaning, and bending the knee,
I adore, and implore that thou liberate me.
Prayer written before her execution (translated by the Reverend James Freeman Clarke)

William Stubbs
[1825–1901]

[x] The worst cause has often been illustrated with the most heroic virtue, and the world owes some of its greatest debts to men from whose memory it recoils.
Preface to The Constitutional History of England

Geoffrey Anketell Studdert-Kennedy ("Woodbine Willie")
[1883–1929]

[y] When Jesus came to Birmingham, they simply passed Him by,
They never hurt a hair of Him, they only let Him die. . . .
And Jesus crouched against a wall and cried for Calvary.
Indifference

[z] God gave His children memory
That in life's garden there might be
June roses in December.
Roses in December

Sir John Suckling
[1609–1642]

[a] Her feet beneath her petticoat
Like little mice, stole in and out,
As if they feared the light;
But oh, she dances such a way!
No sun upon an Easter-day
Is half so fine a sight. *A Ballad upon a Wedding. Stanza 8*

[b] Why so pale and wan, fond lover?
Prithee, why so pale?

Will, when looking well can't
  move her,
Looking ill prevail?
             Song. Stanza 1

[c] 'Tis not the meat, but 'tis the
  appetite
Makes eating a delight.
      Of Thee, Kind Boy. Stanza 3

[d] Long graces do
But keep good stomachs off, that
  would fall to.
        To Lord Lepington

[e] Out upon it, I have loved
Three whole days together;
And am like to love three more,
  If it prove fair weather.
    A Poem with the Answer.
             Stanza 1

[f] 'Tis expectation makes a
  blessing dear,
Heaven were not heaven, if we
  knew what it were.
     Against Fruition. Stanza 4

[g] Success is a rare paint, hides
  all the ugliness.. *The Tragedy
  of Brennoralt. Act I, Sc. 1*

[h] Sleep is as nice as woman,
The more I court it, the more it
  flies me.   *Ibid. Act II, Sc. 1*

[i] But as when an authentic
  watch is shown,
Each man winds up and rectifies
  his own,
So in our very judgments.
       Aglaura. Epilogue

Charles Sumner
[1811–1874]

[j] There is the National flag. He
must be cold, indeed, who can
look upon its folds rippling in the
breeze without pride of country.
If in a foreign land, the flag is
companionship, and country itself, with all its endearments.
      Are We a Nation?
      [November 19, 1867]

William Graham Sumner
[1840–1910]

[k] The Forgotten Man works
and votes—generally he prays—
but his chief business in life is to
pay. . . .
    Essay, The Forgotten Man

Baroness Bertha von Suttner
[1848–1914]

[l] After the verb "To Love," "To
Help" is the most beautiful verb
in the world!   *Epigram*

Charles Swain
[1803–1874]

[m] Let to-morrow take care of
to-morrow,—
Leave things of the future to
fate;

What's the use to anticipate sorrow?—
Life's troubles come never too
  late!
    Imaginary Evils. Stanza 1

[n] Home's not merely four
  square walls,
Though with pictures hung and
  gilded;
Home is where Affection calls,—
  Filled with shrines the Heart
  hath builded.
        Home. Stanza 1

Jonathan Swift
[1667–1745]

[o] So geographers, in Afric
  maps,
With savage pictures fill their
  gaps,
And o'er unhabitable downs
Place elephants for want of
  towns.
    On Poetry, a Rhapsody

[p] So, naturalists observe, a flea
Hath smaller fleas that on him
  pray;
And these have smaller still to
  bite 'em;
And so proceed *ad infinitum.*
             Ibid.

[q] Conversation is but carving!
Give no more to every guest
Than he's able to digest.
Give him always of the prime,
And but little at a time.
Carve to all but just enough,
Let them neither starve nor
  stuff,
And that you may have your due,
Let your neighbour carve for you.
      Conversation

[r] Under this window in stormy
  weather
I marry this man and woman together;
Let none but Him who rules the
  thunder
Put this man and woman
  asunder.   *Marriage Service
  from His Chamber Window*

[s] And he gave it for his
opinion, that whoever could make
two ears of corn, or two blades of
grass, to grow upon a spot of
ground where only one grew before, would deserve better of mankind, and do more essential
service to his country, than the
whole race of politicians put
together.   *Gulliver's Travels.
  Part II, Chap. VII, Voyage to
           Brobdingnag*

[t] Censure is the tax a man pays
to the public for being eminent.
    Thoughts on Various Subjects

[u] Every man desires to live
long, but no man would be old.
             Ibid.

[v] If Heaven had looked upon riches to be a valuable thing, it would not have given them to such a scoundrel. *Letter to Miss Vanhomrigh [August 12, 1720]*

[w] She's no chicken; she's on the wrong side of thirty, if she be a day.
Polite Conversation. Dialogue I

[x] She wears her clothes as if they were thrown on with a pitch-fork.   *Ibid.*

[y] He was a bold man that first eat an oyster. *Ibid. Dialogue II*

[z] Lord! I wonder what fool it was that first invented kissing.
Ibid.

[a] They say a carpenter's known by his chips.   *Ibid.*

[b] The best doctors in the world are Doctor Diet, Doctor Quiet, and Doctor Merryman.   *Ibid.*

[c] I have fed like a farmer: I shall grow as fat as a porpoise.
Ibid.

[d] I always like to begin a journey on Sundays, because I shall have the prayers of the Church to preserve all that travel by land or by water.   *Ibid.*

[e] I shall be like that tree,—I shall die at the top.
Sir Walter Scott's Life of Swift

[f] Ubi saeva indignatio ulterius cor lacerare nequit:
"Where savage indignation can no longer tear his heart."
Inscription on Swift's grave, St. Patrick's, Dublin

Algernon Charles Swinburne
[1837-1909]
[g] Where the wind's feet shine along the sea.
Laus Veneris. Stanza 14

[h] O sad kissed mouth, how sorrowful it is!   *Ibid. Stanza 79*

[i] There will no man do for your sake, I think,
What I would have done for the least word said.
I had wrung life dry for your lips to drink,
Broken it up for your daily bread.
The Triumph of Time. Stanza 12

[j] I wish we were dead together to-day,
Lost sight of, hidden away out of sight,
Clasped and clothed in the cloven clay,
Out of the world's way, out of the light. *Ibid. Stanza 15*

[k] I will go back to the great sweet mother,
Mother and lover of men, the sea. *Ibid. Stanza 33*

[l] O brother, the gods were good to you. . . .
Be well content as the years wear through;
Give thanks for life, and the loves and lures.
Ibid. Stanza 43

[m] Thou hast conquered, O pale Galilean; the world has grown grey from thy breath;
We have drunken of things Lethean, and fed on the fulness of death.
Laurel is green for a season, and love is sweet for a day;
But love grows bitter with treason, and laurel outlives not May.
Sleep, shall we sleep after all? for the world is not sweet in the end;
For the old faiths loosen and fall, the new years ruin and rend.
Hymn to Proserpine: After the Proclamation in Rome of the Christian Faith

[n] For the glass of the years is brittle wherein we gaze for a span.   *Ibid.*

[o] If love were what the rose is,
And I were like the leaf,
Our lives would grow together
In sad or singing weather.

If you were queen of pleasure,
And I were king of pain,
We'd hunt down love together,
Pluck out his flying feather,
And teach his feet a measure,
And find his mouth a rein.
A Match. Stanzas 1 and 6

[p] Take hand and part with laughter;
Touch lips and part with tears;
Once more and no more after,
Whatever comes with years.
Rococo. Stanza 1

[q] The burden of long living. Thou shalt fear
Waking, and sleeping mourn upon thy bed;
And say at night "Would God the day were here,"
And say at dawn "Would God the day were dead."
A Ballad of Burdens. Stanza 4

[r] Despair the twin-born of devotion. *Dolores. Stanza 14*

[s] What ailed us, O gods, to desert you
For creeds that refuse and restrain?
Come down and redeem us from virtue,
Our Lady of Pain.
Ibid. Stanza 35

[t] Venus rose red out of wine.
Ibid. Stanza 39

[u] From too much love of living,
From hope and fear set free,
We thank with brief thanksgiving
Whatever gods may be
That no life lives forever;
That dead men rise up never;
That even the weariest river
Winds somewhere safe to sea.
The Garden of Proserpine.
Stanza 11

[v] Ah that such sweet things
should be fleet,
Such fleet things sweet!
Félise. Stanza 22

[w] Eyes colored like a water-
flower,
And deeper than the green sea's
glass.   *Ibid. Stanza 36*

[x] Two gifts perforce he has
given us yet,
Though sad things stay and
glad things fly;
Two gifts he has given us, to for-
get
All glad and sad things that go
by,
And then to die.
Ibid. Stanza 56

[y] And the best and the worst of
this is
That neither is most to blame
If you have forgotten my kisses
And I have forgotten your
name.
An Interlude. Stanza 14

[z] By the waters of Babylon we
sat down and wept,
Remembering thee.
Super Flumina Babylonis.
Stanza 1

[a] In the grey beginning of
years, in the twilight of
things that began,
The word of the earth in the ears
of the world, was it God? was
it man?   *Hymn of Man*

[b] Poor   splendid   wings   so
frayed and soiled and torn!
A Ballad of François Villon.
Stanza 3

[c] When darkness is half with-
drawn,
And the skirts of the dead night
cover
The face of the live new dawn.
The Last Oracle

[d] The year of the rose is brief;
From the first blade blown to the
sheaf,
From the thin green leaf to the
gold,
It has time to be sweet and grow
old.
The Year of the Rose, Stanza 1

[e] When the hounds of spring
are on winter's traces.
Atalanta in Calydon. Chorus

[f] For winter's rains and ruins
are over,
And all the season of snows and
sins;
The days dividing lover and lover,
The light that loses, the night
that wins.   *Ibid.*

[g] He weaves, and is clothed
with derision;
Sows, and he shall not reap;
His life is a watch or a vision
Between a sleep and a sleep.
Ibid. Chorus

[h] A little while and I shall
laugh; and then
I shall weep never and laugh not
any more.   *Ibid.*

[i] No sweeter thing than chil-
dren's ways and wiles,
Surely, we say, can gladden eyes
and ears:
Yet sometimes sweeter than their
words or smiles
Are even their tears.
A Child's Pity. Stanza 1

[j] All the bells of heaven may
ring,
All the birds of heaven may sing,
All the wells on earth may spring,
All the winds on earth may bring
All sweet sounds together.
A Child's Laughter. Stanza 1

[k] Faith in faith established
evermore
Stands a sea-mark in the tides of
time.   *A Sea-Mark. Stanza 5*

[l] Is not Precedent indeed a
King of men?   *A Word from*
the Psalmist. Stanza 4

[m] Stately, kindly, lordly friend
Condescend
Here to sit by me.   *To a Cat*

[n] A baby's feet, like sea-shells
pink,
Might tempt, should heaven see
meet,
An angel's lips to kiss, we think,
A baby's feet.
Étude Réaliste. I, 1

[o] All our past acclaims our
future: Shakespeare's voice
and Nelson's hand,
Milton's faith and Wordsworth's
trust in this our chosen and
chainless land,
Bear as witness: come the world
against her, England yet shall
stand.   *England, An Ode. II, 5*

[p] To wipe off the froth of falsehood from the foaming lips of in-
ebriated virtue, when fresh from
the sexless orgies of morality and
reeling from the delirious riot of
religion,   may   doubtless   be   a
charitable office.
Under the Microscope

John Addington Symonds
[1840–1893]

[q] Gods fade; but God abides
and in man's heart
Speaks with the clear unconquerable cry
Of energies and hopes that can
not die.
Sonnet, On the Sacro Monte

[r] She smiled, and the shadows
departed;
She shone, and the snows were
rain;
And he who was frozen-hearted
Bloomed up into love again.
Eyebright

Arthur Symons
[1865–1945]

[s] And I would have, now love
is over,
An end to all, an end:
I cannot, having been your lover,
Stoop to become your friend!
After Love. Stanza 3

[t] As a perfume doth remain
In the folds where it hath lain,
So the thought of you, remaining
Deeply folded in my brain,
Will not leave me: all things leave
me:
You remain.   *Memory. Stanza 1*

[u] Life is a dream in the night,
a fear among fears,
A naked runner lost in a storm of
spears.   *In the Wood of
Finvara. Stanza 1*

[v] Kind saint who findest what
is lost, I pray,
Bring back her heart: I lost it
yesterday.   *A Prayer to
Saint Anthony of Padua*

[w] Without charm there can be
no fine literature, as there can be
no perfect flower without fragrance.
*The Symbolist Movement in
Literature. Stéphane Mallarmé*

[x] The mystic too full of God to
speak intelligibly to the world.
Ibid. Arthur Rimbaud

[y] Criticism is properly the rod
of divination: a hazel-switch for
the discovery of buried treasure,
not a birch-twig for the castiga-
tion of offenders.
*An Introduction to the Study
of Browning. Preface*

John Millington Synge
[1871–1909]

[z] What is the price of a thousand horses against a son where
there is one son only?
Riders to the Sea

[a] Bartley will have a fine coffin
out of the white boards, and a

deep grave surely. What more can
we want than that? No man at all
can be living for ever, and we
must be satisfied.   *Ibid.*

[b] May I meet him with one
tooth and it aching, and one eye
to be seeing seven and seventy
divils in the twists of the road,
and one old timber leg on him to
limp into the scalding grave.
There he is now crossing the
strands, and that the Lord God
would send a high wave to wash
him from the world.
*The Playboy of the Western
World. Act II*

[c] A man who is not afraid of
the sea will soon be drownded, he
said, for he will be going out on
a day he shouldn't. But we do be
afraid of the sea, and we do only
be drownded now and again.
The Aran Islands. Page 127

[d] There is no language like the
Irish for soothing and quieting.
Ibid. Page 180

Lee Szilard
[1898–   ]

[e] We turned the switch, we
saw the flashes, we watched them
for about ten minutes—and then
we switched everything off and
went home. That night I knew
that the world was headed for
sorrow. [Describing an experiment in uranium fission made
March 3, 1939.]   *Speech at 80th
anniversary dinner of The
Nation, December 3, 1945*

John Banister Tabb
[1845–1909]

[f] When Christ was taken from
the rood,
One thorn upon the ground,
Still moistened with the Precious
Blood,
An early robin found,
And wove it crosswise in his nest,
Where, lo, it reddened all his
breast!   *Robin Redbreast*

[g] The ghost am I
Of winds that die
Alike on land or sea.
The Fog. Stanza 1

[h] Before a clock was in the
tower
Or e'er a watch was worn,
I knew of night the passing hour
And prophesied the morn;
To man of every age and clime
The oldest chronicler of time.
The Cock

[i] Out of the dusk a shadow,
Then a spark;
Out of the cloud a silence,
Then a lark;

Out of the heart a rapture,
  Then a pain;
Out of the dead, cold ashes,
  Life again.   *Evolution*

[j] With locks of gold to-day;
  To-morrow silver-gray;
Then blossom-bald. Behold,
O man, thy fortune told!
          The Dandelion

[k] Why should I stay? Nor seed
  nor fruit have I,
But, sprung at once to beauty's
  perfect round,
Nor loss nor gain nor change in
  me is found,—
A life-complete in death-complete
  to die.   *The Bubble*

Tacitus
[A.D. 54–119]
*The Oxford Translation. Bohn
Classical Library*

[l] He had talents equal to business, and aspired no higher.
      Annals. VI, 39, 17

[m] Some might consider him as
too fond of fame; for the desire
of glory clings even to the best
men longer than any other passion.   *History. IV, 6, 36*

Genevieve Taggard
[1894–1948]

[n] Drink iron from rare springs;
  follow the sun;
Go far
To get the beam of some medici-
  nal star;
Or in your anguish run
The gauntlet of all zones to an
  ultimate one.
Fever and chill
Punish you still,
Earth has no zone to work against
  your will.
*Of the Properties of Nature for
Healing an Illness. Stanza 2*

[o] Defiant even now, it tugs
  and moans
To be untangled from these
  mother's bones.
      With Child. Stanza 3

Rabindranath Tagore
[1861–1941]

[p] Peace, my heart, let the time
  for parting be sweet.
Let it not be a death but com-
  pleteness.
Let love melt into memory and
  pain into songs.   *Peace*

[q] Come out of thyself,
  Stand in the open;
Within thy heart wilt thou hear
  The response of all the world.
    Sheaves. The Invitation

[r] When I bring you coloured
toys, my child, I understand why
there is such a play of colours on

clouds, on water, and why flowers
are painted in tints.   *The Crescent Moon. When and Why*

[s] I do not love him because he
is good, but because he is my little
child.   *Ibid. The Judge*

[t] I alone have a right to blame
and punish, for he only may
chastise who loves.   *Ibid.*

Sir Thomas Noon Talfourd
[1795–1854]

[u]   'Tis a little thing
To give a cup of water; yet its
  draught
Of cool refreshment, drained by
  fevered lips,
May give a shock of pleasure to
  the frame
More exquisite than when nec-
  tarean juice
Renews the life of joy in happiest
  hours.   *Ion. Act 1, Sc. 2*

[v]   Fill the seats of justice
With good men, not so absolute
  in goodness
As to forget what human frailty
  is.   *Ibid. Act V*

Charles Maurice de
Talleyrand-Périgord
[1754–1838]

[w] Black as the devil,
Hot as hell,
Pure as an angel,
Sweet as love.   *Recipe for Coffee*

Eva March Tappan
[1854–1930]

[x] We drove the Indians out of
  the land,
But a dire revenge these redmen
  planned,
For they fastened a name to every
  nook,
And every boy with a spelling-
  book
Will have to toil till his hair turns
  gray
Before he can spell them the
  proper way.
    On the Cape. Stanza 1

Newton Booth Tarkington
[1869–1946]

[y] Penrod was doing something
very unusual and rare, something
almost never accomplished except
by coloured people or by a boy in
school on a spring day: he was
doing really nothing at all. He
was merely a state of being.
      Penrod. Chap. 8

[z] They were upon their great
theme: "When I get to be a man!"
Being human, though boys, they
considered their present estate
too commonplace to be dwelt

upon. So, when the old men gather, they say: "When I was a boy!" It really is the land of now-adays that we never discover.
Ibid. Chap. 26

Richard Henry Tawney
[1880–   ]

[a] The burden of our civilization is . . . that industry itself has come to hold a position of exclusive predominance among human interests, which no single interest, and least of all the provision of the material means of existence, is fit to occupy.
The Acquisitive Society

Ann Taylor
[1782–1866]
See also her sister Jane Taylor

[b] Oh, that it were my chief delight
To do the things I ought!
Then let me try with all my might
To mind what I am taught.
For a Very Little Child

[c] 'Twas fancied by some, who but slightly had seen them,
There was not a pin to be chosen between them.
Jane and Eliza. Stanza 2

Bayard Taylor
[1825–1878]

[d]   Till the sun grows cold,
And the stars are old,
And the leaves of the Judgment Book unfold.   *Bedouin Song*

[e] They sang of love, and not of fame;
Forgot was Britain's glory;
Each heart recalled a different name,
But all sang "Annie Laurie."
The Song of the Camp. Stanza 5

[f] The bravest are the tenderest.
Ibid. Stanza 11

[g]   The sun has risen; not a vapor streaks the dawn,
And the frosty prairie brightens to the westward, far and wan.
The Bison Track. Stanza 1

[h] The violet loves a sunny bank,
The cowslip loves the lea;
The scarlet creeper loves the elm,
But I love—thee.
Proposal. Stanza 1

[i] Hark how the rain is pouring
Over the roof, in the pitch-black night,
And the wind in the woods a-roaring.
A Story for a Child [A Night with a Wolf]. Stanza 1

[j]   Each little life
Thinks the great axle of the universe
Turns on its fate, and finds impertinence
In joy or grief conflicting with its own.   *Lars, A Pastoral of Norway. Book I*

[k] Learn to live, and live to learn,
Ignorance like a fire doth burn,
Little tasks make large return.
To My Daughter. Stanza 1

Bert Leston Taylor
[1866–1921]

[l] When quacks with pills political would dope us,
When politics absorbs the livelong day,
I like to think about the star Canopus,
So far, so far away!
Canopus. Stanza 1

[m] I meditate on interstellar spaces,
And smoke a mild seegar.
Ibid. Stanza 4

[n] Hate of the millions who've choked you down,
In country kitchen or house in town,
We love a thousand, we hate but one,
With a hate more hot than the hate of the Gun—
Bread Pudding!   *Chant of Hate for Bread Pudding. Stanza 2*

[o] These scoffers, these obstructionists,
These fossils—who are they?
The glad young, mad young futurists
Who prance around to-day.
So Shall It Be. Stanza 6

[p] Everywhere I look I see—
Fact or fiction, life or play,
Still the little game of Three:
B and C in love with A.
Old Stuff. Stanza 3

[q] Consider, friends, this trio—
How little fuss they made.
They didn't curse when it was worse
Than ninety in the shade.
They moved about serenely
Within the furnace bright,
And soon forgot that it was hot,
With "no relief in sight."
A Hot Weather Classic: Shadrach, Meshach, and Abed-nego. Stanza 4

[r] Behold the mighty Dinosaur,
Famous in prehistoric lore . . .
The creature had two sets of brains—
One in his head (the usual place),
The other at his spinal base.

Thus he could reason *a priori*
As well as *a posteriori*.
The Dinosaur

Sir Henry Taylor
[1800–1886]

[s]   His food
Was glory, which was poison to
his mind
And peril to his body.
*Philip Van Artevelde.
Part I, Act I, Sc. 5*

[t] He that lacks time to mourn,
lacks time to mend.
Eternity mourns that. 'Tis an ill
cure
For life's worst ills, to have no
time to feel them.   *Ibid.*

[u]   Such souls,
Whose sudden visitations daze
the world,
Vanish like lightning, but they
leave behind
A voice that in the distance far
away
Wakens the slumbering ages.
Ibid.

Jane Taylor
[1783–1824]

[v] Though man a thinking be-
ing is defined,
Few use the grand prerogative of
mind.
How few think justly of the
thinking few!
How many never think, who
think they do!
*Essays in Rhyme. On Morals and
Manners, Prejudice, Essay I,
Stanza 45*

[w] Who ran to help me when I
fell,
And would some pretty story tell,
Or kiss the place to make it well?
My mother.
My Mother. Stanza 6

[x] One honest John Tompkins,
a hedger and ditcher,
Although he was poor, did not
want to be richer;
For all such vain wishes in him
were prevented
By a fortunate habit of being
contented.
*Contented John [Honest
John Tompkins]. Stanza 1*

[y] "Take a seat," said the cow,
gently waving her hand;
"By no means, dear madam,"
said he, "while you stand."
The Cow and the Ass. Stanza 4

[z] Twinkle, twinkle, little star,
How I wonder what you are,
Up above the world so high,
Like a diamond in the sky.
*The Star [with Ann Taylor].
Stanza 1*

Jeremy Taylor
[1613–1667]

[a] When Abraham sat at his
tent-door . . . he espied an old
man stooping and leaning on his
staffe, weary with age and trav-
elle, coming toward him, who
was an hundred years of age; he
received him kindly, washed his
feet, provided supper, caused him
to sit down; but observing that
the old man eat and prayed not,
nor begged for a blessing on his
meat, asked him why he did not
worship the God of heaven. The
old man told him that he wor-
shiped the fire only, and acknowledged no other God: at which
answer Abraham grew so zeal-
ously angry, that he thrust the
old man out of his tent, and exposed him to all the evils of the
night and an unguarded condition. When the old man was
gone, God called to him and
asked him where the stranger
was; he replied, "I thrust him
away because he did not worship
thee"; God answered him, "I have
suffered him these hundred years,
although he dishonored me, and
couldst thou not endure him one
night, when he gave thee no
trouble?" Upon this, saith the
story, Abraham fetcht him back
again, and gave him hospitable
entertainment and wise instruction.   *The Liberty
of Prophesying. Page 606*

[b] We long for perishing meat,
and fill our stomachs with corruption; we look after white and
red, and the weaker beauties of
the night; we are passionate after
rings and seals . . . our hearts are
hard and inflexible, having no
loves for anything but strange
flesh, and heaps of money, and
popular noises; and therefore we
are a huge way off from the King-
dome of God.   *XXV Sermons*

[c] Every man hath in his own
life sins enough, in his own minde
trouble enough: so that curiositie
after the affairs of others cannot
be without envy and an evil
minde. What is it to me if my
Neighbours Grandfather were a
Syrian, or his Grandmother ille-
gitimate, or that another is in-
debted five thousand pounds, or
whether his wife be expensive?
Holy Living

John Taylor
("The Water Poet")
[1580–1625]

[d] Laugh and be fat.
Title of a tract

[e] God sends meat, and the
Devil sends cooks.   *Works. Vol.
II, Page 85 [ed. 1630]*

Tom Taylor
[1817–1880]

[f] This rail-splitter a true-born
king of men.

How his quaint wit made home-
truth seem more true.

The Old World and the New, from
sea to sea,
Utter one voice of sympathy and
shame.
Sore heart, so stopped when it at
last beat high!
Sad life, cut short, just as its
triumph came!
*Abraham Lincoln Foully Assas-
sinated, Stanzas 5, 6, and 17 [In
Punch, May 6, 1865. (It was at a
performance of Taylor's play,
Our American Cousin, that Lincoln was shot)]*

Sara Teasdale
[1884–1933]

[g] When I can look Life in the
eyes,
Grown calm and very coldly wise,
Life will have given me the Truth,
And taken in exchange—my
youth.   *Wisdom*

[h] Strephon's kiss was lost in
jest,
Robin's lost in play,
But the kiss in Colin's eyes
Haunts me night and day.
The Look. Stanza 2

[i] I must have passed the crest
a while ago
And now I am going down—
Strange to have crossed the crest
and not to know,
But the brambles were always
catching the hem of my gown.
The Long Hill. Stanza 1

[j] Never think she loves him
wholly,
Never believe her love is blind,
All his faults are locked securely
In a closet of her mind.
Appraisal

[k] For better than the minting
Of a gold crowned king
Is the safe kept memory
Of a lovely thing.
The Coin

Sir William Temple
[1628–1699]

[l] When all is done, human life
is, at the greatest and the best,
but like a froward child, that must
be played with and humoured a

little to keep it quiet till it falls
asleep, and then the care is over.
Miscellanea. Part II, Of Poetry

William Temple
(Archbishop of York)
[1881–1944]

[m] There is no structural organization of society which can
bring about the coming of the
Kingdom of God on earth, since
all systems can be perverted by
the selfishness of man.
The Malvern Manifesto

[n] Human status ought not to
depend upon the changing demands of the economic process.
Ibid.

Edward Wyndham Tennant
[1897–1916]

[o] I saw green banks of daffodil,
Slim poplars in the breeze,
Great tan-brown hares in gusty
March
A-courting on the leas:
And meadows with their glittering
streams, and silver scurrying
dace,
Home—what a perfect place.
*Home Thoughts in Laventie.
Stanza 8*

Alfred, Lord Tennyson
[1809–1892]

[p] A still small voice spake unto
me,
"Thou art so full of misery,
Were it not better not to be?"
The Two Voices. Stanza 1

[q] Tho' thou wert scattered to
the wind,
Yet is there plenty of the kind.
Ibid. Stanza 11

[r] No life that breathes with hu-
man breath
Has ever truly longed for death.
Ibid. Stanza 132

[s] O love, O fire! once he drew
With one long kiss my whole soul
through
My lips, as sunlight drinketh dew.
Fatima. Stanza 3

[t] I built my soul a lordly pleas-
ure-house,
Wherein at ease for aye to dwell.
The Palace of Art. Stanza 1

[u] A simple maiden in her flower
Is worth a hundred coats-of-
arms.   *Lady Clara Vere de
Vere. Stanza 2*

[v] Howe'er it be, it seems to me,
'Tis only noble to be good.
Kind hearts are more than coro-
nets,
And simple faith than Norman
blood.   *Ibid. Stanza 7*

[w] You must wake and call me
early, call me early, mother
dear;
To-morrow 'ill be the happiest
time of all the glad New
Year,—
Of all the glad New Year, mother,
the maddest, merriest day;
For I'm to be Queen o' the May,
mother, I'm to be Queen o'
the May.
The May Queen. Stanza 1

[x] There is sweet music here
that softer falls
Than petals from blown roses on
the grass. . . .
Music that gentlier on the spirit
lies,
Than tir'd eyelids upon tir'd eyes;
Music that brings sweet sleep
down from the blissful skies.
*The Lotos-Eaters. Choric Song,
Stanza 1*

[y] All things are taken from us,
and become
Portions and parcels of the dreadful Past.   *Ibid.*

[z] The spacious times of great
Elizabeth.   *A Dream of Fair
Women. Stanza 2*

[a] A daughter of the gods,
divinely tall,
And most divinely fair.
Ibid. Stanza 22

[b] The old order changeth,
yielding place to new;
And God fulfils himself in many
ways,
Lest one good custom should corrupt the world.
Morte D'Arthur. Line 408

[c] More things are wrought by
prayer
Than this world dreams of.
Wherefore, let thy voice
Rise like a fountain for me night
and day.   *Ibid. Line 415*

[d] My first, last love; the idol of
my youth,
The darling of my manhood, and,
alas!
Now the most blessed memory of
mine age!
The Gardener's Daughter

[e] How dull it is to pause, to
make an end,
To rust unburnish'd, not to shine
in use,
As tho' to breathe were life!
Ulysses

[f] In the spring a young man's
fancy lightly turns to thoughts
of love.   *Locksley Hall.
Line 20*

[g] He will hold thee, when his
passion shall have spent its
novel force,

Something better than his dog, a
little dearer than his horse.
Ibid. Line 49

[h] With a little hoard of maxims
preaching down a daughter's
heart.   *Ibid. Line 94*

[i] But the jingling of the guinea
helps the hurt that Honour
feels.   *Ibid. Line 105*

[j] For I dipt into the future, far
as human eye could see,
Saw the Vision of the world, and
all the wonder that would be;
Saw the heavens fill with commerce, argosies of magic sails,
Pilots of the purple twilight,
dropping down with costly
bales;
Heard the heavens fill with shouting, and there rain'd a ghastly
dew
From the nations' airy navies
grappling in the central blue
Ibid. Line 119

[k] Till the war drum throbbed
no longer and the battle flags
were furled
In the Parliament of Man, the
Federation of the world.
Ibid. Line 127

[l] Woman is the lesser man.
Ibid. Line 151

[m] I the heir of all the ages in
the foremost files of time.
Ibid. Line 178

[n] Let the great world spin forever down the ringing grooves
of change.   *Ibid. Line 182*

[o] My strength is as the strength
of ten,
Because my heart is pure.
Sir Galahad. Stanza 1

[p] And wheresoe'r thou move,
good luck
Shall fling her old shoe after.
*Will Waterproof's Lyrical
Monologue. Stanza 27*

[q] But O for the touch of a vanished hand,
And the sound of a voice that is
still!

But the tender grace of a day that
is dead
Will never come back to me.
*Break, Break, Break.
Stanzas 3 and 4*

[r] Cast all your cares on God;
that anchor holds.
Enoch Arden

[s] For men may come and men
may go,
But I go on forever.
The Brook

[t] Insipid as the queen upon a
card.   *Aylmer's Field*

[u] Marriages are made in Heaven. *Ibid.*

[v] Mastering the lawless science of our law,
That codeless myriad of precedent,
That wilderness of single instances. *Ibid.*

[w] Is it so true that second thoughts are best?
Sea Dreams

[x] He that wrongs his friend
Wrongs himself more. *Ibid.*

[y] With prudes for proctors, dowagers for deans,
And sweet girl-graduates in their golden hair. *The Princess. Prologue, Line 141*

[z] A rosebud set with little wilful thorns,
And sweet as English air could make her, she.
Ibid. Line 153

[a] A little street half garden and half house.
Ibid. Part I, Line 211

[b] When we fall out with those we love
And kiss again with tears.
Ibid. Part II, Song

[c] Sweet and low,
Wind of the western sea.
Ibid. Part III, Song

[d] Blow, bugle, blow, set the wild echoes flying,
Blow, bugle; answer, echoes, dying, dying, dying.
Ibid. Part IV, Song, Stanza 1

[e] Sweet is every sound . . .
Myriads of rivulets hurrying thro' the lawn,
The moan of doves in immemorial elms,
And murmuring of innumerable bees.
Ibid. Part VII, Line 203

[f]   Happy he
With such a mother! faith in womankind
Beats with his blood, and trust in all things high
Comes easy to him; and tho' he trip and fall,
He shall not blind his soul with clay. *Ibid. Line 308*

[g] As the greatest only are,
In his simplicity sublime.
Ode on the Death of the Duke of Wellington. Stanza 4

[h] All in the valley of death
Rode the six hundred.

Some one had blundered:
Theirs not to make reply,
Theirs not to reason why,
Theirs but to do and die.

Cannon to right of them,
Cannon to left of them,

Cannon in front of them. . . .
Into the jaws of death,
Into the mouth of hell
Rode the six hundred.
The Charge of the Light Brigade. Stanzas 1, 2, and 3

[i] That a lie which is half a truth is ever the blackest of lies,
That a lie which is all a lie may be met and fought with outright,
But a lie which is part a truth is a harder matter to fight.
The Grandmother. Stanza 8

[j] Flower in the crannied wall,
I pluck you out of the crannies,
I hold you here, root and all, in my hand,
Little flower—but if I could understand
What you are, root and all, and all in all,
I should know what God and man is. *Flower in the Crannied Wall*

[k] Let knowledge grow from more to more.
In Memoriam. Prologue, Stanza 7

[l] I sometimes hold it half a sin
To put in words the grief I feel.
Ibid. Part V, Stanza 1

[m]   Never morning wore
To evening, but some heart did break. *Ibid. Part VI, Stanza 2*

[n] And from his ashes may be made
The violet of his native land.
Ibid. Part XVIII, Stanza 1

[o] 'Tis better to have loved and lost
Than never to have loved at all.
Ibid. Part XXVII. Stanza 4 (also Part LXXXV, Stanza 1)

[p] Her eyes are homes of silent prayer. *Ibid. Part XXXII, Stanza 1*

[q] Whose faith has centre everywhere,
Nor cares to fix itself to form.
Ibid. Part XXXIII, Stanza 1

[r] How fares it with the happy dead? *Ibid. Part XLIV, Stanza 1*

[s] Short swallow-flights of song, that dip
Their wings in tears, and skim away. *Ibid. Part XLVIII, Stanza 4*

[t]   But what am I?
An infant crying in the night:
An infant crying for the light:
And with no language but a cry.
Ibid. Part LIV, Stanza 5

[u] So careful of the type she seems,
So careless of the single life.
Ibid. Part LV, Stanza 2

[v] The great world's altar-stairs,
That slope through darkness up to God. *Ibid. Stanza 4*

[w] So many worlds, so much to do,
So little done, such things to be.
Ibid. Part LXXIII, Stanza 1

[x] Thy leaf has perished in the green,
And, while we breathe beneath the sun,
The world which credits what is done
Is cold to all that might have been.
Ibid. Part LXXV, Stanza 4

[y] God's fingers touch'd him, and he slept.
Ibid. Part LXXXV, Stanza 5

[z] There lives more faith in honest doubt,
Believe me, than in half the creeds. *Ibid. Part XCVI, Stanza 3*

[a] Ring out, wild bells, to the wild sky!

Ring out the old, ring in the new,
Ring, happy bells, across the snow! *Ibid. Part CVI, Stanzas 1 and 2*

[b] Ring in the valiant man and free,
The larger heart, the kindlier hand!
Ring out the darkness of the land,
Ring in the Christ that is to be!
Ibid. Stanza 8

[c] And thus he bore without abuse
The grand old name of gentleman,
Defamed by every charlatan,
And soiled with all ignoble use.
Ibid. Part CXI, Stanza 6

[d] Wearing all that weight
Of learning lightly like a flower.
Ibid. Conclusion, Stanza 10

[e] Faultily faultless, icily regular, splendidly null.
Maud. Part I, II

[f] Gorgonized me from head to foot,
With a stony British stare.
Ibid. XIII, Stanza 2

[g] Come into the garden, Maud,
For the black bat, night, has flown,
Come into the garden, Maud,
I am here at the gate alone.
Ibid. XXII, Stanza 1

[h] She is coming, my own, my sweet;
Were it ever so airy a tread. . .
My dust would hear her and beat,
Had I lain for a century dead.
Ibid. Stanza 11

[i] Ah Christ, that it were possible
For one short hour to see
The souls we loved, that they might tell us
What and where they be.
Ibid. Part II, IV, Stanza 3

[j] Wearing the white flower of a blameless life,
Before a thousand peering littlenesses,
In that fierce light which beats upon a throne.
Idylls of the King. Dedication, Line 24

[k] Eyes of pure women, wholesome stars of love.
Ibid. Gareth and Lynette, Line 367

[l] Lightly was her slender nose
Tip-tilted like the petal of a flower. *Ibid. Line 576*

[m] For man is man and master of his fate. *Ibid. Geraint and Enid, I, Line 355*

[n] The useful trouble of the rain. *Ibid. II, Line 770*

[o] The world will not believe a man repents;
And this wise world of ours is mainly right. *Ibid. Line 899*

[p] Mere white truth in simple nakedness.
Ibid. Balin and Balan, Line 509

[q] As love, if love be perfect, casts out fear,
So hate, if hate be perfect, casts out fear. *Ibid. Merlin and Vivien, Line 41*

[r] It is the little rift within the lute,
That by and by will make the music mute,
And ever widening slowly silence all. *Ibid. Line 386*

[s] Blind and naked Ignorance
Delivers brawling judgments, unashamed,
On all things all day long.
Ibid. Line 662

[t] For men at most differ as heaven and earth,
But women, worst and best, as heaven and hell.
Ibid. Line 812

[u'] But, friend, to me
He is all fault who hath no fault at all.
For who loves me must have a touch of earth.
Ibid. Lancelot and Elaine, Line 132

CHARLES TENNYSON-TURNER—TERENCE 397

[v]   In me there dwells
No greatness, save it be some far-
    off touch
Of greatness to know well I am
    not great.   *Ibid. Line 447*

[w] Sweet is true love tho' given
    in vain, in vain.
            Ibid. Line 1000

[x] As when we dwell upon a
    word we know,
Repeating, till the word we know
    so well
Becomes a wonder, and we know
    not why.   *Ibid. Line 1020*

[y] He makes no friend who never
    made a foe. *Ibid. Line 1082*

[z] The vow that binds too
    strictly snaps itself.
        *Ibid. The Last Tournament,
                    Line 652*

[a] For courtesy wins woman all
    as well
As valor may.   *Ibid. Line 702*

[b] For manners are not idle, but
    the fruit
Of loyal nature and of noble mind.
        Ibid. Guinevere, Line 333

[c] No more subtle master under
    heaven
Than is the maiden passion for a
    maid,
Not only to keep down the base in
    man
But teach high thought, and
    amiable words
And courtliness, and the desire of
    fame
And love of truth, and all that
    makes a man.
            Ibid. Line 475

[d] I found Him in the shining
    of the stars,
I mark'd Him in the flowering of
    His fields,
But in His ways with men I find
    Him not. . . .
For why is all around us here
As if some lesser god had made
    the world,
But had not force to shape it as he
    would?   *Ibid. The Passing
                of Arthur, Line 9*

[e]   The golden guess
Is morning-star to the full round
    of truth.   *Columbus*

[f] The song that nerves a na-
    tion's heart
Is in itself a deed.
        *The Charge of the Heavy
                Brigade. Epilogue*

[g] Charm us, orator, till the lion
    look no larger than the cat.
    *Locksley Hall Sixty Years After.
                        Line 112*

[h] Be patient. Our Playwright
    may show
In some fifth act what this wild
    Drama means.   *The Play*

[i]   A mastiff dog
May love a puppy cur for no more
    reason
Than that the twain have been
    tied up together.
            Queen Mary. Act I, Sc. 4

[j] Old men must die, or the
    world would grow mouldy,
    would only breed the past
    again.   *Becket. Prologue*

[k] Not of the sunlight,
Not of the moonlight,
Not of the starlight!
O young Mariner,
Down to the haven,
Call your companions,
Launch your vessel
And crowd your canvas,
And, ere it vanishes
Over the margin,
After it, follow it,
Follow the Gleam.
    Merlin and the Gleam. Stanza 10

[l] Sunset and evening star,
    And one clear call for me!
And may there be no moaning of
    the bar,
When I put out to sea.

Twilight and evening bell,
And after that the dark.
        *Crossing the Bar. Stanzas 1
                        and 3*

[m] I hope to meet my Pilot face
        to face
When I have crossed the bar.
            Ibid. Stanza 4

Charles Tennyson-Turner
[1808–1879]

[n] The shadow of our travelling
    earth
Hung on the silver moon.
        Eclipse of the Moon

[o] The little moulted feathers,
    saffron-tipt,
The perches, which his faltering
    feet embraced,
All these remain—not even his
    bath removed—
But where's the spray and flutter
    that we loved?
            The Vacant Cage

Terence
[185–159 B.C.]
*Translation by Henry Thomas
Riley. The references are to the
text of the Bohn Classical Library.*

[p] The quarrels of lovers are
the renewal of love.   *Andria.
        Act III, Sc. 3, Line 23 (555)*

[q] Immortal gods! how much
does one man excel another! What
a difference there is between a
wise person and a fool!
    *Eunuchus. Act II, Sc. 2, Line 1
                            (232)*

[r] I have everything, yet have nothing; and although I possess nothing, still of nothing am I in want.   *Ibid. Line 12 (243)*

[s] Jupiter, now assuredly is the time when I could readily consent to be slain, lest life should sully this ecstasy with some disaster.   *Ibid. Act III, Sc. 5, Line 2 (550)*

[t] I know the disposition of women: when you will, they won't; when you won't, they set their hearts upon you of their own inclination.   *Ibid. Act IV, Sc. 7, Line 42 (812)*

[u] I took to my heels as fast as I could.   *Ibid. Act V, Sc. 2, Line 5 (844)*

[v] Many a time a man cannot be such as he would be, if circumstances do not admit of it.
Heauton Timoroumenos. Act IV, Sc. 1, Line 53 (666)

[w] Rigorous law is often rigorous injustice.   *Ibid. Sc. 4, Line 48 (796)*

[x] There is nothing so easy but that it becomes difficult when you do it with reluctance.
Ibid. Sc. 5, Line 1 (805)

[y] As many men, so many minds; every one his own way.
Phormio. Act II, Sc. 4, Line 14 (454)

[z] It is the common vice of all, in old age, to be too intent upon our interests.   *Adelphoe. Act V, Sc. 8, Line 30 (953)*

Tertullian
[A.D. 160–240]

[a] See how these Christians love one another.   *Apologeticus. 39*

[b] Blood of the martyrs is the seed of the Church.   *Ibid. 50*

William Makepeace Thackeray
[1811–1863]

[c] Christmas is here:
Winds whistle shrill,
Icy and chill,
Little care we;
Little we fear
Weather without.
The Mahogany Tree. Stanza 1

[d] Though more than half the world was his,
He died without a rood his own;
And borrow'd from his enemies
Six foot of ground to lie upon.
[Napoleon]
The Chronicle of the Drum. Part II

[e] Werther had a love for Charlotte
Such as words could never utter;
Would you know how first he met her?
She was cutting bread and butter.

Charlotte, having seen his body
Borne before her on a shutter,
Like a well-conducted person,
Went on cutting bread and butter.   *Sorrows of Werther [parody of Goethe]. Stanzas 1 and 4*

[f] This Bouillabaisse a noble dish is—
A sort of soup, or broth, or brew.
The Ballad of Bouillabaisse. Stanza 2

[g] A man—I let the truth out—
Who's had almost every tooth out,
Cannot sing as once he sung,
When he was young as you are young,
When he was young and lutes were strung,
And love-lamps in the casement hung.
Mrs. Katherine's Lantern. Stanza 6

[h] The rose upon my balcony the morning air perfuming,
Was leafless all the winter time and pining for the spring.
The Rose Upon My Balcony. Stanza 1

[i] I'm no angel.
Vanity Fair. Vol. I, Chap. 2

[j] This I set down as a positive truth. A woman with fair opportunities, and without an absolute hump, may marry whom she likes.
Ibid. Chap. 4

[k] Everybody in Vanity Fair must have remarked how well those live who are comfortably and thoroughly in debt; how they deny themselves nothing; how jolly and easy they are in their minds.   *Ibid. Chap. 22*

[l] Mother is the name for God in the lips and hearts of little children.   *Ibid. Chap. 37*

[m] I think I could be a good woman if I had five thousand a year.   *Ibid. Vol. II, Chap. 1*

[n] A comfortable career of prosperity, if it does not make people honest, at least keeps them so.   *Ibid.*

[o] 'Tis strange what a man may do and a woman yet think him an angel.
Henry Esmond. Chap. 7

[p] The book of female logic is blotted all over with tears, and Justice in their courts is forever

in a passion.   *The Virginians.*
                              Chap. 4

[q] Heaven does not choose its
elect from among the great and
wealthy.   *Ibid. Chap. 5*

[r] Women like not only to conquer, but to be conquered.
                              Ibid.

[s] Next to the very young, I
suppose the very old are the most
selfish.   *Ibid. Chap. 61*

[t] 'Tis hard with respect to
Beauty, that its possessor should
not have even a life-enjoyment of
it, but be compelled to resign it
after, at the most, some forty
years' lease.   *Ibid. Chap. 73*

[u] For a steady self-esteem and
indomitable confidence in our
own courage, greatness, magnanimity, who can compare with
Britons, except their children
across the Atlantic?
                    Ibid. Chap. 89

[v] Remember, it's as easy to
marry a rich woman as a poor
woman.   *Pendennis. Chap. 28*

[w] Of the Corporation of the
Goosequill—of the Press, . . . of
the fourth estate. . . . There she
is—the great engine—she never
sleeps. She has her ambassadors
in every quarter of the world—
her courtiers upon every road. Her
officers march along with armies,
and her envoys walk into statesmen's cabinets. They are ubiqui-
tous.   *Ibid. Chap. 30*

[x] The best way is to make your
letters safe. I never wrote a letter
in all my life that would commit
me, and demmy, sir, I have had
some experience of women.
                    Ibid. Chap. 64

[y] The wicked are wicked, no
doubt, and they go astray and
they fall, and they come by their
deserts; but who can tell the mischief which the very virtuous do?
          The Newcomes. Chap. 20

[z] A peculiar sweet smile shone
over his face, and he lifted up his
head a little, and quickly said
"Adsum!" and fell back. It was
the word we used at school, when
names were called; and lo, he,
whose heart was as that of a little
child, had answered to his name,
and stood in the presence of The
Master.
                    Ibid. Chap. 80

[a] A pedigree reaching as far
back as the Deluge.
The Rose and the Ring. Chap. 2

[b] Bravery never goes out of
fashion.   *The Four Georges.*
                              George II

Celia Laighton Thaxter
[1835–1894]

[c] Sad soul, take comfort, nor
forget
That sunrise never failed us yet.
          *The Sunrise Never Failed
          Us Yet. Stanza 4*

[d] Already the dandelions
Are changed into vanishing
ghosts.   *Already*

[e] From wind to wind, earth has
one tale to tell;
All other sounds are dulled, and
drowned, and lost,
  In this one cry, "Farewell."
          Farewell. Stanza 6

Ernest Lawrence Thayer
[1863–1940]

[f] There was ease in Casey's
manner as he stepped into his
place,
There was pride in Casey's bearing, and a smile lit Casey's
face,
And when, responding to the
cheers, he lightly doffed his
hat,
No stranger in the crowd could
doubt 'twas Casey at the bat.

"Strike one," the umpire said.

From the benches dark with
people there went up a
muffled roar,
Like the beating of the storm-
waves on a stern but distant
shore.

With a smile of Christian charity
great Casey's visage shone;
He stilled the rising tumult, he
bade the game go on.

Oh, somewhere in this favored
land the sun is shining bright;
The band is playing somewhere,
and somewhere hearts are
light,
And somewhere men are laughing
and little children shout,
But there is no joy in Mudville,
great Casey has struck out.
*Casey at the Bat [The San Fran-
cisco Examiner, June 3, 1888].
Stanzas 6, 8, 9, 10, 13*

Louis Edwin Thayer
[1878–   ]

[g] I fancy when I go to rest
some one will bring to light
Some kindly word or goodly act
long buried out of sight;
But, if it's all the same to you,
just give to me, instead,
The bouquets while I'm living
and the knocking when I'm
dead.
Of Post-Mortem Praises. Stanza 1

Lewis Theobald
[1688–1744]

[h] None but himself can be his parallel.
The Double Falsehood

Theocritus
[THIRD CENTURY B.C.]
*Translation by J. M. Edmonds,
Loeb Classical Library*

[i] 'Tis peace of mind, lad, we must find, and have a beldame nigh
To sit for us and spit for us and bid all ill go by.
The Harvest-Home. Line 126

[j] O cricket is to cricket dear, and ant for ant doth long.
The Third Country Singing-Match. Line 31

[k] O to be a frog, my lads, and live aloof from care.
The Reapers. Line 52

Theognis
[570?–490? B.C.]

[l] Wine is wont to show the mind of man.
Maxims. Line 500

[m] No one goes to Hades with all his immense wealth.
Ibid. Line 725

Edward Thomas
[1878–1917]

[n] Out of the night, two cocks together crow,
Cleaving the darkness with a silver blow.   *Cock-Crow*

[o] The ideal library in which no book would have disdained its neighbor. Every book indeed seemed just to have ceased talking to his neighbors when I came in.   *Cloud Castle*

Louisa Carroll Thomas
(Mrs. T. Gaillard Thomas)
[1865–   ]

[p] How odd it is that a little Scotch
Can raise Dutch courage to highest notch!
League of Nations

[q] Charm is the measure of attraction's power
To chain the fleeting fancy of the hour,
And rival all the spell of Beauty's dower.
What Is Charm? Stanza 1

Norman Mattoon Thomas
[1884–   ]

[r] The last audience in America to which I would make a serious

address would be a reunion of college graduates. In such reunions men honoring ancient shrines of learning with one accord breathe one prayer: "Make me a sophomore just for tonight." And few prayers are more unfailingly answered.
Commencement Address at Haverford College [1945]

Francis Thompson
[1859–1907]

[s] The fairest things have fleetest end,
Their scent survives their close:
But the rose's scent is bitterness
To him that loved the rose.
Daisy. Stanza 10

[t] Look for me in the nurseries of Heaven.   *To My Godchild*

[u] The innocent moon, that nothing does but shine,
Moves all the labouring surges of the world.
Sister Songs. Part II

[v] Little Jesus, wast Thou shy Once, and just so small as I?
And what did it feel like to be Out of Heaven, and just like me?
Little Jesus

[w] I fled Him, down the nights and down the days;
I fled Him, down the arches of the years;
I fled Him, down the labyrinthine ways
Of my own mind; and in the mist of tears
I hid from Him, and under running laughter. . . .
Across the margent of the world I fled,
And troubled the gold gateways of the stars,
Smiting for shelter on their clangèd bars;
Fretted to dulcet jars
And silvern chatter the pale ports o' the moon. . . .
Still with unhurrying chase,
And unperturbèd pace,
Deliberate speed, majestic instancy,
Came on the following Feet,
And a Voice above their beat—
"Naught shelters thee, who wilt not shelter Me."
The Hound of Heaven

[x] I stand amid the dust o' the mounded years—
My mangled youth lies dead beneath the heap.
My days have crackled and gone up in smoke,
Have puffed and burst as sunstarts on a stream.   *Ibid.*

[y] Ever and anon a trumpet
    sounds
From the hid battlements of
    Eternity.   *Ibid.*

[z] There is no expeditious road
To pack and label men for God,
And save them by the barrel-load.
Epilogue, A Judgment in Heaven

[a] Thou canst not stir a flower
Without troubling of a star.
            The Mistress of Vision

[b] Happiness is the shadow of
    things past,
Which fools still take for that
    which is to be!
    From the Night of Forebeing

[c] The angels keep their ancient
    places;—
Turn but a stone, and start a
    wing!
'Tis ye, 'tis your estrangèd faces,
That miss the many-splendoured
    thing.   *The Kingdom of God.*
                          Stanza 4

[d] Short arm needs man to
    reach to Heaven
So ready is Heaven to stoop to
    him.
    Grace of the Way. Stanza 6

[e] Know you what it is to be a
child? It is to be something very
different from the man of to-day.
It is to have a spirit yet streaming from the waters of baptism;
it is to believe in love, to believe
in loveliness, to believe in belief;
it is to be so little that the elves
can reach to whisper in your ear;
it is to turn pumpkins into
coaches, and mice into horses,
lowness into loftiness, and nothing into everything, for each
child has its fairy godmother in
its soul.   *Shelley* [*The Dublin
            Review, July 1908*]

[f] Children's griefs are little,
certainly; but so is the child, so
is its endurance, so is its field of
vision, while its nervous impres-
sionability is keener than ours.
Grief is a matter of relativity; the
sorrow should be estimated by its
proportion to the sorrower; a gash
is as painful to one as an ampu-
tation to another.   *Ibid.*

[g] Mighty meat for little guests,
when the heart of Shelley was laid
in the cemetery of Caius Cestius!
                            Ibid.

Harold William Thompson
            [1891–   ]

[h] Never speak loudly to one
another unless the house is on
fire.   *Body, Boots and Britches.
                      Page 484*

Maurice Thompson
            [1844–1901]

[i] The sky is like a woman's
    love,
The ocean like a man's;
Oh, neither knows, below, above,
The measure that it spans!
    Love's Horizon. Stanza 1

James Thomson
            [1700–1748]

[j] As those we love decay, we die
    in part,
String after string is severed from
    the heart.
    On the Death of Mr. Aikman

[k] Come, gentle Spring! ethere-
    al Mildness! come.
    The Seasons. Spring, Line 1

[l]   But who can paint
Like Nature? Can imagination
    boast,
Amid its gay creation, hues like
    hers?   *Ibid. Line 465*

[m] An elegant sufficiency, con-
    tent,
Retirement, rural quiet, friend-
    ship, books.   *Ibid. Line 1158*

[n] The meek-ey'd Morn appears,
    mother of dews.
    Ibid. Summer, Line 47

[o] Autumn nodding o'er the yel-
    low plain.
    Ibid. Autumn, Line 2

[p]   Loveliness
Needs not the foreign aid of orna-
    ment,
But is when unadorn'd, adorn'd
    the most.   *Ibid. Line 204*

[q] See, Winter comes to rule the
    varied year.
    Ibid. Winter, Line 1

[r] Cruel as death, and hungry as
    the grave.   *Ibid. Line 393*

[s] The kiss, snatch'd hasty from
    the sidelong maid.
                   Ibid. Line 625

[t] These as they change, Al-
    mighty Father! these
Are but the varied God. The roll-
    ing year
Is full of Thee.   *Hymn. Line 1*

[u] I care not, Fortune, what you
    me deny:
You cannot rob me of free
    Nature's grace,
You cannot shut the windows of
    the sky
Through which Aurora shows her
    brightening face;
You cannot bar my constant feet
    to trace
The woods and lawns, by living
    stream, at eve:
Let health my nerves and finer
    fibres brace,

And I their toys to the great children leave.   *The Castle of
Indolence. Canto II, Stanza 3

[v] When   Britain   first,   at
   Heaven's command,
Arose from out the azure main,
This was the charter of her land,
And guardian angels sung the
   strain:
Rule, Britannia! Britannia, rule
   the waves!
Britons never shall be slaves.
               Alfred. Act II, Sc. 5

James ("B.V.") Thomson
[1834–1882]

[w] Give a man a horse he can
   ride,
Give a man a boat he can sail;
And his rank and wealth, his
   strength and health
On sea nor shore shall fail.
               Gifts. Stanza 1

[x] Give a man a pipe he can
   smoke,
Give a man a book he can read:
And his home is bright with a
   calm delight,
Though the room be poor indeed.   *Ibid. Stanza 2*

[y] Singing is sweet, but be sure
   of this,
Lips only sing when they cannot
   kiss.   *Art*

Henry David Thoreau
[1817–1862]

[z] My life is like a stroll upon
   the beach,
As near the ocean's edge as I
   can go.
   The Fisher's Boy. Stanza 1

[a] Whate'er we leave to God,
   God does
       And blesses us.
         Inspiration. Proem

[b] Any man more right than
his   neighbors,   constitutes   a
majority of one.
The Duty of Civil Disobedience

[c] What a man thinks of himself, that it is which determines,
or rather indicates, his fate.
         Walden. I, Economy

[d] As if you could kill time
without injuring eternity.   *Ibid.*

[e] Most of the luxuries, and
many of the so-called comforts, of
life are not only not indispensable, but positive hindrances to
the elevation of mankind.   *Ibid.*

[f] It is true, I never assisted the
sun materially in his rising; but,
doubt not, it was of the last importance only to be present at it.
                         Ibid.

[g] For many years I was self-
appointed inspector of snow-
storms and rain-storms, and did
my duty faithfully.   *Ibid.*

[h] Beware of all enterprises that
require new clothes.   *Ibid.*

[i] The man who goes alone can
start to-day; but he who travels
with another must wait till that
other is ready.   *Ibid.*

[j] I went to the woods because I
wished to live deliberately, to
front only the essential facts of
life, and see if I could not learn
what it had to teach, and not,
when I came to die, discover that
I had not lived.
         Ibid. II, What I Lived For

[k] Our life is frittered away by
detail. . . . Simplify, simplify.
                         Ibid.

[l] Time is but the stream I go
a-fishing in.   *Ibid.*

[m] Books must be read as deliberately and reservedly as they
were written.   *Ibid. III, Reading*

[n] I never found the companion
that was so companionable as
solitude.   *Ibid. V, Solitude*

[o] If the day and the night are
such that you greet them with
joy, and life emits a fragrance like
flowers and sweet-scented herbs
is more elastic, more starry, more
immortal,—that is your success.
         Ibid. XI, Higher Laws

[p] There is never an instant's
truce between virtue and vice
Goodness is the only investment
that never fails.   *Ibid.*

[q] Every man is the builder of a
temple, called his body.   *Ibid.*

[r] While men believe in the infinite, some ponds will be thought
to be bottomless.
     Ibid. XVI, The Pond in Winter

[s] The setting sun is reflected
from the windows of the alms-
house as brightly as from the rich
man's abode.
         Ibid. XVIII, Conclusion

[t] It is life near the bone where
it is sweetest.   *Ibid.*

[u] I saw a delicate flower had
grown up two feet high between
the horses' feet and the wheel
track. An inch more to right or
left had sealed its fate, or an inch
higher. Yet it lived to flourish
and never knew the danger it in-
curred. It did not borrow trouble
nor invite an evil fate by appre-
hending it.
         Journal. September 1850

[v'] The blue-bird carries the sky
on his back.   *Ibid. April 3, 1852*

[w] The youth gets together his materials to build a bridge to the moon, or, perchance, a palace or temple on the earth, and, at length, the middle-aged man concludes to build a woodshed with them.   *Ibid. July 14, 1852*

[x] Some circumstantial evidence is very strong, as when you find a trout in the milk.
Ibid. November 11, 1854

[y] When the playful breeze drops in the pool, it springs to right and left, quick as a kitten playing with dead leaves.
Journal. April 9, 1859

George Walter Thornbury
[1828–1876]

[z] Get out the hounds; I'm well to-night, and young again and sound;
I'll have a run once more before they put me underground:
They brought my father home feet first, and it never shall be said
That his son Joe, who rode so straight, died quietly in his bed.
The Death of th' Owd Squire

Cyril Morton Thorne
[?–1916]

[a] "My son!" What simple, beautiful words!
"My boy!" What a wonderful phrase!

With double my virtues and half of my faults,
You can't be a stranger to me!
To My Unborn Son.
Stanzas 1 and 2

Hester Lynch Thrale
(Piozzi)
[1739–1821]

[b] The tree of deepest root is found
Least willing still to quit the ground:
'Twas therefore said by ancient sages,
That love of life increased with years
So much, that in our latter stages,
When pain grows sharp and sickness rages,
The greatest love of life appears.
Three Warnings

[c] Johnson's conversation was by much too strong for a person accustomed to obsequiousness and flattery; it was mustard in a young child's mouth.
Quoted in Boswell's Life of Dr. Johnson, Vol. II, Page 396, Everyman edition

Thucydides
[471–401 B.C.]
Translation [1629] by Thomas Hobbes

[d] Because in the administration it hath respect not to the few but to the multitude, our form of government is called a democracy. Wherein there is not only an equality amongst all men in point of law for their private controversies, but in election to public offices we consider neither class nor rank, but each man is preferred according to his virtue or to the esteem in which he is held for some special excellence: nor is any one put back even through poverty, because of the obscurity of his person, so long as he can do good service to the commonwealth.
History. Book II, Chap. 37, Pericles' Funeral Oration over the Athenians who fell in the first year of the Peloponnesian War

[e] To famous men all the earth is a sepulchre. . . .
Their virtues shall be testified not only by the inscription on stone at home but in all lands wheresoever in the unwritten record of the mind, which far beyond any monument will remain with all men everlastingly.
Ibid.

James Thurber
[1894–   ]

[f] Well, if I called the wrong number, why did you answer the 'phone?   *Caption for cartoon*

[g] Humor is emotional chaos remembered in tranquillity.
Quoted by Max Eastman in The Enjoyment of Laughter

Paul W. Tibbet, Jr.
(Pilot of the B-29, Enola Gay, from which the bomb was dropped on Hiroshima, August 5, 1945)

[h] A mushroom of boiling dust up to 20,000 feet.   *Description of drop of atomic bomb*

Thomas Tickell
[1686–1740]

[i] The sweetest garland to the sweetest maid.   *To a Lady with a Present of Flowers*

[j] I hear a voice you cannot hear,
Which says I must not stay;
I see a hand you cannot see,
Which beckons me away.
Colin and Lucy. Stanza 7

John Tillotson
[1630–1694]

[k] If God were not a necessary
Being of himself, he might almost
seem to be made for the use and
benefit of men.   *Sermon*

Henry Timrod
[1829–1867]

[l] Spring, with that nameless
    pathos in the air
Which dwells with all things fair.
          Spring. Stanza 1

[m] There is no holier spot of
    ground
Than where defeated valor lies,
By mourning beauty crowned!
          *Ode, Decorating the Graves of
          the Confederate Dead, Magno-
          lia Cemetery, Charleston, South
          Carolina, 1867. Stanza 5*

John Tobin
[1770–1804]

[n] The man that lays his hand
    upon a woman,
Save in the way of kindness, is a
    wretch
Whom 'twere gross flattery to
    name a coward.
          The Honeymoon. Act II, Sc. 1

Alexis Charles Henri
Clérel de Tocqueville
[1805–1859]

[o] The profession of law is the
only aristocratic element which
can be amalgamated without violence with the natural elements of
democracy, and which can be ad-
vantageously and permanently
combined with them.
          *Democracy in America.
          Vol. I, Chap. 16*

Count Lyof Nikolayevitch
Tolstoi
[1828–1910]

[p] The Frenchman is conceited
from supposing himself mentally
and physically to be inordinately
fascinating both to men and to
women. An Englishman is conceited on the ground of being a
citizen of the best-constituted
state in the world, and also because he as an Englishman always
knows what is the correct thing to
do, and knows that everything
that he, as an Englishman, does
do is indisputably the best thing.
An Italian is conceited from being excitable and easily forgetting
himself and other people. A Russian is conceited precisely because
he knows nothing and cares to
know nothing, since he does not
believe it possible to know anything fully. A conceited German
is the worst of them all, and the
most hardened of all, and the
most repulsive of all; for he imagines that he possesses the truth
in a science of his own invention,
which is to him absolute truth.
          *War and Peace (tr. Constance
          Garnett.   Modern   Library
          Giant). Part IX, Chap. 11*

[q] The most powerful weapon
of ignorance—the diffusion of
printed matter.
          Ibid. Epilogue, Part II, Chap. 8

[r] All happy families resemble
one another; every unhappy
family is unhappy in its own
fashion.
          *Anna Karénina (tr. Nathan
          Haskell Dole). Part I, Chap. 1*

[s] War on the one hand is such
a terrible, such an atrocious,
thing, that no man, especially no
Christian man, has the right to
assume the responsibility of beginning it.
          Ibid. Part VIII, Chap. 15

[t] The whole trade in the luxuries of life is brought into existence and supported by the requirements of women.
          The Kreutzer Sonata. Chap. 9

[u] The only significance of life
consists in helping to establish
the kingdom of God; and this can
be done only by means of the
acknowledgment and profession
of the truth by each one of us.
          The Kingdom of God. Chap. 12

[v] Art is a human activity having for its purpose the transmis-
sion to others of the highest and
best feelings to which men have
risen.   *What Is Art? Chap. 8*

H. M. Tomlinson
[1873–   ]

[w] The sea is at its best at London, near midnight, when you are
within the arms of a capacious
chair, before a glowing fire,
selecting phases of the voyages
you will never make.
          The Sea and the Jungle

[x] How many grave speeches,
which have surprised, shocked,
and directed the nation, have
been made by Great Men too soon
after a noble dinner, words
winged by the Press without an
accompanying and explanatory
wine list.   *Waiting for Daylight*

[y] That figure of Nobody in
sodden khaki, cumbered with
ugly gear, its precious rifle
wrapped in rags, no brightness
anywhere about it except the
light of its eyes, its face seamed

with lines which might have
been dolorous, which might have
been ironic, with the sweat running from under its steel casque,
looms now in the memory, huge,
statuesque, silent but questioning, like an overshadowing challenge. . . .

What is that figure now? The
ghost of what was fair, but was
broken, and is lost.
    Ibid. The Nobodies.
    [November 11, 1918]

Juliet Wilbor Tompkins
[1871–   ]

[z] The hurrying footsteps came
    and went,
And the heart beat thick for the
    great event,
When the Minister came to tea.
    *When the Minister Came
    to Tea. Stanza 1*

Augustus Montague Toplady
[1740–1778]

[a] Rock of Ages, cleft for me,
Let me hide myself in thee.
    Rock of Ages. Stanza 1

Ridgely Torrence
[1875–1951]

[b] Of all the languages of earth
    in which the human kind
    confer
The Master Speaker is the Tear:
    it is the Great Interpreter.
    *The House of a Hundred
    Lights. The Conclusion of
    the Whole Matter*

[c] I was weak as a rained-on bee.
    Eye-Witness. The Tramp Sings

Charles Hanson Towne
[1877–1949]

[d] Youth, there are countless
    stories spread
By gentlemen whose hair is
    gray.
Believe them not, but me in-
    stead—
    The 'Nineties were not really
    gay.
    Ballade of Gentle Denial

[e] I need not shout my faith.

    The hills are mute—yet how
    they speak of God!   *Silence*

[f] How softly runs the afternoon
Beneath the billowy clouds of
    June!
    How Softly Runs the Afternoon

Tom Treanor
[1909–1944]

[g] So many people have an unconquerable instinct to help an
underdog. . . . Many people have a
snobbish instinct to deal only
with topdogs. There are these two
kinds of people in the world, as
unlike as male and female.
    *One Damn Thing After An-
    other. Introduction*

Herbert Trench
[1865–1923]

[h] Last: if upon the cold green
    mantling sea
Thou cling, alone with Truth,
    to the last spar—
Both castaway,
And one must perish—let it not
    be he
Whom thou art sworn to obey!
    A Charge. Stanza 4

Richard Chenevix Trench
[1807–1886]

[i] Lord, what a change within
    us one short hour
Spent in Thy presence will prevail
    to make!   *Prayer*

[j] We kneel, how weak! we rise,
    how full of power!   *Ibid.*

George Macaulay Trevelyan
[1876–   ]

[k] A man and what he loves and
builds have but a day and then
disappear; nature cares not—and
renews the annual round untired.
It is the old law, sad but not bitter. Only when man destroys the
life and beauty of nature, there is
the outrage.   *Grey of Fallodon.
    Book I, Chap. 3*

[l] Education . . . has produced a
vast population able to read but
unable to distinguish what is
worth reading.   *English Social
    History. Chap. 18*

Anthony Trollope
[1815–1882]

[m] He argued that the principal
duty which a parent owed to a
child was to make him happy.
    Doctor Thorne. Chap. 3

[n] How I do hate those words,
"an excellent marriage." In them
is contained more of wicked
worldliness than any other words
one ever hears spoken.
    *The Small House at Allington.
    Chap. 39*

[o] Always remember that when
you go into an attorney's office
door, you will have to pay for it,
first or last.   *The Last Chronicle
    of Barset. Vol. I, Chap. 20*

[p] It is a comfortable feeling to
know that you stand on your own

ground. Land is about the only
thing that can't fly away.
            Ibid. Vol. II, Chap. 58

[q] It's dogged as does it.
            Ibid. Chap. 61

John Townsend Trowbridge
[1827–1916]

[r] Darius was clearly of the
        opinion
That the air is also man's do-
        minion,
And that, with paddle or fins or
        pinion,
        We soon or late
        Shall navigate
The azure, as now we sail the sea.
        Darius Green and His
            Flying Machine

[s] Men are polished, through act
        and speech,
        Each by each,
As pebbles are smoothed on the
        rolling beach.   *A Home Idyl*

[t] Over the hill the farm-boy
        goes,
His shadow lengthens along the
        land,
A giant staff in a giant hand.
        Evening at the Farm. Stanza 1

[u] Mark Haley drives along the
        street,
Perched high upon his wagon-
        seat;
His sombre face the storm defies,
And thus from morn till eve he
        cries,—
        "Charco'! Charco'!"
While echo faint and far replies,—
        "Hark, O! Hark, O!"
        The Charcoal Man. Stanza 1

[v] Our days, our deeds, all we
        achieve or are,
Lay folded in our infancy; the
        things
Of good or ill we choose while
        yet unborn.   *Nativity*

[w] The all-enclosing freehold of
        Content.   *Guy Vernon*

[x] With years a richer life be-
        gins,
The spirit mellows:
Ripe age gives tone to violins,
Wine, and good fellows.
        Three Worlds

Harry S. Truman
[1884–   ]

[y] When they told me yesterday
what had happened, I felt like the
moon, the stars and all the
planets had fallen on me.
        Statement to reporters, April 13,
        1945, the day after his accession
        to the office of President of the
        United States

[z] When Kansas and Colorado
have a quarrel over the water in

the Arkansas River they don't call
out the National Guard in each
State and go to war over it. They
bring a suit in the Supreme Court
of the United States and abide by
the decision. There isn't a reason
in the world why we cannot do
that internationally.   *Speech in*
        Kansas City [April 1945]

[a] Sixteen hours ago an American airplane dropped one bomb
on Hiroshima. . . . It is a harness-
ing of the basic power of the universe. The force from which the
sun draws its powers has been
loosed against those who brought
war to the Far East.
        First announcement of the
        atomic bomb [August 6, 1945]

John Trumbull
[1750–1831]

[b] As though there were a tie
And obligation to posterity.
We get them, bear them, breed,
        and nurse:
What has posterity done for us?
        McFingal. Canto II, Line 121

[c] No man e'er felt the halter
        draw,
With good opinion of the law.
        Ibid. Canto III, Line 489

Martin Farquhar Tupper
[1810–1889]

[d] A babe in a house is a well-
spring of pleasure.
        Of Education

[e] God, from a beautiful necessity, is Love.
        Of Immortality

[f] Error is a hardy plant: it
flourisheth in every soil.
        Of Truth in Things False

[g] It is well to lie fallow for a
while.   *Of Recreation*

[h] A good book is the best of
friends, the same to-day and for
ever.   *Of Reading*

[i] Who can wrestle against
Sleep?
Yet is that giant very gentleness.
        Of Beauty

[j] Never go gloomily, man with a
        mind!
Hope is a better companion than
        fear.   *Cheer Up. Stanza 1*

Ivan Sergeyevich Turgeniev
[1818–1883]

[k] That air of superiority to the
rest of the world which usually
disappears when once the twen-
ties have been passed.
        Fathers and Sons (tr. C. J.
        Hogarth). Chap. 4

[l] That dim, murky period when regrets come to resemble hopes, and hopes are beginning to resemble regrets.
Ibid. Chap. 7

[m] The temerity to believe in nothing.   *Ibid. Chap. 14*

[n] The sensuous joy of magnanimity.   *Ibid. Chap. 17*

[o] Whatever a man prays for, he prays for a miracle. Every prayer reduces itself to this: "Great God, grant that twice two be not four."
Prayer

Nancy Byrd Turner
[1880-   ]

[p] The Bookshop has a thousand books,
All colors, hues, and tinges,
And every cover is a door
That turns on magic hinges.
The Bookshop. Stanza 2

[q] May I have eyes to see
Beauty in this plain room
Where I am called to be.
A Prayer for the Kitchen Wall

[r] Death is only an old door
Set in a garden wall.
Death a Quiet Door

Walter James Turner
[1889–1946]

[s] When I was but thirteen or so
I went into a golden land,
Chimborazo, Cotopaxi
Took me by the hand.
Romance. Stanza 1

[t] If love means affection, I
Love old trees, hats, coats and things,
Anything that's been with me
In my daily sufferings.
Epithalamium. Stanza 3

Thomas Tusser
[1524–1580]

[u] Except wind stands as never it stood,
It is an ill wind turns none to good.   *A Description of the Properties of Wind*

[v] At Christmas play and make good cheer,
For Christmas comes but once a year.
The Farmer's Daily Diet

[w] Who goeth a borrowing
Goeth a sorrowing.
Five Hundred Points of Good Husbandry. June's Abstract

[x] Naught venture naught have.
Ibid. October's Abstract

[y] Wouldst have a friend, wouldst know what friend is best?

Have God thy friend, who passeth all the rest.
Posies for a Parlour

[z] To Death we must stoop, be we high, be we low,
But how, and how suddenly, few be that know;
What carry we then but a sheet to the grave,
To cover this carcass, of all that we have?
Tenants of God's Farmstead

"Mark Twain" (Samuel Langhorne Clemens)
[1835–1910]

[a] This poor little one-horse town.
The Undertaker's Story

[b] They spell it Vinci and pronounce it Vinchy; foreigners always spell better than they pronounce.
The Innocents Abroad

[c] He is now fast rising from affluence to poverty.
Henry Ward Beecher's Farm

[d] A classic is something that everybody wants to have read and nobody wants to read.
The Disappearance of Literature

[e] A powerful agent is the right word. Whenever we come upon one of those intensely right words in a book or a newspaper the resulting effect is physical as well as spiritual, and electrically prompt.
Essay on William Dean Howells

[f] Work consists of whatever a body is *obliged* to do, and Play consists of whatever a body is not obliged to do.   *The Adventures of Tom Sawyer. Chap. 2*

[g] Cauliflower is nothing but cabbage with a college education.
Pudd'nhead Wilson's Calendar

[h] If you pick up a starving dog and make him prosperous, he will not bite you. This is the principal difference between a dog and a man.   *Ibid.*

[i] It is difference of opinion that makes horse races.   *Ibid.*

[j] The reports of my death are greatly exaggerated.
Cable from Europe to the Associated Press

[k] An experienced, industrious, ambitious, and often quite picturesque liar.
My Military Campaign

[l'] The world and the books are so accustomed to use, and overuse, the word "new" in connection with our country, that we early get and permanently retain the

impression that there is nothing
old about it.   *Life on the Mississippi. Chap. 1*

[m] When I'm playful I use the
meridians of longitude and paral-
lels of latitude for a seine, and
drag the Atlantic Ocean for
whales. I scratch my head with
the lightning and purr myself to
sleep with the thunder.
Ibid. Chap. 3

[n] Give an Irishman lager for a
month, and he's a dead man. An
Irishman is lined with copper,
and the beer corrodes it. But
whisky polishes the copper and is
the saving of him.
Ibid. Chap. 23

[o] All the modern inconveniences.   *Ibid. Chap. 43*

[p] War talk by men who have
been in a war is always interesting; whereas moon talk by a poet
who has not been in the moon is
likely to be dull.   *Ibid. Chap. 45*

[q] It was without a compeer
among swindles. It was perfect,
it was rounded, symmetrical, complete, colossal.   *Ibid. Chap. 52*

[r] In Boston they ask, How
much does he know? In New York,
How much is he worth? In Philadelphia, Who were his parents?
What Paul Blouet Thinks of Us

[s] There is a sumptuous variety
about the New England weather
that compels the stranger's admiration—and regret. . . . But it
gets through more business in
Spring than in any other season.
In the Spring I have counted one
hundred and thirty-six different
kinds of weather inside of twenty-
four hours.
*New England Weather. Speech
at dinner of New England Society, New York [December 22,
1876]*

[t] We haven't all had the good
fortune to be ladies; we haven't
all been generals, or poets, or
statesmen; but when the toast
works down to the babies, we
stand on common ground.
*Answering a Toast to the Ba-
bies, Banquet in honor of
General U. S. Grant, Palmer
House, Chicago [November 14,
1879]*

Royall Tyler
[1757–1826]

[u] Father and I went to camp,
Along with Captain Goodwin;
And there we saw the men and
boys
As thick as hasty pudding,
    Yankee Doodle do.
The Contrast. Act III, Sc. 1

[v] Every possible display of
jocularity, from an *affettuoso*
smile to a *piano* titter, or full
chorus *fortissimo* ha, ha, ha!
Ibid. Act V, Sc. 1

John Tyndall
[1820–1893]

[w] It is not my habit of mind to
think otherwise than solemnly of
the feeling which prompts prayer.
It is a power which I should like
to see guided, not extinguished—
devoted to practicable objects instead of wasted upon air.
*Fragments of Science. Vol. II,
Prayer as a Form of Physical
Energy*

[x] Life is a wave, which in no
two consecutive moments of its
existence is composed of the same
particles.   *Ibid. Vitality*

[y] We are truly heirs of all the
ages; but as honest men it behooves us to learn the extent of
our inheritance, and as brave
ones not to whimper if it should
prove less than we had supposed.
Ibid. Matter and Force

[z] The mind of man may be
compared to a musical instrument
with a certain range of notes, beyond which in both directions we
have an infinitude of silence.
Ibid.

[a] To look at his picture as a
whole, a painter requires distance;
and to judge of the total scientific
achievement of any age, the
standpoint of a succeeding age is
desirable.
Ibid. Science and Man

[b] It is as fatal as it is cowardly
to blink facts because they are
not to our taste.   *Ibid.*

[c] Charles Darwin, the Abraham
of scientific men—a searcher as
obedient to the command of truth
as was the patriarch to the command of God.   *Ibid.*

[d] Religious feeling is as much
a verity as any other part of human consciousness; and against
it, on the subjective side, the
waves of science beat in vain.
*Ibid. Professor Virchow and
Evolution*

Edward Smith Ufford
[1851–1929]

[e] Throw out the life-line across
    the dark wave,
There is a brother whom someone
    should save,
Throw out the life-line, throw out
    the life-line,
Someone is sinking today.
    *Throw Out the Life-line
    [Revivalist hymn]*

Evelyn Underhill
(Mrs. Hubert Stuart Moore)
[1875–1941]

[f] I come in the little things,
Saith the Lord:
My starry wings
I do forsake,
Love's highway of humility to
    take.   *Immanence. Stanza 3*

Louis Untermeyer
[1885–   ]

[g] May nothing evil cross this
        door
And may ill fortune never pry
About these windows; may the
        roar
And rains go by.
        Prayer for a New House.
                Stanza 1

[h] Open my ears to music; let
Me thrill with Spring's first
        flutes and drums—
But never let me dare forget
    The bitter ballads of the slums.
                Prayer. Stanza 4

[i] God, keep me still unsatisfied.
                Ibid. Stanza 5

[j] Why has our poetry eschewed
The rapture and response of food?
What hymns are sung, what
        praises said
For home-made miracles of bread?
                Food and Drink

[k]   Lemons
With acid tongues as sharp as
        women's.   *Ibid.*

[l] There is no kind of death to
        kill
The sands that lie so meek and
        still . . .
But Man is great and strong and
        wise—
        And so he dies.
                Irony. Stanza 2

Arthur Upson
[1877–1908]

[m] My days are phantom days,
        each one
    The shadow of a hope;
My real life never was begun
Nor any of my real deeds done.
                Phantom Life

[n] Dig my life deep enough, you
        must
Find broken friendships round its
        inner wall—
Which once my careless hand let
        slip and fall—
Brave with faint memories, rich in
        rainbow-crust.
        *Octaves in an Oxford Garden.
        XXV, Roman Glassware Pre-
        served in the Ashmolean*

[o] Wine that was spilt in haste
Arising in fumes more precious.
        *After a Dolmetsch Concert.
                Stanza 2*

Harold Clayton Urey
[1893–   ]

[p] We need first of all to be
thoroughly frightened.
        Speech on the Atomic Bomb
                [*December 3, 1945*]

[q] This is indeed The Year Atom
Bomb One. It has opened most
ominously. We must waste no
time if we plan to be alive in A.B.
5 or A.B. 10.
        I'm a Frightened Man [*as told
        to Michael Amrine, in Collier's,
        January 5, 1946*]

Paul Valéry
[1871–1945]

[r] A dreamy laziness, a laziness
of enormous reading difficult to
distinguish from study, a laziness
like the repose of a fluid over-rich
with substance and which in its
stillness begets crystals of perfect
form. [Of Anatole France]
        *Discours de Réception, at the
        French Academy* [*1927*], *where
        he succeeded to the chair of
        Anatole France*

Sir John Vanbrugh
[1664–1726]

[s] Much of a Muchness.
        *The Provoked Husband.
                Act I, Sc. 1*

Willard Duncan Vandiver
[1854–1932]

[t] I come from a State that
raises corn and cotton and cockle-
burs and Democrats, and frothy
eloquence neither convinces nor
satisfies me. I am from Missouri.
You have got to show me.
        *Speech at a naval banquet in
        Philadelphia, while a Represen-
        tative in Congress from Mis-
        souri, and a member of the
        House Committee on Naval Af-
        fairs* [*1899*]

Carl Van Doren
[1885–1950]

[u] The first writers are first and
the rest, in the long run, nowhere
but in anthologies.
        What Is American Literature?

[v] The most familiar quotations
are the most likely to be misquoted. . . . Some have settled
down to false versions that have
obscured the true ones. They have
passed over from literature into
speech.   *Introduction to The
        Oxford Dictionary of Quotations*

Mark Van Doren
[1894–   ]

[w] Wit is the only wall
Between us and the dark.
                    Wit. Stanza 1

[x] He talked, and as he talked
Wallpaper came alive;
Suddenly ghosts walked
And four doors were five.
                    The Story Teller. Stanza 1

[y] Grass nibbling inward
Like green fire.
                    Former Barn Lot. Stanza 3

Henry van Dyke
[1852–1933]

[z] If all the skies were sunshine,
Our faces would be fain
To feel once more upon them
The cooling plash of rain.
                    If All the Skies. Stanza 1

[a] This is the gospel of labour,
ring it, ye bells of the kirk!
The Lord of Love came down from
above, to live with the men
who work;
This is the rose that He planted,
here in the thorn-curst soil;
Heaven is blest with perfect rest,
but the blessing of Earth is
toil.   *The Toiling of Felix.
                    Envoy, Stanza 5*

[b] Oh, London is a man's town,
there's power in the air;
And Paris is a woman's town, with
flowers in her hair.
                    "America for Me." Stanza 3

[c] It's home again, and home
again, America for me!
I want a ship that's westward
bound to plough the rolling
sea,
To the blessèd Land of Room
Enough beyond the ocean
bars,
Where the air is full of sunlight
and the flag is full of stars.
                    Ibid. Stanza 6

[d] The lintel low enough to keep
out pomp and pride:
The threshold high enough to
turn deceit aside.
                    *For the Friends at Hurstmont.
                    The Door*

[e] Self is the only prison that
can ever bind the soul.
                    The Prison and the Angel

[f] It is with rivers as it is with
people: the greatest are not always the most agreeable nor the
best to live with.
                    Little Rivers. Chap. 2

[g] The first day of spring is one
thing, and the first spring day is
another. The difference between
them is sometimes as great as a
month
                    Fisherman's Luck. Chap. 5

Pierre van Paassen
[1895–   ]

[h] That detached and baronial
air of superiority the Briton
habitually affects when circumstances beyond his control bring
him into the presence of creatures
of a lesser breed.
                    That Day Alone. Sect. I

[i] It is always growing weather.
Only the ignorant and the blind
believe that the soil ever comes
to rest. Never is it in such intense
travail as in autumn. The heart
of the earth never stops beating.
Scarcely is the harvest home than
the promise of future wheat fields
is visible in the dark clods of
earth.   *Ibid. Sect. VI*

Mariana Griswold (Mrs. Schuyler) Van Rensselaer
[1851–1934]

[j] Sorrow is mine, but there is
no more dread.
The word has come—On the field
of battle, dead.
                    It Is Well with the Child

Bartolomeo Vanzetti
[1888–1927]

[k] I found myself compelled to
fight back from my eyes the tears,
and quanch my heart trobling to
my throat to not weep before him.
But Sacco's name will live in the
hearts of the people when your
name, your laws, institutions, and
your false god are but a dim re-
memoring of a cursed past in
which man was wolf to the man.
                    *Last Speech to the Court [Nicolo
                    Sacco and Vanzetti, Italian an-
                    archists and labor agitators,
                    were executed August 23, 1927,
                    by the Commonwealth of Massa-
                    chusetts on charges, never con-
                    clusively proved, of murder and
                    robbery]*

Anna Jane Vardhill
[1781–1852]

[l] Behold this ruin! 'Twas a
skull
Once of ethereal spirit full;
This narrow cell was Life's retreat,
This space was Thought's mys-
terious seat.
                    Lines on a Skeleton. Stanza 1

Henry Vaughan
[1622–1695]

[m] My soul, there is a country
Afar beyond the stars.
                    Peace. Stanza 1

[n] I saw Eternity the other night
Like a great ring of pure and endless light.   *The World*

[o] Dear, beauteous death, the
jewel of the just!
Shining nowhere but in the
dark;
What mysteries do lie beyond thy
dust,
Could man outlook that mark!
Departed Friends. Stanza 5

Sir Thomas Vaux
[1510–1556]

[p] Companion none is like
Unto the mind alone;
For many have been harmed by
speech,
Through thinking, few or none.
Of a Contented Mind. Stanza 3

Thorstein Veblen
[1857–1929]

[q] The dog commends himself
to our favour by affording play to
our propensity for mastery, and as
he is also an item of expense, and
commonly serves no industrial
purpose, he holds a well-assured
place in men's regard as a thing
of good repute.   *The Theory of
the Leisure Class. Chap. 6*

[r] The womanliness of woman's
apparel resolves itself into the
more effective hindrance to useful exertion.   *Ibid. Chap. 7*

[s] The walking-stick serves the
purpose of an advertisement that
the bearer's hands are employed
otherwise than in useful effort,
and it therefore has utility as an
evidence of leisure.
Ibid. Chap. 10

[t] As felicitous an instance of
futile classicism as can well be
found is the conventional spelling of the English language. English orthography satisfies all the
requirements of the canons of
reputability under the law of conspicuous waste. It is archaic, cum-
brous, and ineffective; its acquisition consumes much time and
effort; failure to acquire it is easy
of detection.   *Ibid. Chap. 14*

William Henry Venable
[1836–1918]

[u] Remember Johnny Appleseed,
All ye who love the apple;
He served his kind by Word and
Deed,
In   God's   grand   greenwood
chapel.
Johnny Appleseed. Stanza 25

Jones Very
[1813–1880]

[v] 'Tis all a great show,
The world that we're in—
None can tell when 'twas fin-
ished—
None saw it begin.
The World. Stanza 1

Victor Emmanuel III
[1869–1947]

[w] The Germans as long as they
have need of us will be courteous,
and even servile, but at the first
opportunity they will reveal themselves as the great rascals they
really are.
*Quoted in The Ciano Diaries
[May 25, 1939]. Page 87*

Queen Victoria
[1819–1901]

[x] We are not amused.
*Comment, upon seeing an
imitation of herself by the
Honorable Alexander Grant-
ham Yorke, Groom-in-Wait-
ing to the Queen*

François Villon
[1430–1484]

[y] Where   are   the   snows   of
yester-year?
*The Greater Testament (tr. D.
G. Rossetti). Ballad of Old-Time
Ladies*

[z] Blonde   or   brunette,   this
rhyme applies,
Happy is he who knows them not.
*Ibid. Double Ballad to the Like
Purport*

[a] There's no right speech out
of Paris town.
*Ibid. Ballad of the Women of
Paris*

[b] If you have money, it doth
not stay,
But this way and that it wastes
amain:
What does it profit you, anyway?
Ill-gotten good is nobody's gain.
*Ibid. Seemly Lesson to the
Good-for-Noughts*

[c] These traitorous thieves, ac-
cursèd and unfair,
The vintners that put water in
our wine.
A Merry Ballad of Vintners

Fred M. Vinson
[1890–   ]

[d] Wars are not "acts of God."
They are caused by man, by man-
made institutions, by the way in
which man has organized his so-

ciety. What man has made, man can change.
Speech at Arlington National Cemetery [Memorial Day 1945]

Virgil
[70–19 B.C.]

[e] Age carries all things, even the mind, away.
Bucolics. IX, Line 51

[f] Love conquers all.
Eclogues. X, Line 69

[g] Be favorable to bold beginnings.
Georgics. I, Line 40

[h] Practice, by taking thought, might little by little hammer out divers arts.
Ibid. Line 133

[i] I fear the Greeks, even when bringing gifts.
Aeneid. Book II, Line 49

[j] Fortunate isle, the abode of the blest.
Ibid. Line 639

[k] Steep thyself in a bowl of summertime.
Minor Poems. Copa: Syrisca, a Dancing Girl, Line 29

[l] Here's Death, twitching my ear: "Live," says he, "for I'm coming."
Ibid. Line 38

François M. A. Voltaire
[1694–1778]

[m] If there were no God, it would be necessary to invent him.
Épître à l'Auteur du Livre des Trois Imposteurs. CXI

[n] A witty saying proves nothing.
Le Dîner du Comte de Boulainvilliers

[o] If this is best of possible worlds, what then are the others?
Candide [Modern Library edition]. Chap. 6

[p] Optimism is the madness of maintaining that everything is right when it is wrong.
Ibid. Chap. 19

[q] For what end, then, has this world been formed? . . . To plague us to death.
Ibid. Chap. 21

[r] In this country [England] it is found good, from time to time, to kill one Admiral to encourage the others.
Ibid. Chap. 23

[s] Let us cultivate our garden.
Ibid.

[t] History is little else than a picture of human crimes and misfortunes.
L'Ingénu. Chap. 10

[u] It is better to risk saving a guilty person than to condemn an innocent one.
Zadig. Chap. 6

[v] The superfluous, a very necessary thing.
Le Mondain. Line 21

[w] Love truth, but pardon error.
Discours sur l'Homme. Discours 3

[x] In the case of news, we should always wait for the sacrament of confirmation.
Letter to Count d'Argental [August 28, 1760]

[y] It seems clear to me that God designed us to live in society— just as He has given the bees the honey; and as our social system could not subsist without the sense of justice and injustice, He has given us the power to acquire that sense.
Letter to Frederick the Great

[z] I disapprove of what you say, but I will defend to the death your right to say it.
To Helvetius

[a] Liberty of thought is the life of the soul.
Essay on Epic Poetry (written in English)

[b] Whoe'er thou art, behold thy master,
He is, or was, or is to be.
On a Statuette of Cupid in the Cirey Gardens

Johann Heinrich Voss
[1751–1826]

[c] Who does not love wine, women, and song
Remains a fool his whole life long.
Attributed to Voss by Redlich in Die poetischen Beiträge zum Waudsbecker Bothen, Page 67. The couplet has also been attributed to Luther.

Charles A. Wagner
[1901–   ]

[d] When I loved you and you loved me,
You were the sky, the sea, the tree.
Now skies are skies, and seas are seas,
And trees are brown and they are trees.   *When I Loved You*

Katharine Kent Child
(Mrs. Edward Ashley)
Walker
[1840–1916]

[e'] However divinity schools may refuse to "skip" in unison, and may butt and butter each other about the doctrine and origin of human depravity, all will join devoutly in the credo, I believe in the total depravity of inanimate things. . . .

The elusiveness of soap, the knottiness of strings, the transitory nature of buttons, the inclination of suspenders to twist and of hooks to forsake their lawful eyes, and cleave only unto the hairs of their hapless owner's head. *The Total Depravity of Inanimate Things [The Atlantic Monthly, September 1864]*

William Walker
[1623–1684]

[f] Learn to read slow: all other graces
Will follow in their proper places.
The Art of Reading

Edgar Wallace
[1876–1932]

[g] 'E doesn't want no pass;
'E's journeying first-class;
'Is trav'ling rug's a Union Jack, which isn't bad at all;
The tune the drummers play
It ain't so very gay,
But a rather slow selection from a piece that's known as "Saul."
Burial of Private Ginger Jones. Stanza 6

[h] Oh God of Battles, Lord of Might—a sentry in the silent night—
I, 'oo've never prayed
Kneel on the dew-damp sands to say:
Oh, keep me through the coming day!
But, please remember, though I pray,
That I am not afraid.
The Prayer by Private Edgar Wallace, R.A.M.C. Stanza 1

Henry Agard Wallace
[1888–   ]

[i] The object of this war is to make sure that everybody in the world has the privilege of drinking a quart of milk a day.
Address: The Price of Free World Victory [May 8, 1942]

[j] The century on which we are entering can be and must be the century of the common man.
Ibid.

William Ross Wallace
[1819–1881]

[k] The hand that rocks the cradle is the hand that rules the world. *The Hand That Rules the World. Stanza 1*

Edmund Waller
[1605–1687]

[l] The yielding marble of her snowy breast.
On a Lady Passing through a Crowd of People

[m] To man, that was in th' evening made,
Stars gave the first delight;
Admiring, in the gloomy shade,
Those little drops of light.
An Apology for Having Loved Before

[n] A narrow compass! and yet there
Dwelt all that's good, and all that's fair;
Give me but what this riband bound,
Take all the rest the sun goes round! *On a Girdle. Stanza 3*

[o] For all we know
Of what the blessed do above
Is, that they sing, and that they love. *While I Listen to thy Voice*

[p] Go, lovely rose!
Tell her that wastes her time and me
That now she knows,
When I resemble her to thee,
How sweet and fair she seems to be. *Go, Lovely Rose. Stanza 1*

[q] The soul's dark cottage, batter'd and decay'd,
Lets in new light through chinks that Time has made.
Stronger by weakness, wiser men become
As they draw near to their eternal home.
On the Divine Poems

John Waller
[1917–   ]

[r] Guns are left to do what words
Might have done earlier, properly used. *In Beirut*

[s] The last time I see people
Is simple as good-bye,
Peter on Weymouth station
Or Kay going home to die.
Good-bye is always a warning.
The Meaning of War. Stanza 3

Horace Walpole
[1717–1797]

[t] The world is a comedy to those that think, a tragedy to those who feel. *Letter to Sir Horace Mann [1770]*

[u] A careless song, with a little nonsense in it now and then, does not mis-become a monarch.
Ibid. [1774]

Hugh Walpole
[1884–1941]

[v] We are so largely the playthings of Fate in our fears To

one, fear of the dark, to another, of physical pain, to a third, of public ridicule, to a fourth of poverty, to a fifth of loneliness—for all of us our particular creature lurks in ambush.
The Old Ladies. Page 149

Sir Robert Walpole
[1676–1745]

[w] The balance of power.
Speech [1741]

[x] Anything but history, for history must be false.
Walpoliana. No. 141

William Walsh
[1663–1708]

[y] Of all the plagues a lover bears,
Sure rivals are the worst. . . .
I can endure my own despair,
But not another's hope.   *Song*

Izaak Walton
[1593–1683]

[z] I have laid aside business, and gone a-fishing. . . .
Angling may be said to be so like the mathematics that it can never be fully learnt. . . .
As no man is born an artist, so no man is born an angler.
*The Compleat Angler.
Author's Preface*

[a] As the Italians say, Good company in a journey makes the way to seem the shorter.
Ibid. Part I, Chap. I

[b] You will find angling to be like the virtue of humility, which has a calmness of spirit and a world of other blessings attending upon it.   *Ibid.*

[c] I remember that a wise friend of mine did usually say, "That which is everybody's business is nobody's business."
Ibid. Chap. II

[d] An honest Ale-house where we shall find a cleanly room, Lavender in the Windows, and twenty Ballads stuck about the wall.   *Ibid.*

[e] Good company and good discourse are the very sinews of virtue.   *Ibid.*

[f] We may say of angling as Dr. Boteler said of strawberries: "Doubtless God could have made a better berry, but doubtless God never did"; and so, if I might be judge, God never did make a more calm, quiet, innocent recreation than angling.   *Ibid. Chap. V*

[g] Thus use your frog: put your hook through his mouth and out at his gills, and then with a fine needle and silk sew the upper part of his leg with only one stitch to the arming wire of your hook, or tie the frog's leg above the upper joint to the armed wire; and in so doing use him as though you loved him.   *Ibid. Chap. VIII*

[h] This dish of meat is too good for any but anglers, or very honest men.   *Ibid.*

[i] Health is the second blessing that we mortals are capable of,—a blessing that money cannot buy.   *Ibid. Chap. XXI*

[j] Oh, the gallant fisher's life!
It is the best of any;
'Tis full of pleasure, void of strife,
And 'tis beloved by many.
The Angler (John Chalkhill)

William Warburton, Bishop of Gloucester
[1698–1779]

[k] Orthodoxy is my doxy—heterodoxy is another man's doxy.
*Quoted by Joseph Priestley:
Memoirs. Vol. I, Page 572*

"Artemus Ward" (Charles Farrar Browne)
[1834–1867]

[l] My pollertics, like my religion, being of an exceedin' accommodatin' character.
The Crisis

[m] The fack can't be no longer disgised that a Krysis is onto us.
Ibid.

[n] I am not a politician, and my other habits are good.
Fourth of July Oration

[o] The prevailin' weakness of most public men is to Slop over. G. Washington never slopt over.
Ibid.

[p] I can't sing. As a singist I am not a success. I am saddest when I sing. So are those who hear me. They are sadder even than I am.
Artemus Ward's Lecture

[q] Did you ever have the measels, and if so, how many?
The Census

[r] He is dreadfully married. "He's the most married man I ever saw in my life."
Moses, the Sassy

[s] Let us all be happy and live within our means, even if we have to borrow the money to do it with.
Natural History

Thomas Ward
[1577–1639]

[t] Where to elect there is but one,
'Tis Hobson's choice,—take that or none.
England's Reformation. Chap. IV, Page 326 [Tobias Hobson, the first Englishman to rent out hackney-horses, made a customer take the horse nearest the door]

Eugene Fitch Ware
("Ironquill")
[1841–1911]

[u] When back into the alphabet
The critic's satires shall have crumbled,
When into dust his hand is humbled,
One verse of mine may linger yet.   *The Rhymes of Ironquill. Preface*

[v] Human hopes and human creeds
Have their root in human needs.
The Washerwoman's Song

[w] The soul of the fact is its truth, and the NOW is its principal factor.   *The Now*

[x] O Dewey was the morning
Upon the first of May,
And Dewey was the Admiral
Down in Manila Bay;
And Dewey were the Regent's eyes,
"Them" orbs of royal blue!
And Dewey feel discouraged?
I Dew not think we Dew.
In The Topeka (Kansas) Daily Capital [May 3, 1898]

[y] Work brings its own relief;
He who most idle is
Has most of grief.   *To-day*

[z] The ballads of the people are the bulwarks of the State.
The Organ-Grinder

[a] Oft the statesman and the saint
Think they're doing good, but ain't.   *Aesop's Fables. No. 17*

[b] When a person knows a story that he thinks he ought to tell . . .
And if no one stops to listen, why
Of course a man will feel
All broke up and dislocated, and uneasy as an eel.
A Romance. Preface

[c] Human beings are like boilers, and the same rules, it would seem,
Have an equal application to affection and to steam.
Making love and putting steam on will entail the same mishaps—

When you get on too much pressure, all is lost by a collapse.
Ibid. Chap. IV

[d] I saw a maxim suitable for monarch or for clown:
"Who openeth a jackpot may not always rake it down."
The Jackpot. Stanza 4

Charles Dudley Warner
[1829–1900]

[e] To plant seeds, and watch the renewal of life,—this is the commonest delight of the race, the most satisfactory thing a man can do.   *My Summer in a Garden. Preliminary*

[f] No man but feels more of a man in the world if he have a bit of ground that he can call his own. However small it is on the surface, it is four thousand miles deep; and that is a very handsome property.   *Ibid.*

[g] What a man needs in gardening is a cast-iron back, with a hinge in it.   *Ibid. Third Week*

[h] Lettuce is like conversation: it must be fresh and crisp, so sparkling that you scarcely notice the bitter in it.   *Ibid. Ninth Week*

[i] In this sort of family discussion, "I will say no more" is the most effective thing you can close up with.   *Ibid. Tenth Week*

[j] There is a good deal of fragmentary conversation going on among the birds, even on the warmest days.
Ibid. Eleventh Week

[k] The plumbers had occasion to make me several visits. Sometimes they would find, upon arrival, that they had forgotten some indispensable tool; and one would go back to the shop, a mile and a half, after it; and his comrade would await his return with the most exemplary patience, and sit down and talk,—always by the hour.   *Ibid.*

[l] Public opinion is stronger than the legislature, and nearly as strong as the ten commandments.   *Ibid. Sixteenth Week*

Sylvia Townsend Warner
[1893–   ]

[m] John Bird, a laborer, lies here,
Who served the earth for sixty year
With spade and mattock, drill and plough;
But never found it kind till now.
Epitaph

Robert Penn Warren
[1905–   ]

[n] Nodding, its great head
    rattling like a gourd,
And locks like seaweed strung on
    the stinking stone,
The nightmare stumbles past,
    and you have heard
It fumble your door before it
    whimpers and is gone:
It acts like the old hound that
    used to snuffle your door and
    moan. *Original Sin. Stanza 1*

[o]   Stands
    like an old horse cold in the
    pasture.   *Ibid. Stanza 9*

[p] The annual sacrament of sea
    and sun,
Which browns the face and heals
    the heart . . .

But the mail lurks in the box at
    the house where you live.
    End of Season. Stanzas 5 and 6

Thomas Warton
[1728–1790]

[q] All human race, from China
    to Peru,
Pleasure, howe'er disguis'd by art,
    pursue.
        Universal Love of Pleasure

[r] All-powerful Ale! whose sor-
    row-soothing sweets
Oft I repeat in vacant afternoon.
        A Panegyric on Oxford Ale

Robert Morris Washburn
[1868–1946]

[s] There is an incongruity in
the death of the young that
shocks, set off as it is in contrast
sharp against life, youth and
vitality. But there is a majesty
and an eloquence in the death of
the aged that nothing can touch.
A link with the far past is gone. A
bridge is broken. A heart which
has throbbed for years has ceased
to beat, like the engines of a
mighty liner when, after a long
and tempestuous voyage, it drops
anchor in its home port.
        On the Death of the Aged

Booker Taliaferro Washington
[1858–1915]

[t] No race can prosper till it
learns that there is as much dignity in tilling a field as in writing
a poem.   *Up From Slavery*

George Washington
[1732–1799]

[u] Labour to keep alive in your
breast that little spark of celestial
fire,—conscience.   *Rule from the
    copy-book of Washington
    when a schoolboy*

[v] That unmeaning and abominable custom, swearing.
        *Orders Against Profanity
            in the Army*

[w] Almighty God, we make our
earnest prayer that Thou wilt
keep the United States in Thy
holy protection; that Thou wilt
incline the hearts of the citizens
to cultivate a spirit of subordina-
tion and obedience to government; to entertain a brotherly
affection and love for one another
and for their fellow-citizens of the
United States at large.
    *Prayer after Inauguration (from
    copy in his pew, St. Paul's
    Chapel, New York)*

[x] It is our true policy to steer
clear of permanent alliances with
any portion of the foreign world.
        *Farewell Address. [Sep-
            tember 17, 1796]*

Nixon Waterman
[1859–1944]

[y] No man can feel himself
    alone
The while he bravely stands
Between the best friends ever
    known—
His two good, honest hands.
        Interludes

Sir William Watson
[1858–1935]

[z] April, April,
Laugh thy girlish laughter;
Then, the moment after,
Weep thy girlish tears.   *Song*

[a] Here are the heights, crest
    beyond crest,
    With Himalayan dews im-
        pearled;
And I will watch from Everest
    The long heave of the surging
        world.   *Shakespeare. Stanza 3*

[b] What is so sweet and dear
As a prosperous morn in May,
The confident prime of the day,
And the dauntless youth of the
    year,
When nothing that asks for bliss,
Asking aright, is denied,
And half of the world a bride-
    groom is,
And half of the world a bride.
        Ode in May. Stanza 2

[c] The seasons change, the
    winds they shift and veer;
The grass of yesteryear
Is dead; the birds depart, the
    groves decay. . . .
Captains and conquerors leave a
    little dust,

And kings a dubious legend of
 their reign;
The swords of Caesars, they are
 less than rust:
The poet doth remain.
Lachrymae Musarum. Stanza 9

[d] Love, like a bird, hath
 perch'd upon a spray
For thee and me to hearken
 what he sings.
Contented, he forgets to fly away;
But hush! . . . remind not Eros
 of his wings. *Epigram*

[e] Too long, that some may rest,
Tired millions toil unblessed.
A New National Anthem.
Stanza 3

[f] Say what thou wilt, the
 young are happy never.
Give me bless'd Age, beyond the
 fire and fever,—
Past the delight that shatters,
 hope that stings,
And eager flutt'ring of life's
 ignorant wings. *Epigram*

[g] Too avid of earth's bliss, he
 was of those
Whom Delight flies because
 they give her chase.
Only the odour of her wild hair
 blows
Back in their faces hungering
 for her face.
Byron the Voluptuary

[h] Strange the world about me
 lies,
Never yet familiar grown—
Still disturbs me with surprise,
Haunts me like a face half
 known.
World-Strangeness. Stanza 1

[i] Five-and-thirty black slaves,
Half-a-hundred white,
All their duty but to sing
For their Queen's delight.
The Key-board. Stanza 1

[j] For still the ancient riddles
 mar
Our joy in man, in leaf, in star.
The Whence and Whither give no
 rest,
The Wherefore is a hopeless
 quest.
An Epistle to N. A. Stanza 4

[k] To dress, to call, to dine, to
 break
No cannon of the social code,
The little laws that lacqueys
 make,
The futile decalogue of Mode,—
How many a soul for these things
 lives,
With pious passion, grave in-
 tent!
While Nature careless-handed
 gives
The things that are more excel-
 lent. *The Things that Are*
More Excellent. Stanza 6

[l] The sense of greatness keeps
 a nation great.
Our Eastern Treasure

[m] Lo, with the ancient
Roots of man's nature,
Twines the eternal
 Passion of song. *England My*
Mother. Part II, Stanza 1

Henry Watterson
[1840–1921]

[n] Things have come to a heluva
 pass
When a man can't cudgel his own
 jack-ass.
*Reply when rebuked for criticiz-
ing the Governor of Kentucky*

Isaac Watts
[1674–1748]

[o] Let dogs delight to bark and
 bite,
 For God hath made them so;
Let bears and lions growl and
 fight,
 For 'tis their nature too.
Divine Songs. XVI

[p] Birds in their little nests
 agree;
 And 'tis a shameful sight
When children of one family
 Fall out, and chide, and fight.
Ibid. XVII

[q] How doth the little busy bee
 Improve each shining hour,
And gather honey all the day
 From every opening flower!
Ibid. XX

[r] For Satan finds some mischief still
For idle hands to do. *Ibid.*

[s] Hush, my dear, lie still and
 slumber!
Holy angels guard thy bed!
Heavenly blessings without num-
 ber
Gently falling on thy head.
A Cradle Hymn

[t] 'Tis the voice of the sluggard;
 I heard him complain,
"You have wak'd me too soon, I
 must slumber again."
The Sluggard. Stanza 1

[u] How proud we are! how fond
 to shew
Our clothes, and call them rich
 and new!
When the poor sheep and silk-
 worm wore
That very clothing long before.
Against Pride in Clothes.
Stanza 3

[v] There is a land of pure de-
 light,
Where saints immortal reign;
Infinite day excludes the night,
 And pleasures banish pain.
Hymns and Spiritual Songs.
Book II, Hymn 66

[w] To God the Father, God the
Son,
And God the Spirit. Three in One,
Be honour, praise, and glory
given
By all on earth, and all in Heaven.
Doxology

John Van Alstyn Weaver
[1893–1938]

[x] Don't you ever try to go
there—
It's to dream of, not to find.
Lovely things like that is always
Mostly in your mind.
Legend. Stanza 7

Charles Henry Webb
("John Paul")
[1834–1905]

[y] Turn out more ale, turn up
the light;
I will not go to bed to-night.
Of all the foes that man should
dread
The first and worst one is a
bed. . . .
Friends I have had both old and
young,
And ale we drank and songs we
sung:
Enough you know when this is
said,
That, one and all,—they died in
bed.
In bed they died and I'll not go
Where all my friends have per-
ished so.

For I've been born and I've been
wed—
All of man's peril comes of bed.
Dum Vivimus Vigilamus.
Stanzas 1 and 2

[z] That 'tis well to be off with
the old love
Before one is on with the new
Has somehow passed into a proverb,
But who follows its teaching
may rue.

Were the proverb not wiser if
mended,
And the fickle and wavering
told
To be sure that they're on with
the new love
Before being off with the old?
Proverbum Sap.
Stanzas 1 and 3

Mary (Mrs. Henry Bertram Law) Webb
[1881–1927]

[a] We are to-morrow's past.
Precious Bane. Foreword

[b] It made me gladsome to be
getting some education, it being
like a big window opening.
Ibid. Book I, Chap. 5

[c] If you stop to be kind, you
must swerve often from your
path.   *Ibid. Book II, Chap. 3*

[d] It's the folk that depend on
us for this and for the other that
we most do miss. So the mother is
more let and hindered lacking the
little creatures clinging to her
skirt than she is when they be
there, for she has no heart for her
work.   *Ibid. Book IV, Chap. 4*

Sidney Webb
(Baron Passfield)
[1859–1947]
and
Beatrice Webb
[1858–1943]

[e] The inevitability of gradual-
ness.
*Presidential address, British
Labour Party Congress* [1923]

Daniel Webster
[1782–1852]

[f] Whatever makes men good
Christians, makes them good citizens.   *Speech at Plymouth, Massachusetts* [*December 22, 1820*]

[g] Mind is the great lever of all
things; human thought is the
process by which human ends are
ultimately answered.
*Address on Laying the Corner-
stone of the Bunker Hill Monument* [*June 17, 1825*]

[h] Knowledge, in truth, is the
great sun in the firmament. Life
and power are scattered with all
its beams.   *Ibid.*

[i] Let our object be our country, our whole country, and nothing but our country.   *Ibid.*

[j] The staff on which my years
should lean
Is broken ere those years come
o'er me;
My funeral rites thou shouldst
have seen,
But thou art in the tomb before
me.   *On the Death of His
Son, Charles, 1826. Stanza 1*

[k] It is my living sentiment,
and by the blessing of God it shall
be my dying sentiment,—Independence now and Independence
forever.
. *Eulogy on Adams and Jefferson,
Faneuil Hall, Boston* [*August 2,
1826*]

[l] He smote the rock of the national resources, and abundant

streams of revenue gushed forth. He touched the dead corpse of Public Credit, and it sprung upon its feet. *Speech on Hamilton [March 10, 1831]*

[m] When tillage begins, other arts follow. The farmers therefore are the founders of human civilization. *Remarks on Agriculture [January 13, 1840]*

[n] America has furnished to the world the character of Washington. And if our American institutions had done nothing else, that alone would have entitled them to the respect of mankind. *Completion of Bunker Hill Monument [June 17, 1843]*

[o] Thank God! I—I also—am an American! *Ibid.*

[p] Liberty exists in proportion to wholesome restraint. *Speech at the Charleston Bar Dinner [May 10, 1847]*

[q] Labor in this country is independent and proud. It has not to ask the patronage of capital, but capital solicits the aid of labor. *Speech [April 2, 1824]*

[r] The people's government, made for the people, made by the people, and answerable to the people. *Second Speech on Foote's Resolution [January 26, 1830]*

[s] God grants liberty only to those who love it, and are always ready to guard and defend it. *Speech [June 3, 1834]*

[t] Inconsistencies of opinion, arising from changes of circumstances, are often justifiable. *Speech [July 25 and 27, 1846]*

[u] A sense of duty pursues us ever. It is omnipresent, like the Deity. If we take to ourselves the wings of the morning, and dwell in the uttermost parts of the sea, duty performed or duty violated is still with us, for our happiness or our misery. If we say the darkness shall cover us, in the darkness as in the light our obligations are yet with us. *Works. Vol. VI, Page 105*

[v] Philosophical argument, especially that drawn from the vastness of the universe, in comparison with the apparent insignificance of this globe, has sometimes shaken my reason for the faith which is in me; but my heart has always assured and reassured me that the gospel of Jesus Christ must be Divine Reality. The Sermon on the Mount cannot be a mere human production. This belief enters into the very depth of my conscience. The whole history of man proves it. *Epitaph (dictated day before his death) on his tombstone*

[w] I still live. *Last words*

Harold Tucker Webster
[1885–1952]

[x] Caspar Milquetoast: The Timid Soul. *Character in Series of Cartoons*

[y] The Thrill that Comes Once in a Life-time. *Title of Series of Cartoons*

John Webster
[1580–1625]

[z] Glories, like glow-worms, afar off shine bright,
But look'd too near have neither heat nor light.
Duchess of Malfi. Act IV, Sc. 2

[a] Heaven-gates are not so highly arch'd
As princes' palaces; they that enter there
Must go upon their knees.
Ibid.

[b] We cease to grieve, cease to be fortune's slaves,
Yes, cease to die, by dying.
The White Devil. Act III, Sc. 6

[c] Vain the ambition of kings
Who seek by trophies and dead things
To leave a living name behind,
And weave but nets to catch the wind.
The Devil's Law Case. Song

[d] The soul was never put into the body,
Which has so many rare and curious pieces
Of mathematical motion, to stand still.
Honorable Employment

[e] I saw him now going the way of all flesh.
Westward Hoe. Act II, Sc. 2

Mason Locke Weems
[1759–1825]

[f] "George," said his father, "do you know who killed that beautiful little cherry tree yonder in the garden?" . . . Looking at his father with the sweet face of youth brightened with the inexpressible charm of all-conquering truth, he bravely cried out, "I can't tell a lie. I did cut it with my hatchet."
The Life of George Washington: With Curious Anecdotes. Equally Honorable to Himself and Exemplary to His Young Countrymen

Winifred Welles
[1893–1939]

[g] My squirrel with his tail
    curved up
Like half a silver lyre.
      Silver for Midas. Stanza 4

[h] Oh all you safe and smooth
    of heart
Listen to song from me,
Whose wooden throat was once a
    part
Of the north side of a tree
      The Violin. Stanza 4

Arthur Wellesley,
Duke of Wellington
[1769–1852]

[i] Nothing except a battle lost
can be half so melancholy as a
battle won.   *Dispatch [1815]*

[j] The battle of Waterloo was
won on the playing fields of Eton.
      *Attributed to the Duke of
        Wellington*

Carolyn Wells
[1869–1942]

[k] Youth is a silly, vapid state;
Old age with fears and ills is rife;
This simple boon I beg of Fate—
A thousand years of Middle Life!
      My Boon

[l] I love the Christmas-tide, and
    yet,
I notice this, each year I live;
I always like the gifts I get,
But how I love the gifts I give!
      A Thought

[m] They borrow books they will
    not buy,
They have no ethics or religions;
I wish some kind Burbankian guy
Could cross my books with
    homing pigeons.
      Book-Borrowers

[n] I don't believe the half I hear,
Nor the quarter of what I see!
But I have one faith, sublime and
    true,
That nothing can shake or slay;
Each spring I firmly believe anew
All the seed catalogues say!
      One Firm Faith

[o] The smile that won't come off.
      Winning slogan in a contest

Herbert George Wells
[1866–1946]

[p] The past is but the beginning
of a beginning, and all that is and
has been is but the twilight of the
dawn. . . . A day will come when
beings who are now latent in our
thoughts and hidden in our loins
shall stand upon this earth as one
stands upon a footstool, and shall
laugh and reach out their hands
amid the stars.
      The Discovery of the Future

[q] Nothing could have been more
obvious to the people of the early
twentieth century than the rapid-
ity with which war was becoming
impossible. And as certainly they
did not see it. They did not see it
until the atomic bombs burst in
their fumbling hands.
      The World Set Free [1914]

[r] Human history becomes more
and more a race between education and catastrophe.
      The Outline of History. Chap. 15

[s] The professional military
mind is by necessity an inferior
and unimaginative mind; no man
of high intellectual quality would
willingly imprison his gifts in
such a calling.   *Ibid. Chap. 40*

[t] Every one of these hundreds
of millions of human beings is in
some form seeking happiness. . . .
Not one is altogether noble nor
altogether trustworthy nor altogether consistent; and not one is
altogether vile. Not a single one
but has at some time wept.
      Ibid.

[u] Our true nationality is mankind.   *Ibid. Chap. 41*

[v] In England we have come to
rely upon a comfortable time-lag
of fifty years or a century inter-
vening between the perception
that something ought to be done
and a serious attempt to do it.
      *The Work, Wealth and Happi-
        ness of Mankind. Chap. 11*

[w] The crazy combative patriotism that plainly threatens to destroy civilization is very largely
begotten by the schoolmaster and
the schoolmistress in their history
lessons. They take the growing
mind at a naturally barbaric
phase and they inflame and fix its
barbarism.   *The Informative
        Content of Education*

[x] The years from thirty to
seventy were formerly a sort of
dump for the consequences of the
first three decades; now they are
the main part of life, the years of
work, expression and complete
self-discovery, to which these
earlier stages are the bright, delightful prelude.
      The Shape of Things To Come

Rollin John Wells
[1848–1923]

[y] A little more tired at close of
    day,
A little less anxious to have our
    way;

A little less ready to scold and
  blame,
A little more care of a brother's
  name;
And so we are nearing our journey's end,
Where time and eternity meet and
  blend.
            Growing Old. Stanza 1

Robert Gilbert Welsh
[1874–1924]

[z] His wings are gray and trail-
  ing,
Azrael, Angel of Death.
And yet the souls that Azrael
  brings
Across the dark and cold,
Look up beneath those folded
  wings,
And find them lined with gold.
            Azrael. Stanza 2

Franz Werfel
[1890–1945]

[a] Yes, death is strong, but look
  you, the strongest,
Stronger is music than death.
  *Poems (tr. Edith Abercrombie
  Snow). The Beyond*

John Wesley
[1703–1791]

[b] Though I am always in haste,
I am never in a hurry.
        Letters. December 10, 1777

[c] Do all the good you can,
By all the means you can,
In all the ways you can,
In all the places you can,
At all the times you can,
To all the people you can,
As long as ever you can.
            John Wesley's Rule

Mae West
[1893–   ]

[d] Come up and see me sometime.   *Diamond Lil* [1932]

Richard Bethell,
Lord Westbury
[1800–1873]

[e] A solicitor, after hearing Lord
Westbury's opinion, ventured to
say that he had turned the matter
over in his mind, and thought
that something might be said on
the other side; to which he replied, "Then, sir, you will turn it
over once more in what you are
pleased to call your mind."
  *Nash: Life of Lord Westbury.
            Vol. II, Page 292*

Edward Noyes Westcott
[1847–1898]

[f] Yes, an' no, an' mebbe, an'
mebbe not.   *David Harum.
                      Chap. 1*

[g] Do unto the other feller the
way he'd like to do unto you an'
do it fust.   *Ibid. Chap. 20*

[h] They say a reasonable number
of fleas is good fer a dog—keeps
him from broodin' over bein' a
dog.   *Ibid. Chap. 32*

Thomas Westwood
[1814–1888]

[i] Storm upon the mountain,
  night upon its throne!
And the little snow-white lamb
  left alone—alone!
            The Pet Lamb. Stanza 1

Edith Wharton
[1862–1937]

[j] There are two ways of spreading light: to be
The candle or the mirror that reflects it.   *Vesalius in Zante*

[k] Somewhere I read, in an old
  book whose name
Is gone from me, I read that when
  the days
Of a man are counted, and his
  business done,
There comes up the shore at evening, with the tide,
To the place where he sits, a
  boat—
And in the boat, from the place
  where he sits, he sees,
Dim in the dusk, dim and yet so
  familiar,
The faces of his friends long dead;
  and knows
They come for him, brought in
  upon the tide,
To take him where men go at set
  of day.   *With the Tide:
                  Theodore Roosevelt*

[l] "Summer afternoon—summer
afternoon; to me those have always been the two most beautiful
words in the English language."
*(Said by Henry James to E. W.)
  A Backward Glance. Chap. 10*

[m] One day when the Sultan
was in his palace at Damascus a
beautiful youth who was his favorite rushed into his presence,
crying out in great agitation that
he must fly at once to Baghdad,
and imploring leave to borrow his
Majesty's swiftest horse.
  The Sultan asked why he was in
such haste to go to Baghdad. "Because," the youth answered, "as I
passed through the garden of the
Palace just now, Death was standing there, and when he saw me he

stretched out his arms as if to threaten me, and I must lose no time in escaping from him."

The young man was given leave to take the Sultan's horse and fly; and when he was gone the Sultan went down indignantly into the garden, and found Death still there. "How dare you make threatening gestures at my favorite?" he cried; but Death, astonished, answered: "I assure your Majesty I did not threaten him. I only threw up my arms in surprise at seeing him here, because I have a tryst with him to-night in Baghdad."

Ibid. Chap. 11

The Reverend Cornelius Whaurr

[n] In this imperfect, gloomy scene
  Of complicated ill,
How rarely is a day serene,
  The throbbing bosom still!
Will not a beauteous landscape bright
  Or music's soothing sound,
Console the heart, afford delight,
  And throw sweet peace around?
They may; but never comfort lend
Like an Accomplished Female Friend!
  The Female Friend. Stanza 1
  (Quoted by E. V. Lucas and
  J. C. Squire; source unknown)

John Hall Wheelock

[1886-   ]

[o] There is a panther caged within my breast,
But what his name there is no breast shall know
Save mine, nor what it is that drives him so,
Backward and forward, in relentless quest.
  The Black Panther

[p] For, as all flesh must die, so all
Now dust, shall live.
  This Quiet Dust

[q] The everlasting song is still unsung,
And the eternal tale is never told:
Earth and the ancient joy are ever young,
It is the heart that withers and grows old.
  The Heart Grows Old

George Meason Whicher

[1860-1937]

[r] How are the mighty withered! You are now
Become your book, and that (O last of woes!)

Shrunk to a school-room bogey.
  Pedants plow
With salt your fields; and there no harvest grows
Save juiceless weeds of grammar. . . .
Butchered to make the school-girl's exercise!   *Ave Caesar!*
  Stanza 3

James McNeill Whistler

[1834-1903]

[s] The masterpiece should appear as the flower to the painter—perfect in its bud as in its bloom—with no reason to explain its presence—no mission to fulfil—a joy to the artist, a delusion to the philanthropist—a puzzle to the botanist—an accident of sentiment and alliteration to the literary man.
  The Gentle Art of Making
  Enemies. Propositions, 2

[t] The imitator is a poor kind of creature. If the man who paints only the tree, or flower, or other surface he sees before him were an artist, the king of artists would be the photographer. It is for the artist to do something beyond this: in portrait painting to put on canvas something more than the face the model wears for that one day; to paint the man, in short, as well as his features.
  Ibid.

[u] Nature sings her exquisite song to the artist alone, her son and her master—her son in that he loves her, her master in that he knows her.
  Ibid. Ten O'Clock

[v] *Wilde.* I wish I'd said that.
Whistler. You will, Oscar, you will.
  Traditional Dialogue

Elwyn Brooks White

[1899-   ]

[w] "It's broccoli, dear."
"I say it's spinach, and I say the hell with it."
  Caption for a cartoon by Carl
  Rose in The New Yorker

[x] Commuter—one who spends his life
In riding to and from his wife;
A man who shaves and takes a train
And then rides back to shave again.   *Commuter*

[y] It is easier for a man to be loyal to his club than to his planet; the by-laws are shorter, and he is personally acquainted with the other members.
  One Man's Meat

[z] Democracy is the recurrent suspicion that more than half of

the people are right more than half of the time.
World Government and Peace

[a] A despot doesn't fear eloquent writers preaching freedom—he fears a drunken poet who may crack a joke that will take hold.
Quoted by Clifton Fadiman

James Terry White
[1845–1920]

[b] If thou of fortune be bereft
And in thy store there be but left
Two loaves, sell one and with the dole
Buy hyacinths to feed thy soul.
Not by Bread Alone [The Century Magazine, August 1907. Adaptation of a Persian theme]

T. H. White
[1906–   ]

[c] Look at the peace of inanimate things,
The sanity of stones,
The probity of pasture fields, dead trees,
Old hills, and patient bones.
Reading Giraldus Cambrensis. Stanza 1

William Allen White
[1868–1944]

[d] Tin horn politicians.
Emporia Gazette, October 25, 1901

[e] "Company" merges into the family when clean towels are not kept in the bathroom every morning. A man is no longer company when they change sheets on his bed only once in two weeks. . . . When sons-in-law come home to visit for years at a time, the question will be seen to have considerable importance.
Ibid. June 4, 1906

[f] A rift in the clouds on a gray day threw a shaft of sunlight upon her coffin as her nervous, energetic little body sank to its last sleep. But the soul of her, the glowing, gorgeous, fervent soul of her, surely was flaming in eager joy upon some other dawn.
Ibid. May 13, 1921. Editorial on the Death of His Daughter, Mary White, aged 17

[g] Consistency is a paste jewel that only cheap men cherish.
Ibid., November 17, 1923

Alfred North Whitehead
[1861–1947]

[h] The deliberate aim at Peace very easily passes into its bastard substitute, Anaesthesia.
Adventures of Ideas. Chap. 20

[i] Youth is life as yet untouched by tragedy. . . . When youth has once grasped where Beauty dwells—with a real knowledge and not as a mere matter of literary phraseology—its self-surrender is absolute. *Ibid.*

Walt Whitman
[1819–1892]

[j] I hear America singing, the varied carols I hear.
I Hear America Singing

[k] I say the whole earth and all the stars in the sky are for religion's sake.
Starting from Paumanok. 7

[l] Nothing can happen more beautiful than death.
Ibid. 12

[m] I celebrate myself and sing myself,
And what I assume you shall assume.
Song of Myself. 1

[n] I loafe and invite my soul.
Ibid.

[o] It [grass] is the handkerchief of the Lord. *Ibid. 6*

[p] And to die is different from what any one supposed, and luckier. *Ibid.*

[q] The orchestra whirls me wider than Uranus flies,
It wrenches such ardors from me I did not know I possess'd them. *Ibid.*

[r] I believe a leaf of grass is no less than the journey-work of the stars. *Ibid. 31*

[s] And a mouse is miracle enough to stagger sextillions of infidels. *Ibid.*

[t] The clock indicates the moment—but what does eternity indicate? *Ibid. 44*

[u] In the faces of men and women I see God. *Ibid. 48*

[v] If any thing is sacred the human body is sacred.
Children of Adam. 8

[w] When I peruse the conquer'd fame of heroes and the victories of mighty generals, I do not envy the generals.
When I Peruse the Conquer'd Fame

[x] Done with indoor complaints, libraries, querulous criticisms,
Strong and content I travel the open road.
Song of the Open Road. 1

[y] All music is what awakes from you when you are reminded by the instruments.
A Song for Occupations. 4

[z] Love like the light silently
wrapping all.
Song of the Universal. 4

[a] Youth, large, lusty, loving—
Youth, full of grace, force,
fascination,
Do you know that Old Age may
come after you, with equal
grace, force, fascination?
*Youth, Day, Old Age and
Night. 1*

[b] Out of the cradle endlessly
rocking.   *Out of the Cradle
Endlessly Rocking. 1*

[c] Give me the splendid silent
sun, with all his beams full-
dazzling!
*Give Me the Splendid Silent
Sun. 1*

[d] Lo, the moon ascending,
Up from the East, the silvery
round moon,
Beautiful over the house-tops,
ghastly, phantom moon,
Immense and silent moon.
Dirge for Two Veterans. 2

[e] Beautiful that war and all its
deeds of carnage must in time
be utterly lost,
That the hands of the sisters
Death and Night incessantly
softly wash again and ever
again, this soiled world.
Reconciliation

[f] When lilacs last in the door-
yard bloom'd,
And the great star early droop'd
in the western sky in the
night,
I mourn'd, and yet shall mourn
with ever-returning spring.
*When Lilacs Last in the
Door-yard Bloom'd. 1*

[g] Come lovely and soothing
death,
Undulate round the world,
serenely arriving, arriving,
In the day, in the night, to all, to
each,
Sooner or later, delicate death.
Ibid. 14

[h] O Captain! my Captain! our
fearful trip is done!
The ship has weather'd every
wrack, the prize we sought is
won,
The port is near, the bells I hear,
the people all exulting.

I with mournful tread,
Walk the deck my Captain lies,
Fallen cold and dead.
*O Captain! My Captain!
1 and 2*

[i] Not till the sun excludes you
do I exclude you.
To a Common Prostitute

[j] I do not think seventy years
is the time of a man or
woman, . . .

Nor that years will ever stop the
existence of me, or any one
else.   *Who Learns My Lesson
Complete?*

[k] To me every hour of the light
and dark is a miracle,
Every cubic inch of space is a
miracle.   *Miracles. 2*

[l] I was thinking the day most
splendid till I saw what the
not-day exhibited,
I was thinking this globe enough
till there sprang out so noiseless around me myriads of
other globes.
Night on the Prairies

[m] Camerado, this is no book,
Who touches this touches a man.
So Long!

[n] I am the Poem of Earth, said
the voice of the rain,
Eternal I rise impalpable out of
the land and the bottomless
sea.   *The Voice of the Rain*

[o] Have you not learn'd great
lessons from those who reject
you, and brace themselves
against you? or who treat you
with contempt, or dispute the
passage with you?
Stronger Lessons

[p] He leaves for America's history and biography, so far, not
only its most dramatic reminis-
cence—he leaves, in my opinion,
the greatest, best, most characteristic, artistic, moral personality.
*Specimen Days. Death of Presi-
dent Lincoln, April 16, 1865*

[q] After you have exhausted
what there is in business, politics,
conviviality, and so on—have
found that none of these finally
satisfy, or permanently wear—
what remains? Nature remains.
Ibid. New Themes Entered Upon

[r] You must not know too much,
or be too precise or scientific
about birds and trees and flowers
and water-craft; a certain free
margin, and even vagueness—perhaps ignorance, credulity—helps
your enjoyment of these things.
Ibid. Birds. May 14, 1881

[s] Political democracy, as it
exists and practically works in
America, with all its threatening
evils, supplies a training-school
for making first-class men. It is
life's gymnasium, not of good
only, but of all.
Democratic Vistas

[t] It is native personality, and
that alone, that endows a man to
stand before presidents or generals, or in any distinguish'd collection, with *aplomb*—and *not*
culture, or any knowledge or intellect whatever.   *Ibid.*

[u] To have great poets, there
must be great audiences, too.
*Notes Left Over. Ventures, on
an Old Theme*

[v] The United States themselves
are essentially the greatest poem.
. . . Here at last is something in
the doings of man that corre-
sponds with the broadcast doings
of the day and night.
Preface to Leaves of Grass [1855]

[w] The proof of a poet is that
his country absorbs him as affectionately as he has absorbed it.
Ibid.

Adeline Dutton Train Whitney
[1824–1906]

[x] God does not send strange
flowers every year.
When the spring winds blow
o'er the pleasant places,
The same dear things lift up
the same fair faces,
The violet is here.
A Violet. Stanza 1

[y] The sun of life has crossed
the line;
The summer-shine of length-
ened light
Faded and failed—till, where I
stand,
'Tis equal day and equal night.
Equinoctial. Stanza 1

John Greenleaf Whittier
[1807–1892]

[z] And ever upon old Decay
The greenest mosses cling.
A Dream of Summer. Stanza 4

[a] Art's perfect forms no moral
need,
And beauty is its own excuse;
But for the dull and flowerless
weed
Some healing virtue still must
plead   *Songs of Labor.
Dedication, Stanza 5*

[b] Heap high the farmer's win-
try hoard!
Heap high the golden corn!
No richer gift has Autumn poured
From out her lavish horn!
The Corn-Song. Stanza 1

[c] When faith is lost, when
honor dies
The man is dead!
Ichabod. Stanza 8

[d] Through the shadowy lens of
even
The eye looks farthest into heaven
On gleams of star and depths of
blue
The glaring sunshine never knew!
All's Well

[e] Search thine own heart. What
paineth thee
In others in thyself may be.
*The Chapel of the Hermits.
Stanza 85*

[f] Blessings on thee, little man,
Barefoot boy, with cheek of tan!
The Barefoot Boy. Stanza 1

[g] Health that mocks the doctor's rules,
Knowledge never learned of
schools.   *Ibid. Stanza 2*

[h] The age is dull and mean.
Men creep,
Not walk.
*Lines Inscribed to Friends under
Arrest for Treason Against the
Slave Power. Stanza 1*

[i] God's ways seem dark, but,
soon or late,
They touch the shining hills of
day.   *Ibid. Stanza 5*

[j] Nature speaks in symbols and
in signs.
To Charles Sumner

[k] For of all sad words of tongue
or pen,
The saddest are these: "It might
have been!"
Maud Muller. Stanza 53

[l] The great eventful Present
hides the Past; but through
the din
Of its loud life hints and echoes
from the life behind steal in.
*The Garrison of Cape Ann.
Stanza 5*

[m] Old roads winding, as old
roads will.   *The Prophecy of
Samuel Sewall. Stanza 6*

[n] The windows of my soul I
throw
Wide open to the sun.
My Psalm. Stanza 2

[o] Once more the liberal year
laughs out
O'er richer stores than gems or
gold;
Once more with harvest-song and
shout
It Nature's bloodless triumph
told.
*For an Autumn Festival.
Stanza 5*

[p] Strike, Thou the Master, we
Thy keys,
The anthem of the destinies!
The minor of Thy loftier strain,
Our hearts shall breathe the old
refrain,
Thy will be done!
Thy Will Be Down. Stanza 7

[q] "Shoot, if you must, this old
gray head,
But spare your country's flag,"
she said.   *Barbara Frietchie.
Stanza 18*

[r] O, rank is good, and gold is
    fair,
And high and low mate ill;
But love has never known a law
Beyond its own sweet will!
                        Amy Wentworth

[s] Shut in from all the world
    without,
We sat the clean-winged hearth
    about.   Snow-Bound

[t] Melt not in an acid sect
The Christian pearl of charity.
                              Ibid.

[u] Alas for him who never sees
The stars shine through his cy-
    press-trees!   Ibid.

[v] Life is ever lord of Death.
                              Ibid.

[w] If woman lost us Eden, such
    As she alone restore it.
        Among the Hills. Stanza 60

[x] Heaven's gate is shut to him
    who comes alone;
Save thou a soul, and it shall
    save thy own!
              The Two Rabbis

[y] God is and all is well.
        My Birthday. Stanza 2

[z] One language held his heart
    and lip,
Straight onward to his goal he
    trod,
And proved the highest states-
    manship
    Obedience to the voice of God.
        Charles Sumner. Stanza 17

[a] With fifty years between you
    and your well-kept wedding
    vow,
The Golden Age, old friends of
    mine, is not a fable now.
    The Golden Wedding at Long-
        wood. Stanza 1

[b] The holiest task by Heaven
    decreed,
An errand all divine,
The burden of our common need
To render less is thine.
        The Healer. Stanza 4

[c] Our fathers' God! from out
    whose hand
The centuries fall like grains of
    sand.
        Centennial Hymn. Stanza 1

[d] Behold in the bloom of apples
And the violets in the sward
A hint of the old, lost beauty
Of the Garden of the Lord!
        The Minister's Daughter.
            Stanza 7

[e] Our first and best!—his ashes
    lie
Beneath his own Virginian sky.
        The Vow of Washington.
            Stanza 14

[f] With the calm patience of the
    woods I wait

For leaf and blossom when God
gives us Spring!
        A Day. Stanza 6

George John Whyte-Melville
[1821–1878]

[g] For everything created
In the bounds of earth and sky
Has such longing to be mated,
It must couple or must die.
                  Like to Like

[h] In the choice of a horse and
a wife, a man must please himself,
ignoring the opinion and advice
of friends.
        Riding Recollections

[i] Education should be as gradual as the moonrise, perceptible
not in progress but in result.
                        Ibid.

Anna Wickham
(Mrs. Patrick Hepburn)
[1883–   ]

[j] The true male never yet
    walked
Who liked to listen when his mate
    talked.   The Affinity

[k] Because of the body's hunger
    are we born,
And by contriving hunger are we
    fed;
Because of hunger is our work well
    done,
And so our songs well sung, and
    things well said.
                    Sehnsucht

Margaret Widdemer
[1880?–   ]

[l] I have shut my little sister in
    from life and light
(For a rose, for a ribbon, for a
    wreath across my hair),
I have made her restless feet still
    until the night,
Locked from sweets of summer
    and from wild spring air.
        The Factories. Stanza 1

[m] Carnations and my first love!
    And he was seventeen,
And I was only twelve years—a
    stately gulf between.
        Carnations. Stanza 1

[n] Well, if the thing is over,
    better it is for me,
The lad was ever a rover, loving
    and laughing and free.
    Mary, Helper of Heartbreak.
            Stanza 1

Albert Edward Wiggam
[1871–   ]

[o] Intelligence appears to be the
thing that enables a man to get

along without education. Education appears to be the thing that enables a man to get along without the use of his intelligence.
The New Decalogue of Science

[p] Statesmanship should quickly learn the lesson of biology, as stated by Conklin, that "Wooden legs are not inherited, but wooden heads are."   *Ibid.*

Kate Douglas Wiggin
[1856–1923]

[q] My heart is open wide to-night
For stranger, kith or kin.
I would not bar a single door
Where Love might enter in.
The Romance of a Christmas Card

Samuel Wilberforce
[1805–1873]

[r] If I were a cassowary
On the plains of Timbuctoo,
I would eat a missionary,
Coat and bands and hymn-book, too.   *Impromptu*

Ella Wheeler Wilcox
[1855–1919]

[s] Talk happiness. The world is sad enough
Without your woe. No path is wholly rough.
Speech. Stanza 1

[t] Talk faith. The world is better off without
Your uttered ignorance and morbid doubt.
Ibid. Stanza 2

[u] Talk health. The dreary, never-ending tale
Of mortal maladies is more than stale. . . .
Say you are well, or all is well with you,
And God shall hear your words and make them true.
Ibid. Stanza 3

[v] It ever has been since time began,
And ever will be, till time lose breath,
That love is a mood—no more—to man,
And love to woman is life or death.   *Blind. Stanza 1*

[w] It is easy to sit in the sunshine
And talk to the man in the shade;
It is easy to float in a well-trimmed boat,
And point out the places to wade.
Practice vs. Preaching. Stanza 1

[x] Laugh, and the world laughs with you;
Weep, and you weep alone;
For the sad old earth must borrow its mirth,
But has trouble enough of its own.   *Solitude. Stanza 1*

Oscar Fingal O'Flahertie Wills Wilde
[1856–1900]

[y] Tread lightly, she is near
Under the snow,
Speak gently, she can hear
The daisies grow.
Requiescat. Stanza 1

[z] Yet each man kills the thing he loves,
By each let this be heard,
Some do it with a bitter look,
Some with a flattering word,
The coward does it with a kiss,
The brave man with a sword!
The Ballad of Reading Gaol. I, 7

[a] I never saw a man who looked with such a wistful eye
Upon that little tent of blue
Which prisoners call the sky,
And at every wandering cloud that trailed
Its ravelled fleeces by.
Ibid. II, 2

[b] All that we know who lie in gaol
Is that the wall is strong;
And that each day is like a year,
A year whose days are long.
Ibid. V, 1

[c] Down the long and silent street,
The dawn, with silver-sandaled feet,
Crept like a frightened girl.
The Harlot's House

[d] Most modern calendars mar the sweet simplicity of our lives by reminding us that each day that passes is the anniversary of some perfectly uninteresting event.   *A Poetic Calendar*

[e] As long as war is regarded as wicked it will always have its fascination. When it is looked upon as vulgar, it will cease to be popular.
The Critic as Artist. Part II

[f] There is no sin except stupidity.   *Ibid.*

[g] Where there is sorrow there is holy ground.   *De Profundis*

[h] All art is quite useless.
The Picture of Dorian Gray. Preface

[i] There is only one thing in the world worse than being talked about, and that is not being talked about.   *Ibid. Chap. 1*

[j] Laughter is not at all a bad beginning for a friendship, and it is far the best ending for one.
Ibid.

[k] The only way to get rid of a temptation is to yield to it.
Ibid. Chap. 2

[l] Children begin by loving their parents; as they grow older they judge them; sometimes they forgive them.   *Ibid. Chap. 5*

[m] When a woman marries again it is because she detested her first husband. When a man marries again, it is because he adored his first wife. Women try their luck; men risk theirs.
Ibid. Chap. 15

[n] Now-a-days we are all of us so hard up, that the only pleasant things to pay are compliments. They're the only things we *can* pay.
Lady Windermere's Fan. Act I

[o] History is merely gossip.
Ibid. Act III

[p] In this world there are only two tragedies. One is not getting what one wants, and the other is getting it.   *Ibid.*

[q] What is a cynic? A man who knows the price of everything, and the value of nothing.
Ibid.

[r] Experience is the name every-one gives to his mistakes. *Ibid.*

[s] They say that when good Americans die they go to Paris.
A Woman of No Importance. Act I

[t] Nothing spoils a romance so much as a sense of humour in the woman.   *Ibid.*

[u] Memory is the diary that we all carry about with us.
The Importance of Being Earnest. Act II

[v] No woman should ever be quite accurate about her age. It looks so calculating.
Ibid. Act III

Thornton Niven Wilder
[1897-   ]

[w] For what human ill does not dawn seem to be an alleviation?
The Bridge of San Luis Rey. III

[x] We come from a world where we have known incredible standards of excellence, and we dimly remember beauties which we have not seized again. . . . The public for which masterpieces are intended is not on this earth.
Ibid. IV

[y] A man looks pretty small at a wedding, George. All those good women standing shoulder to shoulder, making sure that the knot's tied in a mighty public way.
Our Town

[z] The dead don't stay interested in us living people for very long. Gradually, gradually, they let go hold of the earth . . . and the ambitions they had . . . and the pleasures they had . . . and the things they suffered . . . and the people they loved. They get weaned away from earth—that's the way I put it, weaned away.
Ibid.

[a] Every time a child is born into the world it's Nature's attempt to make a perfect human being. Well, we've seen Nature pushing and contriving for some time now. We all know she's interested in quantity; but I think she's interested in quality, too.
Ibid.

Marguerite Wilkinson
[1883–1928]

[b] God bless pawnbrokers!
They are quiet men.
You may go once—
You may go again—
They do not question
As a brother might.
Pawnbrokers

Emma Willard
[1787–1870]

[c] Rocked in the cradle of the deep,
I lay me down in peace to sleep.
The Cradle of the Deep

William, Prince of Orange
[1533–1584]

[d] There is one certain means by which I can be sure never to see my country's ruin,—I will die in the last ditch.
Hume: History of England [1622] and J. R. Green: A Short History of the English People, Chap. 9

Mrs. Bertye Young Williams
[1888-   ]

[e] The inn was full. There was no room.
But certainly I could have done Something if I had known for whom—
Ah, that my door should be the one
To shut out Mary and her Son!
The Bethlehem Innkeeper Speaks. Stanza 3

H. J. Williams
[1874–1924]
and
Jack Judge
[1878–1938]

[f] Good-bye, Piccadilly,
Farewell, Leicester Square,
It's a long, long way to Tipperary,
But my heart's right there!
Tipperary

Oscar Williams
[1899–   ]

[g] One morning the world woke
up and there was no news;
No gun was shelling the great ear
drum of the air,
No Christian flesh spurted be-
neath the subtle screws,
No moaning came from the many
agony-faced Jews,
Only the trees in a gauze of wind
trembled and were fair.
*One Morning the World Woke
Up. Stanza 1*

[h] The prodigious exuberance of
the miniature human beings
Tests the chutes of gravitation,
seventeen trees from the zoo.
The Children's Playground

[i] Get up and out, my man, the
day is bursting with mo-
ments . . .
Rise, my good man, from your
bed of straws in the wind.
The Answer

Wendell Lewis Willkie
[1892–1944]

[j] There are no distant points in
the world any longer. . . . The
myriad millions of human beings
of the Far East are as close to us
as Los Angeles is to New York by
the fastest trains. . . . In the
future what concerns them must
concern us, almost as much as the
problems of the people of California concern the people of New
York. Our thinking in the future
must be world-wide.
Radio Address [*October 26, 1942*]
and One World. Chap. 1

[k] I believe the moral losses of
expediency always far outweigh
the temporary gains. And I believe that every drop of blood
saved through expediency will be
paid for by twenty drawn by the
sword.   *One World. Chap. 4*

[l] Freedom is an indivisible
word. If we want to enjoy it, and
fight for it, we must be prepared
to extend it to everyone, whether
they are rich or poor, whether
they agree with us or not, no matter what their race or the color of
their skin.   *Ibid. Chap. 13*

[m] From the battlefields of Italy
to the gold-star homes here in
America, Negroes have learned
that there is nothing more democratic than a bullet or a splinter
of steel.
*An American Program.
Chap. 2*

[n] The Constitution does not
provide for first and second class
citizens.   *Ibid.*

Dixie Willson
[1896–   ]

[o] He may look just the same to
you,
And he may be just as fine,
But the next-door dog is the
next-door dog,
And mine—is—mine!
Next-Door Dog

Carroll A. Wilson
[1886–1947]

[p] "Familiar quotations" . . .
are more than familiar; they are
something part of us. . . . These
echoes from the past have two
marked characteristics—a simple
idea, and an accurate rhythmic
beat.
*Preface to First Appearance in
Print of some 400 Familiar
Quotations*

McLandburgh Wilson

[q] From out our crowded calen-
dar
One day we pluck to give;
It is the day the Dying pause
To honor those who live.
Memorial Day

[r] 'Twixt the optimist and pessi-
mist
The difference is droll:
The optimist sees the doughnut
But the pessimist sees the hole.
Optimist and Pessimist

T. P. Cameron Wilson
[1889–1918]

[s] Stare Sphinx-like into space,
Nor march the chalky floor all
tousle-haired
When bright boys mention with
a cheerful face
That $(a + a)$ is written down a^2.
*The Mathematical Master to
His Blackboard*

[t] God gives to each man, however beset he may be with the
world, a few minutes at least
daily, when he is utterly alone. I
have read Shelley in a Public
Lavatory, and learnt Rupert
Brooke's war sonnets by heart

while I was doing my morning duty to this body.
Waste Paper Philosophy. IX

Woodrow Wilson
[1856–1924]

[u] There is such a thing as a man being too proud to fight.
Address to Foreign-Born Citizens [May 10, 1915]

[v] The flag is the embodiment, not of sentiment, but of history. It represents the experiences made by men and women . . . who . . . live under that flag.
Address [June 14, 1915]

[w] A little group of willful men, representing no opinion but their own. *Of certain members of the United States Senate [March 4, 1917]*

[x] The day has come when America is privileged to spend her blood and her might for the principles that gave her birth and happiness and the peace which she has treasured. God helping her, she can do no other.
Address to Congress, asking for a declaration of war [April 2, 1917]

[y] The world must be made safe for democracy. *Ibid.*

[z] Open covenants of peace, openly arrived at.
Address to Congress [January 8, 1918]

[a] I have seen fools resist Providence before and I have seen their destruction, as will come upon these again—utter destruction and contempt. That we shall prevail is as sure as that God reigns.
Last public words, to a group of people gathered outside his house on Armistice Day 1923

Duke of Windsor
(King Edward VIII)
[1894–]

[b] At long last I am able to say a few words of my own. I have never wanted to withhold anything, but until now it has not been constitutionally possible for me to speak.
I have found it impossible to carry the heavy burden of responsibility and to discharge my duties as King as I would wish to do without the help and support of the woman I love. . . .
And now we all have a new King. I wish him and you, his people, happiness and prosperity with all my heart.
God bless you all! God save the King! *Farewell broadcast after abdication [December 11, 1936]*

William Winter
[1836–1917]

[c] Who cares for nothing alone is free,—
Sit down, good fellow, and drink with me! *Orgia*

[d] Though all the bards of earth were dead,
And all their music passed away,
What Nature wishes should be said
She'll find the rightful voice to say! *The Golden Silence*

[e] The golden time of Long Ago.
I. H. Bromley

[f] Cold the stars are, cold the earth is,
Everything is grim and cold!
Strange and drear the sound of mirth is
—Life and I are old. *Age*

[g] And, lucid in that second birth,
I shall discern
What all the sages of the earth
Have died to learn. *The Rubicon*

Robert Charles Winthrop
[1809–1894]

[h] A star for every State, and a State for every star.
Address on Boston Common [1862]

[i] The poor must be wisely visited and liberally cared for, so that mendicity shall not be tempted into mendacity, nor want exasperated into crime.
Yorktown Oration [1881]

[j] Slavery is but half abolished, emancipation is but half completed, while millions of freemen with votes in their hands are left without education. *Ibid.*

Owen Wister
[1860–1938]

[k] When you call me that, *smile!*
The Virginian. Chap. 2

Pelham Grenville
Wodehouse
[1881–]

[l] If not actually disgruntled, he was far from being gruntled.
The Code of the Woosters

John Wolcot
("Peter Pindar")
[1738–1819]

[m] Care to our coffin adds a nail, no doubt,
And every grin so merry draws one out.
Expostulatory Odes. XV

Humbert Wolfe
[1885–1940]

[n] Who thought of the lilac?
"I," dew said,
"I made up the lilac
out of my head."
The Lilac. Stanza 1

[o] Like a small grey
coffee-pot
sits the squirrel.
The Grey Squirrel. Stanza 1

[p] Listen! the wind is rising,
and the air is wild with leaves,
We have had our summer eve-
nings,
now for October eves!
Autumn (Resignation). Stanza 2

Thomas Wolfe
[1900–1938]

[q] Which of us is not forever a
stranger and alone?
Look Homeward, Angel!
Foreword

[r] Making the world safe for
hypocrisy.   *Ibid. Part III. 36*

[s] He awakes at morning in a
foreign land, he draws his breath
in labor in the wool-soft air of
Europe: the wool-gray air is all
about him like a living substance
. . . it is in the slow and vital
movements of the people; it soaks
down from the sodden skies into
the earth, into the heavy buildings, into the limbs and hearts
and brains of living men.
Of Time and the River.
Book VII

[t] Where can you match the
mighty music of their names?—
The Monongahela, the Colorado,
the Rio Grande, the Columbia,
the Tennessee, the Hudson (Sweet
Thames!); the Kennebec, the
Rappahannock, the Delaware, the
Penobscot, the Wabash, the Ches-
apeake, the Swannanoa, the Indian River, the Niagara (Sweet
Afton!); the Saint Lawrence, the
Susquehanna, the Tombigbee,
the Nantahala, the French Broad,
the Chattahoochee, the Arizona,
and the Potomac (Father Tiber!)
—these are a few of their princely
names, these are a few of their
great, proud, glittering names, fit
for the immense and lonely land
that they inhabit.
Oh, Tiber! Father Tiber! You'd
only be a suckling in that mighty
land! And as for you, sweet
Thames, flow gently till I end my
song.   *Ibid.*

[u] It is Europeans, for the most
part, who have constructed these
great ships, but without America
they have no meaning. These
ships are alive with the supreme

ecstasy of the modern world,
which is the voyage to America.
There is not one experience that
is remotely comparable to it, in its
sense of joy, its exultancy, its
drunken and magnificent hope.
Ibid. Book VIII

[v] There is no spectacle on earth
more appealing than that of a
beautiful woman in the act of
cooking dinner for someone she
loves.   *The Web and the Rock.*
Chap. 28

[w] If a man has a talent and
cannot use it, he has failed. If he
has a talent and uses only half of
it, he has partly failed. If he has
a talent and learns somehow to
use the whole of it, he has gloriously succeeded, and won a satisfaction and a triumph few men
ever know.   *Ibid. Chap. 30*

George Edward Woodberry
[1855–1930]

[x] O, inexpressible as sweet,
Love takes my voice away;
I cannot tell thee when we meet
What most I long to say.
Song

[y] Where are the friends that I
knew in my Maying,
In the days of my youth, in the
first of my roaming?
Comrades. Stanza 1

John E. Woodrow
[?–1905]

[z] The Church should have a
tapering spire,
To point to realms where sin's
forgiven,
And lead men's thoughts from
earth to heaven.
Spire and Tower

William E. Woodward
[1874–1950]

[a] In the queer mess of human
destiny the determining factor is
Luck. For every important place
in life there are many men of
fairly equal capacities. Among
them Luck decides who shall accomplish the great work, who
shall be crowned with laurel, and
who shall fall back into obscurity
and silence.   *George Washing-*
ton. Chap. 3, Part 2

[b] The turning points of lives
are not the great moments. The
real crises are often concealed in
occurrences so trivial in appearance that they pass unobserved.
Ibid.

[c] Vanity as an impulse has
without doubt been of far more

benefit to civilization than modesty has ever been.
Ibid. Chap. 5, Part I

Samuel Woodworth
[1785–1842]

[d] How dear to this heart are
  the scenes of my childhood,
When fond recollection presents
  them to view.
  The Old Oaken Bucket

[e] Then soon with the emblem
  of truth overflowing,
And dripping with coolness, it
  rose from the well. . . .
The old oaken bucket, the iron-
  bound bucket,
The moss-covered bucket, which
  hung in the well.   *Ibid.*

Virginia Woolf
[1882–1941]

[f] Those comfortably padded
lunatic asylums which are known,
euphemistically, as the stately
homes of England.
  *The Common Reader. Lady
      Dorothy Nevill*

[g] The word-coining genius, as
if thought plunged into a sea of
words and came up dripping.
  Ibid. An Elizabethan Play

[h] The beauty of the world has
two edges, one of laughter, one of
anguish, cutting the heart asunder.   *A Room of One's Own*

[i] Women have served all these
centuries as looking-glasses possessing the magic and delicious
power of reflecting the figure of
man at twice its natural size.
  Ibid.

Alexander Woollcott
[1887–1943]

[j] "Ladies, just a little more
virginity, if you don't mind."
  *Capsule Criticism [Beerbohm
      Tree to the Extras]*

[k] The play left a taste of luke-
warm parsnip juice.
  *Drama review in The New York
      Times*

[l] Inkstained wretches.
  Ibid., of dramatic critics

[m] I must get out of these wet
clothes and into a dry Martini.
  Quoted in Reader's Digest

[n] Babies in silk hats playing
with dynamite.
  *Of diplomats. Quoted by
      Samuel Hopkins Adams:
      "A. Woollcott"*

[o] I am going back to the microphone as a drunkard to his bottle.
  Ibid.

John Woolman
[1720–1772]

[p] Though the change from day
to night is by a motion so gradual
as scarcely to be perceived, yet
when night is come we behold it
very different from the day; and
thus as people become wise in
their own eyes, and prudent in
their own sight, customs rise up
from the spirit of this world, and
spread by little, and little, till a
departure from the simplicity
that there is in Christ becomes as
distinguishable as light from
darkness, to such who are crucified to the world.
  *Considerations on the True
      Harmony of Mankind*

Sarah Chauncey Woolsey
("Susan Coolidge")
[1845–1905]

[q] Every day is a fresh beginning,
Every morn is the world made
  new.   *New Every Morning.
                Stanza 1*

[r] And God, who studies each
  commonplace soul,
Out of commonplace things makes
  His beautiful whole.
  Commonplace

William Wordsworth
[1770–1850]

[s] The Poet binds together by
passion and knowledge the vast
empire of human society, as it is
spread over the whole earth, and
over all time.   *Lyrical Ballads,
      Second Edition. Preface*

[t] All men feel something of an
honorable bigotry for the objects
which have long continued to
please them.   *Ibid.*

[u]   A simple child,
That lightly draws its breath,
And feels its life in every limb,
What should it know of death?
  We are Seven. Stanza 1

[v] And 'tis my faith, that every
  flower
Enjoys the air it breathes.
  *Lines Written in Early Spring.
                Stanza 3*

[w] One impulse from a vernal
  wood
May teach you more of man,
Of moral evil and of good,
Than all the sages can.
  The Tables Turned. Stanza 6

[x]   The sounding cataract
Haunted me like a passion.
  *Lines Composed a Few Miles
      Above Tintern Abbey*

[y] Men who can hear the Decalogue and feel
No self-reproach.
The Old Cumberland Beggar

[z] A primrose by a river's brim
A yellow primrose was to him,
And it was nothing more.
Peter Bell. Part I, Stanza 12

[a] One of those heavenly days
that cannot die.   *Nutting*

[b] She dwelt among the untrodden ways
Beside the springs of Dove,
A maid whom there were none to praise
And very few to love.

A violet by a mossy stone
Half hidden from the eye!—
Fair as a star, when only one
Is shining in the sky.
Lucy: She Dwelt Among the Untrodden Ways. Stanzas 1 and 2

[c]   She shall lean her ear
In many a secret place
Where rivulets dance their wayward round,
And beauty born of murmuring sound
Shall pass into her face.
Lucy: Three Years She Grew in Sun and Shower. Stanza 5

[d] May no rude hand deface it,
And its forlorn *hic jacet!*
Ellen Irwin. Stanza 7

[e] The child is father of the man.   *My Heart Leaps Up When I Behold*

[f] The cattle are grazing,
Their heads never raising;
There are forty feeding like one!
The Cock Is Crowing. Stanza 1

[g] Sweet childish days, that were as long
As twenty days are now.
To a Butterfly. Part II: I've Watched You Now a Full Half-hour, Stanza 2

[h] Ne'er saw I, never felt, a calm so deep!
The river glideth at his own sweet will;
Dear God! the very houses seem asleep;
And all that mighty heart is lying still!   *Lines Composed Upon Westminster Bridge*

[i] The holy time is quiet as a nun
Breathless with adoration.
It is a Beauteous Evening

[j] Men are we, and must grieve when even the shade
Of that which once was great, is passed away.
On the Extinction of the Venetian Republic

[k] Milton! thou should'st be living at this hour:
England hath need of thee! . . .
Thy soul was like a star, and dwelt apart: . . .
So didst thou travel on life's common way,
In cheerful godliness.
London, 1802

[l] Thou unassuming commonplace
Of Nature.
To the Daisy. Part II, Stanza 1

[m] Because the good old rule
Sufficeth them, the simple plan,
That they should take, who have the power,
And they should keep who can.   *Rob Roy's Grave. Stanza 9*

[n] A brotherhood of venerable trees.
Sonnet composed at —— Castle

[o] O Cuckoo! shall I call thee bird,
Or but a wandering voice?
To the Cuckoo. Stanza 1

[p] She was a phantom of delight
When first she gleamed upon my sight;
A lovely apparition, sent
To be a moment's ornament;
Her eyes as stars of twilight fair,
Like twilight's, too, her dusky hair,
But all things else about her drawn
From May-time and the cheerful dawn.   *She Was a Phantom of Delight. Stanza 1*

[q] The reason firm, the temperate will,
Endurance, foresight, strength, and skill;
A perfect woman, nobly planned,
To warn, to comfort, and command.   *Ibid. Stanza 3*

[r]   I saw a crowd,
A host, of golden daffodils.
I Wandered Lonely as a Cloud. Stanza 1

[s]   That inward eye
Which is the bliss of solitude.
Ibid. Stanza 4

[t] Stern Daughter of the Voice of God!
Ode to Duty. Stanza 1

[u] The light that never was, on sea or land;
The consecration, and the Poet's dream.
Suggested by a Picture of Peele Castle in a Storm. Stanza 4

[v]   A mind forever
Voyaging through strange seas of thought, alone.
The Prelude. Book III

[w]   There's not a man
That lives who hath not known
   his godlike hours.   *Ibid.*

[x] Oh! give us once again the
   wishing-cap
Of Fortunatus, and the invisible
   coat
Of Jack the Giant-Killer, Robin
   Hood,
And Sabra in the forest with St.
   George!
The child, whose love is here, at
   least, doth reap
One precious gain, that he forgets
   himself.   *Ibid. Book V*

[y]   How men lived
Even next-door neighbours, as we
   say, yet still
Strangers, not knowing each the
   other's name.
          Ibid. Book VII

[z] Bliss was it in that dawn to
   be alive,
But to be young was very heaven!
          Ibid. Book XI

[a] The world is too much with
   us; late and soon,
Getting and spending, we lay
   waste our powers:
Little we see in Nature that is
   ours.   *The World Is Too
          Much With Us*

[b]   Great God! I'd rather be
A Pagan suckled in a creed outworn.   *Ibid.*

[c] A flock of sheep that leisurely
   pass by,
One after one; the sound of rain,
   and bees
Murmuring; the fall of rivers,
   winds and seas,
Smooth fields, white sheets of
   water, and pure sky;
I have thought of all by turns,
   and yet do lie
Sleepless!   *To Sleep. II, A Flock
          of Sheep*

[d] Blessed barrier between day
   and day.   *Ibid.*

[e] Maidens withering on the
   stalk.   *Personal Talk.
          Sonnet 1*

[f] Dreams, books, are each a
   world; and books, we know,
Are a substantial world, both pure
   and good.   *Ibid. Sonnet 3*

[g] The rainbow comes and goes.
   *Intimations of Immortality.
          Stanza 2*

[h] Our birth is but a sleep and a
   forgetting:
The soul that rises with us, our
   life's star,
   Hath had elsewhere its setting,
   And cometh from afar:
Not in entire forgetfulness,
And not in utter nakedness,

But trailing clouds of glory do we
   come
From God, who is our home:
Heaven lies about us in our infancy!   *Ibid. Stanza 5*

[i] As if his whole vocation
Were endless imitation.
          Ibid. Stanza 7

[j] Though inland far we be,
Our souls have sight of that im-
   mortal sea
Which brought us hither.
          Ibid. Stanza 9

[k] To me the meanest flower
   that blows can give
Thoughts that do often lie too
   deep for tears.
          Ibid. Stanza 11

[l] The monumental pomp of
   age
Was with this goodly personage;
A stature undepressed in size,
Unbent, which rather seemed to
   rise,
In open victory o'er the weight
Of seventy years, to loftier height.
   *The White Doe of Rylstone.
          Canto III*

[m]   The good die first,
And they whose hearts are dry as
   summer dust
Burn to the socket.
          The Excursion. Book I

[n] There is a luxury in self-
   dispraise;
And inward self-disparagement
   affords
To meditative spleen a grateful
   feast.   *Ibid. Book IV*

[o]   I have seen
A curious child, who dwelt upon
   a tract
Of inland ground, applying to his
   ear
The convolutions of a smooth-
   lipped shell,
To which, in silence hushed, his
   very soul
Listened intensely; and his countenance soon
Brightened with joy, for from
   within were heard
Murmurings, whereby the moni-
   tor expressed
Mysterious union with its native
   sea.   *Ibid.*

[p] One in whom persuasion and
   belief
Had ripened into faith, and faith
   become
A passionate intuition.   *Ibid.*

[q] A man he seems of cheerful
   yesterdays
And confident to-morrows.
          Ibid. Book VII

[r]   The gods approve
The depth, and not the tumult,
   of the soul.
          Laodamia. Stanza 13

[s]   Mightier far
Than strength of nerve and
    sinew, or the sway
Of magic potent over sun and
    star,
Is Love, though oft to agony dis-
    trest,
And though his favorite seat be
    feeble woman's breast.
        Ibid. Stanza 15

[t] As thou these ashes, little
    brook, wilt bear
Into the Avon, Avon to the tide
Of Severn, Severn to the narrow
    seas,
Into main ocean they, this deed
    accursed
An emblem yields to friends and
    enemies
How the bold teacher's doctrine,
    sanctified
By truth, shall spread, throughout
    the world dispersed.
    Ecclesiastical Sonnets. Part II,
        XVII, To Wickliffe

[u] Give all thou canst; high
    Heaven rejects the lore
Of nicely-calculated less or more.
    Ibid. XLIII, Inside of King's
        College Chapel, Cambridge

[v]   Where music dwells
Lingering—and wandering on as
    loth to die.   *Ibid.*

[w] Ethereal minstrel! pilgrim of
    the sky!   *To a Skylark.*
            Stanza 1

[x] A Briton, even in love, should
    be
A subject, not a slave!
    Ere with Cold Beads of Midnight
        Dew. Stanza 5

[y] Small service is true service
    while it lasts.
Of humblest friends, bright crea-
    ture! scorn not one:
The daisy, by the shadow that it
    casts,
Protects the lingering dewdrop
    from the sun.   *To a Child,*
        Written in her Album

[z] They called thee Merry Eng-
    land in old time;
A happy people won for thee that
    name
With envy heard in many a dis-
    tant clime.   *They Called*
        Thee Merry England

[a] Wouldst thou be gathered to
    Christ's chosen flock,
Shun the broad way too easily ex-
    plored,
And let thy path be hewn out of
    the Rock,
The living Rock of God's Eternal
    Word.   *Inscription on a*
        Rock at Rydal Mount

[b] How does the meadow-flower
    its bloom unfold?
Because the lovely little flower is
    free

Down to its root, and, in that
    freedom, bold.   *A Poet! He*
    Hath Put His Heart to School

[c] Minds that have nothing to
    confer
Find little to perceive.
    Yes, Thou art Fair. Stanza 2

Henry Clay Work
[1832–1884]

[d] It mus' be now de kingdom
    coming,
An' de year ob Jubilo!
    Kingdom Coming. Chorus

[e] Nicodemus, the slave, was of
    African birth,
And was bought for a bag full
    of gold:
He was reckoned as part of the
    salt of the earth,
But he died, years ago, very old.
    Wake Nicodemus. Stanza 1

[f] Father, dear father, come
    home with me now,
The clock in the steeple strikes
    one;
You said you were coming right
    home from the shop
As soon as your day's work was
    done.
    Come Home, Father. Stanza 1

[g] My grandfather's clock was
    too large for the shelf,
So it stood ninety years on the
    floor.   *Grandfather's Clock*

Sir Henry Wotton
[1568–1639]

[h] Love lodged in a woman's
    breast
Is but a guest.
        A Woman's Heart

[i] Lord of himself, though not of
    lands;
And having nothing, yet hath
    all.   *The Character of a*
        Happy Life. Stanza 6

[j] He first deceased; she for a
    little tried
To live without him, liked it not,
    and died.   *Upon the Death*
        of Sir Albert Morton's Wife

[k] Hanging was the worst use a
    man could be put to.
        The Disparity between
        Buckingham and Essex

[l] An ambassador is an honest
    man sent to lie abroad for the
    commonwealth.
        Reliquiæ Wottonianæ

Sir Christopher Wren
[1632–1723]

[m] Whereas, among labourers
    and others, that ungodly custom
    of swearing is too frequently

heard, to the dishonour of God and contempt of authority; and to the end that such impiety may be utterly banished from these works, which are intended for the service of God and the honour of religion, it is ordered that profane swearing shall be a sufficient crime to dismiss any labourer.
Notice to workmen employed during the building of St. Paul's Cathedral

Ernest Vincent Wright
[1872–1939]

[n] Then all of us prepare to rise
And hold our bibs before our eyes,
And be prepared for some surprise
When father carves the duck.
When Father Carves the Duck. Stanza 1

Frank Lloyd Wright
[1869-   ]

[o] No house should ever be *on* any hill or on anything. It should be *of* the hill, belonging to it, so hill and house could live together each the happier for the other.
Autobiography

John Wycliffe
[?–1384]

[p] I believe that in the end the truth will conquer.
To the Duke of Lancaster [1381]
(Quoted by J. R. Green: A Short History of the English People. Chap. 5)

Elinor Hoyt Wylie
[1887–1928]

[q] We shall walk in velvet shoes:
Wherever we go
Silence will fall like dews
On white silence below.
We shall walk in the snow.
Velvet Shoes. Stanza 4

[r] If you would keep your soul
From spotted sight or sound,
Live like the velvet mole;
Go burrow underground.
The Eagle and the Mole. Stanza 5

[s] I was, being human, born alone;
I am, being woman, hard beset;
I live by squeezing from a stone
The little nourishment I get.
Let No Charitable Hope. Stanza 2

[t] In masks outrageous and austere
The years go by in single file;
But none has merited my fear,
And none has quite escaped my smile.
Ibid. Stanza 3

[u] Farewell, sweet dust; I was never a miser:
Once, for a minute, I made you mine:
Now you are gone, I am none the wiser,
But the leaves of the willow are bright as wine.
Farewell, Sweet Dust. Stanza 4

[v] The clever body five times sensitive
I never have discovered to be kind
As the poor soul, deceived and half-divined,
Whose hopes are water in a witch's sieve.
Angels and Earthly Creatures. One Person. Sonnet VI

[w] I bear a little more than I can bear. *Ibid. Sonnet XVI*

[x] If any have a stone to throw
It is not I, ever or now.
The Pebble

[y] Pity the prickly star that frightens
The Christ Child with its shattered spear.
Pity Me. Stanza 3

[z] The worst and best are both inclined
To snap like vixens at the truth;
But, O, beware the middle mind
That purrs and never shows a tooth!
Nonsense Rhyme. Stanza 2

[a] Honied words like bees,
Gilded and sticky, with a little sting. *Pretty Words*

[b] She'd give the shirt from off her back, except that
She doesn't wear a shirt, and most men do;
And often and most bitterly she's wept that
A starving tramp can't eat a silver shoe. *Portrait in Black Paint. Stanza 2*

[c] Hail, element of earth, receive thy own,
And cherish, at thy charitable breast,
This man, this mongrel beast:
He plows the sand, and, at his hardest need,
He sows himself for seed.

Receive him as thy lover for an hour
Who will not weary, by a longer stay,
The kind embrace of clay.
Hymn to Earth. Stanzas 6 and 7

Thomas Russell Ybarra
[1880-   ]

[d] Oh, the Roman was a rogue,
He erat was, you bettum;
He ran his automobilus
And smoked his cigarettum.

He wore a diamond studibus
And elegant cravattum,
A maxima cum laude shirt,
And such a stylish hattum.
Lay of Ancient Rome

[e] A Christian is a man who feels
Repentance on a Sunday
For what he did on Saturday
And is going to do on Monday.
The Christian

William Butler Yeats
[1865–1939]

[f]   The land of faery,
Where nobody gets old and godly and grave,
Where nobody gets old and crafty and wise,
Where nobody gets old and bitter of tongue.
The Land of Heart's Desire

[g]   When we are young
We long to tread a way none trod before.   *Ibid.*

[h]   Land of Heart's Desire,
Where beauty has no ebb, decay no flood,
But joy is wisdom, Time an endless song.   *Ibid.*

[i] The wrong of unshapely things is a wrong too great to be told.
The Lover Tells of the Rose in His Heart. Stanza 2

[j] The years like great black oxen tread the world
And God, the herdsman, goads them on behind.
The Countess Cathleen

[k] An aged man is but a paltry thing,
A tattered coat upon a stick, unless
Soul clap its hands and sing, and louder sing
For every tatter in its mortal dress.
Sailing to Byzantium. Stanza 2

[l] Consume my heart away, sick with desire
And fastened to a dying animal
It knows not what it is, and gather me
Into the artifice of eternity.
Ibid. Stanza 3

[m] He who is wrapped in purple robes,
With planets in His care,
Had pity on the least of things
Asleep upon a chair.   *The Ballad of Father Gilligan. Stanza 12*

[n] I find, under the boughs of love and hate,
In all poor foolish things that live a day,
Eternal beauty wandering on her way.   *To the Rose upon the Rood of Time*

[o] But I, being poor, have only my dreams;
I have spread my dreams under your feet;
Tread softly because you tread on my dreams.   *He Wishes for the Cloths of Heaven*

[p] She bid me take life easy, as the grass grows on the weirs;
But I was young and foolish, and now am full of tears.
Down by the Salley Gardens

[q] I will arise and go now, and go to Innisfree,
And a small cabin build there, of clay and wattles made;
Nine bean-rows will I have there, a hive for the honey-bee,
And live alone in the bee-loud glade.
The Lake Isle of Innisfree

[r] When I play on my fiddle in Dooney,
Folk dance like a wave of the sea.
The Fiddler of Dooney. Stanza 1

[s] For the good are always the merry,
Save by an evil chance,
And the merry love the fiddle,
And the merry love to dance.
Ibid. Stanza 4

[t] Nor law, nor duty bade me fight,
Nor public men, nor cheering crowds,
A lonely impulse of delight
Drove to this tumult in the clouds;
I balanced all, brought all to mind,
The years to come seemed waste of breath,
A waste of breath the years behind
In balance with this life, this death.   *An Irish Airman Foresees His Death*

[u] What were all the world's alarms
To mighty Paris when he found
Sleep upon a golden bed
That first dawn in Helen's arms.
Lullaby. Stanza 1

Jack Yellen
and
Milton Ager

[v] Happy days are here again,
The skies above are clear again,
Let us sing a song of cheer again,
Happy days are here again!
Happy Days are Here Again [written 1929]. Democratic campaign song, 1932.

Edward Young
[1683–1765]

[w] Creation sleeps! 'Tis as the general pulse

Of life stood still, and Nature
   made a pause,—
An awful pause! prophetic of her
   end.
Night Thoughts. Night I, Line 23

[x] Poor pensioner on the bounties of an hour. *Ibid. Line 67*

[y] Be wise to-day; 'tis madness
   to defer. *Ibid. Line 390*

[z] Procrastination is the thief
   of time. *Ibid. Line 393*

[a] At thirty, man suspects himself a fool;
Knows it at forty, and reforms his
   plan;
At fifty chides his infamous delay,
Pushes his prudent purpose to resolve;
In all the magnanimity of
   thought
Resolves, and re-resolves; then
   dies the same. *Ibid. Line 417*

[b] All men think all men mortal
   but themselves.
             Ibid. Line 424

[c]   Thoughts shut up want air,
And spoil, like bales unopen'd to
   the sun.
        Ibid. Night II, Line 466

[d] How blessings brighten as
   they take their flight!
             Ibid. Line 602

[e] By night an atheist half believes a God.
        Ibid. Night V, Line 177

[f] Our birth is nothing but our
   death begun. *Ibid. Line 719*

[g] The man that blushes is not
   quite a brute.
        Ibid. Night VII, Line 496

[h] Some for renown, on scraps
   of learning dote,
And think they grow immortal as
   they quote.
Love of Fame. Satire I, Line 89

[i]   Be wise with speed;
A fool at forty is a fool indeed.
        Ibid. Satire II, Line 282

[j] For her own breakfast she'll
   project a scheme,
Nor take her tea without a strata-
   gem. *Ibid. Satire VI, Line 190*

[k] Think naught a trifle,
   though it small appear;
Small sands the mountain, moments make the year.
             Ibid. Line 208

[l] One to destroy is murder by
   the law,
And gibbets keep the lifted hand
   in awe;

To murder thousands takes a
   spacious name,
War's glorious art, and gives immortal fame.
       Ibid. Satire VII, Line 55

[m] Oftener chang'd their principles than shirt.
To Mr. Pope. Epistle I, Line 278

George W. Young

[n] The word must be spoken
   that bids you depart—
Though the effort to speak it
   should shatter my heart—
Though in silence, with blighted
   affection, I pine,
Yet the lips that touch liquor
   must never touch mine!
The Lips That Touch Liquor.
             Stanza 5

Roland Young
[1887–   ]

[o] And here's the happy bound-
   ing flea—
You cannot tell the he from she.
The sexes look alike, you see;
But she can tell, and so can he.
             The Flea

Israel Zangwill
[1864–1926]

[p] In how many lives does Love
really play a dominant part? The
average taxpayer is no more
capable of a "grand passion" than
of a grand opera. *Romeo and
Juliet and Other Love Stories*

Zeuxis
[*Circa* 400 B.C.]

[q] Criticism comes easier than
craftsmanship. *Quoted by Pliny
in Natural History*

Hans Zinsser
[1878–1940]

[r] How sweet the Summer! And
   the Autumn shone
Like warmth within our hearts as
   in the sky,
Ripening rich harvests that our
   love had sown.
How good that ere the Winter
   comes, I die!
Then, ageless in your heart, I'll
   come to rest
Serene and proud, as when you
   loved me best. . . .
Then all on earth that Death has
   left behind
Will be the merry part of me
   within your mind. *Sonnets*

OF UNKNOWN AUTHORSHIP

[s] One precedent creates another. They soon accumulate and constitute law. What yesterday was fact, to-day is doctrine.
The Letters of Junius [Attributed, among others, to Sir Philip Francis, Lord Shelburne, Lord George Sackville, and Earl Temple]. Dedication to the English Nation

[t] The liberty of the press is the Palladium of all the civil, political, and religious rights of an Englishman. *Ibid.*

[u] There are some hereditary strokes of character by which a family may be as clearly distinguished as by the blackest features of the human face.
Ibid. XII, To the Duke of Grafton [May 30, 1769]

[v] I do not give you to posterity as a pattern to imitate, but as an example to deter. *Ibid.*

[w] We owe it to our ancestors to preserve entire those rights, which they have delivered to our care: we owe it to our posterity, not to suffer their dearest inheritance to be destroyed.
Ibid. XX, To the Printer of the Public Advertiser [August 8, 1769]

[x] There is a moment of difficulty and danger at which flattery and falsehood can no longer deceive, and simplicity itself can no longer be misled. *Ibid. XXXV, To the Printer of the Public Advertiser [December 19, 1769]*

[y] They [the Americans] equally detest the pageantry of a King, and the supercilious hypocrisy of a bishop. *Ibid.*

[z] We lament the mistakes of a good man, and do not begin to detest him until he affects to renounce his principles.
Ibid. XLI, To Lord Mansfield [November 14, 1770]

[a] The injustice to an individual is sometimes of service to the public. Facts are apt to alarm us more than the most dangerous principles. *Ibid.*

[b] Sumer is icumen in,
Lhude sing cuccu!
Groweth sed, and bloweth med,
And springth the wude nu—
Sing cuccu!
Cuckoo Song. Stanza 1 [Circa 1250. "The most ancient song

that appears with the musical notes attached."—Thomas Warton (1728–1790): History of English Poetry]

[c] When want comes in at the door, love flies out of the window
The Oxford Dictionary of English Proverbs traces this back to J. Clarke: Paroemiologia [1639]

[d] The King of France went up the hill
With twenty thousand men;
The King of France came down the hill,
And ne'er went up again.
Pigges Corantoe, or Newes from the North [A tract printed in London in 1642]. Page 3

[e] Sabina has a thousand charms
To captivate my heart;
Her lovely eyes are Cupid's arms,
And every look a dart:
But when the beauteous idiot speaks,
She cures me of my pain;
Her tongue the servile fetters breaks
And frees her slave again.
From Amphion Anglicus [1700]. [Published in Norman Ault: Seventeenth Century Lyrics]

[f] The United Voice of all His Majesty's free and loyal Subjects in America—Liberty and Property. and no Stamps.
Motto of various American colonial newspapers [1765–1766]

[g] No foe dare molest, where in union are join'd
The plough, loom, and chisel, with commerce combined
Plough, Loom and Chisel Stanza 1 [Ode sung at the Triennial Festival of the Massachusetts Charitable Mechanic Association, Boston, 1810]

[h] An Austrian army, awfully array'd,
Boldly by battery besiege Belgrade;
Cossack commanders cannonading come,
Deal devastation's dire destructive doom;
Ev'ry endeavour engineers essay,
For fame, for freedom, fight, fierce furious fray.
Gen'rals 'gainst gen'rals grapple
—gracious God!
How honors Heav'n heroic hardihood!

Infuriate, indiscriminate in ill,
Just Jesus, instant innocence in-
    still!
Kinsmen kill kinsmen, kindred
    kill.
Labour low levels longest, loftiest
    lines;
Men march 'midst mounds, moats,
    mountains, murd'rous mines.
Now noisy, noxious numbers no-
    tice nought,
Of outward obstacles o'ercoming
    ought;
Poor patriots perish, persecu-
    tion's pest!
Quite quiet Quakers "Quarter,
    quarter" quest;
Reason returns, religion, right,
    redounds,
Suwarrow, stop such sanguinary
    sounds!
Truce to thee, Turkey, terror to
    thy train!
Unwise,   unjust,   unmerciful
    Ukraine!
Vanish vile vengeance, vanish
    victory vain!
Why wish we warfare? wherefore
    welcome won
Xerxes,   Xantippus,   Xavier,
    Xenophon?
Yield, ye young Yaghier yeomen,
    yield your yell!
Zimmerman's, Zoroaster's, Zeno's
    zeal
Again attract; arts against arms
    appeal.
All, all ambitious aims, avaunt,
    away!
Et cætera, et cætera, et cæterā.
    Alliteration, or the Siege of Bel-
    grade: a Rondeau [The Trifler,
    London, 1817]

[i] Howe'er their patients may
    complain,
Of head, or heart, or nerve, or
    vein,
Of fever high, or parch, or swell,
The remedy is Calomel.
    Calomel. Stanza 2 [before 1853]

[j] The sons of the prophet are
    brave men and bold,
And quite unaccustomed to
    fear,
But the bravest by far in the
    ranks of the Shah
Was Abdul the Bulbul Amir.

Now the heroes were plenty and
    well known to fame
In the troops that were led by
    the Czar,
And the bravest of these was a
    man by the name
Of Ivan Petruski Skavar.
    Abdul the Bulbul Amir.
    Stanzas 1 and 3

[k] Oh, the praties they are
    small—
Over here, over here.

Oh, the praties they are small
When we dig 'em in the fall,
And we eat 'em, coats and all,
Full of fear, full of fear.
    Irish Famine Song [1846–1847]

[l] Oh, ye'll tak' the high road
    an' I'll tak' the low road,
An' I'll be in Scotland before ye;
But trouble it is there an' mony
    hearts are sair,
On the bonnie, bonnie banks of
    Loch Lomond.   *Scottish*
    Ballad, Loch Lomond. Refrain

[m] Went out to milk and I
    didn't know how,
I milked the goat instead of the
    cow;
A monkey sittin' on a pile of
    straw
A-winkin' at his mother-in-law.
Turkey in the straw, turkey in the
    hay,
Roll 'em up and twist 'em up a
    high tuckahaw,
And hit 'em up a tune called Tur-
    key in the Straw.
    Turkey in the Straw.
    Stanza 1 and refrain

[n] Sugar in the gourd and honey
    in the horn,
I never was so happy since the
    hour I was born.
    Ibid. Stanza 6

[o] Frankie and Johnny were
    lovers, my gawd, how they
    could love,
Swore to be true to each other,
    true as the stars above;
He was her man, but he done her
    wrong.
    Frankie and Johnny. Stanza 1

[p] All I want of you is a little
see-vility, and that of the commonest goddamnedest kind.
    The New Bedford Classic, as re-
    ported in The History of New
    Bedford [1918] by Zephaniah W.
    Pease. Supposed to be said by
    the mate of a whaler to his ill-
    humored captain

[q] Across the plains where once
    there roamed
The Indian and the Scout,
The Swede with alcoholic breath
Sets rows of cabbage out.
    Quoted by D. W. Brogan in
    The American Character

[r] The lady would remind you,
    please,
Her name is not Lost Angie Lees,
Nor Angie anything whatever.
She hopes her friends will be so
    clever
To share her fit historic pride,
The g should not be jellified.
O long, g hard, and rhyme with
    "yes"—
That's all about Loce Ang-El-Ess
    Los Angeles

[s] Just after the death of the
      flowers,
  And before they are buried in
      snow,
There comes a festival season
  When Nature is all aglow.
      Indian Summer. Stanza 1 [1860]

[t] I pray the prayer the East-
      erners do,
  May the peace of Allah abide with
      you.   *Salaam Alaikum*
          (*Peace Be with You*)

[u] Listen to the Exhortation of
      the Dawn.
  Look to this Day!
For it is Life, the very Life of Life.
  In its brief course lie all the
      Verities and Realities of your
      Existence. . . .
For Yesterday is but a Dream,
  And To-morrow is only a Vision.
      . . .
Look well therefore to this Day!
Such is the Salutation of the
      Dawn.   *The Salutation of
      the Dawn, from the Sanskrit*

[v] The woman was not taken
      From Adam's head, you know,
  So she must not command him,
      'Tis evidently so;
The woman was not taken
      From Adam's feet, you see,
  So he must not abuse her—
      The meaning seems to be.
The woman she was taken
      From under Adam's arm,
  Which shows he must protect her
      From injury and harm.
      Old Scotch Nuptial Song
          [*before 1860*]

[w] Drill, ye tarriers, drill,
  And it's work all day
Without sugar in your tay,
  When you're working for the U.P.
      Railway.   *Laborers' song
      during the construction of
      the Union Pacific Railway*

[x] In the days of old Rameses
  That story had paresis.
      *A familiar saying in the White-
      chapel Club, Chicago.* [*Quoted
      by Kipling in The Ship That
      Found Herself*]

[y] From the halls of Monte-
      zuma,
  To the shores of Tripoli,
We fight our country's battles
  On the land as on the sea.

If the Army and the Navy
  Ever look on Heaven's scenes,
They will find the streets are
      guarded by
  The United States Marines.
      *U. S. Marines' Song.
      Stanzas 1 and 4*

[z] The beauty of the house is
      order;
  The blessing of the house is con-
      tentment;

The glory of the house is hospi-
      tality;
  The crown of the house is godli-
      ness.   *Fireplace Motto*

[a] "I drink to one," he said,
  "Whose image never may depart,
Deep graven on this grateful
      heart,
  Till memory be dead.
To one whose love for me shall
      last
  When lighter passions long have
      passed,
So holy 'tis, and true."
      *The Knight's Toast (to his
      Mother)* [*Attributed to Sir
      Walter Scott but not found
      in his writings*]. *Stanzas 7
      and 8*

[b] Mr. Finney had a turnip,
  And it grew behind the barn,
And it grew, and it grew,
  And the turnip did no harm.
      Mr. Finney's Turnip [*Attributed
      to Longfellow but denied by
      him*]. *Stanza 1*

[c] I'm Terence O'Reilly, I'm a
      man of renown . . .
  If they'd let me be, I'd have Ire-
      land free,
On the railroads you'd not pay
      any fare,
  I'd have the United States under
      my thumb,
And I'd sleep in the President's
      chair.   *Is That Mr. Reilly?
      Stanza 1* [1882]

[d] The Monkey married the
      Baboon's sister,
  Smacked his lips and then he
      kissed her.
      The Monkey's Wedding. Stanza 1
      [*Regimental March of the Ninth
      U. S. Cavalry*]

[e] Reuben, I have long been
      thinking
  What a good world this would
      be,
If the men were all transported
  On this side the Northern Sea.
      Reuben and Rachel. Stanza 1

[f] I loathe, abhor, despise,
  Abominate dried apple pies.
I like good bread, I like good
      meat,
  Or anything that's fit to eat,
But of all poor grub beneath the
      skies,
  The poorest is dried apple pies.
Give me the toothache or sore
      eyes
  In preference to such kind of
      pies. . . .
Tread on my corns, or tell me lies,
  But don't pass me dried apple
      pies!   *Dried Apple Pies*

[g] There is a mystery in human
      hearts,
  And though we be encircled by a
      host

Of those who love us well and are
  beloved,
To every one of us, from time to
  time,
There comes a sense of utter loneliness.

And those who walk with Him
  from day to day
Can never have a solitary way.
  *A Solitary Way. Stanzas 1
  and 3 [1885]*

[h] In the first person, simply
  shall foretells,
In *will* a threat or else a promise
  dwells;
Shall in the second and third does
  threat,
Will then simply foretells a future
  feat.   *Grammar,
      Irish National Schools*

[i] Among the clover-scented
  grass,
Among the new-mown hay,
Among the hushing of the corn
Where drowsy poppies nod,
Where ill thoughts die and good
  are born—
Out in the fields with God!
  *Out in the Fields [St. Paul's
  Magazine, August 20, 1898, re-
  printed in The Boston Globe,
  April 30, 1899]*

[j] The halls of fame are open
  wide
And they are always full;
Some go in by the door called
  "push,"
And some by the door called
  "pull."
  *Quoted by Prime Minister Stan-
  ley Baldwin in a speech, House
  of Commons*

[k] The codfish lays ten thou-
  sand eggs,
The homely hen lays one.
The codfish never cackles
  To tell you what she's done.
And so we scorn the codfish,
  While the humble hen we prize,
Which only goes to show you
  That it pays to advertise.
      It Pays to Advertise

[l] Monday's child is fair of face,
Tuesday's child is full of grace,
Wednesday's child is loving and
  giving,
Thursday's child works hard for a
  living,
Friday's child is full of woe,
Saturday's child has far to go,
But the child that is born on the
  Sabbath-day
Is brave and bonny, and good and
  gay.
  *Birthdays [Quoted by B. L.
  Farjeon, Harper's Weekly,
  September 17, 1887]*

[m] Something old, something
  new,

Something borrowed, something
  blue.   *Wedding Rhyme*

[n] Use it up, wear it out;
Make it do, or do without.
      New England Maxim

[o] Earned a precarious living by
taking in one another's washing.
  *The Oxford Dictionary of Quo-
  tations [1941] says no source
  has ever been traced*

[p] Ladling the butter from
  adjacent tubs,
Stubbs butters Freeman, Freeman
  butters Stubbs.
  *Variously quoted (c. 1890). Al-
  luding to the mutual praise of
  two famous Oxford historians*

[q] God looks after fools, drunk-
ards, and the United States.
      Epigram

[r] Every time I come to town
The boys keep kicking my dawg
  around;
Makes no difference if he is a
  hound,
They've got to quit kicking my
  dawg around. *Champ Clark
      campaign song [1912]*

[s] There is so much good in the
  worst of us,
And so much bad in the best of
  us,
That it hardly behooves any of us
To talk about the rest of us.
  *First printed in The Marion
  (Kansas) Record, owned by
  Governor Edward Wallis Hoch
  [1849–1925], and assumed to
  have been written by him.*

[t] My granddad, viewing earth's
  worn cogs,
Said things were going to the
  dogs;
His granddad in his house of logs,
Said things were going to the
  dogs;
His granddad in the Flemish bogs
Said things were going to the
  dogs;
His granddad in his old skin togs,
Said things were going to the
  dogs;
There's one thing that I have to
  state—
The dogs have had a good long
  wait.   *Perennial Journeys*

[u] Mother, may I go out to
  swim?
Yes, my darling daughter:
Hang your clothes on a hickory
  limb
And don't go near the water.
      Origin dubious

[v] See the happy moron,
  He doesn't give a damn.
I wish I were a moron—
  My God, perhaps I am!
      *Incorrectly attributed to
      Dorothy Parker*

w] Lizzie Borden took an axe
And gave her mother forty
whacks;
When she saw what she had done
She gave her father forty-one.
*Ballad current after the Borden
murder, Fall River, Massachu-
setts [August 4, 1892]*

x] You will eat, bye and bye,
In that glorious land above the
sky;
Work and pray, live on hay,
You'll get pie in the sky when
you die.
*The Preacher and the Slave
[Attributed to Joe Hill in
1927 edition of I.W.W. Songs]*

y] The difficult we do immediately. The impossible takes a little
longer. *Slogan of United
States Army Air Forces*

z] We sure liberated the hell out
of this place.
*American soldier in the ruins of
a French village, 1944. [Quoted
by Max Miller in The Far Shore]*

a] Soldiers who wish to be a
hero
Are practically zero,
But those who wish to be civil-
ians,
Jesus, they run into the millions.
*Army latrine inscription
[Quoted by Norman Rosten
in The Big Road]*

b] Stay with me, God. The night
is dark,
The night is cold: my little spark
Of courage dies. The night is long;
Be with me, God, and make me
strong.
*A Soldier—His Prayer [On a
scrap of paper found in a trench
in Tunisia during battle of El
Agheila. In Poems from the
Desert, by members of the Brit-
ish Eighth Army]*

c] Since wars begin in the
minds of men, it is in the minds
of men that the defences of peace
must be constructed.
*Constitution of the United Na-
tions Educational, Scientific
and Cultural Organization*

d] We are not dealing simply
with a military or scientific problem but with a problem in state-
craft and the ways of the human
spirit.
*Report on the International
Control of Atomic Energy, published March 16, 1946 [Prepared
for the Department of State by
a Board of Consultants: Chester
I. Barnard, Dr. J. R. Oppen-
heimer, Dr. Charles A. Thomas,
Harry A. Winne, and David E.
Lilienthal, Chairman]*

e] After an atomic war no good
will and intelligence will be
needed to bring a permanent
peace to the survivors. They will
get it in the jumbled stones of
their cities.
*One World or None [Edited by
Dexter Masters and Katharine
Way]. Chap. 15, Survival is
at Stake*

f] There's a notable family
called Stein:
There's Gertrude, there's Ep, and
there's Ein.
Gert's writings are punk,
Ep's statues are junk,
And nobody understands Ein.
*Stein Song [Ep = Jacob Ep-
stein, sculptor. Ein = Albert
Einstein, mathematician]*

g] Three faces wears the doctor:
when first sought
An Angel's; and a god's the cure
half-wrought;
But when, the cure complete, he
seeks his fee,
The Devil looks less terrible than
he.

h] How much better if Plymouth Rock had landed on the Pilgrims. *Modern saying, origin
dubious*

Addenda

i] All the brothers were valiant,
and all the sisters virtuous.
*From the inscription on the
tomb of the Duchess of New-
castle in Westminster Abbey*

j] Art and part. *A Scottish
law phrase, an accessory before
and after the fact*

k] Begging the question.
*A common logical fallacy, peti-
tio principii; the first explanation of the phrase is to be found
in Aristotle's Topica, VIII, 13,
where the five ways of begging
the question are set forth*

l] Bitter end. *Somewhat am-
biguous as now used. The older
form, "better end," was used to
designate a crisis, or a moment
of extremity. When in a gale a
vessel has paid out all her cable,
her cable has run out to the
"better end,"—the end which is
secured within the vessel and
little use*

m] Cockles of the heart.
*R. G. Latham, English philolo-
gist, wrote that the most probable explanation of the phrase
lies (1) in the likeness of the
heart to a cockleshell,—the
base of the former being compared to the hinge of the latter;
(2) in the zoological name for
the cockle and its congeners,
Cardium (heart)*

n] Dirty work at the crossroads.
Notes and Queries, London, at-

tributes this to Walter Melville's melodrama The Girl Who Took the Wrong Turning, or No Wedding Bells for Him

[o] Dollar diplomacy. *"Imperialistic activity by the President received another name. Republicans now simply called it 'dollar diplomacy.'" Beard: Basic History of the United States, page 353, discussing the Taft administration. [The expression was used in Harper's Weekly, April 23, 1910]*

[p] Don't sell America short. *Modern Version of J. P. Morgan's saying, "Never be a bear on the United States." [See Mark Sullivan: Our Times, II 318]*

[q] Free soil, free men, free speech, Frémont. *Rallying cry of the Republican Party in 1856, when John Charles Frémont, "the Pathfinder," was the party's candidate for the presidency*

[r] G. I. Joe. *This name, chosen for the soldier in Lieutenant Dave Breger's comic strip for Yank, the Army weekly, first appeared in the issue of June 17, 1942, and was speedily adopted as the popular appellation for all U. S. soldiers in World War II. Writing in Time [February 26, 1945], Lieutenant Breger said: "I decided on 'G. I. Joe,' the 'G. I.' [Government Issue] because of its prevalence in Army talk, and the 'Joe' for the alliterative effect"*

[s] The goose hangs high. *"Originally, perhaps, 'the goose honks high. . . . Wild geese fly higher when the weather is fine or promises to be fine. Hence, the prospects are bright; everything is favourable." Century Dictionary; another explanation is that in some parts of the country a goose is hung high to season, and denotes that a feast of roast goose will soon be ready*

[t] How old is Ann? *This became a popular quotation when The New York Press, October 16, 1903, printed a simple problem: "Mary is 24 years old. She is twice as old as Ann was when Mary was as old as Ann is now. How old is Ann?" It seems incredible that so simple an equation in algebra should have caused so much anxiety, but it did. The answer: Ann is 18*

[u] Nothing succeeds like success. *A French Proverb [Quoted by Dumas in Ange Pitou, Vol. I, Page 72]*

[v] Paying through the nose. *"Grimm says that Odin had poll-tax which was called in Sweden a nose-tax; it was penny per nose, or poll." Deutsche Rechts Alterthümer*

[w] Roland for an Oliver. *These were the two most famous of Charlemagne's paladins, and their exploits are rendered so ridiculously and equally extravagant by the old romancers, that from them arose the saying, to signify matching one incredible lie with another, giving tit for tat, as good as one receives*

[x] Sister Anne, do you see any one coming? *The anxious cry of Fatima, one of the wives of Bluebeard*

[y] Slide, Kelly, Slide. *Title of song by J. W. Kelly [1889]*

[z] Tell 'em Queen Anne's dead. *A phrase which became proverbial for telling in secrecy what everyone knows. [In The Heir-at-Law (1797) by George Colman (The Younger)]*

[a] The public be damned. *William H. Vanderbilt's reply to a newspaper reporter. There are various versions of the occasion of this remark [See Melville E. Stone: Fifty Years a Journalist, Page 116, and Gustavus Myers: History of the Great American Fortunes, Modern Library Giant edition, Page 344]*

[b] The sixty-four dollar question. *Phrase first used April 21, 1940, on a Columbia Broadcasting System program, Take It Or Leave It, a quiz program consisting of seven increasingly difficult questions for which the participant was awarded $1, $2, $4, $8, $16, $32, and $64 respectively for each question correctly answered, but might retire after any question. The $64 question is the climax question*

[c] The woods are full of them. *Alexander Wilson, in the Preface to his American Ornithology [1808], quotes these words and relates the story of a boy who had been gathering flowers. On bringing them to his mother, he said: "Look, my dear ma! What beautiful flowers I have found growing in our place! Why all the woods are full of them!"*

[d] There ain't no such animal. *Comment of a New Jersey farmer looking at a dromedary at a circus. Cartoon in Life November 7, 1907, credited to Everybody's Magazine*

[e] In Adam's fall
We sinned all. *The New England Primer* [As early as 1691, Benjamin Harris, of Boston, advertised as in press the second impression of the New England Primer. The oldest copy known to be extant is dated 1737]

[f] My Book and Heart
Must never part. *Ibid.*

[g] Peter denied
His Lord, and cryed. *Ibid.*

[h] Xerxes did die,
And so must I. *Ibid.*

[i] Now I lay me down to take my sleep,
I pray the Lord my soul to keep;
If I should die before I wake,
I pray the Lord my soul to take. *Ibid.*

Epitaphs

[j] A house she hath, 'tis made of such good fashion,
The tenant ne'er shall pay for reparation,
Nor will the landlord ever raise her rent
Or turn her out of doors for non-payment;
From chimney-tax this cell is free,
To such a house who would not tenant be? *For Rebecca Bogess, Folkestone, August 22, 1668*

[k] It is so soon that I am done for,
I wonder what I was begun for. *For a child aged three weeks, Cheltenham Churchyard*

[l] Here lies John Knott:
His father was Knott before him,
He lived Knott, died Knott,
Yet underneath this stone doth lie
Knott christened, Knott begot,
And here he lies and still is Knott. *Perthshire Churchyard*

[m] A dying preacher I have been,
To dying hearers such as you.
Though dead a preacher still I am
To such as come my grave to view.
Let this to you a warning be
That quickly you must follow me. *Elder Samuel Waldo, South Dover (Wingdale) Cemetery, Dutchess County, New York, September 10, 1798*

[n] A zealous Lock-Smith dyed of late,
And did arrive at heaven gate,
He stood without and would not knocke,
Because he meant to picke the locke. *Epitaph upon a Puritanicall Lock-Smith. Ibid. Page 408*

[o] This is the grave of Mike O'Day
Who died maintaining his right of way.
His right was clear, his will was strong,
But he's just as dead as if he'd been wrong. *Modern*

[p] Fuller's earth. *For Thomas Fuller, D.D., author, and chaplain to Charles II after the Restoration*

[q] Beneath this stone, a lump of clay,
Lies Arabella Young,
Who on the 24th of May
Began to hold her tongue. *British Museum Collection*

[r] Beneath this stone a lump of clay
Lies Uncle Peter Daniels
Who too early in the month of May
Took off his winter flannels. *Medway, Massachusetts, 1746*

[s] Here sleeps in peace a Hampshire Grenadier,
Who caught his death by drinking cold small beer;
Soldiers, take heed from his untimely fall,
And when you're hot, drink strong, or not at all. *Winchester Churchyard, 1764*

Miscellaneous Translations

[t] To resist him that is set in authority is evil. *Adolf Erman: The Literature of the Ancient Egyptians (tr. Aylward M. Blackman). The Instruction of Ptahhotep [Circa 2675 B.C.]*

[u] There it o'ertook me that I fell down for thirst, I was parched, my throat burned, and I said: "This is the taste of death." *Ibid. The Story of Sinuke [Circa 2000 B.C.]*

[v] Go not in and out in the court of justice, that thy name may not stink. *Ibid. The Wisdom of Anii [Circa 900 B.C.]*

[w] Everywhere he feels his Heart because its vessels run to all his limbs. *The Beginning of the Secret Book of the Physician [Circa 1550 B.C.] (tr. Cyril P. Bryan)*

[x] I established law and justice in the land. *Robert Francis Harper: The Code of Hammurabi King of Babylon about 2250 B.C. Page 9 (Prologue)*

[y] If a man destroy the eye of another man, they shall destroy his eye.   *Ibid. Page 73 (Sect. 196)*

[z] Achtung! Schpitfeuer! *"Warning! Spitfires!" Radio message among German planes, always overheard by Royal Air Force flyers during the Battle of Britain*

[a] Dead on the field of honor. *From the death of Latour d'Auvergne at Oberhausen, Bavaria [June 27, 1800] until 1814, his name was retained on the roll of his company of grenadiers, as a mark of honor; at each roll-call the color-sergeant made this response*

[b] Let us learn on earth those things whose knowledge might continue in heaven.   *Motto of Saint Paul's School, Concord, New Hampshire*

[c] Laissez faire, laissez aller (Let it be, let it go; viz., let nature take its course).
    Quoted by Adam Smith in The Wealth of Nations

[d] Never believe the impossible, Never regret the past, Do not long for the unattainable.
    Aucassin and Nicolette [13th century]. Le Lai de l'Oiselet

[e] Nothing equals the joy of the drinker, except the joy of the wine in being drunk.   *Quoted by Maurice des Ombiaux: Nouveau Manuel de l'Amateur de Bourgoyne*

[f] Terrible he rode alone,
    With his Yemen sword for aid;
Ornament it carried none
    But the notches on the blade.
    The Death Feud, an Arab War Song, of an age earlier than that of Mahomet. Anonymous translation from Tait's Magazine [July 1850]

[g] The world is merely a bridge; ye are to pass over it, and not to build your dwellings upon it.
    Inscription on the Victory Gate, Fathepur, India. From Agrapha, Unwritten Sayings of Jesus

[h] There is many a true word spoken in doggerel.
    Czech Folksong

[i] Today all Germany is ours: Tomorrow the whole world.
    Nazi Song

[j] When I am dead let fire destroy the world;
It matters not to me, for I am safe.   *Greek Anthology. Fragment 430 [of unknown authorship]*

THE KING JAMES BIBLE

This Bible is for the Government of the People, by the People, and for the People.

General Prologue, Wycliffe Translation of the Bible, 1384

[k] Among all our joys, there was no one that more filled our hearts, than the blessed continuance of the preaching of God's sacred Word among us; which is that inestimable treasure, which excelleth all the riches of the earth; because the fruit thereof extendeth itself, not only to the time spent in this transitory world, but directeth and disposeth men unto that eternal happiness which is above in heaven.
The Translators

Old Testament

[l] And God said, Let there be light: and there was light.
Genesis. I, 3

[m] It is not good that the man should be alone. *Ibid. II, 18*

[n] They sewed fig-leaves together, and made themselves aprons. *Ibid. III, 7*

[o] In the sweat of thy face shalt thou eat bread *Ibid. 19*

[p] For dust thou art, and unto dust shalt thou return. *Ibid.*

[q] The mother of all living. *Ibid. 20*

[r] Am I my brother's keeper? *Ibid. IV, 9*

[s] And the Lord set a mark upon Cain. *Ibid. 15*

[t] And all the days of Methuselah were nine hundred and sixty and nine years. *Ibid. V, 27*

[u] There were giants in the earth in those days. *Ibid. VI, 4*

[v] And the rain was upon the earth forty days and forty nights. *Ibid. VII, 12*

[w] The dove found no rest for the sole of her foot. *Ibid. VIII, 9*

[x] While the earth remaineth, seedtime and harvest, and cold and heat, and summer and winter, and day and night shall not cease. *Ibid. 22*

[y] Nimrod the mighty hunter *Ibid. X 9*

[z] Babel; because the Lord did there confound the language of all the earth. *Ibid. XI. 9*

[a] His [Ishmael's] hand will be against every man, and every man's hand against him. *Ibid. XVI. 12*

[b] His [Lot's] wife looked back from behind him, and she became a pillar of salt. *Ibid. XIX. 26*

[c] He [Jacob] dreamed, and behold a ladder set up on the earth, and the top of it reached to heaven: and behold the angels of the Lord ascending and descending it. *Ibid. XXVIII, 12*

[d] Mizpah . . . The Lord watch between me and thee, when we are absent one from another.
Ibid. XXXI, 49

[e] They stript Joseph out of his coat, his coat of many colours.
Ibid. XXXVII, 23

[f] Unstable as water, thou shalt not excel. *Ibid. XLIX, 4*

[g] I have been a stranger in a strange land. *Exodus. II, 22*

[h] Put off thy shoes from off thy feet, for the place whereon thou standest is holy ground.
Ibid. III, 5

[i] A land flowing with milk and honey.

Ibid. 8 (and XXXIII, 3)

[j] I am slow of speech, and of a slow tongue. *Ibid. IV, 10*

[k] Ye shall no more give the people straw to make brick.

Ibid. V, 7

[l] This day [passover] shall be unto you for a memorial; and ye shall keep it a feast to the Lord throughout your generations.

Ibid. XII, 14

[m] The Lord went before them by day in a pillar of a cloud, to lead them the way; and by night in a pillar of fire. *Ibid. XIII, 21*

[n] Honour thy father and thy mother. *Ibid. XX, 12*

[o] Eye for eye, tooth for tooth, hand for hand, foot for foot.

Ibid. XXI, 24

[p] I send an Angel before thee, to keep thee in the way.

Ibid. XXIII, 20

[q] He wrote upon the tables the words of the covenant, the ten commandments.

Ibid. XXXIV, 28

[r] The swine . . . is unclean to you. Of their flesh shall ye not eat. *Leviticus. XI, 7, 8*

[s] Love thy neighbour as thyself. *Ibid. XIX, 18*

[t] The Lord bless thee, and keep thee: The Lord make his face shine upon thee, and be gracious unto thee: The Lord lift up his countenance upon thee, and give thee peace.

Numbers. VI, 24, 25, 26

[u] The Lord opened the mouth of the ass, and she said unto Balaam, What have I done unto thee, that thou hast smitten me these three times?

Ibid. XXII, 28

[v] Man doth not live by bread only. *Deuteronomy. VIII, 3*

[w] The wife of thy bosom.

Ibid. XIII, 6

[x] The poor shall never cease out of the land. *Ibid. XV, 11*

[y] As thy days, so shall thy strength be. *Ibid. XXXIII, 25*

[z] The sun stood still, and the moon stayed. *Joshua. X, 13*

[a] At her feet he bowed, he fell, he lay down: at her feet he bowed, he fell: where he bowed, there he fell down dead. *Judges. V, 27*

[b] There was a swarm of bees and honey in the carcase of the lion. *Ibid. XIV, 8*

[c] He smote them hip and thigh.

Ibid. XV, 8

[d] With the jaw of an ass have I slain a thousand men.

Ibid. 16

[e] And Delilah said to Samson, Tell me, I pray thee, wherein thy great strength lieth.

Ibid. XVI, 6

[f] Whither thou goest, I will go; and where thou lodgest, I will lodge: thy people shall be my people, and thy God my God.

Ruth. I, 16

[g] Go not empty unto thy mother in law. *Ibid. III, 17*

[h] Speak, Lord; for thy servant heareth. *1 Samuel. III, 9*

[i′] And all the people shouted, and said, God save the king.

Ibid. X, 24

[j′] A man after his own heart.

Ibid. XIII, 14

[k′] So David prevailed over the Philistine with a sling and with a stone. *Ibid. XVII, 50*

[l′] Saul hath slain his thousands, and David his ten thousands.

Ibid. XVIII, 7 (and XXI, 11; XXIX, 5)

[m′] Tell it not in Gath, publish it not in the streets of Askelon.

2 Samuel. I, 20

[n′] Saul and Jonathan were lovely and pleasant in their lives, and in their death they were not divided. *Ibid. 23*

[o′] How are the mighty fallen!

Ibid. 25

[p′] Thy love to me was wonderful, passing the love of women.

Ibid. 26

[q′] Tarry at Jericho until your beards be grown. *Ibid. X, 5*

[r′] Set ye Uriah in the forefront of the hottest battle.

Ibid. XI, 15

[s′] As water spilt on the ground, which cannot be gathered up again. *Ibid. XIV, 14*

[t′] Would God I had died for thee, O Absalom, my son, my son!

Ibid. XVIII, 33

[u′] The Lord is my rock, and my fortress, and my deliverer.

Ibid. XXII, 2

[v′] The sweet psalmist of Israel.

Ibid. XXIII, 1

[w′] Oh, that one would give me to drink of the water of the well of Beth-lehem, which is by the gate! *Ibid. 15*

[x′] A wise and an understanding heart. *1 Kings. III, 12*

[y′] Many as the sand which is by the sea in multitude.

Ibid. IV, 20

[z] He [Solomon] spake three thousand proverbs: and his songs were a thousand and five.
Ibid. 32

[a] So that there was neither hammer nor axe nor any tool of iron heard in the house, while it was in building. *Ibid. VI, 7*

[b] Once in three years came the navy of Tharshish, bringing gold and silver, ivory, and apes, and peacocks. *Ibid. X, 22*

[c] King Solomon loved many strange women. *Ibid. XI, 1*

[d] I have commanded a widow woman there to sustain thee.
Ibid. XVII, 9

[e] How long halt ye between two opinions? *Ibid. XVIII, 21*

[f] There ariseth a little cloud out of the sea, like a man's hand.
Ibid. 44

[g] A still, small voice.
Ibid. XIX, 12

[h] Hast thou found me, O mine enemy? *Ibid. XXI, 20*

[i] Is thy servant a dog, that he should do this great thing?
2 Kings. VIII, 13

[j] Like the driving of Jehu, the son of Nimshi; for he driveth furiously. *Ibid. IX, 20*

[k] Jezebel heard of it; and she painted her face, and tired her head, and looked out at a window.
Ibid. 30

[l] Set thine house in order.
Ibid. XX, 1

[m] Our days on the earth are as a shadow.
1 Chronicles. XXIX, 15

[n] The Lord gave, and the Lord hath taken away; blessed be the name of the Lord. *Job. I, 21*

[o] All that a man hath, will he give for his life. *Ibid. II, 4*

[p] Night, when deep sleep falleth on men. *Ibid.
IV, 13 (and XXXIII, 15)*

[q] Man is born unto trouble, as the sparks fly upward.
Ibid. V, 7

[r] Thou shalt come to thy grave in a full age, like as a shock of corn cometh in his season.
Ibid. 26

[s] How forcible are right words!
Ibid. VI, 25

[t] My days are swifter than a weaver's shuttle. *Ibid. VII, 6*

[u] He shall return no more to his house, neither shall his place know him any more. *Ibid. 10*

[v] Canst thou by searching find out God? *Ibid. XI, 7*

[w] Clearer than the noonday.
Ibid. 17

[x] No doubt but ye are the people, and wisdom shall die with you. *Ibid. XII, 2*

[y] Speak to the earth, and it shall teach thee. *Ibid. 8*

[z'] Man that is born of a woman is of few days, and full of trouble.
Ibid. XIV, 1

[a'] If a man die, shall he live again? *Ibid. 14*

[b'] I am escaped with the skin of my teeth. *Ibid. XIX, 20*

[c'] Though wickedness be sweet in his mouth, though he hide it under his tongue. *Ibid. XX, 12*

[d'] The price of wisdom is above rubies. *Ibid. XXVIII, 18*

[e'] I caused the widow's heart to sing for joy. *Ibid. XXIX, 13*

[f'] I was eyes to the blind, and feet was I to the lame. *Ibid. 15*

[g'] Great men are not always wise. *Ibid. XXXII, 9*

[h'] He multiplieth words without knowledge. *Ibid. XXXV, 16*

[i'] Fair weather cometh out of the north. *Ibid. XXXVII, 22*

[j'] Who is this that darkeneth counsel by words without knowledge? *Ibid. XXXVIII, 2*

[k'] The morning stars sang together, and all the sons of God shouted for joy. *Ibid. 7*

[l'] Canst thou bind the sweet influences of Pleiades, or loose the bands of Orion?
Canst thou guide Arcturus with his sons? *Ibid. 31 and 32*

[m'] Hard as a piece of the nether millstone. *Ibid. XLI, 24*

[n'] He maketh the deep to boil like a pot. *Ibid. 31*

[o'] I will both lay me down in peace, and sleep. *Psalms. IV, 8*

[p'] Out of the mouth of babes and sucklings. *Ibid. VIII, 2*

[q'] What is man, that thou art mindful of him.
Thou hast made him a little lower than the angels.
Ibid. 4 and 5

[r'] The fool hath said in his heart, There is no God.
Ibid. XIV, 1 (and LIII, 1)

[s'] Keep me as the apple of the eye, hide me under the shadow of thy wings. *Ibid. XVII, 8*

[t'] He rode upon a cherub, and did fly: yea, he did fly upon the wings of the wind.
Ibid. XVIII, 10

[u] The heavens declare the glory of God; and the firmament showeth his handiwork.
Ibid. XIX, 1

[v] Day unto day uttereth speech, and night unto night showeth knowledge. *Ibid. 2*

[w] Sweeter also than honey and the honeycomb. *Ibid. 10*

[x] Cleanse thou me from secret faults. *Ibid. 12*

[y] He maketh me to lie down in green pastures: he leadeth me beside the still waters.
Ibid. XXIII, 2

[z] The valley of the shadow of death. *Ibid. 4*

[a] Thy rod and thy staff they comfort me. *Ibid.*

[b] My cup runneth over.
Ibid. 5

[c] Weeping may endure for a night, but joy cometh in the morning. *Ibid. XXX, 5*

[d] Keep thy tongue from evil, and thy lips from speaking guile.
Ibid. XXXIV, 13

[e] I have been young, and now am old; yet have I not seen the righteous forsaken, nor his seed begging bread.
Ibid. XXXVII, 25

[f] Lord, make me to know mine end, and the measure of my days, what it is; that I may know how frail I am. *Ibid. XXXIX, 4*

[g] He heapeth up riches, and knoweth not who shall gather them. *Ibid. 6*

[h] Blessed is he that considereth the poor. *Ibid. XLI, 1*

[i] As the hart panteth after the water-brooks. *Ibid. XLII, 1*

[j] God is our refuge and strength, a very present help in trouble. *Ibid. XLVI, 1*

[k] Beautiful for situation, the joy of the whole earth, is Mount Zion, . . . the city of the great King. *Ibid. XLVIII, 2*

[l] Wash me, and I shall be whiter than snow. *Ibid. LI, 7*

[m] Oh that I had wings like a dove! *Ibid. LV, 6*

[n] The words of his mouth were smoother than butter, but war was in his heart *Ibid. 21*

[o] They are like the deaf adder that stoppeth her ear; which will not hearken to the voice of charmers, charming never so wisely *Ibid. LVIII, 4, 5*

[p] Surely men of low degree are vanity, and men of high degree

are a lie: to be laid in the balance, they are altogether lighter than vanity. *Ibid. LXII, 9*

[q] Thou renderest to every man according to his work. *Ibid. 12*

[r] We went through fire and through water. *Ibid. LXVI, 12*

[s] He shall come down like rain upon the mown grass.
Ibid. LXXII, 6

[t] His enemies shall lick the dust. *Ibid. 9*

[u'] A day in thy courts is better than a thousand. I had rather be a door-keeper in the house of my God, than to dwell in the tents of wickedness. *Ibid. LXXXIV, 10*

[v'] A thousand years in thy sight are but as yesterday when it is past, and as a watch in the night.
Ibid. XC, 4

[w'] The days of our years are threescore years and ten; and if by reason of strength they be fourscore years, yet is their strength labour and sorrow; for it is soon cut off, and we fly away.
Ibid. 10

[x'] So teach us to number our days, that we may apply our hearts unto wisdom. *Ibid. 12*

[y'] Nor for the pestilence that walketh in darkness; nor for the destruction that wasteth at noonday. *Ibid. XCI, 6*

[z'] The righteous shall flourish like the palm-tree: he shall grow like a cedar in Lebanon.
Ibid. XCII, 12

[a'] As for man, his days are as grass: as a flower of the field, so he flourisheth.
The wind passeth over it, and it is gone; and the place thereof shall know it no more.
Ibid. CIII, 15 and 16

[b'] Wine that maketh glad the heart of man. *Ibid. CIV, 15*

[c'] Man goeth forth unto his work and to his labour until the evening. *Ibid. 23*

[d'] They that go down to the sea in ships, that do business in great waters. *Ibid. CVII, 23*

[e'] Thou hast the dew of thy youth. *Ibid. CX, 3*

[f'] From the rising of the sun unto the going down of the same.
Ibid. CXIII, 3

[g'] I said in my haste, All men are liars. *Ibid. CXVI, 11*

[h'] Peace be within thy walls, and prosperity within thy palaces
Ibid. CXXII, 7

[i'] They that sow in tears shall reap in joy *Ibid. CXXVI, 5*

[j] Except the Lord build the house, they labour in vain that build it. *Ibid. CXXVII, 1*

[k] He giveth his beloved sleep. *Ibid. 2*

[l] Happy is the man that hath his quiver full of them. *Ibid. 5*

[m] Behold how good and how pleasant it is for brethren to dwell together in unity. *Ibid. CXXXIII, 1*

[n] By the rivers of Babylon, there we sat down, yea, we wept, when we remembered Zion.
We hanged our harps upon the willows. *Ibid. CXXXVII, 1 and 2*

[o] If I forget thee, O Jerusalem, let my right hand forget her cunning. *Ibid. 5*

[p] If I take the wings of the morning, and dwell in the uttermost parts of the sea.

[q] I am fearfully and wonderfully made. *Ibid. CXXXIX, 14*

[r] That our sons may be as plants grown up in their youth; that our daughters may be as corner stones. *Ibid. CXLIV, 12*

[s] Put not your trust in princes. *Ibid. CXLVI, 3*

[t] My son, if sinners entice thee, consent thou not. *Proverbs. I, 10*

[u] Wisdom is the principal thing; therefore get wisdom; and with all thy getting get understanding. *Ibid. IV, 7*

[v] The path of the just is as the shining light, that shineth more and more unto the perfect day. *Ibid. 18*

[w] Go to the ant, thou sluggard; consider her ways, and be wise. *Ibid. VI, 6*

[x] Yet a little sleep, a little slumber, a little folding of the hands to sleep. *Ibid. 10 (and XXIV, 33)*

[y] Stolen waters are sweet, and bread eaten in secret is pleasant. *Ibid. IX, 17*

[z] A wise son maketh a glad father. *Ibid. X, 1*

[a] In the multitude of counsellors there is safety. *Ibid. XI, 14 (and XXIV, 6)*

[b] He that is surety for a stranger shall smart for it. *Ibid. 15*

[c] As a jewel of gold in a swine's snout, so is a fair woman which is without discretion. *Ibid. 22*

[d] Hope deferred maketh the heart sick *Ibid. XIII, 12*

[e] The way of transgressors is hard. *Ibid. 15*

[f] He that spareth his rod hateth his son. *Ibid. 24*

[g] Fools make a mock at sin. *Ibid. XIV, 9*

[h] Righteousness exalteth a nation. *Ibid. 34*

[i] A soft answer turneth away wrath. *Ibid. XV, 1*

[j'] Better is a dinner of herbs where love is, than a stalled ox and hatred therewith. *Ibid. 17*

[k'] Pride goeth before destruction, and an haughty spirit before a fall. *Ibid. XVI, 18*

[l'] The hoary head is a crown of glory. *Ibid. 31*

[m'] He that is slow to anger is better than the mighty; and he that ruleth his spirit than he that taketh a city. *Ibid. 32*

[n'] He that repeateth a matter separateth very friends. *Ibid. XVII, 9*

[o'] A merry heart doeth good like a medicine. *Ibid. 22*

[p'] Even a fool, when he holdeth his peace, is counted wise. *Ibid. 28*

[q'] Whoso findeth a wife findeth a good thing. *Ibid. XVIII, 22*

[r'] A man that hath friends must show himself friendly; and there is a friend that sticketh closer than a brother. *Ibid. 24*

[s'] Wealth maketh many friends. *Ibid. XIX, 4*

[t'] He that hath pity upon the poor lendeth unto the Lord. *Ibid. 17*

[u'] Wine is a mocker, strong drink is raging. *Ibid. XX, 1*

[v'] Meddle not with him that flattereth with his lips. *Ibid. 19*

[w'] The beauty of old men is the grey head. *Ibid. 29*

[x'] It is better to dwell in a corner of the housetop, than with a brawling woman in a wide house. *Ibid. XXI, 9 (and XXV, 24)*

[y'] A good name is rather to be chosen than great riches. *Ibid. XXII, 1*

[z'] Train up a child in the way he should go: and when he is old he will not depart from it. *Ibid. 6*

[a'] The borrower is servant to the lender. *Ibid 7*

[b'] Remove not the ancient landmark. *Ibid 28*

[c'] Seest thou a man diligent in his business? He shall stand before kings *Ibid 29* [**d**] Riches certainly make themselves wings. *Ibid. XXIII, 5*

[**e**] As he thinketh in his heart, so is he. *Ibid. 7*

[**f**] Drowsiness shall clothe a man with rags. *Ibid. 21*

[**g**] Despise not thy mother when she is old. *Ibid. 22*

[**h**] Look not thou upon the wine when it is red, when it giveth his colour in the cup; . . . at the last it biteth like a serpent, and stingeth like an adder.
Ibid. 31, 32

[**i**] A word fitly spoken is like apples of gold in pictures of silver. *Ibid. XXV, 11*

[**j**] Heap coals of fire upon his head. *Ibid. 22*

[**k**] As cold waters to a thirsty soul, so is good news from a far country. *Ibid. 25*

[**l**] There is a lion in the way; a lion is in the streets.
Ibid. XXVI, 13

[**m**] Boast not thyself of to-morrow; for thou knowest not what a day may bring forth.
Ibid. XXVII, 1

[**n**] Better is a neighbour that is near than a brother far off.
Ibid. 10

[**o**] A continual dropping in a very rainy day and a contentious woman are alike. *Ibid. 15*

[**p**] He that maketh haste to be rich shall not be innocent.
Ibid. XXVIII, 20

[**q**] There be three things which are too wonderful for me, yea four which I know not: The way of an eagle in the air; the way of a serpent upon a rock; the way of a ship in the midst of the sea; and the way of a man with a maid.
Ibid. XXX, 18 and 19

[**r**] She looketh well to the ways of her household, and eateth not the bread of idleness.
Her children arise up, and call her blessed.
Ibid. XXXI, 27 and 28

[**s**] Vanity of vanities, . . . all is vanity.
Ecclesiastes. I, 2 (and XII, 8)

[**t**] There is no new thing under the sun. *Ibid. 9*

[**u**] He that increaseth knowledge increaseth sorrow. *Ibid. 18*

[**v**] To every thing there is a season, and a time to every purpose under the heaven. *Ibid. III, 1*

[**w**] Better is it that thou shouldest not vow, than that thou shouldest vow and not pay.
Ibid. V, 5

[**x**] The sleep of a labouring man is sweet. *Ibid. 12*

[**y**] It is better to go to the house of mourning than to go to the house of feasting. *Ibid. VII, 2*

[**z**] As the crackling of thorns under a pot, so is the laughter of the fool. *Ibid. 6*

[**a**] To eat, and to drink, and to be merry. *Ibid. VIII, 15*

[**b**] A living dog is better than a dead lion. *Ibid. IX, 4*

[**c**] The race is not to the swift, nor the battle to the strong.
Ibid. 11

[**d′**] Cast thy bread upon the waters: for thou shalt find it after many days. *Ibid. XI, 1*

[**e′**] Rejoice, O young man, in thy youth. *Ibid. 9*

[**f′**] He shall rise up at the voice of the bird. *Ibid. XII, 4*

[**g′**] The grasshopper shall be a burden, and desire shall fail; because man goeth to his long home, and the mourners go about the streets. *Ibid. 5*

[**h′**] Or ever the silver cord be loosed, or the golden bowl be broken, or the pitcher be broken at the fountain, or the wheel broken at the cistern.
Then shall the dust return to the earth as it was; and the spirit shall return unto God who gave it. *Ibid. 6 and 7*

[**i′**] The words of the wise are as goads, and as nails fastened by the masters of assemblies.
Ibid. 11

[**j′**] Of making many books there is no end; and much study is a weariness of the flesh.
Ibid. 12

[**k′**] Let us hear the conclusion of the whole matter: Fear God, and keep his commandments; for this is the whole duty of man.
Ibid. 13

[**l′**] I am the rose of Sharon, and the lily of the valleys.
The Song of Solomon. II, 1

[**m′**] For, lo! the winter is past, the rain is over and gone; the flowers appear on the earth; the time of the singing of birds is come, and the voice of the turtle is heard in our land. *Ibid. 11, 12*

[**n′**] The little foxes, that spoil the vines. *Ibid. 15*

[**o′**] Terrible as an army with banners. *Ibid. VI, 4, 10*

[**p′**] Thy neck is as a tower of ivory. *Ibid. VII, 4*

[**q′**] Like the best wine, . . . that goeth down sweetly, causing the lips of those that are asleep to speak. *Ibid. 9*

[r] Love is strong as death; jealousy is cruel as the grave.
Ibid. VIII, 6

[s] Though your sins be as scarlet, they shall be white as snow.
Isaiah. I, 18

[t] They shall beat their swords into plowshares, and their spears into pruning-hooks; nation shall not lift up sword against nation, neither shall they learn war any more. *Ibid. II, 4*

[u] In that day a man shall cast his idols . . . to the moles and to the bats. *Ibid. 20*

[v] Grind the faces of the poor.
Ibid. III, 15

[w] Holy, holy, holy, is the Lord of hosts: the whole earth is full of his glory. *Ibid. VI, 3*

[x] His name shall be called Wonderful, Counsellor, The mighty God, The everlasting Father, The Prince of Peace.
Ibid. IX, 6

[y] The wolf also shall dwell with the lamb, and the leopard shall lie down with the kid.
Ibid. XI, 6

[z] How art thou fallen from heaven, O Lucifer, son of the morning! *Ibid. XIV, 12*

[a] Like the rushing of mighty waters. *Ibid. XVII, 12*

[b] Watchman, what of the night? *Ibid. XXI, 11*

[c] Let us eat and drink; for tomorrow we shall die.
Ibid. XXII, 13

[d] Hide thyself as it were for a little moment, until the indignation be overpast. *Ibid. XXVI, 20*

[e] Leviathan, that crooked serpent . . . the dragon that is in the sea. *Ibid. XXVII, 1*

[f] For precept must be upon precept, precept upon precept; line upon line, line upon line; here a little, and there a little.
Ibid. XXVIII. 10, 13

[g] We have made a covenant with death, and with hell are we at agreement. *Ibid. 15*

[h] The desert shall rejoice, and blossom as the rose.
Ibid. XXXV, 1

[i] Set thine house in order.
Ibid. XXXVIII, 1

[j] All flesh is grass. *Ibid. XL, 6*

[k] The nations are as a drop of a bucket. *Ibid. 15*

[l] They that wait upon the Lord shall renew their strength; they shall mount up with wings as eagles; they shall run, and not be weary; and they shall walk, and not faint. *Ibid. 31*

[m] They helped every one his neighbour: and every one said to his brother, Be of good courage.
Ibid. XLI, 6

[n] How beautiful upon the mountains are the feet of him that bringeth good tidings, that publisheth peace. *Ibid. LII, 7*

[o] They shall see eye to eye.
Ibid. 8

[p] A man of sorrows, and acquainted with grief. *Ibid. LIII, 3*

[q] All we like sheep have gone astray. *Ibid. 6*

[r'] He is brought as a lamb to the slaughter. *Ibid. 7*

[s'] I am holier than thou.
Ibid. LXV, 5

[t'] Peace, peace; when there is no peace.
Jeremiah. VI, 14 (and VIII, 11)

[u'] Stand ye in the ways, and see, and ask for the old paths, where is the good way, and walk therein. *Ibid. 16*

[v'] Is there no balm in Gilead? Is there no physician there?
Ibid. VIII, 22

[w'] Can the Ethiopian change his skin, or the leopard his spots?
Ibid. XIII, 23

[x'] Written with a pen of iron, and with the point of a diamond.
Ibid. XVII, 1

[y'] Rahel [Rachel] weeping for her children, refused to be comforted. *Ibid. XXXI, 15*

[z'] The fathers have eaten a sour grape, and the children's teeth are set on edge. *Ibid. 29*

[a'] Is it nothing to you, all ye that pass by? behold, and see if there be any sorrow like unto my sorrow. *Lamentations. I, 12*

[b'] A wheel in the middle of a wheel. *Ezekiel. I, 16 (and X, 10)*

[c'] Shadrach, Meshach, and Abed-nego fell down bound into the midst of the burning fiery furnace. *Daniel. III. 23*

[d'] Nebuchadnezzar . . . was driven from men, and did eat grass as oxen. *Ibid. IV, 33*

[e'] Thou art weighed in the balances, and art found wanting.
Ibid. V, 27

[f'] According to the law of the Medes and Persians.
Ibid. VI, 12

[g'] They brought Daniel, and cast him into the den of lions.
Ibid. 16

[h] The Ancient of days.
Ibid. VII, 13

[i] They have sown the wind, and they shall reap the whirlwind.
Hosea. VIII, 7

[j] Your old men shall dream dreams, your young men shall see visions.
Joel. II, 28

[k] Can two walk together, except they be agreed?
Amos. III, 3

[l] And Jonah was in the belly of the fish three days and three nights.
Jonah. I, 17

[m] They shall sit every man under his vine and under his fig-tree.
Micah. IV, 4

[n] Write the vision, and make it plain upon tables, that he may run that readeth it.
Habakkuk. II, 2

[o] The Lord is in his holy temple: let all the earth keep silence before him.
Ibid. 20

[p] Your fathers, where are they? And the prophets, do they live forever?
Zechariah. I, 5

[q] Not by might, nor by power, but by my spirit, saith the Lord of hosts.
Ibid. IV, 6

[r] Have we not all one father? hath not one God created us?
Malachi. II, 10

[s] But unto you that fear my name shall the Sun of righteousness arise with healing in his wings.
Ibid. IV, 2

New Testament

[t] Ye are the salt of the earth: but if the salt have lost his savour, wherewith shall it be salted?
Matthew. V, 13

[u] When thou doest alms, let not thy left hand know what thy right hand doeth.
Ibid. VI, 3

[v] Give us this day our daily bread.
Ibid. 11

[w] Lay up for yourselves treasures in heaven.
Ibid. 20

[x] Where your treasure is, there will your heart be also.
Ibid. 21

[y] The light of the body is the eye.
Ibid. 22

[z] No man can serve two masters. . . . Ye cannot serve God and Mammon.
Ibid. 24

[a] Consider the lilies of the field, how they grow; they toil not, neither do they spin.
Ibid. 28

[b] Take therefore no thought for the morrow; for the morrow shall take thought for the things of itself. Sufficient unto the day is the evil thereof.
Ibid. 34

[c] Neither cast ye your pearls before swine.
Ibid. VII, 6

[d] Ask, and it shall be given you; seek, and ye shall find; knock, and it shall be opened unto you.
Ibid. 7

[e] Or what man is there of you, whom if his son ask bread, will he give him a stone?
Ibid. 9

[f] Therefore all things whatsoever ye would that men should do to you, do ye even so to them: for this is the law and the prophets.
Ibid. 12

[g] Wide is the gate, and broad is the way, that leadeth to destruction.
Ibid. 13

[h'] By their fruits ye shall know them.
Ibid. 20

[i'] The foxes have holes, and the birds of the air have nests; but the Son of Man hath not where to lay his head.
Ibid. VIII, 20

[j'] Be ye therefore wise as serpents, and harmless as doves.
Ibid. X, 16

[k'] The very hairs of your head are all numbered.
Ibid. 30

[l'] Pearl of great price.
Ibid. XIII, 46

[m'] A prophet is not without honour, save in his own country, and in his own house.
Ibid. 57

[n'] If the blind lead the blind, both shall fall into the ditch.
Ibid. XV, 14

[o'] The dogs eat of the crumbs which fall from their masters' table.
Ibid. 27

[p'] When it is evening, ye say it will be fair weather: for the sky is red.
Ibid. XVI, 2

[q'] Thou art Peter, and upon this rock I will build my church.
Ibid. 18

[r'] Get thee behind me, Satan.
Ibid. 23

[s'] What is a man profited, if he shall gain the whole world, and lose his own soul?
Ibid. 26

[t'] Where two or three are gathered together in my name, there am I in the midst of them.
Ibid. XVIII, 20

[u'] What therefore God hath joined together, let not man put asunder.
Ibid. XIX, 6

[v'] Love thy neighbour as thyself.
Ibid. 19

[w'] It is easier for a camel to go through the eye of a needle, than for a rich man to enter into the kingdom of God.
Ibid 24

[x'] For many are called, but few are chosen.
Ibid. XXII, 14

[y] Render therefore unto Caesar the things which are Caesar's. *Ibid. 21*

[z] Blind guides, which strain at a gnat, and swallow a camel. *Ibid. XXIII, 24*

[a] Whited sepulchres, which indeed appear beautiful outward, but are within full of dead men's bones. *Ibid. 27*

[b] As a hen gathereth her chickens under her wings. *Ibid. 37*

[c] Wars and rumours of wars. *Ibid. XXIV, 6*

[d] False prophets. *Ibid. 24*

[e] Wheresoever the carcass is, there will the eagles be gathered together. *Ibid. 28*

[f] Well done, thou good and faithful servant. *Ibid. XXV, 21*

[g] Unto every one that hath shall be given, and he shall have abundance; but from him that hath not shall be taken away even that which he hath. *Ibid. 29*

[h] Inasmuch as ye have done it unto one of the least of these my brethren, ye have done it unto me. *Ibid. 40*

[i] Thirty pieces of silver. *Ibid. XXVI, 15*

[j] The spirit indeed is willing, but the flesh is weak. *Ibid. 41*

[k] All they that take the sword shall perish with the sword. *Ibid. 52*

[l] The potter's field, to bury strangers in. *Ibid. XXVII, 7*

[m] The voice of one crying in the wilderness. *Mark I, 3*

[n] The latchet of whose shoes I am not worthy to stoop down and unloose. *Ibid. 7*

[o] New wine into old bottles. *Ibid. II, 22*

[p] The Sabbath was made for man, and not man for the Sabbath. *Ibid. 27*

[q] If a house be divided against itself, that house cannot stand. *Ibid. III, 25*

[r] He that hath ears to hear, let him hear. *Ibid. IV, 9*

[s] Clothed, and in his right mind. *Ibid. V, 15*

[t] He [Judas] goeth straightway to him, and saith, Master, master; and kissed him. *Ibid. XIV, 45*

[u] There was no room for them in the inn. *Luke. II, 7*

[v] Glory to God in the highest, and on earth peace, good will toward men. *Ibid. 14*

[w] Lord, now lettest thou thy servant depart in peace. *Ibid. 29*

[x] Physician, heal thyself. *Ibid. IV, 23*

[y'] Woe unto you, when all men shall speak well of you! *Ibid. VI, 26*

[z'] No man, having put his hand to the plough, and looking back, is fit for the kingdom of God. *Ibid. IX, 62*

[a'] The labourer is worthy of his hire. *Ibid. X, 7*

[b'] A certain man went down from Jerusalem to Jericho, and fell among thieves. *Ibid. 30*

[c'] A certain Samaritan . . . had compassion on him. *Ibid. 33*

[d'] He that is not with me is against me. *Ibid. XI, 23*

[e'] Wasted his substance with riotous living. *Ibid. XV, 13*

[f'] Bring hither the fatted calf. *Ibid. 23*

[g'] He that is faithful in that which is least is faithful also in much; and he that is unjust in the least is unjust also in much. *Ibid. 10*

[h'] Out of thine own mouth will I judge thee. *Ibid. XIX, 22*

[i'] This do in remembrance of me. *Ibid. XXII, 19*

[j'] The wind bloweth where it listeth. *John. III, 8*

[k'] God so loved the world, that he gave his only begotten Son, that whosoever believeth in him should not perish, but have everlasting life. *Ibid. 16*

[l'] I am the bread of life. *Ibid. VI, 35*

[m'] Judge not according to the appearance *Ibid VII, 24*

[n'] He that is without sin among you, let him first cast a stone at her. *Ibid. VIII, 7*

[o'] Neither do I condemn thee: go, and sin no more. *Ibid. 11*

[p'] I am the light of the world: he that followeth me shall not walk in darkness, but shall have the light of life. *Ibid. 12*

[q'] The truth shall make you free. *Ibid. 32*

[r'] The night cometh, when no man can work. *Ibid. IX, 4*

[s'] I am the resurrection and the life. *Ibid. XI, 25*

[t'] A new commandment I give unto you, That ye love one another. *Ibid. XIII, 34*

[u'] Let not your heart be troubled. *Ibid. XIV, 1*

[**v**] In my Father's house are many mansions.   *Ibid. 2*

[**w**] Greater love hath no man than this, that a man lay down his life for his friends.
          Ibid. XV, 13

[**x**] Be of good cheer; I have overcome the world.   *Ibid. XVI, 33*

[**y**] Now Barabbas was a robber.
          Ibid. XVIII, 40

[**z**] It is more blessed to give than to receive.   *Acts. XX, 35*

[**a**] Much learning doth make thee mad.   *Ibid. XXVI, 24*

[**b**] Almost thou persuadest me to be a Christian.   *Ibid. 28*

[**c**] Wherein thou judgest another, thou condemnest thyself.
          Romans. II, 1

[**d**] There is no respect of persons with God.   *Ibid. 11*

[**e**] Who against hope believed in hope.   *Ibid. IV, 18*

[**f**] Death hath no more dominion over him.   *Ibid. VI, 9*

[**g**] The wages of sin is death.
          Ibid. 23

[**h**] For the good that I would I do not; but the evil which I would not, that I do.   *Ibid. VII, 19*

[**i**] If God be for us, who can be against us.   *Ibid. VIII, 31*

[**j**] Neither death, nor life . . . shall be able to separate us from the love of God.   *Ibid. 38, 39*

[**k**] Hath not the potter power over the clay, of the same lump to make one vessel unto honour, and another unto dishonour?
          Ibid. IX, 21

[**l**] Given to hospitality.
          Ibid. XII, 13

[**m**] If it be possible, as much as lieth in you, live peaceably with all men.   *Ibid. 18*

[**n**] Vengeance is mine; I will repay, saith the Lord.   *Ibid. 19*

[**o**] If thine enemy hunger, feed him; if he thirst, give him drink: for in so doing thou shalt heap coals of fire on his head. *Ibid. 20*

[**p**] Be not overcome of evil, but overcome evil with good. *Ibid. 21*

[**q**] Love is the fulfilling of the law.   *Ibid. XIII, 10*

[**r**] None of us liveth to himself.
          Ibid. XIV, 7

[**s**] Let us therefore follow after the things which make for peace.
          Ibid. 19

[**t**] God hath chosen the foolish things of the world to confound the wise; and God hath chosen the weak things of the world to confound the things which are mighty.   *1 Corinthians. I, 27*

[**u**] Absent in body, but present in spirit.   *Ibid. V, 3*

[**v′**] A little leaven leaveneth the whole lump.   *Ibid. 6*

[**w′**] The fashion of this world passeth away.   *Ibid. VII, 31*

[**x′**] I am made all things to all men.   *Ibid. IX, 22*

[**y′**] Let him that thinketh he standeth take heed lest he fall.
          Ibid. X, 12

[**z′**] If a woman have long hair, it is a glory to her.   *Ibid. XI, 15*

[**a′**] Though I speak with the tongues of men and of angels, and have not charity, I am become as sounding brass, or a tinkling cymbal. . . .
  Charity suffereth long and is kind; charity envieth not; charity vaunteth not itself, is not puffed up.   *Ibid. XIII, 1 and 4*

[**b′**] When I was a child, I spake as a child. . . . When I became a man, I put away childish things.
          Ibid. 11

[**c′**] Now we see through a glass, darkly.   *Ibid. 12*

[**d′**] And now abideth faith, hope, charity, these three; but the greatest of these is charity.
          Ibid. 13

[**e′**] One star differeth from another star in glory.   *Ibid. XV, 41*

[**f′**] The first man is of the earth, earthy.   *Ibid. 47*

[**g′**] In the twinkling of an eye.
          Ibid. 52

[**h′**] O death, where is thy sting? O grave, where is thy victory?
          Ibid. 55

[**i′**] Not of the letter, but of the spirit; for the letter killeth, but the spirit giveth life.
          2 Corinthians. III, 6

[**j′**] The things which are seen are temporal; but the things which are not seen are eternal.
          Ibid. IV, 18

[**k′**] We walk by faith, not by sight.   *Ibid. V, 7*

[**l′**] As having nothing, and yet possessing all things. *Ibid VI, 10*

[**m′**] God loveth a cheerful giver
          Ibid. IX, 7

[**n′**] For ye suffer fools gladly, seeing ye yourselves are wise.
          Ibid. 19

[**o′**] A thorn in the flesh.
          Ibid XII, 7

[**p′**] The grace of the Lord Jesus Christ, and the love of God, and

the communion of the Holy Ghost, be with you all.
Ibid. XIII, 14

[q] The right hands of fellowship. *Galatians. II, 9*

[r] Ye are fallen from grace.
Ibid. V, 4

[s] Every man shall bear his own burden. *Ibid. VI, 5*

[t] Whatsoever a man soweth, that shall he also reap. *Ibid. 7*

[u] Let us not be weary in well doing. *Ibid. 9*

[v] God forbid that I should glory, save in the cross of our Lord Jesus Christ. *Ibid. 14*

[w] Carried about with every wind of doctrine.
Ephesians. IV, 14

[x] Let not the sun go down upon your wrath. *Ibid. 26*

[y] Work out your own salvation.
Philippians. II, 12

[z] Whose God is their belly.
Ibid. III, 19

[a] The peace of God, which passeth all understanding.
Ibid. IV, 7

[b] Whatsoever things are true, whatsoever things are honest, whatsoever things are just, whatsoever things are pure, whatsoever things are lovely, whatsoever things are of good report; if there be any virtue, and if there be any praise, think on these things.
Ibid. 8

[c] I have learned, in whatsoever state I am, therewith to be content. *Ibid. 11*

[d] Let your speech be alway with grace, seasoned with salt.
Colossians. IV, 6

[e] Luke, the beloved physician.
Ibid. 14

[f] Labour of love.
1 Thessalonians. I, 3

[g] Putting on the breastplate of faith and love; and for an helmet, the hope of salvation. *Ibid. V, 8*

[h] Prove all things; hold fast that which is good. *Ibid. 21*

[i] The law is good, if a man use it lawfully. *1 Timothy. I, 8*

[j] Not greedy of filthy lucre.
Ibid. III, 3

[k] Drink no longer water, but use a little wine for thy stomach's sake. *Ibid. V, 23*

[l] We brought nothing into this world, and it is certain we can carry nothing out. *Ibid. VI, 7*

[m] The love of money is the root of all evil. *Ibid. 10*

[n] Unto the pure all things are pure. *Titus. I, 15*

[o] Strong meat belongeth to them that are of full age.
Hebrews. V, 14

[p] Faith is the substance of things hoped for, the evidence of things not seen. *Ibid. XI, 1*

[q'] A cloud of witnesses.
Ibid. XII, 1

[r'] Whom the Lord loveth he chasteneth. *Ibid. 6*

[s'] Be not forgetful to entertain strangers, for thereby some have entertained angels unawares.
Ibid. XIII, 2

[t'] For here we have no continuing city, but we seek one to come.
Ibid. 14

[u'] Let patience have her perfect work. *James. I, 4*

[v'] Blessed is the man that endureth temptation; for when he is tried, he shall receive the crown of life. *Ibid. 12*

[w'] No variableness, neither shadow of turning. *Ibid.*

[x'] Unspotted from the world.
Ibid. 27

[y'] Faith without works is dead.
Ibid. II, 26

[z'] The tongue can no man tame; it is an unruly evil. *Ibid. 8*

[a'] Resist the Devil, and he will flee from you. *Ibid. IV, 7*

[b'] The effectual fervent prayer of a righteous man availeth much.
Ibid. V, 16

[c'] Giving honour unto the wife, as unto the weaker vessel.
1 Peter. I, 7

[d'] Charity shall cover the multitude of sins. *Ibid. IV, 8*

[e'] Be sober, be vigilant; because your adversary, the Devil, as a roaring lion, walketh about, seeking whom he may devour.
Ibid. V, 8

[f'] Bowels of compassion.
1 John. III, 17

[g'] There is no fear in love; but perfect love casteth out fear.
Ibid IV. 18

[h'] A pale horse; and his name that sat on him was Death.
Revelation. VI, 8

[i'] Another book was opened, which is the book of life.
Ibid. XX, 12

[j'] The holy city, new Jerusalem. *Ibid. XXI, 2*

[k'] I am Alpha and Omega, the beginning and the end, the first and the last. *Ibid. 6*

The Apocrypha

[l] How exceeding strong is wine! it causeth all men to err who drink it. *1 Esdras. III, 18*

[m] Ye must know that women have dominion over you: do ye not labour and toil, and give and bring all to the woman? *Ibid. IV, 22*

[n] Great is truth, and mighty above all things. *Ibid. 41*

[o] Now therefore keep thy sorrow to thyself, and bear with a good courage that which hath befallen thee. *2 Esdras. X, 15*

[p] If thou hast abundance, give alms accordingly: if thou have but a little, be not afraid to give according to that little. *Tobit. IV, 8*

[q] Honour thy father and thy mother in law, which are now thy parents. *Ibid. X, 12*

[r] Ye cannot find the depth of the heart of man, neither can ye perceive the things that he thinketh: then how can ye search out God, that hath made all these things, and know his mind, or comprehend his purpose? *Judith. VIII, 14*

[s] Put on her garments of gladness. *Ibid. X, 3*

[t] Our time is a very shadow that passeth away. *Wisdom of Solomon. II, 5*

[u] Let us crown ourselves with rosebuds before they be withered. *Ibid. 8*

[v] In the sight of the unwise they seemed to die: and their departure is taken for misery, and their going from us to be utter destruction: but they are in peace. *Ibid. III, 1–3*

[w] When I was born, I drew in the common air, and fell upon the earth, which is of like nature, and the first voice which I uttered was crying, as all others do. *Ibid. VII, 3*

[x] Who can number the sand of the sea, and the drops of rain, and the days of eternity? *Ecclesiasticus. I, 2*

[y] If his understanding fail, have patience with him. *Ibid. III, 13*

[z] Let not thine hand be stretched out to receive, and shut when thou shouldest repay. *Ibid. IV, 31*

[a] A faithful friend is a strong defence: and he that hath found such an one hath found a treasure. *Ibid. VI, 14*

[b] Be not slow to visit the sick. *Ibid. VII, 35*

[c] Rejoice not over thy greatest enemy being dead, but remember that we die all. *Ibid. VIII, 7*

[d] Forsake not an old friend, for the new is not comparable to him. A new friend is as new wine: when it is old, thou shalt drink it with pleasure. *Ibid. IX, 10*

[e] He that toucheth pitch shall be defiled therewith. *Ibid. XIII, 1*

[f] He will laugh thee to scorn. *Ibid. 7*

[g] A rich man beginning to fall is held up of his friends: but a poor man being down is thrust also away by his friends. *Ibid. 21*

[h] Wine and women will make men of understanding to fall away. *Ibid. XIX, 2*

[i] Whether it be to friend or foe, talk not of other men's lives. *Ibid. 8*

[j] If she go not as thou wouldst have her, cut her off from thy flesh, and give her a bill of divorce, and let her go. *Ibid. XXV, 26*

[k] Gladness of the heart is the life of man, and the joyfulness of a man prolongeth his days. *Ibid. XXX, 22*

[l'] Honour a physician with the honour due unto him. *Ibid. XXXVIII, 1*

[m'] Look upon the rainbow, and praise him that made it. *Ibid. XLIII, 11*

[n'] Let us now praise famous men. *Ibid. XLIV, 1*

[o'] His word burned like a lamp. *Ibid. XLVIII, 1*

[p'] A scarecrow in a garden of cucumbers keepeth nothing. *Baruch. VI, 70*

[q'] It is a foolish thing to make a long prologue, and to be short in the story itself. *2 Maccabees. II, 32*

[r'] Nicanor lay dead in his harness. *Ibid. XV, 28*

[s'] Speech finely framed delighteth the ears. *Ibid. 39*

Douay Bible

The English version of the Old Testament for Roman Catholics was first printed in Douay, France 1609.

[t'] I am the angel Raphael, one of the seven, who stand before the Lord. *Tobias XII, 15*

[u] The faces of them all are as the blackness of a kettle.
Nahum. II, 10

[v] You have sowed much, and brought in little. *Aggeus. I, 6*

[w] He that hath earned wages put them into a bag with holes.
Ibid.

The Koran

Translated [1734] by George Sale

[x] Turn, therefore, thy face towards the holy temple of Mecca; and wherever ye be, turn your faces towards that place.
Chap. 2

[y] Wherever ye be, God will bring you all back at the resurrection. *Ibid.*

[z] O true believers, take your necessary precautions against your enemies, and either go forth to war in separate parties, or go forth all together in a body.
Chap. 4

[a] O men, respect women who have borne you. *Ibid.*

[b] Wheresoever ye be, death will overtake you, although ye be in lofty towers. *Ibid.*

[c] God loveth not the speaking ill of any one in public. *Ibid.*

[d] Let not thy hand be tied up to thy neck; neither open it with an unbounded expansion, lest thou become worthy of reprehension, and be reduced to poverty.
Chap. 17

[e] If God should punish men according to what they deserve, he would not leave on the back of the earth so much as a beast.
Chap. 35

[f] O unbelievers, I will not worship that which ye worship; nor will ye worship that which I worship. . . . Ye have your religion, and I my religion. *Chap. 109*

Book of Common Prayer

American Revision [1928]

[g] We have left undone those things which we ought to have done; and we have done those things which we ought not to have done. *Morning Prayer*

[h] The noble army of Martyrs.
Ibid. Te Deum

[i] Grant us grace fearlessly to contend against evil, and to make no peace with oppression; and, that we may reverently use our freedom, help us to employ it in the maintenance of justice among men and nations.
Prayers and Thanksgivings. A Prayer for Social Justice

[j] The world, the flesh, and the devil. *The Litany*

[k] The kindly fruits of the earth. *Ibid.*

[l] Read, mark, learn, and inwardly digest *Collect for the Second Sunday in Advent*

[m] Renounce the devil and all his works.
Holy Baptism. Of Children

[n] The pomps and vanity of this wicked world. *Offices of Instruction (Catechism)*

[o] To keep my hands from picking and stealing. *Ibid.*

[p] To do my duty in that state of life unto which it shall please God to call me. *Ibid.*

[q] To have and to hold from this day forward, for better for worse, for richer for poorer, in sickness and in health, to love and to cherish, till death us do part.
Solemnization of Matrimony

[r] With this Ring I thee wed.
Ibid.

[s] In the midst of life we are in death. *Burial of the Dead. At the Grave*

[t] Earth to earth, ashes to ashes, dust to dust; in sure and certain hope of the Resurrection unto eternal life. *Ibid.*

[u'] God, in whom we live and move and have our being.
Family Prayer. Morning

[v'] O Lord, support us all the day long, until the shadows lengthen and the evening comes, and the busy world is hushed, and the fever of life is over, and our work is done. Then in thy mercy grant us a safe lodging, and a holy rest, and peace at the last.
Ibid. At Night

[w'] O Heavenly Father, who hast filled the world with beauty; open, we beseech thee, our eyes to behold thy gracious hand in all thy works; that rejoicing in thy whole creation, we may learn to serve thee with gladness.
Ibid. For Joy in God's Creation

Book of Common Prayer, English

[x'] Grant that the old Adam in these persons may be so buried, that the new man may be raised up in them. *Holy Baptism. Of Those of Riper Years*

[y'] With all my worldly goods I thee endow.
Solemnization of Matrimony

INDEX

(For convenience of users, many specific names have been grouped under the general category. *Apple,* for instance, will be found under *fruit, Mississippi* under *river.* If a specific name is not found, look under its general category. Opposites of words are usually to be found together, as *inconsistency* with *consistency.* Cross references have been made to supplementary material. Letters following page numbers refer to position on page; letters run from *a* to *z* throughout book, not *a* to *z* on each page.)

A new concept
in a reference work
designed to help clear
up the two most
troublesome areas of
the English language

Words
Most Often
Misspelled and
Mispronounced

by RUTH GLEESON and JAMES COLVIN

GIANT CARDINAL EDITION GC • 613/60¢

PUBLISHED BY
POCKET BOOKS, INC. pb

A Merriam-Webster

REG. U.S. PAT. OFF.

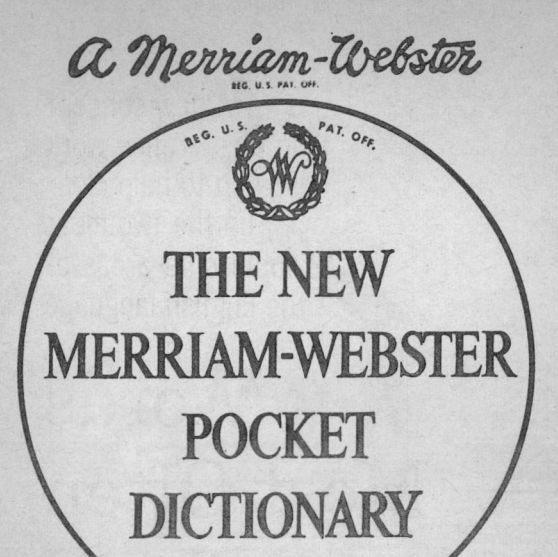

THE NEW
MERRIAM-WEBSTER
POCKET
DICTIONARY

This 640 page pocket-size dictionary has been specially prepared for general use by the recognized leading dictionary makers.

MORE THAN 42,000 VOCABULARY ENTRIES

GUIDES TO SPELLING AND
PRONUNCIATION

SELECTED ETYMOLOGIES GIVING
PRECISE WORD HISTORIES

SYNONYMS

COMMONLY USED ABBREVIATIONS

FOREIGN WORDS AND PHRASES

POPULATION FIGURES
FOR THE UNITED STATES AND CANADA

50010/50¢

If your bookseller does not have this title, you may order it by sending retail price, plus 10¢ for mailing and handling to: MAIL SERVICE DEPARTMENT, Pocket Books, Inc., 1 W. 39th St., New York, N. Y. 10018. Not responsible for orders containing cash. Please send check or money order.

PUBLISHED BY POCKET BOOKS, INC.